LOSING A KINGDOM, GAINING THE WORLD

ALSO BY AMBROGIO A. CAIANI

To Kidnap a Pope: Napoleon and Pius VII

Louis XVI and the French Revolution, 1789–1792

LOSING A KINGDOM, GAINING THE WORLD

THE CATHOLIC CHURCH IN THE AGE
OF REVOLUTION AND DEMOCRACY

AMBROGIO A. CAIANI

First published in the UK in 2023 by Head of Zeus Ltd,
part of Bloomsbury Publishing Plc.

9 7 5 3 1 2 4 6 8

A catalogue record for this book is available from the British Library.

ISBN (HB): 9781800240469
ISBN (XTPB): 9781800240476
ISBN (E): 9781800240490

Printed and bound in Great Britain by
CPI Group (UK) Ltd, Croydon CR0 4YY

Head of Zeus Ltd
First Floor East
5–8 Hardwick Street
London EC1R 4RG

WWW.HEADOFZEUS.COM

In ricordo dei miei nonni Ambrogio,
Laura, Antonio e Anna.
And to my wonderful father Paolo.

'For what shall it profit a man, if he shall gain the
whole world, and lose his own soul?'

MARK, 8:36

Contents

NOTE ON PAPAL
COMMUNICATIONS

The terms used to describe papal letters, communiqués and pronouncements can be confusing. To make matters worse the formats, contents and purposes of these documents were not standardised by the *Curia*, and popes could be a little inconsistent with the terms they used to describe their public announcements. By the eighteenth century, most papal communications were printed and circulated widely. In general, throughout 1700–1903, popes communicated with the Catholic world with the following types of open letters:

- *Papal allocution*: a solemn pronouncement from the papal throne, delivered in secret, or in modern times, in public consistories (meetings) at which a quorum of cardinals are present. It usually concerns some moral or ethical issue.

- *Papal brief*: literally from the Latin term '*breve*', meaning brief or short. These letters constituted relatively straightforward papal pronouncements that were inscribed on vellum then sealed with the fisherman's ring on simple wax.

- *Papal bull*: similar to a brief, but more solemn and closer in appearance and content to letters-patent issued by monarchs. These solemn acts, generally, had legal standing, bestowing powers or rulings on complex matters. These bulls were signed by the pope, monogrammed, countersigned by officials in the Curia and affixed with the great seal of the papacy usually made of lead. The etymology of the term comes from the Latin term '*bolla*' alluding to the melting of lead or other metals used to produce the seal for this document.

- *Papal encyclical*: lengthy circular letters by popes reflecting on specific contemporary questions or offering theological guidance or interpretations on important issues. This practice was introduced by Benedict XIV in 1740 with his encyclical *Ubi primum*. Although these letters were part of the Catholic magisterium, they were not necessarily considered to be infallible statements.

- *Papal decree*: This was a subspecies of papal bull that decreed or ruled on a specific issue that had been referred to the papacy or its courts. It was a solemn and binding decision from the pope.

- *Apostolic constitution*: Another type of papal bull containing the most solemn and important type of legislation issued by the pope in his capacity as spiritual leader of the church. The constitutions *Ineffabilis deus* (1864) on the immaculate conception, *Dei filius et pastor aeternus* (1870) on the results of the First Vatican Council and *Munificentissimus deus* (1950) on the assumption of the Virgin Mary are considered infallible papal pronouncements on Catholic teaching. These texts ranked among the most important written acts issued by the papacy and its Curia.

INTRODUCTION:
PEKING 1705

On 31 December 1705, wind and snow battered the walls of the Forbidden City. An imperial litter, richly decorated with silks, passed through one of the flanking arches of the Meridian Gate; its central archway was reserved exclusively for the emperor. It is likely that a special dispensation had been granted for this mysterious visitor to pass through the Gate of Heavenly Splendour and alight in front of the Hall of Persevered Harmony. Here the sovereign of the Middle Kingdom undertook his most significant court rituals. This ceremonial route was used by the highest-ranking mandarins and members of the imperial clan.[1] Through the sedan chair's screens, horrified Qing courtiers glimpsed a fearsome and bearded barbarian. It was an unprecedented honour for a non-Han dignitary to enter the Forbidden City with such pomp.*

---

* For this European prelate some of the ceremonial of the Chinese court must have seemed familiar. Indeed, to be carried in pomp and deference was hardly shocking to a man who had been educated in the papal court in Rome. On the other side of the globe, (until the 1960s) popes were raised high on the sedia gestatoria to elevate them, both literally and symbolically, above the masses. Some pontiffs who suffered from vertigo closed their eyes, and held the armrests of their chair firmly in terror. Others, like Pius IX, experienced seasickness and terrible nausea due to the wave-like movement that was produced by their carriers. On a richly decorated sedan chair, borne by the great nobles of Rome, the pontiff could be seen by crowds seeking his blessing on St Peter's Square and inside the basilica. See Armand Dubarry, *Histoire de la Cour de Rome* (Paris, 1868), pp. 101–2.

This foreigner had travelled from the other side of the globe and had grave business to transact with the 'Son of Heaven'. Kangxi, emperor of China, had acceded to the 'dragon throne' at the tender age of seven and would reign for over six decades.* As only the third member of his dynasty to rule, he had developed into a wily, energetic and ruthless ruler. The Qing empire was the most populous and economically prosperous power in the world.[2] It controlled the fate and livelihoods of millions in east Asia. Good relations with this superpower remained a top priority not only for its tributary vassals, but also for the European trading empires. Yet this distinguished visitor was neither a merchant nor an emissary of secular power. Charles-Thomas Maillard de Tournon was the first official papal legate (ambassador) to imperial China. He bore the title of Patriarch of Antioch which, according to tradition, had been St Peter's first diocese.[3]

As a prelate, he was dressed in flowing purple robes and might well have passed for a mandarin, but for his dark beard. If tact is the biggest asset for a diplomat, then a robust gastrointestinal system must come a close second. Tournon had started his journey in February 1703 and it took him almost two years to reach his destination. As a native of Piedmont his diet had been rich in dairy foods and red meat. The French East India company ships in which he sailed inevitably passed through India.[4] The cuisine on board changed, becoming more spiced, not to mention covered in flavoursome sauces. The papal legate had always suffered from colitis and Asian food triggered this affliction pitilessly. He spent most of his long journey on ships, canal boats and litters in a far from dignified position. Eventually, he grew feverish and was largely incapacitated for much of his embassy. His arrival in Peking was an anti-climax and he would spend almost three weeks convalescing, unable to attend to his official duties. His first audience in the Forbidden City was delayed to allow him time to recover.

---

* For a remarkable first-person narrative see Jonathan D. Spence, *Emperor of China: Self-Portrait of K'Ang-Hsi* (New York, 1974) and Dominic Lieven, *In the Shadow of the Gods: The Emperor in World History* (London, 2022), pp. 289–99.

This postponement irked Kangxi, who was eager to join the traditional winter hunts at Mukden in Manchuria.[5] Yet the enlightened emperor prided himself on his patience and urbanity. Not only did he wait but he also bestowed on the foreigner the unique privilege of not being obliged to 'kowtow' before him. This custom was mandatory for all persons ushered into the imperial presence. All had to prostrate themselves three times and tap their heads on the ground nine times before the 'Son of Heaven'. Given his gastric turmoil, it was feared that the patriarch of Antioch might not be able to stand again if forced to perform this ritual, yet it was highly irregular for this prostration to be waived.* As a further concession to his health, Tournon was also permitted to sit in the imperial presence, a privilege usually only reserved for those who had passed advanced examinations. The mandarins were furious that this outsider was given honours usually reserved exclusively for their estate.

Tournon's audience with Kangxi came at a crossroads in the history of the church's relations with the Far East. The Italian missionary Matteo Ricci had arrived in China in 1582. He had made an exceptionally good impression by becoming near-fluent

---

* 'Kowtowing' in Europe has been portrayed as grovelling and a mark of 'oriental' submissiveness. Such an assessment is deeply unfair and indeed the practice was hardly as exotic or alien as such hostile descriptions make it appear. Until the twentieth century Catholics were expected to kneel and kiss the pope's silk slippers in deference to his position as Christ's vicar. As Paul VI realised only too well, this was hardly dignified in the modern world and he abolished the practice in the 1960s. See Marina Caffiero, 'La maestà del papa', in Maria Antonietta Visceglia and Catherine Brice, *Cérémonial et rituel à Rome XVIe-XIXe siècle* (Rome, 1997), pp. 281–316. Several decades later, in 1793, the British representative George Macartney's refusal to 'kowtow' doomed his trade delegation to failure. See Eoin McDonnell, *Kowtow: Georgian Britain, Imperial China and the Irishman Who Introduced Them* (London, 2021); James L. Hevia, *Cherishing Men from Afar: Qing Guest Ritual and the Macartney Embassy of 1793* (Durham, NC, 1995), and by the same author, 'Tribute, Asymmetry, and Imperial Formations: Rethinking Relations of Power in East Asia', *Journal of American-East Asian Relations*, Vol. 16, No. 1/2 (2009), pp. 69–83 and Robert Bickers (ed.), *Ritual and Diplomacy: The Macartney Mission to China 1792–1794* (London, 1993).

in Mandarin and well-versed in the works of Confucius.[6] The mnemonic and pedagogical techniques he brought with him were particularly appreciated by Chinese scholars and administrators. His fellow-Jesuits, following his example, became well respected at the imperial court for their Western knowledge. As favoured scientists, astronomers, engineers, and artists, they represented an important conduit for exchanges between East and West.[7] Indeed, their skill as cannon designers and ballistics experts was put to good use by the imperial armies.

Even the collapse of the Ming dynasty in 1644 did not put an end to Jesuit influence in the Middle Kingdom. Their role as cultural intermediaries was highly prized by the Qing emperors who filled the power vacuum left by their predecessors. The learning, artistic abilities, and open-mindedness of the Jesuits deeply impressed Kangxi. Giuseppe Castiglione's paintings and images depicting courtly life in Peking offer a unique Western glimpse into early Qing China.[8] Their lifelike qualities and graphic precision were much prized by the imperial court and demonstrated how well the Society of Jesus had integrated among Chinese elites. In the same way as the Jesuits monopolised the positions of confessors and chaplains for the Catholic monarchies of Europe, on the other side of the world they had the ear of the 'Son of Heaven'. This may explain why, in 1692, Kangxi issued an edict of toleration.[9] He granted Christian churches his protection and declared freedom of worship within his vast domains. Even missionary activity was granted tacit permission to continue and converts could be made, at least discreetly. Unlike Europe's courts, which were sectarian in nature and persecuted heretics, the Chinese emperor fostered a poly-confessional empire so long as his secular authority was unchallenged.

The key requirement of the edict of toleration was that all subjects of the 'Son of Heaven' would continue to participate in Confucian state rituals and ancestor worship.[10] This involved the cyclical commemoration of the great philosopher of the sixth century BC who had provided China with its worldview and ethos. Confucianism has no eschatology (belief in an afterlife) in the limited sense of the term, as it is more concerned with ethics and behaviour in the present rather than with the hereafter.[11] This has allowed it to be seen more as a secular ethos rather than as a theological cosmology. Confucius's teachings provided a guide to a virtuous life and harmonious society, in much the same way as Plato and Aristotle's writing had done in Athens in the fourth century BC.

At different moments of the year the Chinese educated classes burned incense and provided sacrifices of food to their ancestors, who were commemorated in inscribed clay tablets.[12] The Jesuits, with their intellectual agility, had interpreted these practices as secular rather than religious. Did not Europeans honour and evoke their dead in a similar manner with elaborate grave sites? Equally, did not Catholics venerate the memory of the saints whilst, at the same time, maintaining their monotheism? Given that much of Confucianism seemed secular, they assured the emperor that Chinese rites did not conflict with Catholic teaching. But their progressive and tolerant interpretation of Confucian culture was to prove controversial in Europe.

Back in the Vatican, the Curia, or church administration, was none too sure that these Chinese rites were compatible with Catholic teaching. The Chinese ancestor tablets seemed to imply that they were a receptacle that contained the soul of the ancestor being commemorated. Was this not idolatry, rather than mere respect for the dead? Furthermore, there were several Chinese words for God and at least one of them could be conflated with worship of the Emperor.[13] Any deification of the ruler of the Middle Kingdom was difficult for Rome to swallow. During the mid-seventeenth century the papacy had sided with the Jesuits' accommodation of Confucianism because it was understood that some acceptance of local customs was necessary to ease evangelisation. A failure to do so had contributed, in no small measure, to the expulsion of all foreigners and the martyrdom of missionaries and Catholic converts in Japan at the end of the sixteenth century.[14] The goodwill of the Emperor was vital if Europeans were to have any hope of surviving in China.

Other missionary orders in the Far East, such as the Franciscans, Dominicans and Augustinians, accused the Jesuits of having 'gone native'. They were probably jealous of Jesuit success and growth in Peking in comparison to their own meagre results. These rivals to the society of Jesus appealed to the Curia, demanding that Rome intervene vigorously on the question of Chinese rites. They urged the pope to rein in the Jesuits and censure their missionary activities in Peking. Tournon was the first papal legate sent to an Asian emperor and his objective was to negotiate with Kangxi and to explore if a religious *entente* between Peking and Rome might be possible. It was hoped that the 'Son of Heaven' would give permission for the appointment of a 'superior general' who would prohibit the Jesuits' harmonisation of Confucian ritual with Catholic theology. There was also an unrealistic hope that the emperor might be converted to the truth of the Catholic faith. Tournon's mission was driven by anti-Jesuit animus, and he wanted to clip the wings of this powerful missionary order.

Tournon's embassy to the Forbidden City was blighted by ill health and he never acclimatised to China. His erratic behaviour, irritability and lack of courtesy were probably exacerbated by his infirmities. Very much grounded in the aristocratic traditions of Europe, and particularly his native Turin, Tournon refused to take anyone into his confidence except the emperor. He alienated the Jesuits deliberately by refusing their counsel and by complaining, angrily, that the house they provided for him was unworthy of his rank.[15] Equally, the mandarins sent to prepare the groundwork for his audience were insulted by the legate's refusal to reveal the purpose of his mission. The hasty and imperfect translation of his letters of credence from the pope gave the impression that his sole aim was to establish good relations between the Holy Father and the 'Son of Heaven'. Kangxi dismissed this purpose as trivial and was surprised a man might travel nine thousand miles just to seek friendship.

The meeting, on 31 December 1705, between the feverish legate and the emperor was cordial. Indeed, the curiosities, particularly Venetian glass, enamelled objects and musical instruments, sent as gifts by the Holy See, stimulated Kangxi's cosmopolitanism and curiosity about the distant West. Eventually, discussions drifted onto the appointment of a 'superior general' in China to oversee the missions. The emperor saw no difficulty in granting this, but insisted that the person chosen be fluent in Mandarin, proficient in the Chinese alphabet and aware of the cultural realities within his empire. In effect, only the court Jesuits would be eligible for this office. These conditions took the legate by surprise – and in a direction he had hoped to avoid.

Kangxi reassured Tournon that he was informed by the Jesuits that Catholicism and Confucianism were perfectly compatible. The legate regretted that this was not the case. Irritated, Kangxi enquired about specific problems and incompatibilities. Tournon admitted that his knowledge of Confucius's writings was imperfect but that Charles Maigrot de Crissey, apostolic vicar to Fujian (who was an anti-Jesuit French prelate) would be able to answer such queries exhaustively.[16] The emperor grudgingly accepted this and Maigrot was summoned to the capital for a conference. In the meantime, by way of diplomatic reciprocity, fine gifts were collected and despatched on the long journey to Rome. They were precious tokens that would demonstrate that the pope's overtures were welcome while, at the same time, showcasing China's finest silks, porcelains and vases.

During this long interval the legate was invited to witness the fireworks display for the Chinese New Year in February. But, as the weeks turned into months, the patriarch grew increasingly paranoid towards the Jesuits, whom he suspected of turning the imperial court against him. Tournon suspected that he was the victim of a monstrous cabal that had been organised to doom his diplomatic mission. In March matters were exacerbated when over a hundred Chinese Christians came to petition Tournon at his residence. They begged him to tolerate Chinese rites and not condemn ancestor worship. Frustrated and unwell, the legate tried to tear up the petitions but was too weak to do so. Not to be deterred, he trampled the scrolls underfoot in a gesture of contempt for the petitioners.[17]

Appalled by the legate's behaviour, and to get him out of the capital, the mandarins advised Tournon to travel to the hot springs in T'ang'shan.[18] They hoped the mineral and curative properties of these waters would restore the diplomat's health and make him more amenable to compromise. During his time away taking the waters, Tournon became violently ill and he suspected the Jesuits of poisoning him. Despite such tensions, the official despatch he transmitted to the Curia painted his audience with Kangxi in positive colours, giving the impression that it had been a great success. The legate knew that his correspondence was intercepted by the imperial authorities. He avoided using a cypher so as not to give rise to offence or suspicion. In Rome, these words were read prematurely as a triumph. Clement XI was so pleased with this news that Tournon was promoted to cardinal.[19]

After a slow journey along China's complex network of canals Bishop Maigrot arrived in Peking. He carried a list of forty-eight Confucian principles incompatible with Catholicism. An audience with Kangxi was scheduled forthwith. To the emperor's amazement it soon became apparent that the apostolic vicar's Mandarin was poor and that he needed an interpreter to be understood. His arguments failed to persuade Kangxi, who found Maigrot's knowledge of Chinese philosophy deficient. When asked to translate and interpret the inscriptions above the Dragon Throne Maigrot failed to do so. Far from being qualified, this prelate was clearly ignorant of Chinese characters and incompetent to assess Confucian teachings and rituals.[20]

Feeling that he had already conceded too much through his policy of toleration, and was receiving nothing in return, Kangxi's patience became exhausted. The distinct impression he now had was that the papacy wished to interfere in the governance and religion of Qing China. In retaliation, the emperor refused to sanction papal control over the Jesuit missions. Tournon was ordered to leave the empire immediately. Not only that, but the gifts making their way to Rome were recalled and would never reach their destination. The Edict of Toleration was revoked, and Christianity was viewed with growing suspicion. Despite this the Jesuits continued to be treated as esteemed courtiers. Four of them were sent to Rome to try to persuade the pope to change his mind. Most died en route, never to return to Peking.

Tournon's last days were unhappy. He issued a formal condemnation of the Chinese rites from Nanking.[21] The imperial authorities hastened his departure towards the Portuguese enclave of Macau. Here, querulous as ever, he fell out violently with the Europeans who governed this outpost. After a few months he excommunicated the city's authorities over their lack of support for his anti-Confucian stance. In retaliation, the local bishop excommunicated the legate.[22] His premature death in 1710, at the age of forty-two, finally put an end to this diplomatic debacle. Rome came to realise that the mission to Peking had been a dismal failure.

Ten years later, Rome sent another legate, Carlo Ambrogio Mezzabarba, across the world to meet with the now-ageing Kangxi. This mission granted ad hoc permissions for the Confucian rites to be practised discreetly. Yet Mezzabarba failed to persuade the emperor to accept the pope's authority over the small Chinese church within his domains. In many ways Mezzabarba was playing with one arm tied behind his back, for Pope Clement XI, in 1715, had condemned the Chinese rites in his decree *Ex illa die*. Kangxi stated categorically that so long as this prohibition remained in force, Catholicism could not be practised openly in his Empire. A final impasse had been reached, and the hopes of persuading China to accept papal authority had proved evanescent. Growing anti-Jesuit sentiment in Europe pushed Benedict XIV, three decades later in 1742, to confirm Clement XI's condemnation of Confucianism in the bull *Ex quo singulari*.[23] Thus was halted the progress of Catholic evangelisation in China. Only in 1939 did Pius XII finally reverse these myopic decisions with the instruction *Plane compertum*.[24]

The failure to establish relations between the pope and the Chinese emperor was indicative of the Catholic church's growing unease with the secular state's claim to absolute sovereignty.* This book examines how, during the Age of Revolutions (1700–1903), Catholicism came close to the abyss on several occasions.† Emperors, kings, dictators and revolutionaries demanded that the successor of St Peter bend to their will. The popes of this period steadfastly refused to relinquish their political authority and fought hard to retain power over their small Italian kingdom.

---

* The unexpected Vatican–China agreement of 22 September 2018 has done much to defuse long-standing tensions between the Vatican and Beijing. See 'Provisional Agreement between Holy See and China (22 September 2018)', online at www.vaticannews.va/en/vatican-city/news/2018-09/china-holy-see-agreement-appointment-bishops.html [accessed 2 November 2020].
† Eric Hobsbawn prominently defined this period 1750–1850 as 'the age of revolution'. See his *The Age of Revolution: Europe 1789-1848* (London, 1962).

They refused to accept defeat even after 1870, when the walls of Rome were finally breached. For most of its history the Catholic church has considered itself equal in dignity with the state. In Europe a close working relationship existed between the pope and the continent's Catholic sovereigns.[25]

Church and state in the early modern world were bound up in an interdependent 'alliance of throne and altar'. Monarchs and their bureaucracies enforced Catholic teaching, along with its dogmas and moral precepts, over those they ruled. To live in the kingdoms of France, Spain, Portugal and Naples was to be Catholic. To renounce the faith was to become a heretic and an outlaw punishable by 'civil death'. Early modern states were unashamedly confessional.* Catholic princes, in return for their imposition of the one true faith, in most of Southern and Western Europe received legitimation from the papacy. The rewards for keeping the papacy on their side were tantalising. For example, France's ruler held the title of Most Christian King, his Spanish counterpart was proclaimed His Most Catholic Majesty and across the border in Portugal the monarch received the accolade of the Most Faithful King. The Habsburgs were Holy Roman Emperors and as kings of Hungary were styled as Sacred and Apostolic Majesties. Politics and religion cross-fertilised each other before 1700.

These pages tell the story of how this once-comfortable working relationship between church and state disintegrated during the eighteenth and nineteenth centuries. In some ways, the Emperor of China's belief in religious pluralism and his demand that the church be subordinated to the state were signs of things to come in the very heartlands of Catholicism. This process was influenced by several factors such as the scientific revolution of the seventeenth century, whose mantle was picked up by the Enlightenment of the eighteenth. These movements questioned religion's monopoly on

---

* Such arrangements were replicated in Protestant and Muslim polities, although they tended to allow their subjects a greater degree of reluctant toleration. See Bruce Masters, *Christians and Jews in the Ottoman Arab World: The Roots of Sectarianism* (Cambridge, 2001), pp. 16–40; Jacqueline Hill, 'Religious Toleration and the Relaxation of the Penal Laws: An imperial perspective, 1763-1780', *Archivium Hibernicum*, Vol. 44 (1989), pp. 98–109.

the interpretation of the natural world and morality. Having said this, it's worth remembering that the intellectuals who shared this thirst for objective knowledge were not intrinsically anti-Catholic. Many hoped, as Thomas Aquinas had in the thirteenth century, that religion could only be strengthened through the application of human reason to its precepts. Yet the arguments of the Enlightenment did provide the preconditions through which many came to challenge the authoritarian nature of church governance.[26]

Legal, political and humanitarian reform were portrayed as areas which should be freed from the shackles of revealed religion. Tradition had held an iron grip on governments and their administrations for centuries. By 1789 few still believed they inhabited 'the best of all possible worlds', as the unforgettable but hapless Dr Pangloss prematurely concluded in Voltaire's novella *Candide* (1769).[27] Fossilised tradition was lambasted as a barrier to progress and human improvement. This movement would culminate in violent revolution in France during the 1790s.[28] The Catholic church became the great victim of this revolutionary conflagration. This is hardly surprising, given that the alliance of throne and altar was the antithesis of what these revolutionaries wanted to achieve.

Today the term 'theocracy' has exotic if not toxic connotations. A mere google-search of the term will churn up images of the Taliban and Isis. During the eighteenth century, theocracy remained very much alive in Europe's ecclesiastical principalities.* Not only was the pope the head of the 'universal' church and the great custodian of Catholicism's magisterium, but he was also a secular prince. He ruled over the lion's share of central Italy, not to mention several small enclaves in Naples and France.[29] Although his was the largest ecclesiastical principality in Europe, it was by no means unique.

---

* There seems to be no synthetic study of the concept of theocracy in early modern or eighteenth-century Europe. For the best synthesis see William J. Callahan and David Higgs (eds), *Church and Society in Catholic Europe of the Eighteenth Century* (Cambridge, 1979), esp. chapters by Benecke on the Reichskirche (pp. 66–76) and Rosa on the Italian Church (pp. 77–87).

The archbishop-electors of Mainz, Trier and Cologne not only ruled over sizeable and disparate German territories, but they were entitled to vote for the Holy Roman Emperor.[30] Germany, Spain and Poland were littered with prince-bishops who served as secular heads of government. In some cases, prince-abbots, like those of Sankt-Gallen in Switzerland and elsewhere in Germany, were rulers of micro-states.[31] Although such power was largely wielded by men it was not exclusively a male prerogative. Throughout Europe abbesses were some of the most powerful women in the world. They collected rents, acted as community leaders and were appointed judges in manorial courts.[32] Political power in Europe had a decidedly theocratic flavour.

There was growing scepticism, however, over whether priests could be good rulers and honest politicians.* Educated men felt a sense of frustration that in early modern states entry into the priesthood often constituted a fast track towards power, influence and wealth. Priesthood was viewed as a career rather than a vocation by many. The Roman Curia epitomised this tendency and was the source of much frustration. It notoriously played a long game and could be painfully slow in coming to decisions, let alone implementing reform. These lawyer-priests were the bureaucrats of the Middle Ages.[33] To the bright young philosophers of the Enlightenment, such plodding and quibbling was deeply frustrating.

Eventually, the church came under a barrage of criticism. Not all of it came from lay outsiders who detested the privileges of the First Estate (the clergy); sometimes priests and bishops were frustrated by the immobility of their hierarchies and disapproved of their own institutions. Such prelates and clergymen had grown sympathetic to modern theories of social and economic improvement. They engaged with the Enlightenment process and

---

* Jonathan I. Israel, *Radical Enlightenment: Philosophy and the Making of Modernity, 1650–1750* (Oxford, 2001), pp. 197–294; for a synthesis see Jonathan Sheehan, 'Enlightenment, Religion, and the Enigma of Secularization: A review essay,' *American Historical Review*, Vol. 108, No. 4 (2003), pp. 1061–80.

reform by publishing their own visions for a better ecclesiastical future.[34] It was their hope that by internalising such progressive ideals, Catholicism could not only survive present challenges but prosper and renew itself. These were minority voices, who actively and aggressively tried to reshape their parishes and dioceses in the Age of Enlightenment.[35]

The truth remained that the church of Rome had a decided image problem throughout the eighteenth century. The First Estate was the richest and greatest landowner in the continent, after the monarchies of Europe. Bishops and abbots could easily be caricatured as self-indulgent parasites who provided little benefit to the souls they were supposed to save. Monasteries, which had been suppressed in England by Henry VIII during the sixteenth century, were a prime target for reformers who painted monks as wasteful, corrupt and sexually licentious.[36] Calls for the church to be less worldly and powerful multiplied. These reformers, for the most part, were not atheists, let alone modern secularists. They believed in the social utility of religion. For them the priority was a more pastorally engaged and charitable ecclesiastical establishment.

A cost-benefit analysis of the church is not easy even in the present day, and almost impossible when it is applied to the past. The Catholic church provided the only proto-social welfare and healthcare in a society that afforded hardly any state-sponsored assistance to its most vulnerable members. At the opposite end of the spectrum, some bishops and abbots behaved as if the church were an exclusive club that rewarded them bountifully with political and economic privileges. Given such complexity, it is difficult to arrive at an unambiguous assessment of the church's social role during the *ancien régime*. Catholicism protected the weak and poor while simultaneously preying on them. Such ambivalence was at the heart of the church's vulnerability to criticism.

The French Revolution and the Napoleonic Empire opened a Pandora's box in seeking to curb ecclesiastical power. Revolutionaries from the 1790s onwards took it as an article of faith that the church had to be subordinated to the state.[37] They put pressure on the pope and Catholics to yield to the ultimate authority of secular government. Rome's refusal to accept lay tutelage unleashed a culture war that persists to the present day. In the period covered by this book two popes were kidnapped by the French and a third was forced to flee Rome under cannon fire. For the papacy, bitter resistance was the only solution to these direct challenges. The laity had no right to define morality, nor could it interfere in questions of public worship.

Temporal power was the chief battleground in church–state relations during the eighteenth and nineteenth centuries. The preservation of the Papal States in central Italy became the great lost cause of the Catholic church. Defending the 'Papa-Re' (the pope-king) was the *sine qua non* for the papacy's survival. The pope's status as an independent secular prince, it was argued, guaranteed the independence and freedom of the church. It was feared that, if Rome were conquered and the pope expelled from the Eternal City, he would be forced to seek refuge with one of Europe's Catholic princes. If the pope became the subject of a monarch, could this prince not influence the papacy to his advantage? This fear of being subordinated to secular power assumed pathological dimensions as temporal power became imperilled. The maintenance of theocratic government for the papacy and the church was non-negotiable. Catholics were expected to fight and lobby for the independence of the Papal States.

Once the Congress of Vienna in 1815 had redrawn the map of Europe, the pope survived as the last theocrat in Europe.[38] Princely archbishops and abbots of the Holy Roman Empire were divested of their sovereignty. Faced with the mounting forces of revolution, liberalism, socialism and eventually secularism, the papacy realised that it was living in a hostile environment. Napoleon's annexation of Rome in 1809–14 had shown that laymen could govern even the eternal city. Indeed, the populations of the Legations of Romagna had admired the efficient and well-ordered government forced on them by Napoleon.[39] When papal rule was re-imposed, they revolted against the *Papa-Re* with almost cyclical regularity.

The collapse of the Papal States may not have been preordained, but geography certainly did not help the papal cause. Situated right in the middle of the peninsula, the pope was surrounded by salivating neighbours not averse to increasing their domains at his expense. The papal monarchy increasingly found itself a pawn in a delicate diplomatic game between France and Austria.[40] The late arrival of Sardinia-Piedmont onto the scene ultimately proved fatal. Although the papacy would flirt with nascent Italian nationalism, during the 1840s it came to realise that the forces of national identity and cultural patriotism could backfire. In 1848 Pius IX transformed himself from the darling of liberal nationalists to the nemesis of all progress.[41] The pope did not become the figurehead of a federation of Italian states. Instead, he was surrounded by a modern, unitary secular state under the aegis of the Savoyard dynasty.

When Rome, in 1870, was invaded by the troops of the new kingdom of Italy the papacy refused to concede defeat. The pope entered self-imposed confinement in the Vatican, a district of Rome which covers less than a fifth of a square mile.[42] For fifty-nine years the Catholic church refused to acknowledge the existence of the Italian state.* The papacy dispossessed of its statehood would spend many fruitless years condemning and anathemising 'modernism'. If anything was new and progressive, the pope was unlikely to approve of it.[43] From the depths of the Vatican, popes precipitated a crisis of conscience for modern citizens. To whom did they owe ultimate allegiance, Christ's vicar or the nation?

This process was not merely clerical in nature. Pious Catholics across the globe resisted, with vehemence, attempts to confine their faith to the domestic and private sphere.[44] They were convinced that the papacy should be independent, and that the magisterium of the church should continue to have a role in law-making and public morality. As will be apparent, this book is not so much a history of religion, let alone an ecclesiastical history, but a contribution

---

* It could be argued that, until the pontificate of Paul VI during the 1960s, which abolished the papal secular court, the pope continued to behave as if nothing had changed. Paul VI, 'Lettera Apostolica Motu Proprio, Pontificalis Domus, viene cambiato l'ordinamento della casa pontificia,' 28 March 1968, online at: www.vatican.va/content/paul-vi/it/motu_proprio/documents/hf_p-vi_motu-proprio_19680328_pontificalis-domus.html [accessed 4 November 2020].

to the 'politics of religion'. The Protestant Reformation of the sixteenth century had been a theological quarrel about salvation with significant political repercussions.[45] There is an imperfect parallel between Luther's attack on the church and events during the age of revolutions. The revolutionaries had little interest in theology, let alone salvation; they wanted to establish heaven on earth. The control of politics was at the heart of the struggle that pitted the Catholic church against the modern state.

Such stakes were of the highest order and ultimate power the tantalising reward. For Catholics these two centuries were a chronicle of gradual and inexorable political decline and defeat. Having said this, the narrative that unfolds in these pages is not a simple tale of Catholic retreat before a secular advance. It should be remembered that the late-nineteenth-century state was itself riven by factionalism and growing socialist agitation. Catholics diffidently came to play the game by forming political parties and trade unions of their own.[46]

The biggest paradox is that, as the pope lost temporal ground, his spiritual powers became absolute. After 1870 several European countries aspired to a complete separation between church and state. Secular government lost interest in micro-managing the episcopacy and public worship. In the past, monarchs and the nobility had prevented the pope from controlling national church hierarchies and defining church teaching unilaterally. Papal authority, throughout the early modern period, had been diluted by the alliance of 'throne and altar'. The breakdown of this relationship emancipated the papacy spiritually. The culmination of this process was embodied in the First Vatican Council of 1870 which formally declared the pope infallible when speaking on matters of dogma.[47] While the loss of the Papal States was disastrous, it also represented an opportunity which the papacy seized with alacrity.

The process was painful as the loss of state protection significantly damaged the church's economic prosperity. Modern states, which sanction religious pluralism, have tended to confiscate ecclesiastical property and abolish tithes. This ensured that the First Estate no longer had the resources to mount a credible challenge to the authority of the state. Yet the price paid for cutting the umbilical cord that connected the church to the state was significant. Liberal governments could no longer justify interference when it came to religious questions. If freedom of conscience was absolute, then there was nothing to stop Catholics from opposing divorce and other matters that conflicted with the magisterium. Liberals may have deplored Catholic values, but could hardly silence Catholics' right to free speech. The age of revolutions challenged the church but undeniably released it from any allegiance to the state. The waning of monarchical and noble influence gave the papacy unprecedented freedom over the nomination of the episcopacy and clerical hierarchy. After 1903, the crowned heads of Europe finally lost their prerogative to veto papal conclaves (elections).

The nineteenth century reacted against the traumatic experience of revolution and Napoleonic conquest. It witnessed an impressive revival of Catholic fervour and devotion at a grassroots level.[48] For the privileged *ancien régime* clergy, engaging with its flock and ministering to souls had not always been a priority... indeed aristocratic bishops found it mildly distasteful. After 1815, the church rediscovered a 'mass market' for saints, relics, miracles and the re-enchantment of the world. The number of clerical vocations increased exponentially after experiencing a nose-dive during the 1790s.[49] It was a remarkable coincidence that this revival of Catholicism more or less coincided with the second wave of European imperialism during the second half of the nineteenth century.[50] Thousands of young priests, seminarians and missionaries literally marched before the troops that conquered colonies in Africa and the Far East. Catholicism had already been a global religion in the eighteenth century, but by the close of the nineteenth century its coverage reached almost every corner of the globe. It consolidated its pre-existing positions in South America and the Philippines by negotiating concordats with the post-imperial republics that emerged after the Latin American revolutions.[51]

Catholicism's eager collusion with Europe's 'civilising mission' certainly brought about unprecedented expansion. The church's complicity in the dark side and human cost of empire is hard to gauge with precision. To portray Catholicism's relationship with empire as purely evil is unhistorical. On the one hand its pastoral and humanitarian ethos meant that many missionaries were genuinely committed to improving the material conditions of the people they encountered outside Europe. Regrettably their evangelising priorities (with perhaps the exception of the Jesuits who had a proto-anthropological vocation) meant that missionary clergy generally did not believe that the animistic religions and cultures they were supplanting should be preserved, let alone understood.[52] Missionary work often brought medicine, food and education at the cost of compromising indigenous cultures. They simply did not understand, or turned a blind eye to, the fact their missionary activities made them complicit in an imperial project that was far from benign.

It should be clear that the Catholic Church's position during the age of revolutions is not an unambiguous tale of decline and fall nor one of renewal and regeneration. Both these tendencies emerged in the Church of Rome from 1700 to 1903. This book tells the paradoxical story of how the popes lost a kingdom but gained hundreds of millions of souls across both hemispheres. Catholicism burst forth from its European and Latin American heartlands to cover the planet. It was a traumatic experience for the church, which still haunts it today.

2

THE ALLIANCE OF THRONE
AND ALTAR, 1700–73

The Lion of St Mark fluttered in the breeze above Corfu, while its defenders sheltered behind the mighty ramparts of the Scarpone redoubt. They were a motley group of Venetian soldiers, German mercenaries and Greek irregulars. Most fearsome were the Schiavoni, whose colourful tunics and furs gave them the appearance more of a band of desperados than soldiers. Although their name is often translated as 'slave' in English this is a misapprehension. By the early eighteenth century they were Christian Slavs who came from the north-eastern coast of the Adriatic. Most were Dalmatian subjects of the Most Serene Republic of Venice.[1] They had opposed Muslim rule steadfastly for generations and fought in many European armies. Their dream was to expel the Ottoman empire from the Balkans.

In 1716 Venetian galleys had failed to repel the fleet of the *kapudan pasha* (grand admiral) which had penetrated the Corfu channel. The long-standing Venetian colony of Corfu now faced invasion. On 8 July flat-bottomed barges disembarked a large army on the island. According to contemporary sources, which are unreliable, it numbered around thirty thousand. Yet, the most redoubtable unit were the elite imperial Janissaries who were about four thousand strong.[2] Over the next few weeks, supplies and a powerful siege train were unloaded. The defensive walls and forts around Corfu were formidable. Despite this, it was clear that the forces of the Serenissima were severely outnumbered. Field Marshal Johann Matthias von der Schulenburg, who had fought alongside Marlborough and Prince Eugene against the armies of Louis XIV, commanded the defenders.[3] These totalled, at most, four thousand, and their numbers had to be supplemented by the arming of residents of the city. By 3 August, Corfu had been enveloped by the besieging army which, after several assaults, had succeeded in taking the suburbs. Now the engineers of the sultan dug trenches but proved unable to mine the walls of the city. Mortars rained down bombs on the terrified civilian population.

On 19 August 1716, the defenders of the great rampart of the Scarpone realised something was afoot. Venice had invested heavily in improving the defences of Corfu. Indeed, the outer walls of the city were reinforced and designed to be impervious to artillery fire. Yet the odds stacked against Schulenburg and his men were overwhelming. As the morning dawned, great clouds of dust and smoke were observed in the distance. This was followed by an intense artillery barrage. Emerging from the dust cloud could be glimpsed the ornate kaftans of the Janissaries. Their impressive *ak-börks*, or semi-conical hats, were observed getting into line. Then a blood-curdling cry was heard, and the enormous host of the sultan's finest troops launched themselves forward in a murderous frontal assault on the Scarpone.

Canum Hoca, the *kapudan pasha* commanding the sultan's troops, had promised 25 *reales* per Venetian head taken in the offensive.[4] The defenders rained down lethal volleys and used grapeshot to mow down the besiegers but, severely outnumbered, Venice's troops fell back from the ramparts towards the inner walls of the city. Schulenburg realised that a truly dangerous situation had arisen. If the Ottoman troops managed to hold the outer walls, then most of the city, excluding the citadel, was doomed to fall. In the meantime, the Ottomans had raised their crescent banners over the Scarpone, in triumph. Their celebration of victory was premature, however… the Venetians had a surprise in store. Unbeknownst to the Janissaries, the Scarpone had been mined and the fuse was lit. Soon hundreds of Ottomans were killed in a deafening explosion. This not merely led to many casualties but deeply compromised the besiegers' morale. Schulenburg decided to take advantage of the element of surprise. He drew his sword and led a thousand of his men in a desperate counterattack. Hundreds of Venetian soldiers fell in this strike, but they were determined to retake the Scarpone, which was theirs again by nightfall. Thus Schulenburg had commanded one of the few successful sorties and counterattacks in the history of early modern siege warfare.[5]

The Ottomans limped back to their camp and hid behind their trenches. Yet the situation for the Venetians remained grave. The defenders suspected that the fall of Corfu had not been prevented but merely postponed. The next day, menacing storm clouds gathered over the island. By noon the heavens opened, and unleashed a terrible torrential downpour. Soon it was followed by violent lightning strikes. This storm lasted for hours, and was so bad that the Ottoman trenches flooded, and soon turned into streams. Indeed, the besiegers had to abandon their earthworks and take shelter. One stray lightning bolt ignited some munitions, exacerbating the collapse in their morale.

For the next few days Venetian scouts spied a flurry of activity in the *kapudan pasha*'s camp. They feared that yet another assault was imminent.[6] Then, on 22 August, the Ottomans disappeared, having embarked during the night and departed Corfu. Initially Schulenburg, concerned that an ambush was being prepared, sent some Greek raiders on scouting expeditions. They found several stragglers abandoned by the sultan's forces in their haste to leave. These men confirmed that the decision to withdraw had been taken, and that the siege had been lifted. The reason for this move has never been satisfactorily explained. Perhaps Canum Hoca feared that a Habsburg army would soon invade Albania, and that he needed to relocate his army to the Greek mainland? Or was it that he had received reports that Spain, Naples, the Knights of Malta and the papacy had assembled a naval taskforce that would soon reach Corfu?[7] Regardless of the reason for their flight, the Ottomans abandoned their provisions, their munitions and their siege train. The deliverance of Corfu was seen as a miracle, and celebrated as a military triumph by the Serenissima. It was to be their last.

Antonio Vivaldi composed the oratorio *Juditha triumphans* to celebrate this victory. The Old Testament heroine Judith represented Venice's bravery, whereas the monster Holofernes symbolised Ottoman aggression. It ended with a rousing chorus: *Salve invicta Juditha formosa* (Hail unvanquished and proud Judith!).[8] Schulenburg was feted as the republic's saviour, receiving a generous pension and the title of Count of the Holy Roman Empire from Charles VI. On his death a statue of him was erected in Corfu where it still stands in the old fortress.[9]

Halting an Ottoman advance into the Adriatic was hailed as a providential sign of Catholicism's ability to prevail over apparently invincible foes, but as ever the reality was far more nuanced.[10] Schulenburg was a *condottiero* and a sword for hire, thus hardly the idealised hero of Catholic lore – he was a Protestant for starters! – not to mention that large numbers of his followers were Greek Orthodox with a sprinkling of Albanian Muslim irregulars thrown into the mix. Although Venice in its war retained Corfu, it lost most of the Peloponnese, which it had conquered only a few decades previously. This was not quite the unambiguous triumph presented in Vivaldi's oratorio.

Despite this sobering reality, there had been reasons for celebration for the papacy as the world entered the eighteenth century. Rome had weathered the storm of the sixteenth-century Reformation well and had checked the Ottoman advance in the Balkans.[11] Yet this consolidation of power was to prove superficial and brittle when placed under strain. The revolutionary conflagration that would erupt in France in 1789 was not a bolt of lightning from a clear blue sky, but the culmination of a process that had been under way for the better part of a hundred years. Seemingly loyal Catholic polities had been remorselessly and slowly gnawing at the power of the First Estate. Monarchical governments throughout the continent increasingly viewed the privileges and immunities of the clergy with irritation, seeing them as a roadblock to administrative efficiency.

In 1759 Naples' prime minister Bernardo Tanucci wrote of the clergy that: 'They are the cancer of humanity, presently occupied in avarice, laziness, and they make a nonsense of government. It almost seems as if they entered states to destroy them and oppose their fundamental laws.' A year later, his opinion had not improved, and he wrote that all priests and monks were '[t]he excrement of humanity, vicious and generally ignorant with little knowledge of theology or any works of intelligence'.[12] This statesman, despite his energetic prose, was no radical atheist nor an enemy of religion, but somebody who loathed the church's interference in politics and its opposition to rational reforms. During the Enlightenment, there was a growing belief that priests should be priests and stay out of politics.

Yet *ancien régime* popes were not just spiritual leaders but secular princes. During the eighteenth century their duties as rulers of the Papal States occupied much of their working hours. They had little time to be bishops to the diocese of Rome and minister to the faithful.[13] Even within the Papal States it was incredibly rare for ordinary folk ever to glimpse, let alone meet, the Holy Father. Only the citizens of Rome might hope to see the pope carried high above them on his *sedia gestatoria* or as a tiny red-white dot giving the solemn *urbi et orbi* ('to the city and the world') blessing from the loggias of Rome's many basilicas at Christmas and Easter.[14] While, in theory, the spiritual leadership of the church was supposed to consume the pope's every waking hour, in reality the secular responsibility of governing central Italy competed for the pope-king's limited time and resources. Separating the Vicar of Christ from the Italian prince was almost impossible. For early modern popes, these roles were fused and went to the very core of their office.

The papacy's central Italian concerns left the church open to constant accusations of a conflict of interest. Many wondered if, when the pope made policy decisions, they were designed to help the church, or whether he was looking out for the benefit of his own principality. In the world of diplomacy, the Holy See held the senior position of honour in European international relations (something that technically persists to the present day). During the Middle Ages, popes had acted as arbiters in international disputes.[15] Rome's *nuncios* (ambassadors) automatically became the highest-ranking diplomats in Catholic capitals. Given this position of international prestige and responsibility, papal diplomats and cardinal secretaries of state (foreign ministers) had to tread carefully when it came to decisions affecting war and peace. This burden was not something that the church found easy to resolve. Rome found it difficult to play the honest broker in disputes among Catholic sovereigns.

For example, Pope Clement XI had been particularly uncertain how to proceed during the War of the Spanish Succession, which was fought between 1701 and 1714. He initially supported Philip V, the Bourbon claimant to the Madrid throne and its vast South American empire. Midway through the conflict, Clement transferred his recognition to the Habsburg pretender, Archduke Charles, before changing his mind again and returning to Philip V.[16] Such diplomatic flip-flopping did little to reassure the chancelleries of Europe that the papacy had clear diplomatic policies. Decades later, during the 1740s, Benedict XIV found it equally difficult to decide what to do during the War of the Austrian Succession (1740–48).[17] Unlike Clement, he eventually made the wise choice of keeping the Holy See neutral in European conflicts.

Although neutrality today is a legitimate position, and one that is guaranteed by international law, that was not the case during the early modern period. From the perspective of eighteenth-century international relations, neutrality was viewed by princes as cowardly and dishonourable. It was often the case that belligerents refused to respect the immunity of those sitting on the sidelines.[18] Geography was especially unhelpful to the Papal States' desire to remain unaligned. Situated squarely in the centre of the peninsula, the papacy found itself in the unhappy position of forming a buffer zone between the Habsburgs in northern Italy and the Bourbons in Naples. The pope's domains were often devastated by armies on their way to conquer either Milan or Naples.[19] This made the pope's neutrality an impossibility and the economy of the Papal States was much exposed to military predation.

The relationship between Rome and the non-Catholic world remained fraught. The year 1697 had witnessed a notable success with the conversion of the Elector of Saxony, Augustus II (known as 'the Strong') from Lutheranism to Catholicism.[20] During the sixteenth century, the electors of Saxony had been patrons of Martin Luther and champions of the Reformation.* Their return to the Catholic fold in the eighteenth century was a propaganda triumph. Yet the dividends of this conversion turned out to be meagre for the papacy. The subjects of the Saxon elector remained staunchly Lutheran and refused to follow their sovereign's lead.[21] Augustus's conversion had been a matter of politics, rather than of conscience. To put forward his candidature for election to the throne of Poland, he needed Catholic support.[22] To paraphrase Henry IV, it was clear that Warsaw, like Paris, was worth a mass. The conversion of the Wettins of Saxony to Rome was not an isolated case, and thirty other German princes followed their example between 1648 and 1769.[23]

Some princes, like Elector Karl-Philipp of the Palatinate, took their family's Catholicism too seriously. In 1719, Karl-Philipp tried, with some measure of success, to make his Calvinist subjects' lives a nightmare. Their catechism was banned, and he demolished the partition wall that separated Catholics and Protestants in the Church of the Holy Spirit in Heidelberg.[24] This struck at the very heart of an agreement which had ensured that both Christian confessions could continue to use this church after the Thirty Years' War had ground to a stalemate. In response, the Protestant electors of Brandenburg and Hanover started closing Roman churches within their domains. Indeed, Frederick William II of Prussia gleefully sent grenadiers to dissolve the Catholic monastery of Hamersleben near Saxe-Anhalt.[25] The stage seemed set for renewed sectarian conflict in Germany. Sensibly, Charles

---

* Indeed, they emerged, after the Thirty Years War, as directors of the Corpus Evangelicorum, leaders of the Protestant princes of the Holy Roman Empire. See Peter H. Wilson, *The Holy Roman Empire: A Thousand Years of History* (London, 2016), pp. 129, 475; Andreas Kalipke, 'The Corpus Evangelicorum', in J. P. Coy, B. Marschke and D. Sabean (eds), *The Holy Roman Empire Reconsidered* (Oxford, 2010), pp. 228–47.

VI, as Holy Roman Emperor, demanded Karl-Philipp reverse his provocative policies in Heidelberg.

This confessional crisis of the 1720s highlighted just how fragile some of the religious compromises created by the Peace of Westphalia of 1648 remained. Some, though outwardly bizarre, were highly practical. For example, although Lubeck's bishop had converted to Protestantism during the Reformation, six of his cathedral canons were still guaranteed to be Catholics. Another anomaly, from our modern perspective, was the diocese of Osnabrück. Here, the office of prince-bishop alternated cyclically between Catholic and Protestant incumbents throughout the *ancien régime*.[26] This was because the population of this princely diocese was evenly divided between those loyal to Rome and those who looked to the Protestant house of Hanover for leadership. When Catholic incumbents died, Osnabrück tended to devolve to the younger scions of the Guelphic dynasty. Indeed, the last prince-bishop of Osnabrück was George III's son Frederick, the 'grand old' Duke of York (the ineffectual leader of the ten thousand men in the nursery rhyme).[27]

Beyond the continent, the papacy's relationship with the British archipelago was difficult. After 1713, Louis XIV had abandoned his support for the Catholic Stuart's claim to the British throne.[28] The 'old pretender', the uncrowned 'James III', left France and headed into exile in the Papal States, where he was recognised as King of Great Britain.[29] He was to spend the rest of his life in dreary exile, shifting between the ducal palace of Urbino and the fine Palazzo Muti in the Eternal City. For decades, the Curia held on to the forlorn hope that an uprising might be successful in restoring a Catholic monarch to the English throne. These hopes seemed to come to fruition with the accession of the German Hanoverians to the British crown in 1714.[30] This dynastic switch precipitated a Jacobite rebellion within a year. After the death of Louis XIV, this insurrection was suppressed easily as the court of Versailles refused to support the cause of the Catholic pretender with munitions and coin.

Despite this reverse, loyalists in the Scottish Highlands kept the torch of the Stuart claim burning bright. Thirty years later,

1745 saw a spate of highland rebellions, supported by the papacy, and supplied with weapons and cash by the French. This final attempt by James III and his son Charles to regain their lost throne definitively spelled an end to all dreams that Henry VIII's Reformation might ever be undone in Britain.[31] Protestantism was, by then, deep-rooted, and was not going to be overturned. No amount of scheming on the part of papal diplomatic agents was going to persuade the Protestants of Northern Europe to abandon their religious convictions and accept Rome's spiritual authority.

As already intimated, the advance of Islam had been checked. In 1683 the Polish King Jan Sobieski had pushed back a large Ottoman army laying siege to Vienna.[32] Never again would a Muslim power penetrate so deep into the heartlands of Christianity. Indeed, the eighteenth century saw the sultan's empire in retreat from the Balkans. Papal galleys and ships from the Knights of Malta joined the Venetian navy to patrol the Adriatic after the Ottoman empire failed to take Corfu in 1716.[33] Prince Eugene of Savoy's brilliant campaign of 1716–18 against the Turks achieved the Habsburg reconquest of Hungary.* Catholicism's drift southwards into the Balkans, although welcomed in Rome, brought with it logistical and monetary difficulties. The rebuilding of the Catholic Church in Hungary was a delicate process, in which the clergy were given significant representation in the government of the kingdom, and funds were put aside for the re-evangelisation of the patrimony of St Stephen. It was a reconstruction in which the church collaborated eagerly with the Habsburg state.[34]

The Treaty of Passarowitz, signed on 21 July 1718, saw the Austrian annexation of large portions of Bosnia and Serbia to their empire. These mainly Muslim and Orthodox lands resisted conversion to Rome. In the decade to come it became clear that the

---

* The Habsburg monarchy with the Treaty of Passarowitz in 1718 regained all of Hungary and conquered much of northern Serbia. Kenneth Meyer Setton, *Venice, Austria, and the Turks in the Seventeenth Century* (Philadelphia, 1991); Charles Ingrao, Jovan Pesalj, & Nikola Samardžić (eds), *The Peace of Passarowitz, 1718* (West Lafayette, IA, 2011); Karl A. Roider, *Austria's Eastern Question, 1700–1790* (Princeton, NJ, 1982), pp. 38–57; Aksan, *Ottoman Wars 1700-1870*, pp. 89–102.

Ottoman empire was far from a spent force. It had received severe wounds, but was far from vanquished and in fact sought revenge for the humiliations it had suffered in the early eighteenth century. The grand viziers of the Sublime Porte did not have to wait long. Indeed, the Austro-Turkish war of 1737–9 brought a significant resurgence of Ottoman military fortunes.[35] As a consequence of this disastrous conflict, the Habsburgs were forced to return the city of Belgrade and most of Serbia and Bosnia to Muslim rule.

Islam may have been beating a slow retreat from the Balkans, but the situation elsewhere saw little change. Throughout this time, on the shores of the Mediterranean the Barbary pirates continued raiding the coasts of southern Europe and capturing prisoners who were sold in the slave markets of Algiers and Tunis.[36] It must be said that since the mid-seventeenth century Mediterranean slave raids had been gradually declining. The Knights of St John did their best from their island base of Malta to counteract Muslim corsairs with their own acts of piracy and North African raids.[37] Yet both their resources and their galleys proved unequal to the task. It was left to religious orders in Istanbul and other Islamic cities to ransom prisoners and buy back slaves as best as they could from these corsairs.[38] To thwart Mediterranean piracy, the pope repeatedly faced calls for funding and military support. In 1737, Philip V of Spain levied taxes on the South American clergy, with papal approval, to help him in his campaign against the Berbers around Ceuta.[39] These military incursions and skirmishes into North Africa changed little and the population there remained committed to Islam.

Even those monarchies loyal to Rome were to experience significant conflict between church and state. The submission of these Catholic dynasties to the supremacy of the Holy See became increasingly grudging. Since the late seventeenth century, the competition that pitted European states and empires against each other had accelerated and grown more costly. The size of armies, and the bureaucracies needed to maintain them, had expanded exponentially.[40] The privileges of the First Estate were no mere irritant, but threatened to compromise the ability of Catholic states to compete with more fiscally streamlined and centralised Protestant monarchies, like those of Great Britain and Prussia.[41] Statesmen in Lisbon, Madrid, Paris, Naples and Vienna expressed frustration with clerical immunity from prosecution, administrative prerogatives, canon law and tax exemption. In theory, all questions relating to the clergy and canon law could be appealed to Rome. These ecclesiastical freedoms blunted the efficacy of administrative, judicial, tax and social reforms. The cohesion of states was undermined by the existence of a First Estate whose members had few qualms about opposing change.

The Council of Trent (1545–63) had grandiloquently asserted the pope's primacy over the church. Yet Rome's supremacy was accepted by neither the crowned heads of Europe nor the regional episcopates beyond the Alps. The Parlements of France, the appellate courts of the kingdom, had refused to register and approve the canons of Trent; the Spanish monarchy in a similar fashion had quibbled over details of papal control; and the prince-bishops of the Holy Roman Empire in Germany jealously guarded their autonomy from Rome.[42] Indeed many bishops considered the pope to be first among equals, and resented any interference from the Curia within their own dioceses. Not only was the First Estate seen as a roadblock to reform, within the monarchies of Europe, many bishops resented the pope's jurisdiction over their dioceses. This was especially the case when it came to those monastic, mendicant and Jesuit orders who were directly answerable to Rome. The regular clergy's independence from diocesan authorities infuriated bishops.[43] By sidestepping episcopal authority, the Jesuits, in particular, made powerful enemies throughout their existence. This was to have disastrous consequences for them as the papacy and monarchies of Europe wrestled for ultimate control of the church.

For all the confident triumphalism of papal rhetoric, and the apparent magnificence of Rome, the papacy's room for political manoeuvre was in practice very limited. Simply put, the Curia could not afford to alienate the Catholic princes of Europe. For a series of complex reasons, mainly to do with venality such as the sale of public offices, the eighteenth century witnessed a downturn in papal finances.[44] Given that popes had huge spending commitments, not just in central Italy but around the globe, they could not afford to lose support and revenue in Europe. Every acrimonious dispute with a prince could severely damage the church's authority and threaten its financial security. The prime example of such a crisis erupted during the 1680s, between Louis XIV of France and Pope Innocent XI.[45] The Sun King had extended his royal rights, unilaterally, over a small number of vacant dioceses. He claimed the prerogative to administer and distribute the revenues of vacant dioceses pending the appointment of a new incumbent. This led to protests from the Curia and a denial that Louis possessed any such right. Eventually, Innocent IX had refused to confirm the crown's candidates to fill these vacant dioceses.

So incensed was the king by Rome's refusal to invest new bishops, that in 1682 an assembly of the Gallican (French) church was summoned. Here, four articles were proclaimed that ultimately asserted the French church's independence from Rome. This assertion of autonomy was known as Gallicanism, and was by no means a purely French phenomenon. The bishops of France, in their assembly, had reiterated that church councils superseded papal authority, and that the king of France could not be excommunicated by Rome. It was re-emphasised that only royal assent and a national council of bishops could give papal decrees force of law in the kingdom. In 1693, after a decade of mutual recriminations, a new pope, Innocent XII, found a compromise which allowed all parties to climb down. In return for having his episcopal candidates confirmed by Rome, Louis XIV and his bishops agreed to mothball the four Gallican articles.[46] These articles would experience a remarkable afterlife during the Napoleonic empire.

To an extent, this decade-long standoff proved to be a storm in a teacup. After all, in 1685 the French crown had revoked the Edict of Nantes, which had granted limited toleration to Protestants.[47] This gave rise to a vicious campaign of persecution that resulted in a mass exodus of French Huguenot refugees to Britain, Holland and further afield.[48] Despite his dispute with the papacy, Louis XIV showed himself committed to imposing Catholicism on his unwilling subjects. The regalian crisis of the 1680s highlighted the fact that the so-called alliance of throne and altar was not quite an equal partnership. The Gallicanism of the 1682 declaration revivified and awakened the medieval notion of Conciliarism.[49]

The roots of this concept lay in the fourteenth century, when, for complex reasons, a Great Schism had emerged in the West.[50] The Council of Constance (1414–18) had established the principle that an ecumenical council of all bishops superseded the authority of the pope.[51] During the sessions of this council, two popes were deposed and a third was elected to take over the reins of the church, thus putting an end to the Schism. Ever since this time, the papacy had tried to downplay the events at Constance, and indeed the theory of Conciliarism was deemed to be tainted by heresy.[52] One of the key arguments running through this book is that, during the eighteenth century, a neo-conciliarist movement within European Catholicism challenged the authority of the pope and the centralising tendencies of the Curia. Its vision of a more locally accountable church, with limited interference from Rome, appealed to monarchs across the continent. Princes tacitly encouraged such Gallican and conciliarist tendencies among their local episcopates. Neo-conciliarism put sustained pressure on the symbiotic relationship which characterised the *ancien-régime* alliance of throne and altar.

The church legitimated royal rule, and the privileges of nobility, in return for protection, economic benefits, immunity from secular law and a monopoly on public worship. One solution which allowed the church to continue to benefit from this arrangement was to make concessions. This was achieved through a series of concordats and agreements that bestowed on the crowned heads of Europe the right of nomination for vacant dioceses, prestigious benefices and monastic houses. The best example of this was the concordat concluded between Ferdinand VI of Spain and Pope Benedict XIV in 1753. Rome received a massive indemnity of 1.5 million *scudi* in return for eye-watering concessions. Henceforth the king of Spain would have the right of appointment over almost all bishops within Iberia and its empire. Furthermore, papal dues, levies and annuities within the territories of the Spanish monarchy were abolished, sharply reducing the income of the

Holy See.[53] This agreement was by no means unique, and similar arrangements were concluded with Naples, Sardinia, Portugal, Venice and the Habsburgs.

European monarchs used church patronage to reward and maintain the loyalty of their own elites. Reading the surnames of *ancien-régime* bishops in France and under the Habsburg monarchy is a bit like perusing a 'who's who' of the European aristocracy. By 1789, the entire French episcopate was staffed by bishops of noble pedigree.[54] The situation in Germany was similar but the reigning Catholic dynasties were losing their grip on the ecclesiastical electorates and prince-bishoprics of the Reichskirche. By the twilight of the eighteenth century in much of Europe the First and Second Estates had fused together to such an extent as to become indistinguishable. Only Spain and Portugal continued to have an episcopate that was permeable to candidates of common birth.

Prelates still had the ability to wield not just influence and prestige but real power. The seventeenth century was renowned as the age of the great cardinal prime ministers such as Richelieu and Mazarin. Their careers were romanticised when they became the villains of the novels of Alexander Dumas, but clergymen continued to be appointed to ministerial office well beyond 1700: no fewer than three cardinals, Guillaume Dubois, André Hercule de Fleury and Étienne-Charles de Loménie de Brienne, served as principal ministers of the French monarchy.[55] The truffle-munching, culinarily dextrous and militarily astute Cardinal Giulio Alberoni guided the Spanish monarchy's policies for the better part of the 1710s. In 1721, accusations of sodomy put an end to his career.[56] Cardinal József Batthyány, prince-primate of Hungary and Archbishop of Esztergom, was the chief adviser of Maria-Theresa on Magyar affairs. His influence at court and Habsburg politics extended far beyond his family's Hungarian heartlands.[57] Across the continent prelates served as ministers and provincial governors and presided over estates.

Within the church, political influence was not just a matter of ministerial office. Some of the shadiest figures in these realms were the royal confessors.[58] Within the dark confines of the confessional the monarchs of Europe unburdened their consciences, seeking forgiveness for their public and private transgressions. With a sexual athlete like Louis XV, who established his own private brothel in the grounds of Versailles, one imagines that confession must have been an almost full-time occupation.[59] As the Jesuits monopolised the position of royal confessors, they were suspected of unduly influencing royal policies. Such suspicions were not without foundation, as these clergymen often sat on royal councils and advised the monarch on appointments to important offices.[60]

Throughout Europe, reigning dynasties tried to outdo each other in competitive displays of piety and religious fervour. Monarchs needed a dedicated clerical establishment at court to demonstrate their devotion to God. Their royal chaplains and almoners beyond their pastoral office also played significant political roles.[61] The Habsburgs, with their victories against Protestantism and Islam, felt especially beholden to divine providence for their survival and prosperity. The Holy Roman Emperors were one of the most pious dynasties in Europe, creating an endless routine of prayers, masses, worship of relics and processions. Their court was so priest-ridden, and so centred around liturgical celebrations, that its atmosphere was labelled *pietas austriaca* (Austrian piety).[62] Such conspicuous religiosity was meant to underpin the Habsburg claim that they were the pre-eminent dynasty on the continent.

In France, the Bourbons had no wish to be outdone in this race towards piety. They claimed to have been endowed with miraculous powers by God. Their coronation ceremony saw them anointed with holy oil from the ampule of St Remigius. This chrism had the magical property that although it was depleted with each crowning, it would miraculously replenish itself on the eve of each forthcoming coronation. Sceptical *philosophes* suspected, with some justification, that the Abbot of Saint-Remi in Rheims surreptitiously topped up the holy ampule, entrusted to his stewardship, on the eve of royal investitures.

According to legend, this sacred ampule had been brought down from heaven by a dove and used to anoint the barbarian King Clovis as the first Christian king of France.[63] Ever since then the king of France (like the British monarchs until the reign of Queen Anne) had claimed to have the miraculous power to heal a glandular affliction called *scrofula* or the King's Evil.[64] There was one major drawback to this, in that monarchs needed to be in a state of grace, that is absolved of all sin, in order to perform this royal miracle. Given Louis XV's notorious sexual activities outside of marriage, it was often the case during his reign that touching for the King's Evil was postponed. This caused a public scandal and drew negative public commentary.[65]

The growing influence of science and medicine increasingly made the practice seem pointless at best and superstitious at worst. By the 1690s when William of Orange became King of England, he refused to utter the formula 'the king touches you, but God cures you when healing the scrofulous. Allegedly on the only occasion William performed this ritual he declared: 'God give you better health, [...] and more sense.'[66] The last time a French king touched for the King's Evil was at Charles X's coronation in Rheims in 1825, though few were convinced of its efficacy after decades of revolution.[67] But in its heyday, the ritual had displayed the extent to which the crown leant heavily on religion to reinforce its authority and sanction its divine right to rule.

As must be clear, the price paid by the crown for this ecclesiastical legitimation was high and, as the eighteenth century progressed, bureaucrats came to question whether it was worth paying. Not only was the church exempt from all taxation, but it also was entitled to levy tithes on the revenues of the peasantry.[68] In many cases, bishops and monasteries were feudal lords and vast landowners. They held the right to dispense justice on their lands as secular lords of the manor. Church courts like the *officialités, konsistorium, offizialat* and inquisitions imposed canon law on Catholic populations.[69] Everywhere in Europe there was next to no separation between God's law and man's law. Cases like that of the Chevalier de la Barre, whose punishment for blasphemy in 1766 was to have his tongue ripped out of his mouth before he was decapitated, his lifeless corpse being then publicly burnt, certainly made many question why a beneficent god demanded such brutal retribution.[70]

Six days after the chevalier's death, the eloquent philosopher and polemicist François-Marie Arouet, better known as Voltaire, took up the cause. He denounced in print the horrific execution of de la Barre at Abbeville and called for civilisation to reject such barbarism. He sent his pamphlet to the great Milanese penal reformer the Marchese Cesare Beccaria, who had advocated for the abolition of capital punishment and judicial torture.[71] Sadly this plea for humanity did precious little for the unfortunate and very dead Chevalier de la Barre. Freedom of conscience was to develop slowly in this period, and Catholicism always advocated against any toleration of heresy, paganism and, worst of all, atheism. This goal was greatly aided by pre-publication censorship, over which the church wielded much influence. The Index of prohibited books had the force of law in Portugal, Spain and Rome.[72] In Paris, the theologians of the Sorbonne advised the Parlements on which books to condemn and publicly burn.[73] It was expected that every pious Catholic would avoid 'evil' books that went against church teaching.

Thanks to the illicit book trade, which was adept at smuggling across borders, the Index issued by the Inquisition was often seen as a list of interesting and exciting items that should be read, exactly the opposite to its intended purpose. Benedict XIV, who was a notable scholar in his own right, found the business of banning books painful.[74] He was slow to condemn the pathbreaking 'spirit of the laws' by his friend and correspondent, the jurist Charles-Louis de Secondat, Baron de Montesquieu. Even when it came to that monument of sceptical learning, Diderot and d'Alembert's *encyclopédie,* he was hesitant. He admired its ambition to record and catalogue the sum of human knowledge. However, its secular and at times anticlerical entries made tacit toleration of the work an impossibility. But it was also under Benedict XIV's reign that a great miscarriage of justice was corrected. Galileo Galilei's works were removed from the Index, but without fanfare.[75] It would take until the twentieth century for a formal rehabilitation of the Pisan astronomer and his vindication of the Copernican celestial system to come from the Vatican.

Despite Benedict's gentle loosening of censorship, not all governments matched his humanitarian spirit during the Age of Enlightenment. Inquisitions in Rome, Portugal and Spain continued to operate with varying degrees of zeal.[76] *Autos da fé* in which heretics were publicly executed, banished or forced to recant had been important ceremonial occasions in Iberia and its empire. During the first half of the eighteenth century, Portuguese monarchs increased their attendance at these grisly public events.[77] Such elaborate rituals and exemplary punishments were intended to display the restoration of harmony to Catholic society. Audiences watched these awesome spectacles of divine retribution as if God's judgement were unfolding before their very eyes. The church's elites, in conjunction with the crown, restored order and unanimity to the community by removing and punishing those wayward individuals who, inspired by Satan, had challenged the truth and sown dissent amongst the god-fearing. The inquisitor, in the exercise of his duties, was a high-ranking dignitary, as his authority to impose orthodoxy was delegated from the pope.[78] However, throughout the early modern period, the Iberian monarchies tightly directed and supervised these church courts. Papal authority over these tribunals was relatively light and symbolic (except for the Holy Office in Rome).

It is assumed, among scholars, that during the eighteenth century the Inquisition was in terminal decline.[79] While on the whole this may be true, at a regional level the picture is far more complex. In Spain the number of inquisitors, aided by their lay 'familiars' (staff), decreased substantially, but in Portugal the numbers of personnel shot up between the 1750s and the 1770s.[80] Although this increase still awaits an anglophone study, it could be speculated that it might have to do with the fact that Paulo António de Carvalho e Mendonça, the Grand Inquisitor, was the brother of the Portuguese prime minister Pombal. This powerful prelate, who posthumously became a cardinal, used his inquisitorial office to keep in check his brother's enemies and critics.[81]

The turning point came with the great Lisbon earthquake of 1 November 1755. Violent tremors began at 9.40 a.m. and flattened nearly 80 per cent of buildings in the city in minutes. Although many survived this initial catastrophe, wildfire spread throughout the city killing many who were trapped beneath the rubble and asphyxiating many more with its fumes. Panic spread, as much of the population fled toward the docks and open areas of the city centre, unaware that the epicentre of the earthquake had occurred off the coast. Three successive tsunami waves smashed into the beleaguered city, crushing and drowning those unfortunate enough to have headed for the port. It is calculated that as much as a quarter of the city's population of 200,000 perished in this apocalypse.[82]

The randomness and horror of this natural disaster horrified educated Europeans. It seemed impossible to believe that a major European capital could be flattened in a matter of minutes. It inspired Voltaire to write his caustic and biting novella *Candide*. In one famous scene the hero of the story found himself in Lisbon after the earthquake.[83] In a vicious satirical scene the Inquisition was determined to find scapegoats to blame for the disaster. They seized a Basque man who had married his godmother, and two Jews who refused to eat bacon. Candide and his tutor, Dr Pangloss, were also arrested, in the words of the author 'the one for speaking and the other for listening with an air of approval'. Then, this diverse group of unfortunate victims, excluding Candide, were executed in an *auto de fé* to placate the angry God who caused the ground to shake. A fresh earthquake immediately followed the execution of these unfortunates, thus proving either that God had been unimpressed with the human sacrifice offered to him or that natural disasters had little to do with the supernatural.[84] Voltaire's Lisbon sketch, brilliant as it was, exaggerated and was highly unfair in describing the church's reaction. There is little evidence that the Portuguese Inquisition indiscriminately rounded up scapegoats in the aftermath of the earthquake to placate a vengeful God.

In some ways, the opposite occurred as the earthquake gave the secular authorities an opportunity to clip the wings of the clergy. The Milanese Jesuit Gabriele Malagrida had been a missionary in Brazil. Here, his reputation for saintliness and preaching had brought him to the attention of the royal court. He was summoned to Lisbon where his fame and reputation grew. Very unwisely, after the earthquake he began to preach that this disaster had occurred due to the sinfulness of the Portuguese government and the dubious morals of its chief minister Pombal. This denunciation from the pulpit displeased and offended the secular authorities. They soon saw a remarkable opportunity to use this Italian Jesuit's loose tongue to settle old scores, and tighten the government's grip on power. Malagrida had formed a close friendship with the Távora family. Three years after the earthquake King Joseph I was returning home after spending the evening at the Távora palace. Suddenly some masked men approached the carriage in the dead of night and fired three shots.[85] The king escaped this attempted assassination, but he had been injured in the arm and was badly shaken.

Pombal persuaded him to use this event to launch a counter-strike against the restive clergy and nobility of the realm. Under torture, two of the assassins claimed that the Marques of Távora had organised the failed regicide. Malagrida's friendship with this nobleman was enough to persuade the Inquisition to arrest him and interrogate him on suspicion of colluding in the failed assassination. A lengthy period of imprisonment broke Malagrida down, as he reported experiencing a series of visions and disturbing nightmares. The inquisitors used these as proof that their victim held non-canonical views about religion and theology. After a dubious trial, Malagrida was found guilty of heresy.[86] On 21 September 1761 he was garrotted and then burned in the Rossio square of Lisbon.

This affair had little to do with 'real' heresy, but had provided a pretext for Pombal's government to settle old scores against its enemies. Malagrida had the uncanny ability to say the wrong thing at the wrong time in the wrong place, and was too tempting a victim to release. His association with the Távora family and the Jesuit order made him a perfect scapegoat through which the supremacy of the crown over the nobility and clergy could be reasserted. For the rest of his time in power, Pombal and his grand-inquisitor brother reined in the Inquisition. After 1770, it was no longer permitted to investigate the *limpeza de sangue* in Portugal.[87] This dubious legal process had allowed the Inquisition to seek out individuals with Jewish or other non-Christian ancestry. If a person was found to have Jewish blood, they were considered suspect and lost what few legal safeguards they possessed. Their property could be confiscated, and they could be arrested and detained indefinitely.[88] It had been a barbaric instrument of early modern anti-semitism whose abolition was long overdue. In the Iberian peninsula the Inquisition was declining as an independent institution, and would stagger onwards into the nineteenth century.

Elsewhere during the Age of Enlightenment, monarchs gradually dispensed with this ecclesiastical court altogether. Between 1720 and 1780, many princes throughout the Italian peninsula refused to allow the Inquisition to try their subjects and disbanded the court within their domains. The decrees abolishing the Inquisition had little to do with the barbarity of its punishments, let alone enlightened values. The texts which abolished the institution in Italy focused instead on the issue of jurisdiction. For eighteenth-century rulers it was wrong for ecclesiastical laws to be applied independently of the state's secular laws.[89] In the end, it was a question of ultimate authority rather than humanitarianism that sealed the Inquisition's fate. In Spain and Portugal, despite a brief interruption during Napoleon's invasions, the Inquisition would continue to operate throughout the 1820s, only to be finally abolished in 1834 by a liberal government.[90] Within the Papal States, the Holy Office (the local name for the Inquisition) continued to exercise its jurisdiction until 1870, when the fall of Rome to the armies of the kingdom of Italy put an end to its powers.[91]

Although these states reasserted their monopoly power over justice, the imposition of Catholicism's monopoly over public worship was still enforced by them. Failure to keep holy the sabbath or other minor religious infractions could lead to fines and other punishments. With divorce forbidden in Catholic Europe, the only means of exiting an unhappy union was annulment or separation. This process was exceedingly rare, slow and expensive, and one could expect massive delays as these cases often needed to be referred to Rome for final adjudication.[92] In most cases, a legal separation of property and persons was the best that unhappy spouses could hope to achieve. Women were at a distinct disadvantage when it came to retaining custody of children in disputes with their husbands.[93] The only upside was that, before the French Revolution, female plaintiffs in many European jurisdictions retained some control over their dowry through complex marriage contracts.[94]

Another important administrative function that the church undertook was the maintenance of the civil registers. The secular state delegated the task of recording births, marriages and deaths to parish priests. An individual's entire civil existence was contingent on being Catholic. Protestants and Jews living in western and southern Europe had little hope of official recognition in these parish registers. Their baptisms, *bar/bat mitzvahs* and marriages were considered null and void. It was only with the emergence of edicts of toleration during the 1780s in the Habsburg realms and France that non-Catholics started gaining some measure of recognition from the state.[95] Throughout the eighteenth century, ecclesiastical authorities continued to contribute actively to the administration of the state. However, this participation came to be questioned by ministers, bureaucrats and jurists who wondered whether the clergy possessed the competence, and reforming values, necessary to carry this administrative burden. As state power increased, and laws slowly came to be reformed, they freed themselves from the strictures of canon law and ecclesiastical courts.

The other great foundation of ecclesiastical power was landholding. In Catholic Europe the church could own anywhere from 10 to 20 per cent of agricultural land. Given that most European economies of the time were agrarian, it meant that about a fifth of the European economy was tax-exempt and beyond state control. In cities, this per centage was often higher, given that cathedral closes, prebends and confraternities controlled massive real-estate portfolios including houses, buildings and commercial properties. If you were a city tenant in the early modern world, it was likely that your landlord would be holy mother church. Throughout Europe, bishops and archbishops controlled wealth that was the equivalent to the GDP of small principalities. The archbishops of Paris, Rheims and Strasbourg commanded revenues that ran to hundreds of thousands of French livres.[96] This was by no means unique. The archbishop of Toledo had an annual income of millions of *reales* and the bishop of Krakow earned a million *złotys* a year from his properties.[97] But there were significant geographical and regional variations in the First Estate's landholding patterns. In France and Spain about 15 per cent of all arable lands was held by the church but, as this was prime real estate, its economic value was probably much higher than these estimates suggest. These two realms each had a population of 200,000 clergymen.[98] While this may not seem surprising, it should be borne in mind that throughout the eighteenth century the population of Spain was half that of France, so the per capita concentration of priests in Iberia was remarkably high. The situation reached its apogee in Italy: in Bologna, at the heart of the papal legations, up to 10 per cent of the city's population had taken religious vows.[99] You literally could not swing a cat without hitting a priest in this town.

Although the Holy Roman Empire had seen the secularisation of much ecclesiastical property during the Reformation, the church of Rome still held about 12 per cent of all German land. This allowed the Reichskirche, or imperial church, to control the selection of about 10 per cent of deputies sent to the imperial diet.[100] Even in Poland, at the very margins of the Catholic world, the church owned roughly 14 per cent of all land. The Polish church was atypical, possessing around eight thousand parish priests outnumbered by over seventeen thousand monks and nuns, who dominated the clerical landscape on the banks of the Vistula.[101] The *Szlachta* (Polish nobility) paid more in tithes to the church than they did in taxation to the state.

Fiscal immunity, the power to levy taxes and massive property investments made the church an extremely attractive career for ambitious men. Second sons of the nobility, or those unsuited for the military life, were often selected to take holy orders and eventually secure a bishopric. Until the mid-seventeenth century, a handful of families in the Holy Roman Empire monopolised all the top ecclesiastical jobs.[102] By the 1750s, the Wittelsbachs, Habsburgs and other Catholic royal families were experiencing a shortage of sons. This meant that the scions of free imperial knights and other lesser nobles could grab lucrative ecclesiastical preferment for themselves. It was hardly a democratisation of the church, given that proof of nobility in Germany was incredibly rigorous. Even cathedral canons had to prove that all their great-grandparents had been noble before taking their seats in the chapter.[103] But many commoners too sought ecclesiastical preferment. Bright young men used the good education provided by the church to launch brilliant political and intellectual careers. A lack of vocation was no impediment, nor was chastity rigorously enforced. The brother of the last king of Poland, Michał Jerzy Poniatowski, archbishop of Gniezno and primate of all Poland, sired some remarkably successful illegitimate offspring despite his vow of sexual abstinence.[104]

Hierarchies within the regional churches were often murky, and conflicts of authority common. For example, the prince-archbishop of Salzburg, patron of the Mozart family, was not only a sovereign in his own right, he also held the title of *Primas Germaniae* (primate of Germany).[105] This caused much resentment, given that the archbishop-electors of Mainz and of Trier claimed this title too. The incumbent of Mainz also held the honorific position of arch-chancellor of Germany which he claimed made him de facto head of the German church.[106]

Given the autonomy, privileges and complexity of the ecclesiastical principalities on the Rhine it is not surprising that a distinct tradition of independence from Rome emerged. Although the Council of Trent had banned pluralism, that is the holding of more than one diocese by the same man, its practice was common throughout these territories. Across the Rhine in France, the situation was equally fraught. The archbishop of Lyons flaunted the grandiloquent title of Primate of All Gaul.[107] His claims to leadership of the Gallican church were contested by his colleague in Rheims, who styled himself Primate of Belgian Gaul, and the archbishop of Rouen, who held the title of Primate of Normandy. In 1696 the archbishop of Rouen sued his counterpart in Lyons to assert his independence. After years of wrangling, he won his court case in 1703.[108] Despite this, French archbishops failed to establish a clear chain of command during the eighteenth century, and the papacy dared not interfere. Only the challenge of revolution managed to establish an unprecedented unity of purpose and coordination among French bishops, but by 1790, it was too late.[109] Only the pope's title of Primate of Italy seems to have been uncontroversial and accepted by all.

Another major source of power, prestige and wealth was the abbeys scattered across Catholic Europe. Noblemen and women were keen to become abbots and abbesses of these institutions. Through a system known as holding an abbey *in commendam*, they could technically oversee a monastery without ever having to reside with their brother monks.[110] The great abbeys of Melk, Sankt-Gallen, Cluny, St Vaast, Remiremont, Fontevrault and Lubiąż were miniature cities with their own cottage industries. Indeed, champagne and Chartreuse Verte were discovered accidentally by monks during the eighteenth century.[111] Dom Perignon's discovery, that a second fermentation gave white wine a fizz, was perhaps a happier invention than the Carthusian green syrup that produces some of heaviest hangovers known to humankind. Unsurprisingly, the great dynasties of Europe competed to control these monastic organisations. Abbots lived in Madrid, Vienna or Paris enjoying the life of *grand seigneurs* without ever having to submit themselves to St Benedict's strict rule of silence, prayer and toil.[112]

In Spain, monasteries were so highly prized that the king established royal residences in no fewer than a dozen monastic houses. Indeed, Philip II's palace monastery of the Escorial became the prototype for a vision of governance that fused church with state.[113] It was so beloved by the kings of Spain that its crypt became their final resisting place. When the Habsburgs lost Spain after 1713, Charles VI sought to recreate the baroque piety and monasticism of his lost Iberian court. He decided to build a replica that would rival the Escorial at Klosterneuburg.[114] What survives of the monastery today represents only a quarter of Charles VI's final project, and demonstrates just how much value the Habsburgs placed on creating a quasi-monastic royal court. Yet piety did not always guide dynastic calculations over monasteries. Elsewhere, the case of the Comte de Clermont, who died in 1771, emphasises just how much the system could be abused. He was a younger son of the Prince of Condé, who was a cousin of the French king. In recognition of his high birth, he received the abbotship *in commendam* of several monasteries. This included St Germain des Prés in Paris, which was the richest monastic institution in the world.[115] His revenues may have exceeded even those of the archbishop of Paris. Despite his clerical status (which did not permit him to shed blood), Clermont had received a dispensation from Pope Clement XII to lead armies in the field. He was equally renowned for his love of beautiful women and, perhaps more surprisingly, became the Grand Master of all regular freemasons in France. As the ecclesiastical historian John McManners joked, the stone mausoleum he built for his pet monkey was the closest he ever came to exercising his clerical vocation.[116] He further compromised himself by procuring an abbey for one of his illegitimate children. Certainly, such scandal did not serve the church well, and brought the entire system of monasticism into disrepute.

Although the church enjoyed vast wealth, there were huge disparities of income. Some bishops, like those of Vence, Dole, Savona and Sarzana, lived abject lives of near poverty. Lower down the pyramid of the First Estate, innumerable parish priests were only marginally better off than the peasants to whom they preached. Some rural parishes on the peripheries of the early modern state were so poor that bishops and other richer parishes had to make up for the shortfall of funds.[117] These parish priests resented their poverty and their lack of resources when it came to ministering to the souls entrusted to their care. As the century progressed, there was a widening gulf between the episcopacy and monastic elite that monopolised power within the church and the parish clergy and flock on the peripheries, who felt sorely neglected. To make matters worse there was a growing culture clash between the well-educated priests who emerged from well-funded seminaries and their predominantly illiterate congregations. One of the chief aims of the Counter Reformation had been to produce intellectually rigorous priests who would disprove Protestant allegations that Catholic clergymen were theologically ignorant and morally depraved. Under the influence of the sixteenth-century archbishop of Milan, St Carlo Borromeo, new seminaries rose throughout Europe. They aimed to produce less superstitious, more theologically adept and spiritually engaged clergymen.[118]

This attempt to rationalise faith and make it an instrument of self-control against human weakness was hardly popular. Another element of Borromean reforms was to get rid of the 'local boys' phenomenon. Zealous bishops knew that it was a bad idea to send newly trained priests back to the parishes in which they had been born and raised. This could create conflicts of interest in favour of family, friends and local superstitions. The Counter Reformation wanted priests to be the stormtroopers of a rational, disciplined religiosity. The aim was to establish a clergy that would truly instruct congregations in the truths and dogmas of the Catholic faith.[119]

A good example of such reforms was the confessional, a piece of religious technology that only emerged after the end of the sixteenth century. In medieval Christianity confession was a public spectacle.[120] Before receiving communion at Easter, individuals presented themselves before their community and freely confessed their transgressions and sought forgiveness from their neighbours. The sacrament of confession served the anthropological function of restoring peace.[121] It was a ritual whereby resentments and old scores could be settled harmoniously. The physical confessional and its secrecy tried to eliminate such public functions. Here, divided by a screen covered with a grille, the anonymous penitent came to confess his or her sins directly to God. The priests acted as mediators for divine mercy. Penitents were protected by anonymity so that priests would bestow a penance and judge the case impartially.

The diffusion of this practice was slow across Europe and would only become widespread during the eighteenth century. Communities did not really understand the benefits of communing directly with God and resented priests' inquisitorial role in the darkness of the confessional.[122] As every Catholic knows well, the confessor has the right to enquire further if he suspects the penitent is lying or withholding information. By exposing one's secrets and guilt publicly, medieval confession restored harmony to the village cosmos. The Counter Reformation transformed the priest into a living receptacle of one's darkest and most shameful secrets. Although the seal of the confessional is unbreakable, church courts were filled with complaints of gossipy and drunk clergymen who, in a moment of weakness, had let slip what they had heard in secret.[123] Equally, though the priest might not see who he was confessing he could make an educated guess through hearing the voice. Travelling friars-mendicant were popular confessors, since they passed through villages quickly and sinners could unburden their souls unheard by the prejudiced ears of their parish priests. Local clergy deeply resented travelling friars, who took away their near-monopoly in the investigation and eradication of sin.

Such new practices, which sought to internalise the faith, created something of a rift between clergy and congregation. The diary of the eighteenth-century parish priest Christophe Sauvageon epitomises this tension. He was a Doctor of Theology, but due to a lack of patronage was sent to the parish of Sennely-en-Sologne, which was then something of a backwater south of the Loire valley. This village truly represented the Styx for poor Sauvageon, who felt like an anthropologist studying a 'primitive' tribe when he first encountered his fierce-looking parishioners.[124] Their strange dialect, and constant requirement that he bless livestock, tried his patience. He dismissed them as 'baptised idolaters'. For a priest trained in the nuances of the theology of St Paul and St Augustine the superstitions and folk beliefs of his parishioners were close to paganism. When he hid a particularly obscene statue of St Anthony of Padua, his decision proved unpopular and sparked a riot in the parish. Poor Sauvageon was besieged in his rectory for some time.[125] His university education made it difficult for him to relate to the ordinary lives of his parishioners. They wanted him to mediate with those supernatural forces that could bring good harvests and protect their livestock. For ordinary Catholics his task was to forgive their minor transgressions and provide reassurance that salvation awaited them after a life of hard toil. The latest interpretations of Augustinian theology, with its emphasis on predestination, only brought confusion into their prosaic lives. They wanted compassion not rigour.[126]

This seeping friction between many priests and their congregations was symptomatic of a subterranean conflict within the church which had been unleashed a half century earlier. At its heart lay the ideas of Cornelius Jansen, Bishop of Ypres, which were mainly collected in his posthumous book *Augustinus* of 1640.[127] This remarkably dull theological work would set the seventeenth and eighteenth century ablaze. Jansen's aim was to spearhead the spiritual renewal of the church. His words attacked many of the flamboyant rituals and idolatrous practices renewed by Counter Reformation Catholicism. Jansen's ideas about St Augustine's theology of predestination and salvation were extremely contentious. His insistence that God had decided before birth who would be saved and who damned sounded dangerously close to Calvinist Protestantism. Jansen and his followers were very unimpressed with the baroque magnificence and spectacular rituals of Counter Reformation Catholicism. They called for a simple though rigorous faith, in which Christians would avoid all entertainments and mundanities in order to devote themselves almost exclusively to the frequent reception of the sacraments (the mass appeal of such killjoy asceticism is difficult to fathom). This would allow men and women to make manifest the grace that they had received freely from God. Their spiritual battle was for the soul, and to bring about moral improvement. They advocated a simpler, less worldly church that would improve the moral character of society.[128] Cornelius Jansen died in 1638 and did not live to see his ideas grow into a mass movement. He also escaped the formal condemnation of heresy issued against his followers by Pope Innocent X in the apostolic constitution *Cum occasione* in 1653.[129] It was, however, too late as the movement had spread from the Spanish Netherlands (now Belgium) into France and, by the 1750s, had proliferated in every Catholic country.

Jansenists from the outset had one prime target in their sights: the Society of Jesus, founded by St Ignatius de Loyola in 1540. The Jesuit order was one of the great success stories of early modern Catholicism.[130] Their missionary exploits became the stuff of legends; they had even attempted to evangelise China and Japan, though with decidedly mixed results.[131] Across the Atlantic, in the New World, they had ventured further than any other missionaries to bring Catholic teaching to the indigenous peoples of South America. In contrast to the uneven education of diocesan clergy across Europe, the Jesuits undertook a rigorous eighteen-year programme of elite training.* They would rank alongside the PhDs and post-docs of our modern universities today. Armed with such formidable education, they became the vanguard for the renewal of Catholicism in the aftermath of the Reformation. Their 'colleges' monopolised elite secondary education in Europe, Latin America and the Philippines. A remarkably high number of Europe's Catholic nobles sent their sons enthusiastically to these institutions.

At the heart of Jesuit education was *ratio studiorum,* which had renovated the liberal arts of the medieval period. Younger students focused on grammar, humanities and rhetoric. Once these disciplines were mastered, they then moved into philosophy and their education would climax with Christian doctrine.[132] This rigorous education concentrated on the humanities was to remain the staple of elite education during the seventeenth and eighteenth centuries. Their education also promoted genteel extra-curricular pursuits like dancing, horse-riding and fencing, since all were regarded as vital attributes of future Catholic gentlemen. Their boarding schools were renowned for organising magnificent masques, plays and other entertainments which delighted the proud parents of their students.[133] From Warsaw to Lisbon, the cream of the aristocracy and future civil servants of royal bureaucracies entered the gates of these elite boarding schools. By the mid-eighteenth century the Society of Jesus ran about eight hundred colleges across the continent. At the centre of their success was the fact that the Jesuit curriculum was both traditional and practical. It sought to prepare Christian men ready to live in the real world, rather than other-worldly saints. Eighteenth-century alumni of

---

* This still persists to the present day; see William J. McGucken, SJ, *The Jesuits and Education: The Society's Teaching Principles and Practice* (Eugene, OR, 1932) pp. 216–39.

these colleges included Voltaire, Denis Diderot, Giambattista Vico, Lodovico Muratori and possibly Toussaint Louverture was taught to read by a Jesuit,[134] all individuals whose outlook on life betrayed little nostalgia or sympathy for their former teachers. Indeed, the great destroyer of the Society of Jesus, Sebastião José de Carvalho e Mello, later Marques de Pombal, was taught law by Jesuits at the University of Coimbra in Portugal.[135]

The other arena in which the Jesuits excelled was as confessors to the elites of society. These positions were the equivalent of what we would call 'life coaches' today. The confessors were inspired by the sixteenth-century Jesuit academic Luis de Molina, who believed that God's grace could be invoked by all and that a contextual evaluation of sin was vital.[136] Ultimately human beings had free will; they could choose between good and evil. When it came to confession, Jesuits tried to understand the circumstances which had impelled the sinner to commit his or her transgression and to see if there were mitigating factors when deciding on a penance.[137] Their priority was to allow penitents to lead 'well-adjusted' lives free from guilt and sin.

Jesuits' approach to confession left them open to accusations of casuistry. Their enemies accused the followers of Loyola of rejecting Catholicism's strict teachings on sin in favour of permissiveness and laxity. The Jesuits became the therapists, counsellors and psychiatrists of the seventeenth and eighteenth centuries. Through private discussion within the confessional, they probed the psyches of their penitents, and strove to find ways of reconciling their subconscious desires with the reality of their daily lives and moral duties.[138] The elites dropped their old confessors like a bad habit and flocked towards the more sympathetic Jesuits. The Society of Jesus became a favourite of the wealthy and received generous endowments. A visit to the Church of St Ignatius, the chapel of the Collegio Romano in Rome, will confirm this. It embodies the apotheosis of the Jesuits in art, sculpture and architecture.[139]

Success, of course, was not without its price. Rival religious orders responded to Jesuit wealth and power with jealousy, resentment and malice. A black legend emerged that the Jesuits were part of a conspiracy that sought to overturn the rule of law and secular government.[140] More seriously, it was alleged that Jesuit ethics and their confessional style were corrupting public standards. Indeed, the Society's ethical teachings created something of a moral panic between 1650 and 1750. It was claimed that sinners were being encouraged by Jesuits to accept their limitations and not feel unduly troubled about their atrocious immorality.[141] Ultimately, Jesuit confessors were luring the unsuspecting into a false sense of security. They were being told that their sins were minor and would not affect God's grace and their ultimate path to salvation. Cornelius Jansen's followers were outraged by this minimalist approach to sin. They argued that the Jesuits, rather than seeking out an easier road to heaven, were placing people on an express motorway to hell.[142]

This conflict between Jansenists and Jesuits was located at a pressure point in the growing conflict between church and state. The followers of Cornelius Jansen became the victims of an over-reaction on the part of Rome that gained them the aura of martyrdom. Their dismissal as heretics by Innocent X, and Louis XIV's brutal decision to raze the Jansenist hub of Port Royal to the ground in 1711, outraged their followers.[143] One of the biggest miscalculations in this campaign was Clement XI's papal bull *Unigenitus*, issued in 1713, which condemned a new wave of Jansenist writings.[144] To make matters worse, there was a growing debate within the French church about whether Jansenists should be refused the last rites, unless they publicly recanted their heresy.* When the refusal of sacraments became official policy within the archdiocese of Paris during the 1740s, the public fallout against the papacy was spectacular.[145] By over-reacting and persecuting otherwise morally upstanding clergy and Catholics, an obscure theological controversy was transformed into a mass movement. Its adherents called for a radical reform of European Catholicism.

---

* As the historian William Doyle put it, the papacy and French crown had used a sledgehammer to crack an exceedingly small theological nut. See Doyle, *Jansenism*, pp. 45–49; Émile Régnault, *Christophe de Beaumont, Archevêque de Paris*, (2 vols, Paris, 1882), I, pp. 157–79.

As the eighteenth century began, a new generation of Jansenists, or 'reform Catholics', placed the theology of salvation on the backburner, turning instead to ecclesiology (church governance) and the politics of religion.[146] These reform Catholics, ultimately, despised the centralist and ultramontane tendencies of Rome. They believed that parish clergy and local episcopates were better placed to make decisions relating to the welfare of their flocks. It was largely thanks to them that, during the eighteenth century, the dormant, and vexed, question of Conciliarism was resurrected.[147] Ultimately, Jansenist/reform Catholics believed that church councils made of bishops exceeded the authority of the pope. Their subversive vision of church governance put them on a direct collision course with the papacy. Neo-conciliarism was to trouble the sleep of eighteenth-century pontiffs. For their part, monarchs and their ministers sought to use this internal dispute to the state's advantage. Although they could not side openly with heretics, a reduction in papal power, and a more pastorally focused church, very much appealed to the secular powers of Europe.

Jesuits, with their direct allegiance to the pope, had always been the chief object of Jansenist animosity and scorn. The favoured children of the papacy received a better education, more resources and were given remarkable positions of leadership. The campaign of vilification against them was to do significant damage to the public image of the Jesuits. It had already been alleged, during the seventeenth century, that the Society of Jesus's missionary success was not due to their ability but rather to the fact that they had incorporated pagan practices into Catholic doctrine and worship.[148] The followers of St Ignatius were accused of contaminating Catholicism with the rituals of Hinduism in the Indian subcontinent and with Confucianism in China. A myth emerged that the Jesuits were power hungry and greedy. Although the legend for the most part was untrue, it had some verisimilitude, and placed the Society of Jesus on the defensive. It was difficult to avoid the well-targeted campaigns of denigration unleashed by Jansenist publicists. The weekly French periodical *Nouvelles Ecclésiastiques* (*Ecclesiastical News*), which started publication in 1728, became the mouthpiece of the international

Catholic Reform movement.[149] Its articles derided the Jesuits and attacked the papacy's defence of the order.

The first disturbing sign for Rome that the conflict was intensifying and mushrooming out of control occurred in Holland. After the sixteenth-century Dutch revolt against Spain an independent Calvinist republic had emerged. During the 1580s, Catholicism was banned in the Netherlands and dioceses loyal to Rome were dismantled.[150] For the next hundred years the Dutch republic became a Catholic mission territory, much like the forests of Amazonia and China. The congregation of the *propaganda fide*, the chief body that regulated missionary activity throughout the globe, took over responsibility for appointing apostolic vicars to administer the priests and clergy operating clandestinely inside the Netherlands. Several Jesuits were sent to combat Dutch Calvinism. They came into intense conflict with Jansenist missionaries who had crossed from France and concentrated in the former prince-bishopric of Utrecht.[151]

These Utrecht missionaries were supported by Petrus Codde, the apostolic vicar for Holland and an outspoken critic of the Jesuits. This prelate was accused of Jansenism, which he indignantly denied. In 1701 he was summoned to Rome to clear himself and in his place a less Augustinian successor was appointed. He was considered acceptable to the Jesuits, but Dutch Catholics resented him intensely. After decades of failure to reach an accommodation with Rome, the Catholics of Utrecht decided to resurrect the archdiocese of their city unilaterally. In 1723 the clergy of the new cathedral chapter, without papal authorisation, elected Cornelis van Steenoven as their archbishop.[152] To make matters worse, a rebellious French bishop performed the ceremony of investiture and bestowed the apostolic succession on the new archbishop. This empowered the Jansenist-leaning clergy of Utrecht to administer the sacraments without authorisation from Rome.

In this corner of the Netherlands, the rejection of Jesuit missionaries gave rise to an independent Dutch church, which described itself, confusingly, as 'Old Catholic'.[153] Several failed attempts were made during the eighteenth century to heal the schism with the Old Catholics of Utrecht. These Old Catholics have survived to the present day and their theology, liberated from papal authority, diverges considerably from mainstream Roman Catholicism. Indeed, the Old Catholic church, which spread into Germany, Poland and the United States, provides a tantalising glimpse into how a liberal Catholic Church might have developed without the iron grip of papal authority.[154] The survivors of this Utrecht tradition would embrace the ordination of women, lay participation in ministry and sexual liberation in a much swifter manner than most churches did during the twentieth century. Regardless of this future liberal turn, the schism with Utrecht during the eighteenth century highlighted just how far the Jansenists were prepared to go.

The woes facing the successors of St Ignatius de Loyola were hardly confined to Europe. The unravelling of the Society's power intensified in South America, in the most unlikely and remote of places, namely Paraguay. This landlocked Amazonian region had been explored and colonised by the Spanish during the sixteenth century. However, unlike Mexico or Peru, few settlers had ventured there, and the resources devoted to its colonisation were comparatively sparse.[155] The grisly end of Pedro de Mendoza, an explorer and courtier of Charles V, may explain why the colonisation of this remote territory proved unattractive. After trudging up the Paraná, Mendoza lost half of his followers to disease, and most of his supplies to poor transportation. In the end he found hardly any gold or natural resources to justify his adventure, and beat a swift retreat towards the Atlantic. As William Jaenike put it inimitably: 'He probably had [contracted] syphilis. Returning to Buenos Aires in 1536, he embarked for Spain with so few provisions that he had to consume his favourite bitch. He soon went raving mad and died, still en route.'[156] Despite this salutary tale, not all adventurers were deterred by gigantic anacondas, piranha-infested waterways and the alleged cannibalistic practices of the natives of Paraguay.

Initially the rainforests, magnificent but formidable waterfalls and the impenetrable terrain dissuaded settlers from colonising the banks of the Paraná and Uruguay rivers. However, where Spanish settlers refused to go, other Europeans with even more questionable aims eventually arrived. The local Guaraní people, who were indigenous to these jungles, attracted the unwelcome attention of the Portuguese. They realised the potential of the Guaraní to make strong slaves for the plantations of São Paulo. It was calculated that capturing the Guaraní was less expensive than importing and transporting Africans from the Gold Coast.[157] Portuguese slavers, known as *Mamalucos*, became feared and despised for their raids into Uruguay and Paraguay where they captured large numbers of Guaraní. Such incursions from Brazil into this zone of the Amazon basin represented something of a diplomatic embarrassment as these lands were legally Spanish territory.

In 1501, Queen Isabella had recognised the indigenous population of New Spain as her subjects, and thus they could not be enslaved.[158] However, the *conquistadores* established loopholes in this prohibition, through the *encomienda* and *mitayo* systems. The holders of these concessions from the Spanish crown were allowed, through right of conquest, to 'care' for native Americans to expedite their conversion to Christianity. In practice, this meant that the *encomienderos* could exact 'involuntary labour' from their wards who, though theoretically free, were unable to resist their colonial overlords.[159]

Slowly the Catholic Church had come to condemn the enslavement of native people and their transportation away from their homelands.* Paul III's encyclical *Sublimis deus* in 1537 pronounced, patronisingly, that the indigenous populations of South America had souls and were rational beings.[160] The papacy forbade slavery, and insisted instead that the conversion of pagans

---

* Previously Pope Nicholas V, in the papal bull *Dum diversas*, issued on 18 June 1452, had authorised Alfonso V of Portugal to enslave Saracens and unbelievers. This complex bull, which dealt with the legitimacy of Portugeuse trade and maritime expansion, was renewed until the early sixteenth century. The church subsequently changed direction. See James Walvin, *Crossings, Africa, the Americas and the Atlantic Slave Trade* (London, 2013), pp. 21–22 and Anthony John R. Russell-Wood, 'Iberian Expansion and the Issue of Black Slavery: Changing Portuguese Attitudes, 1440–1770,' *American Historical Review*, Vol.83, No.1 (1978), pp. 16–42.

to the truth of the gospels should be the focus of Spain's imperial ambitions. A decade later the Valladolid debates of 1550–1 witnessed the anti-imperialist and abolitionist Dominican Bartolomé de las Casas condemning in the strongest terms Spanish aggression in the New World and arguing against forced conversions. He believed that only through persuasion and reason could people be genuinely brought to Christ.[161] The negative side of this debate was that las Casas endorsed the use of African slaves instead of the indigenous people of South America to alleviate the labour shortfall in the Iberian Empires.[162] This had the cataclysmic effect of incentivising the Atlantic slave trade.

Catholicism's official anti-slavery stance belied a more complex grassroots reality. Clergymen and nuns in the colonial societies of the Americas were slave owners.[163] Within the Papal States themselves, there was a significant population of 'Moorish', or Muslim, slaves who as infidels were constrained to work for the 'universal church' without reward.[164] It would prove difficult for the First Estate to remain entirely uncontaminated by the prevalent attitudes of the societies in which they operated. The Jesuit order's activities on the southern fringes of the Amazonian basin were to be particularly complex and controversial. In Uruguay and Paraguay the Society of Jesus established dozens of *reducciones*.[165] These were huge missions, where the Guaraní people of South America came to live and work. At their height as many as 140,000 people may have lived in them. Anyone who has seen Roland Joffé and Robert Bolt's 1986 film *Mission* will be familiar with its highly romanticised version of these events. Thanks to Hollywood magic, and Ennio Morricone's transcendent soundtrack, the tale is told of the brave Jesuits fighting a losing battle against the forces of slavery and state oppression.[166] Unsurprisingly, the truth was much more intricate than could reasonably be conveyed by a two-hour movie.

The *reducciones* of Brazil, Paraguay, Argentina and Bolivia have been described as theocratic communes.[167] Theoretically, the communities of Guaraní elected their own *corregidor* (mayor) and several *regidores* (councillors). These civil authorities were supposed to coordinate the farming and manufacturing activities within these settlements.[168] The enemies of the Society called them

'Jesuit republics'. Throughout the early seventeenth century, these *reducciones* fought pitched battles against bands of *Mamalucos* sent to enslave their populations. Gradually, the missions were driven further inland, away from the Luso-Brazilian border. Perhaps inevitably, the Jesuits took the controversial decision to arm and provide rudimentary military training to the Guaraní. On 8 March 1641 a Jesuit-led force defeated the *Mamalucos* at the Battle of Mbororé.[169] This amphibious operation fought on the Uruguay river deserves to be better known. Brother Domingo Torres, a former soldier, became the *generalissimo* of the Jesuit-Guaraní army. He commanded a fleet of thirty river vessels and several thousand troops who had been drilled and trained in the latest European combat tactics. The *Mamaluco* forces were astounded to learn that the Guaraní had not only firearms but cannons. The slavers were routed and forced back into Brazil. This victory demonstrated that the Jesuit super-missions of Paraguay had considerable military resources and were there to stay.

The Jesuits did not always have a comfortable relationship with local authorities in Paraguay. Although Madrid had authorised the missions to arm themselves, the colonial authorities were uneasy about this sort of independent militia. Jesuit activities increasingly drew the critical eye of the diocese of Asunción. Its bishops had authorised the creation of these Amazonian missions on the understanding that, once viable parishes had been established, they would be surrendered to diocesan control. This replicated the practice in use with the Franciscans, where, once a Christian community had been set up, it would swiftly be transferred to episcopal authority.[170] Jesuit missions, however, were answerable only to the *propaganda fide* in Rome. They had little desire to relinquish their order's jurisdiction over the prosperous Christian communities that had been built with so much blood, sweat and tears.

When in 1640, without papal approval, the former Franciscan Don Bernardino de Cárdenas usurped the bishopric of Asunción, he ushered in decades of instability.[171] He was constantly struggling with Gregorio de Hinestrosa, the governor of the colony, whom he regularly excommunicated. His relationship with the Jesuits was fraught, to say the least. When Cardenas was experiencing difficulties with the secular authorities he would beg them for assistance. However, once his position was more secure, he would voice his resentment at their economic success and independence from his episcopal rule. In 1644, he issued an anti-Jesuit manifesto accusing them of subverting the authority of both the crown and the church in Paraguay. It claimed that the *reducciones* contained secret mines and denounced the Guaraní catechism as heretical.[172] In 1649 this troublesome bishop bit off more than he could chew when he seized Asunción and tried to expel the Jesuits by force. Eventually, defeated by crown forces, Cárdenas would spend significant time in exile, after which he was sent to the remote diocese of Santa Cruz de la Sierra in Bolivia where he had little opportunity to cause trouble.[173] His anti-Jesuit writings laid the foundations of a black legend that endured well into the eighteenth century.

The whole truth about the *reducciones* is difficult to evaluate, and their depiction as Gardens of Eden in Joffé's film is a decided romanticisation. By the eighteenth century, the missions had drifted southwards out of the rainforests and onto the more open plateaus. The naked innocence of Joffé's Indians is also fanciful.[174] After two centuries of contact with Spanish colonisers, many of the indigenous population had adopted a hybrid culture that mixed European dress and technology with more local traditions and practices. While the Guaraní did enjoy some measure of self-rule, they were subject to rigorous discipline by the Society of Jesus.[175] Their work in the fields and the growing of the lucrative *yerba* crop was hardly voluntary.

The missions did not take kindly to those inmates who did not play according to the rules. Sometimes the Guaraní reverted to shamanic practices and revolted against their Jesuit masters. The *corregidor* of any *reducción* was not an independent politician but was supervised by two Jesuit priests. Indeed, the store-houses were administered by the Jesuits and the surplus produced by the missions was reinvested in the order's many South American projects, with a large portion of the profits going to the general of the Jesuits in Rome.[176] It could be suggested that, rather than counteracting Iberian imperialism, the Society of Jesus was developing its own autonomous version of colonial expansion into South America. It is difficult to know what the Guaraní really felt about their Jesuit overlords but, by the early eighteenth century, the *reducciones* had become their homes.

Some of Cárdenas' list of grievances against the Jesuits were probably justified. They did not pay taxes to the crown and, being directly under the authority of Rome, they refused to contribute to the running costs of the diocese of Asunción. Their title to the lands they governed was dubious, and by raising local militias they appeared to be establishing independent republics in Latin America. One wonders whether the Jesuits had effectively become South American warlords. Other charges were much less likely to be true. Cárdenas accused the followers of St Ignatius of violating the secrets of the confessional to coerce and blackmail the Guaraní. It was also alleged that the Jesuits had silver mines where the native American miners were worked to death. These allegations were libellous. Jesuit priests, like so many missionaries past and present, believed that their relationship with the Guaraní was mutually beneficial. They brought them the word of God, economic progress, effective political leadership and protection from Portuguese slavers. It must also be remembered that, for all their faults, both real and imagined, the Jesuits were intellectuals. They took a great anthropological interest in Guaraní language, customs and beliefs which few other missionary orders replicated.[177] These priests had a complex relationship with the people they proselytised. To portray these relations as either saintly or demonic would be to distort the thorny reality that characterised these enormous missions.

At the heart of the conflict that was about to explode was the power of the state. After all, the Jesuits had established and developed their missions with little recognition of the Spanish and Portuguese empires on whose marches their *reducciones* were scattered. Ultimately the Jesuits looked to Rome for leadership and direction. Disastrously for them, their Superior General and the pope were months away in terms of travel, correspondence and decision-making. These missions, for the modern centralising and reforming states of Iberia, became the incarnation of all that was wrong with an independent church. What right had the Jesuits to establish and administer their own virtual colonies without accepting the primacy of the state? Growing government resentment, combined with a powerful Jansenist-inspired anti-Jesuit campaign in Europe, was to have serious consequences for the Catholic Church in South America and beyond.[178] Already in the 1720s the Jesuits had been attacked and expelled from Asunción by a pro-slavery cabal in the so-called *comuneros* revolt.[179] This temporary expulsion highlighted how the Hispanic settlers of Paraguay were becoming increasingly antagonistic towards the Jesuits. There is a sense that not only the colonial governors and local bishops but now the local planters as well saw the *reducciones* as unfair competition, with access to a virtually inexhaustible pool of cheap labour.

It was a diplomatic deal that spelled the beginning of the end for the Jesuits. In 1750, Ferdinand VI of Spain and John V of Portugal signed the Treaty of Madrid.[180] This agreement, more or less, coincided with the appointment of the Marquis de Pombal as minister of foreign affairs in Lisbon. He was to play a determining role in the growing struggle against the Jesuits but, at this early stage, he was open to compromise. The terms of the Treaty of Madrid sought to end territorial disputes over the Banda Oriental on the Brazilian–Rio de la Plata border. The Spanish would cede large parts of the Amazon basin and the left bank of the Uruguay river to Brazil. In return, the Portuguese would surrender the colony of Sacramento, which had been a centre of smuggling and a threat to the defences of Buenos Aires.[181] The chancellery of Lisbon promised to cease any westward expansion that encroached on Spanish sovereignty. This arrangement was an attempt by the two Iberian empires to reach an entente that would check growing British trade in South America.[182] One of the most crucial and controversial points in the treaty was that it included the transfer of seven *reducciones* to Portuguese control.

Given that slavery was practised openly in Brazil, the Portuguese crown would not offer protection to these missions. Furthermore, it was going to prove next to impossible to relocate thirty thousand

Guaraní into Spanish territory.[183] At this time, the Bohemian aristocrat Franz Retz held the position of Superior General of the Society of Jesus and he intervened against the terms of the Treaty of Madrid. In Rome, the leader of the Jesuits was generally known as the 'black pope', given the enormous power and covert influence it was claimed he wielded over not only the Papal Curia but the courts of Europe too.[184] The Spanish plenipotentiary Don Gaspar de Munive, Marqués de Valdelirios, who had negotiated the treaty, agreed to postpone its implementation until 1753.[185] A joint Hispano-Portuguese commission of ten boundary officers was sent from Europe. They were to sail up the Uruguay and Paraná rivers to visit the seven *reducciones* in question.

The key player in this dispute was the Portuguese jurist and governor of Rio de Janeiro, Gomes Freire de Andrade Conde de Bobadela. He proved reasonable and wanted to avoid violence.[186] Luis Altamirano was the representative of the Jesuit Superior General, and it was left to him to make recommendations to settle this dispute. Altamirano is reviled in Jesuit historiography as a quisling who collaborated with fanatical secularists in the destruction of the Paraguayan missions. In fairness, Altamirano had an invidious choice before him. If he had saved these seven *reducciones* the Jansenists' attacks would have increased and imperilled the very existence of the Jesuit order. Altamirano opted for the least damaging course and sanctioned the new border established by the treaty. He then called on the Jesuit fathers in the seven *reducciones* to obey orders and vacate the settlements.[187]

The fathers refused to do this and instead encouraged the inhabitants in their missions to resist the treaty. This sparked the Guaraní War of 1754–6.[188] During the first eighteen months both sides tried to seek a negotiated settlement but to no avail. The military operations carried out by the *reducciones* proved remarkably effective, especially considering that these missionaries faced the combined might of two of Europe's most powerful empires. Contrary to myth, the Guaraní were not half-naked 'primitives' fighting modern soldiers with bows and arrows. They had been trained in European military tactics, and had operated as irregulars in Spain's colonial conflicts. At the same time, the

Spanish and Portuguese were not the genocidal maniacs depicted by Hollywood. In 1754 the first Hispano-Portuguese invasion of Paraguay was badly coordinated and supplied. Harassed by rising flood waters and native guerrillas, these troops were forced to beat a speedy retreat.[189] Next year, a fresh invasion force set out and clashed with the Jesuit-Guaraní forces at Caaibaté near the San Juan mission. On 10 February 1756 the Guaraní, about 1,700 strong, were routed. Apparently, the invaders' riflemen were instructed to aim for the native officers and thus deprive the militia of the *reducciones* of effective command during the battle. Only five Europeans died in the ensuing confusion, while more than a thousand defenders of the *reducciones* are said to have perished.[190]

It took three years for the Portuguese to complete the 'evacuation' of the seven missions. This was a devastatingly traumatic experience for the Guaraní, who were made homeless.[191] Then international events then led to a remarkable reversal of fortunes. The death of Ferdinand VI in 1759, and the accession of his Neapolitan cousin Charles III, brought about a Spanish realignment with France. This led to the breakdown of the Treaty of Madrid, as the Iberian kingdoms joined opposing sides in the Seven Years' War (1756–63), which was raging in Europe and North America. Suddenly, the Spanish and Guaraní found themselves united in the struggle against Anglo-Portuguese forces in South America.[192] The territories of the seven *reducciones* were reconquered; the surviving Guaraní returned to their ravaged homes and resettled these areas free from the tutelage of their former Jesuit overlords.

Back in Europe, Jansenist-inspired newspapers and pamphlets used these events to pour scorn on the Jesuits and portray them as rebels.[193] Their missions in Paraguay lay on a trembling fault line that divided the Iberian monarchies in Latin America. The weakness of these empires had given the Society of Jesus an opportunity to build a quasi-colonial power base on their imperial marches. By the eighteenth century these Jesuit-run native settlements had become an irritant for both Lisbon and Madrid. The resistance of the *reducciones* against Portugal gave ammunition to Jansenist-inspired publicists and reformers who argued that such native violence was part of a Jesuit conspiracy against the Iberian monarchies. The Paraguayan crisis thus unleashed a chain reaction that ultimately led in the following decades to the destruction of the Jesuits and a weakening of the papacy's authority.

During the wars over the *reducciones,* Antoine de La Valette had been appointed Jesuit Superior in the French Caribbean. He found that his order was deeply in debt on the island of Martinique. The son of merchants, he decided to play the markets and see if he could restore the fortunes of the Society of Jesus in the Antilles. He invested heavily, with leveraged funds, in a triangular scheme that involved slaves, sugar and European goods.[194] Disaster struck in 1755, when the British Royal Navy seized as prizes twelve French vessels laden with luxury goods heading to Bordeaux. This gave rise to a massive financial scandal because these ships carried the cargo on which La Valette had speculated. He was placed in the highly embarrassing position of being unable to honour the order's debts in the Caribbean.[195] The result was a bankruptcy of 2,400,000 *livres* which, in turn, caused a stream of litigation. Panicked creditors appealed to the courts in France, requesting the confiscation of the properties of the Jesuits to repay La Valette's debts. The Jesuits 'lawyered up', and refused to accept liability for La Valette's creative investments. Another public-relations disaster followed, as the Jansenist press denounced the Jesuits not merely for being theologically suspect but also crooked in their financial dealings.[196] When the true extent of the financial black hole he created was revealed, La Valette was removed from office, fled the Caribbean and took refuge in the Netherlands.

Throughout this time, the Jansenist newspaper *Nouvelles Ecclésiastiques* reported with unrestrained glee on Jesuit misdeeds. The attempted regicide of Louis XV of France in 1757, and that of Joseph I of Portugal in 1758, gave rise to hysterical conspiracy theories about a Jesuit plot to destabilise Europe and replace the state with an obscurantist theocratic order.[197] Although the Jesuits had rebelled in Latin America, and produced a financial crash in the Caribbean, the Jansenist allegations of a coordinated plot had no real foundation. The order was certainly guilty of incompetence, but to allege that it wanted to destroy the authority of the state was to twist reality beyond breaking-point. However, the backlash against the Jesuits gave European ministers a good pretext to attack and rein in the power of the First Estate.

Pombal was the first to cross the rubicon in 1759. Already furious with the Jesuit Malagrida's public attack on his ministry, he formally expelled the Jesuits from all dominions of the Portuguese empire.[198] The French followed suit in 1764 in the aftermath of the La Valette affair and other scandals. Not to be left behind in this anti-Jesuit surge, in 1767 the Spanish expelled the followers of St Ignatius from their vast empire.[199] A year later Malta and the duchy of Parma followed suit. The fall of the Jesuits was a complex phenomenon that had little to do with the charges of conspiracy levelled against them. Their loyalty to the papacy, self-promotion, flexible theology and disregard for the state lines made them powerful enemies. For governments increasingly resentful of ecclesiastical exemptions and privileges, the suppression of the Jesuits was a warning shot across the bow of the church.

By 1769 only the papacy and the Habsburg monarchy continued to shelter the society of Jesus in their territories. Carlo della Torre di Rezzonico, Pope Clement XIII, was a Venetian aristocrat sympathetic to the order.[200] As long as he reigned the Jesuits were safe. His bull of 1765, *Apostolicum pascendi,* defended the order, and praised its missionary contribution and educational vocation.[201] The sudden death of Pope Clement in a fit of apoplexy gave rise to one of the tensest and most important conclaves of the eighteenth century.[202] Until the early twentieth century, the crowned heads of Europe had the power to veto papal candidates they judged hostile to their interests. This participation by secular powers in the process of electing the pope shows how far politics and religion were indistinguishable during the eighteenth century.

Although the 1769 conclave, which lasted from 15 February to 19 May, was hardly long by *ancien régime* standards, the question of the Jesuits made it particularly fraught. Those cardinals who were in favour of a centralised and powerful papacy sought to ensure the election of a pro-Jesuit candidate. Non-Italian and moderate cardinals sought to find a compromise candidate, who would defuse the looming conflict between church and state. Cardinal Pierre de Bernis, a favourite of Louis XV's mistress, the celebrated Madame de Pompadour, was instructed to put forward an anti-Jesuit candidate for France. About twenty cardinals were excluded altogether on suspicion of favouring the Society of Jesus.[203]

In the end, the princes of the church, in growing frustration, selected the former Franciscan monk Giovanni Vincenzo Antonio Ganganelli as their candidate. The main reason for their choice was that it was unclear where he stood on the Jesuit issue. Whenever he was asked about his views by colleagues, he expressed them with such sibylline, slippery and complex language that both sides became convinced that he had given an undertaking either to protect or to suppress the order. On 28 May 1769 he was consecrated Pope Clement XIV and was crowned a week later.[204] His pontificate was unhappy, as he found himself cornered by the two factions. He was distrusted by pro-Jesuit cardinals and threatened with schism by the representatives of the Bourbon monarchies of France, Spain, Naples and Parma. The wily old monk became a master of procrastination.

The pressure on Ganganelli was significant, for a year before his election French forces, at the behest of Louis XV, had occupied the papal enclaves of Avignon and the Comtat Venaissin in Provence. If these territories were annexed to France, the papacy's meagre revenues would be compromised even further. It was made clear by Cardinal Bernis that the evacuation of these lands was contingent on the satisfactory resolution of the Jesuit question.[205] Similarly the Bourbons of Naples had occupied the papal enclaves of Benevento and Pontecorvo, showing that the anti-Jesuit coalition was truly trans-European.[206] The other central player in the drama was José Moñino y Redondo, the future Count of Floridablanca, who was Spanish ambassador in Rome. He stooped to bribing important members of the Curia and papal court to bring about the demise of the order.[207] Ultimately, Clement XIV felt outgunned, and feared a schism with the most important churches in Europe. Indeed, there was a real danger that French and Spanish bishops might be appointed without papal confirmation, and that more church lands and monasteries would be seized and secularised. On 21 July

1773 he bowed to this intolerable bullying and promulgated the brief *Dominus ac redemptor* which suppressed the Jesuits.[208]

The events that followed were unedifying. Lorenzo Ricci, the Tuscan Superior General of the Society of Jesus, an indirect descendant of Matteo Ricci, the famous missionary who had evangelised China, was informed that his order no longer existed and that their property was forfeit to the state. To his horror Ricci and his subordinates were arrested, and imprisoned in Rome's grim citadel of Castel Santangelo, which was usually reserved for political dissidents and heretics.[209] Forbidden from celebrating mass or any religious service, Ricci died in the fortress on 24 November 1775. The brief *Dominus ac redemptor* marked a low point in papal power, and showed that the European monarchies could exert significant leverage on the papacy when they acted in concert. This text admitted that the principal reason for the suppression of the Jesuits was to ensure continued unity within the church. Having made enemies of most of the crowned heads of Europe, the Jesuits had become too much of a liability for Catholicism. The brief then listed the many accusations levelled against the society by their Jansenist foes. Their teachings on morality and salvation were far too lax. When it came to missionary work they were accused of insubordination and allowing the toleration of paganism as part of Catholic worship. Worst of all, they were accused of fomenting sedition within Catholic realms like France, Spain and Portugal. This document marked a significant recalibration in the alliance of throne and altar.[210] The throne, which had leant on the altar since time immemorial, now seemed to be crushing it.

Jesuit suppression did untold harm to education across Catholic Europe. Secular authorities gleefully abolished the order's hundreds of colleges throughout the continent, but what to replace them with was far from clear.[211] The abolition of the order provided a big cash injection to the state thanks to the proceeds from the sale of former Jesuit assets and properties.[212] Suppression also compromised the missionary activities of the church beyond Europe. Although several other missionary congregations remained active, they lacked the Jesuits' anthropological knack of understanding the cultures they were evangelising. Indeed,

Bohemian Franciscan attempts to persuade the Ethiopian emperor Iyasu II to enter into communion with Rome in 1751 floundered ignominiously.[213]

The dawn of the eighteenth century had seemed to herald a Catholic resurgence, yet as time moved forward inexorably the church was challenged by the secular state's gradual erosion of its privileges and prerogatives. To make matters worse, the struggle between Jansenists and Jesuits almost amounted to an ecclesiastical civil war. It pitted Jansenist-leaning reform Catholics, who wanted a spiritually rigorous and more democratic church, against the Jesuits, who espoused a centralised baroque church under the uncontested leadership of the papacy. The suppression of the Jesuits in 1773 was a notable victory for reform Catholics and the secular state, but this was only the beginning of the problems that would culminate in the revolutionary conflagration of the 1790s.

2

REFORM CATHOLICISM AND ENLIGHTENMENT, 1773–89

J ean Meslier, parish priest of Étrépigny in Champagne for over four decades, died on 17 June 1729. This obscure clergyman was a diligent but unremarkable priest in his parish, where he was renowned for his charity, austerity and sobriety. Only once did he show some flair, when he denounced the local lord for mistreating his peasants. On that Sunday, Meslier refused to lead the customary prayers for his chatelain. Cardinal François de Mailly, Archbishop of Rheims, disciplined the unruly priest and reminded him of his duty.[1] The curé of Étrépigny was forced to reinstate Sunday prayers for his lord and was ordered never again to challenge the social hierarchy. Meslier had no stomach for open rebellion, so he resumed his dull routine of worship and contemplation for the rest of his uneventful life. When he died, he left his meagre possessions to his congregation. As the local notary inspected his belongings, he found a 600-page manuscript, which nobody suspected Meslier had been writing.[2] Its contents sent a shock wave through the local community. The parish priest of Étrépigny, in its pages, admitted that his life had been a lie and asked forgiveness from his parishioners. It was revealed that, decades earlier, Meslier had lost his faith in God and grown to hate the religion he professed.

He denounced Catholicism's support for a socio-political and economic system that was inequitable and even tyrannical.

The testament quotes approvingly from an unnamed peasant who said: 'He wished [...] that the powerful of this earth and all nobles would be hanged and strangled with the intestines of the last priests' (*Il souhaitait [...] que tous les grands de la terre et tous les nobles fussent pendus et étranglés avec des boïaux de prêtres*).[3] Throughout the text, Meslier painstakingly discredited the Catholic magisterium and sought to prove that God did not exist. This modest Catholic clergyman became for some the father of militant atheism.[4] For him, Christianity and all religions were falsehoods that kept mankind in bondage to powerful interest groups. The discovery of the manuscript plunged the local community into confusion, and the church decided to intervene vigorously. The diocesan authorities ordered that the body of the late parish priest should not be given a Christian burial. The story of Meslier could have ended there, but several copies of his text did not remain in Étrépigny. One version found its way into the private collection of Frederick the Great of Prussia, where this notoriously agnostic monarch read the curé's words with relish.[5]

To the fury of both secular and ecclesiastical authorities, a sixty-page pamphlet entitled *Extrait des sentiments de Jean Meslier* (*Extract of the opinions of Jean Meslier*) was published in 1762.[6] Voltaire had edited the text and decided to have it printed it at his own expense. The booklet caused a sensation, and it sold well. The Parlement of Paris, the largest appeal court in France, seized as many copies as possible, and publicly burned them in its courtyard. Rome's condemnation followed swiftly: the Curia put Meslier's writings on the Index of prohibited books.[7] For all the scandal that this pamphlet had elicited, Voltaire had been careful to expunge Meslier's work of its most subversive content. All his attacks on the nobility and monarchy had vanished as if they had never been there. Despite his criticism of superstition and irrationality, this *philosophe* still believed in social order and dreaded anarchy.[8] Voltaire altered the text so that it transformed Meslier from a diehard atheist into a moderate deist.

Deism was a theory born of the late seventeenth century which accepted that a supreme being had created an ordered universe, ruled by immutable, natural and scientifically discernible laws.[9]

The creator had not tarnished his own creation by breaking his own rules through supernatural and providential interference. Any belief in miracles, magic and direct divine intervention was dismissed as mere enthusiasm and bigotry.[10] To recast Meslier as a deist was to de-claw him and remove any whiff of his radicalism. By publishing less than 10 per cent of the real manuscript's content, Voltaire had attempted to sanitise the curé of Étrépigny for his contemporaries. Few knew the full extent of this priest's denial of God's existence, for Meslier's complete manuscript was only published fully in Holland during the second half of the nineteenth century.[11] Since then, it has created something of a stir amongst academics who seek to celebrate the eighteenth-century Enlightenment as an anti-religious and atheistic movement that helped create our tolerant and prosperous modernity.[12] But in reality, to depict the Enlightenment as overtly secularist and anti-religious is unhistorical.

Admittedly, Voltaire had rejected the Catholic doctrines and beliefs which the Jesuits spectacularly had failed to inculcate into him at the Collège Louis-le-Grand in Paris.[13] Although he detested bigotry and superstition, it would be a leap to portray the doyen of the French Enlightenment as a militant atheist and political radical. He was a civilised moderate who loathed disorder, mob rule and violence. Voltaire wanted to advance human refinement and betterment, but he was no harbinger of revolution.[14]

One should avoid imposing our present values back onto the Enlightenment. The age of reason was also an age of religion.[15] It is true that one obscure priest in provincial Champagne admitted his atheism posthumously. However, there is little or no evidence of other clergymen sharing his mindset. Indeed, Meslier's views are not so much rare as unique. The only comparable example that comes to mind is that of the Polish nobleman and former Jesuit, Kazimierz Łyszczyński, who was executed in 1689 for having written an atheistic tract. He was beheaded, and his remains burned in the old town market square of Warsaw. During his trial Łyszczyński, understandably, had denied being an atheist, claiming that his treatise was unfinished and that the second half would have refuted the anti-religious claims of the first.[16] It seems unlikely this retraction was sincere, and more probably it was a desperate attempt to forestall his barbaric execution.

Throughout the early modern period, accusations of blasphemy and atheism can be found in the records of the Inquisition and other judicial authorities across Europe. Yet they are relatively rare in comparison to denunciations of poor morals, improprieties during confession, and heresy. Unsurprisingly, those accused of rejecting the existence of God denied this dangerous charge.[17] Unlike medieval heresy, which was often supported by a mass movement, a popular secularism failed to materialise during the eighteenth century. There was widespread incredulity and indifference towards revealed religion but this rarely became militant or coordinated.[18] Admittedly, the writings of the Dutch-Jewish philosopher Baruch Spinoza (1632–77) created something of a stir among a small group of committed followers. His scepticism and agnosticism towards revealed religion was expressed in extremely cryptic language, making it difficult to tell whether he was a pantheist or atheist.[19] For Spinoza and his followers, God was not a conscious and intelligent being, but a cold and impersonal force. They denied the Judaeo-Christian notion of a paternal deity who took an interest to the point of interference in the individual lives of men and women. By the mid-eighteenth century there existed a tiny group of Spinoza-inspired atheists in Paris who denied the existence of God and denounced organised religion. Although they have been much studied, it must be understood that they were a decidedly fringe group in comparison to the mainstream *philosophes*.

Perhaps the most famous atheist was Paul-Henri Thiry, better known as Baron d'Holbach, renowned for his fashionable salon and generous hospitality.[20] He published a barrage of texts showing how Christianity put innumerable obstacles in the way of the advancement of European culture and prosperity. He truly hated the clergy, their teachings and how they used superstition to manipulate the masses. Equally extreme, but more anatomically minded, was Julien Offray de La Mettrie, who published, under the patronage of Frederick the Great, the controversial text *L'homme machine* (*Man a Machine*) in 1748.[21] Here, he argued that man was an animal pure and simple, admittedly a complex organism, but one, like any other, driven by chemistry and anatomy. Human thought, the soul and consciousness were by-products of mankind's physicality and had nothing to do with divine intervention. It was noted that if you beheaded a chicken it remained animate for some time after dying. This was a mechanical response and required no assistance from the soul as the engine of the body. Ultimately, life and consciousness had scientific explanations that did not require assistance from theology or divine revelation to be understood. The book was a sensation and was condemned by almost all Christian denominations. Despite the notoriety of Holbach, La Mettrie and their network of friends, they were a minuscule, embattled group in eighteenth-century Europe.[22] Notwithstanding our contemporary fascination with their writings, which appear to us as incubators for the atheism and secularism of our world, their words were hardly representative of their age.

Voltaire may have coined the effective slogan: *Ecrasez l'infâme!* (destroy the infamous one). Yet, his target was not religion as such but the vengeful God of the Bible, and the violent religious institutions of his day. Voltaire's life was dedicated to the promotion of civilisation and the pursuit of human progress. He did not deny religion's role in fostering morality and public cohesion. Indeed, his quip 'If God did not exist one should invent him' was supposed to express the unifying function of religion in human societies. He did not object to Christianity *per se*, but was horrified by the suffering inflicted in the name of religious bigotry.[23]

Even his rival, the Genevan Jean-Jacques Rousseau, did not deny the existence of a creator of the universe. For Rousseau, man needed to abandon the brutality and superstitions inherent in organised cults such as Catholicism, and instead embrace 'natural religion' (a pantheism of sorts).[24] Morality was to be found in nature and was intrinsic to humanity. There was no need for complex theology or law codes, since one could learn so much from primitive societies and even other animals. The cult of nature, and the quest for a natural and undogmatic religion, was to obsess many thinkers and writers during the Enlightenment. Yet when reading Rousseau's many eulogies to nature one suspects he never witnessed a lion hunt a gazelle, a fox slaughter a chicken, or an eagle bear down on a mountain goat.

For traditionalists, cruelty, hatred and violence were as much a part of the natural world as goodness.[25] Rousseau's followers believed that man, in his original state of innocence, was a beautiful and gentle savage. Conservative Christians thought the opposite was the case. Man, in his natural state, was a fallen being, riven with sinister impulses. Catholic theologians had always argued that divine providence had created both the state and the church to safeguard humankind from its self-destructive nature. Authority, both religious and secular, was divine providence's instrument to keep sin and immorality in check.[26] Church and state were divinely instituted to protect society from temptation and evil. Such views were inspired by the book of Genesis, in which Adam and Eve's fall from grace was described so vividly. Only through baptism could humans be saved from original sin and shown the path to salvation in the postlapsarian universe they inhabited.

By the eighteenth century, theological emphasis on original sin and humanity's fallen state were contested. Many *philosophes* believed that God had endowed individuals with intrinsic goodness, but that they were corrupted by tradition and superstition. Only through liberation from the shackles of the church, and the religious bigotry it promulgated, could a regenerated humanity emerge. Freemasonry, one of the Enlightenment's most popular forms of sociability, attempted to humanise religion by instilling notions of brotherhood and equality in those initiated into its mysteries.[27] Inevitably, its secretive, unorthodox and anticlerical views ensured the hostility of Rome. In 1738, Pope Clement XII had banned Catholics from belonging to masonic lodges with the papal bull *In Eminenti apostolates,* which was confirmed in the apostolic constitution *Providas Romanorum* promulgated by Benedict XIV in 1751.[28]

Such prohibitions did little to dissuade many lay Catholics from becoming deeply involved in masonic lodges. Particularly appealing to Catholics was the bizarre order of the knight-mason elect-priests of the universe. This movement, better known as

Martinism, after its enigmatic founders Martinez de Pasqually and the nobleman Louis Claude de Saint-Martin, captivated a generation of conservatives.[29] Its aim was to infuse Catholicism with a new and exciting mysticism inspired by freemasonry. Some of its adherents became the bitterest opponents of progressive enlightenment. The *philosophes* stressed individualism, liberty and intellectual pluralism, whereas these Catholic knight-masons focused on community, duty and tradition.[30] They would become the backbone of a movement known as the Counter Enlightenment.

This movement was by no means unique. A former Jesuit priest called Pio Bruno Lantieri, unhappy with the masonic nature of Martinism, formed groups known as the *amicizie cattoliche,* literally Catholic friendships. These congregations sought to pray together and restore confidence in Catholic worship.[31] They also funded anti-Enlightenment publications that countered attacks on the church and its teachings. This anti-intellectual movement, though popular with young conservatives and traditionalists, was hardly characteristic of Rome's response to the challenges of the age of reason.

There is a tendency to portray Catholicism and the Enlightenment as irreconcilable enemies. In the aftermath of the French Revolution, reactionaries came to see the Enlightenment as a sort of dangerous laboratory from which the virus of revolution had escaped. The former Jesuit and hyper-conservative priest Augustin Barruel published, in 1797, 'memoirs illustrating the history of Jacobinism'.[32] Having witnessed the suppression of the Jesuit order in 1773, and the persecution of the church during the 1790s, this clergyman became convinced that the *ancien régime* had been subverted and destroyed by a secret conspiracy. According to this view, an alliance of freemasons, *illuminati* and enlightened philosophers had created a coalition that had toppled the alliance of throne and altar by stoking the fires of sedition, which had erupted into an uncontrollable revolution.[33] Such paranoid conspiracy-weaving was to have a toxic afterlife that extended well into the nineteenth and twentieth centuries (this compulsive obsession with occult powers is beautifully illustrated in Umberto Eco's last novel *The Cemetery of Prague*).[34] Barruel's pages spewed forth the bitter recriminations of a man whose world had been turned upside down. He could not believe that the Jesuits and the church had been victims of mere circumstance. For him, behind such cataclysms was a satanic influence that had inspired godless radicals and future Jacobins. All Barruel's wild theories were without foundation.

The Roman Curia knew that many texts of the Enlightenment were highly critical of the papacy's authority and Catholic moral teachings. Condemnation of anti-religious texts was swift and immediate. The Index of prohibited books swelled exponentially during this time.[35] Yet, the story of the church's engagement with the *philosophes* was not one of simple rejection. Although many in the church did view the philosophical and scientific treatises that abounded throughout Europe with suspicion, others saw them as an opportunity to reform and strengthen the faith. From 1740 to 1780, Rome's engagement with Enlightenment-inspired theories was one of negotiation and debate, rather than knee-jerk dismissal. One of the quietest revolutions that happened within the church was the removal of Galileo and other Copernican works from the Index of forbidden books, as a result of which one of the greatest scientific injustices perpetrated by the Catholic Church was, discreetly, undone.[36]

Given that the eighteenth century is often described as an anti-Catholic age it is surprising that many clergymen and Catholics more generally engaged so actively with the Enlightenment's pursuit of new knowledge and a better understanding of the natural world. Indeed, the wily and erudite Prospero Lambertini, the future Pope Benedict XIV (1740–58), fostered learning in remarkably progressive ways while he was cardinal-archbishop of Bologna. In a century where prospects for women in public life were dismal, no fewer than three women were admitted to teach at the University of Bologna (the most ancient in the world).[37] In particular, Lambertini encouraged the careers of Laura Bassi to teach philosophy, Maria Gaetana Agnesi, who became a redoubtable mathematician in Milan, and the anatomist Anna Morandi, whose wax anatomical models are unnervingly lifelike, and still can be viewed at the Museo di Palazzo Poggi (formerly the Academy of Sciences) in Bologna.[38] The success of Catholic women, although remarkable, was by no means exceptional, and the church allowed small groups of elite women to pursue knowledge throughout Europe.[39]

During the first half of the eighteenth century, engagement with new forms of learning was fostered.[40] In most universities until the nineteenth century theology was celebrated as the queen of the sciences.[41] Many pious clergymen hoped that Enlightenment's rigour and new methods would strengthen religious truths, rather than weaken them. Scholars now recognise that a Catholic version of the Enlightenment developed during the eighteenth century.[42] During the second half of the century, several Catholics, especially Jansenists, inspired by the Enlightenment, sought to reform the governance of the church.[43] They wanted to move away from the power, worldliness and magnificence of Baroque Catholicism towards a more primitive, rational, pastoral and less superstitious church. According to their vision, priests would have brought Enlightenment ideas to their communities coupled with a more rigorous and austere faith.

The figure of Benedict XIV must loom large in any understanding of the modern Catholic Church's intellectual trajectory. His wit and joviality made him a highly sympathetic figure. When he became a cardinal, he wrote to a friend reassuringly: 'although I have changed colour, I remain the same'.[44] The scion of a noble family in Bologna, it was apparent from an early age that Lambertini had a fine mind. He received a superb education and chose to enter holy orders. Fast-tracked by the authorities, he was given several apprenticeships within the Roman Curia. His knowledge of canon law and theology was extensive. For several years he was part of the 'congregation for rites', the institution responsible for the regulation of worship and liturgy within the church. His time working here made a deep impact on him, inculcating a deep respect for the Catholic notion of *lex orandi, lex credenda*, which held that prayer and liturgy should reflect the beliefs and fundamentals of the faith.[45] There was a growing sense that worship and ceremony should be updated to accommodate the spirit of the age. Reformers wanted less fanfare and spectacle, and more spirituality and self-discipline. Lambertini published a multi-volume treatise in the 1730s providing guidance on the process for the beatification and canonisation of saints. Clearly influenced by the Enlightenment, Lambertini wanted to rid this process of any tinge of superstition. He believed that many events deemed miraculous could be understood through scientific, medical or rational analysis.[46] The future pope did not call into question the notion of sanctity, but believed that modern methods of research would improve canonisation procedures.

A key influence on Lambertini was Ludovico Muratori, one of the greatest intellects and more neglected figures of the Catholic Enlightenment.[47] A remarkable bibliophile and scholar, Muratori was librarian to the Duke of Modena. A scholar-priest, he had published widely on theology and Italian history. Inspired by Enlightenment empiricism, he exposed historical fictions and debunked the legend that the University of Bologna had been founded by the Emperor Theodosius II during the fifth century (it was founded six hundred years later in 1088, still making it the oldest university in the world).[48] Asked to adjudicate in a border dispute between the Este dynasty and the Holy See over the Comacchio region, Muratori's report came out of in favour of the Este claim and not that of the church.[49]

This decision had presented him with something of a crisis of loyalty. After all, Muratori was a priest who ministered to the parish of Santa Maria della Pomposa in Modena. He was suspicious of the pomposity and ostentation of Baroque Catholicism. For him, such exaggerated displays of adoration verged on idolatry. His most important theological works were *On the Moderation of our Intelligence in Religious Matters* (1714) and *The Science of Rational Devotion* (1747), both published under the pseudonym Lamindo Pritanio.[50] He was critical too of excessive religious feasts, pointing out their negative impact on productivity and industry. In 1748 he published a diatribe urging a reduction in Catholic holy days of obligation.[51] Although these works attracted the attention of the Inquisition, they never drew overt condemnation.

Muratori may have had Jansenist leanings, but he was disciplined enough to keep them in check. Throughout his career he recognised the authority of the papacy. He condemned the 'illiterate fervour' and passions of the uneducated for saints, Marian cults, sacred blood and other bizarre practices.[52] For Muratori such devotional practices smacked of neo-paganism. He corresponded with Benedict XIV, who agreed with him that faith could only be strengthened by rational analysis. For him, the sacred trinity and the person of Jesus Christ should be the focus of the faithful's fervour, and all other cults and ostentatious ceremonies were just distractions.[53] Muratori, like many austere reform Catholics, was an erudite theologian but deeply out of touch with his congregation. Most lay folk had tribal instincts that drew them towards ostentatious ceremonies and rituals that fostered a sense of community. The Catholic Enlightenment may have appealed to scholarly clergymen and intellectuals, but for ordinary folk it robbed them of the enchanted world of relics, madonnas, shrines and incense-shrouded ritual.

Cardinal Lambertini left Bologna in 1740 for a conclave that lasted six months (the longest of the eighteenth century).[54] He emerged as pope, a compromise candidate among the European powers. Despite this, his pontificate proved to be a pleasant surprise for both the *philosophes* and the crowned heads of Europe. Indeed in 1745, Voltaire wrote to Benedict to dedicate to him a new play entitled *Fanaticism, or the Prophet Mohammed*, which the pope gratefully accepted, commenting positively on its quality.[55] Lambertini was determined to strengthen the alliance of throne and altar, and to that effect he signed five concordats with Sardinia, Naples, Portugal, Spain and the Habsburgs.[56] He even managed to establish a working relationship with the nominally Protestant Frederick the Great of Prussia. In 1740 Frederick a had annexed the Catholic province of Silesia from the Habsburgs. Lambertini urged him not to interfere with the religion of his new Silesian subjects.[57]

These international treaties, as we have seen, ultimately failed to forestall the growing determination of European monarchies to subordinate the First Estate to their authority. To the annoyance of the Curia, Benedict XIV was in effect a promoter of decentralisation. In his treatise on diocesan synods, published in

1748, he exhorted bishops to take their pastoral duties seriously. He advocated that bishops reside in their sees, provide well-ordered seminaries to train priests and assiduously visit the parishes of their dioceses.[58] He also advocated the use of regular synods of diocesan clergy to reform and reinvigorate local pastoral life. The 1740s were a liberal decade under Benedict's rule. Following Muratori's advice, he reduced the number of feast days in a bid to increase economic productivity.

He also attempted to promote dialogue with Uniate Catholics, who followed the Eastern rite, and Benedict explored the possibility of the Syrian and Armenian churches returning to communion with Rome.[59] He was also the first pope to use the encyclical, which modelled itself on the epistles in the New Testament. It became the key medium through which the papacy issued its reflections and interpretations on complex issues relating to the Catholic magisterium. Henceforth encyclicals were deployed as a medium by his successors to clarify the faith and the dogmas of Catholicism,[60] a tradition that has persisted to the present day.

Lambertini eagerly, though with very mixed results, sought to reform and improve the administrative, fiscal and legal structures of the Papal States. Despite their best endeavours, the popes of the eighteenth century presided over a civil administration that seemed immune to the energy and enthusiasm for reform and efficiency that gripped other European states.[61] As Lambertini entered the 1750s his attitude hardened. He became worried that Catholic states were encroaching too much on clerical prerogatives, and that calls for the toleration of all religions risked endangering the supremacy of the church. The encyclical *A Quo primum*, promulgated on 14 June 1751, showed that Benedict for all his broad-mindedness could not transcend some prejudices. He stated that:

> Credible and trustworthy experts in Polish affairs and the subjects of the kingdom of Poland itself who communicated with Us have informed Us that the number of Jews in that country has greatly increased. In fact, some cities and towns which had been predominantly Christian have now fallen into

ruin and are now practically devoid of Christians. The Jews have so replaced the Christians that some parishes are about to lose their ministers because their revenue has dwindled so drastically. Furthermore, as the Jews control businesses selling liquor and even wine, they are therefore allowed to supervise the collection of public revenues. They have also gained control of inns, bankrupt estates, villages and public land by means of which they have subjugated poor Christian farmers. The Jews are cruel taskmasters, not only working the farmers harshly and forcing them to carry excessive loads, but also whipping them for punishment, so that their bodies are scarred by the lash. So it has come about that those poor farmers are the subjects of the Jews, submissive to their will and power. Furthermore, although the power to punish lies with the Christian official, he must comply with the commands of the Jews and inflict the punishments they desire. If he doesn't, he would lose his post. Therefore the tyrannical orders of the Jews have to be carried out.[62]

This relatively enlightened pope was unable to transcend age-old antisemitic prejudices. The encyclical replicated centuries-old slurs, saturated with unthinking hatred.

The eighteenth century was a time of increasing violence against the Jewish communities of Poland-Lithuania. Although in the fourth paragraph of *A Quo primum* Benedict XIV cautioned Catholics not to persecute nor mistreat Jews, these words sounded hollow, given the venom of the previous statement.[63] The resurgence of the toxic myth of the ritual murders of Christian children by Jews led to several pogroms in the east of the continent. These violent lynchings were, at times, endorsed by Catholic bishops.[64] In his bull *Beatus Andreas,* published in 1755, Lambertini validated the sixteenth-century myth that Andreas Oxner von Rinn, a Tyrolean child, was ritually murdered by Jews in 1462.[65] While the rest of Europe was moving towards the toleration of its Jewish communities, papal Rome showed little or no compassion for a group it still held responsible for deicide (god-killing, i.e. the murder of Christ).

The dialogue with the Enlightenment, tentatively explored especially in its French version, turned to hostility. Benedict XIV became increasingly suspicious of publications crossing the Alps. In 1752 he found himself forced to place Montesquieu's *Spirit of the Laws* on the Index. This eminent jurist from Bordeaux had been a correspondent and friend of Lambertini, so banning his work was particularly distressing. Montesquieu had analysed minutely how societies formed their legal systems under the influence of climate, culture and society. He advocated for a system of checks and balances, not to mention intermediary bodies, which would blunt the arbitrariness of absolute government.[66] However, Montesquieu's view that religion should have little role in the formation of laws struck at the heart of the church's legislative influence. His support for the toleration of all religions was particularly distasteful to Rome.[67]

Between 1753 and 1757, most of the key works of the Enlightenment found their way into the Index. Most famously, the encyclopaedia of Diderot and d'Alembert was included in the list of works Catholics should avoid. This mass compendium had endeavoured to secularise and de-mystify the sum of human knowledge. Its critical perspectives on tradition and superstition made it incompatible with Catholic teaching. Hostile articles on the clergy, missions and church hierarchy were condemned in Rome. Despite the pope's initial flirtation with Voltaire a decade earlier, all this author's many works now found their way into the Index.[68] Benedict XIV was forced to concede that his initial optimism had been premature, and that the Catholic and French versions of the Enlightenment would prove impossible to reconcile. One aimed at modernising religious faith and the other considered religion a matter purely for the private sphere, and conflict was the inevitable outcome.

Despite this clash with the *philosophes,* the eighteen-year pontificate of Benedict XIV deserves to be better known. He was a remarkable pope, who made a sincere attempt to engage constructively with the modern world. His reign was also a time of great cultural and scientific patronage. The collections and structure of the Capitoline museums in Rome were improved considerably.[69] His love of Britain found its incarnation in the English coffee house (*Caffeaus*) which he had built in the gardens of the Quirinal palace (the summer residence of the popes in Rome).[70] Deeply committed to higher education, he reformed Rome's La Sapienza University, and created new scientific academies that sought to create a working partnership between clergymen, intellectuals and scientists rather than muzzling them.

For a time, Benedict XIV took interest in the English scientist Jane Squire's project to discover a means of reading longitude at sea. The system of navigation until the eighteenth century known as 'dead reckoning' was terribly imprecise and could lead to serious navigational errors. In 1707, it had led to the Scilly Isles disaster in which two thousand British sailors lost their lives.[71] In 1714, the British Parliament passed the Longitude Act, which promised to reward handsomely any person able to devise an accurate means of navigation. The members of the Board of Longitude in London refused to even consider a petition from a woman.[72] In contrast, Lambertini believed that gender should be no impediment to the pursuit of knowledge. He referred Squire's project to the Academy of Sciences in Bologna. Regrettably, the system for measuring longitude presented by Jane Squire was impractical, but in papal Rome she received the consideration that had eluded her in London.[73]

Benedict XIV's greatest contribution to keeping peace within the church was his involvement in a renewed crisis that erupted in France between Jansenist parish priests and their bishops. Christophe de Beaumont, the Archbishop of Paris, intervened intransigently against clergymen suspected of harbouring Jansenist tendencies. He commanded the priests of his archdiocese to withhold the sacraments from all those who did not unconditionally accept the papal bull *Unigenitus*, promulgated in 1713.[74] Effectively, this meant that Jansenists were deemed to be heretics in mortal sin who could not be given Christian burial, unless they recanted their theological views.

The French courts challenged the archbishop, and declared his refusal of the sacraments to the dying an abuse of his authority.[75] Louis XV defended the archbishop's decision and briefly exiled the magistrates of Paris to the provinces.[76] Increasingly worried that events were spiralling out of control, Benedict decided, with the help of the French ambassador in Rome, the Comte de Choiseul, to defuse the growing crisis. The encyclical *Ex Omnibus* of 1756 was a masterpiece of conciliation. It postulated that submission to *Unigenitus* was mandatory, but that if in practice some pious Catholics did privately and without scandal refuse to submit to this bull, then such a rejection could not be considered a mortal sin; therefore absolution could not be withheld from crypto-Jansenists.[77] The French monarchy enthusiastically endorsed this encyclical, hoping it would put an end to the conflict within the Gallican church.

Benedict XIV's long pontificate could be seen as a proactive Catholic response to the Enlightenment – an attempt among the intellectual elite of the Roman church to integrate some of the latest methods and insights of science and philosophy into the faith. Men, and some women, from Lisbon to Warsaw were engaged in this project.[78] As ever these efforts struggled against accusations that the church's commitment to reform was superficial, and that it was not going far enough to modernise. If the church's critics had remained confined to a few radical *philosophes* in Paris, then its position would have remained secure. However, in the decades following the death of Benedict XIV in 1758 the church's partnership with the state became dysfunctional. Two processes, firstly the intensification of reform Catholicism and secondly the emergence of Enlightened Absolutism, would eventually combine to chip away at the decaying alliance of throne and altar.

The first involved the transformation of the ongoing Jansenist controversy from a theological into an explicitly ecclesiological/political debate. Benedict's encyclical *Ex Omnibus* failed to satisfy dissenters within the clergy. As the eighteenth century wore on, Jansenism transformed itself ever more into a reformist movement that demanded a more decentralised church, freed from Rome's interference and supervision. As the American historian Dale van Kely has argued, what had started as a Belgian and French phenomenon now became a trans-European reform movement. German, Italian, Spanish and Portuguese Jansenists and reform

Catholics desired greater autonomy from Rome to preach a more austere and unadorned Christian faith.[79]

As we have seen, the suppression of the Jesuit order in 1773 marked a turning point in the history of Catholicism. This notable victory for reform Catholics proved how much could be achieved by allying with state authorities and monarchical governments. With the destruction of the Society of Jesus, these reformers became so emboldened that they turned their attention to an even greater objective: the curtailing of the power of the pope over their local churches. In order to achieve this, the old medieval principle that the church in council exceeded the authority of the papacy was reasserted with vigour. The final decades of the eighteenth century were the heyday of this neo-conciliarist movement, aiming to provide church governance with a more national and democratic flavour.[80]

At the same time, as Jansenism wove itself into reform Catholicism a second important process was taking place in the realm of European politics: the advent of Enlightened Absolutism.[81] Many monarchs came to be influenced by the progressive ideals of the Enlightenment. Inspired by the works of *philosophes* like Montesquieu and Beccaria, they enacted codified and well-structured laws, whose aim was to increase social harmony and stimulate the economic prosperity of their states. Among the most famous reformers of this period were Frederick the Great and Catherine the Great.[82] During the closing decades of the eighteenth century, Catholic Europe was anything but immune from the reforming zeal of these enlightened but still absolute rulers. Monarchs, and their ministers, prioritised the welfare of their subjects, the reorganisation of their administrations and the size of their armies. Naturally, these reforms challenged the privileges of several vested interest groups. The clergy of the First Estate and their exemption from taxation was increasingly seen as a barrier to modernisation. Opposition to enlightened reform from within the church was resented by monarchs and their bureaucracies. In the 1770s and 1780s Enlightened Absolutism and reform Catholicism joined forces informally to curtail the privileges of the papacy and the church.

The man who would face the gathering storm was Giovanni-Angelo Braschi, who adopted the papal title of Pius VI. Born in Cesena in the former exarchate of Ravenna, Braschi came from the provincial nobility of the Papal States. Like so many of his predecessors, he had experienced a successful career in the Curia. Singled out, in his early days, as a competent economist, he had been treasurer of the *camera apostolica* (finance minister) for the Papal States since 1766.[83] Nearly a decade later, in 1775, Braschi ascended to the throne of St Peter after a conclave that lasted five months. Like his predecessor, Clement XIV, he was a compromise candidate and was elected on the understanding, with Europe's monarchies, that he would not restore the Jesuit order.[84] Unlike most eighteenth-century popes, he was neither stout, corpulent nor elderly, but a tall, energetic 58-year-old, with an imposing physique and a full head of blond-grey hair. According to the family history, the Braschi were originally Swedish refugees from the Reformation who had settled in Italy in the early modern period.[85] One could speculate that the new pope's striking appearance had something to do with these Scandinavian roots. The population of Rome seemed much taken with their vigorous and handsome new ruler.

Domestically Pius VI was to influence his capital city and the Papal States in several ways. The most ambitious project he undertook was the draining of the malaria-infested Pontine Marshes. For centuries these swamps had been a source of disease and made large swathes of the Roman *campagna* unsuitable for cultivation. Having spent fourteen years in Velletri, on the outer rim of the marshes, as an auditor for the local bishop, Braschi was very familiar with this insalubrious region. He would spend millions of *scudi*, over two decades, to reclaim thousands of hectares of land for agriculture.[86] It was one of the largest land reclamation schemes in Italian history, an infrastructure project that had been too complex even for the Ancient Romans. Pius's engineering and hydro-geological projects to drain the marshes created immense construction sites. The pontiff enjoyed travelling to Terracina to supervise and witness the progress made on his attempt to reshape this part of Lazio. His was the biggest contribution to the reclamation of the Pontine Marshes until Mussolini completed their drainage during the 1930s.[87]

Braschi was determined to improve and embellish the urban fabric of Rome.[88] He inherited the rudiments for a museum to display the vast papal art collections from his predecessor Clement XIV. This network of rooms near the Vatican library and papal apartments was described by visitors as cluttered and claustrophobic.[89] The precious artefacts amassed by the papacy were not displayed in a way that emphasised their magnificence and uniqueness. Knowing that the collections of antiquities, statuary and paintings drew many visitors, Pius invested heavily in expanding and improving the exhibition spaces in the Vatican palace. The pope wanted to be the instrument through which a splendid and triumphal imperial Rome would rise from the ashes. An artistically and architecturally magnificent capital city would remind all Europe of the power and confidence of Roman Christianity. The Pio-Clementino complex which was built in these decades still forms the backbone of the Vatican museums today.[90] Especially admired were the *sala degli animali* (chamber of the animals) and *sala delle bighe* (chamber of the chariots). Here centaurs, other mythical beasts, the heroes of old, and stone chariots welcomed important visitors. Naturally, there was a charge for admission to view the papacy's treasures. These fees hardly disturbed the deep pockets of travellers on the Grand Tour.

More ambitious still was the plan to complete St Peter's basilica. The mother church of Catholicism was the largest in the world and Michelangelo's dome dominated the cityscape. Bernini's magnificent colonnades and square were an architectural marvel that created the perfect setting for pilgrims to receive the pope's regular *urbi et orbi* blessings. Yet there was something of an architectural imbalance on the square. On the north side lay the Apostolic Palace, the offices of the Curia and the archives and library, whereas to the south there was a space filled by the ancient round church of Santa Maria della Febbre.[91] Remarkably, the biggest church in Christendom lacked what even small chapels seemed to possess: a sacristy, a room where sacred vessels, vestments, incense and other items necessary for divine worship are stored. The architect Carlo Marchionni was commissioned to build a sacristy to be commensurate and adjacent to the basilica. The finished building took eight years to complete and compromised the already fragile papal finances. It was inaugurated in 1784, and Pius VI could claim to be the pope who had finally completed St Peter's.[92]

His ambitions did not stop there, and he also restored monuments throughout the city. Triumphal obelisks were erected in Piazza Montecavallo, Montecitorio and Trinità dei Monti, thus further embellishing public space within the Eternal City.[93] Artists, aristocrats on the Grand Tour and princely rulers flocked to view the rebirth of the city. In 1783 the Vatican was visited by two important monarchs. First came Emperor Joseph II, who travelled incognito under the name Count Falkenstein.[94] The manic and workaholic emperor was the worst house guest in the world. Pius must have breathed a sigh of relief when he left, but there was not much time to rest as the next day, 22 December 1783, King Gustav III of Sweden arrived in the Eternal City using the pseudonym of the Count of Haga.[95] Pius decided to reserve a surprise for the Scandinavian monarch.

He invited him to high mass in the Sistine chapel on 1 January 1784. After the liturgy was complete, Gustav and his courtiers turned north to enter the Pio-Clementino complex. Here the pope met the king, and displayed the treasures of the Vatican to his awe-struck guests. The Swedish king loved the collection so much that he returned four times to the museum. As a parting gift, Pius VI provided a copy of the museum catalogue and a commemorative painting by the artist Bénigne Gagneraux, depicting Pius displaying the collections to his Swedish royal guests. The pose the pontiff assumes is striking, as it is reminiscent of the statue of Apollo of the Belvedere. His right hand stretches out in a demonstrative and creative gesture. It is almost as if the pope has personally managed to fuse Christianity and Antiquity. Pius is represented as an enlightened monarch and a great conservationist.[96]

Clearly the visit had a great impact on Gustav, who returned to Stockholm and based his museum of Haga on the Vatican collections. Meanwhile, the city drew not only monarchs but also antiquarians and artists. The young Johann Wolfgang von Goethe was particularly moved during a stay in Rome which almost felt like a pilgrimage to him. There is a pastoral portrait of him, in a sweeping white cloak and wide-brimmed hat, by his friend Johann Tischbein. Goethe is deep in contemplation of views of the *campagna romana*.[97]

Rediscovery of Rome was by no means confined to visitors from the north, and most great French artists and architects who won the Prix de Rome government bursary spent time at the Académie de France à Rome at Palazzo Mancini.[98] The late-eighteenth-century turn toward neoclassicism owes something to Pius's attempt to reintegrate the antiquities into the cityscape and collections of the Eternal City. The Enlightenment viewed Classical Antiquity almost with veneration. The papacy showcased how the Roman church too sought to preserve and celebrate the vestiges of the Classical past.

Pius's reputation fared less well when it came to the early modern practice of nepotism. During the medieval and early modern period, the most trusted nephew of a pope would often be elevated to the office of cardinal; the practice provides the etymology for the concept of nepotism. These prelates to an extent became the pope's prime ministers until the creation of the position of cardinal secretary of state in 1605. In 1692, Innocent XII abolished the official title of cardinal-nephew.[99] But in Catholic Europe, the advancement of one's blood relations was common. Royal dynasties, the nobility, judges and public servants, all tended to keep things in the family rather than trust strangers.[100] Although the office of cardinal-nephew had been abolished, Innocent XII had permitted at least one papal nephew to be raised to the crimson. Pius VI was close to his sister Giulia's family. He raised his nephew Romoaldo Braschi-Onesti to the dignity of cardinal in 1786. His niece Bendetta, already a nun of the Camaldolese order (a branch of the Benedictines) in Cesena, was made abbess of her convent, despite being, technically, too young for the position.[101] There was nothing unusual in such appointments. In the eighteenth century, only three out of eight popes did not grant family members a seat in the College of cardinals.

Where the situation became decidedly murkier was Braschi's relationship with Romoaldo's brother Luigi, who was showered with donations. His rise would cause great scandal during the 1780s when he received the gift of thousands of hectares of land reclaimed from the Pontine Marshes.[102] Moreover, Pius VI personally took charge of the marriage negotiations for this nephew. Eventually Constanza Falconieri, a rich heiress related to the princes of Santa Croce, was selected. She brought a dowry of 24,000 *scudi*. To further consolidate this union, the duchy of Nemi, worth 90,000 *scudi* a year, was bestowed on Luigi. In all this, Pius had proved himself a generous and ambitious uncle, but his next scheme came close to inheritance fraud.[103]

Don Amanzio Lepri was the scion of one of the richest families of the Papal States. He had inherited an estate worth 1.5 million *scudi*. However, as a professed Knight of Malta, and a priest, he chose not to enjoy his enormous revenues. As he was the last male member of his family, his niece was destined to inherit the Lepri fortune. For reasons that are far from clear, he quarrelled with his heir and decided to disinherit her. His new will left the bulk of his estate to the Order of Malta, and a significant slice to Luigi Braschi-Onesti. In 1782 Don Amanzio decided to alter his will and left Cardinal Romoaldo Braschi the *usufruct* (revenues) of his estate. A few months later, he changed his mind yet again, and decided to donate his estate to the pope with immediate effect. Once the deed of transfer was signed, Luigi and Romoaldo jumped in a carriage with Don Amanzio to visit Villa Lepri and the other properties.

To the immense embarrassment of the papacy, Don Amanzio's niece decided to challenge in court the donation of the Lepri fortune to Pius VI. The judges, unsurprisingly, found in the pope's favour. The niece, who must have been a lady of some determination, decided to appeal the sentence to the tribunal of the Sacra Rota. In 1785 the braver judges of this appeal court reversed the decision of their colleagues, upholding the claim against the pope. Apparently, crowds gathered outside the courthouse to cheer the verdict. On 25 December 1785 Don Amanzio finally gave up the ghost. Yet another altered last will and testament was then discovered. Its content was deeply disconcerting as, in its preamble, it revealed that the dead Knight of Malta had been pressurised by the pope's agents to gift his estate to the Braschi family against his will. He now bequeathed his estate once more to his niece. The only people delighted by this news were the lawyers involved in the case.

This time it was the pope's family who appealed the Lepri testament to the tribunal of the Sacra Rota. In 1787, a settlement was reached in which the niece would retain the bulk of the fortune but pay 400,000 *scudi* to the pope in compensation. Pius VI's French biographer, a loyal Catholic priest, stressed that the pope's actions were well-meaning, and that he had not intended to raid the Lepri fortune. It is hinted in these pages that Don Amanzio was senile and did not know his own mind.[104] Although the full truth of this episode will never be known one could speculate that the pope felt he could not use public funds to endow his nephew Luigi with an estate worthy of the Braschi dynasty. So, cunningly, it was decided instead to plunder the fortunes of a noble family which was heading towards extinction. This whole affair undoubtedly tarnished Pius VI's reputation.

Nor did the story end here, as the building of Palazzo Braschi, next to Piazza Navona, showed that nepotism was alive and well in the 1780s. The architect Cosimo Morelli was commissioned to build this palace on an awkward, tight and overlooked space. He built one of the last great papal palaces of Rome. The grand staircase, liberally decorated with marble and statues of Roman emperors, remains one of the finest in the city.[105] It was a testament to Pius VI's ambition that the Braschi would rise one day to claim their place among the dominant aristocratic clans of Rome. In this instance he showed himself to be a man of the *ancien régime*, following the example of the Borghese, Pamphili, Corsini, Chigi and Albani families. In some ways, Braschi's cupidity was the swan-song for a venal papacy that was destined to disappear in the nineteenth century.

Despite his previous expertise as treasurer for the Papal States, Pius VI's financial and administrative reforms failed to yield significant benefits in terms of new revenues or better agricultural practices. The Curia and farmers of his kingdom remained wedded to the old ways. Although the papacy paid lip-service to reform and administrative improvement, the dividends reaped in the eighteenth century were to be meagre.[106] But it was on the international stage where Pius VI met his greatest failures. His first skirmishes with enlightened monarchs would involve Frederick the Great of Prussia and Catherine, Tsarina of Russia. Both monarchs refused to recognise the abolition of the Jesuit order within their domains. As they were neither Catholics nor subordinate to the pope, they saw no reason why they should abolish a socially useful teaching order. Eventually, Frederick II came to an agreement with the church which allowed the former Jesuits to become ordinary parish priests who could continue to teach in schools. When Frederick died in 1785 residual Jesuit estates in Silesia were sold. Most of the proceeds went to fund local schools, while the surplus was forfeited to the state which used it to fund the Protestant universities of Frankfurt an der Oder, Königsberg and Halle.[107]

Under Catherine the Great the situation proved quite different. She continued to grant the Society of Jesus her protection. The order would survive in Russia until the first decades of the nineteenth century.[108] This led the Bourbon monarchies to protest against the continued existence of the Jesuits in Russia. There was little Pius could do to compel the powerful and orthodox Tsarina to change her mind. Catherine had been born a Protestant but had converted to Russian Orthodoxy out of political expediency on her marriage to the heir to the Russian throne. As a voracious reader of Enlightenment tracts, she had little use for revealed religion. She deployed the church as an instrument to legitimate her rule and extend the power of the state into the furthest reaches of her empire.

Since the first partition of Poland in 1772, large swathes of Livonian and Lithuanian lands had been ceded to Russia.[109] Catherine refused to allow bishops outside of her empire to exercise any jurisdiction over her newly acquired Catholic subjects in these provinces. To solve this problem, she proposed creating a single Catholic diocese that would cover the entire Russian empire – from the Baltic all the way to the Pacific Ocean – creating the largest Catholic diocese in world history. She chose the well-educated, linguistically versatile and somewhat quisling prelate Stanisław Bohusz Siestrzeńcewicz as her preferred candidate for this new see.[110] The Tsarina gave him a salary of 10,000 roubles and established Mogilev in Belorussia as his new diocese with oversight over two million Catholic souls.[111] Rather than alienating the Russian empire, the pope decided to allow this arrangement as an ad hoc measure. In 1782 Catherine unilaterally raised Mogilev to the status of an archdiocese without permission from Rome.[112] Although diplomatic protests were raised the Curia was forced to accept this *fait accompli*.

In some ways, events in Eastern Europe were harbingers of greater challenges that would come from closer to Rome. Since the medieval period, the pope had been recognised as feudal overlord for the kingdom of Naples.[113] Every year, on the eve of the feast of St Peter and St Paul, ambassadors from this southern Italian kingdom presented 7,000 silver ducats and the gift of a *Chinea*, or prize horse, to the pope in acknowledgment of his suzerainty.[114] Bernardo Tannucci, the prime minister of Naples (1754–76), found this subordination to ecclesiastical authority unbearable. Inspired by reform Catholicism and French Gallicanism, his administration quarrelled with the church over questions of property, taxation and ecclesiastical appointments.[115] He levied taxes on the monastic orders, and refused the papacy the right to appoint bishops for vacant benefices within the kingdom.

Tannucci fell into disgrace in 1776, but his successor, John Acton, a French-born English adventurer who was a great favourite of the Neapolitan monarchs, had little sympathy for the church. On 16 March 1782 the jurisdiction of the Inquisition in Sicily was abolished.[116] Acton refused to continue the ceremony of the *Chinea* with the papacy and stopped paying Rome any tribute. In retaliation, the papacy refused to confirm candidates to vacant sees and by the 1780s thirty dioceses lay vacant in Naples. Attempts were made to negotiate a new concordat, but negotiations floundered. In late 1788 the Bourbons suspended diplomatic relations with the Holy See, and the threat of schism loomed large over the kingdom of Naples.[117] Throughout this time, the papacy was involved in a similar dispute with the Republic of St Mark in Venice.[118] Although this quarrel never reached breaking-point as it did in Naples, it did reveal that even in Italy, the centre of global Catholicism, the position of the church was far from guaranteed.

Spain and Portugal, after the expulsion of the Jesuits, seemed satisfied with their success in bringing the church under state control. In 1777, Lisbon saw the accession of the devout, but unstable, Queen Maria. This made Pombal's hold over the government untenable and he was soon removed from power. Maria was a pious Catholic princess who wanted to establish better relations with Rome. Consequently, Pombal's anticlerical reforms were scaled back and the activities of Portuguese Jansenists in seminaries and universities were restrained.[119] Thus ended almost two decades of cold war between the papacy and the Lusitanian empire.

Across the border, in Madrid, the situation was less favourable. Charles III of Spain had, in his youth, reigned as king of Naples, and was deeply influenced by Bernardo Tannucci. Even after acceding to the Spanish throne in 1759, he continued to correspond with and seek advice from his former prime minister until Tannucci's death in 1783.[120] He chose his Spanish ministers from among committed regalists who supported the supremacy of the state. These included men like the Conde de Floridablanca, Pedro Rodríguez Conde de Campomanes and Gaspar Melchor de Jovellanos whose Enlightenment education made them hostile to the church's independence and landholding power.[121] Ecclesiastical estates, common lands and segneurialism made farming inefficient and agrarian reforms difficult. Campomanes stated simply that when the church prospered the state suffered economically.[122]

He may well have voiced his disapproval of ecclesiastical landowning, and complained bitterly about the untaxable wealth in the hands of idle bishops, but there was little he could do about it in the short term. Attacking the church's political and economic power required subtlety and patience. After the expulsion of the Jesuits, Spanish–papal relations remained tense as the monarchy slowly chipped away at the prerogatives of the church during the 1780s and 1790s. The king and his ministers most of all wanted to restrict the Curia's interference in the lives of the Spanish clergy and laity. Campomanes and Jovenallos agreed with the reforming Italian priest Ludovico Muratori's criticisms of the devotional superstitions of peasants and their flamboyant rituals.[123] Like him they wanted to curtail the number of feast days which acted as a brake on the Spanish economy. By the 1790s, a ban on sending matrimonial disputes to Rome was introduced. These were to be heard by local diocesan authorities instead.[124] In 1804, attempts to reform ecclesiastical entails and property mortgages called *mayorazgos* led to fury and passive revolt in the Iberian empire.[125] While neither the Portuguese nor Spanish chancelleries were anti-religious at heart they did aspire, with mixed results, to bring the church under the authority of the secular state.

These attempts paled into insignificance by comparison with events in Vienna under the Habsburg monarchy. Empress Maria Theresa was one of the most remarkable women to emerge during the eighteenth century.[126] On the death of her father Charles VI in 1740, all the great powers saw their opportunity and pounced on what they believed to be a defenceless Habsburg realm. Maria Theresa showed outstanding resourcefulness and tenacity in fighting back against almost all of Europe.[127] It is a remarkable fact that, although the house of Habsburg was militarily outnumbered, facing financial disaster and with no immediate allies, it survived the crisis with the loss of only a single province. This was largely thanks to the energy and initiative of the empress, who galvanised her ethnically diverse subjects to provide money and troops to resist foreign invasion.[128] In her struggle for survival she learned the art of compromise. Her relationship with Catholicism was one of give and take. She was deeply pious, and fulfilled her religious duties assiduously, but had little love for the contemplative and monastic orders.

When it came to the Jesuits, she defended the order within her domains. Complaints from France, Spain and Portugal against the followers of St Ignatius left her unmoved. They had committed no crimes within the Habsburg lands and there was little reason for the crown to act against them.[129] Maria Theresa had largely delegated the education of her children to Jesuit tutors. The care of her own soul was entrusted to the elderly Father Ignaz Kampmiller, a learned Jesuit who felt keenly the responsibility of ministering to the empress' conscience.[130] The Austrian crown had patronised the order for most of its history, and found them useful militants in stopping the spread of Protestantism in the Holy Roman Empire, Bohemia and Hungary.[131] So the empress temporised while dark clouds gathered round the Society of Jesus. It was only after the dissolution of the Jesuits in Spain in 1765 that Jesuit confessors at the Viennese court were discreetly allowed to retire. Maria Theresa did not push actively for the abolition of the order, nor did she put pressure on the beleaguered Clement XIV to do so. Only when the brief *Dominus ac redemptor* was issued in 1773 did she accept that the order would need to be dissolved throughout the monarchy.[132]

During the final decade of her rule, Maria Theresa continued with mixed policies that encouraged gradual reform and compromise. In late November 1780, she contracted a respiratory illness and passed away; her death marked a turning-point for the fate of Catholicism in her domains. She was succeeded by her son, Joseph II, who was already Holy Roman Emperor.[133] Mother and son had a loving relationship, but one that was intense and highly charged. The young Joseph felt frustration when his enthusiasm for enlightened reform was bridled by his formidable mother. Maria Theresa adored her offspring, but she was prone to micro-management: her letters to her thirteen children show a loving parent, but one who controlled their social lives and entertainments with an obsessiveness which must have been grating. In the case of Maria Antoinette, who failed to conceive a child until late into her marriage with Louis XVI, Maria Theresa wrote to her with unwelcome advice on how to excite her husband in bed.[134] In trying to fashion Joseph into a well-educated crown prince, she showered a litany of rebukes on him. In so doing, she succeeded in breeding a deeply neurotic man cursed with absolute power. His mother always advised Joseph to be moderate, patient and open to compromise. After four decades of heeding his mother's admonitions, Joseph was keen to make his own way in the world.[135]

During his ten years as emperor Joseph II promulgated twice as many laws and regulations as his mother had in four decades!

Joseph despised tradition, privileges, exceptions and immunities, seeing them as corrupt practices that compromised the efficiency of the state. He wanted to streamline the administrative infrastructure of his monarchy, and create uniform legislation that would apply to all equally. His inclination was not merely authoritarian, and there was a humanitarian streak in the emperor, who took a great interest in health care and education.[136] The general hospital in Vienna was remarkable, and Habsburg midwifery practices became the most advanced in Europe.[137] Yet his neuroses and obsession with keeping his subjects on their toes could have unpleasant manifestations. Raids on brothels in Vienna to dispense compulsory anti-venereal treatment on prostitutes were a tad over-zealous.[138] He had a prurient fear that aspirant priests would be corrupted by the world, so he advised that the doors of their seminaries be locked shut to ensure they did not succumb to temptation. Joseph II felt compelled to shine the unwelcome flame of the Enlightenment into the startled eyes of his subjects. He expressed to them his view that they were backward and troglodytic bigots.

Under Maria Theresa, the church had cooperated with the monarchy. Christoph Bartholomäus Anton Migazzi, prince-archbishop of Vienna, had been sympathetic to church reform and entered into a partnership with the empress. His seminary became a leading establishment for the preparation of pastorally responsible and diligent priests. Inspired by Muratori, he wanted to create a more austere and socially connected church. He was an ally of the state's attempt to improve the governance of the church.[139] Joseph's attention did not take long to turn to the church, and his reforms were among the most radical to be visited on the First Estate during the late eighteenth century. He complained bitterly that the monastic clergy outnumbered the parish priests in the Austrian lands. Joseph held parish priests in high esteem, as they provided pastoral care and helped in the education of the young, whereas he saw monks as work-shy parasites.[140] It was clear, from his earliest days, that the enormous monasteries of Austria, Hungary, Bohemia, Lombardy and Belgium were in his sights.

His decision to revoke the religious patent of 1778 caused great consternation. His mother had, through this law, renewed the monarchy's commitment to Counter Reformation Catholicism. Under its terms there could only be one religion in the empire, and that was the Church of Rome. Heretics, Orthodox Christians and Jews were decidedly second-class citizens. The legal status of these religious minorities, not to mention their right to hold property, was precarious and they were barred from public service. In 1781, Joseph tore up his mother's patent and introduced toleration for non-Catholic Christians. Catholicism remained the only cult that could be practised publicly, and the only one that was granted state support. However, Protestants and other Christians could now enter government service.[141]

The situation with Jews in the Habsburg monarchy was different, in so far as Joseph wanted to loosen their restrictions to promote assimilation. Communities within the empire would be free to live where they wanted, and the number of professions they could undertake was increased. Yet, their access to public office, ability to build synagogues and own land remained limited.[142] The rules were different for Protestants and Orthodox Christians who were allowed to build discreet chapels. The emperor's toleration edict pained and alarmed Rome. From the perspective of the papacy, how could a Catholic monarch tolerate heresy, error and deicide? The enlightenment argument that toleration and rational argument would win more converts to Rome did little to assuage the Curia's burning doubts.[143] It was simply impossible for Catholicism to turn a blind eye to doctrines and practices that denied God's grace and led individuals to damnation. For the emperor, increasing the population of his lands, and turning them into public-spirited and useful citizens, was a priority. The harsh limitations that had been placed on Protestants and Jews made their ability to contribute to the state impossible. Joseph aspired to their eventual conversion, but his priority was saving them from ignorance and idleness.

Archbishop Giuseppe Garampi, the papal nuncio to Vienna, was aware of the emperor's religious views, and found his planned changes for the church deeply disturbing. The decision by Joseph II to relax censorship laws and allow anti-religious works to circulate in his capital further damaged his relations with the nunciature. To make matters worse, Joseph saw the pope as a minor prince in central Italy who deserved no special treatment. His relationship with Garampi was fraught and he did his best to frustrate the nuncio. He made access to information difficult and his audiences with the archbishop could last as little as fifteen minutes.[144] For his part, the nuncio reported back to the Curia that he despaired of the situation in Vienna, and doubted whether he could give holy communion to the emperor on Easter Sunday 1781. This refusal to grant Joseph the sacraments would have announced Rome's displeasure to the world. Such a diplomatic incident had the potential to lead to a deeply embarrassing breach between the papacy and the Holy Roman Emperor.[145]

Pius, worried that Garampi was overreaching himself, instructed the nuncio to bestow Easter communion on the Holy Roman Emperor without hesitation. But as Joseph's reforms accelerated, the situation seemed to be spiralling out of control. On 15 December 1781, Pius VI wrote to Vienna reminding Joseph that the enlightened Benedict XIV had been his godfather (by proxy) at his baptism. Surely the improvement of the clergy and the promotion of Catholicism within his domains could be achieved through a mutual understanding? The letter hinted that a meeting between the Holy Father and emperor might smooth the way forward.[146] At the same time, Joseph's foreign minister, Prince Wenzel Anton Kaunitz, wrote to the pope protesting against Garampi's interference in secular matters. He was sure the nuncio's lack of tact could not reflect Pius' true attitude towards the Austrian church. After all, the emperor's new laws were designed to improve the organisation of one true religion in the Habsburg lands. There was no intention of interfering with worship or the teachings of Catholicism, which remained the Holy Father's exclusive prerogative. Joseph intended to confiscate monasteries and redistribute their property to the secular clergy and parishes of his realm. As the emperor had stated, several months previously, to Archbishop Migazzi 'the state is not in the church, but assuredly the church is in the state'.[147] This letter from Kaunitz was conciliatory in tone, despite affirming the empire's supremacy. It offered hope that the emperor might be open to negotiation.

Meanwhile, back in Rome, Pius VI, after consulting with the College of Cardinals, put forward an unprecedented proposal. He would travel to Vienna to negotiate directly with the emperor and seek to forestall his more anti-monastic reforms. Everyone was astounded, as it had been over five centuries since a pope had left the Eternal City to travel abroad.* On 28 December 1781, Garampi delivered the papal request to visit the imperial capital to a flabbergasted Kaunitz. Joseph suspected that this was a delaying tactic from Rome rather than a genuine proposal. When Garampi was granted an audience, the emperor interrupted him almost immediately stating that he saw no point in the pope undertaking such a long journey, given that he would not change his ecclesiastic policies. However, Joseph conceded that it would be a prestigious event, and an honour, to receive the pope in Vienna.[148]

As preparations began, it was still far from clear what sort of a welcome Pius VI would receive in Austria. Given that government censorship had been relaxed at the beginning of Joseph's reign, the months preceding the papal visit sparked a pamphlet war on the nature of the papacy and its role in the modern world.[149] The person who made the greatest impact in the public debate was the Jesuit-educated Joseph Eybel, a professor of canon law. His pamphlet *Was ist der Pabst? (What is the Pope?)* caused a sensation. He conceded that the bishop of Rome spoke with the greatest spiritual authority, and that he was the living embodiment of 'unity' within the Christian religion. However, in true Reform Catholic fashion, Eybel set out to prove that the pope was technically the equal of all other bishops. Through the presentation of meticulous historical evidence, he strove to demonstrate that the supremacy of the Holy See (and papal monarchy) were medieval distortions of the church's original governance.[150]

---

* The last time was Pope Innocent IV's trip to the Council of Lyons 1244; Martin V was elected in Constance in 1417 but did not travel again after taking possession of Rome. See Johann von Müller, *The Journeys of the Popes* (London, 1852), p. 37.

In effect, Eybel attacked the Baroque spirituality of the Counter Reformation and took a neo-conciliarist line on papal authority; that is to say that bishops and church councils should retain the right to choose what was best within their lands, and that ecclesiastical appeals to Rome violated the rights of the episcopacy.[151] Eybel's pamphlet (the first of a series of four) became the manifesto of what might be called Josephism. It was clear that the emperor's religious priorities shared much with Catholic reformers who were sympathetic to the suppression of the monasteries, improved education, religious toleration and more austere worship. Over seventy pamphlets emerged in response to Eybel's anonymous work, and showed just how controversial the question of the papacy's position in the Age of Enlightenment had become.[152] Across the Alps, the Holy Office in Rome would not take long to place all of these anti-papal pamphlets on the Index. Pius VI may have intended to travel to the most loyal of Catholic monarchies, but the Habsburg civil service and public opinion were deeply committed to clerical reform.

On 9 February 1782, Pius and a small retinue of prelates, courtiers and attendants left Rome.[153] If he hoped that his visit would avert Joseph II's reforms he was to be disappointed. Legislation on the dissolution of monasteries and the toleration and emancipation of the Jews continued to be implemented. The pope had written that he would reside at the nunciature with Archbishop Garampi, but he was invited to stay at the Hofburg, the palace–government complex that dominated the centre of Vienna.[154] Here, Joseph argued, it would be easier to negotiate through informal discussion. The pope was supposed to travel in secrecy to avoid long-drawn-out ceremonies, questions of etiquette and other delays. In reality, his journey was an open secret. Everywhere municipal authorities disobeyed orders and rang city bells as the pope went by. Crowds of the faithful, clergy and grandees lined the route to cheer him. Once he crossed the border into Carinthia, the emperor's sister Marianne, who was the abbess of a local convent, came to pay her respects to Pius. Joseph and his brother Max Franz, coadjutor to the archbishop-elector of Cologne, travelled beyond the suburbs of Vienna to greet their visitor.[155]

On 22 March Pius VI and Joseph II solemnly embraced each other to great acclaim. They then travelled together in the same carriage. It was estimated that up to one hundred thousand people lined the route from Wiener Neustadt to the Hofburg, cheering the emperor and the pope.[156] In the palace Pius was introduced to the imperial ministers and other royal dignitaries. As this reception concluded the pope proceeded to celebrate a solemn *Te deum* (a hymn of thanksgiving created by St Ambrose in the fourth century), with music possibly composed by Franz Seraph Kohlbrenner, in the chapel. The visit would last a month, but the emperor was ill, with an inflammation in his eyes, which prevented discussions from taking place for nine days. Pius and Joseph eventually negotiated face to face without witnesses; consequently it is difficult to know with certainty what was discussed between them. Having said this, Joseph kept a journal, and the papal master of ceremonies, Dini, did the same.[157] Thanks to these documents, it is possible to gain an insight into the conversations that took place between pope and emperor. In total the two sovereigns spent over thirty hours in each other's company, during which time they debated delicate political, ecclesiastical and theological issues, trying to extract concessions from each other.

From the above-mentioned sources the pope comes across as conciliatory during the preliminary stage of negotiations. He even claimed to understand the reasons that had driven Joseph to publish the Edict of Toleration.[158] Pius' first days in Vienna coincided with Holy Week, and the pope gave daily blessings to vast crowds, who were promised plenary indulgences for their sins. This ensured that the pontiff became a magnet for hundreds of thousands of pious pilgrims who came from throughout the empire to be blessed and forgiven their sins. On Maundy Thursday 1782, the emperor received communion from the pope's hands. In the evening, during the solemn *Cena Domini* mass, the pope washed the feet of twelve paupers in memory of Christ doing the same for the disciples. This ceremony was usually performed by the emperor but he was too ill because of his eye condition. Holy Week was a remarkable event when the entire panoply of Baroque Catholic ceremonies, mystical devotions and arcane rituals were fully deployed, but this Easter in Vienna was even more splendid than usual given the presence of the supreme pontiff.[159]

The widespread enthusiasm for the first papal visit outside of Rome in five centuries showed how much prestige the papacy commanded beyond Italy. Another gradual process that occurred throughout the eighteenth and nineteenth centuries might be described as Catholicism's rediscovery of the 'people'. During the *ancien régime*, the masses were considered savages by many of the upper classes. The condescending Jesuit expression of *nuestras indias* (our Indies) referred to the substandard religious education of many Europeans living in the countryside, whose appreciation of the gospels was little better than that of pagans.[160] Eighteenth-century clergy believed that the people needed discipline and education to curb their superstitious instincts and devotions. As the church entered the nineteenth century, it came to the realisation that devotion, fervour and passion were great assets to be channelled rather than repressed. The post-Enlightenment church would concentrate on emotional and romantic forms of worship that would have disgusted the aristocratic bishops and theologically erudite priests of the previous century.[161] Pius was the first pope to witness the phenomenon of mass Catholicism beyond the Alps. Though moved by the crowds who sought his blessing, he may not have appreciated fully that they were the very bedrock of Catholicism. They were to be an invaluable resource when Europe plunged into revolution a decade later.

Despite initially cordial negotiations with the Austrian emperor, the mood soon changed for the worse. On 12 April the pope became so heated that he stated he would not have given Joseph communion during Easter if he had realised the emperor's true views on religion. Pius even threated to leave Austria early given their lack of progress. Eventually, Joseph agreed to yield six very minor concessions mainly relating to ecclesiastical and judicial appeals to Rome.[162] The language of these concessions was vague and there was no means of ensuring that Joseph II would keep his promises. Despite this the pope felt somehow reassured. As a gesture of goodwill Pius accepted that the emperor would be allowed to nominate candidates for vacant dioceses in the province of Austrian Lombardy. This would be ratified on 20 January 1784 in the Lombard Concordat between the empire and the papacy.[163]

Joseph had the effrontery to demand that the pope instruct the clergy under Habsburg rule to collaborate fully with his ecclesiastical reforms. Even more controversially, Pius was asked to praise, in an open letter, the piety of the emperor and his capital city. These demands went too far, and Pius refused to exhort priests to accept reforms that would interfere with the freedom and autonomy of the church. To defuse the situation, a vague statement was issued, stating that the pope praised the urbanity, generosity and hospitality of the emperor. When it came to the pope's views of Joseph's religious virtue there was a deafening silence. As ever, Pius's greatest weakness, family ambition, was exploited. He accepted the title of prince of the Holy Roman Empire for his nephew Luigi.[164]

On 21 April 1782 the papal convoy left Vienna to travel into the south of Germany. Here he visited sites of Catholic devotion and praised the population's zeal before heading into the Tyrol for the long journey back to Rome. In practice, the conferences between Joseph and Pius changed little. What is remarkable is how lukewarm the pope was in his defence of the monasteries within the borders of Austria. The reason for this lack of resolve is difficult to fathom. One could speculate that, after the suppression of the Society of Jesus in 1773, he felt that the writing was on the wall when it came to the regular orders. Given this lack of papal opposition, the emperor continued his religious policies and reforms with few qualms. Although Pius failed to stem the tide of religious change in the Habsburg monarchy, the results of his trip were hardly trivial. As Joseph II's biographer Derek Beales has put it, Pius VI's journey to Vienna probably forestalled an imperial excommunication and potential schism with Austria.[165] This would have had disastrous repercussions for the Catholic world. In the end Vienna remained in communion with Rome, though tensions persisted. In 1783, to maintain cordial relations and discuss some issues relating to Habsburg Lombardy, Joseph II paid a return visit to Pius where he enjoyed the marvels of Rome in his usual manic way.[166]

In 1780, at the time of the emperor's accession to the throne, there were two thousand convents with around forty thousand monks and nuns in his domains. Inspired by reform Catholicism, the emperor, with the help of his administration, was determined to do away with monasteries which were dismissed as parasitical and wasteful. As early as December 1781, Joseph had decreed the dissolution of all monasteries that were purely contemplative in nature.[167] Their lands, riches and assets would be confiscated by the imperial treasury and sold. The profits from these sales were not appropriated directly by the state but were instead used to support parish clergy. Monks and nuns who served in a medical, educational or welfare capacity were permitted to continue their ministry. In some cases, monastic chapels were transformed into parish churches. Joseph instructed bishops to retrain able-bodied monks and to requalify them as secular priests. The abolition of monasteries under Joseph was not a reprise of the Henrician reformation but rather followed the progressive credo that clergy should benefit and provide pastoral care to the community. In the end, about a quarter of all monasteries, or 530 in total, were abolished. The number of monks and nuns was reduced by over 50 per cent, while the total of parish clergy increased by a quarter.[168]

Joseph's policies showed little or no desire to maintain the old alliance of throne and altar on an equal footing. The determination to establish the state's supremacy over the church was obvious. Catholicism's function was to be reorientated towards utilitarian and practical ends to the detriment of its mystical and contemplative vocation. The funds created by the suppression of the monasteries subsidised new parishes, created an impressive network of schools, and increased the budgets of universities, hospitals and general seminaries. The independence and privileges of the church were curtailed, along with the fees that priests could charge for baptisms, marriages and funerals.[169] Equally, pilgrimages, brotherhoods, cults and holy days of obligation were all placed under strict government control and supervision.[170] These measures may have been popular with Chancellor Kaunitz and the Viennese-educated elites, but elsewhere in the empire they were received with surprise. In the Austrian Netherlands, the decision to impose state-controlled general seminaries and the abolition of monasteries made no small contribution to the Belgian revolt of 1788–90.[171]

What Enlightenment reformers failed to understand was that it was impossible to abolish religious belief with one stroke of the quill. Peasants across the empire continued to take part in processions, and venerate relics and Marian shrines.[172] They wanted trained priests who were close to their communities and facilitated their system of folk beliefs. Well-trained, theologically brilliant and puritanical priests, with a fanatical desire to reform worship, were hardly welcome. Regardless of the emperor's decrees, the faithful continued to cling to their beliefs. Eventually modern states, and their intrusive reforms, met with dogged resistance.

This was certainly to be the case in the Grand Duchy of Tuscany, where Joseph II's brother Leopold reigned. Like the Holy Roman Emperor in Vienna, the Grand Duke was deeply influenced by the Enlightenment and its theories. He wanted to reform his administration and create an efficient and prosperous polity. Leopold, inspired by the writings of the jurist Cesare Beccaria, abolished the death penalty for the first time in human history in 1786.[173] When it came to the church, he shared his brother's contempt for superstitious devotions and the First Estate's tendency to oppose change. He found an ally in Scipione de' Ricci, a prelate who hailed from a noble family which included a saint in its pedigree.[174] Although educated by the Jesuits, Scipione felt drawn, from an early age, by the writings of Jansenists and reform Catholics. When in 1780 he was elevated by Leopold to become bishop of Pistoia and Prato he was a man on a mission.*

De' Ricci was highly sceptical when it came to Baroque Catholicism and its panoply of flashy rituals. As a man of austere Jansenist tendencies, he wanted to return the church to its primitive roots, and excise devotional practices that smacked of neo-paganism. He was sympathetic to the Gallican tradition

---

* For an exhaustive collection of his writings see C. M. F., *Il Vescovo Scipione de' Ricci e le Riforme Religiose sotto il Regno di Leopoldo I* (7 vols, Florence, 1869).

and neo-conciliarist theories of eighteenth-century reform Catholicism. He wished to reduce the interference of the papacy in his own diocese, and sought to increase the Tuscan clergy's autonomy from the Curia.[175] Grand Duke Leopold was deeply sympathetic to these reforming instincts, and encouraged his zealous bishop in his efforts to improve his clergy. Local seminaries were overhauled, and a more rigorous Augustinian training was enforced on aspirant priests. The culmination of de' Ricci's efforts came in 1786, when he summoned a synod in Pistoia.[176] Technically, this assembly of diocesan clergy served as a sort of episcopal forum, where internal reform of the governance of the diocese was debated. Benedict XIV had published in 1748 a tract entitled *De Synodo Diœcesana* in which he encouraged the episcopacy to hold regular meetings where bishops and priests could discuss matters of common concern.[177]

After meeting for over a week, in late September the clergy of Pistoia issued a remarkable set of decrees. These denounced the fact that some bad habits, superstitions and cults had contaminated the Catholic faith. The fathers in the synod wished to return their flock to purer forms of Christianity. The decrees categorically denounced the cult of the sacred heart of Jesus, whose practice was dismissed as idolatrous, because such devotions stressed the physicality of Christ above his divine nature. St Augustine's views on free grace and predestination were reaffirmed (the Calvinist inflection in these articles was troubling for the Curia). Furthermore, it was decided to have the Roman missal translated into the vernacular so that the Italian-speaking population could finally understand the sacred mystery of the mass. The synod delineated the sacraments in simpler language, and tried to establish liturgies that would avoid pomp and magnificence. The fathers of Pistoia recommended that Tuscan seminaries have their curricula renovated to produce priests who were better educated and able to catechise their congregations. Following the example of the Austrian lands and the suppression of the Jesuits, it was deemed desirable that several monastic orders be abolished due to their limited social utility.[178] The synod of Pistoia was the most overt attack on Baroque Catholicism ever attempted within the church. In all its decrees, the authority of the pope was questioned and its tone was decidedly neo-conciliar.

This famous synod did not quite produce the results it intended. The curtailment of the cult of the sacred heart and other saintly devotions proved unpopular with the parishioners in Pistoia. When de' Ricci decided to tear down secondary altars to emphasise the importance of the high altar this was seen as sacrilegious. Riots and protests broke out against the synod's reforms. The people of Prato attacked the episcopal palace after the bishop had proclaimed that the Virgin Mary's girdle, held in the treasury of the cathedral, was fake. Troops were needed to restore order.[179] Luckily for de' Ricci, he had the Grand Duke's support, and it was decided to summon a gathering of all Tuscan bishops to discuss the Pistoian decrees. In 1787 a national council of bishops met in Florence and there was a decidedly lukewarm response to the reforms initiated at Pistoia. A mere three bishops adhered to de' Ricci's reform programme.[180]

The papacy acted slowly, as tensions grew in Tuscany. Only after Joseph II died in 1790, and his brother Leopold had succeeded him as Holy Roman Emperor, did the Curia intervene. De' Ricci had lost his protector, and the pope, in 1794, condemned the synod of Pistoia with the papal bull *Auctorem fidei*.[181] He was confined to his palace and only in 1805 did he agree to abjure the decrees of Pistoia. The situation in Tuscany showed that, even in the heart of Italy, Jansenism had melded with the neo-conciliarist movement into a troubling challenge to the authority of Rome. Yet Pistoia was not a new dawn, but the high point of Italian Jansenism, which crumbled away during the 1790s. The Pistoian decrees foreshadowed many of the decisions taken during the Second Vatican Council of the 1960s.[182] Ultimately, de' Ricci proved to be a man ahead of his times, and the *ancien régime* church was unprepared for such radicalism.

Eventually the gales of neo-conciliarism engulfed the Holy Roman Empire. Since the sixteenth century, papal influence in the Reichskirche had always been controversial.[183] The Jansenist and Gallican traditions crossed the Rhine. Johann Nikolaus von Hontheim, the scion of a noble family who rose to become an auxiliary bishop to the archbishop-elector of Trier, was sceptical of papal claims to supremacy.[184] Like de' Ricci and the Jansenists, he strongly adhered to the notion that the church, when in council, superseded the authority of the pope. A rather turgid multi-volume treatise in Latin with the lumbering title *On the state of the church and the legitimate power of the Roman pontiff* was published in 1763.[185] Its named author was one Justinus Febronius, a *nom de plume* for Hontheim.

For all its density, the content of these books set the Reichskirche alight, and a movement, known as Febronianism, was born. Like so much of reform Catholicism it wanted an ecclesiological revolution and an abandonment of Baroque devotions. What had happened in France, Austria and Tuscany now spread to Germany. Hontheim was particularly sceptical about the pope's claims to supremacy and his demand to exercise authority within the Holy Roman Empire. There is no need to dwell unduly on the contents of this long and tedious work of ecclesiology. Its most immediate effect was to be placed on the index of prohibited books, and, in the 1780s, when Hontheim was discovered to be the author, Rome demanded that he publicly recant his errors.[186] This process was to be a turbulent one, in which Hontheim negotiated and redefined his retraction so often that he elicited the fury of the authorities in the Curia.

Hontheim was no Martin Luther, but his words had certainly given the clergy of the Reichskirche a new arsenal of arguments against the Curia's pretentions in Germany. Matters came to boiling-point when Rome planned to send a papal nuncio to Munich and increase the powers of its nuncio in Cologne.[187] These envoys of Rome were given special powers to hear appeals that sidestepped local diocesan courts and could bestow dispensations without consulting with the local episcopacy. The prince-bishops and archbishop-electors of the empire saw this as a gross usurpation of their prerogatives. In 1786 the archbishops of the Holy Roman Empire met to discuss how to respond to Rome's encroachment on their power. They produced a document known as the *Punctation of Ems*. Its contents bore striking similarities to the decrees of the synod of Pistoia which was taking place at same time.

The *Punctation* categorically demanded that: 'all nunciatures to cease totally, nuncios can be received only in the character of envoys of the pope'.[188] The meeting at Ems also insisted that diocesan boundaries should reflect national borders. The document complained that too many French, Swiss and other non-German bishops had authority over imperial subjects. Initially the *Punctation* met with Joseph II's approval as Holy Roman Emperor, as it sought to increase the powers of the German church against Rome.[189] However, within a year this radical document capsized on the rocks of internal division. The prince-bishops and bishops of the empire felt that the archbishops had arrogated too much power to themselves over the German church. In 1787 the archbishop-elector of Mainz withdrew his adherence to the *Punctation*, followed by the archbishop-elector of Trier three years later.[190] The *Punctation* became the dog that did not bark. The French Revolution presented the papacy, the First Estate and kings of Europe with a challenge that nullified these disagreements.

The second half of the eighteenth century saw an intensification of the internal and external challenges to the authority of the Church of Rome. As already mentioned, the suppression of the Jesuit order in 1773 was hardly an end to the woes of the papacy, but only made ecclesiastical reformers and secular states bolder in their desire to subordinate the church to their authority. With growing success, monarchical governments curbed the privileges and immunities of the First Estate to advance the power of the modern state. As the eighteenth century progressed, many clerics came to see church reform as not merely desirable but essential for survival. Enlightened clergymen and Jansenists coalesced into an informal sodality that sought to redefine the governance of the Catholic Church and reform its devotional practices.[191] Some reformers, like Muratori, focused on ridding the Roman church of its superstitions and folk devotions, but their sobriety and joyless approach to the faith failed to win over their congregations. Meanwhile the episcopacies of France, Tuscany, Austria and the Holy Roman Empire increasingly defended their prerogatives against papal interference. In this they were inspired by the four Gallican articles that had been issued in 1682.[192] There was a growing focus on how church councils were superior to the authority of the pope.

If these trends had continued unabated, one could speculate that a more democratic and devolved Roman Catholic Church might have emerged during the nineteenth century. However, the events of 1789 changed the course of history dramatically for the Roman church.

3

INTO THE MAELSTROM:
THE FRENCH REVOLUTION,
1789–99

D uring the *ancien régime*, the Place de la Nation, on the
eastern side of Paris, was known as Place du Trône. This
name commemorated the triumphal entry of Louis
XIV into his capital after his marriage in 1661. In this square a
ceremonial throne had been erected to celebrate this monarch's
union with Marie-Thérèse d'Autriche. This public space became a
site of memory for the greatest of Bourbon king.[1] Once in power,
the revolutionaries of 1790 decided to obliterate any vestiges of the
monarchical past. First of all, they changed its name to Place du
Trône-Renversé, which translates as 'Square of the toppled throne'.
Then they turned it into a place for public executions during the
Great Terror of 1793–4.[2] A scaffold dominated by a guillotine
occupied the centre of the square. It reminded passers-by of the
fate that awaited the enemies of the Republic. Where once the
monarchy had celebrated its triumphs now counter-revolutionaries
were beheaded before crowds of *sans-culottes*. According to
contemporaries the stench of death and putrefaction that emanated
from this place of execution was nauseating.

On 17 July 1794 several tumbrils ambled their way into this
grim square, one of them carrying sixteen women of varying
ages. To the surprise of the crowd, they sang: *Salve Regina, Mater*

Misericordiæ (Hail Holy Queen, Mother of Mercy).[3] In a time of anti-Catholic fervour, it was inflammatory, and brave, to sing hymns to the Virgin Mary. During the two hours of their final journey from the Conciergerie prison to the Place du Trône-Renversé they sang many hymns, including the office of the dead. These victims of the Terror were all nuns from a convent in Compiègne, about fifty miles from Paris, and had been sentenced to die for the crimes of fanaticism and sedition.[4] In a trial with unreliable witnesses, the jurymen were shown letters to a priest in which the nuns lamented the Revolution's dissolution of their convent and the end of the monarchy. Their moderation and lack of commitment to the Republic's mission to regenerate humanity condemned them.

Silence descended as the nuns dismounted from their tumbril. In a final act of heroism, these women had decided that the youngest novices would die first, comforted by their seniors as they ascended to martyrdom.[5] Madame Lidoine, their leader, watched her subordinates mount the scaffold serenely. To the surprise of the crowd, Lidoine intoned the hymn *Laudate Dominum omnes gentes* (Praise the Lord, all peoples). The prioress took her position at the foot of the steps leading to the guillotine. She offered her hand to help, and comforted her sisters in Christ as they mounted to their deaths. They considered themselves martyrs and were convinced that soon they would see their God face to face. Witnesses to this gruesome spectacle were deeply moved by how the sixteen voices singing slowly petered out as, one by one, the nuns were beheaded. Madame Lidoine's was the last voice heard as she mounted the scaffold, following her flock to execution.[6] Afterwards, their bodies and heads were taken to the nearby cemetery of Picpus. They were thrown into a common grave with 128 other bodies of those executed that day.[7] Ten days later, Maximilian Robespierre, one of the key leaders of the Terror, was toppled and met the same end as the sixteen nuns of Compiègne.[8] Their deaths were pointless, brutal and a mistake.

By chance, three of the congregation had not been in the convent at the time of the arrests on 23 June 1794. They would keep the flame of memory of their martyred sisters burning bright throughout the nineteenth century,[9] a memory that became weaponised as the conflict with Catholicism intensified. In 1905 the French Republic declared a complete separation of church and state.[10] That same year Pope Pius X beatified the martyrs of Compiègne who had given such a venerable example of courage and stoicism for posterity. Their story inspired Gertrud von Le Fort to write a novel, published in 1931, *Die Letzte am Schafott*, loosely based on the events of 1794. Decades later, in 1957, François Poulenc composed a haunting opera entitled *Dialogues des Carmelites*, which honoured the memory of these courageous nuns.[11] The Revolution of the 1790s was the nadir in the fortunes of the modern Catholic Church. Not since the Roman persecution of the first centuries AD had the papacy faced such a threat.

Pius VI and the church had faced significant challenges during the 1770s and 1780s. Yet little could have prepared Rome for the events of the 1790s, which were an extraordinarily violent amplification of the church's conflicts with the Enlightened Absolutists. The regalists and reform Catholics of the eighteenth century wanted to subordinate the church to the power of the state, and aspired to create a more pastorally committed church that would genuinely minister to the needs of its folk.[12] A storm had been gathering round St Peter's dome, but this was hardly unique in the annals of the church. All the Catholic kingdoms had experienced tense relations with Rome. But in France reform Catholicism and Enlightened Absolutism had made less headway in curtailing the power of the church than their counterparts in Spain, Italy and the Habsburg monarchy. It is true that French Jansenists had criticised the power of their bishops and appealed for a more accountable quasi-democratic church.[13] Their newspapers and pamphlets attacking the papacy and the Jesuits had made some impact among the reading public, but had failed to win deep-rooted popular support.[14]

Indeed, if circumstances had been different, the church might have been subject to gradual reform rather than revolution. But the 1780s had been a time of severe fiscal crisis for the French monarchy.[15] Although the eighteenth-century French economy continued to grow, if measured by manufacturing output and colonial commerce, agriculture had stagnated, and the vast majority of French people depended on the land. To make matters worse, Louis XVI found it impossible to reform the excise system to increase revenues, nor could he raise new direct taxes. Powerful vested interests, such as the clergy, nobility, guilds and tax farmers, made raising the crown's revenue impossible.[16] France's intervention in the American War of Independence had brought revenge and victory over Britain in 1783, it had also made France's budget deficit acute.[17] By 1788, the crown was bankrupt, and its attempt to levy new taxes had caused provincial revolts. In November the king and his reforming minister Chrétien-Guillaume de Lamoignon de Malesherbes discussed the escalating crisis. Louis remarked that the situation bore striking parallels with the English civil war. Despite agreeing with the king that the situation was alarming, Malesherbes reassured him that at least 'religious quarrels are not involved'.[18] These words were to prove ironic.

Louis XVI reluctantly summoned an Estates General to Versailles to advise him and rubber-stamp his tax reforms. Not since 1614 had this consultative body been assembled.[19] It encompassed the three estates of the realm: the clergy, nobility and commons. These orders reflected the old medieval notion that society was divided into those who prayed, those who fought and those who did everything else. The king made the decision that the Third Estate (the commons) would have their number of representatives doubled, so that they would equal the First Estate (the clergy) and the Second Estate (the nobles). It was not clear whether this assembly would vote by order or by head. If voting were to take place by order, then the church and aristocracy would always outvote the Third Estate. As part of the election process, each district, and local clerical and noble assemblies, drew up lists of grievances or *cahiers de doléances*. These complaints would act as a sort of mandate on the deputies, who represented the interests and concerns of their locality at the Estates General.[20]

As was perhaps predictable, most of these grievances focused on feudal dues, tithes and taxation which were considered too burdensome by the peasant population of France.[21] Although there was the odd anticlerical complaint or inflection, it can hardly be claimed that an anti-religious *leitmotif* was obvious in the catalogue of grievances. Indeed, in many cases, these lists demonstrated that the people of France were sympathetic to poor parish priests. They were perceived to have suffered much at the hands of a power-hungry episcopacy and corrupt regular clergy, whose monasteries and convents deprived them of vital income. The concerns expressed by the clergy on the whole demonstrated the order's willingness to reform ecclesiastical tax exemptions and tithes. In return for a greater financial contribution, many priests lobbied for a solemn declaration that Catholicism would remain the state's religion and that it should be fostered.[22] Some of the less progressive *cahiers* proposed repealing the Edict of Toleration for Protestants introduced by Louis XVI in 1787.[23] Most parish priests were less militant, and urged the passing of laws that would promote Christian ethics and maintain public morals. The most radical parish priests demanded that the Estates General meet regularly in future and have the power to approve taxation. Unsurprisingly, given their poor relationship with their monastic colleagues, half the secular clergy wanted monastic wealth confiscated and redistributed amongst poor parishes.[24] These documents reveal a church deeply divided between its hierarchy and its priests, but open to some reform.

Elections for the deputies to the First Estate produced a very different result from that of 1614. This time, only 46 were bishops and 56 senior clerics of other kinds, while 231 parish priests and a mere 10 monks made up the total. The last time the Estates had met in 1614, only 10 per cent of clerical deputies could have been classified as parish priests.[25] This sharp division between prelates and priests would become all too apparent after the Estates had assembled and started their deliberations. Indeed, many of the key speakers in the debates would be men who had had noticeable Jansenist leanings under the *ancien régime*.[26] Initially, at least, reform Catholics welcomed the Revolution as a means of furthering their agenda. A desire to restructure the church, and remove its privileges, was something that at first united long-standing reformers with the revolutionaries of 1789.

On 2 May 1789 the Estates General opened with a large religious procession from the parish of Notre Dame de Versailles to the church of Saint-Louis on the other side of town.[27] This pageant, although nobody realised it at the time, was to be the funeral march of the *ancien régime*. It filed past in increasing order of importance. Deputies from the Third Estate headed the procession, followed by the nobility. Members of the royal household in full ceremonial uniforms accompanied them. They included the Grand Falconer of France riding on horseback with a bird of prey held firmly on his glove. At the centre of the procession, the place of honour, members of the royal chapel carried the blessed host in a monstrance to display it to onlookers. Behind the host came the king and the royal family, with the clergy on either side.[28]

When they arrived, the commoner deputies took seats at the front of the church which had in fact been designated for members of the privileged orders. The Grand Master of Ceremonies quickly evicted them from these seats and relocated them to the back of the church. Subordination was manifest even in the uniforms of the different estates. Cardinals and bishops wore splendid violet and crimson robes, while the nobility dressed in black silk suits with silver braid and plumed hats. Third Estate deputies had to make do with a drab black suit without any decoration whatsoever.[29] When delegations of each order were sent to compliment the king, the clergy and nobility were allowed to stand while presenting their homage. Members of the Third Estate kneeled as supplicants in what was seen as a slight to their dignity. The decision to use the same ceremonial procedures and etiquette that had been used in 1614, without any revision to reflect the changed circumstances of the late eighteenth century, turned out to be a major miscalculation. It served to antagonise the Third Estate even before deliberations had begun.

Once the first plenary session, where the king and his ministers outlined the precarious state of French finances, had finished, each Estate retired to a separate assembly room to deliberate on the government's fiscal proposals. The clergy, followed by the nobility, swiftly verified the credentials of each deputy and then began to debate how to reduce the royal deficit. But the Third

Estate refused to accept subordination to the privileged orders. Despite their hostility to their so-called 'betters' they were uncertain about their authority and how to proceed.[30] It was left up to a clergyman, the abbé Emmanuel Sieyès, to break the impasse. Scion of a middle-class family from Fréjus in Provence, Sieyès had shown strong scholastic abilities from an early age. It was decided, despite his lack of a religious vocation, that he should follow a career in the church. Educated at the seminary of St Sulpice in Paris, the intellectual powerhouse of the Gallican church, Sieyès showed a greater aptitude for politics, philosophy and economics than theology. Being a commoner, the abbé could never aspire to become a bishop or a prelate. Despite this handicap, Sieyès became chaplain to the king's aunt Madame Sophie and vicar-general of Chartres. Moving in these circles, he met several grandees who were involved in liberal French politics.[31] Among his most important patrons was Philippe, duc d'Orléans, the king's ambitious cousin.

Although a clergyman, Sieyès was elected as a deputy for the Third Estate for the city of Paris. As soon as it was known that the Estates General would meet in 1789, an explosion of pamphlets and papers demanding different programmes for reform were published. None was to have a greater effect than Sieyès' pamphlet *What is the Third Estate?* The opening lines, 'What is the Third Estate? everything; What has it been hitherto in the political order? nothing; What does it desire to be? Something,' guaranteed that it would be a publishing sensation.[32] The basic premise of the pamphlet was that the privileged orders represented, at most, 4 per cent of the French population. Yet they had the potential to outvote the Third Estate, if voting took place by order. Sieyès denounced the clergy and nobility as parasites, who were sapping the energy of the Third Estate, the only order that performed all the useful and productive tasks of society.[33]

The objective of these polemical pages was not merely to denounce the status quo, but to present a programme for action. Sieyès argued that, as the Third Estate represented 96 per cent of the population of France, it was the embodiment of the nation. Therefore, the first act of this body should be to declare itself a 'national assembly' and arrogate legislative power into its hands. Sieyès argued that the privileged orders could have no role in this deliberative body. Only a national assembly could make legitimate decisions about the future of France. Once the Third Estate had proclaimed itself a national assembly, its next task would be to establish a constitution for the realm.[34] Sieyès did not believe that a constitution was embodied in the traditions and fundamental laws of France. He argued that a new political order could be willed into existence *ex novo* by the deputies. Guided by reason and science, they could establish a fundamental set of rules and principles that would lead to the regeneration of France. Despite these fine words, Sieyès was very much a man of the eighteenth century. He excluded women, children and servants from the right to vote in elections.[35] His pamphlet made it clear that only property-owning elites, who had significant leisure time, could hope to possess the education and wit necessary to represent the national interest. His critics past and present have, with some justification, accused Sieyès of replacing one aristocracy with another.

This pamphlet nonetheless had a galvanising effect on the deputies of the Third Estate, who seized the gauntlet thrown at their feet by the abbé and on 17 June 1789, in a truly historic moment, declared themselves a national assembly. They also decided that it would be their task to give France a modern constitution, fit for a modern and prosperous nation. Louis XVI, fearful that the situation was slipping out of his hands, decided to address the Estates General in a plenary session. On 21 June, the deputies arrived at their regular meeting hall to find themselves locked out by royal troops. Inside, workmen were frantically preparing the room for the arrival of the king. Furious, and suspecting foul play, the Third Estate headed to a nearby tennis court. Here the deputies swore never to disperse until they had given France a constitution. Two days later, on 23 June, the king addressed the deputies directly and commanded them to return to their respective debating chambers. He insisted on the continued existence of the three separate orders. Yet, to sweeten this reactionary pill, Louis did concede that he would not raise any future taxes without the consent of the Estates.[36] He also promised that henceforth the

Estates General would be summoned with regularity. There would be no return to the bad old days of absolutism.

After reading his statement the king left the chamber, and was cheered by the nobility and some conservative prelates. The deputies of the Third and some parish priests of the First Estate sat in stunned silence, not sure how to respond to the royal command to leave the hall. The Grand Master of Ceremonies, the marquis de Breux-Brézé, entered the chamber and reminded the deputies of the king's order to disperse. At this point the fiery and very ugly Comte de Mirabeau, a liberal noble who had been elected as a deputy with the Third Estate, rose to his feet. Everybody waited with bated breath to see what he would say. In his deep booming voice, he exclaimed: 'Go tell those who sent you, that we shall only leave this place through the force of bayonets.'[37] At this moment the deputies broke out in thunderous applause and resumed their deliberations in stark defiance of the king. On learning that his orders had been ignored Louis impotently exclaimed: 'Devil take them, let them stay there.' On 27 June, in a gesture of capitulation, he ordered the deputies of the First and Second Estates to join the National Assembly.[38]

Up to this point, the deputies had followed Sieyès' recommendations with remarkable precision. Soon they would depart significantly from the script he had provided. He had argued for the exclusion of the privileged orders from the parliamentary body's deliberations, and now they were incorporated into the National Assembly. During this time, the Assembly charged a committee of its members, including Sieyès, to prepare a declaration of principles, which would guide the creation of a future constitution.[39] As events moved into July, it was clear the king was deeply displeased with the situation. Forty thousand troops were moved into position in the vicinity of Paris. Many were non-francophone mercenaries, who were considered more reliable than native French soldiers. In an inflammatory gesture, the king dismissed his liberal ministers on 11 July and replaced them with reactionaries.[40]

News that the king had disgraced his liberal ministers, and that troops were closing on Paris, created a panic. Some gun stores were raided, and the Provost of Merchants (the de facto mayor of Paris) was lynched by angry crowds. On 14 July 1789, looking for ammunition, crowds of furious protesters began surrounding the Bastille prison. This medieval fortress was a place where political prisoners and dissenters had been imprisoned since time immemorial.[41] Despite its grim reputation, by 1789 a mere seven prisoners were held in its cells, among them an Irishman called Major Whyte, who believed himself to be Julius Caesar.[42] Of much greater interest were the large stores of gunpowder in its arsenal. Initially the governor of the Bastille, Bernard-René Jourdan, Marquis de Launay, met with a delegation of insurgents. They demanded that the guns be turned away from the city and the reassurance that they would not be used against the people of Paris. Launay agreed and then invited the rebels to lunch. During this time the insurgents changed their minds and demanded that the governor surrender the fortress and its arsenal.[43]

Launay regretted that, without orders from the king, it would be impossible for him to surrender his command. As the crowds surrounding the Bastille surged forward the governor was forced to respond. His reliable Swiss troops and *invalides* (the French equivalent of the Chelsea pensioners) manned the guns, repulsing several waves of attackers. By the early afternoon it seemed as if the defenders of the Bastille were gaining the upper hand. Then a regiment of Gardes Françaises was seen approaching the fortress with field guns in tow. This regiment was notoriously unreliable and, despite being an elite regiment of the royal household, they had famously been routed at the battle of Dettingen in 1743.[44] To the surprise of the defenders, these troops were not approaching to relieve the fortress but had mutinied in support of the insurgents. Outmanned and outgunned, Launey was forced to surrender the fortress and was soon lynched by the crowd. His head was proudly paraded through the streets of Paris in what had been the first bloody day of the Revolution.

The Prince de Broglie and Baron de Besenval, who commanded twenty thousand troops on the Champ de Mars (the present-day site of the Eiffel tower) did not intervene. They feared that their French troops, who had already started to fraternise with the rebels, would mutiny like the Gardes Françaises.[45] The king considered fleeing to the fortress of Metz, about 300 kilometres east of Paris, but he was afraid that this would give rise to a civil war, and decided to remain. His conservative brother, the Comte d'Artois, other reactionary nobles and the Archbishop of Paris fled to the borders, fearing they would be murdered. They hoped their exile would be brief and that they would return once the situation had been rectified. Their hopes were to prove optimistic, to say the least. The archbishop died in exile and it would be twenty-five years before Artois could return to his native country.[46]

On 17 July Louis XVI travelled to Paris from Versailles and capitulated before the insurgents. He recognised the new municipality and national guard created after the fall of the Bastille.[47] The troops surrounding the capital were withdrawn and the liberal ministers recalled. The implosion of government authority in Versailles and Paris gave rise to a series of rural and provincial panics known as the Great Fear.[48] Rumours abounded that aristocrats and bandits were about to launch a counter-revolutionary strike against the people of France. Soon, armed groups of peasants attacked local chateaux, raiding the muniment rooms and cellars of their chatelains. Here they burned all records of feudal dues and obligations to their lords. Not all nobles took such assaults lying down. Although most of the peasantry's anger was aimed at the seigneurial system which had kept them in bondage, they also attacked monasteries and convents, which remained some of the most important landlords in the realm.

Unlike future nineteenth-century revolutions, the events of 1789 had not been planned by professional revolutionaries. They were the result of poor decision-making by the regime, which had led to the collapse of the Bourbon monarchy. Criticism of the church had been voiced in the *cahiers de doléances*, but Catholicism had been a side issue for the deputies of the Estates General. At this early stage, the power of the crown and the privileges of the nobility were the primary targets of these deputies who had to improvise themselves into revolutionaries almost overnight. This situation would not last, as the church came under direct fire and its position of social pre-eminence was eroded beyond recognition.

During the latter half of July, the National Assembly debated a set of principles which would act as a framework for the yet-unwritten constitution. The document they produced, 'the declaration of the rights of man and the citizen' was truly of epochal importance. It is seen today as the founding text for the concept of human rights.[49] Deeply inspired by the American ambassador and future president Thomas Jefferson, each article enumerated the fundamental freedoms of each individual citizen. They enshrined basic guarantees from arbitrary arrest and undue taxation, and freedom of expression. The deputies declared that access to public office was contingent on one's merit rather than caste or order. As far as religion was concerned, article 10 was of the deepest importance:

> No one may be disquieted for his opinions, even religious ones, provided that their manifestation does not trouble the public order established by the law.[50]

This article severed the umbilical cord that had linked church and state for centuries. Catholicism became just one religion amongst many others, and lost its monopoly on public worship. Protestants celebrated their new freedoms, while the situation of the Jewish minority within the kingdom was more complex. The Sephardic Jews of Bordeaux were granted almost immediate emancipation whereas it took longer for the rights of the Ashkenazis of Alsace to be affirmed.[51]

Although today the rights of man are (almost) universally celebrated, at the time they did prove controversial. During the debates, the duke-bishop of Langres, César-Guillaume de La Luzerne, complained it was folly to create unrestricted rights.[52] Others agreed and argued that rights should be counter-balanced by duties, since no freedom could be absolute. For example, freedom of expression needed to be tempered by libel laws.[53] For conservatives, citizens received freedom in return for fulfilling certain obligations towards the state, like taxation or military service or deference to superiors. Driven by their enthusiasm, the deputies ignored the bishop's concerns.

Further bad news for the Catholic Church came in August. On the night of the 4th, several members of the liberal nobility mounted the rostrum of the National Assembly and renounced their pecuniary privileges. Not to be outmanoeuvred, priests and bishops scrambled to relinquish their own immunities and rights. By the end of this long night members of provinces and towns also renounced the ancient rights and exemptions of their localities. The deputies declared that henceforth feudalism had been abolished in France. This parliamentary session was so chaotic that it took the stenographers several weeks to prepare an imperfect record of these eccentric proceedings.[54] The clergy had recklessly renounced the tithe which was the principal source of income for the Gallican church. It has been calculated that France's forty thousand rural parishes collected 120,000,000 *livres* in tithes per year at the twilight of the eighteenth century.[55] This loss of income threatened French Catholicism with financial ruin. Sieyès (somewhat self-servingly), despite his condemnation of privilege, defended the tithe. It was very unclear how clergymen could survive without this vital revenue. But his weak voice and poor oratorical skills ensured that Sieyès' intervention was ignored.[56]

Despite the abolition of the tithe, not all clergymen were at first hostile to the Revolution. The count-canons of Lyons publicly praised the reforms, and appeared at revolutionary festivals.[57] Radical clergymen like Claude Fauchet or Henri Grégoire, who had held Jansenist views in their early careers, emerged as fervent revolutionaries.[58] Long sidelined by a blue-blooded episcopacy, impoverished priests seized the opportunities afforded by the new democratic system inaugurated by the National Assembly. During 1790 some priests would stand for election for municipal office in their villages. Louis XVI even decided to appoint the commoner Jean-René Asseline to the diocese of Boulogne in November 1789.[59] It had been decades since a non-noble had been selected to wear the mitre.

Not all were impressed with the good intentions incarnated in the reforms of the 1790s. Jean-Sifrein Maury, prior of Lihons, became one of the most eloquent counter-revolutionary speakers during debates in the National Assembly.[60] Having been born near

Avignon, which was a papal enclave, he was technically a subject of the pope and defended the rights of the Holy See strenuously in the debating chamber. He often reminded his colleagues that it was madness to ignore completely the wisdom of tradition, and that it was impossible to recast an entire system of government from scratch. He warned that the destruction of the *ancien régime* would lead to lawlessness and mob violence.

Louis XVI played for time and delayed sanctioning the decree of the Rights of Man and noted that the abolition of feudalism would bankrupt the church. This informal veto led to the famous march of the women of Paris on Versailles. A tense standoff developed between 5 and 6 October as the people of Paris and the National Guard surrounded the royal palace. Queen Marie-Antoinette narrowly avoided lynching when some of the crowd gained access to her apartments. They decapitated two of her guards and placed their heads on pikes. Fearing for the safety of his family the king capitulated, signing these decrees and consenting to move his principal residence from Versailles to the Tuileries palace in the centre of Paris.[61] After this event the king was no longer a free agent. He and his court had become prisoners of the radicals.

One essential problem endured throughout the decade. The Estates General had been summoned to solve France's budgetary crisis. Instead of solving this problem the Revolution had accelerated the state's descent into bankruptcy. Abolishing feudalism meant that most peasants and large farmers now believed that they were free from feudal dues and taxation. They disregarded the National Assembly's laws, which prescribed that significant compensation would be paid to former lords for their loss of income.[62] The decree stating that the tithe would continue to be paid until replaced by a general land tax was studiously avoided. As a gesture of desperation, the Assembly appealed to the population to make voluntary tax contributions.* Although some individuals gave generously, there was little hope that these donations could make even a dent in France's spiralling public

---

* Giving money to the state was about as popular an option in the eighteenth century as it is today. AP 9:350–2.

debt. The government attempted to float loans on the international markets, but investors were unwilling to subscribe to bonds issued by a country undergoing a revolution. The finances of the state grew ever more desperate.

On 10 October 1789, Charles-Maurice de Talleyrand, Bishop of Autun, the scion of an ancient princely family, suggested that large swathes of ecclesiastical land be sold to meet France's financial obligations and solve the budgetary crisis.[63] Talleyrand would play a leading role in politics for the next fifty years. He was eloquent, witty, ambitious and utterly unscrupulous. As the result of a congenital defect, he had been born with a club foot and walked all of his life with a limp. Contemporaries referred to him as *le diable boiteux*, or club-footed devil. It was because of this disability that he had been destined for an ecclesiastical rather than a military career (his uncle was the archbishop of Rheims, one of the most important archdioceses in France and responsible for crowning the king).[64] He trembled and wept in despair, as he had no genuine vocation, on the night of his ordination in the Palais du Tau in Rheims. It is hardly surprising he had little loyalty towards the Gallican church into whose service he had been press-ganged by his family.

On 2 November the National Assembly accepted Talleyrand's proposal and voted overwhelmingly to place the church's land at the disposal of the state. Ecclesiastical property made up somewhere between 6 and 10 per cent of all arable land in France, not to mention a vast urban real-estate portfolio.[65] This confiscation gave the national budget a vital injection of liquidity. To further consolidate its position, the Assembly decided to issue a new paper currency, called the *assignat*, which was secured on the future sale of ecclesiastical land. Naturally, bishops, prelates and abbots protested furiously against this confiscation. Indeed, the ambassador for the Knights of Malta died of apoplexy on learning that his chivalric order was to be dispossessed of its immense landholdings in France.[66] Clergymen argued that their property had been the result of bequests and donations. It was therefore deeply unfair that they should be deprived of gifts given by dead benefactors. They claimed that their position as farmers and landlords gave them a better grounding in the lives of their parishioners than if they merely received a salary.

Such complaints fell on deaf ears as radical deputies argued that the clergy had been so under taxed that the state was merely recouping centuries of unpaid dues. More anticlerical speakers saw it as just retribution for the ignorance, superstition and obscurantism into which the clergy had plunged the peasantry for millennia. Although such anticlericalism had always been latent during the eighteenth century, the collapse of the Bourbon regime allowed it to bubble to the surface. Among the orators who spoke most frequently at the Assembly were the lawyers Camus, Bouche, Lanjuinais, Fréteau, Martineau and Goupil who were renowned for their Jansenist allegiances.[67] Although less radical than extremists like Maximilian Robespierre or Isaac René Guy Le Chapelier, they wanted to return to a more primitive church, one shorn of its power and wealth and more engaged with the concerns of ordinary people. They saw this as the moment in which the aspirations of reform Catholicism might be fulfilled.

Having taken the irrevocable step of confiscating all church land the Assembly's attention turned to monasteries and nunneries. On 13 February 1790 the taking of religious vows was prohibited by decree.[68] This certainly echoed the spirit of the age that saw religious houses and convents as parasitical dens of iniquity. Their massive wealth and contemplative vocation left them vulnerable to attack. So too the fact that women were sometimes forced to take religious vows against their will. This did little to endear such institutions to the imagination of a civilised reading public. Denis Diderot's novel *La Religieuse* (*The Nun*), was written in several versions shortly before the author's death in 1784 and was published in 1796 as the Revolution passed its zenith. It told in lurid and exaggerated tones the story of the fictional Suzanne, who was forced by her parents to take religious vows at the age of sixteen. She managed to escape the sadistic abuse of a tormentor called Sister Sainte-Christine only to be transferred to another convent where she became the object of the unwanted lesbian advances of her new mother superior.[69] Diderot indicted the entire convent system as a smokescreen where the weaker members of society were incarcerated and abused. This caricature was certainly powerful, and voiced some of the deepest anxieties about female religious communities.

Commissioners were charged by the National Assembly to take an inventory of monastic lands, goods, treasures and other properties. They also were sent to record whether the inmates wished to remain in their convents or be freed from their vows. In the Convent of St Madelaine in Paris all fifty nuns, including the prioress, slammed the convent gates behind them and did not look back. It is difficult to know whether this was a vote of no confidence in their abbess, the aloof and unfriendly Madame de Montmorency-Laval (the daughter of a duke no less), or whether it had to do with the fact that most of the sisters had been arrested as sex workers and forced to take vows. Perhaps they wanted to discard their current vocation to resume their previous one.[70]

A fascinating, if atypical, case can be found in Rose Lauray, who received the name of Sister Celeste upon taking her vows in December 1769. She would spend the next twenty years in the convent of Notre Dame de Châtellerault near Poitiers. Her father provided Rose with a large sum for the 'dowry to Christ' which was required by the nunnery as an entry fee. This allowed her to join the more affluent sisters of the choir and benefit from a better cell with an ample allowance for linen. Sister Celeste did not perform menial labour, unlike her poorer brethren, but instead taught young girls in the convent's school. Despite this relatively comfortable existence, Rose was not happy. In January 1790 she had challenged her mother superior in a leadership contest, which she lost by just one vote. This defeat seems to have stung her ego deeply. News of the National Assembly's decree freeing nuns from their vows came like manna from heaven. She enthusiastically wrote an open letter claiming her freedom and asking the district authorities to free her from her cell. As the convent gates opened, the former nun became embroiled in a rather undignified squabble over her furniture and linens which her 'vindictive' mother superior refused to return.[71]

This public renunciation of vows caused something of a scandal locally and drew press reactions as far away as Paris. Yet

Rose found it difficult to know what to do with her emancipation. Initially she stayed with her married elder sister, but then moved to nearby Poitiers. Here, thanks to a family connection in the city's revolutionary commune, she was appointed director of the local hospice. Unwisely, the revolutionaries had expelled the experienced nuns who nursed the sick throughout France for refusing to take the civic oath. Although Rose spent almost ten years as director of this medical institute, it was clear she had little aptitude or training for healing the sick. Her movements were monitored, and she was denounced for attending masses celebrated by priests suspected of royalism. She survived such allegations, but during the Napoleonic period she and her nurses were accused more seriously of administering the wrong medicaments to patients under their care. Rose left the hospice and disappeared from the written record until the 1820s when she remerged as the owner of a small primary school for girls, where she taught them to read and write and instructed them in rudimentary Catholic theology. In 1824, while walking with a student to class, she was struck by lightning (tardy divine retribution?). She survived this ordeal and continued to teach girls until 1833 when she retired, with a pension which maintained her until her death two years later at the impressive age of eighty-three.[72]

Understanding Rose's unusual life choices is difficult. Her biographer Gwenaël Murphy suspects that her father, who had remarried after the death of his first wife, was keen to rid himself of the burden of an unwanted daughter and had forced her into a convent at the age of nineteen.[73] Murphy's hypothesis is that for the next twenty years Sister Celeste nursed a deep resentment for her confinement and took the first opportunity to escape. This is certainly plausible, but it is possible her reason for leaving was more political. Her failure in 1790 to wrest control of the convent away from its formidable abbess deeply frustrated the ambitious Rose. Unlike some nuns who left convents, she never married nor started a family.[74] Instead she floated into nursing and teaching, which were jobs typically undertaken by female religious during the eighteenth century. These choices embodied continuity rather than rupture with her previous life as a nun. There is also some evidence that she continued to be a practising Catholic who sought out counter-revolutionary priests to minister to her conscience. While it is true that Rose Lauray's case was not representative of most nuns during the 1790s, it highlights that the reasons why women left convents were complex and diverse.

Once in the outside world, the options available to former nuns in the anticlerical climate of revolutionary France were very limited. For example, Marguerite Jahan, the concierge of Rose's convent in Châtellerault, after leaving her cell walked the streets of Poitiers begging for a meagre living until she froze to death during the bitter winter of 1798.[75] The world opened up to nuns in 1790 proved to be an unsympathetic wilderness, despite the Assembly's rhetoric of emancipation. Indeed, nuns transformed themselves from being perceived as victims of *ancien régime* misogyny to becoming agents of their own destiny. But as Rose's case illustrates navigating life outside of the convent could be fiendishly complex. Not all nuns became the counter-revolutionary fanatics portrayed in the Jacobin press. Infuriatingly for the revolutionaries, most nuns in France demonstrated remarkable commitment to their vows and sought to continue living as sisters in Christ.[76]

In contrast, monks' behaviour seemed to mirror the myths of the black legend that attacked their venality during the eighteenth century.[77] Once their properties had been confiscated, many elected to take the state pension offered by the revolutionaries and leave their monastic houses to their fate. Some, like the disgraced Capuchin friar François Chabot, would make full use of this freedom to marry and take an active role in radical politics. Chabot reinvented himself from a lukewarm monk into a political firebrand during the Terror.[78]

In the course of a single decade, the revolutionaries destroyed a vast network of monasteries, convents and nunneries that had taken a millennium to build.[79] The great symbol of this was the massive abbey of Cluny, the mother hub of the Cistercian order. Its basilica had been the largest church in Christendom until the decision to rebuild St Peter's in Rome during the sixteenth century. The abbey was pillaged in 1793 and then sold, its stone buildings becoming a quarry for property developers. This enormous monastic complex was largely demolished by 1813. Today very little remains of what had been the leading house of the western monastic tradition.[80]

Thus, in a few years the revolutionaries visited destruction on religious institutions that had not been witnessed in Europe since Henry VIII's dissolution of the monasteries in the sixteenth century.[81] Ever since the Reformation, critiques of the regular clergy had remained vigorous. It was not just the laity that condemned their parasitical contemplative lives; even parish priests had become ill-disposed towards communities that provided little social benefit. The monks' loyalty to Rome made them particularly vulnerable to the modern state's desire to subordinate the church to its authority. Politicians wanted no mixed allegiances: Frenchmen were citizens and could have no obligations towards an Italian prince. Religious faith was to be relegated to the private sphere and have little role in public life. Such views ensured that a clash with the papacy was inevitable. On 12 April 1790 Dom Christophe Antoine Gerle, a Carthusian monk and deputy of the National Assembly, proposed the motion that Catholicism be declared the religion of the state.[82] This attempt by the clergy to regain the initiative backfired badly. It led to a stormy debate which further polarised Right and Left in the chamber. The following day, the motion was roundly defeated; Catholicism was to be merely one religion among many.

This barrage of reforms, which effectively disestablished the Gallican church, made the latter's future financially unsustainable. Realising this, the Assembly had charged a committee of deputies, many of whom held Jansenist sympathies, to draw up recommendations proposing the means for the survival of the Catholic religion within a regenerated French state.[83] Throughout the eighteenth century, Enlightened reformers had urged a thorough reorganisation of the kingdom's administration into a uniform and rational system. In deep contrast, the *ancien régime* had been characterised by vast regional disparity and diversity. Each province of the kingdom had had its own laws, tax system and customs.[84] Revolutionaries shared the common goal that in future all of France would be governed the same. The historic jurisdictions of the Bourbon state were abolished and replaced with eighty-three *départements* named after local geographic features like rivers, mountains and the seas.[85] Ancient Burgundy and Provence were replaced with the Côte d'Or and the Var *départements*. Past identities, traditions and superstitions were to be jettisoned in favour of jurisdictions of roughly equal size with similar populations. Many wondered whether these same principles could not be grafted onto the governance structures of the church.

There were 139 dioceses in France. Some in the south, especially Languedoc, were tiny whilst others in the east covered huge swathes of territory that crossed the Rhine and extended into western Germany.[86] Dioceses had grown organically over centuries and were hardly the outcome of rational planning. Some bishops, like those of Paris, Strasbourg and Rheims, were fabulously wealthy, whereas others, like the prelates of Vence, Vienne and Langres, had far more modest revenues. It was with some justification that the politicians of the National Assembly criticised the chaotic structures of the Gallican church. Further down the ecclesiastical pyramid great disparities characterised the parishes. Some were highly prosperous whereas other, destitute priests received a maintenance grant: the *portion congrue*.[87] These *congrueistes* received 700 *livres* a year, which placed them just above the breadline. The ecclesiastical committee of the National Assembly decided to redress these inequities through an unprecedented root and branch reorganisation of the Church. Their proposals would make France's clergymen more independent of Rome than even the Jansenists had ever conceived in their wildest dreams.

Given that all ecclesiastical property had been placed at the disposal of the state it was decided that priests and bishops would in future receive state salaries. The Assembly would redraw unilaterally the boundaries of all French dioceses. This meant that the 139 dioceses of the *ancien régime* would be erased and replaced by eighty-three new dioceses, whose jurisdictions would be congruent with the eighty-three administrative departments established in December 1789.[88] Henceforth the organisation of the church would mirror that of the state. Parishes too were to be reduced, rationalised and amalgamated to reflect the size of their congregations. To be eligible for their salaries, priests and bishops would have to swear an oath of allegiance to the as-yet-unwritten constitution of France.[89] Even more controversially, rather than being nominated by the king, priests and bishops would in future stand for election. They would need the votes of the tax-paying electorate in their districts and departments. This opened the prospect that Jews and Protestants could cast votes in the selection process for Catholic bishops.[90] The decision was made that archbishops in future would invest and consecrate newly elected bishops. This prerogative had been held exclusively by the pope since at least the sixteenth century. The deputies in the assembly rejected the idea that the papacy could refuse to confirm a French bishop. According to their plan, the Curia in Rome would simply be notified that a new bishop had been elected, with a certificate confirming that the candidate had a theology degree and was in full communion with the Catholic faith.

The ecclesiastical committee presented these proposals to the National Assembly for deliberation. This reform was called the Civil Constitution of the Clergy. Bishop-deputies in the Assembly were incensed. They urged that a national council of the Gallican church be summoned to deliberate on these reforms and to refer them to Rome.[91] Not unreasonably, they argued that, as these changes affected the fundamental structures of Catholicism, the papacy should be consulted. Given that the revolutionaries had wrested sovereignty away from the crown the year before and already confiscated all ecclesiastical property, they had little appetite for negotiation. Emboldened by their successes in 1789, the National Assembly had radicalised considerably.

For the radical deputies, the only means of ensuring that the church did not relapse into past corruption was to place it under the tutelage of the state. The National Assembly sought to establish a national church that was economically and politically dependent on government funding. Episcopal and clerical complaints were brushed to one side. On 12 July 1790 the Civil Constitution of the Clergy was passed with the support of a large majority. Ten days later Louis XVI, against his better judgement, sanctioned this law.[92] One suspects that there was some hope that as Pius VI had accepted the reforms imposed on the church by Joseph II, Frederick II and Catherine the Great, he might also capitulate before the Civil Constitution of the Clergy. This was a naive hope.

Rome was caught unprepared for the hurricane that had suddenly hit the Gallican church. Antonio Dugnani, Archbishop of Rhodes, the papal nuncio to Paris, proved to be out of his depth. Although he had warned Rome that the Estates General was filled with seditious and anticlerical minds, he hoped that the crisis would blow over.[93] His despatches expressed the expectation that conservative deputies like the abbé Maury would temper the worst excesses of the National Assembly's ecclesiastical policies. In July 1790 Dugnani obtained a draft of the Civil Constitution of the Clergy, which he forwarded to Rome, warning that this was the worst catastrophe to befall Pius VI's pontificate.[94] Despite the gravity of the situation, the nuncio still believed a diplomatic solution to the church's differences with the revolutionaries might be possible. He exhorted the bishops in the National Assembly to lobby for the toning down of the ecclesiastical reforms, warning that a failure to do so would lead to papal condemnation. The Gallican episcopacy tried hard to find a settlement and forestall schism.

As if the situation were not bad enough, a fresh crisis was brewing in the south of France. Ever since the thirteenth century Avignon and the Comtat Venaissin had been a papal enclave deep in Provence (during the Great Schism of the fourteenth century it had been the seat of the French popes).[95] The residents of these prosperous provinces were papal subjects administered by officials appointed by Rome. The revenues from the territories provided a small but very necessary cash injection to the church's empty coffers. As already mentioned, whenever tensions rose between the Bourbon king and the papacy French troops would occupy these enclaves. Once the dispute was resolved the soldiers would leave and return these territories to the pope.

During 1789 some 'patriots' inspired by revolutionaries across the border started demanding reforms and democratic accountability. The pope's vice-legate (governor) Filippo Casoni,

Archbishop of Perga, was intimidated by the demonstrations and riots. He granted significant autonomy to the radical municipality of Avignon in March 1790 to run its own affairs. An attempt by papal loyalists to regain control of the city prompted an invasion by the French National Guard from nearby Orange. On 12 June, egged on by revolutionary *agents provocateurs*, the radical municipality of Avignon issued a proclamation demanding that the pope's provinces be incorporated into France. To what extent this was an expression of self-determination remains controversial.[96] Casoni fled the city and took refuge in nearby Carpentras which remained under papal control. This caused a crisis whereby the southern part of the pope's Provençal domains had requested formal annexation to France whereas the northern Comtat remained loyal to Rome. Initially the National Assembly in Paris was embarrassed by Avignon's request to be incorporated into France.

Only in August 1790 did news of the Civil Constitution reach Rome. Pius VI charged a special Congregation of Cardinals to express an opinion, or *voto,* on the developing situation in France. The first session consisted of twenty princes of the Church and started its deliberations on 16 September.[97] Its members were mainly high-ranking cardinals who had experience of working in the Holy Office, or Roman inquisition. Their task was to investigate how far the Civil Constitution departed from Catholic teaching. As experts who had made their careers seeking out heresy and disciplining clergymen they seemed ideally suited for the task before them. The Curia was notoriously unhurried in coming to decisions. Each cardinal, with the aid of two trusted theologians, was expected to produce an extensive written opinion on the French situation. At each session the pope would hear the thoughts of each adviser in turn. Then he would chair a debate before coming to an agreed synthesis of the Congregation's collective view. It was then Pius' task to compose, with the help of his theologians, the brief or bull that would respond formally to the reforms of the French revolution. This cumbersome procedure ensured that the Civil Constitution initially was met with a stony silence from Rome.

A key plenary meeting of the congregation occurred on 24 September. The cardinals were thrown into deep consternation on learning that the king had sanctioned the ecclesiastical reforms in France. About a third of those present were open to accepting some of the reforms made by the National Assembly in the structures of the Gallican church. Another group sought to begin negotiations to forestall a schism, whereas the remaining cardinals urged outright condemnation of events across the Alps.[98] In the ensuing discussion these prelates focused on the Declaration of the Rights of Man which they seemed to dislike even more than the Civil Constitution of the Church. Article 10, which sanctioned freedom of worship for all religions, was particularly infuriating for the Congregation. Rome could not countenance equality with other faiths; the truths and teachings of the Catholic Church could not share the stage with heresy.

Following this, the cardinals discussed the contents of the Civil Constitution of the Clergy. Many felt that a reduction and rationalisation of dioceses was not unreasonable. They argued though that the redrawing of the church's internal jurisdiction could not be implemented unilaterally by a secular government. France's bishops would need to be consulted, and the final approval of the Holy Father was vital. It was conceded that bishops and priests had been elected by the laity in the primitive church, but these polls had been merely advisory rather than binding on the church's hierarchy. It was unacceptable that Protestants, Jews and unbelievers would be entitled to elect Catholic clergy. Some cardinals argued that it would be best, once the elections had taken place, if the king nominated the bishop-elect and the pope, if satisfied with his credentials, would invest the candidate. It was certainly out of the question that archbishops, without Rome's sanction, would consecrate new bishops. There was disgust at the notion that, if the National Assembly had its wish, the appointment of bishops would become a purely secular process.[99]

The Civil Constitution aimed to abolish cathedral chapters in the dioceses and replace them with a council of vicars.[100] According to these clauses, bishops would need to submit all important decisions to their vicars for approval. Again, the Congregation in Rome was furious at this proposal. They did not object to the reform of the cathedral chapter system *per se* but felt that this version of reform would destroy the authority of the episcopacy. Under these proposals, the role of bishops would be relegated to the dispensation of the sacraments of confirmation and ordination. According to the doctrines of the church, bishops were the natural spiritual leaders of their community. Their religious authority was subordinated only to the pope and to Rome; the church was not a democracy nor a representative government. Finally, there was a heated discussion on whether the *ancien régime* bishops should meet in a national council of the Gallican church. Some cardinals felt this was pointless, given that the episcopacy was threatened with erasure. Others felt that a national council could allow the bishops to reach a consensus and coordinate their resistance to the reforms of the Revolution.[101]

Many believed that such an assembly of the French episcopacy would greatly confuse the lines of communication. Traditionally, the king had been the natural intermediary between the kingdom's bishops and Rome. The cardinals had mixed feelings when it came to Louis XVI. The more conservative princes of the church deplored his weakness in sanctioning revolutionary legislation, whereas more indulgent members of the congregation argued that the king was now a prisoner in his own capital, deprived of all freedom of action. They failed to reach a consensus on whether to endorse the summoning of a national council or whether to negotiate with the monarch directly. This Congregation was a turning-point of sorts. There was a growing realisation among the cardinals that compromise would be possible, but only if the revolutionaries in Paris would show some willingness to negotiate.[102] These prelates deplored that the pope's role and primacy over the church had barely been mentioned in the text of the Civil Constitution. From a spiritual perspective, the papacy had the right of oversight over the French church and its episcopacy. The Revolution had rekindled with a vengeance the Gallican and Jansenist controversies about the autonomy of the French church with respect to Rome.

To an extent the revolutionaries followed the precedents set during the eighteenth century. Like the monarchs and states of the *ancien régime* they sought to subordinate the ecclesiastical authority to secular power. However, no matter how much the kings of Catholic Europe had slowly eroded the influence of the church, they had never denied the pope's ultimate spiritual authority. One of the great paradoxes of the 1790s was that the French episcopacy had always been jealous of its authority and had resented papal interference throughout its history. For over a century the bishops had defended the four Gallican articles of 1682 which guaranteed it autonomy from Rome.[103] The deputies of the National Assembly had achieved the unthinkable. They had shaken the Gallican foundations of the French monarchy and church beyond recognition, unleashing a process that would lead to their ultimate destruction. Both Louis XVI and his bishops turned to ultramontane Rome for guidance in a manner that would have been unimaginable months earlier.

Emboldened by the silence from Rome, the deputies of the National Assembly pushed forward. As the ecclesiastical historian John McManners put it: 'If there was a point at which the Revolution "went wrong" it was when the [National] Assembly imposed the oath to the Civil Constitution of the Clergy, 27 November 1790.'[104] Through this act the deputies turned allegiance to the Revolution into a matter of religious conscience. Up to this point the counter-revolution had been a minority movement, but now massive numbers of disgruntled Catholics chose loyalty to the pope over allegiance to the Assembly. It took weeks for news of this oath to reach Rome. An emergency session of the Congregation of the Twenty Cardinals was summoned on 16 December. Tearfully the pope informed them that the prospect of a schism with France was looming. Sadly, the documents relating to this session no longer exist. However, a report from the French ambassador in Rome emphasised that, though the cardinals regretted the situation, they condemned without reservations both the oath and those clergymen who acceded to it.[105]

It took the pope a further three months to compose his brief condemning the Revolution's ecclesiastical reforms. On 26 December 1790 Louis XVI signed the decree which demanded that all clergymen in France take an oath to uphold the Civil

Constitution of the Clergy.[106] The next day the radical Jansenist priest and deputy Henri Grégoire was among the first clergymen to take the oath. He was committed deeply to the new constitutional church established by the French Revolution. As a liberal priest, Grégoire was an eager exponent of progressive causes: during the Revolution he would become one of the foremost activists for the abolition of slavery in the French Caribbean.[107] Within months he would find himself in a clear position of leadership for this schismatic church.

Given their loss of power, unsurprisingly, very few bishops took the oath.[108] Talleyrand, together with the bishops of Sens and Orléans, pledged their allegiance to the new constitution. Only three diocesan bishops out of 139 accepted the oath. From the 263 deputies elected for the First Estate in May 1789 only 81 swore allegiance to the constitution in 1791. This elite rejection of the oath did not reflect clerical attitudes towards the Revolution in France. As the year progressed, slightly over half of ordinary parish priests swore the oath, while the rest categorically refused to do so.[109]

Catholicism's role proved to be the most contentious issue of the early years of the Revolution. It caused a deep crisis of conscience in Louis XVI that mirrored the experience of millions of his former subjects. The king's aunts, horrified by this looming religious schism, attempted to travel to Rome for a 'pilgrimage'. On 22 February 1791 they were arrested by the municipal authorities of the town of Arnay-le-Duc in Burgundy. Their *chevalier d'honneur* was forced to gallop back to Paris to inform the Assembly of what had occurred. After a furious debate on the fate of these elderly spinsters, the deputies grudgingly decided to allow them to continue their journey to Rome.[110] Refractory clergymen and their supporters were publicly insulted by radicals in Paris. In some parts of the nation, especially the west and south-east, national guardsmen had to be deployed to evict non-juring priests from their parishes. New incumbents were often treated as usurpers and in some instances were met with hails of stones as they took possession of their churches.

By seeking to redefine the role of Catholicism in society through abstract legislation the National Assembly deeply misunderstood the nature of genuine devotion. For the followers of Christ, the organisation of the church was not a matter of reason but of faith. They respected the pope, their bishops and 'good' priests. The deputies and their pro-revolutionary clergymen were distrusted as outsiders. As many of the constitutional priests were of a Jansenist hue, they came with baggage. Their desire to curtail religious festivals, ostentatious worship and superstitions was hardly going to endear them to their peasant congregations. At best they were humourless killjoys, at worst they were attacked as schismatic heretics.[111]

The tragedy was that the revolutionaries had picked a fight that was completely unnecessary. As the example of Joseph II had shown, the church with time and pressure could be persuaded to accept the supremacy of the state. In contrast, France's revolution put the challenge to institutional Catholicism on steroids. It is worth remembering that these revolutionaries, though undoubtedly anticlerical, were not intrinsically anti-religious, let alone atheists, but they wanted the state to regulate and control religion. Any attempt by clergymen from now on to interfere in politics was met with brutal repression.

On 10 March 1791 Pius VI issued the brief *Quod aliquantum differe*.[112] In it he condemned without hesitation the National Assembly's reforms, especially the Civil Constitution. Above all he accused the revolutionaries of usurping the power and prerogatives that had been vested in the Holy See since time immemorial. Indeed, the pope argued that it was his exclusive right to absolve regular clergy of their monastic vows and he declared the decree of 13 February 1790 abolishing monasteries null and void. Everybody recognised the incendiary potential of this brief. Initially copies were sent to Louis XVI and a few trusted bishops who kept the contents secret for almost a month.

On 13 April another brief entitled *Charitas* was promulgated, condemning the oath to the Civil Constitution as schismatic.[113] It commanded those who had taken the oath to retract their words within forty days under threat of being deprived of all ecclesiastical office. During this time Talleyrand, representing the tiny minority of juring bishops, allowed the consecration of those constitutional bishops elected by their *départements*.[114] This enabled constitutional clergy to receive the apostolic succession. Technically the consecration of these bishops was valid, but it was illicit under canon law as it had not received papal confirmation. Talleyrand's disobedience was deeply embarrassing for the church. Soon afterwards he ceased to wear his clerical dress and did not seek election to any diocese. Now that he was free to choose, he rejected the clerical vocation forced on him by his family. Given his defiance of papal authority, he was named directly in the text of *Charitas* and was suspended from his ministry by the pope. For the church he would never cease to be a renegade bishop. His choices in 1791 would haunt him and pursue him right up to his deathbed.

Pius ended his *Charitas* brief with a final exhortation to the people of France:

> Be careful not to lend your ears to the insidious voice of the fashionable philosophies of this century, they are heralds of death. Keep away from all those usurpers who demand to be called archbishops, bishops or parish priests; have nothing to do with them, avoid them especially in sacred matters. Listen assiduously to the voice of your legitimate pastors, to those who currently live among you and to those who will be sent to you in future. To put it simply, remain united with Us, as nobody can be part of the church of Jesus Christ that does not remain in unity with its visible head, who is seated on the throne of Peter.[115]

Devout Catholics were warned that those who did not retract their oaths to the Civil Constitution of the Clergy were suspended from ministry (but not excommunicated for the time being). With this brief the pope had delegitimised for a significant portion of the French population the church created by the revolutionaries of Paris, as it would now be considered a grave sin to participate in worship with constitutional clergy.

Initially at least non-juring priests tried to move their worship outside of parish churches. Talleyrand advised Louis XVI that

Catholics in communion with Rome could be tolerated as non-conformists and that the king himself could have the freedom to choose which religious rite to observe.* This neat solution ignored the polarisation that the Revolution had introduced around the issue of religion. Between 7 and 11 April 1791, the market women of Les Halles, the main market-place of Paris, assaulted a community of nuns and inflicted on them the sadistic humiliation of being stripped naked and spanked in public. Their alleged crime had been to have admonished students who had attended a 'constitutional mass'.[116] Any dissent from the Civil Constitution was considered treason. To deny the authority of the Roman pontiff became a hallmark of Jacobin radicalism. At Easter 1791 a large group of pious ladies headed to the church of the monastery of the Théatins in Paris. It was their intention to attend a mass celebrated by refractory priests. This gesture proved highly provocative. A large crowd of revolutionary activists attacked the women and drove them from the church. They placed a placard over the door celebrating their victory.[117] The Parisian radicals had no intention of tolerating a conservative Catholic cult in their midst.

At this time, the abbé Jean-Jacques Poupart, priest of Saint Germain l'Auxerrois, the parish of the Tuileries palace, took the oath to the constitution. He had been the king's confessor for many years.[118] Louis as a devout Catholic monarch refused to receive communion from a constitutional clergyman. It was decided that the court would spend Easter at Saint-Cloud, on the western outskirts of Paris. Away from prying eyes, a non-juring priest, François-Louis Hébert, would confess the king and bestow communion on him.[119] Rumours of the king's intentions started circulating around the capital. On 18 April 1791, the royal convoy prepared to leave the Tuileries. A menacing crowd appeared before the palace gates and blocked them. The royal family's carriages were surrounded and insults were hurled at the king.

---

* On 7 May 1791, Talleyrand read a report relating to the issue of religious freedom for non-juring priests which was rather more circumspect than the documents discovered in the Armoire de Fer. AP 25:643–46; AN C 184, no. 204, Talleyrand report to Louis XVI, 1791.

The first gentleman of the bedchamber, the duc de Villequier, was manhandled by the crowd and his frock coat ripped. This confrontation concluded with the rioters unlimbering the horses from carriages. Louis XVI, Marie-Antoinette and their children had to dismount and endure the humiliation of walking back to the Tuileries.[120]

The next day the king protested his treatment to the National Assembly. He received some words of sympathy, but nobody was punished for the insult perpetrated against his sacred person. Louis had already been outraged over his loss of power and liberty. The fact he was now a prisoner, not even allowed to fulfil his religious observances, was the straw that broke the camel's back.[121] A few months later, in the morning of 21 June 1791, Arnaud de la Porte, intendant of the civil list, asked to be admitted to the debating chamber of the National Assembly. He had important news and bore a vital document. After an awkward pause, he informed the awestruck deputies that the previous night the king in disguise, with all the royal family, had departed the capital.[122] The sovereign had left a declaration addressed to the people of France. This lengthy, rambling document was a severe indictment of the Revolution, and listed a litany of grievances against the National Assembly. Louis deplored his treatment, his loss of power and the reforms undertaken in his name. He denounced the laws he had been forced to sanction. This declaration ended with an attack on the Civil Constitution of the Clergy.

Why did the king leave the issue of religion until last in his litany of grievances? Perhaps he considered his loss of power and the constitutional reforms more important issues? The true reason will never be known. It seems, to this author at least, that the king reserved the issue that troubled him the most till last. Indeed, without the looming religious schism, it is difficult to imagine that Louis XVI would have been compelled to flee his capital.[123] He had refused to do so on other occasions in the past. His conscience was of paramount importance to this deeply religious monarch. Without legitimate priests from whom he could receive confession and absolution his life had become unbearable. His escape caused deep embarrassment for the politicians of Paris. To save face, the deputies disingenuously declared that the king had been kidnapped. An early example of fake news.

During their escape, the king was disguised as a valet, while Marie-Antoinette had assumed the guise of a Russian baroness. As they entered Champagne, the small royal party grew complacent, thinking their bid for freedom had been successful. They made the fatal error of stopping for lunch, and slowing down the pace of their flight. Indeed, the king halted at the market town of Saint Menehould to savour its pig's trotters, a delicacy for which it was renowned. He was recognised by the local postmaster, who rode ahead to raise the alarm.[124] Loyal troops had been sent to rendezvous with the monarch. But Louis, who made several unscheduled breaks along the route, failed to appear at the appointed time. Later in the evening, at the town of Varennes in the Ardennes Forest, the carriage was finally halted. Jean Baptiste Sauce, the deputy mayor, a local greengrocer, invited the royal family to rest in his home.[125] A national guardsman called Etienne Radet offered his horse to help the king escape. By now, a large crowd of armed men was gathering in Varennes. It would have been impossible to guarantee the safety of the royals if they had tried to gallop to freedom. The next day, commissioners from the National Assembly came to force the king to return to Paris.[126]

This episode, known to history as 'the flight to Varennes', was the fruit of an international conspiracy which had sought to ensure the liberation of the Bourbon family from Paris. It had been the king's intention to reach the fortress of Montmedy, near the border with the Austrian Netherlands.[127] Here, protected by loyal troops, Louis hoped to negotiate with the National Assembly from a position of strength. His secret diplomatic agents had informed the courts of Europe of his plans to escape. His brother-in-law, the Holy Roman Emperor Leopold II, misled by early reports that the flight had been successful, wrote to Louis to congratulate him. While this episode is famous, it is less well known that the church too knew of Louis's plans to flee Paris. There is inconclusive evidence on whether the Knights of Malta may have set aside funds for the king to draw upon had his flight succeeded.[128] Archbishop Bartolomeo Pacca, the apostolic nuncio to Germany, had been charged by Pius VI to travel to Montmedy. Here he would give Louis XVI a letter of congratulations from the pope.[129]

The king's flight proved beyond all doubt that his loyalty to the Revolution had been exacted under duress and that he was a prisoner. Republicanism, which had been a tiny movement in France, gained significant ground after Varennes.[130] So too did the deputies' distrust of the refractory clergy who were, with some justification, suspected of fomenting counter-revolution. Louis XVI's escape attempt dramatically failed to end the Revolution. On the contrary, it radicalised politics and made the position of orthodox Catholics even more difficult. Emigré nobles and the king's brothers had fled to different European courts, seeking to create an armed concert against the Revolution. It was understood that counter-revolutionary agents abroad were seeking war. Several French radicals in the assembly urged that only a pre-emptive strike could stave off an invasion from *ancien régime* Europe.[131] They proclaimed the slogan: 'War to the chateaux, peace to the cottages.' France's leaders, in a fit of over-confidence, believed that an army of citizen-soldiers fighting for freedom against despotism would be invincible. The chancelleries of Vienna and Berlin were also infected with unrealistic self-confidence. They believed that a nation experiencing revolution would be an easy target for their professional armies.[132]

During this time the pope's woes were hardly at an end. Commissioners, supported by the local National Guard, were sent to the papal enclaves of Avignon and the Comtat Venaissin. Here they held a controversial plebiscite in which, apparently, two-thirds of the population voted for union with France. On 14 September 1791 the National Assembly voted to annex this territory to satisfy the self-determination of the local population.[133] Rome protested vigorously against this violation of its sovereignty but was ignored. The papacy's spiritual and temporal rights were cast aside after less than two years of revolution. The deputies were far from finished: two months later, in November, they passed two decrees which sought to repress suspected counter-revolutionaries. The first enjoined emigrés to return home on pain of having their properties confiscated. The second targeted the non-juring clergy.

It demanded that all priests take the oath or else be declared public enemies. The threat was also made to deport clergy who persisted in their refusal to recognise the Civil Constitution.[134]

Louis was forced to veto these bills before the Assembly. Radicals declared that these vetoes revealed that the king's mask had come off and that his counter-revolutionary loyalties were now manifest. Many agitated for war as news arrived that emigrés were gathering a small army in the territory of the archbishop-elector of Trier.[135] In the early months of 1792, a campaign for war picked up pace and frenzied debates took place in the Assembly urging a pre-emptive strike. Louis XVI was compelled by pressure from both the deputies and public opinion to declare war on the king of Bohemia and Hungary on 20 April 1792.[136] The French armies proved to be highly disorganised and lacked discipline. The capitulation of Porrentruy was followed by the battles of Quiévrain and Marquain between 28 and 30 April. Although these were technically offensive actions the generals felt so unsure about their men that they ordered tactical retreats after little more than skirmishing. After this failure, the troops lynched some of their commanding officers, whom they blamed for these reverses. Defeat on the battlefield radicalised and polarised the French population even more.

Suspicions of the royal family, especially Marie Antoinette, grew exponentially. Not all allegations and rumours about the royal court were false. As the archives in Vienna reveal, the queen had betrayed France's war plans to her Habsburg relations, yet at the time nobody knew that this was the case for certain. In addition, the king's defence of the refractory clergy was a public-relations disaster. To make matters worse, the Duke of Brunswick, the supreme commander of the Allied armies about to invade France, issued a manifesto that threatened Paris with dire retribution should the Bourbon family be harmed.

The threat had the opposite effect. Radicals in Paris started organising a *coup d'état* to topple the monarchy. On 10 August 1792 crowds surrounded the Tuileries palace. Louis XVI proved unable to rally the National Guard to his defence, so he sought refuge with the National Assembly. Eight hundred Swiss Guards loyally resisted the insurgents but were brutally massacred inside the royal apartments. Paris's municipality was replaced by the rebels and the commander of the National Guard was lynched.[137] The deputies suspended the king from office and agreed to summon a Convention to decide and reshape the future government of France. Meanwhile the royal family were transferred to the Temple prison in Paris, which had previously been the headquarters of the crusading Knights Templar. At the same time priests and other suspected counter-revolutionaries were arrested throughout the city and interned.

The Allied armies, on learning this news, continued their inexorable advance towards Paris, soon capturing the fortresses of Verdun and Longwy, which placed them just over a hundred miles from the French capital.[138] The Paris population was gripped by panic and feared that counter-revolutionary fifth-columnists would murder patriots in their beds. They decided to take matters into their own hands. Between 2 and 6 September the prisons, borstals and female houses of detention of Paris were assaulted by rioters. They created kangaroo courts in which people had to prove their innocence from any suspicion of counter-revolution.[139] In one particularly gruesome case, the daughter of the Marquis de Sombreuil was forced to drink a cup of blood to prove her father's innocence. Those found innocent in these staged mockeries of justice were allowed to go free whereas those found guilty were torn to shreds by the angry crowd. At Bicêtre in Paris hundreds of juvenile offenders were killed indiscriminately by the crowds. Among an estimated 1,400 victims of these dark days, three bishops and 220 priests were lynched, including the king's non-juring confessor, the abbé Hébert.[140] There could hardly have been a more emphatic indication that those loyal to Rome were a key target of popular violence.

At the Battle of Valmy on 20 September, the French, thanks to a furious and skilful artillery barrage, succeeded in checking the Allied advance. The Duke of Brunswick and his army were forced to retreat. Next day, the National Convention met for the first time. It deposed the king and declared a republic.[141] This regime was deeply anticlerical and criminalised all non-juring clergy that fell into its hands. A mass exodus of French clergymen and nuns towards the safety of *ancien régime* monarchies, already under way, now accelerated. A large group of bishops headed to London where the British government was receptive and granted them asylum.[142] Others, like the Archbishop of Strasbourg and Bishop of Metz, crossed the Rhine and entered the German side of their dioceses. Unlike so many of their brethren, here at least they were able to retain some of their revenues and dignity.[143] Some went to Spain where, from the great monasteries of Iberia, they longed for the Gothic cathedrals they had left behind them. The Spanish inquisition become a major player in the reaction to the French Revolution. After a decade of dormancy, it was energetically revived to censor writings smuggled across the Pyrenees. An eye was also kept on refugees to ensure that they did not introduce revolutionary heresies into Iberia. This resurrection was temporary and went against the regalist tendencies of the Spanish monarchy.[144] After the 1790s the ministers in Madrid would again try to rein in the power of the First Estate.

Emigrés, whether ecclesiastic or lay, were not always made to feel welcome in their exile. Theirs was an invidious position. From being respected pillars of their communities, they had been transformed into starving ill-dressed refugees. The French Revolution witnessed the largest forced migration of ecclesiastics in modern history. A very conservative estimate, based on official emigration lists drawn up by the revolutionaries, places the number of clergymen who fled France at 24,596.[145] Poor administrative training, incomplete records and mistakes means that the real numbers are bound to have been far higher. Estimates vary from three to seven thousand priests, and a much smaller number of nuns, finding their way to the Papal States during the 1790s.

This created something of a humanitarian crisis as the pope's domain struggled to absorb this large influx of destitute clergy. Pius VI wrote letters to the bishops, abbots and officials of his kingdom beseeching them to be hospitable to the new arrivals,*

---

* See ASV, Segreteria di Stato, Emigrati Rivoluzione Francese, a remarkable archival series which has yet to be studied in any great depth.

who, after all, had suffered persecution for their loyalty to the Holy See. Their steadfastness had cost them their income and banishment from their homes. As the papacy was nearly bankrupt, financial support for those unfortunates was to come from the convents and monasteries of Romagna, Umbria, the Marche and Lazio. Abbots and abbesses were implored to clothe and feed the exiles. France's churches in Rome were transformed into refuges for fleeing clergymen.* Some papal support was given to counter-revolutionary newspapers in Rome which poured scorn on the revolutionary heretics across the Alps.

French priests in the pope's domains did their best to make ends meet. Many sought an income celebrating votive and memorial masses in side-chapels. At Terni, refugees wanted to give French lessons to ordinary folk, but the local authorities feared the spread of the language of revolutionary sedition. Some aristocrats were supportive: Count Monaldo Leopardi, father of the famous romantic poet Giacomo, accommodated several priests in his palazzo at Recanati. At Camerino the abbé Beauchamp was welcomed into the house of the local lord, but Luigi Amici, the local bishop, expressed grave concerns. This noble house was filled with young maids and female servants in the flower of their youth. Such girls, he warned in a letter, were always a danger to a priest but even more so to a young man of twenty-eight years of age. When Beauchamp eventually left, he told the bishop he would never forget Camerino. Why this town proved so memorable remains a mystery.[146]

Others, like the abbé Dorothée, were asked to transit quickly through the Papal States. Though he was a loyal monk, the fact that he brought with him a concubine and three children made the bishop of Commacchio despair.[147] Many of these refugee priests spent their days writing pamphlets denouncing godlessness. Others tried to analyse and understand the causes of the Revolution which had destroyed their Gallican world. Despite

---

* These chuches include: Trinità dei Monti, San Luigi dei Francesi, Sant'Ivo dei Bretoni, Santi Claudio e Andrea dei Borgognoni and San Nicola dei Lorenesi. They exist to the present day. See *Églises françaises à Rome*, online at https://eglisesfrancaisesarome.it/ [accessed 3 March 2021].

being well treated, their nostalgia for their homes was palpable. From being ministers of the richest church in Christendom they were now penniless migrants.

Italian priests and clergymen were not all hostile to events in France. Some found themselves inspired by the Gallicanism and wanted to use it to reform Catholicism at its summit. One of the most intriguing pamphlets to emerge in 1795 was entitled 'Ideas on the organisation of the church hierarchy'. Although published in Italian in Switzerland and by anonymous authors it was probably the work of reform Catholics from Umbria.[148] It called for a new ecumenical council that would act as a sort of constituent assembly for the church, giving it a constitution and imposing limits on papal authority. This document gives an intriguing glimpse into the most radical dreams of reformists who wanted to check the papacy with an ecclesiastical constitution. Its content was never taken too seriously but it did find its way into libraries and archives across Germany and Spain. Soon after that it made its way onto the Index of Rome and Madrid. This text marked the most extreme incarnation of neo-conciliarism in the eighteenth century.

On the other side of the Alps the deputies of the nascent French Republic turned their attention to the fate of the king.[149] The National Convention sat as judge and jury in the trial of Louis XVI, who was indicted for a series of retroactive crimes.[150] The former king was accused of attempting to thwart the annexation of the papal territories of the Comtat Venaissin to France. He was also indicted for fomenting religious riots in Provence and Languedoc during the early part of the revolution in which hundreds lost their lives. His veto of the decree declaring refractory priests enemies of the nation was transformed into a crime,[151] and his loyalty to the church formed a significant part of the litany of accusations he had to face.

In December the Convention, by an overwhelming majority, voted the former king guilty of the crimes of which he stood accused. It then turned to the matter of how he should be punished. Here the situation was much less clear cut. Some wanted the king to pay the ultimate price while others urged imprisonment or banishment.[152] Voting on the king's fate was on a knife-edge: on 17 January 1793, 361 out of 721 deputies voted for the death sentence.[153] Louis XVI was to die by the slimmest of margins, just one vote. As a direct descendant of St Louis, he resigned himself to meet his death bravely and as a fervent Catholic.[154]

His greatest desire was that he be allowed to confess his sins one last time to a non-juring priest. Given that most refractory clergy had been in hiding since the September massacres the Paris municipal authorities had a difficult time locating a confessor. Eventually, they found an Irish priest, the abbé Henry Edgeworth de Firmont.[155] On 21 January 1793, he would accompany the king on his final journey along a route lined with revolutionary troops and silent spectators. When the carriage reached the Place de la Revolution (now Place de la Concorde) the king dismounted and removed his frock coat and necktie. As he mounted the scaffold, the abbé Edgeworth uttered the exhortation: 'Son of St Louis rise to heaven!' The king tried to improvise a speech forgiving his enemies, but this was drowned out by a drumroll.[156] He was taken to the guillotine and beheaded. The crowd gasped and then rushed forward to dip their handkerchiefs in the royal blood. For some this was a souvenir of the death of a tyrant, whereas for others it was a holy relic of a saintly king.

News of Louis XVI's execution caused great consternation across Europe. Britain, Holland, Spain, Naples and Sardinia-Piedmont declared war. France was now completely encircled by powers horrified by its anti-monarchical and anticlerical excesses.[157] Indeed, the Whig politician Edmund Burke had used large portions of his *Reflections on the French Revolution* to attack the religious reforms of the National Assembly. He vindicated the moral leadership that the Gallican church had offered the people of France for centuries. Burke thought it folly to destroy this great institution and, remarkably for an Anglican politician (possibly a crypto Catholic), he even defended the utility of monasteries. By 1792 he advocated the creation of a European armed coalition that would intervene against France.[158] In Rome Pius VI shed tears on learning the news of the king's death. On 17 June 1793 he issued the solemn papal allocution *Quare Lacryme* (*Wherefore the tears*).[159]

Ultimately the example set by Louis XVI was declared worthy of emulation. To this day there are some pious Catholics who continue to lobby for the canonisation of Louis XVI as a saint.*

The war against Europe took a turn for the worse. A series of battlefield defeats was compounded by the defection to the Allies of some high-profile French generals, and the Convention was forced to resort to drastic measures. Between March and August 1793, the mass conscription of one million men was levied throughout France. The peasantry considered it a blood tax, and the result was deep resentment in the Vendée, Brittany and Western Normandy.[160] These *départements* had already been antagonised by the unfair redistribution of church land, and the removal of local priests for their refusal of the constitutional oath poured oil on the fire. Parishioners resented being deprived of ministers who were part of their community and understood their traditions.[161] The replacement of priests in the West with Jansenist-leaning clerics loyal to the new order was often met with violence and boycotts. When the Convention came knocking on the doors of these peasants demanding that they send sons to serve in the army it was the last straw.

These provinces had initially welcomed the Revolution in 1789, but the policies of Paris had alienated them so much that the rebellion in Vendée now spread like wildfire across the region, fanned by refractory clergy. Eventually the rebels formed the Catholic and Royal Army of the Vendée and started a slow march eastwards. Their leaders made contact with emigrés and begged for assistance from Britain. Although poorly equipped and trained, they did score several victories, marching as far as Angers by October. This was the last thing the Republic needed when it faced a European war. Although the Vendean rebels were crushed at the battle of Savenay, a brutal guerrilla war continued throughout the decade, claiming the lives of possibly as many

---

* Due to the absence of a miraculous intercession the process has stalled. See Philippe Boutry, 'Le Roi martyr, la cause de Louis XVI devant la cour de Rome 1820', *Revue d'histoire de l'eglise de France*, Vol. 76, No. 196 (1990), pp. 57–71.

as 200,000 people. Some have claimed it to be an early example of genocide.[162] This interpretation goes too far, as the men of the West were not killed because of their ethnicity. It was their loyalty to the papacy and monarchy that made them targets. Brittany and the Vendée became blood-soaked killing fields for the young republican conscripts, brutal reprisals leading to a spiral of uncontrolled violence. Anti-insurgency tactics used by republican soldiers did little to bring real peace, and strengthened the population's recourse to its traditional Catholic faith. The politicians in Paris accused them of being stupid, bigoted peasants duped by fanatical priests. Such caricatures did not matter to these men who resented interference from a capital that had disdained their Breton tongue, traditions and autonomies.

The Republic's very survival was cast into doubt by war and mass rebellion. Extremist Jacobins felt that half-measures would not be enough to ensure the Revolution's survival. For them betrayal and conspiracy lay at the heart of the Republic's predicament. Enemies needed to be eradicated by the harshest means to win the war. Yet, even this was not enough. For a regenerated society to emerge, the former subjects of the king of France needed to be educated to become virtuous republican citizens.[163] Whether or not they would consent was irrelevant. As Rousseau had said in his *Social Contract*, individuals needed to be forced to become free.[164]

The Terror was not merely an attempt to save the state from military defeat but an ideological campaign to instil republicanism into a largely indifferent population. The attack on traditional Catholicism would accelerate in these months. France's acoustic landscape was refashioned beyond recognition when, in July 1793, church belfries were limited to a single small bell and, a year later, bell ropes were confiscated.[165] Any other bells were seized to be re-cast as guns for the Republic's armies. An eerie silence descended over France as thousands of belfries were rendered unserviceable. Scattered across 300,000 square miles lay 40,000 parishes, whose sense of belonging to a wider religious community had been felt through the reverberations of ringing bells. They announced times for prayer, grief or celebration, and their sound was a unique way of binding communities together. The ominous silence of the revolution marked a new conception of time.

In September 1793 the radical deputy Gilbert Romme mounted the rostrum to give the following speech:

> [The present Gregorian calendar] began amongst an ignorant and credulous people and in the midst of troubles that foreshadowed the impending fall of the Roman Empire. For eighteen centuries, it served to date the progress of fanaticism, the degradation of nations, the scandalous triumph of pride, vice and stupidity, the persecutions and debasements endured by virtue, talent and philosophy at the hand of cruel despots.[166]

He proposed that the new year should start on 22 September 1792 – the exact moment of the proclamation of the Republic.

Fabre d'Eglantine, a former actor, was given the task of devising a new calendar which, like the metric system of weights and measures, would seek to standardise time in a scientific manner. Fabre proposed dividing the year into twelve months of three ten-day weeks known as *décadi*. The months would be named after the weather or seasonal features. What emerged was romantic, with months receiving very evocative labels like *Brumaire, Frimaire, Floreal and Messidor* which roughly translate as 'the misty one', 'the freezing one', 'the blossomy one' and 'the time for harvest'. Days in turn were dedicated to civic virtues, tools and animals. The five days left over from these months were given the label *Sansculottides* and were designated as holidays. The leap-day was to be called *Franciade* and again was a day of celebration for the Revolution.[167]

The calendar was the embodiment of rationalism. Inspired by the new calendar, some wanted to produce decimal clocks that would divide each day into ten-hour segments. Unsurprisingly, these complicated machines were difficult to produce and failed to catch on.[168] This effort to redefine the nature of time was an aggressive attempt to wrest France away from its Christian heritage toward a more natural religion. It echoed the reforms proposed by Muratori and reform Catholics, which had sought to increase productivity by reducing the number of feasts and religious holidays.[169] This new system of timekeeping proved an unexpectedly effective tool in unmasking the Republic's enemies. Those who refused to use it by continuing to observe Sunday, or who bought fish on Fridays, as the church prescribed, could be seen as suspects and denounced as public enemies.[170]

As the Terror accelerated there was a spontaneous surge against Christianity throughout France. In August 1793 the royal necropolis of Saint Denis on the outskirts of Paris was assaulted. Here, since the Middle Ages, the kings of France had found their final resting place in the crypt underneath the basilica built by abbot Suger during the twelfth century.[171] Two months later, these royal remains were exhumed, desecrated, robbed of valuables, and thrown into a communal grave. Even the dead were pursued and punished retroactively for the crime of being royal. In a carnival of iconoclasm, the crowds attempted to destroy the statues and funerary monuments that honoured the kings and queens of France.[172]

Some of the finest sculptors of the Renaissance and Baroque periods had worked on these masterpieces that now risked annihilation. The term 'vandalism' was coined at this time to describe the wanton destruction of beauty and the treasures of the past.[173] According to legend the barbarian tribe of Vandals chanted the disturbing slogan: 'No phoenixes without ashes.' Their philistinism seemed to find a parallel in the aimless modern destruction of heritage. Alexandre Lenoir, who had been appointed a conservator for the many works of art confiscated by the revolutionaries, intervened bravely before the destruction began. He advised that works of art and heritage be preserved for posterity. His depot in the former convent of the Petits-Augustins became the new home for the Revolution's plunder.[174] This site soon was filled to the brim with reliefs, busts and sculptures looted from many of the public buildings, palaces and châteaux of France. This collection would form the backbone of the Museum of French Monuments.

Not all churches, alas, were lucky enough to have a brave Lenoir to protect their art treasures from revolutionary iconoclasm.

Although the attacks on the royal bodies at Saint Denis had been state-sponsored, what occurred next was spontaneous and anarchic. Throughout France fanatics attacked the visible vestiges of Christianity. This campaign is usually described by scholars as 'anarchic de-Christianisation'. The biblical kings of Jesse on the façade of Notre Dame Cathedral were cast down as if they had been French monarchs. Passers-by apparently defecated on them as a supreme act of republican disdain.[175] Such aggressive attacks did untold damage to the hundreds of Gothic cathedrals and churches littered across the hexagon. In Toul Cathedral even to this day the scars of these attacks are plain to see.[176] Empty plinths, damaged statues, destroyed chancels and smashed stained glass are all evidence of the effects of the Revolution on the urban and rural landscape of France.

What is ironic is that most of this symbolic and physical violence was not directed at the refractory priests loyal to Rome. By now, the non-juring clergy had gone underground and ministered, with false identities, to select congregations of traditional Catholics. Their activities were coordinated by a small number of papal agents, known as apostolic vicars, who remained the only connection to Rome. Men like the abbés Salamon and Emery did their best to keep the 'real' Catholic Church alive in this time of persecution.[177] Refractories caught by the authorities risked imprisonment as 'suspects' but they were not the main prey of the de-Christianisation campaign. One of the great ironies of 1793–4 was that the national constitutional church created by the French Revolution came to be one of its greatest victims.

De-Christianisers changed their names to highlight their disdain for the saints. For example, the deputy prosecutor of Pairs, Pierre Chaumette, discarded his first name in favour of Anaxagoras, a classical philosopher who had denied the divinity of the sun.[178] In republican areas children were given the names of classical tyrannicides, like Brutus and Gracchus. In Perpignan, parents of a horticultural bent named their children imaginatively after vegetables such as cabbage, green bean and cauliflower.[179] It is unclear whether these individuals retained the fruit of their parents' republican passions into their adulthood. Such names were certainly testament to the grim determination to consign the Christian tradition to oblivion.

While, on the whole, radicals and *sans-culottes* respected the figure of Jesus Christ, they did not share the same feelings towards institutional churches. Throughout the winter of 1793 constitutional priests were intimidated and maltreated. In many cases they were forced to renounce their priesthood and declare publicly that Christianity was a tissue of lies.[180] In extreme cases constitutional priests, nuns and monks were forced to marry to prove that they had abandoned their vows. In some instances, thirty-year-old clergymen married their sixty-year-old housekeepers. Although to each their taste, it seems unlikely these were love matches. It is difficult to know how many priests rejoiced in their emancipation and wed willingly, but some were bullied and their marriages were political acts to avoid suspicion falling on them.[181]

On 7 November Jean-Baptiste Gobel, the constitutional archbishop of Paris, asked to appear before the National Convention. He entered the debating chamber wearing a red liberty cap, while in his hands he held his mitre, pectoral cross and episcopal ring. Placing these items at the bar of the Convention, he informed the stunned deputies that he surrendered these items, to symbolise his renunciation of his priesthood and vows.[182] It is difficult to judge Gobel's actions. Traditional Catholics accused him of cowardice while radicals were delighted by his apostasy. Gobel may have felt that upholding the cause of the constitutional church had become a thankless task. Unlike Henri Grégoire, who had now been elected constitutional bishop of Blois and defended with vigour the Revolution's church, Gobel seems not to have had the stomach for a fight. After all, during the Terror, state funds and protection for the church had ceased.[183] Grégoire was a man of principle, while Gobel, though also a religious man, did not possess the necessary bravery to stand up to the *sans-culottes* and just wanted to save his life. However, his spectacular renunciation of his priesthood did not save him from the executioner's blade. Denounced as a public enemy, he was guillotined on 13 April 1794. Just before death, he begged forgiveness for his many sins and confessed to one of his vicars-general that he deeply regretted the scandal and harm he had done to religion.[184] After his execution Paris would remain without a resident archbishop for four years.

Jean Meslier's memory was also celebrated during the de-Christianisation campaign. This god-denying priest of the parish of Étrépigny became a hero for radical atheists. Indeed, there was even talk of erecting a column in his honour as the greatest critic of Christianity.[185] Many churches, stripped of their Catholic ornaments, were transformed into temples of reason where deists would celebrate the end of superstition. In 2016, during some restoration work inside the church of Notre Dame de la Daurade in Tarascon, in Ariège, labourers discovered, to the great surprise of the local parish priest, that behind the plaster work lurked tricolour decorations and other symbols dating back to when the building had been repurposed as a temple of reason. It was an almost unique archaeological find which gave a glimpse into the dreams of the de-Christianisers.[186] Even Notre Dame de Paris was affected and an obscene statue of the goddess of liberty with milk flowing from her breasts was placed in the cathedral aisle. Joseph Fouché, a deputy on mission and a former Oratorian teaching brother, caused great consternation when, in the Nièvre *déparetement*, he erected great iron gates over a cemetery with a metal inscription proclaiming that: 'death is but an eternal sleep.'[187] Thus were the pious robbed of the hope of an afterlife.

The winter of 1793–4 marked one of the greatest anti-Christian persecutions ever unleashed. It is true that some deputies and officials had fanned the flames of anarchic de-Christianisation but it was never endorsed as official government policy by the National Convention. Many viewed with horror the anarchy, violence and misery that this campaign had brought to France. No man was more appalled by these events than Maximilian Robespierre. He was now a member of the powerful twelve-man Committee of Public Safety which was the virtual government of France.[188] Although never a good Catholic, he did sense that republicans would need some spirituality to maintain social cohesion and public morality.[189] Robespierre conceived of establishing a brand-new religious tradition that would be tailored to fit the social, cultural and political context of the French Republic. This new cult would instil republican 'virtue' in the population and promote loyalty to Paris.

A proposal was ratified by the Convention to create a 'cult of the Supreme Being'. This new religion came to life at a fraught political moment. Purges and judicial murder had become staples of French parliamentary life. Robespierre was at the peak of his influence, but increasingly distrusted by his colleagues, especially by the de-Christianisers, whose destruction of heritage he had denounced.[190] Through Robespierre's lobbying, the Convention, on 7 May 1794, proclaimed that a special festival, recognising the Supreme Being and the immortality of the soul, would be celebrated in June. It was intended that this new national form of worship would supplant Catholicism. Throughout the republican year thirty-five festivals celebrating virtues as diverse as 'hatred of tyrants,' 'modesty', 'youth', 'agriculture' and, remarkably, 'misfortune' were planned.[191] Inspired by deism, the Convention proclaimed that a supreme intelligence had created the universe. This cult aimed to promote 'virtue', or total commitment to the community, rather than the self, as the core of republican identity. This form of natural religion would act as a cultural and social adhesive for the young republic. It would replace the traditional and religious identities of the *ancien régime.*

The festival that eventually began on 8 June was decidedly odd. The austere neoclassical artist Jacques-Louis David was commissioned to choreograph the spectacle. Robespierre, as current president of the Convention for a two-week term starting on 4 June 1794, presided over these rituals and opened the spectacle by setting alight wooden allegories of atheism before kneeling in front of a statue symbolising wisdom. Then a procession of deputies and officials set out from the Tuileries palace, the seat of the Convention, down an almost straight line to the Champ de Mars (present-day site of the Eiffel Tower). In this open space the Supreme Being would be venerated publicly. Incense burners were strewn throughout the Champ de Mars adding an air of mystery to the event. Robespierre delivered a speech in which he proclaimed solemnly the existence of the Supreme Being and celebrated the French people's triumph over atheism.[192]

A few days after the festival, the Convention passed the Prairial laws, which transferred the burden of proof to those accused of political crimes and deprived them of the right to a defence counsel. The period June to July saw an intensification of the Terror.[193] The fate of the cult of the Supreme Being was inextricably tied to the man who had inspired it. Robespierre had made many enemies and antagonised influential groups. He had contributed to a culture of paranoia and fear that eventually turned on him towards the end of July 1794. He was denounced as a tyrant and declared an outlaw. He tried unsuccessfully to raise a revolt in Paris against the Convention but was wounded in the jaw by a gunshot. It is unclear whether this was an accident or a suicide attempt.[194] Regardless, he was guillotined on 28 July, and the cult he had founded quickly fell into oblivion.

It would be easy to leap to the conclusion that establishing a new religion was impossible. But a few decades later, in the 1820s, Joseph Smith created American Mormonism, which flourishes to the present day.[195] Robespierre had realised that the demolition of the Gallican church had created not just a spiritual void, but a cultural one. His ambition to construct a modern republican system of belief and ethics was compelling. Yet his was a religion of the mind rather than the heart. Faith without recourse to the supernatural and miraculous was utterly devoid of any attraction. Catholics, alienated by the Revolution's ecclesiastical reforms, were hardly likely to find the cold gaze of the Supreme Being enticing.

The fall of Robespierre and the gradual dismantling of the Terror left Catholicism's position in France ever more uncertain. Although the Revolution had always retained an anticlerical streak, it had never been overtly atheist nor secularist. At this time the church loyal to Rome remained a clandestine organisation, forced to go into hiding. For the constitutional church created by the Civil Constitution of the Clergy the situation was hardly better. It had lost its state funding and had suffered persecution from de-Christianisers. In many towns, churches were closed after having been ransacked and these appeared as ruins of a bygone age. One particularly striking phenomenon occurred in

Burgundy. Here, people were loyal to the French Revolution but very religious too. Bereft of clergy, locals began to celebrate mass without recourse to priests. Laymen would ascend the altar and, despite not having received holy orders, proceeded to perform the liturgy.[196] This usurpation of the priest's monopoly of worship drew the surprise and censure of both Paris and Rome, a rare moment of convergence, from two very different perspectives.

It was left to the successor regime of the Jacobin Republic, the Directory, to seek a solution to France's religious woes. What they proposed had only been attempted in the nascent United States of America during the 1790s.[197] There was to be a complete separation of church and state. Henceforth the Republic would support no cult nor its ministers. Theoretically, public authorities would remain staunchly neutral in matters of religious faith. On learning this news, refractory priests started returning to France and began again ministering to the communities they had fled. Some churches were given permission to hold services, but remained the property of the state.[198] Bells stayed still in haunting silence.

For the constitutional church this loss of state support was a severe blow. Yet its leadership showed remarkable resolve, and tried to rebuild what had been lost. At the forefront of this attempt to reignite the constitutional church was Henri Grégoire, Bishop of Blois. He had been one of the few brave men to denounce de-Christianisation in the Convention. Now he became the spiritual leader of the constitutional church created by the Revolution in 1791. His struggle to rebuild this church was nearly impossible. Over 80 per cent of constitutional priests had abandoned their ministry after the Terror.[199] To make matters worse only a dozen out of eighty-three bishops had remained in place during these tumultuous years. Grégoire reached out to these constitutional prelates and urged them to help him reconstruct their church. It was decided in 1797 to convene a national synod in Paris to coordinate the activities of the surviving constitutional clergy.[200] Under Grégoire's leadership new bishops were appointed, seminaries reopened and constitutional priests resumed their ministry throughout France.

Soon the constitutional episcopacy rose in number to fifty-eight and clergy were sent out even to the insurgent West. Here these outsiders remained deeply unpopular and were shunned by a local community that remained loyal to Rome. Yves Marie Audrein, Bishop of Finisterre, was ambushed by rebels on 19 November 1800 and assassinated.[201] This murder highlighted how difficult it would prove to reconcile the ultra-Catholic population of the West with a constitutional clergy perceived as a rabble of usurpers. Despite these failures Grégoire, against all the odds, stopped the Revolution's church from going under.[202]

For all the abuse heaped on the constitutional clergy, they were both liturgically and doctrinally very close to their colleagues loyal to Rome. Indeed, the schism of 1791 was political in nature, and revolved around the authority of the papacy. Unlike the Reformation of the sixteenth century there was little theological disagreement about the path to salvation. This made some wonder whether it might still be possible to heal the divisions between refractory and constitutional clergy.

From 1795 to 1797 the refractories tentatively emerged from hiding and found that the Directorial authorities were willing to grant them limited toleration. The abbé Jacques-André Emery, head of the great Gallican seminary of St Sulpice, and vicar general to the archbishop of Paris, virtually became the pope's administrator for France.[203] The process of rebuilding Catholicism was fraught and eventually overtaken by events. In 1797, the annual elections to the National Assembly returned a monarchist-leaning majority. This spooked the republican Directors who used military force to annul the elections and expel the royalist deputies.[204] A period of brutal repression followed, during which it was decided to impose on all religious ministers a public oath 'proclaiming an eternal hatred of monarchy'. Although Emery opined that this oath might be understood to mean a hatred of tyranny and could be taken, few were convinced by his reasoning. Indeed, the papacy was swift to condemn this new oath. The republican authorities retaliated with brutality to this renewed defiance from Rome. Roughly ten thousand priests were arrested and sentenced to deportation to French Guiana, which had been given the sobriquet of 'the dry guillotine', given the high mortality rate consequent on the insalubrious climate. Around 230 priests were sent to the colonies and a further 700 interned on island prisons in the Atlantic awaiting deportation.[205] Priests in annexed provinces were also subjected to this torment, and thirty Belgian priests ended up in South America.

Up to now the papacy had viewed events from Paris with alarm and horror. At the same time, Rome seemed distant from the turmoil and persecution of the Revolution. Safely on the other side of the Alps, the battles for European supremacy had mainly taken place on the Rhine. The Italian military front had always been a sideshow for the military strategists in Paris. Revolutionary armies had conquered Savoy and Nice from the king of Piedmont and Sardinia but had failed to push their advantage further. The expectation was that the outcome of the war would be determined on the Rhine.[206] Gradually the revolutionary armies had occupied the Rhenish ecclesiastical electorates of the Holy Roman Empire and forced their prince-archbishops to flee. The armies of the Republic thus put an end to the political power of the ancient Reichskirche.[207] Yet here on the banks of the Rhine the offensive stalled and seemed unable to advance further. The appointment of Napoleon Bonaparte to lead the army of Italy was considered a routine change of command. There was little expectation that he would do more than hold the front on the Alpine borders of the Republic or, at most, prepare an invasion of Piedmont. Yet, through sheer vigour and military genius, Bonaparte's troops poured into the northern half of the peninsula, conquering Austrian Lombardy and defeating no fewer than four Habsburg armies.[208]

Napoleon's decision to descend into the papal legations of Bologna, Ferrara and Ravenna caused panic among Rome's ruling elite. Ferdinand IV of Naples had proposed a military alliance and in 1796 urged the pope to declare a war of religion, or quasi-crusade, against the godless Jacobins of Paris.[209] This was a proposal the Curia considered seriously for the better part of the year. Revolution was no longer a remote danger but now had broken down the border fences to the pope's domains.

Realising that military resistance would be impossible for his ramshackle papal army, Pius VI was forced to open peace talks. Republican and Catholic negotiators met at Tolentino where painful discussions began. Here the papacy agreed to cede its Legations in Romagna, its most agriculturally prosperous lands, to the nascent Cispadane Republic (which was to be an Italian puppet state of France). An indemnity of 21 million *livres* would be paid in specie to the French Republic. Even more painful for the pope were the more than one hundred works of art of inestimable value that were transferred from the Eternal City to the museums of Paris.[210] Furthermore, Pius was forced to accept the loss of Avignon and the Comtat Venaissin. Finally, the papacy had to establish diplomatic relations with the French Republic, thus formally recognising its existence.

The treaty was signed on 19 February 1797 and showed that Pius VI was willing to pay any price to forestall the occupation of Rome by revolutionary forces. Soon after there followed the defeat of the Habsburg forces and the Treaty of Campoformio. France, thanks to the triumph of Bonaparte's army, had imposed peace on Europe.[211] As it happened, these accords created a truce rather than a genuine cessation of hostilities. The next year Napoleon would depart on his legendary and militarily catastrophic Egyptian campaign.[212] Joseph Bonaparte, the general's brother, had been sent to Rome as the Republic's ambassador. General Mathurin-Léonard Duphot was part of his diplomatic suite. On 28 December 1797 this youthful military officer organised a republican rally at the embassy in Rome which sparked off a riot. Anti-papal protestors had an altercation with Roman troops. It is not clear how, but Duphot was shot in the chest by an arquebus. He quickly died of his wounds, creating a major diplomatic crisis.[213]

The murder of General Duphot provided French forces with a pretext to invade the Papal States and the Directory commanded its troops to cross Tuscany and head for Rome. Pius VI was begged by his cardinals to flee and take refuge in Naples. The aged Braschi refused to leave his capital and instead awaited his fate. On 9 February 1798 troops commanded by General Louis-Alexandre Berthier approached the Milvian bridge, famously the site of the Emperor Constantine's conversion to Christianity.[214] Berthier demanded the unconditional surrender of the city. The papacy capitulated on 15 February – coincidentally the anniversary of Pius' election as Pope in 1774 – and French troops marched triumphantly into the Eternal City.[215] They proceeded to the Capitoline Hill where they planted a liberty tree. Then a public proclamation deposed the pope as sovereign of Rome and the Papal States. Stunned crowds were informed that, after centuries of tyranny, the people of Rome had regained their freedom. A new Roman republic, modelled on the French Directory, was created.[216]

Next, the French occupied the Vatican and Quirinal palaces, confiscating the papacy's treasures and archives. Pius received the news of his deposition stoically. He was informed that for his own safety he was now in the protective custody of the Republic's troops. On 17 February Pius VI learned that he would have three days to leave Rome and go into exile in Tuscany.[217] Bravely the pope responded that he had no intention of leaving his diocese. However, when threatened with violence, he agreed to leave to avoid bloodshed. Before dawn, on 20 February, the pope heard mass in his private apartments and the blessed sacrament was placed in a pyx which he carried with him. The eighty-year-old pontiff hobbled into the San Damaso courtyard of the Vatican Palace. Surrounded by French troops, he boarded a carriage accompanied only by two prelates and his doctor. Its door was locked from the outside leaving no doubt that the pope was a prisoner. As the carriage pulled away, the pope turned to look at St Peter's dome, which he blessed as tears streamed down his face. He would never see Rome again.[218]

It had been centuries since a reigning Pope had been taken prisoner by a hostile power. Soon after his departure, the College of Cardinals was expelled from the city. The princes of the church were divided into two main groups, one headed for Naples, and the other for Venice. The elderly cardinals Altieri and Antici resigned rather than be forced to leave Rome.[219] February 1798 marked the nadir of Catholicism's fortunes in modern times. The very survival of the church seemed to be at stake. Not only was the pope a prisoner, but the College of Cardinals was scattered and unable to deliberate freely. Many wondered what would happen if Pius were to die. In the meantime, the new Roman Republic began the familiar pattern of confiscating ecclesiastical and monastic property. It also hosted a neo-pagan celebration for the feast of the Federation in St Peter's square. Before the mother church of Catholicism, republicans celebrated the defeat of tyranny and superstition.[220] This spectacle hid from sight the reality that the French were plundering Rome of all its funds and looting its art treasures.

Pius VI had reached Siena and spent several weeks there until he was transferred to the Charterhouse of Florence. In this great fourteenth-century Carthusian monastery, the pope spent nearly ten months.[221] During his time here the pope was technically allowed to write to cardinals and other clergymen to continue administering the church. However, his correspondence was monitored so that it proved impossible for the Holy Father to express himself freely. Furthermore, the absence of the Curia meant that the pope was bereft of the staff and secretaries necessary to govern the church. It was clear that stress and depression were taking their toll on the pontiff. On 24 January 1799 Pius suffered a serious stroke which he barely survived.[222] During this time as a hostage, the pope was assisted by Giuseppe Spina, archbishop of Corinth, an expert canon lawyer and experienced diplomat who became Braschi's closest confidant during his exile.

Events in Europe were turning against the Republic. After the destruction of the French fleet by Horatio Nelson at Aboukir Bay on 2 August 1798 Bonaparte was effectively stranded in Egypt.[223] Russia and Austria launched a counter-offensive in Northern Italy which put pressure on republican troops in Lombardy.[224] In the south, Neapolitan forces commenced an invasion of the Papal States and would slowly push the French northwards. There was a genuine possibility that the pope, if allowed to remain in Florence, would be rescued by *ancien régime* forces. The Directory ordered that the pope be transferred to France. Despite his ill health, which alarmed his doctor, Pius was unable to resist this command. After a slow, month-long journey through frozen and snow-strewn Alpine passes, the convoy carrying St Peter's successor reached the fortified town of Briançon in northern Provence. Here Pius was placed for two months in a modest house next to the local hospital,[225] where the locals brought him meagre food and inadequate supplies. Ominously he was referred to by his French captors as *citoyen pape* ('citizen pope'). His innumerable titles thus disappeared almost overnight.

For some weeks the pope was not allowed to see the prelates and servants who had accompanied him on his journey. Spina and his colleagues were interned in Grenoble as suspected enemies of the Republic. After a month in this lonely border town, the order was given to move the pope, who had now become delirious, feverish and gravely ill, deeper into French territory. On 29 June, the Feast of St Peter and St Paul, unaware of his surroundings, Pius expressed the wish to officiate at the high mass in St Peter's Basilica. Arriving in Grenoble the pope was grudgingly allowed to see his prelates and servants again. In this city crowds of pious Catholics defied the municipal authorities by cheering Pius and asking for his blessing. On 7 July the pope fell into such a deep sleep that his doctor suspected he had suffered another more serious stroke.[226]

Lacking compassion, the Directory commanded the transfer of their distinguished prisoner to Valence. This town in the Rhône valley was to be the final destination of the pope. An old medieval university centre, it was strategically located on the arterial trade route that connected France to Italy.[227] The ailing pontiff was housed in the former governor's residence. Unlike Grenoble, the papal presence in the town was kept secret to avoid mass gatherings. Arriving inauspiciously on 14 July, the anniversary of the French Revolution, Pius settled into a routine. His health seemed to improve with rest and the warm summer weather. In the morning the pope heard two masses, prayed from his breviary, then enjoyed lunch followed by a lumbering walk in the garden. During the afternoon he would take a long period of rest before evening prayers.[228]

The improvement was not to last. The pope suffered a sudden and very severe stroke in early August, after which he drifted in and out of consciousness. Unhelpfully, orders arrived from Paris to transfer the papal suite to Burgundy. Pius's physician informed the authorities that the pope was reaching the end of his mortal existence and forbade all travel. On 27 August in a last fit of energy Pius asked to be dressed and placed in a chair so that he could make his final confession to Spina. After clearing his conscience, the pope recited three times the formula *Domine non sum dignus* ('Oh lord I am unworthy'). He then asked for his servants to pray with him the *De profundis* (the prayer of the dying). The next day he received the sacrament of the dying. According to tradition at midnight he whispered the words '*Domine ignosce illis*' ('God forgive them') which were Christ's words on the cross.[229] At 1 a.m. on 29 August 1799 Pius VI raised his right hand in a feeble gesture of benediction. Fifteen minutes later he gave a long sigh and quietly passed away. Archbishop Spina genuflected and removed the fisherman's ring from his hand. He had promised the dying pontiff to deliver this seal of papal authority to his successor.

Thus died, as a prisoner, the last pope of the *ancien régime*, whose pontificate of twenty-four years and six months had been the longest since St Peter. His death certificate, released by the authorities of Valence, recorded pithily the demise of 'citizen Jean-Ange Braschi exercising the profession of pontiff'.[230] Pius VI's nine-day exequys were performed in a modest chapel of the citadel of Valence. Although the pope had expressed a final wish that his remains be returned to Rome this was refused by the Directory. Spina despatched circulars to all the cardinals of the Roman church informing them of the death of the pope. Where a conclave would assemble to elect Pius VI's successor remained unclear, as was how a church expelled from Rome would weather this revolutionary maelstrom. Though the Revolution cared little for theology, let alone the salvation of the soul, it had shown an unyielding determination to subordinate Catholicism to the power of the secular state. With the death of Pius VI in Valence the church's political power had been brought to its knees. Yet by the autumn of 1799 Austro-Russian forces had succeeded in chasing the French and their erstwhile collaborators almost completely from the Italian peninsula. Rome had been liberated by Neapolitan forces. When it would be returned to papal control, however, remained an open question. Nobody expected that the Catholic Church's resurgence after the experience of revolution and persecution would be easy.

4

THE EAGLE AND THE DOVE: THE NAPOLEONIC EMPIRE, 1800–15

S an Giorgio Maggiore is both a monastery and an island on the Venetian lagoon. Across the water it faces directly onto St Mark's Square. On 14 March 1800 a man in a white cassock appeared on the balcony. A throng of gondolas had cruised down the Grand Canal to gather round the Basilica of San Giorgio to receive his blessing. He was Barnabà Chiaramonti, who had just been elected pope after a three-month conclave.* As a sign of continuity with his predecessor, he chose the regnal name of Pius VII. Like so many eighteenth-century popes, he had not been a first-choice candidate; his election had been a compromise agreed between the pro- and anti-Habsburg cardinals. Through a weird twist of fate, Chiaramonti was a distant cousin to Pius VI and, like him, had been born in Cesena. He was something of an outsider, having spent most of his life away from the machinations of the Curia and papal politics in Rome. He preferred to reside in his diocese of Imola, where he collected a great library of works on the Enlightenment. Although some scholars have suspected that he had Jansenist and reformist sympathies, in reality he was a

---

* The only biography in English is by Robin Anderson, *Pope Pius VII 1800-1823* (Charlotte, NC, 2000).

staunch upholder of papal authority.[1] When the French annexed the papal legations, his diocese of Imola fell under their authority. On Christmas Day 1797, he impressed Bonaparte and others by preaching a sermon that reassured his flock that democracy and Christianity were not mutually exclusive. He expressed the belief that they could work in partnership for the common good.[2] There was a sense that the new pope was a moderate with whom one could do business.

He proved hostile to the Habsburgs in his first months in office. Their claims that they could annex part of the papal territories they had liberated infuriated the College of Cardinals.[3] This led to tensions with the Austrian empire, which refused permission for the papal coronation to be performed in St Mark's Basilica. Instead, Pius VII was crowned inside the massive chapel designed by Palladio in the monastery of San Giorgio Maggiore.[4] The College of Cardinals had been unable to return to Rome. The city had only been reconquered recently by a Neapolitan army. These prelates and the new pontiff remained dramatically short of funds and other essentials. This meant that the coronation needed to take place on a shoestring budget. Even the papal tiara was unavailable. The tiara was a conical headdress surmounted by three crowns, and represented the papacy's spiritual and secular sovereignty. Pius VII's tiara had to be fashioned from papier-mâché then decorated with silver thread and some gemstones donated by pious Venetian ladies.[5] The ceremony took place on 21 March 1800. Chiaramonti was the only pope to be elected and crowned in Venice.*

The church inherited by Pius VII was in crisis. He must have found reports from his cardinals sobering. The Papal States were occupied by Neapolitan and Habsburg troops, while the churches in France and Italy had suffered deeply at the hands of anticlerical revolutionaries. In Germany the situation was hardly better: the

---

* Indeed, it had been almost four centuries since Oddone Colonna had been elected as Pope Martin in Constance in 1417, which was the last time a papal election had taken place far from the Eternal City. See Marzieh Gail, *The Three Popes: An Account of the Great Schism* (New York, 1969).

archbishop-electors of the Holy Roman Empire had been chased from their domains and deposed. It appeared that the old alliance of throne and altar had broken down beyond repair. Catholics could only dream that an Allied victory against the French Republic would allow the First Estate to regain the ground that had been lost during this turbulent decade. By early 1800 the Allied army remained on the offensive, and there was some hope that this year might witness the invasion of France, a breakthrough that had been longed for since 1792, but had spectacularly failed to materialise.

Across the Alps the situation remained confused. On 8 October 1799, General Bonaparte had returned from Egypt, cutting his losses, and seeking to take advantage of the government's weakness in Paris. He adroitly hid the reality of his defeat in the Middle East. Instead, he focused on the scientific discoveries of the expedition.[6] Riddled with political instability and in retreat along all military fronts, the Directory was under significant pressure. During the autumn of 1799 several conspiracies gathered pace, with the aim of toppling this regime which now appeared increasingly feeble and unprepared to meet the Allied offensive expected in the spring.[7] The most influential group of plotters coalesced around the figure of Sieyès, who had been in the political wilderness since 1791. Most of them were intellectuals, high-ranking public servants and disgruntled deputies from the legislative chambers. It was clear that for such a conspiracy to succeed military support would be vital. Sieyès had thought of asking General Joubert to assist them but on 15 August 1799 he was killed in action in Italy. Napoleon Bonaparte, like Chiaramonti, was not the first choice but emerged as a compromise candidate.[8]

On the 18 and 19 Brumaire VIII (9–10 November 1799) the legislative chambers were assembled at Saint-Cloud on the outskirts of Paris. Informed that there was a radical plot seeking to plunge France back into the dark days of the Terror, Napoleon and his confederates tried to persuade the deputies to grant them emergency powers. Things started badly: Bonaparte alienated his audience with a pompous speech, in which he claimed to be Mars the god of war. Deputies surrounded him and threatened him, at which point the general apparently fainted. It was only thanks to quick thinking on his followers' part that the day was saved from disaster. They rallied the troops outside who purged and ejected all the extremist deputies. A rump parliament was then assembled which invested Napoleon and the other conspirators with the executive power. The conspirators, like Sieyès, believed that this general was a nonentity who could be manipulated and used as a straw man. They deeply underestimated Bonaparte who took the initiative and was appointed First Consul of France. A few weeks later a hastily cobbled-together constitution was presented for ratification in a plebiscite. Napoleon's leadership abilities and energy put him at the forefront of the attempts to reorganise and re-galvanise France to meet the armies of the *ancien régime* powers.[9]

Although few lamented the demise of the tottering Directory, it was far from certain that the Consulate that had replaced it was fated to survive. It too faced economic ruin, lawlessness in the provinces and military defeat.[10] Talleyrand, who had risen to become foreign minister, aptly summarised Napoleon's situation when he stated 'if he survives the year he'll do well'.[11] It was clear that everything depended on the outcome of the war. The First Consul assumed personal command of the army and prepared for a counter-offensive in Lombardy. In May 1800 his army of fifty thousand troops crossed the Simplon, Great St Bernard and Gothard passes.[12] This allowed his forces to appear behind the main Habsburg army advancing into Piedmont. General Melas, the Austrian commander, was surprised to find himself cut off from his lines of supply and communication in Lombardy. On 14 June, these Habsburg troops wheeled back and launched a counter-offensive at the village of Marengo. Bonaparte's army was caught by surprise and thrown back in disarray. It was only the miraculous arrival of reinforcements in the afternoon and a stunning cavalry charge that snatched victory from the jaws of defeat.[13] With this success Napoleon could begin to contemplate how to bring domestic peace and tranquillity to France.

It is not often remarked that the First Consul and the new pope shared similar formative experiences. Napoleon, like Chiaramonti, had lost his father at a young age and had been brought up by his deeply religious mother Letizia.[14] On St Helena after his fall from power the former emperor stated that his first communion had been the happiest day of his life.[15] Many of his Bonaparte ancestors had taken religious vows. His crafty and parsimonious great-uncle Luciano was archdeacon of Ajaccio cathedral, and on his father's death had become the virtual head of the family. Napoleon's Italo-Corsican heritage gave him a grudging respect for the traditions and moral teachings of the church. Once he arrived in France for his schooling, his Corsican religious fervour ebbed away as he became exposed to the latest anticlerical publications of deists and Parisian *philosophes*. Yet Napoleon was neither an atheist nor a secularist. Deep down he appreciated the importance of religious belief in cementing and binding complex societies together. As he reportedly once said:

> It is by making myself Catholic that I brought peace to Brittany and Vendée. It is by making myself a Muslim that I established myself in Egypt. If I governed a nation of Jews, I should re-establish the Temple of Solomon.[16]

For him religion was an instrument of social control and a means of legitimation. He had little patience with theology, canon law and least of all mysticism. His understanding of faith was utilitarian, with little space for spirituality.

On the surface, Chiaramonti shared a similar, if rather more aristocratic, pedigree. Under the guidance of his extremely pious mother, Countess Giovanna, no fewer than three of his siblings took holy orders and became committed members of the church.[17] The young Chiaramonti had been deeply marked by his early life as a Benedictine monk. He believed in the power of prayer and contemplation. His intellectual formation was rigidly grounded in theology, self-denial and reflection. For him, the church had a powerful spiritual and pastoral mission. Although he and Bonaparte agreed about the importance of religion in society, their rationales were diametrically opposed. The First Consul was practical and cynical in his views, whereas the pope had an elevated, sublime and idealistic appreciation of the magisterium he had inherited. He was a real priest and not a canon-lawyer of the Curia.

Bonaparte had inherited from the revolutionaries that preceded him a deeply divided France. He was determined to heal all the divisions of the 1790s. None was more damaging than the religious schism created by the Civil Constitution of the Clergy. Within weeks of taking office, he opened negotiations with the Catholic rebel insurgents in the west of France. He promised that religious toleration would be the cornerstone of any future peace.[18] Even during his subsequent second Italian campaign he sought to prove that he was no anticlerical Jacobin. In early June 1800 he recaptured Milan and, before the clergy of the city, he gave a speech in which he applauded religion's contribution to social harmony and peace. Furthermore, the promise was made that, under his leadership, public worship would be guaranteed and protected by the state.[19] Such words were unprecedented for a revolutionary French political leader and caused great excitement in ecclesiastical circles. After the victory at Marengo Napoleon decided to stop in the town of Vercelli, which had a famous seminary that was a hub for reform Catholicism in Italy. Here he met with Cardinal Carlo Giuseppe Filippa della Martiniana. In their discussions, the First Consul expressed his determination to make peace with the Catholic Church. Cardinal Martiniana received this news with jubilation.[20]

These discussions, subsequently known as 'the preliminaries of Vercelli', were a great turning-point in the history of the church. The Cardinal and First Consul discussed at length the key conditions on which Catholicism might be restored in France. They felt that a concordat, or diplomatic treaty, could act as the vehicle for the re-establishment of the church. Its terms were to be a compromise between the Civil Constitution of the Clergy and the Concordat of Bologna of 1516.[21] Bonaparte, unlike the revolutionaries of the 1790s, saw that the pope's consent was vital for such an agreement to work. The refractory clergy's situation was so dire in 1800 that any improvement was greeted by the papacy with enthusiasm. After his meetings with Bonaparte,

Martiniana wrote to the pope outlining the basis on which a new concordat for the French church might be negotiated. Pius VII greeted this letter with excitement and felt that the prospect was worth exploring.[22]

Entering into these discussions was an act of immense bravery for both parties. Many within the French Republic remained hostile to institutional Catholicism and scarcely wanted to see the church resurrected. Napoleon knew he would face internal opposition but believed the rewards would exceed the risks. Equally, many cardinals in Rome hardly relished the prospect of negotiating with a nation who had taken the previous pope captive and put him into an early grave. For them France was a nation that had executed not only its God-given king but also hundreds of priests and nuns. This persecution had transformed thousands of clergymen into refugees and despoiled the church of its worldly possessions. Both Bonaparte and Chiaramonti would have to fight significant internal opposition.

The French requested that an expert negotiator be sent to Paris to open formal discussions on a future concordat. Giuseppe Spina, Archbishop of Corinth, who had followed Pius VI on his final journey to Valence, was seen as an ideal candidate for this mission with his knowledge of canon law and his natural tact.[23] Unbeknownst to the French, Spina had not been granted plenipotentiary powers. He was authorised to undertake informal discussions with the republican authorities, but any final text would need to be sent to Rome for final scrutiny and ratification. The church was horrified at the prospect that Spina would have to negotiate with Charles Maurice de Talleyrand who was now France's foreign minister. As an apostate bishop, who wanted to marry his British mistress Catherine Grand, he was a decidedly unwelcome interlocuter for the church.[24] Craftily, Napoleon decided to appoint a far more acceptable negotiator. Étienne-Alexandre Bernier was a refractory clergymen who had joined the Vendean rebels in 1793. He had spent the revolutionary decade as a warrior priest fighting for God, pope and king. His competence had allowed him to become virtual finance and interior minister to the warlords of the West. His organisational abilities, survival instinct and love of intrigue had earned him the moniker 'Machiavelli in a cassock'.[25] When Napoleon came to power, Bernier perceived him as a man with whom he could work. He quickly rallied to the regime that emerged after the Brumaire coup.

From November 1800 until May 1801 Bernier and Spina were locked in difficult negotiations. It took nine drafts before a settlement that embodied an acceptable compromise emerged. Some points of contention were resolved straightforwardly. It was agreed that the First Consul could appoint bishops to vacant dioceses as the king of France had done since the Concordat of Bologna in 1516.[26] In return, the episcopacy and priesthood would receive state salaries and their freedom of worship would be enshrined in law. Furthermore, it was agreed that the number of dioceses would be reduced to a mere sixty. This was less than half the number than had existed under the *ancien régime*. Although painful, the church promised not to importune nor sanction those individuals who had purchased ecclesiastical property auctioned during the 1790s. Essentially the owners of ecclesiastical land and buildings were no longer condemned to hell.[27] In many ways, Rome accepted that the church of the *ancien régime* was beyond resurrection. There was also a tacit agreement that former priests could have their revolutionary marriages sanctioned.[28] Additionally it was agreed that former monks and nuns be released from their vows if they made a formal application to the church. The only exception was Talleyrand, who was laicised but not permitted to marry his mistress.[29] His schismatic investiture of the bishops of the constitutional church was never forgiven. He ignored the church's disapproval and eventually married his mistress Madame Grand at a civil ceremony in 1802.[30]

There were two major sticking-points in the negotiation of the Concordat. The first related to the surviving hundred bishops of the *ancien régime* church. Bonaparte was adamant that they needed to be removed from their old dioceses.[31] Spina argued that this was exceedingly difficult, as they had committed no canonical crime and it was unheard of that the pope would depose bishops whose only fault had been their unwavering loyalty to Rome. It was left to the wily Bernier to find a solution to this impasse. His prodigious knowledge of church history led him to recall the Donatist crisis of the fourth century in North Africa. In this incident over four hundred bishops had been exhorted to resign their sees to heal a complicated rift within the church.[32] Could not the papacy exhort the Gallican episcopacy to make a similar sacrifice? This solution was eventually enshrined in article 3 of the concordat. In its text Pius VII enjoined the *ancien régime* bishops to resign their dioceses for the good of the church. If they refused their old sees would be abolished. Although this article was supposed to destroy the remnants of the Gallican church it represented something of a revolution in terms of papal authority.[33] Through this provision France implicitly recognised the pope's supremacy over the episcopacy. Such a recognition of Rome's authority to abolish French dioceses would have been unthinkable during the Bourbon monarchy. This article was a milestone in the slow creep toward papal absolutism that would reach its culmination in the dogma of infallibility in 1870.[34]

The second major obstacle was the first article of the concordat. This imposed government supervision and regulation of all church activities.[35] It made manifest the supremacy of the state over the church. Such a concession proved difficult for Rome to swallow. It should be recalled that the First Estate had considered itself for centuries an anointed caste that was both separate from and above the rest of society. Disciplining and monitoring the clergy was a prerogative reserved for the Catholic hierarchy, not secular authorities. During the twentieth century this refusal to accept outside scrutiny was to have disastrous consequences in the child-abuse scandal. Then, as now, the Curia refused to accept that the clergy should be subject to criminal law like all citizens of the state.[36] From Rome's perspective priests could not be supervised by a state that did not accept its magisterium and shared fundamental values. After all, France allowed for divorce (which was forbidden in the gospels) and did not enforce canon law. Worse still, it emancipated Jews and tolerated Protestant heretics within its domain.[37] Having lost its monopoly on public worship, the church felt aggrieved no longer to be the state religion.

Twelve cardinals were charged with scrutinising the different drafts of the concordat and they took some weeks to report back to the pope. Instead of accepting what had been drafted in Paris, they drew up counter-proposals and significantly changed the French document. By May 1801 Napoleon's patience had worn thin and he threw the alternative concordat drafted in Rome into his fireplace. In fury, he threatened Spina with the invasion of the Papal States.[38] As storm clouds gathered in Paris, the church was forced to take an unprecedented step. Cardinal Ercole Consalvi, the pope's secretary of state, who was a brilliant canon lawyer and diplomat, was to travel to Paris to resolve these intractable negotiations. Consalvi was to impress many with his ability to stand up to the French negotiating team and his refusal to be intimidated. His strategy was to seek new partnerships between modernising states and local churches. On the international stage he wanted Rome to remain neutral and avoid getting embroiled in secular conflicts as it had done during the Middle Ages and the Renaissance.

Napoleon realised that Pius's decision to send his principal minister to conclude negotiations meant he was serious about reaching a deal. Consalvi, unlike Spina, had been granted plenipotentiary powers, and thus could sign a binding agreement with the French Republic.[39] This arrival of a distinguished cardinal caused something of a stir as it was the first time in a decade that a prince of the church had been seen in Paris.[40] Bonaparte's reception of the cardinal was frosty, and he pressured Consalvi to conclude negotiations swiftly. After a month of intense discussions and significant re-drafting, a compromise was found for the first article of the concordat. The official signing ceremony was supposed to take place on 14 July 1801. To Consalvi's horror the text of the document presented for his signature had been altered from the version he had approved the night before.[41] As a man of principle he refused to sign a version of the agreement that conflicted with the interests of the church. That evening there was a diplomatic reception whose purpose was to celebrate not only the concordat but also a peace treaty recently signed with the Habsburg empire at Lunéville. Napoleon, embarrassed by the failure to ratify the agreement, greeted the pope's foreign minister with a torrent of verbal abuse and commanded him to leave Paris as soon as possible. At this stage, the Austrian ambassador intervened, reminding the First Consul that only one article remained as a bone of contention. Surely one more round of negotiation could settle this question? Grudgingly Napoleon agreed to give Consalvi another day to reach a settlement.[42]

On 15 July 1801, thanks to some subtle rewording of Article 1, France and the papacy signed a solemn concordat. After a decade of religious turmoil, Catholicism once again received state protection and funding. Yet this agreement only recognised the Church of Rome as the faith of the majority of the French people, not as the religion of state. Pius ratified this treaty in early August despite the protests of several cardinals. Within days he issued the brief *Tam multa* on 15 August 1801. In this open letter he exhorted the *ancien régime* bishops to resign their sees.

About two-thirds of Gallican bishops, over the next two years, acceded to this papal command. The remainder, especially those in exile in London, refused to accept that the pope had the power to deprive them of their episcopal jurisdiction.[43] They neither recognised the authority of the French Republic nor that of the papacy. For them, their spiritual mandate and anointing came from Christ and no one could depose them without just cause. Their followers in France became known as the *petite église*, and rejected the legitimacy of the concordat.[44] This traditionalist sect may have possessed as many as a million members during the Napoleonic period. However, during the nineteenth century their numbers dwindled as their clergy became extinct. Today it is a lay cult with several thousand members concentrated around the Lyons and Angoulême regions.* Nothing could persuade these irredentist Gallicans to accept the authority of either Paris or Rome. They continue to protest the autonomy of their distinctly French brand of Catholicism.

On 5 April 1802 Bonaparte, after some wrangling with deist deputies, persuaded his parliament to ratify the concordat.[45] He

---

* For the Lyonnais see A.N. F7 6376, *Petite Église de Lyons*: a determined campaign of police intimidation and interrogation took place here.

decided to celebrate this milestone with a formal ceremony. Pius VII had sent Cardinal Giovanni Battista Caprara Montecuccoli to be papal legate to France.[46] Caprara was to prove a very weak representative of the pope. He was completely intimidated by Bonaparte and would fail spectacularly to defend the church's rights in the long run. On Easter Sunday 1802 he would preside over a solemn paschal mass and *Te deum* in Notre Dame cathedral. The First Consul rode to the ceremony in Louis XVI's coronation coach. His decision to profess his Catholicism publicly drew negative comment from many army officers and intellectuals. To avoid awkwardness, he had refused to undergo confession and take communion during this ritual. Despite some scepticism about the rebirth of Catholicism, the people of Paris turned out enthusiastically to welcome the official resumption of religious services in the capital.[47]

Many royalists came back to France, encouraged by this gesture of *détente*, and the government even returned émigré properties that had not been sold. The most famous exponent of this trend was the writer and intellectual François-René de Chateaubriand. In 1802 he published his elegiac multi-volume work *Génie du Christianisme* (*Genius of Christianity*).[48] These tomes were a staunch defence of Christianity's contribution to human civilisation. Chateaubriand defended the church's magisterium, rituals and history against the critiques of Enlightenment and revolutionary opponents. As a reward, the First Consul appointed him to be a secretary to the French embassy in Rome.[49] His honeymoon period with the consular regime was to prove short-lived.

Bonaparte's half-uncle, Joseph Fesch, had been a priest during the *ancien régime*. Although it is not entirely clear whether he had taken the oath to the Civil Constitution of the Clergy, his vocation was genuine and, after a period in hiding during the Terror, he had resumed religious ministry.[50] Like many Italians, Napoleon recognised the utility of having a priest in the family. He appointed his relative to the archdiocese of Lyons which made him primate of all Gaul.[51] Further pressure was exerted on Pius VII, who agreed to elevate Fesch to the position of cardinal. It was decided that this member of the Bonaparte clan would make the ideal French ambassador to Rome.[52] Unfortunately for his nephew, Fesch was no yes-man. He always found it difficult to make up his mind on whether his ultimate loyalty lay with his nephew, who had fast-tracked his ecclesiastical career, or with the pope, who was the spiritual head of the church. His tenure of the embassy in Rome was to be fraught with tension and conflicts of interest.

Despite its promise to bring peace, the concordat had still left significant unresolved issues. For the papacy it was supposed to mark the beginning of the rebirth of Catholicism in France. Vatican officials hoped that it might herald a return to the old alliance of throne and altar. This was certainly not the understanding of the politicians and administrators of the French Republic. They saw the concordat as a capitulation on the church's part. By ratifying this treaty, Rome, for them, had accepted the supremacy of the state over religious belief. The French government, in the years following its ratification, took every opportunity to stretch the concordat's terms to breaking point.

To the papacy's fury, when the agreement was published in France, the government tagged an additional seventy-seven organic articles onto the text of the concordat. These set out the rules for the supervision and regulation of Catholic worship.[53] Rome resented not having been consulted over these articles, and was further provoked when ten former bishops loyal to the Revolution were appointed to vacant dioceses. These appointments were an expression of Napoleon's policy of *amalgame* (amalgamation). Its objective was to fuse the winners and losers of the French Revolution into a semi-permanent elite.[54] For the government it seemed sensible to extend this conciliatory policy to ecclesiastical nominations. It was expected that refractory and constitutional clergy could both be persuaded to let bygones be bygones and work together to rebuild the church. Pius and his cardinals were unimpressed, but not entirely surprised. Rome demanded that these schismatic clergymen make a public retraction of their past oaths and errors dating back to the 1790s.[55] The authorities in Paris argued that any clergyman who accepted the concordat implicitly repudiated the Civil Constitution of the Clergy. Bernier, now Bishop of Orléans, met with these controversial candidates individually and gave written reassurance to Rome that they deeply regretted their past misdemeanours.[56] Pius was hardly satisfied, but there was little that he could do about it.

Amalgame as applied to the post-concordat church was more an aspiration than a reality. In Rouen and Lyons 'constitutional' clergy were kept away from important positions and parishes. Ultramontane congregations refused to attend services where the celebrant was known to have sworn the detested oath to the Revolution. In Angoulême, Toulouse, Besançon and Strasbourg the constitutional bishops refused to denounce publicly their past actions and favoured their former pro-revolutionary brethren.[57] While the concordat may have ended the outright persecution of the church, French Catholicism remained deeply divided.

Yet a new generation of clergy did emerge. The priests who were trained during the Napoleonic decade were very different from those who had preceded them. Gone for good were the aristocrats who had once monopolised the bishoprics. Most future parish priests were 'country lads' with a moderate standard of education, who were deeply sympathetic to the folk beliefs and superstitions of their congregations.[58] They had little nostalgia for the Gallican and Jansenist traditions of the past. In many cases, the complex theology of the eighteenth century went over their heads. For this generation of clergymen, most of whom had been cast adrift during a decade of revolutionary persecution, they instinctually turned to Rome for leadership and guidance.[59] These priests accepted papal authority in a fashion that would have been unthinkable during the eighteenth century. Napoleon's expectation that he could incubate a state church loyal to his regime was to prove forlorn.

For the Consular regime, the concordat was a template for near-perfect church-and-state relations, whereas Pius VII viewed the treaty as an exceptional measure that reflected circumstances unique to France. Its terms were supposed to allow the Gallican church to rebuild after the turmoil of revolution. Bonaparte wanted to export this agreement to all the territories ruled from Paris. The extension of the concordat to Piedmont in north-western Italy, after its annexation in 1803, deeply upset Rome. After all, this region had not experienced the devastation of revolution, so the unilateral changing of diocesan boundaries and the confiscation of monastic property seemed to show that the French were determined to make further destructive demands on the Catholic Church.[60]

Napoleon insisted that a concordat be negotiated for the Republic of Italy. This French satellite state, of which he was the president, covered Lombardy and the former papal legations of Romagna. Rome very grudgingly accepted this request, and the treaty was very similar to the agreement reached with France in 1801. The main difference was the concession that Catholicism was to be the state religion of the Italian republic. This turned out to be meaningless in practice, as Catholicism was not granted a monopoly on public worship. Yet the Italian concordat was less invasive than its French counterpart, as only two dioceses were abolished in Lombardy whereas on the other side of the Alps over eighty sees had been eliminated.[61] Once again, organic articles and police regulations were unilaterally tagged onto this document without consulting the local ecclesiastical authorities. Such underhand tactics irked the papacy and the church's discomfort grew.

Despite these forebodings, hope for further reconciliation emerged in May 1804 when, after a series of failed assassination plots, Napoleon was offered the imperial crown by the French senate.[62] His collaborators and supporters believed that a secure male line of succession would bring increased stability to the French state. Inspired by the example of Caesar Augustus in antiquity, he seized this opportunity eagerly and agreed to become the hereditary emperor of the French Republic. Yet there was a worry that such a freshly minted dynasty, bereft of religious sanction, would lack legitimacy alongside the other crowned heads of Europe. Re-establishing the precedents and rituals set by the Bourbons was dangerous. Such a return to the immediate past would seem like a rejection of the French Revolution in favour of a restoration of the ancien régime, and would have caused consternation among the republican elite. Napoleon's advisers instead looked to the Carolingians of the eighth and ninth centuries for inspiration.[63] After all, Charlemagne had successfully established a trans-European empire that dominated the western half of the continent. Its territory paralleled France's current hegemony over the Low Countries, the Rhineland and Northern Italy.[64]

Napoleon's counsellors advised him (incorrectly) that a new dynasty needed to be anointed by the papacy to enjoy real legitimacy. They cited the example of Pope Stephen II, who had travelled to Paris in 754 and crowned Pepin the Short in Saint Denis; and Pepin's son Charlemagne was crowned emperor of the West on Christmas Day 800 by Pope Leo III.[65] The decision was taken by the council of state to invite Pius VII to travel to Paris to anoint Napoleon with holy oil during a solemn coronation mass. News of Bonaparte's assumption of the imperial title was greeted with surprise by the Curia but there was also hope that it was another sign that France was putting its revolutionary past behind it. Pius was unsure of how to respond when Cardinal Fesch informed him of the French government's invitation to preside over the coronation mass in Notre Dame. Pius argued that a pope could not travel so far merely to crown the new emperor. Fesch became very red-faced and had to explain that this ritual was to be very different from previous investitures. He was forced to reveal that Napoleon would place the crown on his own head in a gesture that the source of his sovereignty was principally secular. Pius's role would be relegated to anointing the emperor with holy oil to highlight that Napoleon's elevation had divine sanction as well.[66]

That this ceremony was to be a 'self-crowning' was hardly ideal, but the pope could accept this arrangement in return for other concessions. Members of the Curia explained that when Pius VI had travelled to Vienna in 1782, it had been to negotiate with Joseph II on the future of Catholicism within the Habsburg monarchy.[67] Only the promise to reopen discussions on the constitutional bishops, the organic articles and divorce would induce the pope to travel to Paris. A demand was made too for the return of the papal legations of Romagna be placed on the table. Their loss in the Treaty of Tolentino had severely compromised the economic viability of the Papal States. Fesch intimated disingenuously that it would indeed be possible to open discussions on these matters once the pope had arrived in Paris and spoke face to face with Napoleon.[68]

Despite the concerns of his cardinals, Pius VII accepted the invitation and agreed to undertake the journey during the cold month of November. Four convoys carried the papal entourage, requiring 146 horses to draw their carriages.[69] It would take twenty-three days for the pope to reach the palace of Fontainebleau to the south of Paris. To avoid the rigid ceremonial of a formal meeting, Napoleon staged an impromptu encounter. He decided to go hunting in the nearby forests. Though this was a sport he did not enjoy, he wanted to mimic the prime passion of the other crowned heads of Europe.[70] The imperial hunt intercepted the pope's carriage at the crossroads of the Croix Saint Herem. In the chilly, damp autumnal weather, Chiaramonti was forced to descend from his carriage in his white silk slippers into a quagmire as he approached the emperor. They embraced and travelled on together to Fontainebleau.[71] Here Pius was introduced to the imperial family and ministers of state. A few days' rest were allowed before the journey to Paris.

Once in the capital, many hours were spent in private discussions and preparations for the coronation service. Napoleon and Pius were cordial with each other but their personalities were not well matched: Chiaramonti was reserved, gentle, taciturn and languid in his movements whereas the emperor was a volcano of energy, imperious and agitated. The cynicism of the secular ruler grated against the spirituality and delicacy of the former Benedictine monk. During Pius's stay in the Tuileries palace, crowds assembled beneath the papal apartments to seek a blessing. Napoleon, fearful of being upstaged by the pope, decided to appear on the balcony side by side with the pontiff as he blessed the throngs below.[72] A first stumbling block emerged when it came to the issue of the constitutional bishops. Napoleon assured the pope that matters would soon be brought to a satisfactory conclusion. Pius VII angrily declared that he would refuse to attend the coronation until these former schismatics retracted their oaths and admitted their errors in writing. Though he was furious, the emperor was forced to accept this request or face a scandal.[73]

Another storm was brewing but it came from a very unexpected quarter. On the eve of the coronation the Empress Josephine asked to speak with the Holy Father urgently. In a tearful audience, she revealed that she and Napoleon had only undergone a civil marriage before a registrar in 1796.[74] The pope was horrified to learn that in the eyes of the church the future imperial couple were unmarried. Pius insisted to a highly irritated Napoleon that he and Josephine would need to take part in a religious wedding if he was to be anointed emperor the next day. Grudgingly he consented, and Cardinal Fesch was summoned to perform the ceremony in the imperial apartments. The pope granted special dispensations to allow this sacrament to be bestowed so speedily. According to the records, Talleyrand and Marshal Berthier stood as witnesses.[75] Whether they were actually present remains unclear, and this was to have important consequences in future. For Bonaparte's siblings this was a bitter blow, as they loathed Josephine, whom they saw as a disloyal adventuress.[76] Given that her marriage had now been blessed by the church it would be difficult to dissolve.

On 2 December 1804 processions of dignitaries and distinguished guests marched solemnly to Notre Dame cathedral, the exact centre of historic Paris. Pius's solemn entry down the nave was a deeply moving and impressive moment. As he progressed towards the altar the choir intoned the hymn *Tu es Petrus* (You are Peter).[77] There was a sense that the divisions of the French Revolution had been healed. No monarch had been crowned in Notre Dame since 1431, when the 10-year-old Henry VI of England had been invested as king of France during the Hundred Years War.[78] This ceremony marked a sharp departure from the *ancien régime*, since the Bourbons had always been crowned at Rheims and never in their capital city.[79]

This coronation was not just a simple investiture but was intended to solemnise the Bonapartes' rise as the fifth dynasty to rule France legitimately. The heart of this ceremony was a high mass during which the emperor was anointed, received the badges of his office and then crowned himself. Pius VII's dignity and piety in celebrating the liturgy impressed spectators. Indeed, the painter David, who was later to immortalise this scene, apparently exclaimed: 'There is a real priest.'[80] The story is often told that Napoleon snatched the crown from the pope's hands and crowned himself. This is simply untrue. The self-crowning had been agreed in advance. Once the emperor had placed the crown on his own head, Pius moved forward, kissed him twice and then blessed him. Subsequently he turned to the congregation and proclaimed: *Vivat imperator in aeternum*! To which all replied 'Long live the emperor.'[81] The most delicate part of the ceremony related to the coronation oath. As Napoleon was to promise to defend all the laws of France, including a guarantee of past sales of church property, and to protect all religions equally, the pope was not willing to be present at this part of the ceremony. As the mass ended, he made a speedy retreat into the sacristy, while Napoleon headed to the rear of the nave, where he took his secular oath of office.

While it is true that this papal coronation added lustre and prestige to the imperial regime, it did not create a closer relationship between France and the Church of Rome. Although the ceremony was filled with pomp and circumstance it was too complicated for its message to be understood easily. Napoleon had tried to weave popular election, constitutionalism and traditional ideas of monarchy together with divine sanction. The result left those present feeling bewildered.[82] The emperor's gratitude to the pope for giving his regime a modicum of religious legitimacy was wafer thin. Despite all his promises to open discussions on divorce, the organic articles and the question of the papal legations of Romagna, he conceded nothing. Indeed, the pope's trip yielded very few concrete dividends. There was a promise that the emperor would fund new French missions to China. The Sisters of Charity were allowed to minister as nurses in hospitals, and Napoleon's mother became their patron, somehow acting as a personal guarantor for the order.[83] There were attempts to open discussions on a concordat for Germany, but Pius refused to entertain such negotiations as this was a matter for the Holy Roman Emperor, Francis II, and his episcopacy. The only exception to this refusal to modify the German episcopacy occurred during a solemn consistory in Paris. Here, Pius VII translated the former archbishop-elector of Mainz, Theodore Dalhberg, to the prince-archbishopric of Regensburg. This former leader of the Reichskirche had rallied to the French with enthusiasm. He would become Napoleon's most important ecclesiastical client in Germany.[84]

The French had promised that the pope and his entourage would be showered with gifts, and some apparently generous gestures were made. Pius's nephew Scipione Chiaramonti was rewarded by being elevated to the position of chamberlain in Napoleon's new satellite realm of Italy.[85] A newly manufactured papal tiara, fashioned by the ablest goldsmiths of Paris, was presented to Pius VII as a souvenir of his trip to France. On closer inspection it was discovered that most of the gems that adorned it had been looted from Rome by the Directory in 1798.[86]

Given that so little headway was being made in the negotiations, Pius decided to take his leave from the emperor. Departing from Paris, the papal convoys took a slow route out of the country. Chiaramonti and his suite visited the great Gothic cathedrals of eastern France and met local clergymen. After crossing the Alps into Piedmont, in April 1805, the convoy made for the great hunting lodge of Stupinigi, just outside Turin. Here, Pius and Napoleon had another encounter. The emperor was on his way to be crowned king of Italy, and the content of their conversations was not recorded. They would not see each other again for almost eight years. Meanwhile, Bonaparte's assumption of the royal title for the Italian peninsula highlighted his expansionist aims. It cannot have been reassuring that the arms of the Papal States appeared inside the coat of arms of Napoleon's Italian kingdom.[87] France asserted, far from subtly, that it was the new hegemonic power in Italy. Such claims were something the pope and Curia categorically refused to acknowledge.

His expedition to Paris deepened Pius's distrust of France's new emperor. Events would prove him right. Although Napoleon wanted to restore domestic harmony to France, he remained a son of the Revolution. He wanted a church subordinate to the power of the state and retained a visceral hatred of monasteries and convents. The French empire's growing territorial ambitions brought it into conflict with Britain, Russia, Naples and the

Habsburgs. Consalvi advised the pope that a strict neutrality was the best course of action as Europe again became engulfed in constant warfare.[88]

For Napoleon the Papal States clearly lay within his sphere of influence. He claimed that, as the foremost Catholic monarch in the world, the pope should ally himself to France and follow his lead. This was something that both Pius VII and Consalvi wanted to avoid at all costs. Their neutrality would be violated repeatedly by French troops in 1805 and 1806. The ports of Ancona on the Adriatic and of Civitavecchia just outside of Rome were occupied and garrisoned by the French to shut off these trade hubs from British shipping and commerce.[89] Imperial armies then crossed the Papal States on their way to conquer Naples. During these marches they requisitioned food and lodgings with little regard for the pope's sovereignty. Once southern Italy had been conquered, the papal enclaves of Benevento and Pontecorvo were annexed unilaterally without compensation. To add insult to injury Talleyrand was given the title of Prince of Benevento.[90] In retaliation, Pius VII refused to recognise Napoleon's brother Joseph as king of Naples. During this time, the pope's patience was put to the test, and in November 1805 he issued a formal diplomatic protest against French violations of his territory.

This letter was badly timed, as Napoleon would win his greatest military victory on 2 December 1805 at Austerlitz. Despite being severely outnumbered, he crushed the combined armies of the emperors of Austria and Russia. This led to the Peace of Pressburg, which resulted in the dissolution of the Holy Roman Empire and the French annexation of Venetia in north-eastern Italy.[91] This was only the beginning. In 1806 Prussia, with monumentally bad timing, declared war on France when it was at the zenith of its military might. The armies of Frederick the Great's once invincible war machine were smashed at the twin battles of Jena and Auerstedt.[92] A Russian counter-offensive in the east initially made some headway but was decisively defeated on 14 June 1807 at the Battle of Friedland, which was yet another Napoleonic triumph. Alexander I of Russia sued for peace at Tilsit.[93] On a raft in the middle of the Niemann river, he and

Napoleon entered a formal alliance. It seemed as if the French emperor really was set to create a neo-Carolingian empire in Western Europe.

French encroachments against the church's authority continued unabated during this time. A new imperial catechism was imposed on congregations throughout the empire. Since the sixteenth century, the church had used such texts to teach the Catholic faith in an easy-to-follow question and answer format.[94] It was the duty of every parish priest to inculcate the children of their parish with the catechism's lessons. Napoleon's version of this text was hardly heretical. It did, however, play down the pope's supremacy over the universal church and the sections on salvation and redemption were abridged. More irksome was the demand that Catholics should pray for Napoleon. This new catechism specified, in no uncertain terms, that imperial subjects owed their emperor military service, obedience and taxation. Praying for the monarch and the royal family had been a staple of *ancien régime* political culture. Rome did not object to prayers being said for the welfare of the emperor, but the catechism also presented Napoleon as the instrument of divine providence in restoring order and the fruits of religion.[95]

Nor was this all. Enemies of Bonaparte had often argued that his first name had pagan origins. Cardinal Fesch denied this was the case. He made the dubious claim that the name Napoleon had origins in St Leo of Naples. It was left to the more intellectually acrobatic librarians of the Ambrosian library in Milan to find a saint for the emperor. After an in-depth scouring of their records, they discovered a reassuringly obscure Egyptian saint called Neapolis, whose martyrdom in ancient Rome was shrouded in a convenient veil of mystery.[96] He seemed the perfect empty vessel into which to pour a new imperial cult. In a brilliant propaganda coup, the feast day of St Neapolis of Egypt was found to coincide with the emperor's birthday of 15 August. For pious Catholics this day also commemorated the Assumption of Mary into heaven, a holy day of obligation. The key feast of the French empire was thus grafted onto the church's most important Marian celebration. Catholic and imperial worship were fused together to buttress the religious legitimacy of the regime. This improbable saint's day caused bemusement mixed with irritation in the Curia.[97]

Once the peace treaty was signed at Tilsit, Pius VII was informed in no uncertain terms by the French emperor that he was most displeased with his conduct during the recent wars. Napoleon's priorities had shifted since his creation of the continental system in late 1806. To win the war he needed to bring the British economy to its knees by closing off the continent to its goods. The Papal States steadfastly refused to accept this self-blockade and British residents were left unmolested. In 1807 the emperor informed the pope that, if he did not enter into a defensive and offensive alliance by the end of the year, dire consequences would follow.[98] Pius despatched a cardinal to negotiate, but the French demanded that the Adriatic seaboard of the Papal States be annexed to the kingdom of Italy. This was a condition impossible for the church to accept.

Pius held several crisis meetings with his cardinals to discuss the imminent invasion of his domains. All agreed that military resistance with the minuscule papal army was impossible. Some suggested that the pope take flight and seek the protection of other European powers. Although this solution had its benefits the only real possibility was to seek asylum on board a Royal Navy vessel in the Mediterranean. This meant the pope would have to seek refuge from a Protestant power, which would be deeply embarrassing. The more innovative solution proposed was passive resistance. For months, the Curia had been coordinating a concerted campaign to refuse all collaboration or aid to occupying forces. Secret sealed letters had been transmitted across the Papal States to regional governors instructing them on how to behave should French soldiers appear in their territories. It was considered vital that no papal official, whether civil or ecclesiastical, swear any oath to France. Pius resigned himself to the possibility of becoming a French prisoner. It was possible that the emperor might allow him to travel to Germany to seek protection from a German Catholic prince.[99] Yet this was to prove a forlorn hope.

In December 1807 troops from the kingdom of Italy occupied the north-eastern half of the Papal States.[100] A diplomatic protest from the papacy enraged Paris and the irrevocable decision to launch an invasion was taken. On 2 February 1808 an expeditionary force led by General Sextius Miollis appeared at the gates of Rome. He claimed his troops had been sent to ensure law and order within the pope's domain and that his occupation was to be temporary. Papal forces immediately capitulated. Napoleon's forces flooded into the city across the Milvian bridge. It was almost exactly a decade since the revolutionary armies had entered the Eternal City and deposed Pius VI. General Miollis was no anticlerical firebrand; his brother was Bishop of Digne (a man with a saintly reputation who inspired Victor Hugo's character Mgr Myriel in *Les Misérables*). As a veteran of many campaigns, including the American War of Independence, he wanted to ensure a smooth occupation and avoid antagonising the local population.[101]

Initially, relations were cordial and Miollis was even granted an audience by Pius VII. The general hosted receptions and gave balls to woo the elites of the Eternal City (even some cardinals attended these events). But when it became clear that the French had no intention of leaving, the pope ordered his subjects to avoid all contact with the occupiers. Wherever Miollis went in the city a vacuum formed around him. This did not bode well as the regime would need popular consent to create a working administration that could collect taxes and impose conscription.[102] From the depths of the Quirinal, the pope orchestrated this campaign of passive resistance against the invaders.

The French tried to recruit a civic guard to entice Romans into collaboration. Most of those who joined came from the local *sbirri*, rough-and-ready men who were often local thugs and former bandits. They had been recruited by the papal authorities for centuries to impose order in the areas surrounding the capital. They were a classic case of poachers turned gamekeepers. Their officers were drawn from the ranks of renegade papal aristocrats, several of whom had supported the Roman Republic of 1798.[103] Luigi Braschi, duke of Nemi, was the most high-profile case of a papal aristocrat who supported the Napoleonic occupation. His willingness to work with the invaders allowed him to become the first *maire* (mayor) of Rome. Given that he had been the beneficiary of his uncle Pius VI's patronage this betrayal was deeply scandalous.[104] Yet for the most part the pope's prelates and nobles staunchly adhered to his instructions. Festivities, concerts and church services organised by Miollis were boycotted by Roman high society.

One group however did welcome the French as liberators. The Jews of the Roman ghetto had lived for centuries as second-class citizens of the papacy. They were mistreated, discriminated against and forced to endure annual sermons persuading them to convert to Christianity. Inspired by the Enlightenment, Napoleonic administrators broke open the gates of ghettos wherever they went and granted full civic rights to the Jews of Europe.[105] In Rome they greeted the French as emancipators and enjoyed their rights as citizens, much to the fury of their former persecutors. Sadly, the freeing of the Jewish population in Rome did not destroy centuries of Catholic anti-semitism, but confirmed the worst fears of bigots. Freedom of conscience was as seen a dangerous seditious doctrine and prelates were appalled by the drive to allow religious pluralism even at the centre of the Catholic world.

In an effort to show the pope that they meant business, the occupiers ordered all Italian cardinals who were subjects of Napoleon or his brother Joseph, King of Naples, to depart from the city.[106] Very soon Pius found himself isolated and attended by a rump of less than half the College of Cardinals. French requests for an alliance, and demands that the papacy surrender its central Italian kingdom, were rejected contemptuously. Deprived of his most trusted advisers, it was around this time that Pius appointed Cardinal Bartolomeo Pacca as acting secretary of state.[107] Pacca would urge the pope to resist the empire's demands zealously.* In September 1808 an attempt was made to arrest Pacca in his apartments in the Quirinal palace. Only Pius's decision to interpose himself physically between the cardinal and the soldiers who had come to arrest him saved his foreign minister from

---

* As already mentioned in the previous chapter, Pacca was a conservative diplomat who had been given the mission of rendezvousing with Louis XVI if his flight to Varennes had been successful.

immediate deportation. After this incident crowds of Romans gathered underneath the windows of the palace cheering '*Bravo il papa!*'[108]

During this time Napoleon had much else to distract his attention. He had embarked on his disastrous Spanish adventure.[109] The attempt to transfer his brother Joseph from the throne of Naples to that of Madrid was to be among the biggest miscalculations of his career. As ever, the French invaders confiscated monastic property, abolished the Spanish inquisition and brought the Iberian church under the iron control of the state. More so than anywhere in Europe this led to mass popular resistance against the invaders.[110] Indeed, some of the most famous guerrilla leaders, such as Jerónimo Merino, known as *el cura* (the vicar), were priests who led a holy crusade against the godless French.[111] Napoleon hired writers and scholars to publish books listing the crimes of the papacy and the Spanish inquisition, but this had little effect on loyal Catholics.[112]

It is difficult to overestimate the religious dimension to the rise of armed guerrilla movements against the Napoleonic empire. In 1809, supported by their clergy, peasants rose in open rebellion in Spain, southern Italy and the Tyrol. These irregular forces fought for their region and their faith with remarkable zeal. Their violence and brutality horrified the imperial authorities in Paris. Although these *guerrilleros* could not hope to defeat the empire by themselves, they were a debilitating ulcer on French manpower and resources.[113] It showed just how hollow claims that the empire was bringing peace, stability and progress sounded to those invaded by imperial troops. The situation became graver still when the Habsburgs, who had been rearming since 1806, launched a pre-emptive strike into southern Germany, hoping that this offensive would give rise to a mass anti-French insurgency.[114] Napoleon was forced to divert his forces swiftly from Spain into Germany to defeat the Austrians.

It was during this time that he took the fateful decision to annex Rome and make it the second city of his empire. On 10 June 1809 the papal standard was lowered throughout the Eternal City. Pius looked out of his study window in the Quirinal to observe the French tricolour being raised over Castel Sant'Angelo, the city's citadel. He sighed *'Consummatum est!'*,[115] the very words Christ had uttered just before he died on the cross. It was clear that such an affront to the pope's sovereign rights could not go unanswered. During the night, a solemn papal bull was affixed to the doors of all the major basilicas and churches of Rome. This text deplored the violation and the annexation of the Papal States. It excommunicated and cursed all those who had ordered or collaborated in the seizure of the Eternal City and the papacy's domains.[116] Although Napoleon was not named, it was clear that he was the target of this text. Excommunication, or the denial of all sacraments, from the church was the highest sanction that St Peter's successor could inflict on a secular ruler. A hand-picked committee of theologians was promptly summoned by the imperial government in Paris. Its members advised that the Gallican articles of 1682 could be invoked in this circumstance. This text stated categorically that the king of France could not be excommunicated for political reasons.[117]

For Pius his central Italian kingdom was no relic of a bygone medieval past. He refused to surrender the domains that his predecessors had assembled and defended at such great cost. Being a secular ruler in his own right was the pope's only means of guaranteeing his spiritual independence. Should the papacy be subjected to the political authority of a European power there was a danger that a secular ruler could force the pontiff to take decisions that contradicted church teaching. Pius VII's unyielding defence of papal sovereignty in central Italy represented the opening shot in a battle for survival that would last for most of the nineteenth century. Unluckily for the papacy, the domains of the church were surrounded by powerful and covetous neighbours.

Meanwhile, news of the excommunication reached Napoleon after he occupied Vienna. In May 1809 he had suffered a severe military reverse at the Battle of Aspern-Essling, the first battle he had personally lost, so his humour was dark and preoccupied with the forthcoming offensive. The *Grande Armée* was poised to cross the Danube and fight a decisive battle against the armies of the Habsburg empire.[118] He was furious when he learnt that he and his officials had been condemned by the church. Napoleon wrote to his brother-in-law Joachim Murat who had recently succeeded Joseph as king of Naples.

> If the Pope, against the well-being of his office and the gospels, preaches revolt and hides behind his immunity in order to publish circulars and sow dissent, he must be arrested; the time for games has passed. Philip the Fair had Boniface [VIII] arrested, and Charles V kept Clement VII in prison for a long time; and he had done far less [than Pius VII]. A priest who preaches disorder and war instead of peace to the powers of the earth abuses his office.[119]

Although the wording of this letter was ambiguous both Murat and Miollis understood it to mean that the pope was to be removed from Rome. Administering central Italy and encouraging collaboration would be impossible while Pius remained in the Quirinal fanning the flames of discontent.

Given the delicacy of this mission it was decided to seek out a specialist in covert operations. General Étienne Radet of the imperial gendarmerie was a veteran of many campaigns and one of the best bandit-chasers in the empire.[120] He was summoned to the Eternal City from Tuscany. Here he was informed that the emperor wished that the pope be taken into custody and removed from the city. Radet must have swallowed hard when he heard his orders. He observed that extracting the pope from Rome in broad daylight was impossible. What was needed was a night-time operation in which gendarmes would, like modern commandos, penetrate the Quirinal palace. Once inside they would kidnap the pope before anyone realised or raised the alarm. Miollis, as military governor, approved the operation and asked the general to make preparations. Radet proposed dividing his seven hundred men into three columns. One column would climb over the walls of the papal gardens and gain entry to the palace through the servant's quarters. Radet would lead a second column that would scale the roof of the Quirinal. Both columns would meet in the main courtyard of the pope's summer residence and open the gates to the remaining forces waiting on Piazza di Monte Cavallo.

This daring scheme was scheduled to take place on the night of 5–6 July 1809. Needless to say, things did not quite go according to plan. The first column went astray in the shrubbery of the Quirinal gardens and thus lost valuable time. Radet led his men up the scaling ladders and was keen to be the first on the palace roof to direct operations. However, as he climbed upwards it soon became clear that the ladders requisitioned in Rome were of appalling quality. Very soon they disintegrated, causing Radet and his men to fall in a heap, making an ungodly racket in the process. Soon flickering candles started appearing inside the Quirinal. The element of surprise had been squandered. The prelates and guards inside shouted 'to arms' and 'treason'. Soon the bells in the bell tower of the main courtyard started tolling and the sound reverberated across the dark cityscape. Hundreds of Rome's belfries replied, flooding the city with the sound of tolling bells. Radet, not one to be diverted from his mission, picked up an axe and started hacking at the main gate to the papal residence. Given that these gates had been reinforced with steel, the general merely made himself dishevelled and sweaty.[121]

After several minutes of fruitless exertion noises emerged from inside the Quirinal. The first column had finally found its way into the courtyard and now unlocked the palace gates for their comrades. Gendarmes flooded the interior and quickly disarmed the Swiss guard, who had been ordered not to resist. Radet asked to be shown to the pope's apartments. He was led down a long dark corridor where a faint light glimmered at the end. Pius, woken abruptly from his slumber, had dressed and was ready for this remarkable encounter. He was seated in his study with Cardinal Pacca at his side. Radet was asked why he had interrupted the pope's rest. Very embarrassed, and looking increasingly like a guilty schoolchild, the general explained that he had the unpleasant duty of demanding that Pius renounce his sovereignty over central Italy. According to one account the pope's reply was categorical: '*Non debemus, non possumus, non volumus*' (We must not, we cannot, we will not).[122]

Radet expressed his regret, but in the event of such a refusal he was under orders to escort the pope out of the city. Departure was to be immediate and Pius was asked to bring his most essential possessions with him for the journey. Disdainfully the pontiff replied he only needed his breviary and asked to be accompanied by Cardinal Pacca. As the pope descended the grand staircase that led to the main courtyard of the Quirinal, the gendarmes presented arms as a mark of respect to their distinguished prisoner. Once the convoy was ready to depart the carriage door was locked from the outside.[123] Like his predecessor Pius VI, Chiaramonti was now at the mercy of his French captives. Only once did he turn his head to bless the Eternal City, unsure if he would ever see it again, and his eyes welled with tears as he caught a glimpse of St Peter's dome in the distance. Crowds lined the route out of Rome, their ashen faces betraying their fury at the pope's kidnappers.

The journey was shambolic, as no orders had been issued about where the prisoner should be taken. As the convoy raced through Tuscany, Chiaramonti's health, which had become fragile in recent years, began to falter as stress triggered a recurring inflammation of his bladder. During the journey he was often feverish and unwell. His carriage was frequently driven at such speed that on one occasion an axle broke. The vehicle capsized and the pope was flung to one side. Although shaken, he was unharmed, but soon the local population gathered round and hurled insults at the gendarmes accompanying the pope.[124] Radet thought it best to resume his journey in haste and deliver his prisoner to the authorities in Florence. Napoleon's sister Elisa, Grand Duchess of Tuscany, wanted to avoid holding such a controversial prisoner and ordered that Pius be moved out of her domains. After two weeks, the convoy crossed the French border and settled in Grenoble to await further instructions. On the same night as Pius was seized, Napoleon had a won a costly victory against the Habsburgs at Wagram, close to Vienna. On learning the news that the pope had been kidnapped he wrote the following letter to his minister of police:

I am upset that the Pope has been arrested, it is madness! One should have just detained Cardinal Pacca and left the Pope in peace in Rome. But ultimately one cannot do anything about it; what's done is done. I have no idea what prince Borghese has been up to, but it is my intention that the Pope does not enter France. If he is still on the Genoese riviera the best place for him is Savona. It has a large house where he can be accommodated decently until one decides what to do with him. I have no objection, if he desists from his insanities, that he be sent back to Rome. If he has entered France, make him head back toward Savona and San Remo. Make sure you intercept all his correspondence.[125]

Historians have debated at great length whether the order to kidnap the pope had emanated from Napoleon.[126] Although written instructions were never sent directly, either to Murat in Naples or Miollis in Rome, there can be little doubt that they correctly interpreted the emperor's intentions. Pius was to be isolated from the Curia and put under pressure to surrender the Papal States to the French empire.

Chiaramonti would reside in the remote port of Savona on the Ligurian coast for the next three years. This town had been the home of the della Rovere family which had given the Catholic world two popes: Sixtus IV and Julius II, who had been the great patron of Michelangelo.[127] Pius VII lived in the episcopal palace, which was adjacent to the cathedral and possessed its own, rather modest, Sistine chapel. Although this town had been an important trading centre during the late Middle Ages it had gone into steep decline after its conquest by Genoese in 1528.[128] It had become a sleepy backwater where one did not venture without good reason. For the French, Savona's deep harbour was of strategic importance and thus the citadel was well garrisoned with troops.

Initially Pius VII was given a generous stipend and his palace underwent significant refurbishment. Although not allowed to meet with high-ranking prelates and Roman officials, the pope could interact with ordinary folk. In these early days, his prison routine was far from rigid. He granted audiences to the local population and bestowed weekly blessings from the balcony of the episcopal palace on the crowds below. Often the pope could be found celebrating mass in the town's cathedral. The only place outside Savona that Pius visited during his confinement was the sanctuary of Nostra Signora della Misericordia (Our Lady of Mercy) in the nearby St Bernard valley. According to a local tradition, which persists to the present day, the Virgin Mary had appeared to Antonio Botta in 1536. She informed him that her son was angry with the sins of the world and urged repentance. In subsequent apparitions the Madonna appeared less wrathful and informed Botta that she came to bring the world 'mercy not justice'.[129] For centuries this shrine had been a site of fervent Marian devotion. It was especially popular with sailors who came to give thanks for deliverance after escaping savage storms. Pius travelled as a pilgrim to this sanctuary and prayed before the statue of the Virgin in the crypt. He vowed secretly to the Holy Virgin that, if he ever was released from his ordeal, he would return to crown her statue.[130]

Revolutionary persecution and the struggle against the Napoleonic empire taught the church that its greatest source of support was to be found among rural Catholics. By all accounts Pius VII was deeply touched by the simple, though fervent, faith of ordinary people. He understood how important ceremonies, traditions and saints' cults were for people whose health and livelihoods were fragile in a world filled with uncertainty. Reform Catholicism and Jansenism had a deep disdain for such folk beliefs, which they considered superstitious. Now the attack on popular religion came from Paris, rather than from within the church itself, Catholic peasantries across Europe vehemently resisted any intrusion into their belief system. This experience of revolutionary turmoil followed by French imperial expansion, which imposed 'modern rationalist values' on unwilling populations, led to the emergence of a grassroots movement for religious renewal.[131] The papacy learned that it was unwise to curb popular enthusiasm, but rather that it should form the bulwark of its defence against an increasingly anticlerical world. Throughout the nineteenth century the church came to realise that its greatest asset was not the support of monarchs and great nobles but the fervour of the masses. After the defeat of Napoleon, Rome made every effort to foster devotions to saintly and Marian cults. Processions, magnificent liturgical celebrations, and jubilees became essential elements in the reinvigoration of Catholic worship. The eighteenth-century rationalistic reforms would be played down in favour of a centralised papal monarchy that encouraged, rather than repressed, popular devotion. This was the most important lesson learned by Pius VII during his exile.

Back in Paris, in 1810, Napoleon's attention turned to the issue of dynastic succession. It was clear that the Empress Josephine was past childbearing age. The decision to divorce the empress became unavoidable. There was a sense that a new union with one of Europe's great ruling dynasties was needed to cement the Bonapartes' legitimacy. The first candidate was Grand Duchess Catherine, the Tsar's sister, but this was rejected by Russia's dowager empress.[132] Imperial diplomacy shifted its focus to the Habsburgs, as Francis I had an unmarried and healthy daughter, the Archduchess Marie-Louise.[133] Repeatedly vanquished by France, the Austrians needed to end their isolation, so they welcomed this opportunity for *détente*.

Although arranging a divorce in civil law was simple, receiving an annulment from the church was much more complicated. It was a papal prerogative to dissolve the matrimonial unions of reigning monarchs. Clement VII's refusal to annul Henry VIII's marriage to Catherine of Aragon in 1527 had led to the breach with Rome and the establishment of the Anglican Church.[134] Given that Pius was a prisoner it was impossible that he would agree to an annulment. The emperor was forced to seek out the ecclesiastical courts of the Gallican church in Paris, known as *officialités*. The petition claimed that Napoleon had been coerced by the pope and Josephine into a religious marriage against his will on the eve of his coronation. Furthermore he alleged that there had been no witnesses to the marriage, and that it had been celebrated without the consent of the local parish priest. Fesch, who had officiated at these events, found himself embarrassed by his nephew's convenient rewriting of history. The eyebrows of the canon lawyers and judges of the *officialité* must have risen when they read that the most powerful man in Europe claimed that he had been coerced into marriage. Such grounds were usually invoked by girls beaten by their fathers into marrying old men, but the judges of the *officialité*, fearing that a refusal to accept the imperial petition would result in their imprisonment granted the annulment.[135]

With all impediments lifted Napoleon's Habsburg match could proceed. Since the annexation of Rome, most of the College of Cardinals had been transferred to Paris. So too had the Vatican archives, ecclesiastical tribunals and many art treasures. To embarrass the papacy, Napoleon insisted that his archivist find the papers relating to the trial of Galileo and publish the most embarrassing documents relating to this miscarriage of justice.[136] Ultimately, the emperor wanted to show that statecraft and priestcraft were incompatible. The secular needed to have supreme authority over the spiritual. Paris was not merely to function as the administrative summit of a vast European empire, but it was to be the seat of future popes and the centre of the Catholic world. The palace of the archbishops of Paris was being enlarged and refurbished to become the new seat for future pontiffs.[137]

To add legitimacy to his dynastic union with the Habsburgs, the College of Cardinals was invited to attend both the civil and religious wedding ceremonies. Many princes of the church, led by Consalvi, protested that they could not attend a marriage which was, technically, bigamous. Only the pope had the authority to annul and allow the remarriage of reigning sovereigns. Despite their remonstrances, the cardinals were none too subtly urged to attend the wedding celebrations. On 2 April 1810 dignitaries from across the empire arrived at the Louvre. Here they watched the emperor process down the Gallerie de Diane in full ceremonial dress, and with great pomp. This great gallery of the Louvre had been transformed temporarily into a chapel by the neoclassical architects Percier and Fontaine.[138] As the imperial gaze turned to the stalls reserved for the cardinals, Napoleon's face turned red with fury. Only half of the invited cardinals were present. Their absence cast deliberate doubt on the legitimacy of this dynastic union. The next day the emperor ordered that the thirteen cardinals who had refused to attend the ceremony in the Louvre be sent into exile in provincial France. They were to be deprived of their distinctive crimson robes and became known as 'black cardinals'.[139] These men would form the die-hard ecclesiastical opposition to the empire. They would spend the next three years in backwaters, deprived of funds. Pius deeply missed the counsel of his most trusted advisers. It was very difficult for any pope to come to a decision without first placing it before a congregation of cardinals for deliberation. The emperor hoped he could break Chiaramonti's spirit by isolating him.

This growing crisis created a major problem for the empire. Napoleon's candidates for the vacant dioceses could only take office once papal confirmation had been granted. Since 1807 Rome had steadfastly refused to confirm any candidates nominated by Paris.[140] Gallican theologians, canon lawyers and administrators desperately tried to find a way of bypassing the papal confirmation process. They uncovered a precedent used by Louis XIV during the 1680s when he was engaged in a dispute with the papacy. Cathedral chapters had been persuaded to elect the king's episcopal nominees as vicars capitular to the diocese. This meant that royal candidates could administer their sees without papal approval.[141] Napoleon decided to resurrect this solution and pilot it in Paris, Florence and Asti. For archbishop of Paris, he nominated Jean Siffrein Maury who had been elevated to cardinal as reward for his opposition to the French Revolution. This prelate had staunchly rejected the revolutionary reforms of the 1790s and supported the Bourbon pretender Louis XVIII during his almost two decades in exile. Yet his resolve had waned, and he decided to rally to the empire.[142]

Although Pius was supposed to be kept in the dark of all outside developments a highly sophisticated clandestine communications network had been set up in Savona. During audiences, those admitted to the ceremonial kissing of the pope's feet would smuggle scraps of paper into the seams of his white cassock. At night the pope would reassemble and read these letters. He would then write a reply which was smuggled out in the papal laundry by brave washerwomen.[143] Through Catholic *amicizie* (brotherhoods) and other pious congregations these missives were trafficked into

Turin, then Lyons and finally Paris. Very daring Catholic nobles, priests and women all conspired to help the pope communicate with the outside world from his Ligurian prison.[144]

To the horror of the imperial government, a formal condemnation of Maury's acceptance of the Paris archdiocese was published and circulated clandestinely in December 1810. The emperor commanded his police to discover how this papal brief had been smuggled out of Savona. After a complex investigation it emerged that the abbé Paul-Thérèse-David d'Astros, vicar general of Paris and a high functionary in the ministry of religions, was responsible for the covert communications network. On New Year's Day 1811 Napoleon showered Astros with verbal abuse and ordered his imprisonment in the fortress of Vincennes, where he would languish for the next four years.[145] All those found to be involved in the network were either incarcerated or sent into exile. Priests in the former Papal States who persisted in refusing the oath to the imperial government faced harsher measures. Several thousand Roman clergymen were deported to the Alpine fortresses, the Piacentino and Corsica.[146]

Pius VII himself was punished for his defiance of the emperor. One day in January 1811 as he walked in the gardens of the episcopal palace of Savona, imperial gendarmes broke into his bedroom, confiscated all of his books, with the exception of his breviary, and removed all writing utensils. Access to the pope was restricted and weekly audiences with the local population forbidden.[147] Savonese tradition has it that, during these dark days of persecution, the pope performed a series of miracles. The most spectacular was a levitation that occurred during the consecration of the blessed host during high mass. Stories abounded around the town about the extraordinary acts of piety that the pontiff performed during his exile.[148] Indeed, there is an ongoing attempt by priests in this Ligurian diocese to have Pius VII canonised. There was certainly much popular sympathy for the plight of the pope and he became an object of intense veneration. The imperial authorities with their persecution had succeeded in transforming him into a martyr.

Since 1810 two committees of theologians had gathered in Paris under the chairmanship of Cardinal Fesch to discuss potential solutions to the investiture crisis. They believed it was impossible for metropolitan archbishops to bypass papal authority and confirm new bishops. Their advice was to send a delegation to Savona to negotiate with Pius and see if he might be amenable to compromise.[149] This deputation of bishops was made up almost entirely of Gallican diehards, carefully selected by the emperor. They set out in April 1811 and would spend the better part of a week trying to persuade the pope to yield to imperial demands. It was clear that such blackmail was having its desired effect. Pius was plagued with insomnia and stomach problems due to the pressure exerted on him to reach an agreement. His gaolers reported that he often sat in a chair staring into the abyss. Catatonic and depressed, he became impervious to the outside world. [150] Despite all this pressure, he refused to renounce his sovereignty and confirm imperial candidates in their sees.

Fesch's committee had one other solution to offer, whose roots lay deep in the reform Catholicism of the previous century. Conciliarism seemed to provide the only means of circumventing papal authority. It was clear that it would be impossible to summon an ecumenical council of the entire church without the pope's authorisation. Such a body, consisting of the entire Catholic episcopacy, theoretically could overrule the papacy. Such a large meeting had not been called since the Council of Trent (1545–63), which reformed and galvanized the church to meet the challenge of Protestantism.[151] With the pope a prisoner, the only recourse open to the imperial authorities in Paris was to summon a national council. Its membership would include all the bishops of greater France, those of northern Italy and some from Germany. Cardinal Fesch stressed that this national council could not overrule the pope's prerogative powers. But the bishops could issue a decree, exhorting the pope, after a six-month pause, to authorise archbishops to invest candidates for the episcopacy. Feeling that this was the only road open to him, the emperor decided to invite all the bishops of his vast empire to meet in Paris in June 1811.[152]

This great assembly offered a pretext to use the clergy to legitimate the imperial dynasty. On 20 March 1811, after a difficult delivery, the Empress Marie-Louise gave the Bonapartes a male heir, who was named Napoléon-François.[153] He was immediately proclaimed King of Rome and showered with honours. This title was reminiscent of that of 'King of the Romans' which the Holy Roman Emperors had bestowed on their designated heir. In some ways the emperor of the French was positioning himself to succeed the Holy Roman Empire and create a neo-Carolingian empire concentrated on the banks of the Rhine and Po rivers. On 9 June a lavish baptism for the infant king of Rome took place. Cardinal Fesch, as the Emperor's grand almoner, presided over this ritual. All the bishops of the empire were present, which added weight and prestige to the imperial christening. After Napoléon-François was cleansed of original sin, the imperial couple headed to the Hôtel de Ville, where a lavish public banquet had been prepared to celebrate the arrival of a crown prince. Here the emperor and empress dined in state observed by great dignitaries, prelates and less mighty subjects. The day ended with a spectacular firework display.[154] With Napoleon there was always the suspicion that such magnificence, ceremonial formality and flaunting of power hid from sight his deep-seated lack of confidence in the solidity of his regime. As Napoleon reminded his brothers, they had not inherited their thrones. They did not have the patina of centuries of dynastic succession to cement their legitimacy. Their regime was not built on any historical tradition but rather on popular consent, expressed through plebiscites and military victories. These were fragile foundations.

On 17 June, a week after the king of Rome's christening, the bishops of the empire processed solemnly to Notre Dame for the opening mass of the National Council. Cardinal Fesch, as primate of all Gaul, was to preside over this gathering of the empire's episcopacy. It was apparent from the sermon preached by the bishop of Troyes that these prelates had mixed feelings about the council. Their Gallican instincts conflicted with their loyalty to the pope as supreme leader of the church.[155] After the initial roll call, Fesch asked that all those present swear allegiance to Pius VII individually. Then the imperial minister of religions, Félix Julien Jean Bigot de Préameneu, read a letter from the emperor outlining his programme for ecclesiastical reform. The language chosen was deeply undiplomatic and accused Pius of the worst excesses of the medieval papacy.[156] From the very first day many bishops were alienated by the anti-papal tone of proceedings.

A subcommittee chaired by Fesch was appointed to draft a reply to the emperor's letter. Several bishops gravitated towards Maurice de Broglie, the bishop of Ghent, who became the leader of the opposition. Broglie hailed from an *ancien régime* princely dynasty that had a venerable tradition of military and ecclesiastical service.[157] He had initially rallied to the empire, but had become increasingly uncomfortable with attempts to suppress the freedom of the church. To the immense fury of the imperial administration, he had refused to accept his elevation within the Legion of Honour. This was his protest against the emperor's kidnapping of the pope and the occupation of Rome.[158] Blessed with a genuine priestly vocation, de Broglie was independent and fearless in pursuit of what he felt was a just cause. Indignantly he persuaded the committee to refuse to answer the emperor's letter in obsequious language. Instead, he advised that the National Council should urge the immediate release of Pius VII. It was essential for the bishops to communicate freely with the supreme head of the church to resolve the delicate and vexed question of episcopal investiture. For two weeks de Broglie's followers clashed with Napoleonic loyalists.[159] Fesch's conscience was deeply torn between loyalty to his emperor and his priestly duty. It was becoming clear that he was losing control of the National Council.

Napoleon was surprised that the acquiescent reply he had expected from his bishops had not arrived. He summoned Fesch to report on progress and to explain why his orders had not been executed. The cardinal infuriated his uncle by explaining that the bishops wanted the pope to be freed and did not believe that they could empower archbishops to invest candidates for vacant dioceses. Furious, the emperor hurled abuse at his uncle, even accusing him of being ignorant when it came to theological matters.[160] Fesch stood firm, saying that he would prefer martyrdom to subverting the authority of the papacy. This protest impressed Napoleon, who mellowed and became more conciliatory. He decided to compromise, and agreed that any decree issued by the council would require the consent of the pope. Content with this concession, Fesch returned to his brethren, believing he had found a way out of the impasse. His colleagues greeted this vague compromise with little enthusiasm and continued to argue against the imperial reforms. On 10 July the Council met in a plenary session and rejected any attempt to bypass the pope's control over episcopal investiture.[161]

Fesch travelled to the Tuileries, expecting a turbulent audience with his nephew; however Napoleon greeted the news calmly and betrayed little surprise. Two days later, in the dead of night, de Broglie and two of his brother bishops were arrested as ringleaders of the anti-imperial opposition. Their apartments were searched, and some anti-imperial documents were unearthed. These included treatises on the authority of the popes and Pius's condemnation of Maury's acceptance of the archdiocese of Paris. The errant bishops would spend the next few months in the fortress of Vincennes, before being sent into internal exile.[162] The Council was dissolved but the bishops were ordered to remain in Paris, where they were subjected to a campaign of intimidation from the police. Threatened with incarceration and other punishments, many promised to support the emperor's reforms. On 5 August, once the minister of religions was sure that he had majority support, the Council was reconvened. Here, in a streamlined plenary session, without any debate, they proceeded to vote on a decree that would empower archbishops to invest new bishops. Out of the ninety-three present, only thirteen voted against. Years later, Cardinal Pacca lamented to a friend who had attended the National Council of 1811 that so many bishops had forgotten their duty. 'Even the best horse sometimes bolts, your eminence,' said his friend. 'That may be,' replied the Cardinal, 'but that the entire stable should bolt!'[163]

True to his word, Napoleon authorised the council to send a delegation to the pope and seek his approval for their decree. Soon the usual group of reliable Gallicans was rushing towards Savona. Pius was appalled by the outcome of the Council, which would short-circuit, and ultimately bypass, his authority over episcopal appointments. To put further pressure on the pope he was handed several letters from French and Italian bishops. These amounted to little more than emotional blackmail. In hysterical terms these prelates beseeched him to accept the Council's decree and thus end the conflict with the empire which threatened to tear the church apart. Pius grew fearful that a refusal to negotiate might give rise to a schism reminiscent of the one unleashed by the Civil Constitution of the Clergy. So the pontiff reluctantly agreed to discuss the decree issued by the National Council with the delegates sent to Savona. For weeks he debated its content. He was prepared to make concessions on condition that he be permitted to receive counsel from his cardinals and return to Rome.

Pius eventually prepared a brief in response to the National Council's decree.[164] He appealed directly to the bishops in Paris, thus creating the impression that the National Council had acted under papal, rather than imperial authority. The emperor rejected the brief as insufficient. He wanted a complete capitulation from the pope, as if he had been defeated in battle. When informed of this rejection, Pius was furious with the Gallican delegates sent to negotiate with him. He argued that he had shown good faith and now refused any further concession. In January 1812 the episcopal delegation departed Savona. Their mission had been an abject failure.[165] The National Council of 1811 brought neo-conciliarism, one of the key tenets of reform Catholicism, into disrepute. Napoleon's cynical appropriation of church councils showed how dangerous they could be in the wrong hands. In contrast to the eighteenth century, few Catholics would advocate the use of conciliarism to limit papal power during the following two centuries. It was the papacy that eventually reappropriated conciliarism and deployed it to strengthen its leadership over the universal church.

By early 1812, Napoleon was deeply concerned by the collapse of his alliance with Russia. This breach with St Petersburg had the potential of creating a massive back-door through which British contraband could flow into Europe and nullify his continental system.[166] He resolved to break Russian power, and organised one of the largest concentrations of troops ever witnessed in the history of warfare. Around six hundred thousand soldiers, from over twenty nations, started marching into Poland. On 24 June, imperial forces crossed the Nieman river and began the disastrous invasion of Russia.[167] During this time, the emperor had not forgotten his captive in Savona. Alarming reports were arriving of Royal Navy vessels navigating dangerously close to the harbour. There was some fear that the British might launch an amphibious operation to rescue Pius from his captors. From imperial headquarters in Dresden the order arrived to transfer the pope to the palace of Fontainebleau, south of Paris.[168]

A colonel of the gendarmerie, Antoine Lagorce, was assigned to accompany and guard the pontiff on his journey into France. Rumours had it that this soldier had started life as a priest but abandoned his vocation during the Revolution and married. Now he had divorced his first wife and was devoted to the regime he served with great military efficiency.[169] He kept his prisoner under extremely tight surveillance. On the evening of 9 June 1812, the pope was informed that departure for France was imminent. He greeted this news with resignation and deep sadness. Strict secrecy surrounding the papal departure was to be maintained at all costs. Pius was dressed in a large grey overcoat, his white slippers were dyed with black ink and his pectoral cross was removed. Despite the fact it was unoccupied, the episcopal palace was illuminated and guarded as if nothing had changed for several days after the departure.[170]

Pius was not in a fit state for this arduous and rapid journey after the stress of three years of detention. As the convoy galloped into Piedmont, the distinguished passenger became feverish and deeply unwell. His recurrent inflammation of the bladder flared up, becoming acute and causing some bleeding. In the small hours of 11 June 1812 the convoy pulled into the hospice-convent of Montcenis. This large complex had been built in the middle of one of the great arterial mountain passes of the Alps. It was an essential transit point between France and Italy. The function of this hospice was to offer nourishment, medical assistance and shelter to weary travellers.[171] By now Pius was extremely unwell. He was unable to stand and could only pass a few drops of blood-stained urine. The monks had been instructed to prepare a room for a distinguished visitor. To their immense shock, they dropped to their knees when they recognised that their mysterious guest was the pope.

During the night Chiaramonti's health deteriorated to the extent that the monks gave him the last rites. Lagorce wrote to the authorities in Turin asking for a surgeon to be sent with all possible haste. To his surprise he received an order to continue the journey into France without delay. Chiaramonti refused to proceed any further and his entourage also insisted that he be given time to recover. A local surgeon called Balthazard Claraz was summoned to the pope's bedside. As a good Catholic, Claraz was astounded to discover that his patient was the supreme leader of the church. Lagorce wanted the surgeon to insert a rudimentary version of a catheter to relieve the inflammation of the bladder. Claraz stated that the operation was dangerous and refused to carry it out. He insisted the pope not be moved for at least a day or two.[172] The situation was so grave that Lagorce was forced to inform the minister of police in Paris that the pope was near death.[173] Chiaramonti's brush with mortality in the hostel at Moncenis must rank as one of the great 'what ifs' of history. Had he died, in all likelihood, Napoleon would have assembled a conclave in his empire at which loyalist cardinals would have elected a pro-French candidate to the papacy. One could speculate that a counter-conclave of independent cardinals would have assembled elsewhere and proclaimed a rival pope. Events at Montcenis brought Catholicism to the brink of a new Great Schism in the West.

This outcome was avoided thanks to Claraz's sound medical advice. After a few days' rest, the inflammation subsided and the pope started sleeping more restfully. Lagorce, fearful of disobeying his orders, insisted that the journey resume. On 15 June the convoy departed Moncenis and rode into Savoy. The pontiff's carriage was modified so that a mattress could be placed inside it. This allowed the gravely ill passenger to lie horizontally and rest. Although travelling in this fashion was far from comfortable, the pope eventually arrived at Fontainebleau on 19 June where, to Lagorce's immense surprise, the gatekeeper had not been informed of their arrival. The convoy was refused entry until orders arrived from Paris confirming the identity of the travellers.[174]

The next morning an audience was requested by Napoleon's ministers of state to present their compliments to the pope. Fontainebleau was one of the great palaces of the French Renaissance. It had hundreds of rooms, and was surrounded by acres of ornamental gardens and hundreds of acres of woodland filled with game. The palace library had a fine collection of books on profane subjects but relatively few works on theological and spiritual matters.[175] Through the summer and autumn of 1812 Pius spent many months of boredom in this gilded cage. There was little to do but await developments. The situation in Russia had not gone according to the emperor's grand design. He had anticipated a decisive battle in Lithuania, but the Russians withdrew ever further into the interior of their vast empire. As their supply lines shortened, those of the French became ever more overstretched. The largest battle of the campaign took place at Borodino at the very gates of Moscow on 7 September. It was sheer carnage, even by Napoleonic standards, with combined casualties on both sides of 70,000 dead and wounded.[176] Although there was no clear victor, the Russians evacuated Moscow.

Napoleon expected that peace negotiations would follow soon but with each passing week there was no sign of an emissary from Tsar Alexander I. Realising that his supply situation was becoming untenable, he ordered a retreat. It would be seen as one of the greatest military disasters of modern history. Harassed by Russian irregular forces, a harsh winter and the absence of supplies, the army that had begun the invasion in June 1812 was slowly reduced to shreds on its way back to the Polish border.[177] At Smorgoni in Lithuania, on 5 December, Napoleon decided to leave his crumbling army and return to Paris to raise a new force of troops.[178] His priority was to return home to reassure public opinion that he had not been defeated by the Russians but rather by winter. Upon reaching the Tuileries he began building another army of 800,000 men from raw conscripts.[179] It was his intention, in the spring of 1813, to enter Germany and start a counter-offensive against his enemies.

He had not forgotten his eminent prisoner languishing in Fontainebleau. Napoleon was determined, while he was back in Paris, to settle the religious question that so undermined his regime. Catholic clergy were encouraging civil disobedience against his authority. A new settlement with the pope was needed to restore stability within France and its European empire. On the pretext of going hunting, the emperor decided to stage another meeting with the pope. On the evening 19 January 1813 Pius was resting after dinner in his salon when suddenly the doors opened, and Napoleon appeared before him.[180] It was over eight years since their last meeting. Chiaramonti had aged significantly; he had lost weight, he stooped slightly and his eyes had sunk into his skull. Bonaparte too was no longer the svelte and youthful leader who had invited the pope to crown him in 1804. He had grown stout, his hair had thinned and he tired more easily than in the past. Yet his gaze and expression remained fiery.

He embraced the pope and they greeted each other cordially. It was agreed that the next few days would be spent in negotiation. For six days they were locked in secret negotiations and nobody was admitted into their presence. The writer Chateaubriand alleged that Napoleon grabbed the pontiff by the hair and dragged him across his study, forcing him to sign an agreement.[181] Months later in a letter to his friend, the bishop of Cervia, [182] Pius denied that the emperor had ever assaulted him nor physically mistreated him, though Napoleon did once, out of frustration, grab the pope's cassock so strongly that his entire body shook.* The negotiations were painful for Pius as Napoleon was determined to extract important concessions from his captive.

On 25 January 1813, a document that became known as the Concordat of Fontainebleau was signed.[183] Its terms represented an implicit renunciation by Pius VII of his central Italian principality. In return he would receive a generous pension, the use of several palaces and the right to communicate freely with

---

* This description almost entirely reprises the dialogue invented in Alfred de Vigny, *Servitude et Grandeur Militaires* (Paris, 1864), pp. 244–61, esp. pp. 255, 258.

foreign diplomats. Napoleon promised to pardon those cardinals and bishops who had defied him in the past, and it was agreed that the pope would be allowed to consult the College of Cardinals. Pius also made the unprecedented concession that archbishops would be authorised to invest new bishops if the pope refused to do so after a deferral of six months. Essentially, the pope had surrendered the most jealously guarded prerogative of the Holy See. In return, he would be allowed to appoint ten Italian bishops, not including the suburban dioceses around Rome which would remain dependent on the papacy. The agreement sealed the triumph of the state over the church.

In truth the remarkable aspect of this agreement was not that Pius VII, after almost four years of isolation, capitulated to the emperor's bullying, but rather that he had resisted so long. Some sources dismiss Chiaramonti as a senile old man. This was extremely unfair. After all, he was undergoing a terrible mental strain, which had made him irritable and prone to psychosomatic illnesses. Despite this, his approach to French demands had remained consistent throughout. Events in January 1813 proved to be an aberration, not at all typical of this iron-willed pontiff. Pius regretted signing the Concordat of Fontainebleau within days of doing so.[184] His sleep and digestion became unsettled. Once reunited with loyalist cardinals like Consalvi, he began preparing a written retraction of his agreement. This had to be done in secrecy because every time he left his apartments to celebrate mass, dine or go for a walk his papers were searched by the imperial gendarmerie. The pope's letter disowning the Concordat of Fontainebleau was sent to the emperor on 23 March.[185]

Napoleon received it a week later at his imperial headquarters in Dresden, to which he had returned. He greeted it with uncontained fury and regretted he had not established a new Christian church in 1801 instead of opening negotiations with the papacy. But the fate of the empire and the church would be determined by the outcome of the campaign in Saxony. At the battles of Lützen and Bautzen in May Napoleon, despite his huge reverses in Russia, inflicted bloody defeats on the armies of Russia and Prussia. Indeed, if Marshal Ney had not misread his orders and become lost, the Tsar's army might have been encircled and annihilated.[186] These victories demonstrated that the French emperor remained a formidable force to be reckoned with. Orders were given for the *Te deum* (a liturgical hymn of praise) to be sung in all the churches of the empire to give thanks to the Lord God of Hosts for victory. Such successes proved to be pyrrhic. A truce was called at Pleischwitz and Austria offered its services as a mediator. Between June and August 1813 Count Klemens von Metternich, now Austrian Chancellor, tried to persuade Napoleon to accept a reduced empire concentrated in France with some territories in Italy.[187] This offer was indignantly refused and it is said that in his last meeting with the French emperor Metternich sighed: 'Sire, you are lost.'

These words would prove prophetic. Given the obstinate French desire to pursue the war against Prussia, Russia and England, the Habsburgs decided to throw caution to the wind and join the anti-Napoleonic coalition.[188] For the first time since 1793 France was at war with almost every nation in Europe. Soon minor German states like Bavaria and Württemberg started to switch allegiance from France to the Allies. The situation was becoming desperate for French forces in Germany, yet Napoleon was able to inflict a significant defeat on Austria at the Battle of Dresden on 26–27 August 1813.

Following the advice of the Habsburg chief of staff General Joseph Radetzky, the coalition developed what was known as the Trachenberg plan.[189] This authorised Allied commanders to fight individual engagements with France's marshals but to avoid an all-out battle with the *Grande Armée*. By September, several French corps were surrounded and virtually wiped out. Napoleon was now outnumbered and had positioned himself in Leipzig where he hoped to launch an offensive either towards Berlin in the north or Prague in the south. Seeing that the French were in a vulnerable position the Allies decided to launch a combined attack on Leipzig. Beginning on 16 October the Battle of the Nations was fought over three appallingly bloody days. Half-a-million troops clashed to decide the fate of Europe. Such carnage would not be seen again until the Battle of the Somme during the First World War.[190]

Outnumbered and outgunned, the French suffered a decisive defeat. The remnants of the shattered *Grande Armée* limped back towards the French border, harassed by their former German allies. The question was no longer if Napoleon would be defeated, but when and what shape the European map would now take. Although the emperor of the French was offered generous terms on multiple occasions in the autumn of 1813, he continued to refuse them.[191] By January 1814 even his brother-in-law Joachim Murat, King of Naples, switched sides. Realising that his hegemony over Italy was crumbling, Napoleon despatched Etienne Fallot de Beaumont, Bishop of Piacenza, to Fontainebleau. His mission was to negotiate the restoration of the Papal States with Pius VII.[192]

The Government was keen that those who had collaborated with the occupation and annexation of Rome would be left unperturbed or, at least, allowed to resettle in France. Pius VII was no fool and refused to enter negotiations with Fallot de Beaumont. Chiaramonti stated that he would renounce none of the church's prerogatives and renewed the papacy's claims even to the Avignon and Comtat Venaissin in the heart of Provence.[193] It soon became clear that this formidable pope would never yield. As a former Benedictine monk Chiaramonti seemed to possess inexhaustible self-discipline and patience. Bowing to the inevitable, the empire's ministers advised that the pope should be sent back to Rome. Cynically they hoped that he would sow discord among the Allies by pressing his claims to the Papal States. Although the Habsburgs had committed to restoring the papal kingdom in central Italy, the exact details of how much territory would be returned to the papacy remained unclear.[194]

Lagorce started to prepare for the pope's return home. On 23 January 1814 two large postal carriages pulled out of the palace of Fontainebleau. They carried Pius VII, who bid a tearful farewell to his cardinals, enjoining them never to negotiate with the collapsing French empire. Bizarrely, the return journey to Rome was to be C-shaped. The convoy headed west into the interior of France then southwards before steering west towards Nice.[195] Although Pius was supposed to be travelling incognito, large crowds gathered to cheer the liberated pope and wish him well. Lagorce became worried as the crowds he encountered were enormous and could easily have overpowered his gendarmes. Once beyond Nice the convoy headed along the Ligurian coast and the pope would spend nearly two weeks in his former prison, Savona's episcopal palace. Eventually orders arrived from the minister of police to hand over the pope to the Habsburg army near Parma. On 25 March 1814, on the banks of the Taro, after two months of travel, Lagorce surrendered Pius to Austrian forces.[196] The pope apparently blessed his former gaoler and gifted him a grey mare called Cocotte which he had kept with him since his kidnapping in 1809.

That night the pope received the full military honours due to a sovereign and slept in the Farnese ducal palace in Parma.[197] Henceforth he was free and his slow return to Rome was cheered by enthusiastic crowds. The problem remained that the Eternal City was occupied by the troops of Murat, King of Naples. It was impossible to return until these soldiers had been evacuated. The long-awaited news arrived on 6 April 1814. Napoleon, having been deposed by the French senate, had signed an act of abdication at the palace of Fontainebleau.[198] The war was over. The news caused mass jubilation throughout Italy as the pope proceeded to his native Cesena. Here, in the Chiaramonti palace, he would create a provisional government for the Catholic Church. Slowly cardinals, prelates and other dignitaries travelled to this town in Romagna to pay homage to the pope. Initially Archbishop Annibale della Genga was given the task of negotiating the restoration of the Papal States with the Allies.[199] Once Cardinal Consalvi was freed by the French, Pius reappointed him to the position of secretary of state to the Holy See. Della Genga was an arch-reactionary who wanted to turn the clock back to 1789. The next decade would witness an intense rivalry between him and the secretary of state for control of the Curia. Consalvi demanded that della Genga be recalled and sent to Paris instead. The secretary of state would spend the better part of the year in several European capitals, lobbying the Allies for the restoration of the Papal States.[200]

Pius VII saw the hand of divine providence in his liberation. It seemed to confirm the righteousness of his cause in defending both the church and the papacy's sovereignty over central Italy.

Yet Pius would not grant amnesty and oblivion for past crimes, though his encyclical *Il trionfo* of 4 May 1814 (unusually for the time published in Italian rather than Latin) beseeched his subjects not to lynch nor raise a violent hand to those who had collaborated with the invaders. He promised that just retribution would follow his restoration according to the rule of law and God's will.[201] Pius had been plucked from Rome in 1809 with a gentle and affable disposition. Five years of imprisonment had marked his personality deeply. He now suffered from neuroses, distrusted outsiders and had developed a deep contempt for modernity. His original openness to intellectual argument and philosophy had evaporated. During his exile he had learned to admire the simplicity of the faith of peasants and ordinary people he had encountered in Liguria and provincial France. During the twilight years of his papacy he would oversee the first stirrings of Catholic renewal. This movement sought to re-evangelise the peoples of Europe and allow them to rediscover the mystery, enchantment and charisma of divine worship and ritual. After almost two months of temporising in Cesena, the troops of Murat finally evacuated Rome.

On 27 May 1814 the papal cortege approached the Milvian bridge. Twice in the previous fifteen years French armies had invaded and conquered Rome through this access point. Unlike his predecessor Pius VI, the pope did not return to Rome in a coffin, but in triumph. He proceeded directly to St Peter's basilica, where he would officiate over a solemn *Te deum*. Once this was accomplished, Pius VII descended into the crypt. Here he knelt in silent prayer before the tomb of St Peter, the prince of the apostles and according to tradition the first pope. Although his thoughts were never recorded, he must have contemplated the dramatic reversals of fortune he had experienced during his pontificate.

After bestowing his blessing on the crowds in St Peter's Square the pope departed for the Quirinal palace.[202] To his surprise the sons of prominent Roman families unlimbered the horses from his carriage. They then proceeded to pull the coach themselves through the Eternal City amidst crowds of joyful citizens. On entering the Quirinal, Pius for the first time shed some tears, remembering that horrible night when General Radet had kidnapped him. The palace was much changed, as Napoleon had given orders to transform it from a Christian monastic complex into an imperial palace, decorated in the latest neoclassical fashion. Many rooms had been knocked through to create long galleries. Statues of saints had been taken down to be replaced with Roman gods. An eerie Jupiter bore an uncanny resemblance to Napoleon.[203] It is remarkable that the emperor who had so shaped the destiny of Rome and sought to make it the second city of his empire had never visited it.

Pius found an enormous backlog of unresolved business awaiting him on his return to his capital. Among his first actions was to appoint Cardinal Pacca acting secretary of state, in Consalvi's absence. This arch-reactionary immediately set up a commission of enquiry with the unwieldy title 'Special congregation charged with the general investigation into all disorders that occurred in the recent and very painful events with special reference to clergymen, be they secular, or regular, both in Rome and within the Papal States so as to advise His Holiness on appropriate actions to be undertaken'.[204] This commission of enquiry, made up of five cardinals, would investigate hundreds of clergymen who had collaborated with the French occupiers. Most were ordered to publish a full retraction of their past errors. Others were forced to resign and most had to make a full confession of their misdemeanours. There were few incarcerations of former collaborators, though many did lose their livelihoods and status.[205]

The person singled out for exemplary punishment was Cardinal Maury. His acceptance of the archdiocese of Paris without papal confirmation was an egregious example of disobedience. He would spend several months in a cell in Castel Santangelo and then die a penitent in a monastery in Rome. Given that he had been rewarded so lavishly for his resistance to the French Revolution during the 1790s his decision to rally to Napoleon was disturbing.[206] Those clergymen who had collaborated with the usurper could have little hope of advancement. The treatment of lay collaborators was more lenient as it was considered a lesser betrayal than that of priests who had taken more solemn vows of submission to the papacy.

Pius VII's first major decision was to prove controversial. Many priests and conspiracy theorists saw Clement XIV's decision to disband the Jesuit order in 1773 as the beginning of the church's woes. The belief was that the papacy's abandonment of these loyalists had opened the floodgates to freemasons and *philosophes* to undermine religion.[207] In consequence Pius decided on 7 August to issue the bull *Sollicitudo omnium ecclesiarum*. After forty-one years the Jesuit order was restored by papal decree. Although some Jesuits had survived in Russia and Sicily it would take many decades for St Ignatius' followers to rebuild their organisation.[208] Very soon, liberals across Europe interpreted this restoration as a reversion to the church's interference in politics. The nineteenth century would reprise the eighteenth-century myth of a Jesuit conspiracy to undermine secular authorities.[209] The church in post-Napoleonic Europe would seek to regain the initiative and became pathologically distrustful of modern governments. The decision by the restored Portuguese and Spanish monarchies to resurrect their inquisitions, after the French had abolished them, was unwise.[210] Rome seemed determined to fight new ideas and institutions with every means at its disposal.

Some of the reactionary measures bordered on the bizarre. Cardinal Pacca insisted that the Papal States abandon the modern time-keeping system used in the rest of Europe. In its place they returned to the complicated *Ora Boema* or *Ora Italica* system of time keeping. Under this system the date changed at sunset and the length of hours varied according to the season. Restoration Rome was literally in a different time zone to the rest of the world.[211]

While Pacca was turning the clock back, Consalvi had been trying his best to persuade the monarchs of Europe to restore the pope's domains. His mission initially met with failure. With the first Treaty of Paris signed on 30 May 1814 France was returned to its 1792 borders. The Allies accepted that Avignon and the Comtat Venaissin were an integral part of France, and would not be returned to the papacy nor would compensation be provided. But Consalvi did settle one question definitively in Paris. In meetings with the restored Louis XVIII he managed to persuade the king of France to uphold the 1801 concordat. There was a lot of pressure to abrogate this treaty, but the papal secretary of state managed to persuade the French government to honour it.[212]

This was important as Article 3 enshrined the pope's absolute right to remove bishops from French dioceses. Gallicanism would suffer terminal decline during the nineteenth century.[213] France's clergy, excluding a small minority, would henceforth turn to Rome for leadership. Consalvi, after these meetings in Paris, headed to London. Here he tried to persuade the British government to support the restoration of the Papal States. The cardinal charmed London's elites, including the Prince Regent who was impressed with the tact, affability and intelligence of the pope's foreign minister. Consalvi presented the prince with some trinkets and mementos left to him in the will of the late Cardinal Henry Stuart,[214] the last pretender to the Jacobite throne of the United Kingdom. His death put an end to any even forlorn hope of a Stuart restoration. So delighted was the prince by these gifts that when later he became George IV he contributed financially to Canova's monument in St Peter's commemorating the three Stuart pretenders to the British throne.[215]

More seriously, Consalvi persuaded Robert Stewart, Viscount Castlereagh, the British Foreign Secretary, that a papal restoration would help create a stable equilibrium in the Italian peninsula. The pope's domains would act as buffer keeping in check Habsburg and Bourbon desires to dominate Italy. To further elicit Castlereagh's goodwill Consalvi, although initially hesitant, promised to support Britain's campaign for the abolition of the slave trade. There was a vague commitment to negotiate, at a future date, some resolution of the thorny question of the rights of Catholics in the United Kingdom, especially in Ireland.[216]

Despite his ability to charm the Allied monarchs, Consalvi left London without any concrete undertakings. His next port of call would be Vienna, where a congress had been summoned to discuss the future of Europe. Although it was expected that this international summit would take four weeks, the negotiations proved so intricate that it took nearly nine months before it concluded its work. There was very little appetite among the sovereigns of Europe to restore the ecclesiastical electors, prince-bishops and lord abbots of the *ancien régime*.[217] During Napoleon's occupation and administration of these territories significant gains had been made in solidifying the authority of the state over the church. In so doing, he had achieved gains that exceeded even Joseph II's wildest dreams. Outside of the papal domains the primacy of secular authority would be reaffirmed without limitation by the victorious Allied powers. The Reichskirche and the ecclesiastical principalities of the Holy Roman Empire were gone forever.

Consalvi's position at the Congress of Vienna was delicate. There was an Allied undertaking to restore the Papal States, but several provinces had still not been returned to papal control. He heard rumours that the Legations of Romagna, centred around the agriculturally rich cities of Bologna, Ferrara and Ravenna, might be given to Napoleon's wife, the former Empress Marie-Louise, as an Italian principality.[218] Indeed the populations of these regions had been under Napoleonic rule since 1797, and approved of the efficient administration introduced by the French. Local elites were lobbying against being returned to the papacy.[219] More ominously, the king of Naples had been slow in evacuating Umbria and the Marche. Murat had been promised territorial enlargement at the expense of the pope's domain, as the price for his switching sides to the allies in January 1814. Consalvi was advised to be patient and await the results of the work of Metternich and Castlereagh.

Much to the cardinal's chagrin, Talleyrand had been appointed France's chief negotiator by Louis XVIII. He proved deeply unsympathetic to the papacy's demand for full restoration. This apostate bishop was ubiquitous whenever the future of the Catholic Church was at stake. The former papal enclaves of Benevento and Pontecorvo, inside Neapolitan territory, remained a bone of contention too. Consalvi insisted that they be returned to the pope who was their rightful owner and had never relinquished his sovereignty. Talleyrand, as prince of Benevento, without hesitation demanded monetary compensation for the loss of a principality he had never legitimately held. While Murat remained in control of Naples, it proved difficult for Consalvi to make headway. As already observed, the cardinal had a progressive vision of international relations. He thought the papacy should avoid at all costs acting as guarantor for any agreements reached in Vienna.[220] The Catholic Church did not possess any significant military forces, and could not hope to compete on the plane of great-power politics. Neutrality was the best means of avoiding becoming embroiled in international conflicts. It was not an unreasonable stance, since prosperous Switzerland and Sweden flourished as the neutral states *par excellence* during the nineteenth century.[221] Alas, Rome's geographic position at the centre of the Italian peninsula made remaining aloof from international conflict more difficult. The Papal States were surrounded by covetous neighbours.

By February 1815 negotiations in Vienna had stalled. Unexpectedly, events in the Mediterranean catalysed the situation. Napoleon had been exiled after his abdication to the island of Elba, off the Tuscan coast. Here he had become the emperor of his own Lilliputia. Fearing that the Allies would transfer him to a more distant place of exile, he decided to stake everything on a last gamble. On the evening of 26 February 1815, with one thousand troops on a flotilla of small vessels, he set sail from Elba.[222] Their ultimate destination was unknown, and this caused panic throughout Europe. Reports reached Cardinal Pacca in Rome that the former emperor was heading for Naples.[223] However, it soon became clear that this rumour was false, and that Napoleon had landed in France. As he marched northwards, regiments of troops mutinied and joined the imperial cause. On 19 March the former emperor entered Paris and resumed residence in the Tuileries.[224]

Murat impulsively declared himself for Napoleon and decided to attack the Austrians in northern Italy. As his troops approached the borders of the Papal States the Curia and College of Cardinals were thrown into a state of great agitation. Pius, unlike in 1809, decided to flee his capital as a safety measure and seek refuge in the kingdom of Piedmont-Sardinia. He reached the safety of Genoa on 3 April 1815.[225] While waiting for the military outcome of Napoleon's final adventure, the pope expressed the desire to return to Savona. A month later, accompanied by the king of Sardinia, Pius headed to the Sanctuary of Nostra Signora della

Misericordia. Here, to great applause and acclaim, he placed a golden crown on the statue of the virgin.[226] This was in fulfilment of his vow that should he ever be freed from captivity he would return to this shrine to honour Mary the mother of God. In so doing he inaugurated a century of renewed enthusiasm and devotion to Marian shrines across Europe.

Events in France and Naples played into Consalvi's hands. He received a commitment from Metternich that, once Napoleon and Murat had been defeated, the Papal States would be restored in full. Little was left to do for the cardinal but to wait. Between 2 and 3 May 1815 near the town of Tolentino (which had witnessed the disastrous treaty of 1797) Murat was decisively defeated by the Austrians. He tried to issue a manifesto to rally Italians to expel all foreign troops, but his appeal fell on deaf ears.* He was forced to escape Naples disguised as a Danish sailor, but was captured in Corsica and executed by firing squad.[227] Italian nationalism was the dog that did not bark in 1815.

Napoleon's One Hundred Day rule in France saw him trying to re-invent himself as a liberal emperor. He granted a new constitution which guaranteed individual rights and freedom of the press. Such promises rang hollow to priests loyal to the Bourbons, or those who criticised his regime, as they would continue to be placed under surveillance, arrested and harassed.[228] Only two bishops turned out to the Champ de Mai ceremony he had organised to celebrate the new constitution.[229] His episcopacy now saw him as the enemy rather than as the restorer of the church. On 12 June 1815, the Final Act of the Congress of Vienna that restored the Papal States was signed. Six days later, on the blood-soaked plains of Waterloo, Napoleon was decisively defeated by Anglo-Prussian forces.[230] This time the Allies exiled him to the remote island of St Helena in the South Atlantic where he would remain until his death on 5 May

---

* See Jean Tulard, *Murat* (Paris, 1999), pp. 363–6. Tulard's biography is truly excellent but he is wrong about the date of the proclamation of Rimini, which he otherwise reproduces faithfully.

1821, unable to disrupt the peace of Europe, though his ghost did continue to haunt the continent.[231]

Consalvi's achievements in Vienna were enormous. Through patient diplomacy he was able to secure the full restoration of the pope's domain, including the return of the enclaves of Benevento and Pontecorvo.[232] In early October 1814 such an outcome had seemed difficult. Pius wrote to his secretary of state expressing his confidence and satisfaction. Despite this, Consalvi was instructed to lodge a formal protest against the failure to return Avignon to the papacy and the same position was taken in regard to the ecclesiastical principalities of the Holy Roman Empire. Consalvi did not sign the Final Act of the Congress of Vienna,[233] as he wanted the Holy See to remain independent of all international commitments.

After Murat's defeat, Pius VII slowly journeyed back to Rome, where he was greeted once again triumphantly. The Catholic Church had come to its lowest ebb during the French Revolution and Napoleonic period. One pope had died a captive and the other had spent almost five years as the prisoner of Napoleon. Countless artworks and the entire Vatican archives had been transferred to Paris.[234] Under the terms of the second Treaty of Paris, Louis XVIII was forced to restore all plundered art and archives to their rightful owners.

Pius VII, Consalvi and the Curia now prepared for the arduous task of restoring papal government over disparate provinces that had been deeply disrupted by the experience of Napoleonic rule. Many, like Cardinal Pacca and Archbishop della Genga, wanted to return to the pre-revolutionary status quo, pretending that the past two decades had never occurred. Others, like Consalvi, sought to modernise the state and make it fit to meet the challenges of the nineteenth century.[235] The lessons to be drawn from the papacy's recent ordeals were not obvious. One impulse was to deploy reactionary measures and repression to restore papal authority. There was a sense that Europe would need a mass campaign to re-embed the Catholic magisterium into the fabric of society and politics. A minority, foremost among them Consalvi, urged limited administrative reform and liberalisation as the best means of preserving the Papal States from the perils of revolution. Repression, renewal and grudging reform would be the *leitmotif* of nineteenth-century Catholicism. The equal partnership of throne and altar that had characterised the *ancien régime* was gone forever, but what would replace it was far from clear.

5

RESURRECTION:
THE CHURCH AFTER THE
CONGRESS OF VIENNA, 1815–46

On 16 September 1810, at 2 a.m., some horsemen galloped into the town of Dolores, two hundred miles north of Mexico City. They were breathless and sweating profusely, and their faces betrayed grim determination. Their destination was the rectory. Here, they pounded on the door to rouse the parish priest. Although startled, Miguel Hidalgo y Costilla was not surprised by their arrival. He let them in and the first to speak was Ignacio Allende, a tall military officer with prominent sideburns. His words were a call to immediate action: 'Gentlemen we are lost, there is no other option but to go seize the Spaniards [*gachupines*].'[1]

Hidalgo had been involved for months in a conspiracy to topple the viceroy of New Spain, Francisco Javier Venegas, Marqués de la Reunión. The intention was to replace the imperial government with a junta made up of Creole elites who, once in power, would introduce 'home rule' to Mexico. They knew that the failure of their plan would see them branded as traitors and executed on the gallows. Hidalgo and his confederates decided to strike first. During the night, they arrested the sub-delegate and other municipal authorities of Dolores. They were particularly delighted to apprehend Father Francisco Bustamante. He was sacristan to the parish, and for years had acted as the eyes and ears of the local inquisition.[2] The conspirators realised that they needed weapons, so they headed to the local militia barracks to seize what armaments they could. Their next decision was momentous. Mexican society, like so many colonial cultures, was arranged around a strict social hierarchy. At the top stood the Peninsular Spaniards, who had crossed the Atlantic Ocean, and who governed the king's American possessions. They had privileged access to public office and the levers of power. Next came the *criollos*, or Creoles, who were the descendants of the *conquistadores* and colonists who had built the economy of New Spain for centuries. These men resented their exclusion from the machinery of government. At the bottom of the pyramid stood the native population and those of mixed heritage, disparagingly dismissed as *indios*.[3] Hidalgo argued that their conspiracy had no hope of succeeding without widespread popular support. As 16 September was a Sunday and a market day, there would be large crowds in town. It seemed a good opportunity to launch a call to arms against all Spaniards.

As hundreds gathered in Dolores to hear mass and attend the market, they were surprised that their priest was not inside the church making preparations as was usually the case. Their curiosity was piqued further when the town's bells started tolling at a strange hour. Soon Hidalgo appeared on the porch of his church. Here he gave a rousing speech, calling on his parishioners to rebel against the Spaniards. Although no undisputed version of his words has survived, enough sources remain for an educated guess as to the content of his diatribe. Hidalgo reminded the assembled peasants of their oppression and mistreatment at the hands of the Spanish. The speech probably ended with the words: 'Long live Ferdinand VII! Long live America! Long live Religion! Death to Bad Government.'[4] These words had a galvanising effect and became known as the *grito de Dolores* (the cry of Dolores). Every year, on 16 September, the Mexican president still re-enacts a version of these words on the country's national day.[5] Soon seven hundred peasants on foot and horseback were in open rebellion against the imperial state.

Within hours they raised Our Lady of Guadalupe as their battle standard. This icon was associated with the alleged apparitions of the Virgin Mary to the Chichimecan peasant Juan Diego Cuauhtlatoatzin in December 1531. The mother of God had appeared to him instructing him to build a shrine on the hill of Tepeyac, on the northern fringes of Mexico City. This hill, prior to the Spanish conquest, had been an Aztec temple where the earth goddess had been worshipped. On Juan Diego's cloak a miraculous image of the virgin appeared and, ever since, this site and relic have held a special place in Mexican religious life.[6] Guadalupe allowed for a remarkable synthesis to emerge between pre-Colombian spirituality and Catholicism. The Virgin of Guadalupe was a contrast to the statue of Our Lady of Los Remedios, which Cortes had carried with him during the conquest of Mexico City.[7] The *criollos* and native Mexicans followed the local Marian cult, whereas the Spaniards were committed to the *conquistador*'s version of the Mother of God.

Events in Dolores would spread like wildfire throughout Latin America. Their immediate cause had been Napoleon's invasion of Spain and the forced abdication of the Bourbons in favour of his brother Joseph.[8] Peninsular elites in the colonies refused to recognise the Bonaparte dynasty. They decided to support an insurgent Junta Central that had emerged in Cadiz in defiance of the French invaders, and they aspired to rule Spanish America for the king as if nothing had changed. The vacuum of power left by Napoleon's invasion allowed centuries of tensions between *criollos* and *peninsulares* to bubble to the surface.[9] Catholicism was to play a complex role in the unfolding drama.

The period between 1815 and 1846 is often seen as one of reaction, during which Catholicism put up a futile attempt to turn the clock back to the world as it was before 1789.[10] Events in Mexico reveal that the situation was not that simple. It is true that the papacy adapted to the post-Napoleonic world with great difficulty, but not everybody in the church was so fearful of change and revolution. Hidalgo's revolt, and the clergy's involvement in the Latin American wars of independence, were harbingers of the twentieth century's liberation theology.* Unlike Europe, in South

---

* Liberation theology refers to a Catholic Marxist movement that was popular in South America and was eventually criticised by John Paul II. See Christopher Rowland, *The Cambridge Companion to Liberation Theology* (Cambridge, 2007).

and Central America revolution was fuelled by a defence of local religious traditions against the Spanish monarchy's attempts to subordinate the church to the imperial state. The abolition of the Jesuits had been unpopular in these provinces.[11] Furthermore, in Mexico the church had been a vital source of credit for poor farmers, miners and entrepreneurs. Increases in taxation and an attempt to regulate the credit market had damaged the church's position as a lender during the Napoleonic wars.[12] This had made life harder for many farmers in Mexico.

Hidalgo seized the opportunity afforded by the growing unpopularity of the viceregal government. As he marched out of Dolores, his numbers swelled and he appealed to fellow *criollos* to join him. Although Hidalgo was highly educated and attracted to Enlightenment ideals, his followers resembled the peasants of the Vendée who had rebelled against the French Revolution.[13] They wanted to protect their local economy, ensure a fairer distribution of agricultural land and defend their religious traditions against outside interference. Their battle cries of 'Long live Ferdinand VII, the Virgin of Guadalupe and Religion!' demonstrated that they were hardly Jacobins. As the father of several illegitimate children, it must be admitted that Hidalgo's own religious vocation was rather lukewarm.[14] His message was that Mexico needed to defend itself from the Spaniards who were the servants of the godless Napoleon, and from the heretical English who coveted their land. This appeal to terrifying images of foreign meddling proved compelling.

Within weeks a horde of twenty thousand was on the march. Many were riding mustangs or ponies and most were armed with little more than spears or bows and arrows. This force probably contained only a hundred or so militia-men trained in regular warfare. They made for Guanajuato, the second city of Mexico with a population of nearly seventy thousand. Juan Antonio Riaño was the intendant of this prosperous mining city. Aware that his command was Hidalgo's target, he started fortifying the Alhóndiga (the granary/arsenal of the town), and transferred there the treasure, archives, valuables, food and grain of the Spanish elites. The calculation was made that these supplies could allow five hundred defenders to endure a three-month siege. On 24 September 1810, in a gesture of over-confidence, Riaño abandoned the city's outer defences and took shelter inside the Alhóndiga. The inhabitants of Guanajuato felt abandoned by the elites, who had taken shelter in this improvised citadel. They quickly joined Hidalgo's forces as they poured into the city.[15]

The Spanish had underestimated the numbers they were facing. A murderous hail of stones damaged the roof and killed many defenders, and Riaño was one of the first to die, adding further uncertainty for the defenders.[16] The Spaniards fired volleys and launched grenades at their assailants but were overwhelmed. A siege that was supposed to last three months barely lasted five hours. In the aftermath the violence was unimaginable: not only were the three hundred defenders killed, but their bodies were mutilated and castrated. White *peninsulares* and *criollos* were rounded up indiscriminately; some were imprisoned while others were massacred.[17] The lack of discipline led to the ransacking of shops and liquor stores. Soon the native insurgents were dressed in fine clothes and very inebriated.

Hidalgo proved unable to gather the funds and supplies stored in the Alhóndiga as they had already been looted.[18] This lack of discipline was frightening and ultimately Hidalgo realised he could not control his followers, who had become a horde. Three hundred Spaniards had perished in the attack but so, soberingly, had over two thousand insurgents. Many rebels had been trampled to death rather than killed by bullet wounds. The victory at Guanajuato had been costly enough in terms of casualties, but its real significance was as a public-relations disaster. It damaged the rebel cause by destroying any chance of widespread *criollo* support for the rebellion. Very few colonial elites were willing to join what they saw as a murderous mob. In the aftermath, Hidalgo was excommunicated by Manuel Abad y Queipo, Bishop of Michoacán.[19] Although they had been friends and shared a fascination with Enlightenment literature, the bishop could not condone indiscriminate violence and lynching.

By October, the numbers of Hidalgo's followers had swollen to eighty thousand. They were hardly an army; these men lacked any organisation, let alone training or modern drill. To add to the confusion, they included children and women, who followed their husbands into battle.[20] On 30 October 1810 the rebels were only thirty kilometres west of Mexico City. Félix María Calleja del Rey, in command of the royalist forces, sent two thousand regulars to meet the invaders. At the Monte de las Cruces a pitched battle was fought between the horde and the Spanish regulars. Hidalgo's insurgents, under the banner of the Virgin of Guadalupe, attacked in three waves. The defenders sought the protection of Nuestra Señora de los Remedios (Our Lady of Remedies) as they held firm under the murderous onslaught.[21] Although hugely outnumbered, the discipline of the regular troops repulsed the attackers with well-coordinated volleys. Yet the third and final assault forced them to withdraw in good order back to Mexico City.[22]

This first engagement with a modern military force shook the confidence of the insurgents. In the following days almost half deserted the ranks and returned home. For reasons that have never been clear, Hidalgo decided to return to his heartlands.[23] There is some speculation that the viceroy of New Spain had promised to meet him to discuss his demands for *criollo* representation. More likely, the rebel officers did not feel confident that their ill-disciplined followers could take Mexico City. This retreat allowed General Calleja to prepare a counter-offensive. A week later seven thousand Spanish troops intercepted the horde. Unwilling to engage in an open battle, Hidalgo ordered a withdrawal, but under sustained cannon fire the rebels were routed and fled the field in disorder.[24] Given the worsening situation there was an attempt to win the hearts and minds of the *criollos* by publishing a rebel newspaper, *El Despertador* (*The Alarm*). Here Hidalgo published his programme of reforms, which included the abolition of tribute, involuntary servitude, and excise duty on alcohol.[25] He also promised to create protected native reservations to galvanise his native American followers. It was too late; the massacres at Guanajuato had been a godsend to the royalists in Mexico City. This newspaper only succeeded in heightening the alarm of criollo elites.

As Calleja drove ever deeper into rebel territory, eventually re-taking Guanajuato, the violence increased exponentially. Spanish hostages were massacred brutally by the insurgents. In retaliation Calleja executed those who had collaborated with Hidalgo's men. The day of reckoning between the Madonnas of Guadalupe and de los Remedios arrived on 17 January 1811. At the bridge of Calderòn, 400 miles north-west of Mexico City, royalist troops massacred the rebel horde.[26] The leaders tried to regroup, but the situation was desperate, as now even the native Americans had turned against the insurgency. Impatient to evade the royalists, Hidalgo and his officers rode toward Texas. As they traversed this desert region they were met by hostile counter-revolutionary crowds. The convoy was heading towards a town, ironically called Nuestra Señora de la Guadalupe de Baján. Here the fugitives hoped to use local wells to replenish their water supplies. Unbeknown to them their destination had been betrayed to royalist forces. On 21 March Hidalgo was ambushed and taken prisoner with his remaining supporters.[27]

The captives were taken to Chihuahua to await their fate. Although eager to end the rebellion, the Spanish imperial authorities were fascinated as to why these men had taken up arms. Their interrogations were thorough and searching. While most of his followers were put before military tribunals, and eventually shot, Hidalgo's status as a priest posed a dilemma. Inquisitors from Mexico City had to travel to Chihuahua to interrogate the rebel vicar under canon law. On 27 July 1811 Hidalgo was stripped of his priestly status and presented to the secular arm of justice for trial.[28] Although he proved himself brave throughout his ordeal, he did admit that the military action and the organisation of the rebellion had been a mistake.

A retraction published in his name has proved controversial, given that Hidalgo remains a martyr and the founding father of modern Mexico.[29] He did not so much renege on the promise of Mexican nationhood as realise that he had failed in his mission to regenerate colonial society. On 30 July he appeared before a tribunal composed of nine *criollo* judges. They unanimously sentenced the parish priest of Dolores to death by firing squad. At the former Jesuit college of Chihuahua he was executed. He was posthumously decapitated and his head sent to Guanajuato, where it was displayed as a warning to anyone who should challenge the authority of Spain in the New World.[30]

Yet this was hardly the end of it. Latin America was to be the site of a brutal struggle between rebel and royalist forces for the next sixteen years. Bishops condemned the rebellion. They had been appointed by the crown under the *patronado* system. This resembled the system in Europe whereby monarchs appointed episcopal candidates and Rome confirmed them. It is hardly surprising that the Latin American episcopacy remained loyal, for the most part, to the crown on which it relied for patronage.[31] Given the turmoil, most clergy tried to avoid taking sides and ministered to their congregations as best they could. Yet a small core of radical priests, over four hundred according to official records from this time,[32] continued to incite their flock to rebel against their Spanish overlords.

Another Mexican priest, José María Morelos, an acquaintance of Hidalgo who participated in his insurrection, picked up his mantle. Morelos, though less intellectual and charismatic than Hidalgo, was a born guerrilla commander. His bands, made up of ranchers and Puebla Indians, were three thousand strong and operated in the lowlands of Michoacán and Guerrero.[33] A man of very few words, unlike Hidalgo, he imposed a rigid discipline on his men and planned daring raids. Like so many Latin American revolutionaries he believed in the necessity of authority, a love of the fatherland and religion. His key aim was to rid New Spain of the detested peninsular elites. An attachment to the Virgin of Guadalupe showed that in terms of political culture his rebellion was a continuation of Hidalgo's horde. But this time the *guerrilleros* were organised and disciplined.

Between 1813 and 1815 they fought a brutal irregular war against the authorities of Mexico City. Although Morelos had fathered two children from a mistress, he seems to have had a genuine vocation.[34] He defined himself as a servant of the nation, and his vision of the Mexican future had a decidedly theocratic hue. Parish priests would be natural leaders of the community.

While imperial taxes were to be resisted, tithes paid to the clergy were to be paid assiduously and in full. Once the Guerrero region was under his control, he summoned a representative assembly that became known as the Congress of Anáhuac, in 1813.* This congress declared independence from Spain and gave Mexico its first (of many) constitutions: *Sentimientos de la Nación*, which established a sectarian Catholic state that placed priests in a significant position of leadership.[35] While this short text of twenty-two articles did establish a separation of powers and the abolition of slavery, it was far from the Jacobin constitution of 1793. Article 19 stated that:

> this Constitutional Law establishes that 12 December will in all towns be dedicated to the celebration of María Santísima de Guadalupe, the patroness of our freedom and all people will be encouraged to monthly devotions [towards her].[36]

The devotion to this Mexican Virgin Mary was thus constitutionally enshrined. The next article abolished all interference in foreign lands except missionary work to spread the faith. It is true that, in general, the age of revolutions disrupted traditional monarchical authority and challenged European imperialism. Yet, as the Mexican example highlights so well, it was not intrinsically anticlerical let alone anti-religious.

A significant minority of clergymen responded to the French revolutionary and Napoleonic challenge with their own radical vision of a future society. In much of Latin America religion was to be the foundation of the new state. Their plan was not to abandon politics, but rather to fuse religion and the state together.[37] This challenge to Spanish sovereignty could not go unanswered and General Calleja pursued a relentless pacification campaign in the Guerrero region. His counter-insurgency techniques worked, and gradually the irregulars were disarmed and executed.[38] Like

---

* They chose this term as it was the ancient Nahuatl word used by the Aztecs to describe their heartlands. See John Chasteen, *Americanos, Latin America's Struggle for Independence* (Oxford, 2007), pp. 104–105.

Hidalgo, Morelos was captured in 1815 and tried in Mexico City. It is fascinating to note that Morelos reacted with horror when interrogators from the Mexican inquisition accused him of being a proponent of Rousseauan and Jacobin ideals. This priest was keen to emphasise his doctrinal purity and refutation of all heresy. Unfrocked, Morelos retracted his errors and was allowed to receive the last rites before he was executed on 22 December 1815.[39]

Although the Mexican Revolution was more religious in nature than other South American rebellions, the latter shared many of its aspirations. In Buenos Aires, at the General Congress of 1810, out of a total of twenty clerical deputies sixteen voted for severing all links with Spain.[40] Indeed, many Argentinian priests supported the independence struggle in the Rio de la Plata region. In Peru, twenty-six out of fifty-seven deputies in their constituent congress were priests.[41] Similarly, in Simón Bolívar's Venezuela and in Colombia most of the parish clergy supported independence.[42] Although El Libertador, as Bolívar was known, was a deist with little belief in divine intervention, he understood Catholicism's potential when it came to bestowing legitimacy on his regime. His policy was to court the lower clergy. Indeed, the Dominican friar Ignacio Mariño fought as a guerrilla leader with Bolívar in the Llanos region.[43] Anti-Spanish catechisms were issued to urge Americans to fight against Spanish imperialism as a God-given duty.[44] Certainly, by the 1820s, the growingly anti-monarchical tone of these insurrections was of great concern to the Inquisition and church authorities.

Pius VII, traumatised by five years of detention by Napoleon, found events in South America troubling. He had little time for rebels, even those who fought to defend the church. On 30 January 1816 he issued the brief *Etsi longissimo terrarum* in which he expressed concern over the rebellion across the Atlantic. In no uncertain terms the pope declared to the colonial episcopacy:

On earth We are the representatives of He who is the God of Peace, that was born to redeem mankind from the tyranny of the devil, and who proclaimed peace to mankind through his angels. We believe it to be part of Our apostolic function,

which We exercise unworthily, to encourage you with this
letter to redouble your efforts to uproot and annihilate
completely the disastrous riots, sedition, and discord which
one man [Bolívar] has sown among you.[45]

Initially the bishops were quite happy to support the
royal government. Rebels were denounced in cathedrals and
excommunicated by diocesan authorities. From 1815 to 1820
reinforcements arrived from Spain to restore order in Venezuela
and Mexico. They made significant headway in the pacification
of the rebel colonies. It seemed the Spanish empire might regain
control of South America.[46] In 1820, however, there was a dramatic
reversal of fortune.

Additional regiments of regular troops destined for America
were ordered to Cadiz to await embarkation. Here, an outbreak
of yellow fever spread through the ranks like wildfire. Liberal-
minded officers, concerned about disease and fighting for a cause
they did not support, began to plot. Captain Rafael del Riego
issued a *pronunciamento* (proclamation) against the absolutist
government in Madrid. He placed himself at the head of a mutiny
that soon controlled the army. King Ferdinand VII was forced
to restore the liberal constitution of 1812.[47] The revolutionaries'
decision to expropriate much of the church's property and lands
raised alarm bells in the Curia. The Cortes (Spanish parliament)
summoned by the liberals in Madrid called for unity across the
Spanish empire and promised greater freedoms to all Spaniards in
both hemispheres. The rebels in Latin America saw this turmoil
as an unmissable opportunity to regain the initiative. They knew
that the South American royalists could now expect no supplies or
reinforcements from the mother country.[48]

In March 1821 Rafael Lasso de la Vega, Bishop of Mérida, met
with Bolívar for informal discussions. He was one of the few
bishops who had remained in Venezuela and not fled.[49] Bolívar
insisted that Catholicism would enjoy freedom from state
interference in the republics of South America. He reassured the
bishop that he was no Jacobin and that he appreciated the benefits
of religion. Lasso de la Vega wrote to Pius VII on 21 October 1821.[50]

He outlined the dreadful situation in Venezuela and how most bishops had been forced to flee their dioceses. Remarkably the one-time loyalist bishop wondered if the church might not be able to reach an accommodation with the new Latin American republics. If the Spanish had achieved constitutional government thanks to Riego's mutiny, why then should not the *criollos* of America?

Spain's liberal revolution, and its anticlericalism, put the Holy See in a difficult position. Should Rome support the revolutionaries in Madrid or those in Caracas? Cardinal Consalvi advised caution, and reiterated his belief that neutrality was the best position for the papacy. During this time, a canon of the cathedral of Santiago in Chile, José Ignacio Cienfuegos, arrived in Rome. He was an emissary of the Chilean head of government Bernardo O'Higgins.[51] Cienfuegos met secretly with the pope and then with the cardinal secretary of state. He impressed on them how South America's new republics would accept the pope's authority over local churches. The argument was made that Chile's republicans had treated the church better than Spain's liberals. Indeed, Article 1 of the Chilean constitution proclaimed Catholicism as the state's religion in perpetuity. Consalvi saw this as an opportunity to place the church on a solid footing in South America and urged the pope to open a dialogue. After months of temporising, on 7 September 1822 Pius VII replied to Lasso de la Vega. The ageing pontiff stated:

> We do not wish to meddle in affairs that touch on state policy; but care only for religion, for the church of God over which We preside, and for the care of the souls entrusted to Our ministry, while We bitterly lament the many wounds that are inflicted on the church in Spain, We also ardently desire to provide for the needs of the faithful in the American regions.[52]

This letter stopped short of a recognition of the new Latin American republics. Yet it showed that the pope had little liking for the liberal revolution in Spain and its ecclesiastical reforms. At the urging of Cienfuegos and Consalvi the momentous decision was taken to send a papal emissary to open discussions with the

South American revolutionaries. In many ways this decision mirrored the one taken in 1800 to negotiate a concordat with Napoleonic France. Rather than plunge the church into a direct confrontation with the new regimes of Latin America it would be much better to find a compromise. Unlike Europe's revolutions, the Mexicans, Peruvians, Venezuelans and Chileans had shown themselves committed to their Catholic faith.

The man selected for this mission was Mgr Giovanni Muzi. Born in 1772, he came from a modest family background. His father had been a porter and menial labourer. Although born in modest circumstances, the young Muzi was clever and won a scholarship to study in some of the best institutions in Rome. His career as a hospital chaplain was brief, and he was appointed censor to the prestigious La Sapienza university. In 1812 he took the unfortunate decision to take the oath of allegiance to Napoleon, which placed him in a minority of priests who collaborated with the French invaders. As a reward, he was given the chair of moral theology at the Collegio Romano, one of the premier seminaries in the Catholic world. Pius VII's return interrupted Muzi's ascent and he was in the wilderness for some months. He appeared before the 'congregation of disorders' headed by Cardinal Pacca and was asked to retract publicly his oath to the French. After being forgiven he was reinstated in the Curia and made secretary to the nuncio in Vienna, where he served with distinction as a diplomat from 1815 to 1819.[53]

Given his experience in an important European capital and his theological acumen he was seen as the ideal candidate to go to South America. He was given the title of Apostolic Vicar and raised to the honorific position of Archbishop of Philippi. His remit included the authority to nominate caretaker bishops in Chile and Rio de la Plata (basically both sides of the tip of South America). Under no circumstances was he to appoint permanent bishops to vacant dioceses. Consalvi wanted to avoid giving offence to either the *criollo* revolutionaries or the liberal government in Spain. The ultimate question of whether the king of Spain or the new republics held the right to appoint to vacant dioceses would remain unresolved for the time being.[54]

Muzi brought with him as his deputy a thirty-year-old cleric named Giovanni Maria Mastai Ferretti, a man of average height with a tendency towards corpulence, and an amiable, smiling face. This young aristocrat from Senigallia, on the Adriatic coast, was to be the key protagonist in the story of Catholicism during the age of revolutions. In 1846 he would be elected by his fellow cardinals as Pope Pius IX, better known as Pio Nono.[55] The idealistic Giovanni Maria saw his mission to Chile as a missionary adventure, which would enable him to bring the word of God to the furthest reaches of the southern hemisphere. Little did he realise that this would be his first apprenticeship in the murky world of the politics of religion. On 28 June 1823 Pius VII took the step of extending Muzi's power to encompass all of South America and Mexico, excluding Portuguese Brazil.[56]

This apostolic delegation heading to Latin America was to be joined by Cienfuegos, whose expertise would prove essential in briefing Muzi and Mastai Ferretti about Chile. When the travellers reached Genoa, they learned that Pius VII had passed away. In the subsequent conclave at the Quirinal, Consalvi's great rival, Annibale della Genga, was elected Pope Leo XII.[57] He dismissed his adversary from the position of secretary of state. But despite his detestation of revolution, della Genga reluctantly confirmed Muzi's mission to the Americas. With continued support from the new papal administration, the travellers set sail on 5 October for Buenos Aires.[58]

In the Atlantic their ship was so badly beset by storms that it was impossible for Muzi and Ferretti to offer mass because of the violent pitching caused by the waves. In early January 1824, green around the gills and unsteady on their legs, the prelates landed in Buenos Aires and were given a triumphal welcome by the locals. The pious population were deeply touched that the pope had sent an emissary to the southern hemisphere. Yet not everybody felt the same. The government minister Bernardino Rivadavia, inspired by Benthamite and utilitarian ideals, had issued laws on freedom of worship for all faiths, which had upset Rome.[59] There had also been attempts to police the clergy and curtail the tithe. To make matters worse, priests who preached against these ecclesiastical reforms were threatened with expulsion. Muzi was greeted with froideur and suspicion by the civil authorities of Argentina. The revolutionary press of the city accused Muzi of being an agent of reaction.[60] Given the hostility of the Argentine elites, the apostolic vicar decided not to linger but push onwards to Chile.

It would take over two months to travel through the Rio de la Plata region and eventually cross the forbidding Andes. While they were making this long journey, Bernardo O'Higgins had resigned from power to be replaced by Ramón Freire, who was much less sympathetic to the church.[61] The president of the Chilean senate was Camillo Henriquez, a priest deeply imbued with the works of the French Enlightenment. His progressive ideas had brought him to the unwelcome attention of the Spanish inquisition in 1809. Appalled by the brutality of the royalist authorities in Chile, he had become a convert to revolution and an eloquent radical journalist. During the wars of independence, he had been excommunicated and was not surprisingly unsympathetic to the Catholic hierarchy. He presided over a senate that was hesitant, if not hostile, to opening negotiations with Rome.[62]

When papal mission arrived, Freire was on the frontline fighting the *peninsulares* in the north. He wrote to his officials asking them to bestow full honours on his distinguished visitors. They were housed in the Palacio de La Moneda in Santiago. Given that the war with Spain was raging, the apostolic vicar was left to fester for two months without much contact from government ministers. During this lull, Cienfuegos made it clear he wanted to be appointed by Muzi as a caretaker bishop. When this failed to occur, he abandoned the delegation and went into a sulk. In June, Freire returned from military operations and gave the papal delegation a cordial audience. Yet it proved difficult to pin down the general and open negotiations.[63]

Little did they know that Freire had other fish to fry. On 19 July, a coup was launched, after which Freire assumed dictatorial powers and abolished the pro-Catholic constitution of Chile.[64] One of the first acts of the new government was to request Muzi to approve the reduction of religious festivities to increase productivity. To ingratiate himself with the new administration, the apostolic vicar accepted this request, limiting the holy days of obligation to a mere sixty-three![65] Regardless of this gesture of goodwill, new laws on press freedom had given rise to a concerted attack on Catholic teaching. This alarmed the clergy of Santiago. To make matters worse, Freire deported the bishop of the capital and appointed Cienfuegos in his place, ignoring the papal preorgative to confirm all episcopal candidates. Cienfuegos started administering his diocese with little regard for the niceties of ecclesiastical law.[66]

Worse was to come. On 22 September 1824 commissioners were sent to all the monasteries and convents of Chile to make an inventory of their property. Many suspected that this was a prelude to the confiscation of monastic lands, whose sale could help pay off the national debt of Chile.[67] Furious at these provocative acts, Muzi decided to leave and asked for his passport. The government asked if the apostolic vicar might be willing to appoint caretaker bishops before departing. At first the pope's emissary was willing to consider governmental candidates. The first three names proved unacceptable and were rejected. The government said that it would be satisfied if Cienfuegos were made caretaker bishop of Santiago. Muzi refused, given that the true bishop of the city was still alive and was a loyal Catholic.[68] With this standoff, the mission to Chile ended in dismal failure.

On 19 October the delegation again crossed the Andes. Their next destination was Montevideo, the future capital of Uruguay. During his four months there Muzi was well received and ordained four new priests. He wrote a long open letter placing the blame for the failure of his mission squarely on the Argentine and Chilean authorities.[69] On 18 February 1825 the first apostolic vicar to South America departed on board the *Colombia* for Genoa. Muzi has sometimes been criticised for his rigidity and intransigence. Although he may not have risen to the occasion, the truth is that he was not empowered to negotiate a concordat, nor could he appoint legitimate bishops. His instructions from Consalvi tightly restricted his room for manoeuvre. Equally, the refusal of the Chilean government to propose moderate churchmen for the role of caretaker bishops made his position impossible. With hindsight, his biggest mistake was to travel to the most radical and revolutionary parts of Latin America. Had Muzi and his party landed in Mexico or Venezuela the outcome of the mission might have been very different. The Curia deplored that in eighteen months Muzi had only sent two despatches back to Rome. He was scapegoated for the failure of the mission and this ended his diplomatic career.[70] After his return, he was appointed bishop of the small Umbrian town of Citta di Castello, where he served in obscurity until his death in 1849.[71]

Yet for the young Mastai Ferretti, the journey gave him a reputation within the Curia as a well-travelled and competent prelate. More importantly it gave him a glimpse into revolutionary government and he showed little sympathy for the reformers he met in Chile. On his return he was made director of the hospice of San Michele a Ripa Grande, one of the largest institutions for the care of the elderly, foundlings and fallen women in the Papal States.[72] Here he showed himself an active priest and deeply committed to the pastoral wellbeing of his unfortunate charges. Impressed by his achievements, Leo XII decided to appoint Mastai as archbishop of Spoleto at the tender age of thirty-five. In 1832 he was transferred to the important diocese of Imola, which had been Pius VII's see before his ascent to the papacy. This appointment marked him out as the rising star of the church. Few doubted his piety and pastoral priorities, yet the new bishop stressed that he was a priest and not a politician.[73] He wanted to avoid the limelight. As will be apparent in the next chapter, he did not get his wish.

Even before the failure of the Muzi mission, Leo XII had confirmed his predecessor's disapproval of the rebellions in Latin America. In 1823 a French army had invaded Spain, put an end to its liberal revolution and restored Ferdinand VII to absolute power.[74] On 24 September 1824, in the papal brief *Etsi iam diu*, the pope exhorted and advised the bishops in hispanic America to remain steadfast in their loyalty to the crown in Madrid.[75] It is difficult to imagine a more misguided attempt to rally the church in Latin America around a discredited divine-right monarchy. Leo's brief was addressed to an episcopacy that was either dead, in exile or had been deposed. Indeed, this letter backfired badly, by proving to the leaders of the wars of independence that the Catholic hierarchy was hostile to them.

It would take a new pope, Gregory XVI, to implement the solution Muzi had failed to execute. By the late 1820s it was clear that the Spanish had been ejected from South America, except for the islands of Cuba and Puerto Rico. An imperial *reconquista* was an impossibility. In the bull *Sollicitudo ecclesiarum* of 1831, Gregory XVI stated that the Holy See could enter into pragmatic agreements with de facto governments that did not possess legitimate authority.[76] Such compromises were necessary to give stability and leadership to the church. The pope then appointed six caretaker bishops to Mexico. They could administer pre-existing dioceses and dispense all normal episcopal functions.[77] However, Spain still claimed the *patronato* over these dioceses, and threatened sanctions if the papacy formally recognised the new republics. As a result of this last-ditch imperial tantrum, these bishops could not be given full title to their dioceses and, technically, could only act as apostolic administrators for a limited time. The death of Ferdinand VII in 1833 brought about a decided change in the atmosphere.[78] In the wake of his passing, Spain descended into the chaos of the Carlist civil wars and the government in Madrid now had no hope of ever recovering its colonies.[79] In 1835 the papacy recognised Venezuela and a year later the republic of Mexico. The Catholic Church signed no fewer than ten concordats with Latin American states between 1852 and 1889. All but two of these treaties were signed by Pius IX who, all those years before, had been a young secretary to the Muzi mission.[80]

The liberation struggles of South America were a remarkable episode in the age of revolutions. Once Napoleon had invaded Spain and cut off the colonies from the metropole a vacuum of authority emerged. The viceroys tried their best to maintain royal authority, but their position in Mexico City and Lima was constantly under challenge. Like the North American, Haitian and French Revolutions these uprisings attacked traditional authority and the legitimacy of empire.[81] The *criollos* wanted to wrest sovereignty away from Spain and place it in the hands of the colonial elites of these successor states. They sought to create new national identities, political cultures and traditions that would suit their hispano-American environments. Unlike Europe, where religious pluralism and the subordination of the church to the state had been of paramount importance during the 1790s, in Latin America Catholic identity was irrenounceable. A substantial minority of priests participated actively in the revolution and encouraged the religious zeal of the insurgents. Most of the countries created after 1825 recognised themselves as confessionally Catholic.[82]

While the church may have declined financially and socially in Peru, this was an exception.[83] The reverse was the case in Mexico, where the cult of the Virgin of Guadalupe became an icon of national resurgence. Hidalgo and Morelos were elevated as national heroes and are feted to the present day.[84] Admittedly the dominance of Catholicism in South America was challenged by the anticlericalism of some revolutionaries during the 1820s.[85] Monasteries and church lands were plundered, yet such attacks proved transient. The Caudillos of the Americas were no Jacobins. In Columbia and Venezuela, Bolívar sought to establish a working arrangement with the clergy.[86] He was content to allow a privileged position to the Catholic Church as long as the legitimacy of his regime was not challenged. So, despite some anti-ecclesiastical rhetoric in Chile and Argentina, Rome consolidated its hold on the continent during the first half of the nineteenth century. After all, with the Spanish monarchy's authority gone, the papacy could deal directly with the Latin American church in a way that would have been unthinkable during the eighteenth century.[87] In most Latin American republics Rome kept a solid grip over education and a rudimentary system of social welfare. Where the nascent state was weak, the church could use its network of dioceses and parishes to strengthen its influence over the local population.

In this region of the southern hemisphere revolutionaries proved decidedly tolerant towards Catholicism. While they may have exiled royalist bishops *en masse*, they were sympathetic to the parish priests who ministered to grassroots communities. This spirit of openness was not reciprocated in Rome. Almost as a reflex, the papacy issued condemnations against the rebels, showing that Rome failed to understand that what was occurring on the other side of the Atlantic was not a continuation of the French Revolution. Left to its own devices Rome might well have succeeded in alienating *criollo* Catholics and igniting a new schism. It was thanks to charismatic priests and the indigenous people's incorporation of Catholicism into their culture that the church survived. South America demonstrated that the anticlerical banner unfurled in Revolutionary France and the Napoleonic empire was not an inevitable consequence of rebellion. Radical priests transformed the Virgin Mary and Jesus into revolutionary icons that would cast a long shadow on South American Catholicism.

Back in Europe, the period after the Congress of Vienna is often dismissed as an age of restoration. Such a label gives the misleading impression that the statesmen of the old world turned the clocks back to before 1789 and pretended that the French Revolution had never happened.[88] Historians exaggerate the reactionary nature of the papacy during the first half of the nineteenth century. It is certainly true that the popes of this period (Leo XII, 1823–9; Pius VIII, 1829–30; Gregory XVI, 1831–46) were deeply conservative enemies of revolution.[89] But regardless of these men's illiberal views, there has been a tendency to embellish their reactionary stances.

Historians regularly state that Leo XII condemned vaccination because it had been invented by the Protestant Edward Jenner. This pope was quoted in 1829 announcing that 'whoever allows himself to be vaccinated ceases to be a child of God. Smallpox is a judgement of God, the vaccination is a challenge toward heaven.'[90] The problem is that Leo XII never said any such thing.[91] There is not a shred of evidence that he resisted the inoculations that were carried out in the Papal States. It is certainly true that, once elected, della Genga did roll back the administrative and legal innovations established by Consalvi.[92] These attempts to modernise the Curia and bring efficient government to the pope's domains proved transitory. Having said this, to focus on the pontiffs that followed one another in grim succession after 1823 would be to ignore how many Catholic clergymen and laymen wanted the church to assume a new, and in some cases radical, role in society. The privileged First Estate of the *ancien régime* had been erased by the revolution of 1789. It was beyond resurrection. How the relationship between church and state was to be defined in post-revolutionary Europe was an open question.

Catholic intellectuals and mystics provided several solutions to this dilemma. They were influenced by the artistic and cultural movement known as Romanticism.[93] Unlike the neoclassical intellectuals of the eighteenth century, Romantics sought the truth not in nature but within their own genius and immortal souls. They sought the terrifying incommensurability of the sublime rather than delighting in orderly beauty and form. Hegel described the goal as 'absolute inwardness'.[94] For many, Romanticism was a rebellion against the stolid world of Enlightenment rationalism. These artists and philosophers were fascinated by emotion, medievalism, mysticism and history in a manner that would have been alien to *philosophes* of the *encyclopédie*. Further down the pyramid, ordinary believers proudly reinvigorated the baroque rituals, processions and cult of saints that had been vehemently attacked by the reform Catholicism of the previous century.

These believers felt that the church had abandoned its social vocation during the *ancien régime*. The First Estate had positioned itself above rather than within society. There was a feeling that the 1790s had unleashed a torrent of religious indifference and egotistic individualism. The revolutionaries had taught men to look after themselves, rather than each other. These Catholics were appalled by economic liberalism's lack of interest in the vulnerability of the poor before the cruel whims of market forces. Society had become atomised and brittle due to the collapse of solidarity among people. They idealised the Middle Ages as a time in which corporate identities had bred social cohesion and solidarity. The fact that such views were a distortion of the past mattered little. It allowed radical Catholics to redefine the church's position in both the present and the future. For them, only by ministering to the poor and assuming a leadership role at the centre of society could the church heal the evils of the post-revolutionary order.[95]

It should be noted that these young men had matured during the Napoleonic period, and had witnessed the emperor's persecution of the Roman church. They had seen how Bonaparte unscrupulously manipulated France's traditions of Gallicanism, Jansenism and conciliarism to divide the episcopacy and weaken the authority of the pope.[96] Feeling betrayed by Napoleon's Gallican collaborators, such thinkers were drawn toward more ultramontane perspectives. A key inspiration on their thinking was the counter-revolutionary Savoyard intellectual Joseph de Maistre (1753–1821) who, in a book entitled *Du Pape* (*On the pope*) published in 1819, reinvigorated the concept of papal infallibility and supremacy.[97] Given that the pope could not err in his judgements, de Maistre argued that he should hold a sort of supranational sovereignty over Europe, that the Holy See should act as the supreme court of appeals for the entire continent in matters of international law and morality. What this younger generation took from de Maistre was the importance of the papacy in regenerating European society. They felt little sympathy towards his paternalistic and authoritarian disdain for the masses. His pessimism about human nature and its propensity towards sin proved controversial among those who had reached maturity at the fall of the Napoleonic empire.

Yet there they shared his longing that the pope and his successors might help shape the post-revolutionary order for the better. This younger generation of Catholics urged the church not to fear the masses but to help provide solutions for the social woes of the age. In a time of individualism, exploitation and ideological chaos, they believed that Catholicism and its ethical teachings could restore unity of purpose and harmony to European society. Only a rediscovery of the social mission of the Catholic Church could allow selfish individuals to be reintegrated into a moral community of believers (something de Maistre had ignored).[98] Such thinkers and activists laid the groundwork for a movement within the church known as social Catholicism, which would reach its culmination at the end of the nineteenth century.

The clergyman who most epitomised Catholicism's flirtation with Romanticism and new social thinking was Hugues Felicité Robert de Lamennais. His vision of a regenerated society in which religion would hold centre stage failed to materialise. Yet his barrage of publications highlighted how a younger generation of Catholic thinkers from the 1820s and 1830s, far from sharing the papacy's nostalgia, looked to the future with hope rather than despair. Lamennais was born into a prosperous, deeply religious and recently ennobled Breton family of merchants and shippers. The loss of his mother at the tender age of five left the young Felicité with a deep sense of anxiety.[99] He dealt with this by seeking to please others and impress them with his charisma. One suspects that behind Lamennais' passionate writing style lay a human being probably afflicted by some form of bipolar disorder. Felicité went through cycles of elation that quickly descended into doldrums of despair. After a youth spent reading the works of the Enlightenment and embracing deism, he experienced a damascene conversion. Probably under the influence of his brother Jean-Marie, who was ordained a priest in 1804,[100] Felicité rediscovered the power of Catholic teachings and the history of the church.

Lamennais developed a disdain for the *ancien régime* episcopacy and came to see the First Estate as a selfish corporation, more interested in worldly power and wealth rather than the material well-being of its congregation. He denounced the Gallican articles of 1682, which he blamed for the lack of unity within the eighteenth-century church. During the Napoleonic empire he witnessed the persecution of the church and learned of the imprisonment of Pius VII. In collaboration with his elder brother Jean-Marie, Felicité wrote a treatise entitled *Reflections on the State of the Church in France in 1814*.[101] This text criticised Napoleon's attempts to arrogate the pope's power to confirm bishops in their dioceses. It was also very anti-Gallican and advocated a restoration of papal power. Unsurprisingly, these early writings were banned by the imperial censor and made little public impact. So critical was Lamennais of the Napoleonic regime that, during the Hundred Days in 1815, he fled to London.[102]

After Waterloo Felicité returned to France, where he was ordained a priest. In 1817 he published his 'Essay on Indifference in Matters of Religion' which caused a sensation. It argued that the scepticism and agnosticism of the Revolutionary order had deeply damaged European civilisation.[103] The Bourbons, who had returned to rule France in 1814, had inherited from Napoleon a modern and secularised administration, which claimed neutrality when it came to matters of religion. Lamennais accused the state of being, in effect, atheistic and asserted that its failure to recognise the truth and pre-eminence of Catholicism had deeply harmed society and the bonds of solidarity. At this early stage one could be forgiven for thinking that he was advocating a return to the alliance of throne and altar of the eighteenth century, yet nothing could have been further from Lamennais' mind.

During the 1820s, his unyielding belief was that Catholicism should be placed at the centre of European culture and society. Between 1817 and 1845 popes entered into concordats with Bavaria, Sardinia, Naples, Russian Poland, Prussia, Hanover, Belgium and Switzerland.[104] In theory, these deals brokered with European states were supposed to demarcate clearly the boundaries that defined the ecclesiastical and secular spheres. Yet Lamennais and others feared that, through these deals, the church was compromising its social and ethical pre-eminence. Ultimately the church should not be subservient to non-religious states that did not share its moral imperatives.[105] Could the Calvinist king of Prussia and the Orthodox tsar of Russia really have the best interests of Catholicism at heart? Catholic monarchs limited by reforming ministers or liberal constitutions were little better.

For Lamennais it was necessary to go back to basics. The crown and state were important players in regenerating society, but the papacy and clergy should be the protagonists of Europe's future. It was for priests to reanimate communities damaged by the revolution's individualism and agnosticism.[106] During this time, wandering missionaries, including Felicité's brother Jean-Marie, toured France. They tried, as the Jesuits had done in Paraguay or in the Far East, to convert those tempted away from the Catholic fold by the Revolution.[107] Their preaching exhorted the lost sheep of the 1790s to return to the church. These missionaries had a disturbing tendency to engage in book-burning rituals. During these sessions bonfires were erected and the works of Voltaire and Rousseau were consigned to the flames.[108] It was in the context of these Catholic missions and religious revivals that Lamennais' ideas solidified. It was not so much a question of restoring a lost golden age; for Lamennais it was important to jettison the Gallican past in favour of an ultramontane future.

In 1824, thanks to his staunch defence of papal supremacy, Felicité was invited to Rome. He quickly fell in love with the majesty of the Eternal City, and was excited to meet eminent cardinals. One of the less wholesome aspects of Lamennais' character was his self-promotion and solipsistic nature. He craved attention. His moment of glory arrived when he was granted three audiences with the pope.[109] Although Leo XII provided Lamennais with encouragement, he found him to be an *esaltato*, or fanatic. He cautioned the young priest to curb his enthusiasm and work with the French episcopacy. Leo advised the French hierarchy to handle Lamennais with care, as he might be liable to go off the rails if not guided by moderation. The pope's words were prophetic.[110]

A portrait of Lamennais, from 1826, by Jean-Baptiste Paulin Guérin, depicts a well-dressed, if somewhat effete, clergyman with handsome features and fiery eyes. The portrait captures well the intensity but also the underlying fragility of the man. As time passed, Lamennais' attachment to the Bourbon dynasty waned. He now saw it as a lost cause. The kings of France had placed themselves at the head of an irreligious and non-confessional state that had inherited administrative structures that were intrinsically anti-Catholic from Lammenais' ultramontane standpoint.

He set out his case in a new book entitled *On Religion in Relation with the Civil and Political Order*, published in 1825. He still saw the papacy as the greatest hope for moral reawakening and social cohesion. Felicité, in almost Napoleonic fashion, desired to centralise the pope's control over the church. Gallicanism had made the church divided and vulnerable. His attacks on the autonomy and prerogatives of French bishops became ever more vituperative. His new dictum, paraphrasing Montesquieu, was 'no pope, no church; no church no religion; no religion, no society'.[111] His denunciations of the four Gallican articles of 1682 landed him in trouble with the French courts. At his trial in 1826, Lamennais stated in his defence:

I owe it to my conscience and to the sacred character with which I am invested to declare to this court that I remain

unshakably attached to the legitimate head of the church.
That his faith is my faith, that his doctrine is my doctrine and
that up to my last breath I will continue to profess and defend
[these precepts].

Unwilling to create a martyr, the judges ordered the confiscation
of his most recent book and fined him thirty francs.[112]

The following years were to be a time of soul-searching for
Lamennais. He wanted to move from the position of an armchair
theorist into active political engagement and to put his ideas into
practice. So in 1828, with his brother Jean-Marie, he founded
the Congregation de Saint Pierre.[113] This association aspired to
become an even more ultramontane version of the Jesuits. Its
mission was not only to cement papal authority over the church
but to foster the church's magisterium in Europe and the globe.
Combining former missionaries and activists, this order of priests
was to serve in the front line in a battle to establish a new Catholic
social order.

Lamennais' aspirations evolved significantly as the 1820s
drew to a close. Appalled by the elitism and indifference of the
restoration regimes to poverty and inequality, Lamennais warned
that Europe was sitting on a powder keg of popular discontent. In
yet another book, this visionary priest now argued that revolution
needed to be understood rather than opposed.[114] In a remarkable
volte-face, he contended that the church had nothing to fear from
liberty. Quite the reverse: if the state upheld freedom of worship
and tolerance of all religions, Catholicism would prosper and
rediscover its social mission to help the poor and defend the
weaker members of the community.

Outside France events seemed to be proving him correct. In
1828 the Irish Catholic lawyer and orator Daniel O'Connell stood
for a by-election in County Clare.[115] He defeated the Protestant
and Unionist incumbent to great acclaim. A constitutional crisis
quickly followed as his Catholicism, especially his adherence to
the doctrine of transubstantiation, precluded him from taking
his seat in Westminster.[116] This event catalysed the campaign
for the emancipation of Catholics and their enfranchisement

across the United Kingdom. It seemed as if Ireland was on the brink of insurrection against the Protestant ascendancy. Fear of civil unrest forced the Duke of Wellington's very reluctant Tory government to concede Catholic emancipation in 1829.[117] This was a truly historic turning point. For the first time since the reign of William III and Mary II, British subjects loyal to the papacy were granted civic equality within the British Isles.

There were several qualifications, though, which significantly tempered the effects of the Roman Catholic Relief Act of 1829. For example, religious orders like the Jesuits were severely curtailed in their ability to operate in the United Kingdom. Furthermore, the property qualification for electors was raised. This meant that most middle-income Catholics would not be wealthy enough to vote in elections.[118] Despite these stings in the tail, reformism had allowed the Roman Catholic Church to re-emerge within the British archipelago, which had been such a bastion of Protestantism during the early modern period. The repercussions in Ireland were momentous. O'Connell's success in the cause of emancipation emboldened him to seek the repeal of the 1801 Act of Union which had brought the island of Ireland under direct rule from London.[119] This repeal movement, which ultimately ended in failure in the 1840s, fused religion and Irish national identity tightly together. It set the tone for the future, whereby the adherents of the union and those who opposed rule from Westminster came to be divided along increasingly sectarian lines.[120]

Lamennais interpreted events in Britain as a sign that political liberty and religious freedom could only strengthen the position of Catholicism.[121] For him, cutting any remaining cords that connected the church to the state would be beneficial. This epiphany represented an almost complete abandonment of the theocratic and monarchical priorities that had guided his early thinking. In 1829 he published *On the Progress of Revolution and the War Against the Church*. Lamennais outlined how the ongoing war between monarchical despotism and liberal anarchism had reached a crisis point. He warned that: 'everything rushes towards a catastrophe long foreseen by men capable of foresight for whom it will come as no surprise. The people already have an inkling of it.'[122] He expressed the hope that from the embers of this revolution and turmoil would spring a regenerated Catholic society.

His predictions proved all too well founded. Paris, Brussels and Warsaw all descended into violent revolution between 1830 and 1831. Lamennais' immediate reaction was to create a newspaper, *L'Avenir* (*The Future*), which would preach the new gospel of liberal Catholicism.[123] A generation of young idealists joined him on the editorial board of this paper. They included Charles Forbes René, comte de Montalembert, the Dominican friar Jean-Baptiste-Henri Lacordaire and the young priest Philippe Gerbet. In the prospectus of 1830 the editors proclaimed: 'We demand firstly freedom of conscience, full, universal, without qualification, without privilege, and in consequence for all that concerns we Catholics [we demand] the total separation of the Church and the State.'[124] This was followed by appeals for freedom for the church to teach its magisterium, freedom of the press, freedom of association, elections for the masses and an end to bureaucratic centralisation.[125]

It would be a mistake to see all this as a straightforward attempt to reconcile liberalism and Catholicism. Liberal Catholicism was distinct from classical liberalism, it saw absolute freedom as a route to anarchy and moral turpitude. Liberal Catholics, instead, believed that a church emancipated from the control of the state would prosper, and return to its original social mission of spreading the gospel message. Clergymen would go into communities to help the poor and weak without any state-imposed restrictions. Lamennais' ideas would prove inspirational in the late nineteenth century and for future generations of social Catholics.

In Brussels, Lamennais' journalism inspired some of the Catholic elites of the Belgian Revolution. The Comte de Merode and Marquis de Beauffort wrote letters, published in *L'Avenir,* expressing their conviction that Catholic values were at the heart of their revolution, which they felt had liberated the church from the bondage of the Dutch tyranny.[126] They could now regenerate society and reinvigorate its Christian foundations. A pamphlet they published in the last weeks of 1831 gives the measure of their idealistic radicalism:

Catholics you are summoned not just to free one or two peoples but to liberate the entire universe! Oh! If those who resist your doctrines could only understand the love that you bear them! You take them away from an imperfect and transient freedom, toward a liberty that is complete and stable. You invite them to remain in the bosom of a great family, to be seated at the banquet to which providence has called all its creatures. The social sovereignty of the Church which you venerate, frees the mind from error, the heart from passion, daily life from oppression. It establishes a singular alliance between a power that is infallible and beneficent with a complete liberty of the mind, the soul and life.[127]

This passage bursts with the enthusiasm and raw energy of religious Romanticism. Elsewhere these Belgian aristocrats praised the achievements of their Catholic brethren in France and Poland in casting off the yoke of despotism and deistic indifference. Yet, if one reads between the lines, it is possible to see what divides these two Belgian noblemen from Lamennais' social thinking. They saw the church as having the authority and wisdom to curb the worst excesses of democracy and populism. Their vision was ultimately paternalistic. It was endowed with little optimism or desire for the participation of the masses in politics. Merode and Beauffort were closer to the classically liberal position of a limited rather than a universal franchise.

Indeed the 1831 Belgian constitution was a finely balanced document that sought to create a moderate settlement that would distribute power in the new state to property owners, while taking into account the regional complexities of these provinces.[128] Although the majority of Belgians were Catholics, the Lutheran Leopold of Saxe-Coburg-Gotha had been invited to become their king. Married to a French princess, the new king of the Belgians had already given an undertaking that his offspring would be raised in the Catholic faith.[129] In terms of religion, the constitution of 1831 is sometimes interpreted as heralding a modern separation of church and state in Europe. This is not quite the case, as the document merely established the state's neutrality in matters of religion. The government of Brussels decided not to interfere in the internal administration of any recognised faiths.[130]

Henceforth, the papacy would have a completely free hand when it came to appointing bishops in Belgium. Despite this, the state would continue to pay the salaries of all priests and pastors who ministered to local communities. The biggest limitation was that Catholics would have to undergo a civil marriage to ensure the validity of their church wedding. Despite this minor inconvenience, the Belgian church emerged strengthened by the terms of the constitution of 1831. Catholicism was emancipated from the tutelage of the state while still receiving public funding. This arrangement, clearly, favoured a revival of the Roman church in the southern Netherlands where, in less than fifteen years, the religious orders more than trebled in size.[131]

Although Gregory XVI initially greeted the Belgian revolution with suspicion, he remained true to his pragmatism. It took a decade for diplomatic relations to become normalised between the Papal States and this new country. Among the first nuncios sent to an independent Belgium was a Mgr Vincenzo Pecci (he served 1843–5). This slender diplomat with an aquiline nose impressed all with his moderation.[132] Through his 'broad-church' approach, he was able to keep priests inspired by Lamennais in check by means of compromise and patience. Although unassuming and bookish, Pecci would come to play a key role when he was elected Pope Leo XIII in 1878.[133] As will be discussed, he was the pope who would engage most seriously with social Catholicism. Lamennais had been among the first to emphasise the church's social mission in ministering to the poor and to those who were exploited by industrial capitalism. Pecci had observed such inequities in Belgium, one of the first European countries to industrialise on a mass scale. Whereas most popes had argued that the social structure of society was God's will, the future Leo XIII thought the church should bring justice to the downtrodden and marginalised.[134]

Yet this opening towards social Catholicism lay in the future. Lamennais' liberal and radical Catholicism of the 1830s collided with the traditions of the French church. L'Avenir vehemently denounced the Gallicanism of the French episcopacy, and rejected all appeals to conciliarism.[135] In February 1831 a riot broke out in Paris. The republicans behind it attacked the church of Saint Germain l'Auxerrois, a site of veneration for the now deposed Bourbon dynasty. To make matters worse they ransacked the palace of the archbishop of Paris.[136] The church hierarchy blamed *L'Avenir* for having inflamed the passions of the people against the episcopacy. Most Gallican and royalist bishops wrote pastoral letters to their flock denouncing Lamennais' ideas and banned them from reading *L'Avenir*.[137]

Lamennais had come to believe that the papacy, if shorn of political power, would enjoy a huge rise in moral authority. For these radicals, the pope had nothing to lose from renouncing his sovereignty and everything to gain in terms of prestige. Liberal democracy would allow the Holy See to regain complete authority over the church, which had been usurped by absolute monarchies since the early modern period (during the first half of the nineteenth century kings still appointed 555 out of the total of 646 bishops in Europe).[138] These ideas touched a raw nerve for the church.

In other circumstances Rome might have tolerated or tempered these young idealists' initiatives to rejuvenate the church, but now revolutionary contagion had spread to the pope's own kingdom. In February 1831 the people of Modena rebelled against their duke,[139] and this uprising spread into nearby Parma.[140] The insurgents soon entered the papal legations of Bologna, Ferrara and Ravenna, provinces that had fared well under Napoleonic rule and had been reluctant to return to papal government in 1815.[141] Its elites needed little incentive to rebel. They deeply resented the administrative inefficiency and reactionary nature of theocratic rule. Embarrassingly most of the pontifical troops joined them in a mutiny and hoisted the Italian tricolour (the flag of Napoleon's north Italian realm). The eruption of revolution within his own kingdom made Gregory XVI suspicious of all attempts to reconcile the church with liberalism.

The revolutionaries declared themselves the Province Unite Italiane. They set up a provisional government which deposed the pope in Romagna and declared independence.[142] Gregory XVI, alarmed that over half his kingdom was in open rebellion, begged the Austrians to provide military support. In April 1831 Habsburg troops crossed the frontier and restored papal government in the legations at the point of their bayonets.[143] The reliance on foreign troops was a stark reminder that many of the pope's subjects deeply resented his government. While on the surface these revolutions proclaimed liberty as their rallying cry, there was also a growing nationalist feeling emerging in Belgium, Poland and Italy. During the first half of the nineteenth century, the link between nationhood and the state remained unclear.[144] The revolutionaries of the 1830s had a vague sense that rulers should share the language and culture of those they governed. This incipient sense of nationhood was spreading, especially among the educated liberal elites of European cities. The church in the nineteenth century was to have a vexed relationship with the passions aroused by nationalism.[145]

Seeing the monarchies of Europe challenged, and the church's doctrines called into question, Gregory XVI felt hostile towards the apostles of change. The papacy would deal with new states pragmatically, but would not recognise their legitimacy. Unlike the revolutions in Belgium or France, the Polish rebellion ended in bloody repression, as Tsar Nicholas I poured troops into his defiant Polish kingdom.[146] The Poles were routed in battle, their revolutionary leaders either executed or forced into exile. As ever, the tsar treated the church as subordinate to his authority and gave few concessions to the Catholic minority in his empire. Rome's initial temporising over events in Warsaw proved a deep disappointment to Europe's liberals.

Lamennais began to realise that Rome was increasingly alienated by his politics and teachings. His ultramontane stance, which had won him so many plaudits with the Curia during the 1820s, had now been transformed by his endorsement of liberalism, democracy and the prioritisation of the social question. By mid-1831 it was clear that the Gallican episcopacy had closed ranks against him and condemned his doctrines. Subscriptions to L'Avenir dropped by half as pious Catholics obeyed the order of their bishops to stay away from this heterodox publication.[147] The last number appeared on 15 November 1831. In it Lamennais had a surprise for his readers: 'It is said, that we have been condemned in Rome. So be it! It is to Rome that we will go to listen to our verdict and prostrate ourselves before the chair of Saint Peter.'[148] He concluded this final editorial with the ultramontane exhortation: 'Rome, Rome, Rome!'

Travelling with Montalembert and Lacordaire, Lamennais set off on the journey to the heart of Catholicism. For his friends (with whom he shared a deep sense of spiritual intimacy), Felicité's mental health was a growing cause for concern. During the journey, he was assailed by panic attacks and manic delusions.[149] He became convinced, in fits of paranoia, that the Austrian Chancellor Prince Metternich had turned the pope against him.[150] On 30 December 1831 the travellers reached Rome and were greeted by indifference. Most cardinals refused to receive them or listen to their pleas. It seemed as if a papal audience might prove impossible.[151]

The man who ultimately broke this impasse was Cardinal Pacca. This reactionary, now seventy-five years of age, was cardinal vicar of Rome and as such exercised the pope's spiritual authority over the city. He received the petition of these French visitors asking to have their ideas judged positively by the church. On 3 February 1832 the pope accepted a long report from the deputation outlining their views on the politics of the church. The promise was made that a committee would examine the document and respond to it. However, as this would take many months Pacca advised the travellers to return to Paris and await the verdict there.[152]

The papacy had other, larger problems. It was facing an unexpected international crisis. There was lingering resentment in the legations of Romagna after the forcible reimposition of papal rule in 1831. Once the Austrian army withdrew, the local population refused to pay any taxes. This situation escalated after the murder of some papal officials. It was clear that the local authorities were failing to reimpose order. Gregory XVI requested that the Habsburg field marshal Josef Radetzky return with troops to repress the simmering rebellion.[153] France feared that this move constituted a power grab by Austria in Northern Italy.

During the night of 22 February, the residents of the Adriatic port of Ancona woke to witness the disembarkation of a regiment of French soldiers, who occupied the citadel and harbour. France's government proclaimed that they would remain in this papal port for as long as Habsburg troops garrisoned the legations. More alarming still, the naval commander in charge of the operation proclaimed to the local population that he was part of an advance army that would free Italy from foreign rule. He disbanded the papal administration and raised a local civic guard.[154]

Lamennais was unlucky to be in Rome at a time when the Curia felt that liberal France was out of control. His timing could not have been worse, and his decision to remain, despite Cardinal Pacca's hints that he should return home, caused embarrassment. But his persistence paid off. In March, after almost three months, he was finally granted an audience. On 13 March the delegation of three from *L'Avenir* entered the Vatican. To Lamennais' profound chagrin he discovered that he would be introduced to Gregory XVI by the Cardinal-duc de Rohan, who had publicly condemned him in France.[155] The audience was a deep and humiliating disappointment. The pope was kind, offering them snuff and enquiring about the visitors' impressions of Rome. He asked about affairs in France and their opinion of the occupation of Ancona, and apparently joked that: 'The French will either all go to hell or to heaven but there is no purgatory for them.'[156] Whenever Lamennais tried to turn the conversation to *L'Avenir* and its doctrines, the pope awkwardly changed the subject. In a moment of bizarre banality, he asked if the group had yet had the chance to visit St Peter's. After fifteen minutes the audience ended, the visitors were ushered out, and presented with medals depicting St Gregory the Great. *L'Avenir's* mission to Rome had been a dismal failure.[157] Given this disappointing result, Lacordaire returned to Paris, while Felicité walked the ruins and catacombs of the city like a ghost.[158]

On 9 June 1832 the pope issued the brief *Cum primum* to the Catholic bishops of Poland reminding them of their allegiance to their God-given sovereign, the Russian tsar.[159] Liberals across Europe viewed the pope's condemnation of the insurrection as a betrayal of the persecuted Poles. Lamennais wrote to his brother Jean wondering if this was a sign that he should resume publishing *L'Avenir* in defence of persecuted liberal Catholics.[160] In a moment of self-delusion he wondered whether Rome's silence over his ideas amounted to a tacit encouragement to resume his work. On 9 July Lamennais and the young Comte de Montalembert decided to return home at leisurely pace, making a detour to Bavaria.

It was now that his Gallican enemies decided to unite. Paul d'Astros, the archbishop of Toulouse, resented the arrogance of this band of youths. He himself was above reproach, as he had suffered imprisonment during the Napoleonic empire. As vicar general of Paris in 1809–10 he had helped Pius VII smuggle documents out of Savona. D'Astros had also played a key role in coordinating clerical opposition to the emperor.[161] Incensed by Lamennais' liberal Catholicism, and his continued denigration of Gallicanism, d'Astros issued the 'censure of Toulouse' against fifty-six propositions to be found in Lamennais' writings of the previous fifteen years. This document was countersigned by a dozen Gallican bishops. It arrived in Rome on 28 July and influenced those sitting in judgement of *L'Avenir's* doctrines.[162]

Felicité and Montalembert were blissfully unaware that the Gallican episcopacy had united to denounce *L'Avenir* and its editor as heretical. The weary travellers reached Munich on 12 August. They arrived during a furious thunderstorm, which seemed portentous to Lamennais' unsettled mind. In this great city, a group of liberal Catholics from Paris had gathered to greet their master. The group included many German admirers, foremost among them the theologian Ignaz Döllinger.[163] After some sightseeing Felicité was invited to enjoy a banquet in his honour. Towards the end of the meal, some Bavarians, who had imbibed generous quantities of alcohol, apparently decided to give a performance of boisterous alpine yodelling to entertain their distinguished guest. Unexpectedly a waiter bearing a note on a silver platter approached him. He informed the editor of *L'Avenir* that an official from the nunciature in Munich wished to speak to him. Whilst the yodelling continued Lamennais briefly disappeared from the table, returning pale and trembling with a forced smile, holding a packet of papers. The yodelling abruptly ceased as Felicité slumped into his seat.[164]

His friends enquired what had happened. He replied that he had been given a copy of a new encyclical from the pope, entitled *Mirari vos*. It was a direct condemnation of liberalism, which implicitly rejected *L'Avenir* and its doctrines. In it Gregory XVI rejected, point by point, the programme of reform advocated by Lamennais in the pages of his newspaper. He stated unequivocally:

> Nor can We predict happier times for religion and government from the plans of those who desire vehemently to separate the Church from the state, and to break the mutual concord between temporal authority and the priesthood. It is certain that that concord which was always was favourable and beneficial for the sacred and the civil order is feared by the shameless lovers of liberty.[165]

As if the contents of *Mirari vos* were not bad enough, there was also a letter from Cardinal Pacca. This stated explicitly that His Holiness disapproved of Lamennais' doctrines, reforms and ideas as expressed in *L'Avenir*. In the light of the French thinker's great talent and former services to the church, Gregory had decided not to name him, nor his newspaper, in the encyclical.

His friends noticed that he entered a catatonic state and sat motionless in his chair in the Munich restaurant. Later, Lamennais described his condition as a kind of spiritual death. As he limped out of the restaurant, all he could say to his friends was: 'the encyclical has now appeared, it condemns us, we must submit to it'.[166] He was agonised at not being able to defend the Polish people from the despotism of tsarist Russia. Yet, with Montalembert, he agreed that *L'Avenir* would not resume publication. This undertaking was solemnised in a letter written to Cardinal Pacca on 10 September 1832.[167] Lammenais could not stomach staying in Paris, where the conservative press rubbed salt into his gaping wounds. He retired to the manor house of La Chênaie in Brittany, which he and his brother Jean had inherited from their grandfather in 1799.[168] Here he spent months brooding and praying for inspiration. It would take significant self-sacrifice for Lamennais to swallow his pride and renounce his ideas.

What followed was to be a comedy of errors. As was predictable, at La Chênaie Felicité fell into a profound depression. He read the book of the Apocalypse feverishly, and St John's visions of Armageddon haunted his waking dreams. He began to believe that humans faced a similar battle in which democracy and liberty would have to battle against the forces of despotism and industrial slavery.[169] His own imagination filled with visions of evil reigning supreme in the world. To distract him, Montalembert sent Lamennais a translation of Adam Mickiewicz's *Books of the Polish People and of the Polish Pilgrimage*. During his time in Rome Lammenais had written a poem in honour of the Polish Revolution. It was agreed with Mickiewicz's French translator and publisher that his ode would be added to the *Polish Pilgrimage*.[170] Once it went to press it was clear that Lamennais' retraction of his liberal Catholicism had not been authentic.

In the spring of 1833 d'Astros decided to reopen the issue and crush this restless dissident once and for all. In a letter to Gregory XVI the archbishop of Toulouse insisted that Lamennais needed to issue a more convincing and sincere retraction. On 8 May 1833, the pope replied that he agreed with d'Astros, and that he was concerned about recent publications and voices emerging from Paris.[171] Rome decided to press Lamennais for a full, public and unequivocal retraction of all his errors. Between the summer and winter of 1833 Lamennais sent no fewer than three declarations to Rome, but each time the pope considered them insufficient and replied that an unconditional renunciation of his doctrines was required.[172] Those who knew Lamennais well could see that the strain he was undergoing was severely damaging his mental health. During this time, he received a stream of famous visitors. These included renowned authors like Victor Hugo, Alphonse de Lamartine and Pierre Simon Ballanche.[173] He was fast coming to be seen as a martyr persecuted by the church establishment. After months of correspondence and fruitless negotiation, on 11 December 1833 Lamennais sent his fourth, final and briefest declaration to Gregory XVI. He unequivocally renounced all past errors and promised obedience.[174] After many months the case seemed to be closed.

In Rome his note recanting his ideas was received in triumph, and the Curia thought it had scored a complete victory against this troublesome and rebellious priest. On 28 December 1833 a papal epistle, jubilantly welcoming Lamennais back into the bosom of the church, was despatched to Paris.[175] On 10 January 1834 the carriage of the archbishop of Paris drove down the rue de Vaugirard, the street where Felicité lived in Paris. He walked into the apartment and embraced the former rebel, giving him two kisses on his cheeks. He announced that all was well, and that the pope had enthusiastically received his declaration. After Lamennais had read the letter from Gregory XVI he smiled bitterly. The archbishop offered to help him compose a letter of thanks for what he called the 'pope's clemency'. Lamennais wondered if this was truly necessary and joked that his words could be misinterpreted, and that he would be forced to write several versions of his note of thanks.[176] The archbishop accepted that now was not the right time but emphasised that an obedient priest would soon thank his sovereign pontiff for his forgiveness.

Far from settling the issue, Lamennais found his retraction hard to swallow. He spoke wildly about travelling to the Orient and leaving his woes behind him. Those who knew him soon became aware that Felicité was up to something. In March 1834 he was seen giving his friend, the literary critic Charles Augustin Sainte-Beuve, a manuscript to take to his publisher.[177] Lamennais then returned to La Chênaie and waited. Paris was filled with rumours that an incendiary book was about to appear. In late April, when Felicité met with his brother the abbé Jean, he had much to tell him. He admitted to Jean that he had refused to sign a letter of thanks to the pope. Graver still, he had written a booklet in which he revealed how despotism and evil pervaded the modern world. He simply could not remain silent. It was his duty to denounce the individualism and the authoritarian nightmare under which people were forced to live.[178] Jean begged his brother to relent and not publish his new text. According to family tradition, Felicité relented and gave his brother written instructions for his publisher to withdraw the booklet. Jean ran to the nearest postal town of Dinan and sent a courier to the publisher, Renduel, ordering him to stop the presses – but it was too late.

The next day, 30 April 1834, the shelves of Paris bookshops were filled with a work entitled *Paroles d'un Croyant* (*Words of a Believer*). It was to become a publishing sensation, with rough estimates stating that over 100,000 copies sold within the first two months!* Within months pirated editions and translations appeared in Brussels, London, Amsterdam and Geneva. This 200-page booklet was inspired by the book of the Apocalypse in its content and style, full of infernal visions and forebodings.[179] Lammenais argued in this prophetic text that all systems of politics and organised religions were a tissue of lies that hid selfishness, oppression and exploitation. True Christianity was not to be found in Rome and the corruption of the Curia, but in a future that would be built through liberal revolution. Charles Saint-Beuve and other liberals praised the lyricism and visionary power of *Paroles d'un Croyant*.[180] For the Gallican episcopacy and royalist clergy, it was proof that at last the mask was off! Behind the ultramontane Lamennais lay a hypocrite who had been happy to preach loyalty to the pope only so long as it gave him fame and public adulation.

Lamennais had externalised the inner conflict that ravaged his soul. He came to the bitter realisation that his personal convictions clashed with the institution he had served for most of his life. For him, the priority for all political systems and religions should be to build a moral community cemented in social solidarity. By rejecting the authority of the papacy, he created a breach with his brother Jean that proved irreconcilable. Even his friends Montalembert and Lacordaire no longer could support him. *Paroles d'un Croyant* cemented his reputation as a brilliant author but ended his ecclesiastical career.[181]

Rome's reaction was swift. On 25 June 1834 Gregory XVI issued the encyclical *Singulari nos*. It condemned Lamennais'

---

* Anywhere between 100,000 and 300,000 copies were sold, according to Villefosse, *Lamennais, ou l'occasion manquée*, p. 173.

newest publication forcefully and without reservation, stating that: 'though small in size, it is enormous in wickedness'.[182] The pope was scandalised by its subversive content and demonic visions. He denounced its attempt to dissolve all political and ecclesiastical authority that would lead to anarchy. The encyclical ended, somewhat disingenuously, by leaving the door open for Lammenais to return to the church on condition he accept its authority. Although he was not excommunicated, the author of the *Paroles* had gone too far to return to Catholicism.

After 1834, Lamennais was not merely a schismatic but an apostate priest. He would embrace Christian socialism as his new cause and produce a great many works denouncing the conditions of the poor and of factory workers. He published a deeply influential essay entitled 'Modern Slavery' in 1839.* This showed how the capitalist economy had created a new and insidious type of bondage. Catholicism was now part of the problem rather than the solution.[183] He would spend the rest of his life involved in socialist politics. After the 1848 revolution he was elected to the National Assembly, where he supported the national workshops which provided paid work for the unemployed.[184] He eventually died in 1854 and was buried in the Père Lachaise cemetery in Paris. According to his wishes, he was placed in a common grave without any ritual or Christian liturgy, to be mourned by a new generation of writers and socialists, who saw him as a role model.[185] His family and the friends of his youth stayed away, his abandonment of the church too painful to contemplate even twenty years later.

It is tempting to dismiss Lamennais as the road not taken by nineteenth-century Catholicism. While there is some truth in this, it should not be forgotten that his pre-1834 writings provided for a very different type of liberal Roman church. This was a project that Lamennais himself abandoned by becoming a radical Christian socialist. His early writings were not the end but rather the beginning of new currents in Catholic thinking. Liberal and

---

* An English translation can be found in Richard A. Lebrun and Sylvain Milbach (eds), *Lamennais: A Believer's Revolutionary Politics* (Studies in the History of Political Thought, Vol. 13) (Leiden, 2018), pp. 279–98.

social Catholicism survived Lamennais' condemnation by Gregory XVI, and his subsequent apostasy.[186] Although the papacy and the Curia remained hostile to the teachings and legacy of his early writing, Lamennais remained an inspiration for others. Followers like Montalembert, Lacordaire, and his brother Jean continued to pursue a progressive form of Catholicism that would oppose the individualism and materialism of the nineteenth century.[187] They never saw their friend Felicité again, but although they continued the legacy and work of the liberal Catholicism enshrined by *L'Avenir,* the *Paroles* of 1834 created rifts that would never heal. He had gone too far.

His former travelling companion, Lacordaire, in 1835 and 1836 gave a series of Lenten homilies inside Notre Dame cathedral which may have been attended by as many as six thousand people. It reinvigorated the idea of preaching to the masses of Paris which had been neglected since the revolutionary conflagration of the 1790s.[188] He appealed to priests to mix persuasion, philosophy, poetry and emotion in their weekly sermons. Although Lacordaire had broken with his former master he continued to believe, as a Dominican friar, that teaching the faith to the masses was fundamental to his vocation. A young university student, Frédéric Ozanam, who had been friendly with Lamennais during the years of *L'Avenir,* founded the St Vincent de Paul Society in 1833.[189] This association encouraged its members to organise themselves to promote prayer and contemplation, but at the heart of the society was an emphasis on good works. Its members have a particular mission to minister to the hungry and homeless.* Nothing could represent better the sense of social solidarity and community that lay at the heart of Lamennais' social vision.

Even some who had been hostile to the radicalism of *L'Avenir* came to appreciate its social mission. The former royalist prefect Alban de Villeneuve Bargemon had been a vocal opponent of

---

* According to its website the society today has almost two million members in 150 countries and ministers to thirty million people in need. See International Confederation of the Saint Vincent de Paul Society, online at https://www.ssvpglobal.org/about-us/ [accessed 21 June 2021].

revolution throughout his career.[190] Yet out of a sense of paternalism and *noblesse oblige,* he argued that both state and church had a duty to provide for the needs of the most indigent members of society. Conservatives and Catholics were active in advocating a paternalistic welfare state during the 1820s and 1830s. They did so not out of a belief in equality and social justice, but because they saw helping the needy as part of their divinely ordained duty. Classical liberals saw poverty as the outcome of bad life choices and inevitable market outcomes and made little provision to assist the poor.[191]

Prior to the emergence of Marxism, throughout the nineteenth century several elite Catholics urged the state to provide food, medical care, education and pensions for the weakest and poorest members of society. Villeneuve Bargemon published a three-volume study entitled *Christian Political Economy* in the same year as Lamennais issued his *Paroles.*[192] It was a mixture of statistical analysis, describing the condition of the poor, with proposals for charitable institutions that would minister to their needs. Unlike liberal laissez-faire economists, Villeneuve Bargemon urged the state to introduce reforms that would assist the indigent. He particularly believed in education as the keys means of escaping poverty. In 1841 he would collaborate with Montalembert to introduce a law restricting child labour in factories.[193]

Their mantle would be picked up by Albert, Comte de Mun during the 1870s, when he created, with other aristocrats, the Catholic worker circles. These associations sought to provide succour and education to the downtrodden workforce of modern industrial systems. They hoped to create a mass movement which would support an ultramontane church, aristocratic paternalism and French royalism. As we will see, such movements revived social Catholic priorities, but failed dismally to persuade workers that monarchy would protect their interests better than democracy.[194] Such reformers, like the former editors of *L'Avenir,* were deeply critical of the exploitation of workers by factory owners. Although Lamennais had left the church, his legacy in France was picked up by Catholics who prioritised social issues and the evangelisation of the masses.

Lamennais' influence was not confined to France. After 1834, many Catholics in Belgium, Germany and Italy were drawn to his early writings. They recalibrated his ideas to their own tastes and local contexts. Those inspired by him in Italy emphasised his ultramontane tendencies and his liberal ideas about nationalism. The 1830s had been a decade of crisis for the Papal States in its international relations. France's occupation of Ancona only ended in 1838, after Habsburg forces withdrew from Ferrara and crossed the north bank of the Po.[195] There was a sense that the Papal States would find it difficult to maintain their position of neutrality as long as their inefficient and unpopular government was so deeply resented by their subjects. The constant threat of domestic rebellion necessitated regular foreign military intervention.

The people of Emilia-Romagna loathed Gregory XVI's government, which refused any reform, let alone representative government. In 1843 Rimini was taken by a group of insurgents, who tried to seize nearby Ravenna as well, but were repulsed.[196] Although papal troops eventually restored order, Field Marshal Radetsky had once again placed Austrian regiments and warships at the ready. There was a sense that Chancellor Metternich's goodwill was all that stood between the papal government and its disgruntled subjects in Romagna.

The papacy's appreciation of nascent Italian nationalism prior to 1848 was ambivalent. Italy's sense of nationhood was far from well established throughout the peninsula. The term *campanilismo* describes the loyalty felt towards the bell tower of the local town. For many Italians, municipal loyalties were often stronger than national bonds (something that persists to the present day).[197] Most of the peasantry had little interest in the romantic and intellectual nationalism of the elites of the towns and cities. Their priorities were more prosaic, focused on subsisting in a preindustrial world where the supply of food was never guaranteed. Catholicism provided a far stronger identity in this rural world than any ethnocentric nationalism.

Even among patriotic elites there were major disagreements about how a united Italy might be achieved. A Jacobin minority dreamed of a unitary republic, while others believed only a federal Italy would work.[198] The term *risorgimento* (rebirth or resurrection) came to describe this Romantic movement striving for Italian nationhood. In its earliest incarnation it had noteworthy religious elements. Perhaps the most significant figure here was Vincenzo Giobèrti, an intellectual Piedmontese priest who had published widely in the fields of philosophy and theology. He had been made a court chaplain in Turin.[199] He was inspired, to an extent, by Lamennais' vision of a regenerated Christian society, but disagreed vehemently with him when it came to extreme liberalism.[200] At first, he was on good terms with King Charles Albert and was much respected at the Sabaudian court. However, by the late 1820s Gioberti was beginning to show sympathy for the revolutionary Giuseppe Mazzini and his Giovane Italia (Young Italy), a secret society of republican revolutionaries.[201] Although there was little direct evidence of his collusion with this organisation, Gioberti was arrested and held without charge for four months in 1834. He was then exiled to Paris and eventually settled in Brussels, where he taught philosophy and wrote for a living.[202]

Although a reader of liberal Catholic literature, Gioberti was much closer, in theological terms, to the Jansenists and reform Catholics of the eighteenth century. He disliked what he saw as the ostentatious, irrational and idolatrous worship of Counter Reformation Catholicism. He published a five-volume work entitled *Il Gesuita Moderno* (*The Modern Jesuit*, 1845–6) in which he sought to revivify the black legend of the Jesuit order.[203] He claimed that they were behind all the evils that afflicted both the church and the state. In its tone and style it was an early example of the sort of conspiracy theory which was rife among more traditionalist nationalists. In his convoluted and dense prose, Gioberti indicted the Jesuit order as part of a dark plot against modernity and progress. In contrast to Lamennais' Romanticism, Gioberti was a child of the eighteenth-century Catholic Enlightenment. However, unlike the Jansenists, he was not quite so Gallican in his tendencies.

The most important work he published during his exile was *Il Primato morale e civile degli Italiani* (*The Moral and Civil Primacy of the Italians*), a historical, literary, philosophical and cultural vindication of Italian genius throughout the centuries, listing the accomplishments and achievements of Italian culture. [204] Its pages place the thinkers, artists and philosophers of the peninsula at the forefront of European liberal progress. For Gioberti, at the heart of this Italian cultural ebullience lay Catholicism and the presence of the papacy in the very centre of Italy. This school of thought came to be known as the Neo-Guelphs, named after the faction that supported the papacy's rights in Italy during the medieval period against the power of the emperor.[205] For Gioberti the great strength of Italy was that the papacy made it at once culturally homogenous and cosmopolitan. This paradox was at the heart of Italy's relationship with the pope. As he put it:

> Italy and the Holy See are certainly two distinct and essentially different entities. It would be an absurd, not to say a wicked and sacrilegious, endeavour to confound them. Nevertheless, a marriage of eighteen centuries has united them in brotherhood to the extent that if one can be Catholic without being Italian (indeed it would be ridiculous to suggest otherwise), one cannot be a perfect Italian without being Catholic. One cannot merit the first title without participating in the splendour of the second. And in religious terms the pope does not belong to Italy any more than he belongs to any other nation and is a cosmopolitan figure. Yet in civil society [the papacy] created Italian genius and is indissolubly linked to it. One can say in truth that Italy spiritually is of the pope, as the pope is materially inside Italy. This relationship is akin in psychological terms to the body being in the spirit whereas philosophically the spirit is in the body.[206]

Ultimately Italian cultural unity and progress could be attributed to the beneficent influence of the papacy. Equally, the cosmopolitan ability to relate to other nations was inherent in the pope's mission as Christ's vicar to the universal church. Gioberti expressed the belief, or hope, that the best chance for Italian unity lay in a federation of the princes of the peninsula, operating under the presidency of the pope.[207] Only the papacy could provide the guidance and moral authority to unite Italians.

Gregory XVI was not taken with Gioberti's vision. He distrusted the true motives of liberal and reform Catholics in Italy. He had a sneaking suspicion that those who desired national unity were in fact crypto-revolutionaries and republicans. For this traditionalist pope, upholding his sovereignty in central Italy against the encroachments of European powers and radicals remained the priority.[208] Unlike Lamennais and Gioberti, Gregory believed that the problems of the present could be solved with solutions from the past. There was little hope for movement on liberalism and nationalism as long as this conservative pontiff remained at the helm of the Papal States.

A different source of inspiration for liberal Catholicism was offered by Antonio Rosmini-Serbati, from Trento, on the southern fringes of the Tyrolian Alps. Rosmini was much taken with Lamennais' vision of using the church to revitalise social solidarity in post-Napoleonic society. During the 1820s Rosmini had met Lamennais, whom he found fascinating, and had asked to stay in touch with the leader of the ultramontane movement in France. Yet when Rosmini wrote to him in Paris he was rebuffed by a curt note stating that Lammenais was too busy to write. Although irked by this refusal, the young Antonio formed an important network of ecclesiastical and literary friends in Milan and Rome. These included the future Gregory XVI and Alessandro Manzoni, whose novel *The Betrothed* remains one of the pillars of the modern Italian language.[209] Like Gioberti, Rosmini was a Neo-Guelph who saw the papacy as the foundation of Italian identity and a force for progress.

In 1828 he founded the Institute of Charity, otherwise known as the Rosminians.[210] This religious congregation was supposed to combine the monastic quest for self-perfection with charity for the poor and active ministering to the spiritual needs of the community. It sought to fight the individualism and materialism of post-revolutionary society by instilling a sense of solidarity within communities. The order was quite successful in northern Italy, especially at the Monte Calvario, near Domodossola in

Piedmont, which became its mother hub. The order would become especially prominent in its attempts to minister and provide relief to the Irish peasantry, in particular during the horrific potato famine of 1847.*

Rosmini, like Lamennais, was a critic of laissez-faire economics. He believed that the church, once liberated from the allure of power and the temptations of wealth, would increase its moral authority. This placed him squarely in the camp of the liberal Catholics. During the 1830s he secretly wrote a treatise entitled *Delle Cinque Piaghe della Santa Chiesa (On the Five Wounds of the Church)*, which would only be published openly in 1848.[211] In it he argued that five ills deeply afflicted the church:

1. The gulf that divided the clergy from the laity.
2. Poor clerical education.
3. Divisions among the episcopacy.
4. The crown's power to appoint bishops to most vacant dioceses.
5. The abuse and mismanagement of ecclesiastical wealth.

Rosmini hoped that the papacy could act as a driving force in improving the clergy, de-politicising the episcopacy and leading to the moral reinvigoration of society.[212] Gioberti, Rosmini and Manzoni shared the Jansenist focus on sobriety and austerity in worship, but they did not share the eighteenth century's scepticism of papal claims to primacy. There is little in their writings about conciliarism. They wanted the shy and grudging Gregory XVI to move from a siege mentality to active engagement with liberal Catholics in Italy, France, Belgium, Germany and Poland.

The pope not only gave them a cold shoulder, but when it came to the civil wars raging in Spain and Portugal, in both cases favoured the reactionary (and losing) sides.[213] To the Curia's chagrin both conservative claimants, Dom Miguel of Portugal

---

* Francesco Zavatti, 'Charity as Social Justice: Antonio Rosmini and the Great Irish Famine', *Journal of Ecclesiastical History*, Vol. 72, No. 3 (2021), pp. 573–89.

and Don Carlos of Spain, were defeated and would spend the rest of their reactionary lives in exile. This gave the liberal governments in Madrid and Lisbon the pretext to unleash a wave of anticlerical legislation, which stepped up state control over the Iberian clergy. The number of dioceses was reduced and there was also some violence against monastic clergy in Madrid during the riots known as the *matanza de los frailes* (massacre of monks) of 1834, and more widely in Catalonia.[214] Despite the inauspicious decades of the 1830s and 1840s, however, the Spanish clerical establishment did recover and would experience remarkable growth later in the century.

Gregory's conservativism was tempered by pragmatism. In December 1845 Tsar Nicholas I visited Rome to meet with the pope. He attempted to persuade Gregory to consent to the marriage of his daughter, Grand Duchess Olga, to a Catholic Habsburg prince. Given that Gregory XVI had urged Polish bishops to accept the tsar's legitimate authority, all observers expected that this Habsburg match would be easy to secure. The tsar was received on two occasions in private audiences,[215] in which the ageing pontiff surprised Nicholas by severely criticising his tyrannical repression of Polish national aspirations. Gregory reminded the tsar that he would be accountable to God for his actions and urged him to treat his Polish subjects more leniently. The audiences ended in failure and the tsar failed to receive permission for his daughter's marriage.[216]

The church in the decades following the Congress of Vienna has been often criticised for following a reactionary and counter-revolutionary line. There is some truth in this and it is difficult to deny that popes Leo XII, Pius VIII and Gregory XVI could be described as 'grumpy old men' in their responses to modernity. Napoleon's kidnapping of Pius VII and the annexation of the Papal States had left a deep psychological scar on the papacy. It felt under threat from the modern state and became paranoid whenever its prerogatives were threatened. Nineteenth-century popes were determined to maintain their temporal sovereignty unwaveringly. Without Habsburg muscle, the temporal power of the popes was unviable. So the papacy was forced to rely on the protection of monarchies and empires. It had neither the inclination nor the incentive to change. A policy of conservativism was seen as the best hope for the preservation of the Papal States.

Many Catholics, as distinct from the papacy, did not share this backward-looking mentality. A radical new generation of religious men and women felt alienated by the post-Napoleonic world. For them, the French Revolution had atomised society and the Catholic Church was not the problem but the solution. They argued that the church and the new order could help each other. The revolutions in South America were not intrinsically anticlerical. Progress did not have to be anti-religious or Jacobin in flavour. Inspired by their re-reading of Catholic history and culture, these activists believed that a streamlined church, led by the papacy, could regenerate society and create new forms of social solidarity. To an extent, it was liberal Catholics who made the welfare state conceivable through their paternalistic impulse to provide charitable institutions for the poor. If Lamennais had been more patient, these new initiatives might have transformed Catholicism beyond recognition. The papacy's outright condemnation of *L'Avenir* was exacerbated by the demand that he provide an unconditional retraction of his liberal views. Such severity pushed Lamennais onto a collision course with an ultramontane movement he had once eulogised. His eventual apostasy placed him beyond the pale and even his closest friends abandoned him. Despite this, liberal Catholicism and social Catholicism, although defeated in the 1830s, were not dead. They would remain in suspended animation within the church throughout the rest of the nineteenth century.

Counterintuitively, the Restoration was a time of intellectual ferment and rejuvenation of religious culture and practice for the Roman church. After the maelstrom of revolution and the persecution of clergy in France, Belgium and Italy had ended, the number of men in holy orders and women in convents grew rapidly. When Napoleon fell there were approximately 30,000 secular priests in France; by 1830 this had risen to 40,000, and would reach a peak of 58,000 in 1878.[217] Similar trends could be seen in the regular orders: after 1814 there were about 13,000 female religious in France, but by 1880 this number had grown to a peak of 100,000.[218] Such numbers were mirrored, although not matched, by male monastic congregations and mendicant orders. The male return to contemplative life did resume, but the numbers were far short of those of the *ancien régime*.

Outside of France this phenomenon, known as the Catholic revival, accelerated significantly during the second half of the nineteenth century. A rise in clerical and religious vocations was matched by the laity's rediscovery of the mystery and magnificence of baroque Catholicism. There is some evidence that congregations took to flamboyant processions and ornate rituals with relish.[219] In 1831 the visions of the Virgin Mary experienced by Catherine Labouré, in her convent in the rue du Bac in Paris, emphasised how, in this Romantic age, many longed for the solace offered by the supernatural.[220] The miraculous medal given to Catherine by the mother of God became an emblem of religious rebirth. Thousands of these ornaments were worn around the necks of the faithful who through them rediscovered the immanence of the sacred in their daily lives. This thirst for divine intervention would only become greater as the century evolved. Catholicism, for Romantics, seemed to provide answers where science and rationalism could not. It transformed the cold realities of fatality into redemption and hope.

Although Gregory XVI focused on preserving the Papal States and forestalling revolution, his policies outside Europe were more accommodating. He gradually recognised and accepted the emergence of a post-imperial church in South America with the bull *Sollicitudo ecclesiarum* in 1831. As already indicated, this allowed Catholicism to consolidate its position and, in many instances, especially in Mexico, to grow in power and influence. He also presided over a church whose missionary objectives around the globe were much more ambitious than ever before. Apostolic vicars were established in Korea, Sri Lanka and Calcutta. The church had not given up the idea of gaining converts in the Far East.[221]

New religious orders were created to keep up the missionary momentum and the propagation of the faith in Africa, too. Admittedly, expansion proved to be slow during these decades.

The nineteenth century, especially after 1870, was to be an age of vast missionary expansion for Western Christianity, coinciding with the acquisition of new territories by European empires.[222] Gregory XVI laid the groundwork for this future attempt to bring Catholicism to non-Europeans. As ever, the results of these initiatives left a mixed legacy.

On 3 December 1839, Gregory reiterated in the bull *In supremo apostolatus fastigo* the papal ban on the Atlantic slave trade and the mistreatment of native peoples. This renewed confirmation of Catholicism's proscription of slavery was long overdue.[223] Brazil had avoided revolution because the Portuguese royal family had relocated to this colony during the Napoleonic wars.[224] It was a unique case in history where the colony became the metropole for almost a decade. In 1822 independence was achieved with the creation of a Brazilian empire under the constitutional rule of a Portuguese royal. This allowed for a peaceful separation between the metropole and the colony, thus avoiding the bloody conflict which had torn hispanic America asunder.

Given this non-violent transition to independence, Brazilian society experienced far less change than elsewhere on the continent. At the heart of its economy lay the plantation complex, which was built on the misery of African slaves.[225] The local Luso-Brazilian church not only failed to criticise this arrangement, but on the contrary profited from it. Religious orders and convents were massive slave owners; the Benedictines alone owned thousands of displaced Africans. Despite being the largest Catholic country in the world (in terms of expanse), with 14 million inhabitants, the local church was tiny. A mere seven hundred secular priests ministered to hundreds of thousands of souls.[226] These religious were generally members of the colonial elite rather than outsiders and were little disposed towards missionary work, or seeking to change their society. In reality, the clergy did not venture far from the coastline into the Amazon basin. They mainly cared for the planters, rather than those kept in bondage. So, despite the papal proscription of slavery, this noxious practice continued well into the closing decades of the nineteenth century.

By the 1840s Catholicism had tried to deal with the challenges it faced through a mixture of failed innovation and more concerted reaction. After the unfortunate state visit of Nicholas I, the ageing Gregory XVI clung to life for another six months. When he passed away on 1 June 1846, many wondered in which direction his successor would lead the church. Liberal Catholics hoped forlornly that the cardinals might elect a pope who would be their ally, a man of God who would accept a less powerful Roman church and be far closer to the weak, poor and oppressed. A regenerated and morally triumphant Catholicism remained their aspiration. The conclave of 1846 would give them a glimmer of hope that their vision might be realised.

6

REVOLUTION IN ROME: PIO NONO AND THE ROMAN REPUBLIC OF 1846–50

Pellegrino Rossi, the third layman to hold the office of minister of the interior for the Papal States, ascended the grand staircase of Palazzo della Cancelleria. This building, which had been the seat of the Roman Curia, boasted a beautiful courtyard whose design was attributed to the great Renaissance architect Donato Bramate. Since March 1848, it had served as the first secular parliament in the history of the church.[1] Rossi, despite being surrounded by hostile crowds calling for his death, maintained his dignity and calm. He was a slender figure of average height, clean shaven with a slightly receding hairline. On 15 November 1848, the late autumn in Rome was very mild, and Rossi was not wearing an overcoat as he made his way up the marble steps. Suddenly a man rushed past the security cordon and struck the minister on his left side. He swooned, stumbled and was visibly dazed. Before he had a chance to recover another assailant, a short man with a moustache, surged forward and plunged a dagger into the right side of his neck. Blood gushed profusely from an artery and, within minutes, Rossi lay dead.[2]

The papal chamber of deputies, unperturbed, decided to continue with the order of business. Outside, the crowds rejoiced at the death of the hated and unpatriotic minister. His body was paraded through the streets as a trophy. Members of the revolutionary and patriotic club met in the Piazza del Popolo. There were cries of 'Blessed be the hand that struck Rossi!'[3] The next day, ten thousand armed men, accompanied by several mutinous civic guards, marched towards the Quirinal palace. They held pikes and muskets and were dragging some cannons. They demanded a popular head of government, independence for Italy and a wider suffrage. Arriving in Piazza di Monte Cavallo the crowd found the palace doors shut. They turned their artillery towards the main gates and opened fire. Soon, a side entrance of the Quirinal was burning. In the palace, the pope was in his state rooms, surrounded by the diplomatic corps and trusted advisers. Monsignor Giovanni Battista Palma, who edited the pope's pronouncements, edicts and briefs into courtly Latin, was standing by a window that looked on to the square below. Suddenly the men in the chamber heard the simultaneous sound of a gunshot and glass shattering and Palma fell backwards, mortally wounded.[4]

Mastai Ferretti, who all those years ago had accompanied Mgr Muzi to Argentina and Chile, was now Pius IX, supreme pontiff of the Catholic world. His loyal Swiss guards had been dismissed on 17 November and the Quirinal's security had been entrusted to unreliable civic guards (volunteers from Rome's bourgeoisie).[5] The situation was hopeless. As a man of peace, the pope wanted to avoid all bloodshed. With crowds becoming ever more menacing, concessions had to be made. It was agreed to appoint ministers acceptable to the revolutionaries in Rome. When it came to Italian independence, the issue was, in classic parliamentary fashion, referred to a committee.[6] This allowed for precious extra time in what was a truly critical situation for the papacy.

The prefect of the sacred palaces, Cardinal Giacomo Antonelli, had been preparing for the pope's flight for some time. His plan was audacious. Antonelli was among the last cardinals of the Roman church to take minor orders but he was never ordained a priest. He had risen through his administrative skills, and was a wily politician. His personal morality (he may have fathered a daughter) and cupidity were the stuff of legend, but he was at least competent. A mere forty-two years old – a stripling for a cardinal – with dark brown hair and of average build, he was to show remarkable zeal and energy in rescuing the pope from the revolution that was now engulfing his domains.[7] In coordination with the ambassadors in Rome and the chancelleries of Europe, Antonelli had devised a plan, whose full details were known only to himself and Pius IX.*

On the evening of 24 November 1848 the French ambassador, Eugène duc d'Harcourt, arrived for one of his regular audiences with the Holy Father. He spent an hour talking very loudly about the situation in Europe and the Papal States.[8] Unbeknown to the guards and his own entourage, during his visitor's discourse Pius IX had changed into a black cassock, put on a dark hat, and tinted spectacles. Antonelli had chosen this moment for the pope's flight, as it coincided with the changing of the guard. Pius left the palace through a back passage to find the carriage of Count Karl von Spaur, the Bavarian ambassador, awaiting him.[9] Inside was his wife, Teresa Giraud, a Roman aristocrat and one of the great beauties of the age, and the couple's son. The pope pretended to be the boy's tutor. Sometime later, Giraud would publish her reminiscences of the daring escape from the Papal States.[10] The Bavarian minister's carriage quietly left Rome with diplomatic passports for the occupants. Harcourt had been told by Antonelli that the pope would head for Civitavecchia and embark onboard a French naval vessel, the *Ténare*, sailing to Marseilles.[11] This was a deliberate lie. Antonelli wanted to ensure that if Harcourt fell into the hands of the revolutionaries, he would have no idea of the pontiff's real destination. On the same night Antonelli fled to the Spanish embassy, from which he escaped the city under a counterfeit passport.[12] To further confuse any hostile observers, quantities of clothes and effects belonging to the pope had been shipped out of the city in boxes described as charitable donations to the orphanages of southern Italy.

---

* In October the pope had received as a gift from the bishop of Valence a pyx that had belonged to Pius VI. This vessel had carried the holy eucharist when that luckless pontiff died a prisoner in revolutionary France. His successor, half a century later, treasured the relic, but was determined not to share the same fate as Pius VI. See Giacomo Martina, *Pio IX*, Vol. I: *1846–1850* (Rome, 1974), p. 298.

The civic guard were flabbergasted to find that the Quirinal palace had been abandoned and that Rome's diplomatic corps had fled. Initially, some suggested that the people should be told the pope had been kidnapped. In the end a proclamation announcing the pope's flight was circulated throughout the city. The radical deputy Carlo Luciano Bonaparte, a descendant of Napoleon's brother Lucien, put forward the motion that a constituent assembly be summoned to give central Italy a constitution. Not since Napoleon's annexation of Rome in 1809 had the Papal Sates experienced secular rule.[13] This time it was not imposed by a foreign power but was the fruit of a domestic revolution. It consummated the irreconcilable breach that had emerged between the pope's theocratic administration and his subjects.

Yet this dramatic outcome was entirely unforeseen. On 14 June 1846 Cardinal Mastai Ferretti, Bishop of Imola, had entered the conclave to elect the successor of Gregory XVI. This was the last papal election to take place in the Quirinal palace (after 1870 it became the official residence of the king of Italy), considered a more salubrious venue than the Vatican itself, which was too close to the humidity and stink of the River Tiber.[14] Mastai was renowned for his great piety and emphasis on the pastoral care of his flock. Although he was not bookish, apparently he had been presented with a copy of Gioberti's nationalist manifesto, the *Primato*, just before leaving Imola for the conclave.[15] A year before he had himself written a reform proposal for the administration of the Papal States. With his usual moderation he had advocated an end to violent repression but, at the same time, denounced liberalism and religious indifference. His pamphlet promoted a gradualist reform agenda, whose aim was to improve the administration of the church and the state.[16]

Mastai was not considered a likely candidate for the papacy, and had a reputation for being liberal. Most conclaves of the early nineteenth century lasted at least a month. It was a great surprise when white smoke wafted from the Quirinal roof after a mere three days. Mastai appeared on the balcony to great acclaim from the crowds below. He took the name Pius IX in honour of Pius VII, his predecessor at Imola. Unbeknown to him he would face similar challenges.[17]

As he was the first pope ever to be photographed, there is no doubt that the fifty-four-year-old Pius IX was somewhat corpulent, but this aspect of his physique was counterbalanced by a kindly and gentle face. He was keen to be loved by his new subjects, and began his pontificate with several measures aimed at pleasing the people of Rome. On 17 July he issued a full amnesty for political prisoners, as was traditional at the accession of a new pontiff. Although this pardon was technically open to all, the 'fine print' severely limited who was released from prison.[18] Nevertheless, crowds in Rome cheered the new pope's clemency and the mistaken impression was created that this new Pius was progressive. The decision to allow the installation of gas lighting and to begin railway construction in the Papal States was a marked contrast to Gregory XVI's obstinate refusal to accept new technology.[19] Commissions were appointed to overhaul and modernise the civil and criminal codes in central Italy. Programmes to stimulate the local economy and create new industries were authorised.

There seemed hope that Mastai might be the liberal pope predicted by Gioberti who would unify Italy. This promise seemed to be confirmed by Pius's emotive response to the cheering crowds. What the people of the Papal States did not realise was that their new sovereign was not a political animal. He was hungry to be popular, but he was emphatically not a radical revolutionary. His priorities were spiritual, and he certainly was not the national messiah foretold by the Neo-Guelphs. Yet this was not how the crowds perceived him. They regularly cheered him with the words 'Viva Pio Nono!'[20] On 9 November 1846 he issued his first encyclical *Qui pluribus*. Unlike his progressive administrative measures, this text was characterised by its great continuity with Gregory XVI's previous pronouncements. It roundly condemned new ideas of progress and religious indifference. It called on Catholics to be wary of those who advocated change.[21] Anyone who read the encyclical carefully should have realised that this pope was not Gioberti's unifier who would chase the Austrians out of Italy. Yet few took his wordy encyclical at face value, and instead, most continued to view the pontiff as a progressive. Liberal Britain was so impressed with this pope, seemingly so different from his reactionary predecessors, that they sent the Earl of Minot to lend Pius British support for his modernisation programme. Even the United States established a permanent diplomatic legation in Rome for the first time.[22]

In 1847, as already mentioned, Gioberti's *Gesuita Moderno* had appeared in print in Lausanne and caused a sensation. These volumes accused the Jesuits of being behind a cabal whose aim was to shackle the freedom of Italy to the despotism of Austria.[23] The Congregation of the Index underestimated the potential impact of this conspiracy theory. It refused to ban the work as it did not display any flagrant theological errors.[24] As a result the prefect of the Index remained silent about Gioberti's anti-Jesuit stance. This emboldened attacks on the order, which was accused of being an Austro-Jesuit faction in Italy. In response the superior general, Peter Jan Beckx, declared the order's complete submission to the papacy. As protests grew, Pius was forced to inform the Society of Jesus that he could no longer guarantee their safety and on 28 March 1848 they were advised to leave the Papal States.[25]

The myth of Pio Nono, the liberal pope and unifier of Italy, spread like wildfire across the peninsula,[26] especially amongst educated urban liberal elites, who wanted to enjoy constitutional and representative government as the French and southern Germans had done since 1814.[27] Despite his silence on the issue, the pope became an anti-Habsburg emblem. Admittedly, Pius had encouraged the Curia to implement administrative and economic reforms that would ameliorate conditions within the Papal States. When it came to constitutional government, the ambassadors of Austria and Bavaria pressured the pope to stay away from any concessions that would inflame the situation.[28] One man who urged reform and wanted to grant more concessions was the French ambassador, Pellegrino Rossi. He came from a modest Tuscan family, had been a senior official in Murat's provisional government of central Italy in 1814 and had then become a professor of political economy in Paris.[29] Given his piercing intelligence and tact, France's king, Louis Philippe, had appointed him ambassador to Rome. He would be a close and valued confident of the pope until his assassination. There was growing pressure on Pius to dismiss reactionary clergy from government posts and replace them with competent laymen.[30] The Curia and much of the diplomatic corps, meanwhile, were deeply concerned that constitutional concessions would destabilise the Papal States.

Among the first acts undertaken by the reforming Pius was the relaxing of press censorship on 15 March 1847.[31] Rather than calming spirits, this allowed for an explosion of pamphlets and broadsheets demanding ever greater freedoms. The emergence of patriotic circles hardly restored tranquillity. Men met in these gatherings to discuss and debate the politics of the age. They became a key forum in which radicalism gathered pace.[32] In April 1847, the pope created a *consulta* (consultative assembly) to advise the papacy. Ecclesiastical governors for each province in the Papal States would nominate three deputies to travel to Rome to deliberate on those matters referred to them by the Holy Father.[33] The people of Rome celebrated wildly. They marched from the Piazza del Popolo down the Corso to the Quirinal where Pius IX appeared on the balcony to bless thousands in the Piazza di Monte Cavallo. His words were drowned out by the shouts of 'Viva Pio Nono!'[34] If Pius believed that these limited concessions would satisfy the growing radical movements in Rome and the legations, he was mistaken.

Perhaps one of the most remarkable figures to emerge at this time was Angelo Brunetti, known as Ciceruacchio (Fatso), from the popular Trastevere quarter. He came from modest circumstances, had no formal education and as a youngster went to work as a carter specialising in bringing wine from the Castelli region into Rome. Those who peddle alcohol tend to be popular, and Ciceruacchio made a reputation for himself as a colourful, charismatic and friendly leader of Rome's popular classes. He became wealthy enough to own a house, along with several horses and carts. Cicerauacchio was generous with his wine and was often asked, like a mafia boss, to mediate in disputes.[35]

During the early part of Pius IX's reign, he was to 'call the shots' at a grassroots level in Rome. He was a great supporter of the new pope, whom he believed had a liberal agenda. Very provocatively, in the spring of 1847, he had helped tear down the ghetto gates and then organised a mass picnic where the Jews and Christians of Rome could fraternise as equal citizens.[36] This scandalised conservative opinion in the Curia and confirmed fears that concessions merely made people bolder in their demands. On 1 January 1848 Ciceruacchio headed a delegation from the patriotic circles of Rome. He marched to the Quirinal and presented no fewer than twenty-four demands for reform to the cardinal secretary of state. On receiving this list, the cardinal exclaimed: 'So you'll never be happy? You are insatiable.'[37]

Against his better judgement, the pope was persuaded to allow the formation of a civic guard. This citizen's militia was supposed to reinforce law and order in the city.[38] On 12 June the pope introduced the first cabinet in the history of the church, but to mass disappointment all eight of the ministers were cardinals. Ultimately, the priesthood wanted to retain control of the state.[39] The situation was inflamed considerably when, in July 1847, Field Marshal Radetzky reinforced the Habsburg garrison in Ferrara with a thousand troops.[40] As part of the Congress of Vienna settlement the citadel, at the heart of the city, had been manned by Austrian troops since 1814. Given the growingly revolutionary climate, the decision to increase foreign troop numbers in Romagna proved incendiary.[41] Ciceruacchio and his fellow radicals cried that the Papal States had been invaded by foreign troops. In August the nuncio in Vienna delivered a protest against the reinforcement of the garrison in Ferrara.

The crowds in Rome lobbied for war with the Habsburgs. Pius wanted to avoid propelling his kingdom into a war with Austria which his poorly equipped army and the disorganised civic guard could not hope to win. A peaceful outcome to this crisis was the top priority. It was decided to investigate the creation of a customs union with Tuscany and Sardinia-Piedmont.[42] This was seen as a preliminary attempt to create a pan-Italian league under the presidency of the papacy, in line with Gioberti's vision. Mazzini published an open letter beseeching Pius to lead the movement for Italian unification.[43] Despite hopes that Italy was on the verge of nationhood, slow progress was made in coordinating the commercial and diplomatic policies of these Italian states, whose administration, politics, ethos and internal configuration were so different. On 2 October a papal decree created a municipal council to administer the city of Rome. All its members were co-opted by the government.[44] For the first time since Napoleon's rule Rome had some measure of local government.

On 15 November 1847 the twenty-four deputies of the Consulta di Stato headed to the Quirinal to be presented to the pope. It was a festive occasion witnessed by Florence Nightingale, the future founder of modern nursing, who, like many British people, was in Rome to enjoy the mild winter.[45] For the first time the laity was given a forum in which to make its views known to the papacy. Pius warned the deputies to avoid utopianism and assist him in the administration of the state. Ultimately, sovereignty resided in him as pope-king and not in the people. This equivocal statement on the pope's part was hardly going to fulfil the heightened expectations of the population of Rome. For them, Pio Nono had become the emblem of Italy's Neo-Guelph aspirations for cultural, social, religious and national renewal.

The year 1848 – and few would have predicted this – was to witness a trans-European revolution.[46] Only Iberia, England and Russia were left unscathed by the general insurrections that swiftly spread through Europe's cities. This was remarkable in a pre-industrial age, where communications were still so slow. Most of Europe had very rudimentary rail and telegraph networks. News travelled at the speed of a horse. The term *quarantotto* (the number 48) still means a great upheaval or mess in contemporary Italian. Perhaps the Arab Spring of 2010 and the protests in Tahrir Square come closest to mirroring these events of the mid-nineteenth century.[47] Yet their scale, rapidity and coverage is where the resemblance begins and ends.

In nineteenth-century Europe, bad harvests, repressive political systems and a generalised sense of cultural malaise proved to be powder kegs for social discontent.[48] Localised insurrections in Milan, Palermo and Paris were contagious. Their message of freedom circulated to Naples, Vienna, Budapest, Berlin and most of Germany. Crowds forced reluctant monarchs to grant constitutions and parliaments. In Turin and Copenhagen concessions were made to forestall revolts.[49] In these early days, these revolutions were accompanied by demands for national self-determination and the period became known as the 'springtime of the peoples'.

It was hardly surprising that Rome was not spared the blaze of revolutionary excitement engulfing the continent. By February 1848 crowds were marching down the Corso with grim determination. They still cried 'Viva Pio Nono!' But this slogan was now accompanied by demands for a liberal constitution and freedom of the press. Rather than containing the disorder, the civic guard, which counted Prince Carlo Bonaparte among its officers, seemed to be encouraging the crowds. Ciceruacchio and his men started chanting 'Down with the ecclesiastical ministers!' On 12 February Pius reluctantly appointed four laymen to join his cabinet.[50] In a proclamation, issued a few days previously, the pope had used the words: 'Bless, great God, Italy and preserve for it the precious gift of faith!' Although the text warned against agitators who were pushing Italians towards sedition and war, those who read these closing lines came to the mistaken conclusion that Pius wanted national unity.

As the revolution accelerated across Europe, Pius decided, on 14 March 1848, to issue a *Statuto fondamentale* for the Papal States. It remains the only written constitution of the Catholic Church. Never before or since has any Roman pontiff accepted any limitation of his authority or sovereignty. The preamble established a bicameral legislature consisting of an appointed high council and elected council of deputies. Pius wanted to make his position clear:

> Within our Sacred Principality We cannot separate the temporal goal of establishing internal prosperity from the vital priority of maintaining the political independence of head of the Church, which is why this portion of Italy has remained independent [for centuries]. We therefore reserve for Us and Our successors the supreme sanction and promulgation of all laws that will be deliberated upon in Our chambers. Furthermore We will maintain the full exercise

of Our sovereign authority in all areas not covered by this
statute which encompass the Catholic religion and morality.[51]

Although this was hardly a liberal democracy by twenty-first-
century standards, the pope had agreed to share *some* legislative
power with a parliament which included *some* elected individuals.

The document was impressive, guaranteeing many individual
rights and abolishing pre-publication censorship. It established
intellectual property and copyright for authors, something
which few constitutions enshrined at the time.[52] Although the
suffrage was limited by property qualifications, it was generous
by nineteenth-century standards. The pope reserved for himself
and the College of Cardinals the power to negotiate treaties and
maintain diplomatic relations with the rest of Europe. Overall,
the pope followed the principles set by the liberal constitutions
published in Piedmont, Tuscany and Naples.[53] During this time
Cardinal Antonelli was appointed cardinal secretary of state, a post
he would hold for thirty years despite a brief interruption during
1848 (when he was made prefect of the apostolic palaces). He had
been one of the guiding lights behind the *Statuto fondamentale*
and, at this stage of his career, he was not averse to reform.[54]

Far from satisfying the radicals of Rome, there were demands
on the pope to proclaim a crusade to expel all 'barbarians'
from Italy. The situation reached breaking-point when on 24
March, under pressure from popular opinion, Charles Albert of
Piedmont declared war on the Austrian empire.[55] Ciceruacchio
and his associates demanded that the papal government follow his
example. After basic training, the patriots were turned into units
of volunteers and marched to Romagna on the northern frontier
of the Papal States. Although Pius authorised the recruitment
of these troops, he refused to bless their flags and ordered them
to remain within his borders.[56] Two military divisions were
established: the first, consisting of a mixture of regular and poorly
equipped troops, numbering about seven thousand men, was
placed under the command of the Piedmontese general Giovanni
Durando. The other, ten thousand ill-disciplined volunteers,
was led by the Neapolitan general Andrea Ferrari.[57] Pius was

categorical in demanding that his troops maintain a defensive posture and under no circumstances invade Austrian Lombardy. He knew that many of his subjects wanted to assist the insurgent provisional government in Milan, which had managed to expel the Austrians during a five-day pitched urban battle. Marshal Radetzky had withdrawn from the cities and, ominously, the peasants of Lombardy cheered him on his way.[58] Clearly not all Italians felt the same way as the revolutionaries. Habsburg forces were preparing to meet the Piedmontese. The papacy's amateur soldiers would be no match for these well-trained veterans.

On 5 April, Durando issued orders to exterminate the enemies of God and Italy.[59] Without papal approval, his army joined the Piedmontese in the struggle against Austria. Furious, Pius IX demanded that the general justify himself, but Durando persisted in ignoring his commander in chief.[60] A few weeks later, on 17 April, a formal congregation of the College of Cardinals was summoned. The first question was whether the Papal States should join the war. A unanimous 'no' was uttered by the princes of the church. When the pope asked what was to be done if his principality descended into chaos, the ambiguous answer that God would protect the church was hardly reassuring.[61]

Pressure grew, day by day, for the pope to declare war on Austria, but Pius refused to throw the Papal States into a nationalist adventure on the coattails of Charles Albert's Piedmont. On 29 April 1848, he made his views known in the papal allocution *Non semel*.[62] Pius reiterated that his policies were in keeping with those of his predecessors, and reminded them how he had tried to reform his kingdom for the better. But he also wanted to dispel any doubts about the papacy's ultimate allegiance, which was to God, rather than any nation. He described how rumours were circulating that the pope was anti-Austrian and pro-Italian in his sympathies.[63] Pius, as the heir to the prince of peace, could not enter a European war without betraying his Christian ministry. This allocution marked a turning-point in his reign.

Diplomats representing the Italian states who had formed a league to fight Austria protested bitterly against Pius's refusal to join the war. The radicals of Rome were even more infuriated, as they believed that the mask was now off. The pope was no liberal, but a friend to Habsburg counter-revolution. This allocution damaged the myth of the reformist Pio Nono. On 1 May a procession traversed the city and headed to the Quirinal demanding a lay government. The next day Count Terenzio Mamiani, who was one of the political prisoners freed on Pius IX's accession in 1846, was appointed the first lay minister of the interior of the Papal States.[64] To the great scandal of the devout, he refused the oath of allegiance to the pope. In the meantime, efforts were made by the church to offer its services as a mediator between the Italian league and Austria. While these talks were ongoing, General Durando merged his forces with those of Charles Albert of Piedmont.

On 9 June news arrived of a decisive defeat of the nationalist forces at the Battle of Vicenza. Durando and his miniature army were encircled by Habsburg columns and forced to capitulate.[65] This further confirmed that an amateur army, fired by a spirit of nationalism, was no match for professionally trained soldiers. Ciceruacchio and Carlo Bonaparte, who had once praised Pio Nono, now became his bitter critics. They wanted a more energetic and radical solution to the question of unification. Matters were made worse when Radetzky's forces reoccupied Ferrara and foraged for supplies. This was tantamount to invasion, cried Roman patriots.

Gioberti had become the man of the hour as his Neo-Guelph prophecies had seemed to be coming to fulfilment. At the start of the war, he had been recalled from exile and appointed speaker to the Piedmontese parliament and minister without portfolio in Turin.[66] It was probably thanks to his influence that Antonio Rosmini, the other leading light in Italy's Neo-Guelph movement, was despatched by Charles Albert to Rome to try to persuade Pius to join the war.[67] He arrived in the Eternal City on 15 August. Two days later he was received in audience at the Quirinal. Pius responded positively to the idea of an Italian federation. There were discussions about negotiating a new concordat with Piedmont to protect the church from anticlerical reformers. The pope admired Rosmini and enjoyed their conversation. Apparently, he offered to elevate this liberal priest to the cardinalate, but Rosmini demurred. It was during this time that he published his treatise *On the Five Wounds of the Church*, an appeal for a poorer, less powerful and more socially engaged church.[68] The printing of this text won Rosmini very few friends in the Curia and cooled the pope's attitude to Charles Albert's envoy.

A draft proposal, probably written by Rosmini, in which the papacy held the presidency of a new Italian federation consisting of Piedmont, the Papal States and Tuscany, met with Pius's favour. It was agreed that this new political entity would have a customs union, a common currency and a permanent assembly in Rome.[69] On receiving news of these preliminaries, Charles Albert was deeply unhappy, and insisted he should hold the presidency of the federation, not the pope, as he was fighting on the front line. But by now the impetus that had propelled the spring revolutions had reached its climax. In Paris, General Cavaignac bloodily repressed a socialist uprising in June 1848. With the threat from the Left disarmed, a more conservative republic emerged in France.[70]

In Naples, Ferdinand II, having been forced to concede a constitution and elections, decided to regain the initiative. The new liberal regime found it impossible to maintain law and order. Revolution had brought with it an economic depression that made the regime unpopular with the population of the capital. On 15 May royal forces massed around Naples and the liberal revolutionaries and national guards threw up hastily constructed barricades. After a bloody day of fighting led mainly by Ferdinand's Swiss mercenaries, the Neapolitan Revolution ended in blood.[71] Now in control of his capital, Ferdinand sought to repress the rebellion in the rest of his realm. In July his forces crossed the straits to Sicily and mercilessly bombarded Messina. This act of indiscriminate shelling gained him the sobriquet of *Il re bomba* (The bomb king).[72] By September, royal forces had regained control of Sicily, the starting-point of the 1848 revolutions. Neapolitan contingents and ships sent to assist Charles Albert were recalled.

Meanwhile, in Rome, Pius IX decided to replace the volatile Mamiani with a more moderate minister of the interior. Since the July Monarchy had been toppled in February 1848, Pellegrino Rossi had been replaced as French ambassador in Rome by

Harcourt, and he was now a private citizen.[73] His relationship with the pope had been close, and he was seen as a wise head in difficult circumstances. He was appointed minister of the interior on 10 September, and soon after the ministries of finance and police were added to his responsibilities.[74] His stated aim was to achieve an Italian federation peacefully. In his vision, each Italian state would retain its sovereignty in a supranational confederation.[75] This union would strive to harmonise gradually the different economic and administrative systems of the peninsula.

Rossi was an efficient administrator and zealous reformer. He immediately made enemies in the Curia by taxing the clergy and outlawing the bribes habitually taken by ecclesiastical civil servants.[76] Under his guidance an ambitious programme to build a large rail and telegraph network was put in place. Rossi's liberal vision meant that he was resented by all those whom his reforms affected. As the situation reached boiling point, Rossi, as described at the start of this chapter, paid the ultimate price.[77] He had embodied the hope that the Papal States could be administered by laymen. His brutal murder in broad daylight shocked European opinion and deeply marked Pius IX. As he sat in Count Spaur's coach riding southwards he regretted the many concessions he had made to his subjects.

His escape journey, during the early morning of the 25 November, went smoothly for the most part. A hiccup occurred when Spaur changed horses at an inn in Terracina. Here, two gendarmes walked toward the carriage and enquired who the travellers were and where they were heading. Informed that the leader of the group was the representative of the king of Bavaria the gendarmes offered to act as an escort. Some quick thinking allowed the Countess Spaur to claim that there was no danger for travellers in the daytime, and they were in a hurry. Thanks to these lies, a few hours later the coach crossed the southern frontier of the Papal States without incident. They were now in the domains of the king of Naples and the pope in his carriage seat sang the *Te deum* for his deliverance.[78]

The fugitives' destination was the naval fortress of Gaeta, fifty miles south of Rome. Here the pope arrived in the afternoon.

His first stop was the Albergo dei Giardinetti, where rooms had been reserved under an assumed name. Little did the hotel owner suspect that his guest was the Holy Father.[79] What happened next was farcical. The *Ténare* arrived in the port carrying the Duc d'Harcourt, who offered to take the pope to Marseilles. Shortly thereafter, a Spanish vessel carrying Cardinal Antonelli sailed into Gaeta and proposed to take Pius to the Balearic Islands. Not be outdone, a Royal Navy vessel followed on their tail extending an invitation to travel to Malta.[80] In the meantime, Count Spaur reported to the commander of the citadel, Major Gross. This Swiss mercenary, who spoke the local dialect of his canton, could not understand the count's South German accent. As a precaution, sentries were dispatched to the Albergo dei Giardinetti,[81] while messages were sent to Naples seeking instructions.

On learning that the pope had arrived in his kingdom, *Il re bomba* and several members of the Bourbon royal family immediately embarked on the royal yacht and sailed to Gaeta. The pope had now changed into a white cassock. When the king and queen of Naples came before him, they fell to their knees. Pius had tears streaming down his face and clasped the king's hands in his own and thanked the monarch for granting him asylum. For Ferdinand II the pope's presence in his domains was a sign of divine approbation. He had just ordered the royal gazette to announce the happy news of the arrival of his distinguished guest and asked his subjects to give thanks.[82] Pius was accommodated in the royal palace, built by Charles III in Gaeta. Here he would be joined by cardinals, officials and diplomats. For several months this Neapolitan naval base would become the seat of the Catholic Church, and the exiled government of the Papal States. On 4 December a diplomatic note was issued to all the powers of Europe, asking them to help restore Pius to his principality.[83]

The month of December was one of uncertainty. The revolutionaries in Rome selected Mamiani as minister of foreign affairs. He had the thankless task of reassuring Europe that the pope was safe to return to his capital city and that Rossi's murderers would be punished.[84] In the meantime Carlo Bonaparte, Ciceruacchio and his patriot followers pushed for the deposition of the pope-king. This was a high-risk strategy, as the wheel of fortune was turning inexorably against the revolutionaries. On 20 December, the results of the French presidential elections were announced. In a landslide, Louis-Napoleon Bonaparte, a nephew of the late emperor and Carlo's first cousin, won three-quarters of the vote.[85] Ever since the defeat of the socialist insurrection in June, the French republic had been steering towards a more conservative and authoritarian safe harbour. Louis-Napoleon, like his uncle, had little religious faith but he realised that the Catholic Church could legitimise his regime and reconcile the divisions of the past.[86] As the new president of the republic, he expressed his displeasure at the pope's treatment and exile.

On New Year's Day 1849, Pius issued the proclamation *Da questa pacifica*. In it he reacted with unrestrained fury against the revolutionaries' summoning of a constituent assembly to give central Italy a republican government. Unlike most other papal briefs, this was published in Italian and not archaic Latin. Rosmini, who had arrived in Gaeta, begged the pope to temper his words and adopt a more conciliatory tone. The Neo-Guelph priest was dismissed with irritation and the Curia ensured his advice was not heeded. Pius by now was convinced that conciliation had been a grave mistake. Only a hard line could win back his kingdom and restore the papacy's political and spiritual independence. He thundered:

> We hereby forbid all, regardless of their station, or condition, to take any part in those electoral assemblies that would dare select individuals to attend the previously condemned [constituent] assembly. At the same time, We remind you that failure to observe this absolute prohibition will incur automatic major excommunication for whosoever would dare make themselves guilty of any challenge to the temporal sovereignty of the supreme Roman pontiffs.[87]

All those who dared defy the authority of the pope-king were excluded from the church and forbidden the comfort of the sacraments. The liberal pope and unifier of Italy now

Emperor Kangxi ruled his vast Empire from 1654 to 1722. He was a model of enlightenment and tolerance. Catholicism could well have put down roots in China but for the Curia's intransigence.

Carolus Thomas Maillard de Tournon Taurinensis, Patriarcha. Antiochenus, Visitator Generalis Apostolicus in Sinarum, et alijs Indiarum Orientalium Regnis, cum potestate Legati de Latere. S. R. E. Presbyter Cardinalis creatus in Consistorio secre. to die 1 Augusti 1707. Obijt Macai die 8 Iunij 1710.

Dominicus de Rubeis haeres Io: Iacobi, ad Templu. S. M. de Pace cum Privil. S.P. et Sup: perm.

Charles-Thomas Maillard de Tournon had the delicate mission of establishing diplomatic relations between the Holy See and the Chinese Empire. His poor health and hostility to the Jesuits doomed his mission to failure.

View of the fortifications of Corfu in 1700. The Serenissima had invested heavily in protecting this gateway into the Adriatic.

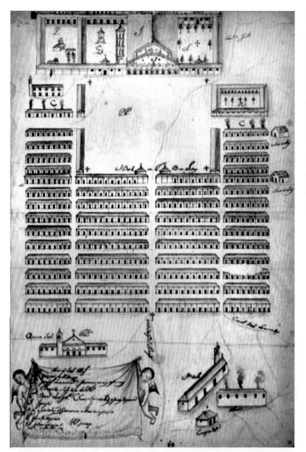

This plan of a *reducción* in modern-day Brazil shows the scale and ambition of the Jesuits to transform these missions into prosperous model towns and economic hubs for the native population. The order kept a tight oversight over the administration and finances of these settlements.

As these ruins show, the Jesuits' success brought them into conflict with both Iberian monarchies. Once papal protection was lifted, these 'mega-missions' were easy prey to the rapacious empires that surrounded them.

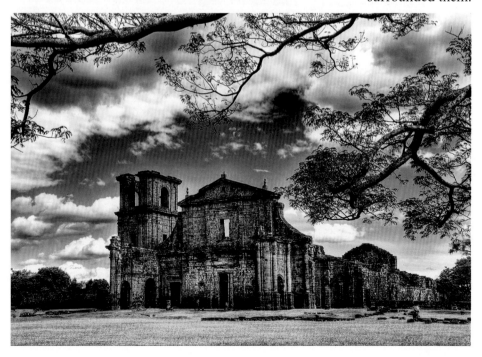

Sebastião José de Carvalho e Melo, better known as the Marquis de Pombal, was a moderniser and reformer influenced by the Enlightenment. He was determined to make the church subservient to the state.

The Lisbon earthquake of 1755 was a major catastrophe. It inspired Voltaire to write his deeply pessimistic novella *Candide* and gave Pombal a pretext for reining in the Jesuits.

The encyclical *Ex Omnibus* tried desperately to put an end to the Jansenist controversy in France. It was a clever compromise on the part of Benedict XIV but neither party really desired a reconciliation.

Pope Benedict XIV was one of the most enlightened and sympathetic popes in history. A highly learned prelate and endowed with a sense of humour, he demonstrated that Catholicism's struggle against Enlightenment was not inevitable.

Satirical print showing Clement XIV signing the brief *Dominus ac Redemptor* in 1773 abolishing the Society of Jesus (Jesuits) to satisfy the secular states of Europe.

Pius VI was a great patron of the arts who did much to beautify and restore the Eternal City. He was equally determined to drain the Pontine Marshes. His attempts to forestall the political decline of the Catholic Church all ended in failure.

The meeting between the Pope and Joseph II was one of the first in centuries to occur outside of Rome. The Curia had high expectations that Pius VI could persuade the emperor to compromise and roll back his anti-monastic reforms. Despite the enthusiastic welcome the trip extracted virtually no concessions from the Habsburg Emperor.

A scene depicting the execution of the Carmelites of Compiègne during the French Revolution. Their unnecessary death would later inspire Francis Poulenc to compose his magnificent opera *Dialogues des Carmélites* (1956).

The rising in the Vendée demonstrated the power of religious belief when it came to resisting the modernising reforms of the French Revolution. Counter-revolutionary rebellions such as these drained the modern state of resources and manpower it could not spare.

Napoleon Bonaparte's Concordat of 1801 seemed to have finally reconciled the Church with the modern state. Yet it was the fruit of miscommunications and would prove to be a truce rather than a permanent peace.

When Napoleon was proclaimed Emperor of the French it was a huge bonus that Pius VII agreed to anoint him. Bonaparte's self-crowning had been agreed in advance but the two men's personalities clashed and this trip bred great distrust.

Pius VII spent almost five years as Bonaparte's prisoner after his kidnapping in 1809. On his return to Rome in 1814, he forgot very little and showed little inclination to compromise with modernity.

Miguel Hidalgo y Costilla shown here in a highly romanticised portrait hoisting high the standard of the Virgin of Guadalupe. The revolutionary currents that saw Spain lose its South American possessions were not intrinsically anti-clerical.

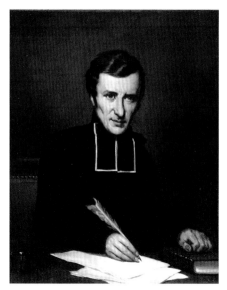

Félicité de Lamennais was the spiritual guru of his age and saw the revival of Catholicism as essential in a world of individualism and growing industrialisation. His attempts to reconcile liberalism and the magisterium of the church eventually brought him into conflict with Rome.

Pius IX, elected in 1846, seemed at long last to be the liberal and nationalist pope predicted by Italian nationalists like Gioberti. His early reforms made him the darling of the liberals for the first two years of his pontificate.

An eerie scene by the painter Caffi showing a nocturnal blessing by Pius IX from the Quirinal balcony during the stormy events of 1848.

Despite the French constitution renouncing aggressive war, Louis-Napoleon sent an expeditionary force to restore Pius IX's absolute power over the Papal States.

Louis-Napoleon, the nephew of the first French emperor, was something of an unknown quantity in 1848 when he was elected president of the Second Republic. He understood well the political power of the church and its hold over the Catholic electorate in France.

A cannon ball from a French mortar in 1849 that became lodged in the marble staircase of the Colonna Palace's world-renowned gallery. It has remained there to the present day.

Colonna Gallery

Giuseppe Garibaldi, who had fought in the Uruguayan Civil War, returned to take command of the doomed defenders of the Roman Republic in 1849. His defense of the Eternal City became the stuff of legend.

Angelo Brunetti, nicknamed Ciceruacchio (Fatso), was a wine merchant who effectively became the principal leader of the Roman popular movement of 1848–9.

The kidnapping of the illicitly baptised little Edgardo Mortara shocked the sensibilities of European liberal public opinion. Pius IX's refusal to return this little boy to his Jewish parents caused outrage throughout the continent.

Edgardo Mortara grew to become an outstanding and committed priest. He took on the name Pio in honour of the pope who forced him to renounce his Jewish heritage. This picture shows him meeting his mother in later life. How far his conversion was genuine, or a form of Stockholm syndrome, remains unanswered.

This statue depicts the apparition of the Virgin in La Salette in 1846. Unlike elsewhere, this Mary heralded many punishments from a vengeful angry God and called humanity to repentance. Such miraculous events tended to occur in places where the conflict between church and state was heating up.

As Rome was surrounded on all sides by the newly unified Italian state Pius IX summoned all the bishops of the Catholic world to the Vatican in 1869. Here, after much pressure, not to say bullying, the dogma of papal infallibility was proclaimed.

While the pope was being proclaimed infallible, the Italian army was poised to breach the walls of the Eternal City. On 20 September 1870 the temporal power of the popes was ended and Rome became the capital of Italy.

Pius IX retired to the Vatican and became its so-called prisoner. He waged a silent and futile war against modernity from behind the mighty walls of his last citadel. He died in 1878 and was buried with some difficulty in the church of San Lorenzo *fuori le mura*.

Cartoon from the 1875 *Kulturkampf* showing Bismarck playing chess with Pius IX.

A view of Marpingen today, where the Virgin Mary hoax occurred in 1876.

Regardless of the loss of the Papal States, Catholicism saw an opportunity to gain converts during the second age of European imperialism. It had particular hopes that King Mutesa I of Buganda might be a conduit for the conversion of the Great Lakes region. He proved on the contrary to be a wily politician who played the great monotheistic religions off against each other.

Cardinal Lavigerie was one of the first prelates to rally to the French Republic. In return, the order of White Fathers, which he founded, received government protection for their activities throughout the French empire in Africa.

The aristocratic diplomat Vincenzo Pecci was elected Leo XIII in 1878 at the age of sixty-eight. Few expected a long pontificate… he was to become one of the longest serving and most important popes in the history of the church.

The Conclave of 1903 was the last time a secular power used its power of veto. Here the Emperor Franz-Josef vetoed the election of Cardinal Rampolla. After this date the use of a veto during papal elections was prohibited on pain of excommunication. In many ways this conclave marked the final demise of *ancien régime* Catholicism.

metamorphosed into the enemy of modernity, transformed from being one of the most beloved pontiffs in church history to one of the most reviled by liberals, reformers and the press. [88] Indeed, the very liberals who, a few months previously, had celebrated him as Italy's salvation, now denigrated him as a public enemy. The psychological repercussions on Pius, who was very impulsive and emotive, were considerable. He would henceforth refuse all accommodations with and concessions to liberalism and representative government.

Rosmini himself would pay the price for his vision of a spiritually renewed and primitive church. On 30 May 1849, the Congregation of the Index forbade Catholics to read *On the Five Wounds of the Church*.[89] This was agonising for a priest who remained obedient and committed to the papacy. He pledged publicly his submission to Catholic teaching, then retired to Stresa on Lake Maggiore, where he died a disappointed man in 1856.* In the maelstrom of revolution, Pius turned the church backwards and, rather than sailing out of the storm into clear waters, set his course firmly into the tempest.

Da questa pacifica radicalised the situation in Rome beyond recognition. Ciceruacchio whipped the Roman crowds into a frenzy with ominous cries of '*Viva l'Italia!* And death to the rich and priests.' On 21 January 1849 a quarter of a million people took part in the vote to elect the constituent assembly. Excluding Napoleon's indirect ballots of the first decades of the nineteenth century, these were the first popular elections in the history of Italy.[90] A week later, the great composer Giuseppe Verdi premiered his opera *La battaglia di Legnano* at the Teatro Argentina in the capital. The score and libretto recast the struggle of the northern Italian city states against the German emperor Federico Barbarossa during the twelfth century in

---

* His rehabilitation would have to wait until 2001, when the congregation of the doctrine of the faith declared that the condemnation of his work had been due to misunderstandings. See 'Note on the Force of the Doctrinal Decrees, Concerning the Thought and Work of Fr Antonio Rosmini Serbati', online at https://www.vatican.va/roman_curia/congregations/cfaith/documents/rc_con_cfaith_doc_20010701_rosmini_en.html [accessed 6 July 2021]

a highly nationalistic light. Each of the four acts ended with a rousing appeal to Italians to repel these barbarous invaders. The opera ended orgasmically with the finale '*è salva Italia*' ('Italy is saved!') Members of the audience went wild and invaded the orchestra pit to embrace the musicians.[91]

On 5 February the newly elected deputies gathered on the Capitoline hill followed by a procession of enthusiastic Romans. Ciceruacchio and Carlo Bonaparte were elected to the provisional government. The radicals had won, or so it seemed. The mighty bell of the Capitoline rang out in triumph.[92] Priests, obedient to the will of their sovereign, kept well away from proceedings. Four days later, the pope was deposed as ruler of central Italy. The papacy's spiritual independence was guaranteed in law by the deputies, but all political power was taken away from the pontiff.

Citizenship was extended to all, regardless of religion, and all faiths were allowed. Suffrage was extended to all male adults. Critically, on 9 February, Rome was proclaimed a republic, the cutting of the last umbilical cord linking Rome to the papacy. The republicans wanted to celebrate a solemn *Te deum* in St Peter's, but the canons of the basilica categorically refused. Less scrupulous priests were found to officiate,[93] but it was clear that the new state was born on the modern fault-line that pitted church against state.

In March 1849, the republican nationalist Giuseppe Mazzini arrived in Rome. Together with other two 'straw men' he was appointed a triumvir.[94] This mystical nationalist would exert unprecedented authority over the fledgling republic. He was an austere, almost Robespierrian figure in his asceticism, but an able administrator who galvanised the Romans to create a modern state. Soon he was joined by the warrior Giuseppe Garibaldi, who had fought in the wars between Brazil and Uruguay. His knowledge of guerrilla warfare, together with his flair for the unexpected, would make him a vital supporter of the revolution.[95] The general was accompanied by the highly eccentric Barnabite priest Ugo Bassi from Bologna, who wore a black cassock with a red shirt and carried weapons. He would act as the military chaplain to the irregular forces of the new state.[96]

The real tragedy of 1849 was that the Roman republic was born at the precise moment when the European counter-revolution was gaining momentum. The revolutions in Paris, Naples, Vienna and Berlin had been crushed by military repression.[97] In Italy the creation of the republic sowed discord amongst the proponents of an Italian federation. In Tuscany the Grand Duke was ousted by radicals, and a short-lived republic was proclaimed in Florence.[98] Gioberti was appointed prime minister of Sardinian Piedmont in December 1848. He advised Charles Albert not to ally with the republics of central Italy and to go on the offensive alone against the Habsburgs.[99] Between 22 and 23 March 1849, Field Marshal Radetzky routed the forces of Charles Albert, outnumbered two to one, at the Battle of Novara. On the same day, the king abdicated in favour of his son who became King Victor Emanuel II.[100] The following month Russian forces poured into Hungary and restored it to Habsburg rule.

The Roman revolution was only beginning when all the other democratic movements in Europe had already been subdued. Apart from Venice, which stubbornly endured a Habsburg siege for many more months, most of Italy had been restored to the rule of its traditional monarchs.[101] President Louis-Napoleon of France viewed the situation with some alarm. It seemed as if Austria's forces under Radetzky were destined to reconquer the entire peninsula, and place Italy under Habsburg hegemony. He was unsure how to react. On the one hand, he viewed papal rule as a vestige of the dark ages and was unsympathetic to it. At the same time, he did not want to abandon centuries of French influence over Italy. On 16 April, a motion was put before the French National Assembly to provide the government with the funds necessary to send an expeditionary force to take Rome. The French Left accused the government of seeking to destroy the Italian people's right to self-determination. Despite these bitter recriminations, the motion was passed by a majority of 395 to 283.[102]

A force of twelve thousand men, led by General Charles Oudinot, the son of one of Napoleon's marshals, set sail on 21 April for Civitavecchia. Expecting no resistance and an easy victory, these troops were not equipped for a sustained siege. At Gaeta,

Harcourt and the French diplomatic team informed the pope that Louis-Napoleon expected him to issue a manifesto guaranteeing liberal institutions in return for this military assistance. Pius categorically refused to make any such undertaking until he had returned to Rome.[103] Three days later Oudinot landed in Civitavecchia and took the port with ease. Although the general claimed to be a friend of the Romans, he imprisoned the city's authorities and hoisted the French tricolour. It was very clear that his force had little intention of allowing the republic to continue in its present state.[104]

Mazzini took the initiative and ordered his armed forces to repel the invaders. The Roman assembly issued a proclamation on 25 April urging resistance to the death.[105] As the French expeditionary force began its march toward St Peter's dome, the defence of the city was entrusted to Garibaldi and his irregulars. Faced with overwhelming odds against a professional army, the generalissimo of the republic was in his element. He had about 1,500 legionnaires, many of them veterans who had followed him into battle in South America. They were sunburnt rednecks, who wore large felt hats decorated with thick black grouse feathers. Although these volunteers who had fought in Uruguay had worn red shirts, they don't seem to have adopted them in Rome, apart from Ugo Bassi.[106]

As they marched through the city, crowds threw their hats in the air and cheered: 'Viva la Repubblica!' Garibaldi with his deep cobalt eyes, long beard and poncho was the epitome of heroism (or at least this was the carefully cultivated image he wanted to broadcast). Sitting astride his grey charger he was an inspiring sight, communicating confidence and calm – the quintessential guerrilla leader. Behind him rode Andrea Aguyar, a black former slave from Uruguay who had joined Garibaldi's band in South America, his striking athletic physique and tall stature adding to the general's mystique. The freed slave acted as an aide de camp to Garibaldi, whom he served with veneration.[107]

On 28 April the generalissimo reviewed his forces. Apart from his own legionaries, he could count on the remnant of the pope's regular army, the civic guards and some volunteers from northern Italy who had fought with Charles Albert. A delegation was sent to General Oudinot who was marching towards Rome from the south. The commissioners of the republic tried to persuade him to call off his attack, but the over-confident general stated that he would dine at the best hotel in the city that very evening.[108] At five in the morning Oudinot ordered his troops to approach Rome's city walls. What confronted them were the Janiculum walls built by Pope Urban VIII during the seventeenth century to complete the defensive encirclement of the city.[109] Despite French confidence, these walls were tall and thick and had been constructed to withstand artillery. In their arrogance the invaders approached these defensive structures without a siege train.

As the soldiers approached Porta Pertusa, they realised that the gate had been walled up decades previously – a fact that had not made it onto the general's maps. The defenders rained down murderous volleys and used their defensive artillery on the blue-coats below. Without scaling ladders this first attempt to take Rome was doomed to failure. The attackers decided to try two other gates of the city, but found that these entrances were equally well defended. Then they attempted to set up camp in the leafy suburbs of the Janiculum, where many Roman princely families had their villas. Garibaldi had anticipated that this area might be used as a staging ground for an assault on the city, so he had filled it with snipers and sharpshooters who harassed the French. Embarrassingly, Oudinot was forced to order a general retreat to Civitavecchia. His Roman dinner would have to wait.[110] A courier was sent to Paris requesting urgent reinforcements, heavy artillery and a siege train.

The defenders broke into applause and cried, among other things, 'Down with Pius IX and no more government of infamous priests.' But the situation was far from rosy for the defenders of the republic. Austria's forces were occupying the legations in the north, while a Neapolitan army had arrived in Albano, about fifteen miles from Rome, on 5 May.[111] Garibaldi, daring as ever, launched a pre-emptive strike and pushed back the Bourbon forces. But the French were preparing for a second strike, and a large contingent of Spanish troops landed in Fiumicino near Rome on 9 May.[112]

For Louis-Napoleon the situation was delicate, as many deputies on the Left of the French National Assembly had denounced the expedition to Rome. They were inspired by Garibaldi's resistance. It was difficult for the government to sustain the lie that the expedition was to assist the people of Italy, rather than attempting to quench the fires of revolution in Rome. Ferdinand de Lesseps, a career diplomat and future builder of the Suez Canal, was sent to negotiate with Mazzini. He was warmly welcomed when he announced that he was authorised to place Rome under the protection of French troops and guarantee that its people would in future be allowed to choose their own system of government.[113] Given that these proposals did not recognise the legitimacy of the Roman Republic, Mazzini rejected them as insufficient. On 20 May, Ciceruacchio led a mob into the Piazza del Popolo, where they proceeded to tear down Pius IX's coat of arms which decorated the churches at either end of this magnificent square – a clear sign that the radicals considered the pope their enemy.

De Lesseps became frustrated with Mazzini, whose mystical dreams of Italian unity struck him as utopian. Many Romans did want to be rid of their theocratic government, but this did not mean that they viewed Venetians or Sicilians as brothers joined in a common struggle. These other Italians were still referred to as *forestieri* (outsiders) by the people of the Papal States.[114] Mazzini's fantasies about Italians gaining a sense of national consciousness and seizing their independence were not as widely shared as he thought. Indeed, the Italian peasantry thought more about their subsistence than of the tricolour or nationhood.

On 29 May, de Lesseps transmitted the French government's final offer of military protection from other foreign powers and a guarantee that the people of Rome would be allowed to choose their own system of rule. Mazzini sent a counter-offer citing the French constitution's promise that France would never threaten the freedom of other peoples.[115] An angry Oudinot prepared for his assault against the city walls. In a last-minute attempt to stave off the attack, de Lesseps had persuaded Mazzini to withdraw his counter-proposal. It was too late, since elections in France had returned a crushing conservative majority in the national assembly.[116] The emboldened President Bonaparte had lost all patience, and ordered Oudinot to take Rome without delay. He hoped this would please Catholic voters in France.

By 2 June a force of over thirty thousand French troops had emerged from the malaria-ridden and sweltering heat of the Roman *campagna* and positioned themselves for the siege. Behind the walls eighteen thousand volunteers, troops and civic guards prepared to meet the onslaught. The next day, after many hours of bloody fighting, Oudinot's men seized a key position on the Janiculum hill. They captured the villa Doria-Pamphili, which faced Porta San Pancrazio, and from which vantage point they could see the city of the Caesars stretched out before them.

For the next few days, the French bombarded the city walls. Some cannon balls fell on the Trastevere quarter, which housed many of Ciceruacchio's followers, as it was just beneath the Janiculum on the west bank of the Tiber. A stray cannon ball went through the roof of the Colonna palace. It embedded itself in the magnificent gallery housing one of the best collections of Old Masters in Europe. The princes of Colonna decided not to repair the marble steps damaged by the projectile, and the canon ball is still proudly implanted in the marble floor to this day. By 20 June the siege cannons were so close that the Janiculum walls started to crumble under the impact of the shells. Inside the city dissent grew between Mazzini, who wanted to launch a suicidal counterattack, and Garibaldi, who favoured a defensive stance and the setting up of barricades within the city itself.[117]

Once the outer walls collapsed Oudinot was faced with a dilemma. A generalised bombardment of the city risked damaging the archaeological remains and monuments of one of the most important cultural sites in the world. To make matters worse ten foreign consuls inside Rome signed a petition protesting any further bloodshed or destruction within the city. It was decided to concentrate fire in a straight line, toward the Capitoline hill and Palazzo della Cancelleria, which were the nerve centres of the republican government.[118] On 26 June Garibaldi informed the government that the situation was hopeless. He advised that the defenders attempt a sortie and head for the hills to the east of Rome. Here they could continue a guerrilla war against the foreign powers and the papacy. Mazzini rejected the plan. It was only the pleading of volunteers and civic guards that stopped Garibaldi from leaving in disgust.[119]

Four days later, French forces stormed the breaches they had made in the city walls and poured through the outer defences. Garibaldi led a desperate charge in a bid to repel the attackers, but it failed, and his loyal comrade Aguyar was killed in the melee. After the bloody fighting on 30 June a truce was declared.[120] Mazzini came to the constituent assembly, which was presided over by Carlo Bonaparte. He informed them that further resistance was futile. The options open to the republican government were martyrdom, surrender or a flight to the provinces, where the fugitive government could incite a guerrilla war against the foreign troops. It was agreed to end immediate armed resistance and to flee to the hills.[121] Delegates were sent to Oudinot to discuss terms for the surrender. There was still some hope that the French might protect the people of Rome from reactionary government and repression. Garibaldi summoned his men to St Peter's Square where he proclaimed: 'To those who follow me I demand great love of the fatherland [...] I can promise no pay but only hardship, hunger, thirst and all the rigours of war.'[122] Despite this unappetising offer, four thousand men cheered and agreed to follow him into exile.

Members of the constituent assembly worked furiously, knowing that the arrival of French soldiers was imminent. As one of their last acts, they published the constitution of the Roman Republic on which they had been working for months. It was one of the most republican and democratic texts of the age of revolutions.[123] While the constitution was read on the Capitoline hill, Oudinot's men were marching through the Corso. They soon dissolved the assembly and the political clubs, removed the Italian tricolours and began dismantling the barricades.[124] Mazzini kept a low profile, and eventually escaped using a false passport issued to him by the United States consul. The British consulate in Rome issued over five hundred passes to help former revolutionaries flee from papal repression.[125]

The French occupiers had little wish to engage in reprisals and turned a blind eye to much of what was happening in the immediate aftermath of the fall of the city. Garibaldi and his followers were soon encamped on the bleak hills of the Abruzzi. By late July 1849, they realised that the guerrilla army they had hoped to raise would have little hope of succeeding. Garibaldi decided to push on to Venice and help the city resist the Austrians.[126] Harassed by Austrian troops, he tried to embark his brothers in arms, including his pregnant wife Anita, on the Adriatic coast. Habsburg naval vessels pushed them back on to land. He decided to split his force into smaller detachments, hoping that at least a few would make it to Venice. His wife Anita became dangerously ill and was unable to continue the journey. She soon died, seven months pregnant.[127] Distraught, Garibaldi was led by sympathisers to Tuscany, and eventually set sail from Genoa into exile, vowing never to rest until Italy was united.

His other companions, the Barnabite chaplain Ugo Bassi and Ciceruacchio, were captured by Habsburg troops. On 8 August, Bassi was taken to Bologna where, as an excommunicate, he was not allowed to receive the last rites before he was shot by firing squad.[128] Ciceruacchio, together with his two young sons, met the same fate. Carlo Bonaparte, as a first cousin of the president of France, was allowed to set sail for Marseille. He would spend a dreary exile in Paris. His main achievement of note was to become the president of the French capital's botanical garden in 1854, a year before his death.[129]

On 4 July, an emissary from General Oudinot reached Gaeta and the royal palace. Here he deferentially presented Pius IX and his government in exile with the keys to the city of Rome.[130] Eleven days later papal rule was officially restored and a *Te deum* held in St Peter's to celebrate the event. Pio Nono had little appetite for the conciliation and reform the French president had demanded. He felt that his liberal concessions, at the start of his reign, had emboldened the revolutionaries in their demands. It became his iron determination to fight modernisation and punish those who had challenged his authority. He issued a manifesto in which he charged a commission of cardinals to govern the capital under French occupation, investigate recent events and punish wrongdoers.[131] The Jews who had been liberated by the revolution were immediately returned to the ghetto and forbidden from owning property outside its precincts.[132] Catholic antisemitism was to reach another low point under Pius IX's restored regime. The restoration of the Holy Office, or Inquisition, scandalised European liberal opinion too. French diplomatic agents in Gaeta were told unambiguously that the pope had no intention of granting his people a constitution, let alone resuming the experiment of lay government. He argued that innovations confused people and needlessly excited their spirits.[133]

Back in Rome, the consuls noted the angry faces of the people of Trastevere who had sympathised with Ciceruacchio. Published proclamations from the commission of cardinals were ripped from the walls.[134] Papal rule was reimposed through force. Not everyone was upset by these events. Merchants, the nobility, the families of clergy and civil servants were relieved that the siege was over. The restoration of law and order had reestablished normality and their livelihoods. French troops and officers meanwhile were appalled that they had become accomplices in restoring the worst aspects of papal control. In their minds, they had come to release Rome from anarchy and restore liberal government. Their mission had been a failure.

For the French negotiating team, the aim of persuading Pius to make concessions was thwarted by the ambassadors of Austria, Spain and Naples, who fanned the flames of repression and reaction.[135] On 27 August a copy of an open letter from Louis-Napoleon to the military governor of Rome reached Gaeta. It read like an ultimatum. It lambasted the wicked advisers who surrounded Pius and condemned the authoritarian restoration of papal power in Rome. The letter made clear that the French had not come to Italy to reimpose despotism and that a failure to implement liberal reforms might lead to the withdrawal of troops from the Papal States. If Bonaparte had hoped this would pressure the pope into concessions it had the opposite effect.[136] On 4 September, incensed by French demands and emboldened by the surrender of Venice to the Austrians, the pope left Gaeta for the palace of Portici in Naples. With the fall of Venice, the Italian revolution was over.

Mount Vesuvius had been dormant since 1839, but recently the volcano had given alarming signs of reawakening. According to local lore, Pius IX extended his arm and blessed it. Immediately all tremors and noises ceased. The people of Naples praised the pope and were convinced that having him in their city was lucky.[137] Those who tell this story forget to add that the blessing only worked for a few months, as Vesuvius erupted in February 1850 releasing two million cubic metres of lava, but at least with no recorded fatalities. On 17 September the pope issued a long-awaited manifesto in which he thanked the Catholic armies which had liberated Rome. Republican France's role was deliberately underplayed. Papal sovereignty was jealously guarded, and precious few concessions were made. Pius accepted the need for a council of state, a consultative chamber, an advisory tax assembly and some elected municipal councils.[138] It was very little in comparison to the articles of the Roman constitution of 1849. Indeed, the papal *Statuto fondamentale* of March 1848 had been more generous in its terms. Among the cardinals there was little stomach for resuming liberalisation. A rather parsimonious amnesty was issued in which those who had not participated in the recent revolution were forgiven. Unlike in 1846, however, the pope was not in a forgiving mood.

While at the palace of Portici, Pius played the tourist. He was particularly fascinated by the archaeological excavations at Pompei and Herculaneum, which he visited on several occasions. King Ferdinand presented the pope with several artefacts as gifts. The supreme pontiff visited Naples itself, where he presided over religious festivals and rituals in many of the magnificent baroque churches which adorned the Parthenopean city.[139] One might speculate that the pope wanted to prolong his stay here so as not to be compromised by the repressive measures being visited on the population of the Papal States.

After three months in Naples, the encyclical *Nostis et nobiscum* appeared. It was a blistering and unwavering condemnation of a modern plot against the God-given authority of the clergy. This interminable encyclical interpreted socialism and communism as new forms of Protestantism. There was a specific condemnation of the activities in Italy of Protestant bible societies, which Pius accused of spreading heresy.[140] Who was behind this heretical conspiracy, and what their ultimate aim might be, was very unclear. Yet, the solution was transparent. The members of the clergy needed to be better educated to be able to assume a frontline role in correcting these errors and deviations. Priests, friars and monks, all had a part to play in saving Europe from the dangers of new ideas and their potential to fracture society. The pope exhorted bishops to reorganise their diocesan clergy and seminaries, and to encourage confident preaching against the errors of the day. *Nostis et nobiscum* was an impressive denunciation of revolutionary ideas, and a rallying cry for the clergy to unite.

While the pope stayed in Portici throughout the Christmas festivities, he was in no hurry to return to Rome. To further the objective of improving the Catholic clergy, and educating the masses to accept the church's magisterium, Pius approved the creation of the Jesuit periodical *La Civiltà Cattolica*.[141] After distancing the Society of Jesus from his domains, the pope invited them back. Their high-powered education and loyalty to the Holy See was seen as an asset. This new journal's prospectus was circulated to over 120,000 individuals.[142] It would become the mouthpiece of ultramontane and hyper-conservative Catholicism for the latter half of the nineteenth century. Relentlessly anti-modernist in tone, it flirted with modern antisemitism.[143]

Despite re-establishing the ghetto walls, the pope was keen to secure a loan from the Rothschild bank. Since the reign of Gregory XVI the major Jewish bankers had helped prop up the ever-fragile finances of the papacy.[144] They would do so again, but used this opportunity to lobby insistently for an improvement in the conditions of their co-religionists in the Papal States. Rather than receive the loans gratefully, and listen to the humanitarian concerns of the Rothschild family, the papacy deeply resented all interference in its domestic affairs. The disingenuous argument was made that ghettos were not prisons, but rather protected the Jewish populations from violence and exploitation.[145] This age-old justification rang hollow to those forced to live in overcrowded confinement behind iron gates.

As 1850 dawned, it was clear that Rome, with its French garrison, was now under the firm control of the church's authorities. Despite the trauma of the previous year, Pius decided the time had come to return to his capital. On 4 April he began the slow progress home, accompanied by *Il re bomba* and the Neapolitan royal family. Two days later, at the border, they parted company, latter receiving a fulsome blessing and the gratitude of the pope for sheltering him during the revolution. Once the pope entered his realm, he found a warm welcome and some triumphal arches erected to celebrate his return.[146] When the papal carriage entered Velletri he was met by the military governor of Rome, General Achille Baraguey d'Hilliers. Here again effigies, decorations and local officials all gathered to cheer their returning sovereign.

On 12 April, after an absence of almost eighteen months, Pius re-entered his capital. He was greeted by cheering crowds of loyalists and curious onlookers. Solemn masses of thanksgiving were offered at the basilicas of St John Lateran and St Peter. Once the pope was back in the Vatican, an impressive 101-gun salute burst out from Castel Santangelo.[147] Unlike his predecessors, he would from now on prefer the greater security of the walls of the Vatican to the Quirinal palace, which held unpleasant memories for him. That evening Rome was illuminated, as fireworks lit the sky. Every year thereafter 12 April became a public holiday. While the crowds did come out to celebrate Pius's return, it was impossible not to notice he was now escorted by French troops. Inside the basilicas where he celebrated mass rows of blue-coated armed soldiers stood guard.[148] Pius had been restored to his kingdom by military means. He came to loathe politics and would increasingly delegate the task of governing the Papal States to Cardinal Antonelli, who had organised his successful flight and restoration.[149] Pius IX would focus much more on his pastoral mission and on fostering a revival of Catholic worship.

In 1846 he had hoped gradually to modernise and liberalise Catholicism. The explosion of revolution two years later had deeply scarred the pope. He now felt under siege, and wanted Catholics to avoid contamination from liberal and progressive forms of thinking. The historian Hugh Macleod has called this process the ghettoisation of Catholicism.[150] This gradual closure to the world saw those loyal to Rome being encouraged to avoid contact with modernity. There was an explosion of Catholic publications, schools and societies that would allow those with a conservative and ultramontane disposition to meet, without fear of encountering individuals who thought differently. While the fortunes of the Papal States would, ultimately, depend on the vagaries of European geopolitics, the spiritual supremacy of the papacy would be strengthened beyond recognition.

The tragedy for Pius was that he was never able to disentangle his position as a secular Italian prince from his spiritual mission as head of a global religion. His decision to pull up the drawbridge marked the death knell for the Papal States. However, the centralisation of his spiritual stewardship over Catholicism was crucial for the modern papacy. His encouragement of mass piety and ostentatious devotion would yield enormous dividends. If any event made the modern Catholic Church what it is today, then it was the trauma of the revolution of 1848. The church, once bitten by Napoleon in 1809, and now by its own people, was outraged. It was a case of 'twice bitten four times shyer'. Pius declared war on the modern world on behalf of millions of Catholics. To this day, the papacy has a deeply dysfunctional relationship with those who urge it to change. This resistance to modernity derives from insecurities unleashed after *il quarantotto*. For the church, concessions became a sign of weakness, the beginning of the end, rather than a means of creating a new working relationship with post-revolutionary society.

7

CAN THE POPE ERR?
THE FIRST VATICAN COUNCIL,
1851–78

Loud pounding interrupted the stillness of the night. The date was 23 June 1858. Soon heavy footsteps could be heard ascending a staircase. A papal carabiniere and a police inspector entered the first floor of a flat in Bologna. Marianna Mortara opened the door, surprised and uncertain why her home had come to the attention of the authorities. Her husband Momolo came back from a short stroll and was shocked to find unwelcome visitors. This Jewish family knew that the pope's officials rarely brought good news. The inspector said he had come on the authority of the local inquisitor to see their children and, despite protests from Marianna and Momolo, he entered the bedroom where the young Mortaras were fast asleep. He and his colleague ordered that all the children except the six-year-old Edgardo should be removed from the room. Horrified, the parents obeyed, wondering what was happening. They were informed that, some years previously, the young Edgardo had been baptised clandestinely when he had been ill (this had been done without the Mortaras' knowledge by their Christian servant Anna Morisi). It was impossible for the papal authorities to allow a Christian child to be raised by Jewish parents. In what must have been a waking nightmare, Marianna screamed and threw herself on her child. She physically interposed her body between her six-year-old son and the police, making it impossible to extract the child without injuring the mother.[1]

At 11 p.m. friends of the Mortaras went to the San Domenico convent. They were received by the city's inquisitor, the Dominican friar Pier Feletti. He confirmed that Edgardo had been baptised in secret. When they protested loudly Feletti gave the invertebrate justification that he had no choice in the matter, he was merely following instructions. Under canon law, a Christian could not be raised by non-believers. To defuse the situation, Feletti decided to allow the child to stay in the flat for the time being.[2] Two policemen remained in the apartment to make sure that the child was not secreted away or (following Catholic antisemitic legend) murdered for his Christian blood.*

The next day, a Jewish delegation asked for an audience with Cardinal Giuseppe Ferretti, the apostolic legate who was the highest authority in Bologna.[3] They were told that His Eminence was out of the city and unable to receive them. Returning to the Mortara flat they told the family to prepare for the worst. Momolo, seeing that his wife Marianna was broken with grief, advised that she be taken elsewhere to spare her the sight of Edgardo being taken away. It proved extremely difficult to persuade her to let go of her six-year-old offspring but, eventually, the crying and screaming mother was taken to a place of safety.

On the afternoon of 24 June, Momolo, with his brother-in-law, begged the inquisitor to relent. Feletti was unwavering: the child had to be taken away. On his return home Momolo noticed that a large contingent of *carabinieri* had arrived, along with a carriage with darkened windows. Momolo was forced to watch as the officers grabbed his crying son and spirited him away from his family. Grief-stricken, he lost consciousness, exhausted by the trauma and the lack of sleep, and fell to the ground.[4]

---

* Sadly, the myth of the blood libel had persisted into the nineteenth century. Magda Teter, *Blood Libel: On the Trail of an Antisemitic Myth* (Cambridge, MA, 2020), pp. 374-84; and for medieval versions see Alan Dundes, *The Blood Libel Legend: A Casebook in Anti-Semitic Folklore* (Wisconsin, 1991); and Hannah Johnson, *Blood Libel: The Ritual Murder Accusation at the Limit of Jewish History* (Michigan, 2012).

Europe was scandalised by such inhumanity. Many saw it as a monument to Catholic self-delusion that kidnapping a child from his family could be squared with the precepts of Jesus Christ. Liberal newspapers excoriated the church for its inhumanity and violation of the rights of parenthood. Public opinion in France and England was particularly appalled by this cruel action.[5] Through the global Jewish diaspora, the Mortaras lobbied indefatigably for the return of their boy. Young Edgardo in the meantime had been taken to the House of Catechumens in Rome. These institutions were devoted to the conversions of non-Christians to the faith and had a mixed reputation to say the least.[6] Many of them, founded by the Jesuits, had the purpose of instructing Jewish converts in the Catholic faith prior to baptism. In Edgardo's case, given he had already been baptised, his evangelisation was fast-tracked. Having endured the trauma of being kidnapped, the young boy was by all accounts treated well. But he was subjected to a form of brainwashing and forced to undergo an unremitting programme of intense catechesis.

Late in July, Momolo travelled to Rome and sought the assistance of a Christian lawyer to plead his case. Cardinal Antonelli, as a wily politician, could not ignore that the growing press storm had turned the kidnapping into a public-relations disaster. The Jesuit newspaper La Civiltà Cattolica, the voice of anti-modernist Catholicism, perversely declared: 'He [Edgardo] was separated from his father to safeguard his liberty and to prevent his father from abusing his paternal rights to violate [his liberty].'[7] Few were convinced by the moral suppleness of this Jesuit periodical. Antonelli met with Momolo, promising to raise the matter with the Holy Father. Permission was granted for the father to see Edgardo, but how many times Momolo saw his son and what was said remains uncertain.[8] The liberal press stated that the boy wanted to go home, whereas Catholic reports stressed how happy the boy was to have become a Christian. The fact remains that the parent was not allowed to see his son alone. He was always supervised by the rector of the House of Catechumens. Momolo was informed that the solution was simple: if he himself converted to Catholicism his boy would return home. Unmoved by this cruelty, Mortara hoped that he could retain his faith and recover his son.[9]

A press war was waged in the months that followed in which Catholic newspapers like *L'Univers* and *La Civiltà Cattolica,* presented Edgardo as a Christ-like child, blessed with a sublime intelligence. They portrayed him as wise beyond his years and eager to persuade his fellow Jews to follow him on the path of conversion. It was even alleged that Pius IX had visited the young child several times.[10] On these occasions he imparted paternal affection and praise on the child. Indeed, the priests of the Catechumens encouraged the six-year-old to view the pontiff as his real father. The positive gloss put on the story to make the young Edgardo seem like a child saint is deeply disturbing. Little could hide the fact that the papal authorities had deprived parents of their child for spurious reasons.[11]

Jewish communities in the United States marched in protest in San Francisco and Boston. Protestants and evangelicals supported their righteous indignation.[12] In 1860, this tale of woe inspired Victor Séjour, a Franco-American playwright, to stage the *Soothsayer, or Tarot Card Reader,* which was loosely based on the Mortara affair and brought it to the attention of theatre audiences on both sides of the Atlantic.[13] Ambassadors from France, Piedmont, London and even reactionary Naples pleaded with the pope to return the boy to his family.[14] Pius IX reacted with extreme irritation, arguing that he was a great protector of the Jews and had done much to improve their condition.[15]

Further attempts to persuade the pope soon emerged. The Rothschilds wrote to their agents in Rome and directly to Pius demanding that, in the name of humanity, Edgardo be returned to his parents.[16] Their generous past loans were ignored, and their appeals met with a firm refusal. Sir Moses Montefiore, one of the United Kingdom's most prominent Jews, not to mention a financier and philanthropist, travelled to Rome in April 1859 to plead with the papacy for the release of the young boy. He was politely received by Cardinal Antonelli but his request to for an audience with Pius was denied.[17] This led to a firestorm in the European press.

The Mortara affair added to the Papal States' international isolation. This meant that, when the wars of Italian unification erupted, Pius had few allies to defend him in Europe. His principality was gradually swallowed up by the kingdom of Sardinia-Piedmont, which came to lead the movement for Italian unification. After 1859 the pope's domains were reduced to Rome and Lazio. Bologna, the starting point of this story, became an Italian city and Momolo's family gained full civil rights. Given the bad memories associated with this city they decided to relocate to Turin.[18] During the 1860s the Mortara affair took on a new meaning, when Pius declared open war on modern ideas and nationalism. Although he had lost most of his kingdom, he was determined not to admit that the kidnapping of Edgardo was a mistake. This Jewish boy became a symbol of the redemptive qualities of conversion.

The new Italian government issued arrest warrants for those responsible for the abduction of Edgardo. Pier Feletti, the former inquisitor, was one of the few papal officials not to flee Bologna. He was arrested on 31 December 1859. The hunter had become the prey.[19] Feletti had little empathy for the family he had torn asunder. It was decided that the inquisitor would stand trial for the kidnapping. Catholic opinion was incensed that a clergyman who had merely performed his duty could be tried like a common criminal. It confirmed all the church's worst fears about the liberal state's attitude towards priests.[20]

Feletti claimed ecclesiastical immunity from secular courts. Informed that clerical privilege had been abolished, the former inquisitor's resolve faltered. His defence became that he was only obeying the directives of a higher canonical authority. The witnesses cross-examined during the trial confirmed that the legate in Bologna, the archbishop of the city, and the Holy Office in Rome had all played important roles in this affair. After three months in detention, Feletti awaited his verdict on 14 April 1860. The judges found that the Dominican inquisitor had acted under the authority of the previous regime and not of his own accord. He was acquitted of all criminal charges and freed.[21] In Rome, Pius showed no sign of wishing to release Edgardo from his captivity. As time went on, the boy seemed to develop a deep and dependent relationship with his captors. On New Year's Day 1861, when the Jewish delegation was granted their regular audience with the pope, they noticed that next to him was a young boy. He was dressed in a seminarian's cassock and had clearly taken vows to enter the priesthood. To their horror they realised he was Edgardo![22]

In 1865 the young seminarian became a novice of the canons regular of the Lateran, friars who focused their energies on the pastoral care of souls and urban missionary work. He took the name Pio in honour of his 'benefactor'.[23] Within the gates of the monastery the fourteen-year-old convert had little hope of being rescued by his family. These canons wore white cassocks and a white skull cap which made them almost indistinguishable from the pope. By all accounts, Edgardo was a conscientious friar. When Rome fell to the Italian army in 1870, the young Mortara was interrogated by the military officers who took the city. He stated that he had no wish to return to a family, who, after thirteen years, were strangers to him. As a man of nineteen years of age Edgardo was free to do as he wished.[24]

Pius IX, fearing that his showpiece Jewish convert might be in danger, decided to ship Mortara abroad, to a convent in the Austrian empire. Meanwhile Momolo and Marianna had moved to Florence, broken by their failure to retrieve their son. On 3 April 1871, a servant in their household plunged to her death from an open window. The cause of this fatality has never been clear. Given the suspicious circumstances the Italian authorities indicted Momolo for murder. According to local reports he had a troublesome and possibly sexual relationship with the dead woman. In a bizarre verdict, the judges stated that due to a lack of evidence, they could not convict a specific culprit. Momolo was acquitted, but under a dark cloud. Completely humiliated and exhausted from a life of misfortune, he died a few months later in 1872.[25]

In 1878 Marianna, now a widow, visited her son on hearing that Edgardo was preaching in Roussillon on the Franco-Catalan border. It was a sad reunion and it marked how far mother and son had drifted after a life of separation. Although both were kind to each other and showed affection, Edgardo put pressure on his mother to convert to Christianity and follow his example – something this pious Jewish lady steadfastly refused to do. They remained in touch, and the young priest visited his family in Italy, but his siblings did not appreciate the invidious position in which Edgardo had been placed and resented his attempts to convert them to Christianity. Marianna died in 1890 and rumours circulated that she had converted on her death bed. Edgardo himself denied these murmurings, lamenting his failure to persuade his mother to embrace the 'true faith'. Although he did return regularly to Italy to preach the joys of Catholicism and devotion to the Virgin Mary he would spend the remainder of his life in a convent in Belgium. It was to be a long life: Father Pio-Edgardo, as he became known, eventually died in 1940.[26]

Mortara's plight proved emblematic of Pius IX's reign after 1849. Once his sovereignty was restored, he resisted all appeals for compromise or accommodation with progressive ideals with unremitting stubbornness. Although forced conversions of Jews in Catholic Europe were admittedly rare, Edgardo's case was not unique.[27] What made it especially painful was the extreme youth of the child in question. The defenders of the church point to the fact that Father Pio-Edgardo found fulfilment as a clergyman and embraced his new faith with enthusiasm. This may be hard to deny, but what alternative lay open to an impressionable child of six? By all accounts he was treated well in the House of the Catechumens. It must have been exciting to be received frequently in audience by Pius IX who entertained and treated the young boy as a family member. To meet and be complimented by the head of the largest religion on earth must have turned Edgardo's young head: how could it do otherwise?

Due to his forced conversion he was able to lead a life that would have been impossible as a member of a persecuted minority in Bologna. His captors transformed him from the offspring of a 'race of deicides' into a living manifestation of the Christian God's redemptive power. Yet if one lifts the veil of moral self-delusion behind which the church and its defenders hid, the fact remained that the Papal States, in a spasm of theological self-righteousness, deprived a family of one of their children. In so doing, they removed all agency, all freedom and all humanity from Edgardo. He became a pawn in the battle that pitted papal reaction against liberalism.

After his restoration in 1850, Pius set his kingdom on a defiant collision course with modernity. In a world beset by new ideas, political turmoil, revolution and moral ambiguity Catholicism promised certainty. Choice and freedom bred heresy and confusion. In their place the church offered rules, routines and spectacle. Whereas science and reason offered death as oblivion, the successor of St Peter promised redemption, salvation and eternal life. While the French revolutionaries and Napoleon had sought to subordinate the church, the new liberal governments that emerged after 1850 wanted to privatise and remove any public recognition for religion. Indifference proved a much greater threat to Catholicism than Napoleon's attempt to incorporate the church into his imperial edifice. The states of Europe threatened to cut the umbilical cord that had tied Catholicism to the state ever since Constantine's conversion to Christianity in the fourth century. Popes would resist this attempt to deprive them of political power with every weapon at their disposal.

Domestically, Pius IX wanted to demonstrate that even without representative government, or democracy, his subjects were governed humanely and efficiently. The truth of this is difficult to ascertain. Defenders of the church point to the fact that taxes were relatively low in the Papal States, whereas detractors point to the fact that indirect taxes in Rome made it one of the most expensive cities in Italy. For all its faults, Pius's administration did achieve one miracle. In 1858, for the first time in centuries the government of the Papal States balanced its books and was not in deficit.[28] The permanent presence of an Austrian occupying force in the legations of Romagna and the French garrison in Rome made it clear that, without foreign intervention, papal rule would prove impossible. There were certainly attempts to improve the infrastructure of the Papal States, but these proved ineffective. By 1859, a hundred kilometres of railway had been laid in central Italy whereas in Piedmont almost a thousand kilometres of track had been constructed.[29]

More serendipitous was an incident that occurred on 12 April 1855 near the church of St Agnese in Rome. After a ceremony in the church, the pope attended a reception for the Collegio di Propaganda. Halfway through the reception, creaking and disturbing sounds wafted upwards from the floorboards. Before an evacuation could take place, the floor collapsed, and the pope and his 130 admirers descended unexpectedly to the floor below. Remarkably nobody was harmed in the disaster. All cried out that a veritable miracle had saved Pius from certain death.[30] The pope vowed that he would go to Loreto to give thanks to the blessed virgin for his deliverance.

He decided to use the occasion to visit the northern provinces of his realm. In 1857 the convoy of papal carriages set off for a four-month excursion in which he would meet an enthusiastic reception from locals. He met the Grand Duke of Tuscany and spent many hours in dialogue with an emissary of King Victor Emanuel of Piedmont.[31] He paid particular attention to Bologna. It was imperative that he woo his most rebellious subjects and convince them of the benefits of papal government. During his stay, the pope had several meetings with his old liberal acquaintance Count Giuseppe Pasolini. This intellectual observed to Pius that the lack of a written constitution, not to mention the alliance with Austria, contributed to the international isolation of his principality. Liberal states, like France and Piedmont, could easily depict the papacy as a tyrannical theocracy.[32] Pasolini advised gradual reform and liberalisation to his sovereign. His unwelcome opinion was politely received and ignored.

Counterintuitively, during the 1850s the pope did make some headway in Protestant countries. British Prime Minister Robert Peel provided additional funding for Catholic seminaries in Maynooth, in Ireland, in 1845.[33] The aim was to facilitate the integration and pacification of this unruly minority. Emboldened by this, the Holy See decided to increase its activities in Protestant countries, and lobbied for religious toleration. In Holland and the United Kingdom, the Catholic episcopacy was re-established for the first time since the Reformation.[34] In England this proved deeply controversial, and the government, through an act of parliament, forbade Catholics from using the same titles as Anglican bishops. There were cries in the press that the pope, by re-establishing a Catholic hierarchy, was undermining the religious settlement which had governed Great Britain since the Glorious Revolution of 1688.[35] In the Low Countries there were attempts to reconcile with the Old Catholics of Utrecht, but these initiatives did not get very far. For better or worse, England and Holland were no longer mission territories and witnessed the re-establishment of Catholic hierarchies for the first time in almost four hundred years.

The rebirth of Catholicism in Britain reignited age-old debates about whether ritual, tradition or scripture should be paramount within the Anglican protestant tradition.[36] Some high-profile conversions to Rome, like those of John Henry Newman and Henry Edward Manning, raised alarm bells within the Anglican establishment. Yet the feared mass exodus never occurred. England and Scotland remained staunchly Protestant. The nineteenth century saw an evangelical revival in Britain that dwarfed any rediscovery of Catholicism.[37] Despite Rome's daydreams the English, Welsh and Scots had no intention of resuming communion with the papacy.

Across the Irish Sea, the situation in the pre-famine church was decidedly different. Though the Protestant ascendency continued to dominate elite culture and the public sphere on the island, it had failed to convert its tenantry and the labouring classes to its anti-Papist creed. The Roman Catholic clergy, like its European counterpart, was characterised by Gallican tendencies towards autonomy and a flexible adherence to Rome's distant authority.[38] During the first half of the nineteenth century there was a great shortage of priests, nuns and ecclesiastical buildings. As little as a third of the population were estimated to be regular churchgoers receiving the sacraments.[39] Such lax religious observance coincided with an accelerating abandonment of the Irish language and customs that had begun in the seventeenth century. Paul Cullen's appointment first as archbishop of Armagh in 1849 and then Dublin three years later, to become Ireland's first cardinal in 1866, was to prove a watershed moment for Irish Catholicism.[40]

A supporter of Pius IX, and former rector of the restored Irish College in Rome, Cullen had spent thirty years training priests at the heart of Italy. He now demanded that the Irish clergy toe the ultramontane line.

His reforms after the synod of Thurles in 1851 were instrumental in creating a resurgent and highly centralised, not to say authoritarian, version of Catholicism in Ireland.[41] It was a system that would survive unchallenged until the 1960s. Despite the disastrous decline of the Irish population due to the 1846–8 potato famine, Irish men and women flocked to take religious vows. In 1800 there were only 1,850 priests and 122 nuns to minister to four million souls; by 1870 numbers had risen to 3,200 priests and 3,700 nuns for the same population. Numbers of primary school pupils attending British-funded Catholic national schools rose from 100,000 in 1850 to 500,000 in 1900.[42] Illiteracy declined from 40% to a mere 15% during this same time. The church's tentacular grip on Irish society and culture was manifest in the realm of education. Cullen created what could be termed an Irish imperial church that gave unsolicited advice and direction to Irish prelates who held dioceses as far away as the US, Canada and Australia.[43]

The Hibernian episcopacy presided over a deep change in Irish identity at home and abroad. The ancient customs of the Gaels had been devasted by the penal laws and the cultural hegemony exercised by the Anglo-Irish ascendancy. Catholicism imbued Irishness with a new sense of coherence and confidence that filled the cultural and linguistic vacuum inherited from the eighteenth century. Yet Cullen was instinctually cautious, as he had witnessed the radicalism of the Roman Republic and Mazzini. He detested the Young Ireland movement and condemned the violence of Fenianism from the pulpit.[44]

Instead, the Irish church he moulded was Connellite to the marrow. During the 1840s, O'Connell's repeal association had coordinated its political campaigning with Father Theobald Mathew's total abstinence society, which worked successfully to reduce the consumption of whiskey and beer.[45] For the church, it was not just a question of political nationhood but of regenerating society morally. Cullen's episcopacy supported constitutional nationalism and sought a partnership with the British establishment rather than its overthrow. At the same time the Irish clergy championed land reform against Protestant landlords and the redistribution of farms to poor tenants, supporting land agitation but always a little uneasy about Michael Davitt's Land League (1879–81) and its radicalism.[46]

The Irish Catholic Church would change beyond recognition from 1800 to 1900. Under Cullen the clergy flourished and hundreds of new churches were constructed across the island with British subsidies. Religious observance became the norm as mass attendance rates reached 90 per cent. The sacraments, processions and pilgrimages became a visible manifestation of Irish communal identity. Historian Emmet Larkin has described this process as a 'devotional revolution'.[47] Fear of social ostracisation or clerical censure forced Irishmen and women into a passive acceptance of religiosity. Ultramontane Catholicism fostered social cohesion with its focus on baroque display and a puritanical commitment to the family as the building block of society.

The British state's near-surrender of education to the Church of Rome meant that Irish people could not hope to escape poverty or advance socially without being indoctrinated in Catholic dogma.[48] While the growth of the Irish church was a success story for nineteenth-century Catholicism, its strengths hid from sight its contradictions. The near-perfection demanded by Cullen of his clergy and their congregations meant that the Irish episcopacy developed an almost pathological phobia of scandal and public immorality. Difficult moral questions were relegated to the private sphere where, far from being resolved, they festered.

Equally public denunciations of Protestantism and all its works hid from sight the reality that Irish Catholic bishops were committed collaborators with the British empire. Catholics who worked for the civil service in Dublin Castle did so with the benediction of their clergy.[49] One of the great success stories of this time was Lord Russell of Killowen who, educated exclusively in Irish establishments, rose to become the first Catholic chief justice of England and Wales in 1894.[50] The Irish church shared Catholicism's love of power and its protean ability to adjust to seemingly hostile environments. As the twentieth century dawned, republicanism, socialism and secularism were considered bigger foes than the British establishment.

The situation was similar in much of Europe, where 1848 had convinced many conservatives that reforms and concessions were necessary for the preservation of social and political order. Constitutions and parliaments had survived in Germany, Scandinavia, Spain, and Portugal. Italy was the exception, in that only Piedmont had maintained the *Statuto Albertino,* while the other pre-unitary states remained absolutist. This constitution de facto abolished the ghetto of Turin, and allowed all religions to be tolerated. Its text heralded the disestablishment of Catholicism in the principality. Camillo Benso, Count of Cavour, came to prominence as a liberal prime minister of King Victor Emanuel II. Although he was a man of some Catholic faith, he was deeply impressed with the achievements of liberal France and England.[51] Only by curbing the church's power, he believed, in this corner of north-western Italy, could political, social and economic progress be achieved. Cavour was not a modern secularist, being closer to the eighteenth-century regalists and the ideas of Joseph II. In his view, the church must serve the state and provide social utility.[52]

As a liberal, Cavour proposed the formula of a 'free church within a free state', which deeply displeased Pius IX. Cavour's reforms of the 1850s sent shock waves through Italy, and led to the accusation that he was a godless anticlerical. The first big measure, the Siccardi law of 1850, involved the *Foro ecclesiastico.* This measure removed the privilege that exempted clergymen from the jurisdiction of ordinary courts of law.[53] Given that the *Statuto* had established equality before the law, it was offensive that ordained ministers could benefit from a separate system of justice. In response to the abolition of the *Foro,* the archbishop of Turin instructed his clergy not to collaborate with the police or courts of law. As punishment, this prelate spent some time in the grim Fenestrelle fortress in the Alps before being exiled from Piedmont.[54] The church's refusal to accept the jurisdiction of secular courts to try priests was to prove a public-relations disaster, one whose effects are still being felt a century and a half later.

These early disagreements ensured a highly dysfunctional working relationship between the Holy See and the state of Piedmont. This might have been avoided if the Savoyard monarchy had renounced its right to appoint bishops so as to induce the papacy to accept compromises. Instead, mistrust escalated with the Rattazzi law of 1855, which ordered the closure and seizure of monastic land on a scale not seen since Joseph II seven decades earlier.[55] Out of 604 convents, 334 were suppressed. In retaliation, Rome decided to excommunicate those responsible for the law.[56] Many of the locksmiths, masons and labourers charged with seizing monastic property refused to carry out government orders.

Indeed, the question of monastic confiscations led to a brief conflict between Cavour and the king, who was increasingly uncomfortable with the anticlerical direction of travel his government was taking. The prime minister briefly resigned but, as nobody else was able to form a cabinet, Cavour was quickly back in office.[57] In order to reduce further the church's influence on electoral politics,[58] he then enacted a law which made clergymen ineligible for public office. These anticlerical measures highlighted how times had changed for the church, even in Italy. Sardinia-Piedmont had been one of the most theocratic and fiercely loyal Catholic states in the world. Such a sharp turn towards liberalism and anticlericalism should have made it clear to the papacy that it could not rely even on its former heartlands.

Pius reacted against secular encroachments on the church's authority with a belligerent reassertion of religious truth. During his reign, some of the profoundest dogmas of the modern papacy would be defined and grafted onto the very marrow of Catholic identity. Mary the mother of Jesus had always been the object of fervent veneration in the Roman church. Yet for all the ardent veneration, the statues, apparitions, medals and Marian cults, the theological status of Mary was not clear.[59] The key issue revolved around the way in which God chose this ordinary woman as the vessel through which he became incarnate as Jesus Christ. It was unthinkable that a person contaminated by original sin and sexual intercourse could have given birth to God. Yet gospels and other sources were silent as to why Mary was selected for this singular honour. The archangel Gabriel in Luke's gospel had announced that she was 'full of grace' (Luke 1: 26–38) but this added to the mystery rather than clarifying it.

Since the Middle Ages, theologians had speculated that Mary had been born into the world without the taint of original sin.[60] This hypothesis became known as the 'immaculate conception'. Many Catholics had believed in it fervently and propagated the cult. Yet there was no consensus on the issue. The great St Thomas Aquinas had contested this theological hypothesis.[61] But the Council of Basel of 1431 believed that it was consistent with scripture and, by the sixteenth century, 8 December had come to be celebrated annually as the feast of the Immaculate Conception.[62] Yet there was no clear definition of this remarkable concept. The Catholic obsession with Mary's feminine purity sits very well with the church's almost exclusively masculine culture. According to Catholic tradition, only men could act in *persona christi* during the sacrifice of the mass. Jesus chose male form and only appointed men as his apostles. The assumption was made that only men could be channels for the miracle of transubstantiation (the moment at the consecration when bread and wine are transformed into the body and blood of Jesus).

This of course left a problem for the church, as women like Mary Magdalen or Martha were key disciples of Christ; indeed, they played important roles in the early church.[63] Mary the mother of Jesus provided a solution to this problem of female invisibility. By elevating her to semi-divine status it made her femininity the highest symbol of purity. In practice, women now had a role model but one that was impossible to emulate: a divine woman free from contamination, desire or temptation. The immaculate conception was an effective means of celebrating women, whilst simultaneously subordinating them. Only nuns, hidden from the world and shielded from concupiscence, could come close to fulfilling the Marian ideal.

Pius IX, as a fervent practitioner of the cult of Mary, was determined to clarify her position from a theological standpoint. He consulted the bishops of the Catholic world about whether the immaculate conception should be defined as dogma. Over 90 per cent responded positively that it should become one of the pillars of Catholic belief.[64] Upon returning to Rome from his exile he created a commission of theologians, to transform the immaculate conception into a dogma.[65] It took these men of learning almost four years to prepare a text which would fulfil Pius' dream. On 8 December 1854 the papal bull *Ineffabilis deus,* which raised the Virgin Mary above all the saints of the church, was promulgated.[66] The church, guided by Pius, affirmed that it was the custodian of all divine revelation, which had ceased upon Christ's ascension into heaven. Catholicism claimed that it had received from God a finite 'deposit of faith'. This implied that Rome alone had complete authority to interpret divine scripture and define ecclesiastical tradition. Reason and research could not elucidate such mysteries. Only faith, guided by the papacy, could aspire to do so. This text threw down the gauntlet and directly challenged the assumptions and worldview of modernity. Liberals, socialists and scientists, with their ephemeral intellectual fashions, could not compete with the church, which alone had the power to reveal eternal and immutable truths.

The bull ended with the grim admonition that to deny the immaculate conception of Mary was to incur automatic excommunication.[67] Despite this dire warning the dogma proved to be popular amongst grassroots Catholics, who for centuries had believed in Mary as a powerful intercessor in their daily lives. The mother of God had fulfilled their desires, hopes and expectations for generations. She had been there for them in times of despair, hardship, and death.* With this bull, the papacy effectively endorsed the passionate enthusiasm of Marian congregations that extended from Spain all the way to Poland.

In theory, this was entirely an internal matter, pertinent only to the church's magisterium. It is nevertheless difficult not to resist analysing the dogma of the immaculate conception from a political perspective. In highly romantic terms, it sought to reassert

---

* Some Madonnas were also believed to punish; see Michael P. Carroll, *Madonnas That Maim: Popular Catholicism in Italy since the Fifteenth Century* (Baltimore, 1992).

tradition, mysticism and papal authority above reason, liberty, individualism and science. In it, Pius launched a thunderbolt against the complacent politicians of Europe's capitals. One suspects that many well-educated elites read *Ineffabilis deus* with wry smirks of contempt. Little did they know how quickly the masses in the remote countryside would make the Virgin Mary the symbol of their rejection of an increasingly intrusive state. Most Catholics were peasants throughout the period covered by this book. The modern state brought unwelcome taxes, conscription and surveillance into the countryside.[68] It is little wonder that religion offered forms of solace to ordinary people that liberal politics could not.

Almost a decade before, on 19 September 1846, two teenage children, Maximin Giraud and Mélanie Calvat, were minding some cows close to the town of La Salette in Dauphiné on the foothills of the French alps. Suddenly they came upon a mysterious lady who was seated in a state of some distress and weeping uncontrollably. Her dress was white and gold and covered with pearls. At her feet lay roses. She wore a crucifix and an ornate headdress that resembled a coronet. Initially shocked, the children froze as she turned toward them and said: 'Do not be afraid.' She brought glad tidings that, although her son had been angry with the world for turning away from God, there was still time to repent and convert. She knew that potato blight and poor harvests had devasted the local community. In both French and the local Occitan dialect she advised the locals not to plant seeds until the next year. She recommended that people pray more, reciting the Lord's Prayer and the Hail Mary. Each child then received a secret to guard in their hearts. After this admonition the Lady, depending on the children's different versions of the encounter, rose into the clouds or disappeared up a mountain.[69]

The local parish priest was much taken with this revelation and broke into tears, though sceptics wondered how far he was delighted to have some distraction from the monotonous duties of a parish situated in a dull provincial backwater. Shortly afterwards, on the ground where the Virgin had appeared, a miraculous spring of clear water burst forth. Five years later, the local bishops authenticated the apparition,[70] which replicated patterns of Marian manifestations that had occurred through the centuries. The virgin tended to appear to innocent, marginalised children. Her appearance coincided with a period of economic hardship and the onset of political revolution. The message, generally, was one of hope and redemption to be followed by a prediction of economic prosperity.[71]

Very soon pilgrims and the curious flocked to see the site of the apparition in La Salette. After several years, the diocese invested a considerable sum to build a large sanctuary which could house the pilgrims coming to this holy site. In later years Mélanie became a nun and Maximin became a Papal Zouave after dropping out of medical school. They both eventually published the secrets entrusted to them by the Virgin. In both accounts Mary stated that France would be punished for having corrupted the world. Apocalyptic times awaited humanity, and the church would be persecuted. In Maxim's case the lady had informed him the redemption of the world would begin in a Protestant country. As was often the case, the mother of God expressed her deep disgust at a world that was turning away from religious traditions and public devotions. Throughout the nineteenth century, the Virgin Mary was to appear with some regularity as Table 1 indicates.

Table 1 Apparitions of the Virgin Mary during the nineteenth century

Title	Visionary	Place	Year
Our Lady of the Miraculous Medal	Catherine Labouré	Paris, France	1830
Madonna of the Miracle	Marie-Alphonse Ratisbonne	Rome, Papal States	1842
Our Lady of La Salette	Mélanie Calvat Maximin Giraud	La Salette, France	1846
Our Lady of Lourdes	Bernadette Soubirous	Lourdes, France	1858
Our Lady of Licheń	Nicholas Sikatka	Licheń, Poland	1850
Madonna Addolorata del Cerreto	Veronica Nucci	Cerreto, Italy	1853

Our Lady of Good Help	Adele Brise	Champion, Wisconsin, USA	1859
Our Lady of Pontmain	Eùgene Barbadette Joseph Barbadette Jeanne-Marie Lebossé Françoise Richer	Pontmain, France	1871
Santa Maria Ausiliatrice	Angela Berruti	Feglino, Italy	1874
(False) Marian apparitions in Marpingen	Margaretha Kunz Katharina Hubertus Susanna Leist	Marpingen, Trier, Germany	1876
Our Lady of Pellevoisin	Estelle Faguette	Pellevoisin, France	1876
Our Lady of Gietrzwałd	Stanisława Samulowska Justyna Szafryńska	Gietrzwałd, Poland	1877
Our Lady of Knock	Fifteen people	Knock, Ireland	1879
Maria Santissima Addolorata di Castelpetroso	Fabiana Cicchino, Serafina Valentino	Castelpetroso, Italy	1888
Our Lady of Donglü	Seven hundred people	Donglü, Hebei, China	1900

It would be incorrect to state that these manifestations were extraordinary. The sixteenth and seventeenth centuries probably experienced an equal number of such apparitions. What is striking, however, is that, out of the fifteen Marian events listed above, eleven occurred during Pius IX's reign. Even more enlightening is the fact that Mary appeared in France five times, Italy four times and Poland twice. As epicentres of conflicts between church and state, the mother of God's appearance seemed to vindicate (somewhat conveniently, it might be said) the church's newfound confidence in her intercession, centrality and power.

One of the reasons why Lourdes, the most famous of all Marian miracles, was so striking were the words of the Virgin. Bernadette Soubirous shared many of the characteristics of the women and children who experienced such visions. She was vulnerable, in ill health and possibly the victim of domestic abuse. Her father had been an unsuccessful mill owner with a drinking problem. As an illiterate and neglected child who spoke a Pyrenean dialect rather than French, she seemed an unlikely medium through which the divine would manifest itself. Regardless, on 11 February 1858 this teenager experienced the first of eighteen apparitions. The Virgin at Lourdes was more child- and fairy-like in her appearance, and decidedly less loquacious, than the crying Lady at La Salette. She was rather friendlier, and less apocalyptic in her messages.[72] The denouement came, on 25 March, with the sixth apparition. Local priests had instructed Bernadette to ask who the mystery lady was? The intention was to discover whether this entity was the Virgin Mary or a demon in disguise. The answer came in the local patois: 'Que soy era Immaculada Counceptiou' (that I am the Immaculate Conception).[73]

This, for the clergy, confirmed the veracity of Bernadette's claims to have communed with God's mother. How could a theologically ignorant peasant girl understand such a complex idea as the immaculate conception? The answer was probably simpler than these men might have imagined. This fragile and unschooled girl could easily have stirred from her boredom during Sunday homilies and heard the term 'immaculate conception' explained to her congregation in church. In a rural world where reproductive sex was omnipresent, it must have been remarkable to learn that God had procreated asexually with a perfect woman. Pius's redefinition of Mary's role in the church was something that not merely appealed to elites, but had captured the imaginations of ordinary folk. Rome's perspective on the immaculate conception and Ineffabilis deus had received its vindication on the foothills of the Pyrenees.

Further confirmation occurred when another miraculous spring bubbled up at the site of Bernadette's visions. This one claimed to cure from all afflictions those endowed with a pure faith. In the years to come, on average, anywhere between sixty to ninety cures per annum were declared.[74] Yet the healing narratives of the sick focused far more on the nature of their faith, and how it had been strengthened by bathing in and drinking the miraculous waters. Little actual medical evidence was considered or analysed in the first decades of Lourdes. It was only during the 1880s that Catholic elites and intellectuals asked for the medically trained to examine and certify the miracles, as Benedict XIV had urged as far back as the 1740s.[75] The creation of a medical bureau at the shrine hardly convinced sceptics and atheists. For radical secularists it underscored the urgent need for the church to stay well away from sick patients, not to mention its tendency to understand disease as a manifestation of sin and the supernatural.[76]

Much of what happened in this Pyrenean town was dismissed as mass auto-suggestion by the medical establishment in Paris. In contrast, religiously inclined doctors tried to certify the curative powers of faith and divine intercession.[77] The chasm dividing believers and unbelievers was impossible to bridge. Mary remained the border guard on the frontier that separated the secular citizen from the devout peasant. These Marian sites were spaces where divine immanence could be felt and experienced. Liberal states provided only individualism and isolation, whereas the miraculous bestowed a sense of community and meaning on life. For ordinary Catholics, Lourdes became a sacred site of pilgrimage and hope – a place where a distant God sent his beloved mother to bestow comfort and healing. It certainly turned this sleepy Pyrenean village into a bustling town with a major shrine, hotel businesses, teeming souvenir shops and, eventually, its own airport. Observers who were less than charitable wondered about the extent to which Marianism was big business for the church.

A troubling and analogous case occurred in Marpingen, near Saarbrücken in Germany. The events of 1876 followed a recognisable pattern. Three young pre-pubescent girls experienced a visitation from the Virgin while out in some woodland. Very leading questions were put to them by Father Jakob Neureuter, the local parish priest. Excited by the prospect that he might have his own personal Lourdes on his hands, this clergyman let his enthusiasm get the better of him. Instead of asking the girls what they had witnessed or been told, he sought confirmation that Mary had declared she was the immaculate conception. The three girls repeated what the priest asked them with enthusiasm. All further answers to Father Neureuter's questions vindicated *Ineffabilis deus* and the church's Marianisation. Soon a miraculous spring with curative properties was discovered, and thousands flocked to this Germanic Lourdes seeking cures.[78] It was embarrassing for all involved when, in 1889, Margaretha Kunz, one of the eight-year-old visionaries and now a novice nun, wrote a confession in which she revealed that the apparition had been a lie.[79] The young girls, having heard about Lourdes, wanted to imitate Bernadette. As events spiralled out of control, Kunz admitted that she and her confederates had enjoyed the limelight. Fake apparitions are nothing new, and the church has debunked many, but this one came close to fooling the church authorities.

Despite its eventual discrediting as a hoax, Marpingen in 1876 had attracted crowds of thousands of pilgrims seeking solace and cures. Mary's appearance, during a time of economic hardship and religious renewal, seemed providential. It captured the imagination of the rural masses of the Saarland. As will be discussed later in this chapter, Germany was experiencing a significant conflict between the Vatican and Bismarck's freshly unified state known as the *Kulturkampf* (struggle for civilisation).[80] The sudden appearance of such Catholic fervour on the banks of the Saar troubled the local authorities, and the local mayor decided that these mass gatherings were disturbing public order. Gendarmes were sent to scatter the pilgrims, but proved to be too few to convince people to leave.

On 13 July 1876 the 8th company of the 4th Rhenish regiment arrived in Marpingen. As the crowds became hostile and unsettled, the decision was made to fix bayonets and disperse the unarmed pilgrims. Although one gendarme was almost thrown from his horse, none of the soldiers were injured during these scuffles; however, more than sixty Catholic pilgrims suffered cuts and injuries in the melee.[81] After this event there was a serious press battle. The controversial decision was taken to place the three eight-year-old visionaries on remand. Several individuals, including the parish priest, were indicted with disturbing the peace and other public-order offenses. Liberals portrayed the believers as bigoted, ignorant and credulous peasants. It was argued that the state had every right to police and prohibit such backward superstition. In response, the eminent Prince Edmund von Radziwill, a monk and member of the Catholic Zentrum party, came out in defence of the pilgrims. He declared that states had no business regulating the religious beliefs and observances of minorities.[82]

German Catholics argued, with some justification, that they were being hounded and sidelined because of their loyalty to Rome. On 16 January 1877 there was a furious parliamentary debate in the Reichstag, in which the Zentrum party and liberals skirmished for five hours on whether the local authorities in Marpingen had overreached themselves. The denouement of the entire affair occurred in a trial before the supreme court of Saarbrücken in March 1879. Although the judges and prosecution sneered at the unsophisticated credulity of the rural inhabitants of this town, the verdict found that the state authorities had been heavy-handed in their approach. All those indicted of disturbing the peace were acquitted and the government was forced to pay their legal costs.[83] In the end the authorities in Germany had used a sledgehammer to crack a very small nut. Marpingen might well have vanished into history as an elaborate hoax. Yet, the political mismanagement of this affair highlighted the lengths to which the liberal state might go in order to thwart Catholic popular devotions.

Mary's tendency to reappear during Pius's reign was notable. Public debates over the church's role in influencing the visionaries could be vicious. So too were scientific and medical debates on whether any cure could be described as miraculous. The phenomena of Lourdes and later Marpingen were interpreted by politicians as a direct challenge to the authority of the state and modern science. Simply put, those who sought solace and healing as a community of believers put their Catholic faith above their citizenship, to the deep disturbance of middle-class elites in France, Italy and Germany. Primary schools, factories and the army would become key institutions in which superstition was to be eradicated.[84]

Emile Zola, the novelist, had visited Lourdes during the 1880s and seemed impressed by what he observed. However, to the indignation of the Catholics who had hosted him in this Pyrenean valley, he published a hostile novel entitled *Lourdes* in 1894. He dismissed the women who experienced cures as hysterics and hinted at possible sexual frustration in those touched by the divine. More damning still was the interpretation that the Marian apparitions were largely caused by the power of mass suggestion.[85] Although the dogma of the immaculate conception accelerated and galvanised the Catholic revival of the nineteenth century, it further increased the gulf that divided church and state.

Pius IX's greatest priority, the retention of his kingdom, was to prove his deepest disappointment. It was the lost cause of Catholicism during the nineteenth century. Without either allies or an international guarantee of neutrality, the Papal States were in diplomatic terms a sitting duck. During these years, however, conservatives and reactionaries from across Europe volunteered to serve as soldiers for the Holy Father. Legitimists from France, Carlists from Spain, pious Neapolitans, Irish Catholic nationalists (recruited by Cardinal Cullen), along with Belgian and Swiss mercenaries, all travelled to serve the cause. The Papal Zouaves, with their remarkable long mustachios, blue shirts and white baggy pantaloons, looked like a band of desperados.[86] Their fearsome appearance added to the mystique of these international defenders of Pius's divine right. Given that they were poorly armed, badly equipped and ill-supplied, they were hardly a formidable fighting force against modern armies. Pio Nono would need all the external help he could get.

Cavour and Victor Emmanuel II had been desperate to extricate Piedmont from the diplomatic isolation in which this tiny kingdom had languished since Charles Albert's defeat in 1849. Sometimes Cavour is presented as a Machiavellian genius, who was busily planning Italian unification from 1854 onwards.[87] Such a view is far too simplistic. Like any statesman, the Piedmontese prime minister could hardly see into the future, but he could recognise an opportunity when he saw one. His decision to join Britain and France in the Crimean war in 1855 gained this corner of north-eastern Italy some powerful friends.[88]

Other events came to his aid as well. On the evening of 14 January 1858 Napoleon III and the Empress Eugenie were on their way to the Paris Opera to enjoy Rossini's extravaganza *William Tell*. Out of the crowd, three masked terrorists emerged and hurled bombs at the imperial convoy. Windows were shattered, eight people were killed and over one hundred were wounded. Although unharmed, the imperial couple were badly shaken.[89] An Italian revolutionary, Felice Orsini, was captured and found to be the mastermind behind the assassination attempt. Louis-Napoleon met with his would-be murderer and expressed sympathy for the Italian cause. Before being guillotined Orsini wrote an open letter to the French emperor begging him to support the Italian nation's desire for unity. Given Louis-Napoleon's experience as a revolutionary *carbonaro* in Italy during his youth, he was inclined to be sympathetic. Once the letter was published, the emperor replied, cryptically, that the youth of the peninsula and their national aspirations were close to his heart.[90]

Plombières-les-bains is a spa town in southern Lorraine renowned for the curative properties of its mineral waters. In July 1858, many visitors dressed in fine suits turned up in this sleepy holiday destination. Two gentlemen, one clean-shaven and stout, the other with Mephistophelian whiskers, an over-sized chest and bandy legs, sat in animated conversation. They were none other than Cavour and Napoleon III, who had come to discuss the Italian situation. Victor Emmanuel, who was famous for his mercurial nature, had remained at home; he was unlikely to be of any help in the world of patient diplomacy. During these secret meetings in Plombières, Piedmont and France signed a secret alliance. This stipulated that if Piedmont were to be attacked by the Habsburgs, France would swiftly cross the Alps to join the struggle and fight for the creation of a northern Italian kingdom. France demanded the provinces of Nice (Garibaldi's birthplace) and Savoy as compensation for its military assistance. Given that these border areas were on the wrong side of the Alps, and mostly French-speaking, Cavour agreed.[91]

The plan had been that an insurrection would be triggered in the duchy of Massa and Carrara in northern Tuscany. Unhelpfully, the denizens of these remote Tuscan provinces failed to oblige Cavour and failed to rebel, and it seemed that the longed-for war would not materialise. Napoleon III wanted to avoid appearing as the aggressor in a conflict, so he suggested an agreement in which both Piedmont and Austria would stand down. Unexpectedly, on 23 April 1859 the Habsburg ambassador in Turin delivered an ultimatum demanding that the Piedmontese army disarm unilaterally.[92] Cavour could not believe his luck! According to legend he whistled the famous and rousing aria from Verdi's *Trovatore* 'Di quella pira'. Six days later Vienna declared war, playing straight into the hands of the secret alliance sealed at Plombières.[93]

Field Marshal Ferenc Gyulay, Radetzky's successor, invaded Piedmont. If he had delivered a knockout blow to the small army of Victor Emmanuel the campaign might have ended before it began. Unfortunately for Gyulay, he hesitated and tried to manoeuvre his army along the axis of the Mincio river where Radetzky had scored some of his greatest victories in 1849. This wasted valuable time, allowing French forces to arrive swiftly by railway. In June, at the battles of Magenta and Solferino, Franco-Piedmontese forces defeated the Habsburgs, but at the price of almost fifty thousand casualties on both sides.[94] Horrified by these losses, Napoleon III signed an armistice with the Habsburgs on 12 July at Villafranca. To Cavour's chagrin he annexed the Lombardy region to France and then agreed to transfer the province to Piedmont.[95] Humiliatingly, Venetia remained part of the Austrian empire, in breach of the Plombières agreement.

Although Piedmont felt betrayed by its French allies, the rest of Italy met the news from the north with enthusiasm. Cavour temporarily resigned from the government in protest over the violation of the terms of the Plombières agreement, but was soon back in office.[96] Carefully staged insurrections now occurred in central Italy. The dukes of Tuscany, Parma and Modena were literally sent packing in bloodless revolutions. More ominously for Pius, the same treatment was reserved for the three papal legates of Romagna. Although the fate of central Italy hung in the balance for some time, the acquiescence of the French and British governments allowed for plebiscites to be held in these duchies, resulting in an overwhelming vote to join Piedmont in 1860.[97] France agreed to recognise this enlarged northern Italian kingdom if it received Nice and Savoy in compensation.

Pius protested the loss of Romagna in the most vehement terms; little did he know that worse was to come. The year 1860 certainly epitomised the law of unintended consequences. Napoleon III had wanted to help Piedmont conquer only the Austrian provinces of Lombardy and Venetia. According to the terms agreed at Plombières, the pope, the central duchies and the Bourbons of Naples were supposed to be left in peace.[98] As hostilities in the northern theatre ceased, Garibaldi and a thousand red-shirted volunteers embarked from Genoa in May 1861.[99] Their destination was Marsala in Sicily. The plan was to incite a local rebellion and unseat the Bourbon dynasty. Few, especially Cavour, thought that his plan had much chance of succeeding.

Neither the Piedmontese navy nor the Royal Navy made much effort to stop Garibaldi.[100] After all, the thousand red-shirts were going to face a modern and well-equipped army of a hundred thousand Bourbon troops. However, due to appalling generalship, possible collusion and lack of resolve, these professional solders retreated under the pressure of the irregular volunteers, and Garibaldi proclaimed himself dictator of Sicily on behalf of Victor Emmanuel II, whom he described as king of Italy.[101] With astonishing rapidity, the volunteers crossed the Strait of Messina and started a triumphal progress northward. Large concentrations of Bourbon troops capitulated to Garibaldi, whose reputation as a military genius destroyed their will to resist.

Since the death of *Il re bomba* in 1859, his son Francis II had sat precariously on the throne of the Two Sicilies. On 5 September 1860, the king lost his nerve and evacuated Naples. To Garibaldi's complete astonishment the city's garrison and the Neapolitan navy anchored in the bay capitulated to him without firing a shot.[102] Despite this, the war was not over yet, and the red-shirts marched north to meet the still-formidable remnants of the Bourbon army. The final battle, fought between 26 September and 2 October, centred on the southern bank of the Volturno river, north-west of Naples, where Francis II's men outnumbered the volunteers two to one. It was a hard-won victory for the red-shirts and one that determined the future of the south within a united Italy. With mixed feelings Garibaldi met with Victor Emanuel II at Teano, to the north of Gaeta, where Francis and his remaining troops had retreated. Here the great guerrilla leader surrendered his conquests in southern Italy to the king of Piedmont, whom he recognised as sovereign of the entire peninsula.[103]

The Neapolitan monarch held out for four months in the great fortress in Gaeta, which had once sheltered Pius IX after he had fled the revolution in 1848. On 13 February 1861, despite the king's courage and the heroism of the garrison, the remaining Bourbon forces capitulated, overwhelmed by the Piedmontese artillery barrages from both land and sea. Francis II decided to spend his exile in Rome as a personal guest of the pope.[104]

The Papal States did not escape from being sucked into the military vortex that had enveloped Italy. Patriots from Tuscany made an incursion into central Italy and briefly captured Perugia. A column of Zouaves assaulted the town and retook it for their pope-king.[105] The brutal seizure of this university town, and the lowering of the Italian tricolour, incensed nationalist sensibilities throughout Italy. By early 1860 volunteers flocked from Catholic Europe to aid in the defence of the pope's principality. Among them were Baron Athanase Charette de la Contrie and Henri de Cathelineau, both of whom had served with the Austrian army and were experienced soldiers. Their arrival seemed providential, and it was remarked that they were descendants of famous Vendean guerrilla leaders from the 1790s.[106] These regions, which had fought for their religion and priests against the French Revolution, transmitted this vocation to later generations. Another large contingent was made up of Irish aristocrats and adventurers who, encouraged by Cardinal Cullen, like the 'wild geese' of the eighteenth century had come to fight for Catholicism.

The most famous of this Irish contingent was Myles Walter

Keogh from County Carlow. After his tour of duty with the papal army he travelled to America where he met his death during Custer's last stand at the Little Big Horn in 1876.[107] Less wholesome was John Surratt, an American with long whiskers, who joined the papal forces in 1866. He had been an associate of John Wilkes Booth and participated in planning the assassination of President Lincoln. When the American minister Rufus King discovered that this man was serving in the papal forces, a long-drawn-out extradition process was initiated. Ultimately Surratt was expelled to the United States, where he stood trial and was acquitted.*

By mid-1860, almost twenty-five thousand volunteers had arrived in Rome to defend what remained of the kingdom of the church in central Italy. Facing these assorted foreign troops were over seventy thousand crack Piedmontese soldiers. In September, a carefully planned insurrection broke out in the Marche and Umbria regions. Cavour sent an ultimatum demanding that all military forces in these eastern provinces of the papacy be evacuated. This demarche was never answered.[108] The Italian invasion of the Papal States was to be two-pronged. One column would invade the Marche and the other Umbria. Despite some gallant resistance in Orvieto and Spoleto the papal forces were forced to capitulate quickly in Umbria.[109]

Refusing to be intimidated, a large contingent of Swiss and Irish Zouaves marched to reinforce the citadel of Ancona. This key strategic port on the Adriatic had been occupied many times during the nineteenth century by hostile powers. On the approaches to Ancona a pitched battle was fought at Castelfidardo near Loreto. Here the pope's troops, though badly outnumbered, tried to slow down the Piedmontese advance towards this stronghold on the Adriatic. It was hopeless. On 18 September 1860, the encirclement of the port and its walls was completed. Artillery from ground forces and from the Piedmontese navy fired shells into Ancona

---

* His mother had not been so lucky. She was hanged the previous year for having sheltered Booth in her boarding house. See Frederick Hatch, *John Surratt, Rebel, Lincoln Conspirator, Fugitive* (Jefferson, NC, 2016), esp. pp. 85–129.

from all angles. After an eleven-day defence the Zouaves and their commanders surrendered. The walls of Ancona looked like Swiss cheese and the defenders' cannons had been destroyed.[110] Pius's volunteers had faced overwhelming numbers and modern artillery. The hundreds of men who died for the Papal States had only delayed the inevitable. Soon plebiscites were organised in the Marche and Umbria region. They voted overwhelmingly to be annexed to Italy.[111] Pius now reigned over a miniature kingdom that compromised only Rome and Lazio.

When the legations of Romagna voted for annexation, an almost immediate condemnation was issued. On 26 March 1860 the brief *Cum Catholica ecclesia* had denounced all violations of papal sovereignty and pronounced excommunication on all those who were responsible. The brief specified that all 'mandatories, accomplices, supporters, counsellors, followers or promoters' of the annexation of papal territory were to be considered outside of the church.[112] *Cum Catholica ecclesia* specified that the excommunication included not just those Piedmontese and Italian officials currently in office, but also their successors and future appointees.

It was one of a dozen or so documents issued against the Piedmontese government during these years. When, in June 1861, Cavour suddenly became gravely ill, it was clear he was dying. He asked a friend of his to hear his final confession and bestow the last rites. Giacomo da Poirino, a Franciscan priest, arrived at the Cavour palazzo in Turin and gave absolution to the great enemy of Pius IX.[113] Cardinal Antonelli summoned this insubordinate confessor to Rome. Pius received him in a private audience. He asked if Cavour had made a public retraction of all his sins against papal sovereignty. When it became clear that no written retraction existed the pope was very angry. Poirino was censured by the Inquisition and had his right to hear confession suspended. The archbishop of Turin later deprived him of his parish.[114] However, he was rewarded by the Italian government with the order of St Maurice and Lazarus and provided with a pension.

Pius was traumatised, wrathful and unrealistic in his expectations. He hoped that the divine providence that had restored him to power in 1850 would perform the same miracle during the 1860s. It was a decided irony that the liberal Pio Nono of 1846, the great hope of the Neo-Guelph movement, was now perceived as the biggest barrier to the completion of unification.[115] Pius complicated matters by enacting some highly damaging fiscal policies in the aftermath of unification. Although he had lost most of his realm, the pope refused to default on, or transfer, his public debt to the new kingdom of Italy. Such an action would have been an implicit recognition and legitimation of the new unitary state. The bondholders for the Papal States had to be repaid, despite a collapse in revenue. To survive, the practice of Peter's pence was revived. This involved an appeal, throughout the parishes of Europe, for voluntary contributions to help the papacy maintain Rome and its fiscal commitments. Catholics gave generously and millions of *scudi* flowed into the coffers of the church. French legitimists gave prodigally, and their contribution amounted to almost 40 per cent of the total.[116]

The survival of the Papal States was to be the key question for the peninsula during the 1860s. On 17 March 1861 Victor Emmanuel II was proclaimed king of Italy in Florence. Ten days later the new Italian parliament published the declaration *Roma Capitale*, which proclaimed that national opinion demanded Rome be the capital of a united Italy.[117] Not all Italians were pleased with unification. Many were disillusioned by the centralising ambitions of the new state while others, loyal to the old dynasties of the peninsula, rose in anger. This guerrilla-style insurgency in the former Papal States and Naples came to be known as *brigantaggio*. The phenomenon mixed elements of organised crime with outbursts of guerrilla war. Sometimes their raids were political, at other moments criminality was cloaked in anti-risorgimento rhetoric. These irregular attacks severely compromised public order. Military might, counterinsurgency and martial law were needed to arrest the rebels. In some cases, family members of brigands were taken hostage by the government to force their criminal brethren to give themselves up.[118]

As 1859 closed, Napoleon III had tried to persuade the pope to renounce his temporal power. In return, he promised that Cavour's liberal and anticlerical legislation would be withdrawn, and that a constitutional guarantee of the papacy's independence would be proclaimed.[119] Pius sent diplomats to discuss this proposal, but had little intention of considering it seriously. On the contrary, he was offended that the French emperor had even suggested it. However, Pius began to feel the pressure of his position, so much so that he collapsed in the Sistine chapel, feverish and exhausted, during Holy Week 1861.[120] Those who suspected this was a sign of ill health thought a conclave was imminent, but such speculation proved premature. Despite fainting, this pontiff was blessed with an iron constitution. Many Catholics around the world sympathised with the pope's indignation over the deprivation of his lands by force. Even some of Lamennais' former associates, like Lacordaire and Montalembert, defended the papacy's right to a temporal state. Despite this, they blamed the pope's obstinate refusal to grant a constitution in 1850 as the cause of all his woes.[121]

There had been some negotiations between Victor Emmanuel II and Napoleon III about replacing the French garrison in Rome with Neapolitan troops, but Garibaldi's conquest of the south made this impossible. Reluctantly the French emperor was forced to leave the French garrison in the Eternal City, as it was feared that its evacuation would lead to an immediate Italian attack. To maintain the support of his Catholic electorate, the French emperor could not abandon the pope.[122] Garibaldi had publicly stated his intention to move on the city as soon as feasible, and liberate it as Italy's capital. Hungry to avenge the fall of Rome in 1849, in 1862 he gathered two thousand of his volunteers in Sicily and began a march towards the Eternal City. Fearful that this aggressive action would lead to a war with France, the Italian government decided to send regular troops to check his advance.

On 29 August at Aspromonte, in the Calabrian hills, the volunteers and Italian *bersaglieri* (sharpshooters) met face to face. Garibaldi commanded his men to hold fire and apparently some Italian soldiers changed sides and joined the red-shirts. A sudden panic occurred, and the volunteers opened fire. Shots were exchanged and Garibaldi himself was wounded, while a dozen men died on both sides. It was disturbing for the red-shirts to recognise that many in the regular army were former companions of theirs, with whom they had served in the 1860 campaign to liberate the south. Wanting to avoid a fratricidal blood bath, Garibaldi ordered his men to stand down. He was given immediate medical treatment; then he and his two thousand men were arrested. They spent a few weeks in prison before receiving an amnesty. Garibaldi was released to his home on the island of Caprera off the Sardinian coast. Here, in this barren rock, he brooded over the failure of unification and wrote Mills-and-Boon-style romance novels.[123]

This debacle at Aspromonte only served to make Garibaldi's myth grow even stronger. Liberal newspapers across Europe described the event in deeply emotive language. They reported how this romantic hero had cried 'Rome or death!' when he rallied his troops and urged them onwards towards the Eternal City.[124] When he visited London in 1864, he was given a triumphant hero's welcome, and feted by the great and the good of British society. The man who had, on two occasions, tried to put an end to the temporal power of the popes was seen in Protestant Britain as the perfect hero of modern times.[125] Needless to say, he had not given up. Garibaldi would ride again!

The Roman question remained a great pressure point for European politics through the 1860s. There was little agreement on the pope's position as a temporal ruler. A solution of sorts was reached in September 1864 when a convention was signed between France and Italy whereby the French emperor agreed to withdraw his troops from Rome in return for an Italian guarantee that the integrity of papal territories would be maintained. For his part, Victor Emmanuel II promised not to attack Rome, and undertook to transfer the capital city of Italy from Turin to Florence.[126]

This September Convention of 1864 confirmed for Pius the precariousness of his position. Without the troops of Napoleon III, or at least an international guarantee of his neutrality, he was defenceless. To make matters worse, it was unclear how, without significant coercive force, his subjects could be prevented from rebelling. The people of Trastevere and the Ghetto had shown enthusiasm for the revolution fifteen years before. If the pope had felt under siege ever since 1849, the ongoing unification of Italy only made his pain worse. He felt that only a show of strength and confidence could make clear that the church would not compromise its teachings or principles for the sake of political expediency.

Pius had a sense that the growth of religious incredulity, revolution, liberalism, socialism and individualism had drawn people in Europe away from respect for legitimate authority and the acceptance of traditional Catholic teaching. In June 1862, he charged a commission of theologians to draw up a list of the worst errors of the age.[127] Some of his closest advisers believed this was a mistake, as those loyal to the church already knew which modern notions were regarded as errors. The few atheists in Europe were hardly going to take much heed of a papal condemnation. Furthermore, any perceived papal condemnation of democracy had the potential to backfire.[128] Pius haughtily overruled such concerns, feeling that the assertion of his version of the truth was essential.

During that same summer, hundreds of bishops gathered in St Peter's Square to witness the canonisation of the Japanese martyrs who had died in the twilight of the sixteenth century.[129] After the pope had personally elevated these twenty-six Jesuits and Franciscans to glory, he asked the bishops of the Catholic world for their opinion on a formal condemnation of modern errors. A total of 96 bishops failed to reply, while 159 stated it would be a bad idea;[130] American bishops especially believed that a condemnation of democracy would be counterproductive in the United States. This meant that roughly four hundred prelates, or two-thirds of those consulted, were in favour.[131] The pope pressed on with his plan (he never took much notice of advice in any case).

Unwisely, correspondence relating to this list of errors had been leaked to the French government and from there to others within the church. Montalembert seems to have been aware of this list and was appalled. He was invited to speak in the Belgian city of Malines at a conference of three thousand priests and theologians. Loyal to his earlier years at L'Avenir, he argued that Catholicism and modernity could be reconciled. He endorsed Cavour's notion of a 'free church within a free state'.[132] For him, political interference weakened rather than strengthened Catholicism. Ignaz Döllinger, a professor of ecclesiastical history in Munich, made a speech defending similar ideas.[133] Thus the list of errors was controversial even before it was published, but Pius was determined to declare all modern ideologies as evil, and exhort Catholics to steer clear from them.

This syllabus (or list) of errors was appended to an encyclical: *Quanta cura*. It was no coincidence that this vital document was issued on 8 December 1864, the feast of the Immaculate Conception. Pius restated his authority to define doctrine and curse the false claims of the modernity that had led millions away from Catholic teaching. The letter opened with remarkable confidence: the source of the woes of the modern world was to be found in the French Revolution of 1789. The encyclical quoted reverentially Pius VI's *Diu satis* brief, which had condemned the attacks on monasteries and the church during the 1790s. Humankind's rebellion against legitimate authority and religion was the expression of diabolical machinations whose aim was to subvert all civil and political order.[134] For Pius IX, a society unmoored from traditional authority was rudderless and bound for shipwreck. It was a determined declaration of war on the values of post-revolutionary Europe. Although the encyclical was explosive, few but theologians and intellectuals actually read this complicated text and fully understood its denunciation of the modern world.

Of much more interest to most readers was the list of eighty intellectual positions which were condemned as errors. This compendium has been criticised, with some justification, as lacking coherence and structure. It reads more like a shopping list of modern ideas Pius disliked rather than a sustained critique of anti-Catholic thinking. Amongst the key errors condemned were religious indifference, toleration of false religions, rationalism, naturalism, freemasonry and pantheism. Modern ideologies such as communism, socialism and liberalism were also considered unsuitable for Catholics. Bible reading, the translation of sacred texts and Protestantism unsurprisingly were anathemised (cursed for eternity). Any proposition that denied the legitimacy of the temporal power of the popes and church teaching was denounced without appeal. Most glaring of all was the condemnation of the absolute sovereignty of the state over civil and political affairs. Pius and his theologians steadfastly refused to accept that heads of government and legislative assemblies could adopt secular laws that conflicted with religious truth. This was particularly glaring in articles 65–74 which attacked state interference in the sacrament of marriage. Divorce was impossible in Catholic teaching, and only the church could annul imperfect unions. The most controversial was article 80, which condemned as a grave error the proposition that: 'The Roman Pontiff can, and ought to, reconcile himself, and come to terms with progress, liberalism and modern civilization.'[135] This declared publicly that the papacy was fundamentally opposed to the modern world.

Educated European elites were quick to appreciate the implications of this list of errors. It is much less clear that the peasants who were so enthused by the cult of Mary cared much about the syllabus. Liberal Catholics such as Montalembert, Döllinger and the historian Lord Acton in Britain felt marginalised in an intransigent church that had set itself on a collision course with the nineteenth century.[136] The man of the hour was Félix Dupanloup, Bishop of Orléans. Despite a difficult start as an illegitimate child, he had become a kind, erudite and passionate educator. Slim, with an attractive face and long white hair, he looked like a patriarch of old. As a young priest, he had managed to reconcile with the church the apostate bishop and former minister of Napoleon, Talleyrand, who, under his guidance, made a full deathbed confession.[137]

Dupanloup's task now was even harder. His goal was to soften Pius's intransigent language to allow liberal Catholics to read his syllabus with some flexibility. He published a pamphlet in which he delicately and painstakingly reinterpreted the syllabus of errors.[138] His reasoning at times had to be acrobatic. That each proposition listed in the syllabus was condemned by the church was undeniable according to Dupanloup. Yet this did not imply that the church endorsed the opposite to each proposition as true. For example, proposition 63 condemned the notion that: 'It is lawful to refuse obedience to legitimate princes, and even to rebel against them.' Dupanloup felt strongly that this did not mean that Catholics should give their rulers unthinking obedience. There were theoretical circumstances in which tyrannical or impious princes could and should be resisted.[139] Ultimately Catholicism condemned disorder, but did not champion tyranny. Similarly, article 80 seemed to imply that the pope denounced all of modernity. For Dupanloup nothing could be further from the truth. The syllabus criticised the bad aspects of modernity but by no means every aspect of contemporary society. His exegetical aerobics won the bishop of Orléans no fewer than six hundred letters of admiration. Apparently, on studying Dupanloup's pamphlet, even Pius XI exclaimed, 'He has explained and clarified the encyclical in the manner that one should understand it!'[140]

Despite the pope's efforts, the syllabus hardly achieved its goal. Those who embraced radical politics, denied the existence of God, or believed in individual freedom were unlikely to be swayed from their cause just because the Roman pontiff disapproved of it. The syllabus turned out to be a lesson in the politics of futility. As was often the case, Pius was preaching to the converted. It was left to Catholic liberals to deal with the fallout, and try to persuade public opinion that their pope was less obscurantist than he appeared. Regrettably for Dupanloup, Acton, Montalembert and Döllinger, the problem remained that their supreme leader was a man of the *ancien régime*. His bonhomie and good nature concealed the sheer extent of his reactionary nature. There seemed to be no unpopular cause with which Pius IX did not flirt.

From 1861 to 1865 the United States had erupted into civil war.[141] In general, both Washington and the Confederacy were staunchly Protestant. Despite this, they both had significant Catholic minorities within their zones of control. This was especially the case in Louisiana, Florida, Kentucky, Maryland, Texas and South Carolina in the slave-owning South. Some Jesuits had owned slaves in Baltimore until the abolitionist movement persuaded them of the necessity to offload their embarrassing property.[142] The Confederacy, although smaller, had fifteen Catholic dioceses, which compared favourably with the North's twenty-two.

Catholics had certainly acclimatised to the deep South and shared the mores of their white-supremacist neighbours. Augustin Verot, Bishop of Savannah, published a treatise in 1861 that failed to condemn the institution of slavery. He claimed that it was an evolutionary practice that would decline as justice became more firmly established in the South.[143] He also claimed that slavery was divinely sanctioned, which did not square with Catholic teaching.* At least Verot admitted that the slave trade was immoral and that those held in bondage should have basic rights, such as living free from violence, starvation and sexual exploitation. He also argued for the validity of slave marriages and against the breakup of families. Appeals for the good treatment of those in bondage were meaningless in practice. Verot showed how Catholics in the South could downplay papal pronouncements against slavery to blend into the political culture of their environment. They did not much trouble the consciences of slave-holders.

The southern government wanted to keep its Catholic minority on side, and needed all the friends it could find. Given the diplomatic isolation facing the Confederacy, Jefferson Davis was desperate to build international goodwill. France and the United Kingdom had refused to recognise the legitimacy of this slave-owning polity.[144] Davis decided to send Patrick Lynch, Bishop of Charleston, and Father John Bannon to represent Confederate interests in Rome. Both were native-born Irishmen, extremely religious, and in Bannon's case had served as a chaplain in the Confederate army in no fewer than four battles. This mission to Rome was a long shot, given that no European government was willing officially to receive Confederate diplomatic agents.

Bannon was the first to arrive in Rome in 1863. Pius received him to discuss spiritual matters, but did not recognise his diplomatic status. Bannon made every effort to charm the pope

---

* John Francis Maxwell, *Slavery and the Catholic Church: The History of Catholic Teaching Concerning the Moral Legitimacy of the Institution of Slavery* (London, 1975). The practice of course was different from the theory, cf. Maura Jane Farrelly, 'American Slavery, American Freedom, American Catholicism', *Early American Studies*, Vol. 10, No. 1 (2012), pp. 69–100.

and explain how the Confederacy was much more tolerant of religious freedom than the godless Union. Pius clumsily praised Bannon's passionate character, describing him 'as a magnificent fellow'.[145] He even condescended to receive a letter and an appeal for recognition from Jefferson Davis. It claimed that the American South merely fought a defensive war against Northern aggression. Given the wars of Italian unification, and the violation of papal sovereignty, Pius showed some sympathy with this line of argument. In a surfeit of chivalry the pope replied to Davis in a letter of thanks. Although not an official diplomatic note, it created excitement among the politicians in Richmond, Virginia (the Confederate capital).[146]

In December 1863 Bannon was joined by another Confederate agent, Ambrose Dudley Mann, who was received in private audience but again with no official status. He wrote overly optimistic reports, stating that Catholic recognition of the Confederacy was imminent. Antonelli, as cardinal secretary of state, had reiterated, time and again, that the church remained neutral in civil wars. No matter how sympathetic Pius might appear, he could not sanction the Confederacy.[147] To Mann's discomfiture, during a papal audience he was informed that President Lincoln claimed the war was being fought over the question of slavery. Pius advised that if Jefferson Davis took a lead by emancipating slaves this would help the Southern cause.[148] For all his clumsiness, the pope had come to the heart of the matter, and called the Southern bluff; ultimately, he had found the one concession the Southerners could not make. Mann's reply – that slavery was an issue of states' rights rather than one which a national government could decide – was disingenuous. Pius smiled awkwardly, which Mann chose to believe meant that the pope conceded the point. Confederate diplomats overestimated the papacy's sympathy, but it certainly did Pius no favours elsewhere that Confederate newspapers portrayed these audiences as a de facto recognition of the South.

Davis then made the decision to send Lynch as an official Confederate diplomat to the Holy See. Lynch's progress was slow, due to a tour of his native Ireland and some time spent in England; he only arrived in Rome in 1864, by which time the defeat of the

Confederacy was certain.[149] Antonelli received Lynch, but informed him that the Curia would only deal with him in his capacity as a bishop, and would not recognise any diplomatic role. Perhaps ironically, Lynch met the pope on 4 July 1864 in solemn audience. Although the pope expressed a great interest in the condition of the diocese of Charleston, he confirmed in no uncertain terms that the Holy See would not recognise the Confederacy. More meetings followed. Pius offered to mediate, but knew that the Union would not accept this. He also urged the gradual abolition of slavery. Again, the Confederate press hailed these meetings as evidence that the Vicar of Christ was on their side. Despite all this diplomatic gaucherie, Antonelli had told Rufus King, the US representative in Rome, that the Holy See considered the South's secession a violation of the American constitution.[150]

Although the Confederate missions in Rome were failures, it is difficult to explain why Pius entertained these diplomats in a way that few nations in Europe had done. The Southern press coverage could have damaged the papacy's relationship with Washington. Thankfully Cardinal Antonelli and Rufus King's pragmatic diplomacy made clear that, although the church was neutral, it favoured an outcome that would hasten the demise of slavery.[151] This allowed the Northern press to mock the Southern missions. Through good fortune rather than deliberate calculation, Pius's audiences did not add to America's traditional anti-Catholicism.[152] But they highlighted the pope's cavalier and romantic instincts when it came to politics. He had a deep sense of solidarity with the underdog. Although this description fitted the Confederacy's military situation, its moral putrefaction due its slave economy should have rung far more alarm bells in the papal court.

As the 1860s progressed, the syllabus of errors won Catholicism few friends. When the Habsburgs went to war against Prussia in 1866, Italy joined the fray. It used an alliance with Berlin as a pretext to fight for Venetia, which it had failed to gain in 1859. Although the campaign produced mixed results, Garibaldi's irregulars fought well.[153] As ever he was obsessed with avenging the memory of Bassi, Aguyar, his wife Anita and so many others who had perished in defence of the Roman Republic in 1849. By

September 1867 Garibaldi was lobbying for an invasion of the Papal States. He travelled around Liguria and Tuscany seeking to raise ten thousand volunteers. Everywhere he went he was met with cheers and young men eager to sign up to the cause. The Italian government, fearing that the red-shirts might jeopardise relations with France, decided to return Garibaldi to his home on Caprera, where he was placed under house arrest.[154]

Despite this, his sons Menotti and Ricciotti gathered bands of red-shirts on the Tuscan borders. As could have been predicted, the regular Italian army ignored these violations of international law. By October 1867, raiding parties crossed into the Papal States, harassing the local authorities and police. Since 1861, the Badenese general Hermann Kanzler had become inspector general of Pius's troops. He was a proud career soldier, deeply loyal to his sovereign.[155] His shake-up of the regular army and the volunteer Zouaves had transformed them into a real, if poorly equipped, fighting force. Whenever these troops confronted Garbaldian volunteers the red-shirts were soundly thrashed. It was decided to ignite a popular uprising within Rome itself. On 22 October, Rome's city gates were closed to prevent the entry of agitators. The papal police fought against the clock to prevent terrorist incidents. At 7 p.m. a bomb exploded in Piazza Colonna, shattering the windows of the buildings nearby but harming no one. Later, inside Castel Santangelo, Rome's citadel, two artillery officers carrying torches were spotted. Inside the arsenal, they were seen preparing to ignite the gunpowder stores.[156] The papal police had a tip-off and forestalled a cataclysmic explosion.

As members of the police congratulated themselves on a job well done, and on the quality of their intelligence, there was suddenly a massive explosion. Palazzo Serristori, a large edifice used as a barracks for Papal Zouaves in Borgo Santo Spirito, almost adjacent to St Peter's Square, partially collapsed and burst into flames. Twenty-five men, mainly from the regimental band, died in the explosion.[157] Revolutionaries had brought several barrels of gunpowder into the cellars of the palazzo and set them alight. It was later discovered that the bricklayers Gaetano Tognetti and Giuseppe Monti were responsible for this act of terrorism. They had fought in the Italian army, and were followers of Garibaldi. Captured and eventually tried, they were sentenced to death for the crimes of *lese majesté* and mass murder. On 24 November 1868 they were beheaded near the Circus Maximus. This was the last time that an execution with the papal guillotine took place in Rome.[158] They became martyrs for Italian nationhood.

By now, the French were becoming increasingly concerned. There were reports that the Italian army was providing the red-shirts with logistical support and weaponry. Napoleon III decided to ship a French expeditionary force from Toulon to thwart any attempt to seize Rome. Garibaldi gave the police the slip in Caprera, and joined his volunteers in late October 1867.[159] He was determined to try to take Rome before the arrival of French reinforcements. It was too late. On 29 October Napoleon III's men disembarked at Civitavecchia and marched to support General Kanzler. They were armed with deadly new Chassepot rifles. These breach-loading firearms were much more effective, accurate and had longer range than any weapon used in Italy up to then.[160]

On learning of this, many volunteers in Garibaldi's ranks started to desert. His ten thousand volunteers shrunk to half that number by 1 November. At Monterotondo, about fifteen miles from Rome, the volunteers decided to withdraw. For reasons that remain unclear, they took the road southwards towards Tivoli. The red-shirts were marching into the heart of papal territory with very few cavalry units to provide intelligence or protect the infantry. Kanzler could not believe his luck, and decided to destroy them. He stopped the enemy at the walled town of Mentana on 3 November. A furious battle erupted in the late morning. The papal troops secured some high ground, which allowed their artillery to bombard Garibaldi's force.[161] However, some surprisingly well-timed counter-attacks slowed the momentum of the papal army's onslaught. It was only the arrival of French reinforcements that allowed Kanzler to claim a significant victory by nightfall.

Garibaldi asked to be given a safe conduct to leave the Papal States. The French granted this request on the proviso that the volunteers surrender their armaments. It was an embarrassing defeat: the red-shirts had lost about a thousand men whereas the Franco-Papal force had suffered just thirty-six casualties.[162] It was the only major military victory that Pius IX achieved during in his reign. Garibaldi's final attempt to wrest Rome from papal rule had failed. He was arrested on the Tuscan border and sent to brood in the fortress of Varignano for three weeks.[163] Never again would this dashing guerrilla commander trouble the eternal city. Mentana was undoubtedly a papal victory, but a pyrrhic one. It highlighted yet again how Kanzler's ten thousand men had to rely on French support.

As his temporal authority waned Pius was determined to solidify his spiritual power. He decided to call a general ecumenical council to discuss the vexed question of the pope's authority over the church and its teachings. There had not been such a council since Trent, which took place from 1545 to 1563.[164] Then, Catholic bishops had formulated a response to the challenge of the Protestant reformation. The Catholic Reformation allowed the Roman church to regain the initiative. Councils were viewed, however, as a high-risk strategy. In the medieval period they had been used to oust popes.[165] Throughout the early modern period conciliarists continued to argue that the church in council superseded the authority of the papacy. Napoleon's attempt to use a council of bishops to short-circuit papal authority had brought it into disrepute among more devout Catholics.[166]

Pius wanted to use the council as a vehicle to reinforce his authority. The notion that the papacy had the final word in doctrinal matters had been around since the thirteenth century. Early Franciscans, pleased with a litany of papal pronouncements in their favour, wanted to ensure that these would not be overturned in future.[167] They came up with the notion of 'infallibility', that is to say that the bishop of Rome, on matters pertaining to teaching and the faith, could not err. This was a controversial concept. It was contested throughout the Middle Ages and the early modern period. Many popes were uncomfortable with infallibility since it meant that they themselves would be bound by the decisions of their predecessors. Indeed, what if two popes contradict each other? If they both cannot be mistaken, how can it be they do not agree? Perhaps wisely, the papacy has decided to let sleeping dogs lie for most of its history.

Only Pius IX could have wished to reawaken this vexed issue, and he felt the circumstances were ripe.[168] Since the earliest days of his pontificate he had considered convening a council, but it was only after the syllabus of errors, and its contested reception, that he took this idea forward. In March 1865 he charged a central commission of cardinals to draw up a rigid agenda of issues that the council might discuss. This was a notable departure from what had happened previously; in the past, bishops decided on the agenda only once a council was in session.[169] The Tridentine precedent of free debate needed to be avoided at all costs.

Indeed, the secret Vatican archives contained the papers of Trent, which clearly showed how, in the sixteenth century, the bishops had taken the lead in fixing the agenda for reform. Few were aware of this, as the church's archives were amongst the most difficult to access in the world;[170] indeed anyone violating the secrecy of the archives could incur excommunication. The prefect of the archives was Augustin Theiner, a former Silesian Protestant and a meticulous scholar who, on meeting Lamennais, had converted to Catholicism. He had refused a pay rise because it meant that he would have been required to attend services in St Peter's basilica, and this would have interfered with his studies. His published work on the French Revolution, Napoleon and the Reformation had done much to increase the reputation of the church.[171] He was a loyal if pedantic bookworm. During the 1850s he had proposed that the church publish the proceedings of the Council of Trent. A commission of cardinals and Dominicans, charged with investigating this matter, decided against it. The records of Trent highlighted how the bishops had been divided and had debated issues that were now dogma. The church much preferred that only the canons and decisions of this council be published, rather than the transcripts of the sessions.[172]

Theiner was bitter about the decision, and sulked in his apartment in the Tower of Winds, just above the Vatican archives. With little evidence, he suspected that the Jesuits were behind this move, and he nursed a strong grudge. The matter might have rested there but, in 1867, he was visited in his apartment by the liberal Catholic Lord John Emerich Acton. Acton, as an eminent historian, believed in making sources widely available, so he wanted the proceedings of the Council of Trent to appear in print.[173] Letters from the ecclesiastical historian Ignaz Döllinger urged him to reveal the historical truth, rather than follow the church's official line. Theiner was not a politically savvy creature and did not realise that behind Acton and Döllinger's flattery lay a determination to thwart papal infallibility at all costs. To Pius's great fury, during 1870 the files relating to Trent were circulated widely, and enemies of the concept of infallibility used them to argue that the new council should be given more autonomy.

A very annoyed Pius IX summoned Theiner for an epic tongue-lashing. On his knees, the archivist swore he had not leaked any documents, and that he had not allowed Acton into the archives. Few believed him, but there was insufficient evidence to condemn him. Theiner was allowed to remain an archivist, but he was no longer allowed access to the files entrusted to his care. The door connecting his apartments to the archives was bricked up.[174] Only in the Roman church could there be an archivist barred from his own archives! Theiner, understandably, resented this to his dying day. Shortly before his death he travelled to Zagreb and deposited his transcripts of the proceedings of the Council of Trent with the sympathetic local bishop. They were published posthumously. On his way home, the ailing Theiner died in Civitavecchia. This whole episode made Pius even more determined that the archives should remain closed to the public.

Although bishops and cardinals were lukewarm when it came to defining papal infallibility as dogma, Pius was determined that his supremacy should be recognized by the 'universal church'. Dupanloup argued that the question of infallibility should be kept off the agenda.[175] Instead a commission of cardinals decided that the council, in fact, needed to examine six items: church and state, infallibility, the Papal States, faith, marriage and new political ideologies. Behind this agenda lay the hand of Pio Nono himself.[176] Even his secretary of state, Antonelli, thought this course of action misguided. The announcement of the council was made in the solemn bull *Aeterni patri,* on 29 June 1868 (the feast of Saints Peter and Paul). Its mood was one of unbridled gloom:

> The Catholic Church, its salutary doctrines, its venerable sovereignty, and the supreme authority of this Apostolic See are challenged and opposed by the haughty enemies of God and men. All things holy are derided, ecclesiastical property is plundered, and bishops & virtuous men of Catholic sentiment are vexed in a thousand ways [...].[177]

The pope's radical solution was then unveiled:

> Following the illustrious footsteps of our predecessors We have judged it timely to summon a general Council, something We have desired for a long time, all Our venerable brother bishops on this Universal Catholic orb are called to share in Our concerns.[178]

The council would meet in the Vatican on 8 December 1869, the feast of the Immaculate Conception. The date reminded the faithful that he already had defined Catholic teaching, single-handedly, on this aspect of the faith. Pius IX considered himself de facto infallible; the council was to recognise this reality *de jure* too. An open letter to Protestants and non-Catholics invited them to observe at the council. It urged them to repent of their errors and rejoin the unity of the church. Needless to say, most of those who read this letter considered it pathetic at best, insulting at worst.[179]

If any one event set the future pace for the modern Catholic Church, and all the problems which afflict it to the present day, that event was the first Vatican Council. Over seven hundred bishops and thousands of pilgrims flocked to Rome. Unlike the sixteenth-century gathering at Trent, the monarchs and heads of state of Europe were not invited.[180] Another departure with tradition was the presence of the entire College of Cardinals. Cardinals Manning and Luigi Bilio were among the key leaders of the infallibilist party. They wanted to ensure that nothing was left to chance when the council met. It was agreed that bishops should be allowed to speak, but not to debate. The language of the council was to be Latin, and twenty-four hours' notice was required prior to presenting a speech. Bishops were not allowed to form caucuses nor to respond to each other's speeches.[181]

The council was held in the north transept of St Peter's basilica. Whether this was a strategic choice or sheer incompetence is anyone's guess. The acoustics of the mother church of the Catholic world were notoriously poor. This ensured that the proceedings were inaudible for most of the participants, apart from the secretaries who sat beneath the pulpit where speeches were made. The restrictions on discussion and debate ensured that the pope and the Curia kept control of the proceedings. It was their intention to pilot the council towards an unconditional acceptance of their agenda.[182]

On the opening day of the council, a crowd of spectators assembled in St Peter's Square, including the Empress Elisabeth of Austria, Queen Olga of Wurttemberg and the deposed King Francis II of the Two Sicilies.[183] They witnessed the solemn procession of 49 cardinals, 11 patriarchs, 6 prince-bishops and 680 bishops. They were followed by 28 abbots, 29 superior generals of religious orders, over two hundred Roman priests, senior members of the Knights of Malta and the pope's guards. At the very rear of the procession, high on the *sedia gestatoria*, carried by magnificently dressed nobles and with two fans made of ostrich feathers on either side, was Pius IX. He always complained that the *sedia gestatoria* made him seasick. His blessings from this mobile throne were always quite rapid, for he was afraid that more flamboyant movements might allow his nausea to get the better of him. Over two-thirds of those present were European. The church in the wider world, mainly represented by the Americas, was in a minority at the council.[184] This grand opening ceremony for the first Vatican Council was the last grand procession of the *ancien régime* church. Never again would such a spectacle be seen.

The council was opened by a solemn pontifical mass followed by a *Te deum*. Manning, Bilio and the Curia had years to prepare the ground; they had no intention of letting it slip from their grasp. Dupanloup and Henry Maret, professor of dogmatic theology at the Sorbonne, led a Gallican group of French bishops who strongly opposed any formal definition of infallibility.[185] They were joined by a group of German Febronian bishops inspired by Döllinger in Munich. These prelates, at a generous estimate, numbered about 150.[186] Against them stood a mass of over five hundred infallibilists. But what the minority of bishops who opposed infallibility lacked in numbers they made up for in their access to news media.

Lord Acton and his family had moved to Rome so that he could write newspaper articles and inform the world of the outrageous events occurring in the basilica. Fluent in German, he penned the 'Römische Briefe vom Konzil' (Roman letters from the Council) which he signed as 'Quirinus' and published in the *Augsburger Allgemeine Zeitung*.[187] This incensed Pius IX, who had ordered his bishops to maintain absolute silence and secrecy on the council's proceedings. Cardinal Manning was given permission to leak the papal side of events to Louis Veuillot, the editor of the Catholic newspaper *L'Univers Réligieux*.[188] It was hopelessly naïve of the minority to believe that the pope's determination to force through infallibility could be swayed by public opinion. Pius deplored how 'some leaders among the opposing bishops are effeminate, others are sophistical, or frivolous or heretical. They are all ambitious, boastful and obstinately attached to their own opinion.'[189] He was incensed when Archbishop de Mérode, one of the pope's personal almoners, joined the minority. Apparently, when Mérode broke his leg during the council and could no longer participate, Pius remarked 'it would have been better if he had broken his tongue'.[190]

Dupanloup and the Gallicans wanted to delay proceedings for as long as possible so the bishops in Rome could fraternise and share points of view, but Manning and Bilio saw the potential danger of this socialising. If the minority persuaded others to join the opposition this could seriously delay the business of the council. It was also decided that the officers and subcommittee members of the council should be elected immediately. To nobody's surprise, only candidates with infallibilist credentials were elected to these key positions.[191]

For the first few months, the council dealt with broader questions about the nature of God, faith and reason. The result of these deliberations was the Apostolic constitution *Dei Filius* promulgated on 24 April 1870 and declared dogma. Most of the document merely reaffirmed long-standing Catholic teaching: God was the source of all creation; he could be known not through experience, but only through revelation; the totality of all revealed truth was contained in holy scripture and tradition; the church was the custodian and interpreter of this great body of faith (known as the deposit of faith); for an individual to read texts, history and tradition independently of Catholic teaching was a grievous error. Each canon in *Dei Filius* anathemised anyone who should contradict the council's statements.[192] This Apostolic constitution proclaimed that revelation, and its interpretation, had remained fixed and immutable since the year AD 33, when Christ had died on the cross.

The great victim of *Dei filius* was history. Any hint that Christianity had evolved or changed in the past two thousand years was implicitly denied. This is why Döllinger's book, published in August 1869 under the pseudonym Janus and entitled *Der Papst und das Conzil* (*The Pope and the Council*) was immediately placed on the Index.[193] This erudite historian and theologian showed how the papacy had evolved from being a bishopric that was merely first among equals to becoming a medieval bully with unbridled territorial ambitions. Döllinger attacked papal claims to infallibility and sovereignty, while upholding the conciliarist foundations of the church. Catholicism's magisterium had not emerged on the morning of Christ's resurrection complete and incontrovertible. Rather it was the production of accretions, traditions, politics and fashion like any other body of human knowledge.

Döllinger's words proved all too transparently that historical thinking was the biggest danger to Pius IX's version of the truth.[194] Nothing could have been further from Pius' own understanding of religion. *Dei filius* censured religious historicism but, in contrast, had nothing to say about Darwin's *Origin of Species* (1859), which was already seen as a profound challenge to traditional ideas about time and nature.[195] Pius showed remarkably little interest in hard science. In this respect, Catholicism did rather better than Protestantism, which in its more evangelical form still tears itself apart over the conflict between Darwin and scripture.

The European press took little notice of *Dei filius* which was impenetrable in its language and for much of the text merely reaffirmed medieval Thomistic theology. The question that dominated public debate in newspapers, coffee houses and educated salons was infallibility. Confident that he was now in control of the council, Pius decided to move papal infallibility to the top of the agenda.[196] The reasons behind this move are not altogether clear. Perhaps the looming Franco-Prussian war added urgency to the situation? Napoleon III and Bismarck were in dispute over a candidate for the Spanish throne, and the threat of war was growing on the Rhine. If this occurred, France would be forced to withdraw its Roman garrison. One could speculate that the pope wanted the council to finish its work before an Italian invasion of his domain. A military occupation of Rome was sure to interrupt and delay the business of the council.

The fact that infallibility rose to the top of the agenda revealed the weakness of the opposition. Pius, it is said, once exclaimed: 'I am so determined to go forward with this matter that if I knew the council was going to be silent on it, I would dissolve it and define it myself.'[197] The pope here spoke more truth than he realised. Bishop Henri Maret, on 3 June 1870, made the point in open session that if the pope was infallible why did he need a council to sanction it? Did this not imply that the council was in effect superior to the infallible pope? This intervention caused a massive storm, and the censure of Maret by Cardinal Bilio.[198] The French bishop had touched on a sore point, and one which the preparatory commission itself had discussed throughout 1868–9. It was an unanswerable objection. Another curious issue brought up by the minority was the remarkable case of Pope Honorius I, who had been condemned for heresy by the Third Council of Constantinople in the seventh century.[199] If at least one pope had been deemed to be heretical, how could infallibility apply to any pope? A contradictory situation could emerge in which the utterances of Honorius would be both infallible and heretical at the same time! The responses to this objection argued that this was the exception that proved the rule.[200] To an extent, there is something to this argument, in so far as it is understandably difficult to identify heretical popes in the annals of Catholicism.

One of the most important events in the council was a speech made by Cardinal Filippo Maria Guidi, a former Dominican who had been appointed by Pius as archbishop of Bologna. Due to differences with the new Italian state, he was unable to take up his office and reside in his archdiocese. As he had kept a low profile during the early sessions of the council, most assumed that he was a papal loyalist. When, on 18 June 1870, he ascended the pulpit of the north transept of St Peter's, most expected a dull and learned disquisition on infallibility. He was to surprise everybody. His speech began with two rhetorical questions. Is the pope *personally* infallible? And if so, is this power separate from the church? Guidi was categorical that the power to define dogma was not personal, but intrinsic to the pope's prerogatives. He stressed that the office of the papacy was dependent on the church and not separate from it.

Although members of the Curia were irked, many applauded and kissed Guidi's hands.[201] It seemed as if he had solved the problem by placing the pope's authority back within the council. Pio Nono was incandescent with rage. That same day, Guidi was summoned to a private audience, where the bishop of Rome screamed at the surprised cardinal that his speech had been an attempt to curry favour with the Italian government. Guidi replied that he had merely tried to follow the tradition and history of the church. Pius, according to some sources, hissed: 'I! I am tradition! I am the church!'[202]

For all of Pius' determination to have the council acknowledge his infallibility, some qualifications were included. The notion of *ex cathedra* appeared in the draft of the definition. The pope was considered infallible only when he spoke, as it were, from the chair of St Peter. This meant, in practice, that not all papal statements were automatically immune from error. It was only when the pope stated explicitly that he was about to make an infallible statement that the power of infallibility was activated. To put it simply: only when the pope put on his infallible hat was he infallible.[203] His other pronouncements, though authoritative and binding, were not immune from potential error. This proved to be a pyrrhic victory. On 16 July the infallibilists scored an important point by rewording the text, which now stated that infallibility was intrinsic to the papacy, and not the fruit of consent from the assembled church.

As the final vote would take place two days later in the presence of the pope, many of the minority bishops asked to be excused and return to their dioceses. They wanted to avoid at all costs voting against Pius in his presence. Permission was given and, on 17 July, trains filled with two hundred exhausted and disgruntled bishops leaving Rome and heading northwards.[204] This departure was the final defeat of Gallicanism and Febronianism. These currents of Catholic thought had been vanquished by the very council that they had sought to convene with such vehemence throughout the eighteenth century. It was a decided irony that an ecumenical council, rather than limiting Rome's authority, was about to bestow spiritual and theological absolute power on the papacy. Neo-conciliarism, which had been dying a slow death since Napoleon's national council of 1811, was given the *coup de grace* in 1870. It would never trouble Catholicism again. By now, in France priests had begun to abandon their Gallican robes and rites in favour of a more ornate Roman style. Thus regional variations in the dress, liturgy and practices of Catholic clerics evaporated after 1870. They were supplanted by Roman cassocks, birettas and wide-brimmed hats which became the norm across the Catholic globe. It was in these decades that the ornate threads and patterns which decorated chasubles and stoles (until Vatican II) became standardised and ubiquitous in Catholic churches in all of Europe.[205] Pius IX was for Catholicism what Napoleon had been for the state, an indefatigable centraliser.

On 18 July, 530 bishops, slightly over half the bishops of the Catholic world, processed into St Peter's. They then individually cast their votes on infallibility. Nobody doubted the outcome: all but two prelates voted in favour of the new dogma. Once balloting was completed, the heavens opened and a deluge hit Rome. Apparently, a lightning bolt struck St Peter's dome to great effect and the consternation of all present![206] Infallibilists took this as sign of divine approbation, whereas the minority saw it as confirmation that God was angry. Pius promulgated the

Apostolic constitution called *Pastor aeternus,* which granted him spiritual mastery over the church. He then adjourned the council until October. This constitution was a short document, divided into four chapters. The first three dealt with the primacy of Rome over the church, defining the scriptural basis upon which the pope claimed his supreme authority. Not much in these sections was controversial or particularly surprising. The key innovation was that no Catholic in future was to be allowed to question the evidence and assertions put forward in *Pastor aeternus.*

In contrast, the fourth chapter 'on the infallible magisterium of the Roman Pontiff' was incendiary. It proclaimed, in an age of intellectual exploration and scientific progress, that:

> The spirit was not promised to the successors of Peter to reveal, through his inspiration, new doctrines, but rather, to guard scrupulously and make known faithfully with his assistance the [divine] revelation transmitted to the Apostles, that is to say, the deposit of faith.[207]

History and the very idea of the mutability of the church were denied in this passage. A myth was propounded here that Christ had given Peter and his successors a finite, self-contained and invariant truth, which was to be restated eternally for the benefit of humanity – a denial of the changing nature and the ecclesiology of Christianity over two millennia. The definition of infallibility was, appropriately enough, absolutely certain in its language:

> The Roman Pontiff, when he speaks *ex cathedra,* that is to say, when he exercises his supreme office of shepherd and teacher of all Christians, and with the full force of his supreme Apostolic power he defines doctrine in matters of faith and morals thus binding the entire church, he possesses through that divine assistance, promised to him in the Blessed Peter, that infallibility which the Divine Redeemer bestowed on his church to define doctrine relating to faith or morals. In consequence this definition is intrinsic, and not consented to by the church, nor subject to change.[208]

To contradict this doctrine would incur an automatic anathema. Centuries of conciliarism, ecclesiology, and the idea of the church as a community of equals, died on 18 July 1870. Catholicism became a spiritual autocracy, whereby no one could contradict the authority of the Holy See in doctrinal matters. Despite this arrogation of supreme spiritual authority to themselves, the Roman pontiffs since Pius IX (who only deployed it for the dogma of the immaculate conception in 1854), have used this power sparingly. Only Pius XII in 1950 intentionally invoked infallibility when he proclaimed the assumption of the Virgin Mary into heaven to be an undebatable dogma.[209]

Shortly after the definition was made public in Rome, an apocryphal story tells us that an anonymous placard appeared near Piazza Navona, taunting the episcopacy: 'You came to Rome as shepherds, but left as sheep!' The First Vatican Council was a tactical masterpiece. The Curia skilfully manipulated the assembly, and opposition remained ineffectual throughout. Pius wanted infallibility and he got it. Strategically, it was a disaster for the church. It endowed the papacy with an authority it was loath to deploy. Worse still, it made both the Catholic clergy and laity completely dependent on Rome for guidance. Little room was left for personal initiative within a church that prized obedience over intellectual integrity. Bishops were absolved from thinking for themselves, and became automata. Infallibility made Christian dialogue impossible. Protestant and Orthodox churches could not reasonably deal with an institution that dogmatically dismissed them as heretical rebels.

From a diplomatic point of view, infallibility meant that the church could hope for little international sympathy. The day after the promulgation of *Aeternis pastor,* Napoleon III declared war on Bismarck's Prussia. As French troops suffered catastrophic defeats, the garrison in Rome was withdrawn, and this time it would not return. On 2 September 1870, the French emperor and a substantial part of his army surrendered at Sedan.[210] The one European empire committed to defending the temporal power of the papacy had been destroyed. In Florence, the Italian government saw the dream of *Roma Capitale* within its grasp.

Garibaldi's obsession with ending the temporal power of popes was, in the end, to be accomplished by others.

Although news arrived that the Italian army had started mobilising in August, Pius was convinced that no Catholic army would dare desecrate Rome. General Kanzler had concentrated all his forces on the Aurelian walls and had received alarming reports that at least thirty thousand Italian troops were mustering. They were commanded by General Raffaele Cardorna, and counted amongst their number General Nino Bixio, one of Garibaldi's leading comrades during the Roman Republic of 1849. He was determined to be among the first to storm the walls and liberate the Eternal City.[211] Following the example of Pius VII in 1808, Pius IX gave orders not to resist overwhelming military might. The pope, thinking of himself as the successor to the prince of peace, wanted no bloodshed. Kanzler observed that it would be dishonourable to surrender Rome without even firing a shot. This persuaded the Holy Father that at least some symbolic resistance against the Italians was necessary.[212]

Unable to guarantee the integrity of his realm through military means, the seventy-eight-year-old pontiff sought supernatural assistance. He had himself taken to the Lateran basilica, where the *scala sancta* was located. These marble steps were reputed to have once led to Pontius Pilate's praetorium or headquarters in Jerusalem. According to tradition, it was here that Jesus Christ had been mocked and eventually condemned to death. Devout Romans and foreign pilgrims would ascend and descend these stairs on their knees, as a penance for their sins, or to seek divine assistance. The trembling pope, supported by two sturdy footmen, knelt like a common pilgrim. He then ascended and descended the *scala sancta*, imploring God to spare Rome from the Italian onslaught.[213]

On 8 September 1870 Count Gustavo Ponza di San Martino brought an ultimatum from the Italian government, demanding free access to the Eternal City. He also carried a letter from Victor Emmanuel II, informing the Holy Father that, despite his own personal devotion, he was forced to deploy his troops to safeguard law and order. Only Italian soldiers could ensure Pius's personal safety. San Martino carried a draft treaty of ten articles which defined the future of papal sovereignty in Rome. Pius was offered full rights over the Leonine city, a walled rectangle containing several districts including the future Vatican City.[214] The Count of San Martino assured Pius that he would receive a generous stipend from the Italian government. Provocatively, the pope used the exact same words Pius VII had used when General Radet demanded in Napoleon's name that he renounce his kingdom: 'Non possumus' (We cannot!).[215]

Three days later, Italian troops appeared before the walls of Rome. General Kanzler issued a manifesto declaring the city to be in a state of siege. The last hope for the papacy was an appeal sent to the Emperor Franz-Josef of Austria-Hungary asking him to send military assistance. Given recent Habsburg defeats at the hands of the Prussians, this Catholic dynasty had no stomach for military adventures. The Austrian minister in Rome reported that Vienna could offer Pius IX no help.[216] On 16 September Italian troops occupied Civitavecchia, cutting Rome off from the sea. Cadorna sent a plea to Kanzler to surrender without bloodshed, but he refused. Two days later the ministry of war ordered the general to prepare the attack on Rome.

At 5 a.m. on 20 September 1870, Italian batteries opened fire on the Aurelian walls to the northeast of the city. An hour later, the diplomatic corps were summoned to the Vatican to be close to the pope.[217] By 6.30, it was clear that the guns were concentrating their firepower on the weaker sections of the walls, near Porta Pia. Within an hour, a breach had formed in one section of the wall. Two hours later, a furious Italian assault, led by an elite *bersaglieri* regiment, charged through the breach. The young Zouaves on the other side did their best to repel them, but were soon overwhelmed by the sheer force of numbers.[218] For a further forty-five minutes, Italian artillery put pressure on other gates of the Eternal City. Feeling that honour had been satisfied, Kanzler was commanded by the pope to raise the white flag of surrender. In the confusion of battle, it took the defenders some time to realise that the order to stand down had been issued.

All of Rome, apart from the Leonine city, was occupied by Italian troops. The Eternal City was no longer ruled by the pope, but had become the capital of the kingdom of Italy. That evening a solemn diplomatic protest was sent by Cardinal Antonelli against the violation of the church's capital.[219] After toying with the idea of leaving for exile, Pius decided to remain behind the high walls of the Vatican. The council, which was supposed to reconvene in October, was adjourned indefinitely (it was formally dissolved only in 1960!).[220] There was some talk of transferring to the Belgian town of Malines, but this was considered inexpedient. This great ecumenical council never completed its business.

Soon, the volunteers and Zouaves were placed on trains and given safe passage to their country of origin (France for the vast majority). Gangs of youths, radicals and liberals gathered in St Peter's Square to shout insults outside the deposed pontiff's windows. The residents of several districts adjacent to the Vatican had started agitating against remaining under theocratic rule, and demanded to be allowed to join modern Italy. With the departure of the pope's army, Cardinal Antonelli was forced to ask General Cadorna, with great embarrassment, to occupy the Leonine city to ensure law and order.[221] On 2 October the more than 200,000 inhabitants of greater Rome were invited to vote in a referendum on whether they wished to be annexed to Italy. Within the city walls 40,785 voted in favour of joining Italy and 46 against.[222] Although this was a landslide by any definition, those loyal to the pope had refused to participate in the plebiscite. The results were inflated, but gave the incorporation of Rome into Italy some much-needed legitimacy.

Outside of the Leonine city, monasteries, public buildings, and papal palaces were confiscated. The Quirinal, the site of Pius VII's kidnapping and of four nineteenth-century conclaves, became the seat of the king of Italy.[223] Victor Emmanuel II, as a Catholic, was much perturbed by the violation of the pope's rights and never felt comfortable in Rome. He spent most of his time in his native Turin and Piedmont.[224] The encyclical *Respicientes ea*, issued on 1 November 1870, predictably denounced the seizure of Rome and excommunicated all those responsible. Pius IX was rigidly determined not to accept the legitimacy of the new Italian state.[225]

Pius had declared himself dramatically 'a prisoner in the Vatican' (*captivus Vaticani*) before the assembled diplomatic corps when Rome fell to the Italian army. Uneducated Catholic peasants across the world on learning this horrifying news had visions of the poor pope in a prison cell chained to his bed. This did not quite fit the splendour and comfort of the Apostolic palace, although humid and malodourous in the summer months. Pius refused ever again to appear on the balcony, or loggia, overlooking St Peter's. The faithful would have to enter the basilica to see the pope and receive his blessing. It was an example that his successors would follow for six decades.

Several months later, on 13 May 1871, the Italian parliament passed the law of guarantees. The Holy See was offered the Vatican, the Lateran palace and Castel Gandolfo, overlooking Lake Albano, as extraterritorial residences for the pope to enjoy. Pius's right to communicate freely with the church and the diplomatic corps was assured. The Italian state promised to pay 3 million *lire* annually for the upkeep of the papacy.[226] Two days later in the encyclical *Ubi nos* Pius repudiated the law of guarantees. He called on the European powers to restore him. He never accepted, nor drew on the stipend offered by the Italian government, as this would have been an implicit recognition of the Italian state.[227] The position of the papacy, within Italy, would remain unresolved for nearly seventy years.

During his remaining years, the pope reinforced the policy of *Non expedit* which had emerged in 1868. This exhorted Catholics not to participate in Italian politics and elections. It was an 'own goal' for the church, as it delayed the formation of a Catholic political party in Italy until 1919.[228] Pius' final years were a melancholy time. Most Catholic countries underwent a gradual process of deconfessionalisation. Belgium, Luxembourg, the Netherlands and Switzerland all implemented legislation that removed much of the church's privileged position over education, welfare and politics.[229] Even the Habsburg monarchy introduced equality among all religions. This led to the emancipation of the Jews, much to the chagrin of the Holy See.[230] Spain had undergone a republican revolution in 1868 that led to a raft of anticlerical legislation. The restoration of the Bourbon monarchy in Iberia in 1873 slowed the drift against the church.[231] Most liberal politicians, after the embarrassment caused by reactionary measures like the syllabus of errors and infallibility, wanted to cut any remaining links between state and church. It was a quiet revolution, in which the church was relegated gradually to the private sphere of personal belief.

More serious problems emerged in Bismarck's Germany. Unlike in Italy, the process of unification had created a federal empire in which most princes were allowed to retain nominal sovereignty, if not much power.[232] The difficulty was that, confessionally, Germany was divided in two: a Lutheran-Calvinist north, and a Catholic Rhineland and south. Given that the Prussian monarchy had been instrumental in the process of national unity, Bismarck was keen that Germans should not suffer any conflicts of loyalty. He was worried that the doctrine of infallibility, Catholic trade unions and the Zentrum party meant that he had fifth columns in the midst of his new polity.[233] He wanted to ensure that Catholics would be brought to heel, and accept their incorporation into the new state. The pope must be dissuaded from interfering, or disturbing, the political settlement that had emerged after 1870.

Bismarck and the conservatives found unlikely allies in the German liberals, who believed that the fight against the papacy was symbolic of the fight that pitted progress against reaction. A progressive scientist, Rudolf Virchow, described this process as a *Kulturkampf*.[234] Although the chancellor did not use this term himself, he would, for the better part of the next decade, enforce a series of anti-Catholic measures. He started by appointing Cardinal Gustav-Adolf von Hohenlohe as German ambassador to the Holy See. Given that this prince of the church had been an opponent of infallibility, the pope refused to accept him in Rome.[235] Hohenlohe, to make matters worse, was a friend of Döllinger, who had been excommunicated in 1871.[236]

Bismarck decided to escalate the conflict with the Falk law of 1872, which opened all schools to governmental scrutiny and purged them of Catholic clergy. The following year, all clergymen were required to have graduated with a proper university degree or risk being removed from office. The church's refusal to accept this meant that many bishoprics and parishes lay empty as the state refused to accept Vatican appointees. The 'pulpit law' of 1875 allowed imperial prosecutors to pursue priests who made inflammatory political statements. Religious orders, especially the Jesuits, were expelled from Germany, the only exceptions being those monks and nuns who ministered in hospitals.[237] Pius inflamed the situation by ordering Catholics to disregard all German anticlerical legislation.

Soon, dozens of priests and several nuns were detained by the imperial authorities. The key flashpoint was Marpingen in 1876,[238] as we have seen, where the Marian visionaries, together with thousands of pilgrims, were dispersed by imperial soldiers. The German government's overreaction and heavy-handedness strengthened, rather than weakened, Catholic solidarity. The *Kulturkampf* increased the number of Zentrum party deputies in the Reichstag to ninety-six.[239] By the end of the decade, Bismarck needed these Catholics votes to pass legislation. Anti-Catholic laws were toned down. The *Zentrum partei* formed an unholy alliance with the imperial conservatives to thwart the growth of German socialism. Thus the ferocity of the *Kulturkampf* had strengthened the church somewhat.[240]

By 1878, Pius had ruled the Roman Catholic Church for over thirty-one years. His was the longest pontificate in history apart from St Peter's legendary thirty-four years as Christ's direct successor. The liberal pope of 1846 was still physically recognisable in his rotundity and good humour. Yet his ability to compromise had vanished, replaced by a stubborn, paranoid and reactionary mindset. He lived out his declining years in the Vatican. He denied the reality of Italian unity and expressed the certainty that one day God would restore his vanished kingdom. His physical decrepitude became noticeable; he gained weight and his legs were covered in painful sores. Disconcertingly for those around him, Mastai had developed a tendency towards narcolepsy. His impromptu naps could lead to embarrassing delays in meetings and audiences. Yet one thing which he did retain was an almost youthful voice. Contemporaries were surprised by his continued charisma and inspiring speeches.[241]

By January 1878 he had weakened considerably, and was barely able to stand. His last official engagement was at Candlemas on 2 February. He was visibly frail and unwell during the service. Five days later, as he drifted in and out of consciousness, it was thought wise that he should make his final confession and receive the last rites. Towards the evening of 8 February he breathed his last.[242] Before his lifeless corpse stood Cardinal Bilio, one of the key authors of the syllabus of errors and infallibility; next to him was Cardinal Pecchi, Bishop of Perugia and *camerlengo* (chamberlain) of the Holy See. It was their duty to tap the pope's head gently with a silver hammer to certify his death.

Pius's body lay in state for nine days and over 300,000 mourners thronged to St Peter's. Some came to pay their respects, others were there out of curiosity. The numbers were so great that the College of Cardinals grew concerned about public order. They instructed the chief treasurer of St Peter's to write to the Italian government to request troops inside the basilica to maintain the peace.[243] A formal recognition of the authority of the Italian state was avoided.

The pope had requested that he should be buried in the crypt of the beautiful primitive basilica of San Lorenzo Fuori le Mura. Underneath the altar, according to tradition, lay the bones of St Stephen, the first Christian martyr.[244] It took almost two years for the crypt to be made ready for the pope's remains. Fearful that a solemn procession would cause trouble, it was decided to transfer the coffin to San Lorenzo during the night. Late on 12 July 1881, large hostile crowds of liberals and radicals gathered to hurl curses at the hated remains of the last pope-king. Stones were thrown at the priests and dignitaries accompanying the corpse. At one point, some rioters seized the coffin and shouted that they were going to throw Pius into the Tiber. Only the arrival of mounted *carabinieri* prevented the desecration of the pope's remains.[245]

Pius IX's pontificate was the most important in the history of the modern Catholic Church. He radically reshaped the institution he governed. After the revolution of 1849, his foremost priority was the retention of the Papal States. This was an abject failure, and he could not stem the tide of Italian unification. Despite his declaration of war on liberalism and modernity, politics did not bend to the pope's will. Yet the paradox was that the pope who lost a kingdom gained a spiritual mastery over the church that his predecessors could only have dreamed of achieving. His relentless insistence on declaring infallibility and spiritual autocracy bolstered the institution of the papacy beyond recognition.

Young Lamennais and the liberal Catholics had hoped that a strengthened papacy would create a more progressive and socially aware church. The increased influence of the papacy did quite the opposite, though Pius did give Catholicism a spiritual impetus and popular enthusiasm that it had not achieved in centuries. The cult of the immaculate conception, the Marian apparitions, and the flamboyant reassertion of baroque spectacle all pleased the Catholic masses. Yet it seems unlikely that the peasants of Europe much cared about infallibility, or the theological controversies that had raged in the Vatican. For them, statues, apparitions and miracles brought the divine to their villages and parishes. It provided hope and enchantment where liberalism, socialism and science could only offer fatality and cold reason. This spiritual renewal touched the lives of millions of ordinary people. Yet the refusal to negotiate with the modern state set the tone for the future of Catholicism. The dysfunctional relationship that was established between the Vatican and modern politics owes a lot to the stubbornness and recalcitrance of Pio Nono. A less volatile pope would have served the church better.

8

'THE NEW THINGS':
LEO XIII AND THE SOCIAL
QUESTION, 1878–1903

On 15 November 1875 the *Daily Telegraph* of London published a letter by the explorer Henry Morton Stanley, purporting to be written on behalf of King Mutesa of the Baganda, a Bantu people in what is now Uganda.[1] It called on Christian missionaries to travel to the heart of the Great Lakes region of eastern Africa. Here evangelisers would be granted royal protection and every encouragement in spreading the word of God. It was not clear to readers of the *Telegraph* why the king should extend this invitation. No mention was made of the fact that the king had just been criticised by some Egyptian imams for the laxity of his religious observances. This censure had infuriated him, and to signal his displeasure, he had ordered seventy converts to Islam burned alive.[2]

Stanley's announcement that huge areas of unexplored jungle were now open to Christianity caused great excitement. European do-gooders scrambled to be the first to reach Buganda. Perhaps their enthusiasm might have cooled if they had been aware of the king's explosive temper. But these men of God followed a higher calling that came from the mouth of Christ himself. Jesus in the gospels had given all Christians the 'great commission' of preaching the 'good news' so as to convert all the peoples of the world to the truth.* Within two years, members of the Anglican Church Mission Society (CMS) had established a mission station in Buganda. This organisation, founded in 1799, was one of the largest missionary institutions in the world,[3] and while revolution engulfed Europe they sent out thousands of Protestant volunteers to spread the gospel and lobby for the abolition of the slave trade.[4]

Catholics were painfully aware that, by the second half of the nineteenth century, they were lagging behind in the missionary 'great game.' The French Revolution's destruction of ecclesiastical institutions had led to a chronic shortage of funds and vocations. Napoleon had promised to fund missions to China after his coronation.[5] However, his dispute with Pius VII ensured that this pledge was a dead letter. By 1822, outside Europe and the Americas, there were only a few hundred missionary clergy. Recapturing the momentum was going to prove difficult. Gregory XVI, before becoming pope in 1831, had been prefect of the *Propaganda Fide* (Congregation for the Propagation of the Faith). His time heading this institution, which was charged with the dissemination of Catholicism throughout the planet, had been instructive. Although Gregory had never travelled outside Italy, he understood that regalvanising the missions should be a priority.[6] During his reign, some effort was made to reorganise, fund and improve the education of the orders whose vocation it was to spread the gospel to the non-Christian world. During the first half of the nineteenth century the results achieved were mediocre at best.[7]

Beyond South America, the Philippines and Portuguese Goa, where the Iberian monarchies had forced Catholicism on their subjects, there was little hope of making progress. Until the 1880s, Britain was the key driving force behind the second age of European imperialism. The only exception was Algeria

---

* According to St Mark's Gospel Jesus 'said unto them, go into all the world and preach the gospel to every creature. He who believes and is baptised will be saved; but he who does not believe will be condemned' (Mark 16:14–18, KJV).

which had been conquered by France in 1830.[8] Understandably Anglican Britain had little incentive to spread Catholicism in its distant empire. Yet Catholic emancipation in 1829 meant that Roman clergy were tolerated within its colonies. There is an aphorism which states that 'first comes the missionary, then the trader and finally the gunboat'. This remark seems to be truer for Protestant empires than for Catholic ones.[9] Ever since the reign of Constantine in the fourth century, the church had co-opted the power of the imperial state to solidify its unity and promote conversions.

The Berlin Conference of 1885 unleashed the second great age of imperialism. Under the wily stewardship of Prince Otto von Bismarck, Europe's great powers drew arbitrary lines to divide Africa into spheres of influence.[10] Spurious reasons were given to justify such aggressive expansionism: chancelleries argued that they wanted to end the African slave trade, bring education, technological advances and welfare to these 'barbaric' lands. These humanitarian justifications thinly concealed motives of economic exploitation, imperialist 'prestige' and cultural desolation. The Catholic Church exulted in the potential spread of Christianity to the so-called 'dark continent'. It had been a dream of the papacy ever since Portugal had tried to colonise Angola and had experienced some success in converting the kingdom of the Kongo during the seventeenth century.[11]

For the Curia the fear remained that the modern separation of church and state might be exported to Africa. After all, article 6 of chapter 1 of the Treaty of Berlin emphasised that the great powers would: 'without distinction of creed or nation, protect and favour all religious, scientific or charitable institutions'. This passage upset the papacy, as it placed all religions on the same footing within the colonies. Yet the next clause was sympathetic to missionary endeavours, stating that: 'Christian missionaries, scientists and explorers, with their followers, property and collections, shall likewise be the objects of especial protection.'[12] Imperial states saw missionaries as vital to their project of bringing European civilisation and values to Africa. After 1885, the 'scramble for Africa' would see Britain, France, Belgium, Germany and Italy racing to carve up the continent.* A surge in Catholic missionary activity would follow in the wake of this expansion into Sub-Saharan Africa. The truly unexpected outcome of the scramble for Africa was that, by 1910, Catholic missionaries outnumbered their Protestant rivals.[13]

Although missionaries aspired to improve the lives of Africans, they had, to say the least, ambivalent feelings about the local cultures, religions and societies. Some clergymen became amateur anthropologists and linguists;[14] for others, it was simply a case of transplanting European Christianity onto local realities, which for them were valueless. Catholics still clung to the imperative *extra ecclesium nulla salus* (outside of the church no salvation). Animism, tribalism, immodest dress, non-European family structures and polygamy were viewed as 'barbaric' practices to be extirpated. Yet for all that, missionaries, especially Protestant ones, could become whistle-blowers denouncing the worst excesses of imperialism.[15]

Unfortunately the Catholic Church was often hoodwinked by the humanitarian rhetoric of imperialists, whereas Protestant evangelicals understood better that behind 'nice words' often lay such atrocities as forced migrations, genocide, neo-slavery, inter-tribal war and savage mutilations. As long as the imperial state protected its missionaries, Rome had an unfortunate habit of not asking too many embarrassing questions. As a white settler in Rhodesia put it in 1911: 'Of all the missionaries the Roman Catholics did the least harm, for they never preach equality nor allow the natives to approach the level of equality in any way.'[16] Given that many missionaries (especially those from France) had some crypto-royalist sympathies, it is hardly surprising that egalitarianism was not a Catholic priority. Obedient to Pius IX's exhortations, they denounced modernity as satanic. They were concerned that the French Republic would bring secularism to its growing African empire. On occasions, when the gospel of *la république* was preached instead of that of Jesus Christ, recriminations could follow between the men in white colonial uniforms and those in

---

* For a classic narrative, see Thomas Pakenham, *The Scramble for Africa* (London, 1992).

cassocks.[17] Yet such tensions tended to be the exception rather than the norm. The Catholic Church did collude with Europe's second age of imperialism and certainly did not oppose it. On the contrary, it was viewed as an opportunity to gain more souls for God.

Cardinal Charles Lavigerie, Archbishop of Algiers, was a notable proselytiser and adventurer. He had developed a deep passion for evangelisation when he was stationed in the Middle East. In Lebanon he had defended the Christian minority against the depredations of the Ottoman authorities.[18] Yet he realised that there was very little progress in making actual converts. Muslims seemed very happy with the Quran and viewed Christ as a great prophet but not a divinity. One of the pretexts for the Crimean war (1853–6) had been the protection of the holy shrines of Jerusalem.[19] France's victory gained the custodianship of these sites for a Catholic Church that was woefully unprepared to assume this responsibility. The Latin patriarchate of Jerusalem had only been resurrected in 1847 to give the Catholics in the Holy Land some coordination.[20] The Order of the Holy Sepulchre was revitalised the same year, as a sort of cash-for-honours scheme that funded some fledgling missionary activities in Palestine.[21] Yet in the birthplace of Christianity only a few local people showed an inclination to abandon Islam or Judaism for the gospel. The Middle East proved a disappointment for Catholic missionary hopes.[22]

Throughout his later career, expanding the church and gaining souls became an obsession for Lavigerie. On arriving in Algiers in 1868, he founded the Missionnaires d'Afrique, better known as the White Fathers, an order dedicated to the conversion of Africans.[23] His missionary methods were controversial to say the least. During his first year as archbishop, Algeria was beset by a terrible famine and cholera epidemic. Lavigerie proposed collecting all the orphans created by these catastrophes into villages where they would be nourished, educated and taught a craft.[24] Unsurprisingly, the price paid for such assistance was conversion to Catholicism. This policy was akin to creating villages full of little Edgardo Mortaras in which young boys and girls would become Catholics with little real choice in the matter. Fearing Maghrebi and Arab outrage against these proselytising initiatives,

Marshal McMahon, the governor of French Algeria, demanded that Lavigerie cease his activities.[25] The archbishop refused, saying that he was the pastor of all, not just Christian colonists. Another contentious plan involved encouraging missionaries to purchase slave boys and girls in the African interior. After these youths had been converted, they would be emancipated and encouraged to form Catholic communities.[26] Informed consent was not high on Lavigerie's list of priorities when it came to converting natives.

When King Mutesa's letter inviting missionaries made its way to Algiers it electrified the archbishop.[27] He felt that it was vital not to abandon Sub-Saharan Africa to Protestants and Muslims. The *Propaganda Fide* in Rome was sent an ambitious plan that included several maps for the evangelisation and creation of a Sub-Saharan church. Africa was divided into enormous squares indicating the location of future dioceses and metropolitan provinces.[28] The Curia was so impressed by these grand designs that Lavigerie's jurisdiction was expanded to include all the Sudan, and the Great Lakes region. Although the White Fathers had not yet received canonical confirmation as a religious order from Rome, they were authorised to establish mission stations in this new territory.

The first expedition, composed of ten missionaries, was planned for 1878.[29] The leader of this mission was Léon Livinhac from the Aveyron *département*, situated deep in the Massif Central of France. A studious though fragile child, he was an unlikely candidate for missionary work. Like his brethren, he hid his effete and fragile frame behind a luscious beard.[30] The real powerhouse in the expedition was Father Simeon Lourdel from northern France. In contrast to most missionaries, he was blond, blue-eyed, clean-shaven and boyish in his looks.[31] This Viking stood out like a sore thumb in African society. Both men came from farming stock, and had dominant mothers who had inculcated an iron faith into their souls. Hardship was second nature to them.

Lavigerie was very proud of his missionaries. As preparations began for the mission to equatorial Africa, he reassured them that it would be arduous, difficult and that the expedition was bound to result in some deaths. Those martyred for the faith were guaranteed entry to paradise (apparently not a disincentive among missionaries). On 17 April 1878 the expedition departed Marseille on board the *Yang-Tse* steamer heading for China.[32] They sailed through the Suez Canal which had been completed in 1869 and made a stop in Aden where they changed vessels.[33] By 30 May the intrepid missionaries landed in the sultanate of Zanzibar. They would spend the next weeks collecting provisions and learning Swahili, the *lingua franca* of East Africa. Lourdel complained of the high salaries for porters and the need to hire armed *askaris* (African irregulars) to protect the convoy. For weeks the caravan travelled at a snail's pace. Impassable quagmires, malaria-infested jungles and other perils made the terrain difficult to traverse. Another problem consisted in payments of the *Hongo*, a toll exacted by the local tribes for safe passage through the region.

After three months, the travellers approached the banks of Lake Tanganyika.[34] By now they had almost been completely deserted by their bearers and *askari*. New recruits needed to be hired to proceed onwards towards Buganda. At this point, the missionaries divided in two, one group headed for Tanganyika, the other for Lake Victoria (Nyanza). To the north lay territories held by a fearful warlord called Mirambo (which meant 'corpses' in the Nyamwezi dialect).[35] Lourdel recklessly attempted to negotiate with this warrior for permission to cross his domain. Luckily the tribe had left on a raiding expedition, so the missionaries speeded on their way.[36] When on 30 December 1878 the team reached the banks of Lake Victoria the *askari* fired shots of joy in the air while the missionaries knelt to give thanks to the Virgin Mary for their deliverance.

However, for the White Fathers the real adventure lay ahead. They had reached the northern frontier of modern Tanzania and now Mutesa awaited. Crossing the lake would prove easier said than done. A local chief provided a canoe to allow a delegation to travel to pay homage to the king. It was only on 17 February 1879, nearly a year after they left Marseille, that Lourdel disembarked in Buganda. Mutesa wondered why they had come. As was becoming clear by the late nineteenth century, Africans could expect little good from white visitors.[37]

They were not the first to have arrived. Alexander Mackay was a dour, humourless, and terribly earnest presbyterian Scot. After years as a draughtsman and engineer in Germany, following a damascene conversion he had joined the Church Missionary Society.[38] His arrival at the Bugandan court the previous year marked the beginning of Christian missions in this corner of Africa. Technical expertise, and a rigid work ethic, qualified him to teach advanced carpentry and farming to the locals. Soon ambitious Bagandans flocked to him, but the price they had to pay was to listen to his sermons. He was vehemently opposed to the White Fathers and urged the king to expel them.[39] Mutesa was far too curious to heed Mackay's anti-Papist sentiments and gave Lourdel permission to come to his court on Rubaga (a hill overlooking modern Kampala). During months of travel, these intrepid priests had learned some Swahili and were thus able to communicate directly with the king and his officials during a public audience.

Mackay accused them of idolatry and misinterpreting the Bible. Soon Lourdel and the Scotsman entered into a furious argument about the true nature of Christianity. Mutesa was a canny politician and decided to play the Catholic missionaries off against the Protestant ones. Thus, he remained in control by dividing and manipulating the different religious sects in his realm.[40] He ensured that they were all kept hoping that they would be given preferment, but none was ever given the upper hand. Mutesa consented that the White Fathers establish themselves in Rubaga. The process of transferring the remaining missionaries and their baggage to this site took four months.

Once installed in the capital, four large, interconnected huts were constructed for the Catholic mission. This structure resembled a convent with a refectory and a chapel for the White Fathers. Lourdel described how the diet of cooked bananas and sweet potatoes was plain but nutritious.[41] Unlike the people of Tanzania whom he disparaged, the elites of Buganda impressed him with their manners and dress. Soon, a very uneasy triangular relationship emerged between the different faiths in Buganda. The Muslims loathed the British, and Mackay detested the Catholics (although it seems the other Anglican missionaries were better disposed towards the Papists).

Mutesa, in his almost daily discussions with Livinhac and Lourdel, made it clear that politics, rather than theology, was his prime concern. He was worried about Arab-Egyptian incursions to the north of his realm. Having sent messages of friendship to Queen Victoria, he was surprised that she had not replied. To test the waters with France, he requested the White Fathers negotiate on his behalf with Paris to make Buganda a protectorate.[42] Stunned by this unexpected demand, the priests answered that they had no authority to discuss political matters. Mutesa was disappointed and wondered whether Catholic missions were useful to his government after all. Then the king fell ill. He called on Father Lourdel to minister to him and provide modern medicine. Although this blond priest was not a qualified physician, he did what he could, dispensing home remedies. Luckily, the monarch recovered and praised, perhaps a little too generously, the benefits of Western medicine.

Lourdel and his brethren were invited to preach at court. One of the most contentious discussions with Buganda's leaders revolved around the position of the Virgin Mary. If she was the mother of God, then was she a divinity? Indeed, the doctrine of the immaculate conception deeply perplexed these African elites who argued (reasonably) that it made little sense. Yet, the king expressed his admiration for Catholic eschatology. He seemed taken with the notions of heaven, purgatory and hell.

Whether Mutesa was genuine in his appreciation or politically motivated is anybody's guess.[43] His sudden request to be baptised in October 1879 astonished the White Fathers. Lourdel responded that, to be received into the church, the king would need to select one wife and send away the other 'concubines'. This condition did not impress the Bugandan court, as marriages were not purely romantic but were part of vital dynastic alliances. Almost immediately, the pagan and Islamic factions at court reassured the monarch that their faiths positively encouraged polygamy. One can only wonder if Mutesa's request for baptism was an attempt to ignite the religious divisions within his court and keep everyone guessing as to his ultimate intentions.

Regardless, Christian norms on monogamy and chastity ensured that the elites of the capital, who had dozens of wives, would be unwilling to convert. It was from the ranks of the younger generations, keen to learn more about Western knowledge, that the first catechumens were recruited. Thanks to this influx, the White Fathers gradually learned to speak Luganda. In time, they would produce the first dictionaries of this hitherto-unstudied Bantu language.[44] More problematic was the missionaries' practice, inspired by Lavigerie, of purchasing child slaves, whom they converted and then freed. This led to suspicions that they were trying to create a militia of Christian boy-soldiers. During the early 1880s the White Fathers would have to tread carefully, as their activities elicited curiosity and hostility in equal measure.[45]

The year 1881 saw the Rubaga mission grow exponentially as over one hundred catechumens joined. The first Catholic community in Uganda, though small, was beginning to take root. Some of these converts were described as *basomi* or 'readers'. This reflected their growing mastery of the magisterium of the church and Western knowledge.[46] Several of these *basomi* were 'pages' at the royal court. The White Fathers hoped that, by converting the future generation of Bagandan elites, Catholicism would flourish on the northern shores of Lake Victoria. But trouble was brewing, as these conversions gave the appearance that the White Fathers were building their own powerbase at court.

A meteorological accident reversed the fortunes of the Bugandan mission. During a storm, a bolt of lightning struck Mutesa's palace, burning it to the ground.[47] This disaster was interpreted by the pagan faction as an ill omen. Tensions grew as the Arab traders spread allegations that the White Fathers were buying slaves and arming them with Remington rifles. To make matters worse a cholera epidemic broke out in the kingdom. Given that the Christian God seemed ineffectual in preventing these disasters, the king toyed with the idea of making Islam the state religion to placate heaven. The death of the queen-mother in the autumn of 1882 was yet another bad portent. Growing xenophobia amongst the Baganda prompted Lourdel and his associates to evacuate the mission at Rubaga. With royal assent these priests left Buganda in January 1883.[48]

Mutesa had been ill for some time and succumbed to his infirmities a year later. He was succeeded by his son, who became Mwanga II and was a controversial ruler from the start. Mackay described him, rather hysterically, as a 'black Nero' and vicious tyrant.[49] Little documentation survives giving a glimpse into Mwanga's psyche, but where Mutesa had been skilful in dividing and ruling the different faiths of his kingdom, Mwanga does not appear to have equalled his father in keeping pagan, Muslim, Protestant and Catholic influences balanced.

The impending arrival of James Hannington, the new Anglican bishop of East Africa, created a crisis. This clergyman from Sussex was an idealist; sporting a prominent beard, he was determined to bring light of Christ to the Baganda. There was a prophecy at the court in Kampala that their nation would be conquered by invaders from the east. Hannington was determined to enter Buganda from this direction. He was clearly a man with a death wish. Mwanga, feeling his authority under threat, ordered the arrest and execution of the hapless bishop in 1885.[50] The new monarch was determined to use force to cement his unsteady authority.

It was at this time that, unwisely, Lourdel returned to Rubaga to pay homage to the new king. Mwanga greeted the returning White Fathers positively. He stated that it was his intent to reject paganism and Islam in favour of Christianity. To the missionaries' surprise the number of catechumens had grown from one hundred to over eight hundred since their departure two years previously. The *basomi* had kept the flame of Catholicism burning during their absence.[51] It is here that the story gets complicated.

The standard hagiographical account narrates how Mwanga II was homosexual and wanted to take advantage of his Catholic *basomi* and Anglican pages. These young men bravely refused the advances of the furious monarch. An enraged Mwanga ordered around forty of these Christian boys be burned alive,[52] a move that cemented his reputation as an ogre. This persecution gave Rome its first Bantu martyrs, who were eventually canonised as saints in 1964.[53]

This narrative is a little too neat. Homosexuality remains the worst accusation that can be made against a man in African culture. To scapegoat Mwanga as a wicked, weak, and homosexual king who squandered Buganda's independence seems convenient. It privileges the role of one corrupt individual in placing Uganda at the mercy of European colonisation. This story papers over the religious and political divisions that were already tearing Bagandan society apart. One wonders whether post-colonial Ugandans (especially as the country became majority Christian in the twentieth century) rewrote their history so that the loss of their independence was attributed to the shenanigans of one 'sexual deviant' rather than recognising that internal divisions made pre-colonial Buganda vulnerable to foreign interference. This tale had its uses for the Catholic Church too. For Rome it was better, in terms of publicity, to have been persecuted not just by a standard tyrant, but by one with homosexual tendencies. So, for the Vatican, the martyrs who were burned alive in 1886 not merely resisted the encroachments of the state but heroically refused to surrender to 'sexual perversion' too. These martyrs were double heroes. Yet the truth was more complex, and was linked to the growing turmoil that characterised Bagandan court politics.

In 1887, the arrival of German forces, determined to colonise Dar es Salaam, to the south of the realm, caused much concern for the king.[54] There were increasing recriminations between the Islamic and Catholic factions. Mwanga was forced to make a choice between these groups. He chose the Quran over the Bible at first. The martyrdom of the Christian *basomi* was a harbinger that his allegiances were shifting towards the Muslim traders at his court.[55] Worryingly for the king, armed militias started forming along sectarian lines. Soon, Christians and Muslims had thousands of men under arms. Unhappy with this growing threat to his authority, Mwanga hatched a plot to restore pagan worship and to expel all the monotheistic religions.[56]

The missionaries, Muslims and their armed followers united to resist Mwanga. They succeeded in temporarily dethroning him and replaced him with his brother, and Buganda entered a virtual state of civil war for the remainder of the 1880s.[57] To end this conflict and cement his restoration, King Mwanga sought British assistance. In 1894 Buganda became a British protectorate; despite this, Mwanga found his loss of autonomy unbearable and he launched an attack on British forces in East Africa. Defeated in 1897, he became a prisoner and would die in the Seychelles islands in 1903, at just thirty-five years of age.[58] Although the Ugandan protectorate that emerged after 1900 privileged Protestant evangelisation, the missions of the White Fathers did not vanish but, on the contrary, prospered. By 1914 there were over 100,000 Roman Catholics on the banks of Lake Victoria, which prompted Rome to fund the construction of St Mary's Cathedral on Lubaga Hill, the very site where Lourdel had begun his work four decades previously.[59]

For all its oddities, the adventurous story of the White Fathers in Uganda epitomised how, from 1878 to 1903, Catholicism expanded into Africa. Rome gained ground rapidly after almost a century of missionary neglect. Not all missionaries were quite as subtle as the White Fathers in their approach, however. Father Guillemé, stationed in upper Congo, came across a village besieged by a troop of rapacious monkeys. He took out his rifle and shot the largest one which promptly fell to the ground from his perch. The other monkeys beat a hasty retreat and the local villagers celebrated Gillemé as the man who had delivered them from their tormentors.[60] Opening a dialogue with the unconverted was not always so easy, and Catholicism tended to prosper most in territories under direct colonial rule.

Rome's collusion with Leopold II of Belgium was a particularly dark episode in the history of Catholic missions in Africa.[61] His acquisition of the enormous Congo basin as a private fief presented proselytisers like Cardinal Lavigerie with mouth-watering opportunities for the mass conversion of souls. Although many Catholic Belgian politicians were anti-colonialist they were roundly ignored by both monarch and the Vatican in a relentless bid to penetrate sub-Saharan Africa.[62] Leopold's rhetoric, that he wanted to fight slavery from within Africa and bring humanitarianism and civilisation to 'barbarism', was vacuous. Concealed behind these pieties lay genocidal violence, new forms of slavery, economic depredation and unspeakable cruelty.

For the population of the Congo basin the failure to fulfil ivory and rubber production quotas led to savage *razzias*, burnings and mutilations.[63] The misery visited on the Congo was genocidal. Industrialists, and adventurers put much pressure on the church to support Leopold's Congo Free State as a model of European colonisation. Cardinal James Gibbons of Baltimore praised the Brussels monarchy in public, and attacked those who denounced the brutality of the *force publique* in Congo.[64] He even urged the papacy to give every support to evangelising this part of Africa.

Many White Fathers, Belgian Scheutveld fathers, Mill Hill fathers and other congregations mounted expeditions to the Free State.[65] Yet, given Lavigerie's commitments elsewhere in Africa, progress was sluggish. Only by the early twentieth century did missionaries begin their work in earnest and, by 1912, there were about 100,000 converts.[66] When humanitarians like Edmund Dene Morel and Roger Casement blew the lid off the atrocities committed by Belgium, the Jesuits and other religious orders flocked to deny that this was the case. Catholics defended Leopold, stating he was waging a brutal war against Arab slavers, and seeking to pacify inter-tribal warfare. The fact that this was done through trading monopolies and the enslavement of vast numbers was ignored. There is some evidence that the *force publique* in the Congo specifically avoided committing atrocities in areas near missions.[67] Yet it seems an odd coincidence that evangelicals were able to uncover the truth whereas Catholics pleaded ignorance. Worse, the papal nuncio in Brussels, along with several cardinals in London, claimed that Protestant whistle-blowing was a form of jealousy. While their attempts to convert Congolese souls floundered, Rome's missions prospered.[68]

In 1905, Leopold commissioned an independent enquiry to answer domestic and international outcry against his activities in Congo. The members of this panel published a damning indictment, not only of the king's colonial agents, but also of the Catholic missions.[69] Given this outcome, Rome's discomfort grew considerably, and relations with Belgium became chilly. Somewhat cravenly, Catholic missionaries now defended their work and turned on the Free State authorities. Arthur Vermeersch, a Flemish Jesuit, in 1906 published *La Question Congolaise*.[70] He broke ranks with the church, criticised Leopold's exploitation of his colonial fiefdom and advised that the Belgian state should annex the Congo and transform it into a colony.

Far from being beyond repair, the coolness between the Vatican and Brussels lasted a few months. In May 1906, the Congo Free State and the Catholic Church signed a concordat which guaranteed the missions' freedom, [71] and promised each station at least one hundred hectares of land (two hundred for larger establishments). In return, the Vatican agreed to submit detailed statistics on the missions' activities and their educational curriculum to the Governor General of the colony for approval. This was the only concordat ever signed between the Catholic Church and a European colony in Africa. The agreement was shameful, proving that the Roman Catholic Church was all too willing to close its eyes before the serial violence and exploitation inflicted by the *force publique* on its unfortunate subjects.

There was a sense that the nuncio in Brussels seemed much more ill at ease with Leopold II's sexual laxity and his extramarital affairs than with the monarch's brutal abuse of his African fiefdom.[72] The eventual annexation of the Free State by Belgium in 1908 may have been a step in the right direction. Yet the colonial authorities in Brussels put the needs of empire over those of the locality. Throughout the Belgian presence in Congo, the Roman church was to remain a powerful interest group which provided education and basic welfare to the Congolese.[73] In this colony the relationship between the church and the imperial state was quasi-symbiotic.

This would have been difficult to achieve in those territories controlled by the largest European empires, namely Britain and France. Here the collaboration with a Protestant behemoth and a secular republic was more guarded. In these imperial domains Catholicism was never granted a concordat, or the favoured position enjoyed in the Congo Free State. Yet, even here impressive inroads were made in persuading African souls to convert and make the metaphorical journey to Rome.

Such success was ironic, given that, at the same time, modern secularism was accelerating in Europe.[74] Indeed, the old continent was being ravaged by a renewed conflict between church and state. In 1878, within the National Assembly, Leon Gambetta, the future radical French prime minister, had declared: 'Clericalism! There is the enemy!'[75] Counter-intuitively, European attitudes to religion within their imperial peripheries were totally at odds with those of their heartlands. When Gambetta wrote to colonial officials, he reminded them in no uncertain terms that 'anticlericalism is not for export'.[76] Given this greater freedom to evangelise, educate and control souls outside of Europe it is little wonder that the Vatican chose the path of least resistance.

The French empire did not merely cover large swathes of Saharan and equatorial Africa, but included Indochina and some Caribbean islands. During Napoleon III's reign, France's policy-makers grew concerned about Britain's commercial expansion into east Asia during the Opium Wars.[77] There were fears that Laos, Cambodia and Vietnam risked falling under the sway of the Union Flag. Since the seventeenth century, French missionaries had experienced some success in finding converts to Christianity in this corner of the world.[78] Yet much depended on the good will of the Nguyen dynasty that ruled Vietnam. Catholics in the southern part of the state had risen in revolt during the 1830s, and faced brutal repression. Hanoi became wary of missionary activities within its domains.

The accession of the Emperor Tự Đức in 1847 seemed auspicious. He had a reputation as an educated, cultured, and gentle monarch. It was hoped he would promote toleration and protect clergymen in his domains. This apparent honeymoon did not last long, as the emperor began to suspect Christians of disloyalty. He felt missionaries undermined his rule by preaching rebellion and, as a result, religious freedom was curtailed; he persecuted converts, burnt down churches and arrested missionaries. As many as thirty to forty thousand may have been massacred in Tonkin.[79] When, in 1858, two French Jesuits were executed, the situation reached boiling point. This incident provided Paris with the pretext it needed to gain an imperial foothold in Indochina. As a reprisal, a French naval force bombarded Da Nang, and then seized the

Mekong delta. French forces occupied the provinces of Biên Hòa, Gia Định and Định Tường in south-eastern Vietnam. In 1862 Tự Đức was forced to admit defeat by signing the Treaty of Saigon which accepted France's annexation of this region.[80]

The French government came to realise that the Mekong River was not the gateway to Chinese trade that they had hoped, making this imperial foothold far less lucrative than anticipated. French officers in Saigon took the initiative and, without consulting their government, invaded the north. In 1872 Hanoi was seized, much to the satisfaction of the local bishop, Paul Puginier.[81] Another treaty guaranteed the freedom of missionaries and their protection by the Viet authorities. Twelve years later, with the Treaty of Paternôtre, Vietnam, Laos and Cambodia became French protectorates.[82] As with Africa, the French foreign and colonial offices funded missionary expansion in these regions.

All seemed to be going well until an incident caused deep embarrassment for both the Catholic clergy and the imperial state. Marie-Charles-David de Mayréna was an adventurer and a swindler who, fleeing Paris because of debts, travelled to Indonesia,[83] where he bored his listeners with fake stories of his exploits in the Franco-Prussian war and at times hinted that he was tasked with some secret government mission. These tall tales did not get him very far, until he arrived in Indochina in 1888. Here he befriended two priests in the highlands of Annam. Thanks to their good offices Mayréna met with village chiefs. Abusing their credulity, he pretended that he was a government emissary empowered to sign commercial agreements. He soon regulated trade, tribute and religion in these remote imperial marches.

On 3 June, in the village of Kon-Gung, Mayréna's megalomania was unleashed as he proclaimed himself King Marie I of the Sedangs. As a token of gratitude to the missionaries, he declared that Catholicism was the state religion in his constitution. His elaborate uniforms, etiquette and stationery drew the attention of journalists. They reported back to Europe with bemusement about the creation of this pseudo-principality. Marie I's expenses soon far outstripped his income, and he desperately sought to sell his kingdom to France. When he was rebuffed, he threatened to offer it to Britain or Germany.[84] This was treasonous and soon France's colonial authorities blockaded his kingdom. The governor refused any contact with this eccentric self-styled king.

By November, Mayréna and his royal guard, dressed like a light-opera chorus, landed in Hong Kong.[85] Unable to sell his kingdom or mining concessions, he returned to Europe. In Paris he tried to set up a Sedang embassy but was ignored by President Sadi Carnot. Depressed, he frequented the cabarets of the capital and was often seen importuning the chorus girls of the Moulin Rouge. More seriously, he tried to sell Sedang titles of nobility to the unwary. Having duped a poor naïve Belgian investor, Marie I tried to sail back to his kingdom on the proceeds. However, in his absence his realm had been retaken by French forces. He was forbidden to land in Indochina, and was offered a small pension if he left quietly. Mayréna eventually settled on a Malaysian island abandoned by all apart from his dog. He died of unspecified causes on 11 November 1890.[86]

Mayréna's legacy on the missions in Indochina proved damaging. The missionaries involved claimed not to have colluded in the creation of the kingdom of Sadang, yet their signatures were on documents negotiated by Marie I and the village chiefs. In one instance, a punitive expedition had been arranged against a tribe that had attacked the missions. These clergymen had fallen under the spell of Marie I. An investigator sent to examine the Sadang kingdom and the missions was struck by how powerful Catholic institutions had become. They taught the gospel aggressively, and sought to gain considerable property for themselves in the process. This official wondered how far the missions really were aiding in the spread of French language, republican culture and civilisation in these remote provinces.[87]

Gambetta may have been sure that missionaries could act as the stormtroopers of French imperialism, but his successors were less sanguine about their effectiveness in spreading civilisation. Colonial officials were trained in the highly centralised, secular and rationalistic *grandes écoles* in Paris. *Laïcité* (secularism) was the creed of these future generals and governors of colonies.[88] Many of them joined masonic lodges that were overtly hostile to the church.[89] They could not deny that in terms of education, welfare and hospitals Catholicism provided on the cheap what the state could not hope to finance, but were these missionaries preaching the correct creed or were they keeping native minds in bondage and obscurantism? During the 1890s, the French empire answered this question by cutting public funding to missions as a secularisation campaign directed from Paris picked up momentum.[90] After two decades of relative tranquillity in the colonies some of *la république*'s anticlericalism seemed ready for export.

In 1870, the Catholic Church lost its central Italian kingdom with the result that there was a concerted effort, and a highly successful one at that, for the church to regain the initiative in missionary territories. About 80 per cent of the priests and nuns who headed out into Africa and Asia were French.[91] The final decades of the nineteenth century saw much of the groundwork laid which led to Christianity's transformation, by the end of the twentieth century, from a minor sect to Africa's largest religion.[92] Spectacular growth was also experienced in Asia, especially Indochina. By 1900, there were a million Catholics in France's east Asian possessions, up to 700,000 in China, probably 50,000 in Japan and even Korea, untouched in the early modern period, may have gained as many as 20,000 converts.[93]

North America too witnessed exponential growth in its Catholic population. The potato famine of the 1840s had created a mass influx of Catholic migrants on the east coast, inflaming even further the hatred of the white Anglo-Saxon Calvinists of the US.[94] These white descendants of Protestant settlers described themselves as 'native Americans' who did not wish to be contaminated by popery. The 'know nothing' movement unleashed a notorious wave of anti-Catholic feeling in the United States, and encouraged crowd violence and electoral intimidation against Catholics.[95] Although anti-Catholicism was to remain a powerful trope in American culture right into the twentieth century, after the civil war US citizens loyal to the pope were no longer the beleaguered minority they had been in the 1840s.

Vast influxes of German, Italian and Irish Catholics continued unabated throughout this time. In 1880 there were about 4 million

Catholics in the United States. By 1906 this number was nearly 11 million.[96] Given these numbers, they became a significant minority in municipal politics. The Society of Tammany Hall in New York State was an important Democratic party association which mobilised its grassroots activists, seeking to provide leadership and assistance to the party's rank and file. It became a magnet for ambitious Irishmen who wanted to make their way in the world. At times it operated more as a racketeering, protection and mafioso-style organisation. In the 1870s, one of its leaders, 'honest' John Kelly, a former New York sheriff, became a king-maker in the city's politics.[97] His nickname was a play on the fact that Kelly was 'as crooked as a nine-bob note'. He was related through marriage to America's first cardinal, John McCloskey. No candidate seeking election in the districts of this bustling metropolis could hope to get elected without the goodwill of honest John. Counter-intuitively William Russell Grace, the first Irish Catholic mayor of New York in 1881 and in 1885, was elected on a ticket to clean up Tammany Hall – something which he tried but failed to do.[98]

The Irish stranglehold over the North American church, after five decades of immigration, was impressive and owed much to Cardinal Cullen's encouragement. Between 1850 and 1918 all archbishops of New York were of Irish descent. The situation in Boston was identical. By 1884 thirty-five out of sixty-two bishops were Irish Americans; the Germans held fifteen dioceses and the Italians none![99] Ethnic tensions did lead to a minor schism in 1907 when the Polish National Catholic Church in America broke away from Rome and joined the old Catholics who opposed the dogma of infallibility.[100]

Away from Europe, the Roman church in the United States sought to champion progressive causes and was friendly to nascent trade unionism. A rather eccentric organisation, known as the Knights of Labour, a cross between a masonic lodge and a trade union, had recruited over 100,000 members by 1884.[101] Many wanted this organisation condemned, but Cardinal James Gibbons proved sympathetic. Just as he had unwisely supported Leopold II's Congo Free State, now Gibbons more shrewdly defended the dignity of labour and the right of workers to associate. In 1886 the police had fired on strikers and rioters in Chicago.[102] The prefect of the *Propaganda fide* wanted to ban Catholics from joining the Knights of Labour. Appalled by this plan, Cardinal Gibbons intervened to defend the Knights and argued that they had nothing to do with events in Chicago. The archbishop of Baltimore thus highlighted publicly the plight of modern industrial workers. This support for the Knights allowed the Vatican to retain significant working-class support in the United States.[103]

Despite this growth all was not well. The hibernianisation of the American church was not viewed positively by all and drew the resentment of Germans and Italians, who wondered why members of their community could not gain ecclesiastical preferment. A movement known as Cahenslyism, named after the German philanthropist Peter Cahensly, emerged in opposition to the hibernian monopoly over Catholic worship in North America. The adherents of this cause claimed, misleadingly, that Irish bullying had led ten million German, Latin and Slav Catholics to convert to Protestantism. So Cahenslysists lobbied for US parishes to be organised along national lines. There was a proposal that floating German bishops should be created to minister to the Teutonic communities in America.[104] The Curia dragged its feet. Eventually some parishes and schools organised along national lines did emerge, after the First World War. Yet a firm 'no' came from the Vatican over creating national dioceses. Bishops were the fathers of all their flock.[105] Universalism lay at the heart of Catholicism.

What worried the papacy more was the indebtedness of American churches to banking houses. They also deplored the autonomy of priests from their bishops. Lay interference in the management of parishes and dioceses on the eastern seaboard was considered irregular. The final decades of the nineteenth century saw a determined effort from the Curia to rein in the American church. Following the first Vatican Council there was a determination that even the non-Europeans follow the orders of the centre.[106] Since 1858 when the first transatlantic cables had been laid it was possible to communicate instantaneously between Kerry in Ireland and Newfoundland off the coast of

Canada.[107] Technology like the telegraph and eventually wireless communication made the connection between the Vatican and its spiritual empire across the globe closer than ever before.

Leo XIII issued the encyclical *In plurimis* on 5 May 1888. It was addressed to the bishops of Brazil and praised them for their increasingly abolitionist stance. In these pages he urged them to lobby more outrightly for the abolition of human bondage in this large empire. The encyclical was a theological deconstruction of the wrongs of slavery. It affirmed that it was the fruit of original sin rather than part of divine providence. Despite its progressive tone, there was a puzzling paragraph on the kindness and superiority of Christian masters which hardly reflected the reality of slavery in the Americas. *In plurimis* focused on Brazilian slavery but also condemned the Muslin slave trade in Zanzibar, Sudan and Egypt, which preyed on Ethiopians. Although this encyclical was a step in the right direction, the subtext – that Christian slavery was more benign than its Muslim counterpart – was convenient.[108]

Eight days later, Brazil promulgated what was known as the *lei áurea* (golden law). This finally abolished slavery within the empire and manumitted all those held in bondage.[109] In the Western world slavery was now universally abolished. Emancipation signalled a period of intense change in Brazilian history and church-and-state relations. On 15 November 1889 a military coup exiled the emperor and proclaimed a republic in Rio de Janeiro;[110] a secular regime was established with the determination to modernise the state. As ever the church's monopoly on worship and its privileged position was perceived as an obstacle to reform. A year later, laws for the separation of church and state were passed in quick succession. Freedom of worship, civil unions, secular education, and an end to the subsidies for the Catholic Church heralded the arrival of European-style secularism in South America. The bishops protested, but had little real choice but to adapt to the new reality. Despite losing its established status, Catholicism in Brazil continued to prosper.[111] An influx of foreign clergy, new missionary funds, and reforms to the administration of the church meant that

Brazil would become home to the largest Catholic population in the world.

By the twilight of the nineteenth century the church was beginning to cast its nets more widely beyond the Old World. Beset by revolution, secularism, modernism and indifference, Europe seemed a dead-end for the Church of Rome. In comparison Africa, Asia and the Americas were fertile grounds in which the seeds of the Catholic magisterium could be planted and eventually produce millions of converts. To all intents and purposes, therefore, the pope lost his kingdom in 1870 but gained the world.

This did not prevent the Curia in Rome, and the successors of Pius IX, from coveting central Italy. On 20 February 1878, after a mere three ballots, the College of Cardinals elected Vincenzo Gioacchino Pecci, the papal Camerlengo, as Pope Leo XIII.[112] It had been a strange conclave as the cardinals had initially voted to leave Rome and find a neutral location to elect the new pontiff. Yet, the impracticalities of relocating the college to an unspecified location proved too cumbersome and the princes of the church remained in the Vatican. There is an old Roman expression that 'a fat Pope is usually followed by a thin one'. This was certainly true in terms of the physical appearance of the new pope! Leo was svelte and aristocratic, with a prominent aquiline nose; he was also cerebral and aloof,[113] whereas Pius IX had been rotund, warm, jovial and stubborn. Yet, the old saying in fact alluded to the superstition that a long pontificate was usually followed by a short one. Pecci, on his elevation to St Peter's chair, was sixty-eight years of age and frail. Nobody would have guessed that he was to live a further twenty-five years, making his reign the fourth longest pontificate in history.

As already described, Pecci had started his career as nuncio in Belgium, where he had shown himself open-minded and willing to compromise. His promotion to the archdiocese of Perugia, where he remained for decades, was seen as a means for the Curia to sideline a progressive voice. Cardinal Antonelli disliked him because he was not a yes-man.[114] During his time at Perugia Pecci read voraciously and perfected the art of writing pastoral letters to the faithful in his diocese. Throughout his pontificate he wrote no fewer than eighty-eight encyclicals, making him by far the most prolific pontiff in terms of his ability to write and communicate with the universal church. He was also the first pope to be filmed, giving a blessing, by the newly invented kinetoscope.[115] Although many in the Curia suspected him of liberal tendencies, they need not have worried. Leo XIII was a conservative and a moderate who immediately emphasised that his reign would follow the legacy set by his larger-than-life predecessor Pius IX.

The breach with Italy remained unresolved. Indeed, Leo refused to appear in St Peter's Square for his coronation. No pope could bear to cast his gaze on the Eternal City which the Italian state had illegitimately seized from the church. Plans for the crowning to take place in the basilica were scrapped for fear of a stampede or public disorder. The new pontiff had to make do with the splendour of the Sistine chapel.[116]

Once in office, Leo would vacillate between gestures of conciliation and reactionary measures. He willingly negotiated the end of the *Kulturkampf* with Bismarck. From 1881 new bishops started to be appointed for vacant sees in Germany and, a year later, the Vatican resumed formal diplomatic relations with the German empire.[117] Things were more complicated in France. After the fall of Napoleon III, a temporary republic was proclaimed. To the horror of conservatives, Paris erupted into a bloody insurrection, known as the Commune, where the archbishop of Paris, Georges Darboy, was executed by communard insurrectionists.[118] The Third Republic, in Versailles, was forced to suppress this revolution at the cost of much blood. This conservative regime was expected to be transitional, a sort of waiting room to see which dynasty would be invited back to reign over the hexagon.[119] On the hill of Montmartre permission was granted to build a neo-byzantine basilica. It was constructed so that France could expiate the many sins that had led to its defeat in 1870.[120]

In the beginning, at least, the Third Republic was not anticlerical. Too many of its ministers were dukes for the republic to even contemplate a frontal attack on the church. Adrien, Comte de Mun, was a pioneer of social Catholicism in France. He believed that, as a nobleman, it was his vocation to build social cohesion and harmony. This could only be achieved through a grassroots movement that would inculcate the love of God and monarchy in the working masses.[121] With several associates, he created the *œuvre des cercles catholiques d'ouvriers* (Catholic worker circles). By 1878 there were forty thousand members in France, with eight thousand elite sponsors that covered over three hundred branches. An Italian equivalent, the *opera dei congressi,* was founded in 1875 by Count Giovanni Grosoli, and would prove highly successful.[122]

These associations provided their members with honest diversion, religious worship, education and charity. They were paternalistic, in that the nobility and upper middle class monopolised the levers of power. Such workers' circles were probably as close as France ever came to the notion of what the British call 'one nation conservativism'.[123] In Britain this concept held that a harmonious society could only be established when everybody could flourish and develop gradually from their station in life. The late nineteenth century was to be an age of mass democracy and free choice; given that such Catholic associations fostered paternalism and submission to authority, after the 1880s the numbers of adherents and activists went into a steep decline.[124] Simply put, there were more sympathetic and less elitist organisations to energise the working classes.

In France during the 1870s, hopes for a monarchical restoration floundered as the Legitimist and Orleanist factions proved unable to reach a mutually agreeable compromise. Matters were not helped by the Comte de Chambord who was as stubborn as a mule. The Bourbon pretender's refusal to accept the tricolour as his flag doomed his cause. His rather lame protestations, that the principle he incarnated could not be compromised, fell on deaf ears.[125] In 1875 the decision that the president would be elected by the senate and chamber of deputies de facto made a monarchical restoration very difficult. By the 1879 elections, the republicans had taken control of both chambers and the presidency.[126] All hopes of a Bourbon or Bonapartist return to the throne of France were gone.

Gradually Leo XIII counselled Catholics, through a policy known as *ralliement,* to rally to the republic and accept the new regime. On 12 November 1890 Cardinal Lavigerie received the civilian and military authorities of French Algeria in his palace for a banquet. As dinner ended, the moment for toasts arrived. In a prepared speech, Lavigerie lifted his glass expressing the hope that the divisions of the past could be forgotten, and that good Catholics would be willing to sacrifice themselves for the good of the fatherland.[127] To everyone's surprise a choir of White Fathers entered the dining room and sang the *Marseillaise* with brio. This act was met with stunned silence. Many of the officers and civil servants in the room had royalist sympathies, so were appalled by what they had witnessed. As a form of gesture politics, Cardinal Lavigerie's toast became an eloquent symbol that France's monarchical past needed to be jettisoned by church leaders.[128]

This incident became known as the toast of Algiers, and caused a media storm of remarkable proportions. The bishop of Angers anonymously published an article criticising the cardinal for his treachery. Ultimately, though somewhat gradually, the pope made his support for Lavigerie known, which prompted even a staunch legitimist like Albert de Mun to accept the legitimacy of the republic in 1891. The papacy abandoned French royalism with the encyclical *Au milieu de sollicitudes* of 1892.[129] Extraordinarily, this was published in French, rather than Latin or Italian. It affirmed that it was not for the church to condemn any regime established by a European state. Only anarchy and disorder were intrinsically bad. Therefore, French Catholics should be less intransigent, and the pope urged them not to plot against or seek to topple the republic – this of course did not mean that the faithful should accept anticlerical legislation, let alone the separation of church and state.

Although Leo did not endorse the formation of a French Catholic party, he believed that the faithful could support conservative parties that aimed to reverse anticlerical legislation through constitutional means. This was a major contrast to the policy of *non-expedit* which did not allow Italians to vote or stand for election.[130] This *détente* was not mirrored by republicans across the Alps. Jules Ferry's governments sponsored laws to prohibit priests from teaching in schools. Legal divorce, abolished by the Bourbons in 1816, was reinstated in 1884, much to the scandal of the church.[131] *Laïcité,* France's extreme brand of secularism, it was argued, was the new religion of the state. Modern rationalist values based on empirical science needed to be inculcated in the population of the republic at large. Radicals felt that only by bringing a secular credo to education could the noxious effects of clericalism be exorcised from French society.[132] Despite these heavy blows, the Vatican preferred to stay silent, rather than open a breach with Paris. After all, republican France was the most populous Catholic power in the world.

In 1887 a pamphlet entitled 'Conciliation' was published by the Vatican deputy-archivist, Father Luigi Tosti.[133] This well-connected socialite was credited with preventing the confiscation of much church property in Rome during the Italian invasion of 1870. His friendship with government officials made him a sort of go-between for the Vatican and the Quirinal palace. Many suspected that his latest pamphlet had received tacit approval from Leo XIII. It expressed the hope that the ongoing dispute between Italy and the papacy would be resolved.[134] The pope, in Tosti's view, was a diplomat, a good patriot and the heir to the prince of peace.

It was in everybody's interest to find a solution that would allow both parties to end these two decades of crisis, and emerge with their pride unbesmirched. Tosti met with Sicilian Francesco Crispi, the Italian minister of the interior, at his home. The priest alleged that his proposals had Vatican approval, and went on to state that, in return for a guarantee of papal sovereignty and independence, Leo would venture outside the Vatican in 1888, and would even receive the king of Italy, Humbert I, in formal audience. Crispi made encouraging noises and felt these moves went in the right direction.[135]

Several factors militated against this peace-making initiative. Firstly, the appointment on 2 June of the conservative Cardinal Mariano Rampolla del Tindaro as secretary of state made many wonder how far Tosti's plan did in fact have papal support. Rampolla was known to favour an alliance with France rather than any rapprochement with Italy.[136] Matters were made worse by an editorial printed in the newspaper *L'Osservatore Romano,* the official mouthpiece of the Vatican. It denounced Tosti, and demanded that it be made clear that his pamphlet on conciliation did not have papal support. This crisis, rather than effecting a rapprochement, only served to emphasise the distance that continued to separate both parties. It is not clear how far the anticlerical Crispi had been sincere about his desire to negotiate peace. Leo XIII reiterated that only the restoration of temporal power would bring an end to the crisis. Poor Tosti was hung out to dry and forced to publish a retraction.[137] Shortly after this event, Crispi became Italian prime minister.

Ever since France had failed to deliver on the commitments made at Plombières, Italy had prioritised its diplomatic efforts to the north of the Alps. In 1882, it signed a defensive treaty of alliance with Germany and Austria-Hungary.[138] As a member of this triple alliance, Italy undertook to join any conflicts where France was the aggressor. Five years later a tariff war heightened Franco-Italian tensions. The state visit to Rome in 1888 by Kaiser Wilhelm II was highly controversial. He was the first crowned head to make the journey since the breach of Porta Pia in 1870. Wilhelm visited the Italian royal family first at the Quirinal, and then travelled to the Vatican to compliment the pope. This was interpreted by the Curia as a deliberate snub. Further offence was caused when Bismarck and the emperor's brother unexpectedly entered unannounced the papal study and interrupted the imperial audience. Wilhelm II refused to discuss the Roman question, let alone support the return of temporal power to the papacy. Apparently, Leo XIII was so upset by this insult that his eyes welled with tears.[139] That evening, at a state banquet, the Kaiser raised his glass and toasted Rome as the capital city of a united Italy. This was considered a great triumph for Italian diplomacy and an insult to the church.

The following year, as a courtesy, the Italian king Humbert I paid a return state visit to Berlin in May. Here, unwisely, he promised to review German troops in the formerly French territories of Alsace-Lorraine. When this was leaked to the press, mass demonstrations erupted, and the trip to Strasbourg was cancelled.[140] Humbert's *faux pas* deeply antagonised the diplomats of the Quai d'Orsay. The situation in Europe was tense that summer. Francesco Crispi was something of a gambler. His failure during the Tosti negotiations had reawakened the anticlericalism of his youth. He was a Sicilian who had enthusiastically joined Garibaldi's one thousand volunteers in their conquest of the Kingdom of the Two Sicilies in 1861.[141] He had little commitment to Catholicism and detested clericalism.

So uncomfortable did the pope feel about Crispi's policies that he often told diplomats that they would force him to leave the Eternal City. That same year the unveiling of a statue to Giordano Bruno in Campo dei Fiori, in the centre of Rome, infuriated the papacy to unprecedented heights.[142] This free thinker, friar and philosopher had been burned at the stake as a heretic in 1600.[143] Italy now celebrated him a hero, and a martyr who been the victim of clerical fanaticism. When the statue was unveiled, thousands of freemasons marched through Rome chanting anticlerical slogans. This caused massive concern within the Vatican as it was interpreted as a deliberate insult. Édouard Lefebvre de Béhaine, the ambassador of France, encouraged Leo to prepare for the worst.

Several secret meetings between the French ambassador, the pope and Cardinal Rampolla examined the threat of an imminent war between France and Italy. Béhaine shared his belief that, given the circumstances, a general European conflagration was inevitable. There was a suggestion that a departure from the Eternal City was the only means of guaranteeing the pope's independence. On 30 June 1889, Leo XIII summoned all cardinals to a secret consistory. He claimed that, if a war were to break out, his personal safety could not be guaranteed in Italy. It was announced that Leo and the College of Cardinals would need to prepare to leave the Vatican. It was the pope's intention to stop first in Monaco and then decide where to go. Malta, Salzburg and the Balearic Islands were proposed as possible places of temporary exile.[144] Despite the injunction to maintain the strictest secrecy over these plans, news of the meeting leaked out to the European press. Soon letters from Europe's episcopacy arrived, inviting the pope to settle in their diocese or episcopal palaces.

More damagingly, Cardinal Hohenlohe had disclosed the news and decisions made by this consistory to his friend Crispi.[145]

Although the prime minister had made a speech just before the parliamentary summer recess, claiming that he was unconcerned about the international situation, in reality he was unnerved. Sabre-rattling from France and Leo XIII's threat to flee the Vatican made him fear a plot against Italy. There were discussions with Humbert I and the minister of war on whether it would be wise to begin mobilising the Italian army. French military manoeuvres on 17 July, near the Alpine border heightened Italian paranoia.[146] Crispi telegrammed Berlin, Vienna and London to warn them that Europe was on the brink of war.

Cardinal Hohenlohe was asked informally by the Italian government to make it known to Leo that he was free to leave Rome, but warning that his departure could spark a murderous international war. Crispi reminded the pope that Pius IX's recourse to foreign troops to defend his sovereignty had ended in abject failure.[147] Leo refused to receive Hohenlohe, as he detested the German prince-cardinal. In the end, Bismarck informed Crispi that he was unconvinced that France wanted a conflict. German diplomacy did its best to defuse the situation. No one really wanted war. Ultimately, the war scare of 1889 proved to be a storm in a teacup. Both Leo XIII and Crispi reacted somewhat hysterically to the diplomatic tensions with Paris. The pope allowed himself to be manipulated by the French embassy in Rome, becoming involved in a crisis that could have been easily avoided. It seems doubtful that the Curia was serious about the threat of leaving the Vatican. They had too much to lose.

Crispi's political gambling was eventually to lead to his undoing. In 1896, a disastrous Italian attempt to conquer Ethiopia led to the Battle of Adua, which proved to be the first decisive defeat of a colonial power by an Africa army.[148] Crispi's career ended with the folly of this imperial disaster. If anything was true about the Italo-Vatican crisis of 1889 it was that it shattered any hope of conciliation with Leo XIII.

During the 1890s, the pope's attention turned to more manageable problems. Since his election in 1878, Leo had tried to reverse some of the worst intransigence of his predecessor. As a trained diplomat, he wanted a dialogue with the modern world rather than mere condemnation. He was torn between a desire to be reconciled with modernity and his impulse to continue the policies of Pius IX. Unlike his predecessor this pontiff wanted Catholics to participate actively in learning and science. He felt that they should not fear opening their minds. During his reign the Vatican archives were opened to scholars for the first time, albeit with severe restrictions. There was also encouragement for rigorous scientific biblical and scriptural study.[149] One of the most crucial policies of the pope was to advocate a rediscovery of St Thomas Aquinas. Neo-Thomism, it was argued, could provide Catholicism with the confidence to respond to the modern world, especially as this Catholic sage had argued that the correct application of reason was not in conflict with religious faith. Leo's love of Aquinas was first outlined in his encyclical *Æterni patris* of 4 August 1879, which served as a manifesto for his reign. Secular scientists and philosophers ridiculed the papacy for believing that the solutions to the modern world could be found in the scholastic writings of a thirteenth-century monk.[150]

This typified Leo XIII's dilemma: he wanted to move the church out of a siege mentality, but his conservative instincts made it difficult for him to trust those outside the Catholic fold. As a pope he tended to blow hot and cold. Often, a progressive and open-minded encyclical would be followed by one that was a reactionary condemnation of modern ideas. Yet for all that Leo did, ultimately, move the church forward. In 1885 he accepted in his encyclical *Immortale dei* that governments could tolerate other faiths but only to forestall other evils such as civil war, violence or persecution.[151] Such reasoning was a step forward in comparison to Pius IX's carpet-bombing of religious pluralism.

On 20 June 1888, the encyclical *Libertas præstantissimum* appeared. It stated that the Catholic Church was not intrinsically hostile to liberty. God had endowed man with free will, which was the ultimate freedom. What the church objected to was the misuse of liberty to preach falsehood and immorality. Ultimately, the church could accept 'good' liberty, but condemned license. This letter indicated that governments should limit the freedom of the press and opinion if they spread error. Yet for all its reactionary language, *Libertas* affirmed that the church was not anti-democratic or against constitutionalism. Although according to scripture authority came from above, in certain circumstances popular participation could be a moral good, especially when it promoted Christian values.[152]

In many ways, these two encyclicals laid the groundwork for the concept of Christian democracy, which would become so influential in the twentieth century. Indeed, the expression was used by Leo himself, though sparingly.[153] The pope admired American democracy but was concerned that in Europe it would lead to revolution and anarchy if left unrestricted.

As the nineteenth century entered its twilight, Europe remained divided into two camps. A religious and highly clericalised countryside remained loyal to the papacy and accelerated the Catholic revival that had begun in the 1820s.[154] There was little sign that the rural world's attachment to religion was waning. On one side of the divide could be found industrial workers, bourgeois liberals, urban-dwellers and scientists who were deeply hostile to organised religion.[155] Although Bismarck's *Kulturkampf* had been resolved diplomatically, its ethos spread through Europe. Unlike in the eighteenth century, the state no longer wished to subordinate the church to its authority. On the contrary, secularisers wanted to confine religion to the private sphere, where it would dwindle into insignificance. In stark contrast, they believed the modern scientific, medical and rational progress offered by the secular state would become the dominant culture of the future.

To an extent the church was retreating from the cities and exiling itself in remote agricultural hamlets. In Belgium, the Ruhr, Silesia, Bilbao, Catalonia, eastern France and northern Italy, millions of workers were abandoning a church that appeared to have little concern for the industrial slavery in which many of them languished.[156] All that these wage-slaves seemed to receive from the church was blanket condemnation of freemasonry, socialism, communism and trade unions. Given that Europe was experiencing a sustained period of demographic growth many in the Curia felt complacent that their flock would continue to increase. After all, the number of Catholics was growing, thanks to medical advances and missionary work. New churches were being built, and the seminaries were full of ambitious peasant ordinands.[157] The late nineteenth century did not appear to herald a crisis of faith.

Leo XIII was not sure that this was the correct attitude to adopt. Although it had taken Europe far longer than Britain to urbanise and industrialise, the process had inexorably crept forward and there was no going back. It seemed myopic and perilous for the church to ignore the 'social question' which now pitted conservatives and liberals against socialists in European politics. The encyclical *Rerum novarum* (Of new things) published on 15 May 1891 was perhaps the most progressive papal document published in modern history.[158] It resuscitated and reinvigorated the moribund social Catholicism which Lamennais and those of his ilk had pioneered during the 1820s and 1830s. This encyclical implicitly, endorsed the activities of the *cercles catholiques, opera dei congressi* and Knights of Labour.

Even that arch-conservative and architect of papal infallibility, Cardinal Manning, deplored the greed of modern capitalists. In 1889 a major strike erupted between the dock-workers of London and their bosses. The cardinal praised the dignity and restraint of the striking workers. When negotiations began between the workers and the bosses in September of that year, Manning was asked to mediate in the wage dispute.[159] Many of the dockers' requests were met and this prince of the church became a hero of the labouring poor in London. The cardinal's pleas that Leo think more practically about the social question were heeded.

The *Rerum novarum* remains relevant to the concerns of our present world. In one of its more heartfelt passages, it reminded employers that:

Their principal duty is to provide everybody with their due. Doubtless, before deciding whether wages are just, many factors need to be taken into account; but capitalists and owners should be mindful that human laws do not permit them to oppress the indigent and the destitute for the sake of avarice or convenience, in order to collect profit on the

back of other peoples' misery. To defraud people of their
wages is a great evil, one which cries out for vengeance in the
sight of God. [...] Lastly, it is the responsibility of the rich
not to cut down working men's savings, whether by force, by
fraud, by manifest, or concealed, usury; this responsibility is
all the more important when the working man is weak and
undefended, thus his slender assets should be considered
sacrosanct.[160]

To drive the point home, the Roman church reminded capitalists
and bankers that they could not behave as they liked towards
their employees. The encyclical reminded them that women and
children could not be expected to do the same jobs and work
the same hours as men. Furthermore, it was part of the Ten
Commandments that all working people be allotted a day of
rest. Finally Christian workers' associations, whose goal it was
to improve the moral and material conditions of proletarians,
were authorised and encouraged. Essentially, the *Rerum novarum*
sanctioned the creation of Catholic trade unions.

For all the encyclical's openness towards the plight of the
oppressed, Leo XIII was by no means an unreconstituted social
Catholic, let alone a radical. He blamed the social question on
the destruction of the medieval guilds and corporations that had
regulated the manufacturing sector during the medieval and early
modern period.[161] Papal nostalgia for a golden age of apprentices,
journeymen and master craftsmen was hopelessly naïve. Leo's
anachronistic hope for a return to the guild system betrayed a lack
of understanding of modern industrial economics.

A large portion of *Rerum* was devoted to the condemnation of
socialism and godlessness. This was hardly surprising. Leo XIII had
done the same in several prior encyclicals. For him, work should
allow fathers of families to provide the materials necessary for the
survival of a Christian family. The promise of the next life should
be the most important thing for a Catholic. The state could assist
the indigent, but any notion of a welfare state that would interfere
in a father's right to manage his own homestead was deplored.
Laws could regulate wages and fairness, but not the Christian

family. Leo preferred Christian charity to welfare. Although strikes could be justified in extreme circumstances, they were best avoided. Finally, a very large portion of the *Rerum* is a vindication of the right to private property. In these pages the right to enjoy the legitimate fruits of one's labours, ingenuity and inheritance was given a scriptural basis.[162] The Catholic Church saw property as a right for all, though one that should not be abused.

The *Rerum novarum* was not a liberal – let alone socialist – document, as it is often portrayed, but it was a definite step in the right direction. Almost every twentieth-century pope cited it, or updated its teaching, to reflect modern economic, political, and environmental concerns.[163] It made manifest that the church now understood and was sympathetic to the plight of working Catholics. It allowed the social Catholicism inspired by Lamennais and others a new lease of life. Those interested in alleviating the suffering of workers and the poor were welcome in the church. Like Lamennais' writings, the *Rerum* was the beginning of a wider debate within the church, rather than a clear solution to the problem of industrial capitalism. Its immediate impact was mixed at best. Christian trade unions did not find much acceptance amongst the mainstream workers' movement; rather, there was resentment that religiously based associations divided factory employees and damaged their bargaining power.[164] After 1891, it took several decades for Catholic trade unions to grow. Austria, Belgium and Mexico were the polities that took the precepts of the *Rerum novarum* most to heart. Here they built Catholic associations whose memberships reached hundreds of thousands of workers.[165]

In Italy and France attempts were made to pry the *cercles catholiques* and *opera dei congressi* away from aristocrats like Grosoli, de Mun and la Tour-du-Pin. Clergymen of humbler origins, such as Don Romolo Murri in Italy, argued that such movements should elide aristocratic paternalism, delegating real power to workers. Unlike Leo XIII, Murri, though a pious Catholic priest (something of a radical firebrand in his later years), was a determined believer in Christian democracy. He supported strikes, even to the point of violence, to allow workers to gain their rights.[166] To an extent, the *Rerum* caused excitement and mobilised some Catholic workers, but it did not precipitate an immediate surge in Christian trade unionism. Socialists were right that the fragmentation of workers' associations into different camps weakened their bargaining power rather than strengthening it. While the *Rerum novarum* did reiterate the church's condemnation of socialism without reservation, it did attempt to replace it with a Christian defence of workers' rights before the vagaries of modern capitalism.

Given this spirit of *détente* towards democracy and the social question, many Catholics wanted to push the Vatican further in its concessions to modernity. For example, Mgr John Ireland, the first archbishop of Saint Paul, Minnesota, undertook a European-wide tour in 1892.[167] His task was to showcase the remarkable progress that had been made in establishing Catholicism on the western frontiers of the United States. He described how thousands of his fellow Irishmen had left the poverty-stricken bogs of Connemara to find freedom and prosperity in the United States. The speeches he made at banquets and other functions were translated and published in French by the abbé Félix Klein, a republican and liberal cleric who was determined to accelerate the church's conciliation with the modern world.[168]

Apparently, Archbishop Ireland had proclaimed that:

This is the century of democracy where the people, dissatisfied with the absolute power of sovereigns, have become sovereign themselves, and now exercise more or less directly the natural [political] rights that have been bestowed on them through God's will. The Catholic Church, I am certain, does not fear democracy, nor the efflorescence of the sacred principles of equality, fraternity, and liberty for all mankind in and through [the teachings of] Christ. These principles suffuse every page of the Gospels.[169]

One suspects that he came to regret these injudicious words quickly. Intransigent members of the Curia and conservative journalists were appalled by this endorsement of the French Revolution.

The figure who became a hero for liberal and republican Catholics was Father Isaac Hecker, the founder of the missionary society of Saint Paul. This exemplary priest had died in 1888; safely dead, there was little danger that he would contradict the progressive doctrines that his latter-day followers attributed to him. In 1891, an English priest, Walter Elliot, produced a biography in which Hecker was portrayed as a modernising hero. Matters were made worse by the book's translation into French by the abbé Klein, which radicalised Hecker's original considerably.[170] A foreword by Mgr Ireland claimed he was a great mystic and democrat. The biography gave the impression that Hecker considered contemplation, mortification of the flesh and obedience outdated medieval virtues. It was alleged that he believed instead in good old American values like enterprise, honesty, thrift and associationism. Ultimately the individualist, independent and anti-monastic message that emerged from this biography came to be known as Americanism.[171] Many in the United States and France embraced its precepts. Conservatives deplored it.

The Chicago World Fair of 1893, like the universal exhibitions of Paris, London and Barcelona, wanted to showcase the best in global manufacturing and luxury products to a public of rich consumers.[172] These month-long extravaganzas were also moments for cultural exchange. The world fair celebrated, with great pomp, the third centenary of the Columbian discovery of America. Exhibitions and reconstructions were supposed to commemorate the triumph of white American nationhood and democracy. The plight of native Americans was all but ignored, and little was said about slavery.[173] Unexpectedly, the fair hosted a parliament of world religions, which turned into a great three-week ecumenical summit. Here, Protestant pastors, Orthodox priests, Islamic mullahs and Buddhist monks met for one of the first inter-faith exchanges in the history of humanity.[174] Many of Hecker's followers, including Father Elliot and Archbishop Ireland, were present. The key representative for Catholicism was Cardinal Gibbons of Baltimore who, a little prematurely, called the world parliament one of the most felicitous events in the history of the young American republic. Plans were set in motion to host a world congress of religions in 1900.

Although Leo XIII, throughout his pontificate, had expressed admiration and encouragement for the North American church, he could not remain silent before such developments. The Curia was concerned about Americanism's push towards ecumenism, its unconditional endorsement of democracy, and its attack on the monastic contemplative life. The highly conservative abbé Charles Maignen wrote a pamphlet in 1898 entitled 'Was Father Isaac Hecker a saint?'[175] In it he condemned the biography and its principles. This acted as a catalyst in the reaction against Americanism and its supporters. Regardless of his own personal misgivings, Leo was forced to address a papal brief to Cardinal Gibbons, the *Testem benevolentiae* published on 22 January 1899.[176] Although it praised the North American church, it condemned as heretical the doctrines attributed to Hecker and his followers. Americanism became a modern heresy that the church anathemised without reservation. There were fears that American values would promote moral laxity (they weren't entirely wrong about this). Both Cardinal Gibbons and Archbishop Ireland wrote grovelling letters to Leo XII, assuring him that they did not hold any of the precepts condemned as heretical by the brief.[177] Americanism turned out to be another storm in a very small teacup, but it did show the conservative pope's discomfort in the face of Christian democratic values, ecumenism and individualism. Another clash with political modernity would soon damage the church's reputation further.

Captain Alfred Dreyfus' conviction for treason in 1894 was one of the greatest political crises in French history. Through this miscarriage of justice, antisemitism's dark history in Europe was revivified, just as the twentieth century dawned.[178] New racialist theories and distortions of Darwin's writings coated historic hatred of the Jews in pseudo-scientific garb. Artur, Comte de Gobbineau's *Essai sur l'inégalité des races humaines* (Essay on the inequality of the human races) was a stomach-churning and morally bankrupt attempt to ground racism in science. Édouard Drumont's book *La*

France juive (Jewish France) claimed erroneously that although the Jews were significantly less than 1 per cent of the population, they owned a quarter of the nation's wealth. The Antisemitic League, founded in 1889, lobbied for the exclusion of Jews from public life.[179]

Conspiracy theorists started to connect freemasons, revolutionaries, and Jews in outlandish plots that aimed to overturn the socio-political order in Europe. They pointed accusatory fingers toward the financial meltdown of the Union Générale in 1882. This mismanaged Catholic bank, and its board, made high-risk investments and manipulated the price of stocks on the Paris markets. The corrupt ineptitude of its directors led to some going to prison for fraud. Many of the account-holders and shareholders of this banking union were French royalists and supporters of the Comte de Chambord. Some aristocrats and ultra-Catholics were left with their fingers badly burned in the ensuing bankruptcy.[180] In the end, it was the Camondo, Cahen d'Anvers, and Rothschild families which organised a rescue package for the failed bank. Instead of being praised for their intervention, these Jewish financiers became the target of a concerted press campaign that blamed covert Semitic forces for the collapse of an upstanding Catholic bank. Similarly, in 1888 Jews were blamed for the failure of the Panama Canal venture, in which French financiers had invested heavily. Admittedly the Jewish capitalist the baron Jacob Adolphe Reinach had been involved in the collapse, but the press unfairly overplayed his hand in the affair.[181]

Traditional antisemitism, infested by pseudo-scientific ideas and conspiracy theories, was to make an unholy alliance with reactionary French Catholicism. In 1847, some followers of Lamennais created the congregation of the Augustinians of the Assumption with the aim of teaching, missionary work and the creation of a Catholic public sphere. They became so influential that, in 1864, they were granted formal papal sanction to continue their activities.[182] Unlike Lamennais, this splinter group became deeply disillusioned with liberal Catholicism, and spearheaded the attack on modernity. They were ultramontane and royalist to their teeth, to the extent that the assumptionists were behind the campaign that led to the construction of the Sacré Coeur on Montmatre to expiate the sins of France after its defeat by Prussia in 1870.

The true power of the organisation came from the creation of a publishing conglomerate, known as *la bonne presse* (the good press).[183] Through periodicals, magazines, digests and pamphlets they sought to turn society away from godlessness and religious indifference. In terms of circulation, their biggest 'hitter' was a newspaper, *La Croix* (*The Cross*), founded in 1883, which was edited by Father Vincent de Paul Bailly who had been a chaplain to the Papal Zouaves during the 1860s.[184] By the 1890s the paper had hundreds of thousands of subscribers and many local branches. Its pages vomited forth a litany of virulently antisemitic articles that far exceeded anything its Italian equivalent, *La Civiltà Cattolica,* had ever been able to muster.[185] Yet, unlike secular antisemites, the paper resurrected the old Catholic tropes of deicide and even republished early modern prints showing images of Jews murdering Christian children for their blood.[186] The paper was deeply vexed by Leo XIII's policy of *ralliement,* which it decried as defeatist.

The opportunistic alliance of secular and religious antisemitism during the 1890s was to have truly noxious effects. In 1894, a military court-martial had found Captain Alfred Dreyfus, a Jewish officer serving in the French army, guilty of betraying military secrets to the German embassy. This case appeared to confirm the allegations made by the haters of Jews. The *école militaire*, a key officer-training institution for the French army, was situated on Champ de Mars.[187] Here Dreyfus was publicly and humiliatingly degraded for treason. All emblems of his rank were ripped from his uniform and thrown to the ground. His sword was snapped in two. Throughout his ordeal, with great dignity, the Jewish officer asserted his innocence and his loyalty to France. He was then sentenced to imprisonment on Devil's Island off the coast of French Guyana.[188]

On the surface, it seemed a simple case of the army having detected a bad egg and dealt with him accordingly. Lieutenant-Colonel Georges Picquart was a dashing professional soldier and came from an ardent Catholic family. He had little love for Jews and was convinced that Dreyfus was a traitor.[189] In 1895 he became the head of French military intelligence. As he looked over the evidence, he became increasingly uneasy with the material used to incriminate the Jewish captain. Most of it had been marked 'top secret' and kept away from court. As Picquart investigated, he discovered that some documents had been forged and that the man betraying French secrets was in fact Ferdinand Walsin Esterhazy. When Picquart brought this horrific truth to the attention of his superiors he was told to keep quiet, and that the army had found their man. He refused to do so, and Esterhazy was tried and acquitted of treason. One traitor was more than enough for the French army.[190] After this the lieutenant-colonel was transferred for an almost two-year tour of duty in North Africa where it was hoped he might die in an insurrection. On his return Picquart refused to stay quiet. So he was court-martialled and forced to resign from the army.[191]

During this time, the Dreyfus family, along with moderate French republicans, had been lobbying on behalf of the unjustly convicted captain. In 1898 the famous author Emile Zola, who had previously attacked the Marian apparitions in his novel *Lourdes*, published an open letter entitled 'J'accuse' (I accuse) in *L'Aurore* newspaper.[192] It caused a sensation, since it indicted the elite of French politics and the army of colluding to convict an innocent and loyal Jewish officer. The Catholic press, especially *La Croix*, took it as a sign that this enemy of the immaculate conception was part of a wider masonic and Jewish plot to undermine France's traditional order. Zola's attack could not go without answer.

He was sued for libel by the French government. The trial took place between 7 and 23 February 1898. Outside the Palais de Justice, antisemitic mobs hurled abuse at the defenders of Dreyfus, while the supporters of the captain responded in kind. It appeared as if France might descend into civil war. *La Croix* noted that the trial took place on 11 February, the anniversary of the apparition of Mary in Lourdes. The Assumptionists were sure that Zola would be punished for his blasphemies against the mother of God.[193] Notables of the republic and the most prestigious names of the French general staff appeared as witnesses in the trial.

Lieutenant-Colonel Picquart appeared for the defence but made little impact. Only Zola's 'libellous accusations' could be examined in the trial. The substance of the Dreyfus affair itself could not be discussed. Given this restriction, it was clear that the court was out to secure a conviction. Zola was found guilty and sentenced to one year in prison and a 3,000-franc fine, the highest penalty for this type of crime. Embarrassingly Zola fled to London to avoid arrest. Antisemitic riots and violence became endemic throughout France, much of it fuelled by conspiracy theories and *La Croix's* venom.[194]

After the May 1898 parliamentary elections, a more moderate republican majority was returned.[195] The new minister for war decided, once and for all, to launch an enquiry that would prove Dreyfus guilty and end the controversy. This backfired badly when Lieutenant-Colonel Hubert-Joseph Henry, who had collected much of the evidence for the captain's original trial, was interrogated by the minister and several generals about some inconsistencies in the case against Dreyfus. To the horror of the enquiry Henry broke down and admitted that he had forged the evidence, a confession that led to his arrest. He was sent to the Mont-Valérian fortress accused of forgery, where he committed suicide on 31 August 1898.[196] Anti-Dreyfussard newspapers, especially *La Croix*, claimed that the colonel was a martyr who had been hounded to his death. One of the fathers of French fascism, Charles Maurras, published a eulogy in the *Gazette de France,* praising this devoted servant of the French state. Others printed the letters written by Henry to his wife, claiming his innocence, to portray him as a victim rather than a liar. Henry's suicide precipitated the resignation of some high-profile generals who had been witnesses for the prosecution in Zola's libel trial.

In 1899, France's anti-Dreyfussard president Félix Faure died suddenly after a tryst with his mistress in the gardens of the Elysée palace. He was replaced by Emile Loubet who was sympathetic to a retrial for Dreyfus. During the funeral of his predecessor a clumsy attempt at a military coup occurred. Some reactionary officers tried to persuade troops to march on the Elysée palace and seize control.[197] It was clear that this miscarriage of justice was tearing France apart. Clerical and conservative France clashed with secular and progressive France over the question of this Jewish officer's innocence or guilt. This same year Dreyfus was tried again in Rennes and the usual cast of characters appeared in the witness box. Again, the court-martial found the captain guilty, but this time two out of five judges dissented from the verdict, and his sentence was reduced to ten years. This ruling caused outrage and international condemnation.[198]

For the next six years a concerted campaign lobbied for the rehabilitation and vindication of Dreyfus. It coincided with the French government's implementation of increasingly anti-Catholic legislation, which culminated in the 1905 law for separation of church and state. This abrogated Napoleon's concordat and privatised Catholicism.[199] The next year France's supreme court quashed the judgements against Dreyfus, and totally exonerated him of wrongdoing. He went on to have a distinguished career in the army and fought with valour during the First World War.[200]

The affair left a rancid taste in the mouth and compromised the Catholic Church in France. The Assumptionist espousal of strident antisemitism, and its persecution of the unfortunate Dreyfus, showed how little the church had evolved since the Mortara affair. Leo XIII had intervened in 1899, demanding that Father Bailly tone down his antisemitic attacks in *La Croix*.[201] Yet despite this attempt de-escalate the conflict the church remained unsympathetic to the plight of Jews in Europe.[202] It would continue to condemn them as deicides and pray their conversion to the one true faith.

On the other side of the globe, Spain's grip on her few remaining colonial possessions was slipping. For decades Madrid had faced insurgencies in Cuba and the Philippines. The solution had been to flood troops into these areas to keep the guerrillas at bay.[203] Hawks and imperialists in Washington, especially the under-secretary to the Navy, the colourful Theodore Roosevelt, saw in the crumbling Spanish empire as an opportunity for expansion.[204] When the USS *Maine* exploded in Havana harbour in 1898, with the loss of 258 sailors, it provided a *casus belli* for the United States. Although at the time engine explosions were not uncommon in ships, US imperialists cried foul play, and accused Spain of causing the accident. The United States declared war, claiming that it would not annex Cuba, but instead fight to free this colony from Spain.[205]

What would happen to the Philippines, which had been a secondary concern in US foreign policy, was uncertain. Apparently, President McKinley had to be shown on a map of the Pacific where this archipelago was located.[206] Republican politicians, hungry to participate in the second age of imperialism, and give America an empire of its own, were keen to seize this territory. It was a moment of great pride when Commodore George Dewey sank the obsolescent Spanish Pacific squadron without any loss of life.[207]

Madrid's governor in Manila attempted to appeal to his Filipino subjects to rise and defend the island against the invaders. After centuries of oppression and racist disdain, few locals were sad to see the Spanish being chased out. The US navy transported the exiled Emilio Aguinaldo, who had already led a guerrilla campaign against Spain in 1896, back to the Philippines.[208] Soon a revolutionary insurrection destroyed the governor's authority beyond Manila. Knowing that the situation was hopeless, the Spanish negotiated that the city would be surrendered to American forces. It was agreed that to preserve honour a mock bombardment and some token Spanish resistance were to be enacted. Things did not quite go according to plan. Some of Commodore Dewey's guns scored direct hits on Spanish soldiers causing several dozen casualties. Nevertheless, Manila was occupied on 13 August 1898, thus ending the war.[209]

Catholicism had taken root in the culture of the Philippines. Colonisation had supplanted the original animist religion of the islanders three centuries previously. Much of the arable land was owned by the Augustinian, Dominican and Franciscan orders. As already mentioned, through the *patronato* system, the Spanish monarchy made ecclesiastical appointments subject to papal confirmation for all its imperial domains. This meant that peninsular Spaniards monopolised the episcopacy in the Philippines and all positions of power. The 830 Filipino priests present in the colony held menial positions as curates.[210] This hispanisation of the church of the Philippines led to much resentment amongst the local clergy.

The defeat of Madrid in the Spanish American War of 1898 put the episcopacy of the Philippines in a vulnerable position, given that their imperial protectors had been expelled.

Many Filipino priests felt the moment had come not merely to throw off the imperial yoke but to send their Spanish bishops packing. Father Gregorio Aglipay was a tall, articulate, and handsome priest. Although he had been an average seminarian, there was something in him that inspired others to follow. His opportunity for leadership was about to come. Aguinaldo had been assured by American forces that the Philippines would be granted independence. When the Treaty of Paris of 1898 ceded the Philippines to the US government, tensions between US military forces and Filipino freedom fighters grew.[211]

Aglipay was appointed *vicario general castrense* (supreme military chaplain) on 20 October. The next day, he issued a manifesto to the church in which native-born Filipino clergymen were encouraged to join Aguinaldo's forces to minister to *guerrilleros* under his command.* These pages reiterated the Philippine church's submission to the Holy See, but demanded that the pope appoint native-born bishops. The publication of a second manifesto, that same week, heralded that further ecclesiastical turbulence was on the way. In these pages Aglipay announced that his goal was to create a powerful and independent Filipino national church. Catholicism would be the state religion but, for this concession, Aglipay intimated that the local church should be given autonomy to administer its own properties and hierarchy. It was a decided paradox that while most of the Catholic world had become ultramontane, the Philippines were proposing their own version of Gallicanism. In the months that followed, Father Aglipay devised a very daring plan. He knew that the bishop of Vigan was held prisoner by revolutionary forces. Pressure was placed on this prelate to appoint Aglipay as his vicar for the diocese of Nueva Segovia, on Ilocos Norte (the island of Luzon). Soon, the new vicar

---

* This paragraph follows Pedro S. de Achútegui and Miguel A. Bernard, *Religious Revolution in the Philippines: The Life and Church of Gregorio Aglipay 1860–1940* (2nd edn, Manila, 1961), pp. 2–75.

travelled to Vigan, where he installed himself in the episcopal palace and issued pastoral letters to the local clergy.

Meanwhile, the tensions in Manila between American troops and Filipino freedom fighters were at breaking point. In early January 1899 all hell broke loose. A Chinese resident of the city tried to kick a dog, but his shoe flew off and hit a native resident in the face. This was the spark that set off mass violence. Soon the streets were deserted as the guns came out. By February American forces were forced to engage in street-by-street conflict as a bloody battle unfolded, but their superior weaponry put Aguinaldo's forces to flight.[212] Hundreds of young US servicemen perished and thousands of *guerrilleros* were slaughtered in the fighting.

Americans had to settle down for what became a sanguinary counter-insurgency against the Philippine liberation forces.[213] Aglipay was excommunicated by the archbishop of Manila and was soon driven from Vigan by American forces. He joined the guerrillas, and became an effective commander. At Paniqui the priests in the Filipino revolutionary army vowed never to accept the authority of foreign bishops. For the next two years, Aglipay would spend his time in hiding, leading daring assaults against American soldiers and then retreating into the jungle. He was accused of atrocities against Spanish monks and other colonial officials. The Vatican sent a decree in 1900 forbidding priests from engaging in guerrilla warfare, but this was roundly ignored.[214] When Aguinaldo was captured by Americans, in March 1901, it was clear that the insurgency was losing the war. Two months later, Aglipay surrendered to US forces in the hope of clemency.

When the war ended in 1902 a general amnesty was granted. Soon Filipino intellectuals and journalists started agitating for a national church. Isabelo de los Reyes, a writer who had lived for much of his life in Madrid, became one of the key intellectual fathers of Philippine nationalism. He used newspapers to advocate for the confiscation of all land held by religious orders. On 3 August forty-two notables met under the stewardship of Reyes with the goal of creating a national church – Iglesia Filipina Independiente (IFI).[215] Aglipay was offered the position of Obispo Máximo (supreme bishop), something he initially refused. It took little persuasion to change his mind. He was now the leader of a nationalist church that was heading towards a schism with Rome. The new supreme bishop was installed in the Tondo district of Manila on 26 October 1902. He celebrated his elevation with a solemn mass and blessed many sacred objects. Afterwards there was a massive procession accompanied by brass bands. At this late stage in his ministry Aglipay still rung a note of conciliation and wanted to forestall a schism.[216]

An apostolic delegate from Rome, Giovanni Batista Guidi, arrived in November, though he had little hope of changing the ecclesiastical direction of travel. On 17 September 1902 the Vatican had promulgated the apostolic constitution *Quae mari sinico* which sought to reorganise the Philippine church after the evaporation of the Spanish *patronato*. Ultimately a commitment was made to increase the number of native-born Filipinos in the church, but central control by the papacy was emphasised.[217] This document was filled with good intentions, but it would be impossible for Aglipay and his followers to accept such a meagre concession. The IFI formally rejected Leo XIII's constitution, thus opening a formal schism with Rome. On 18 January 1903 the national church of the Philippines consecrated its new bishops, violating canon law as only an existing bishop could consecrate new prelates.

The population of the Philippines in 1903 was seven million. Aglipay claimed about three million adherents to his church, but these numbers were greatly inflated and the true figure was probably closer to one million.[218] Although the IFI declared it wanted to remain Catholic in all things, apart from its obedience to the pope, its members soon developed theological positions that conflicted sharply with Catholicism. Aglipay denied the trinity, and assumed a unitarian understanding of God. The liturgy of the mass was translated, and the clergy allowed to marry.*

---

* This, eventually, led the IFI into full communion with the episcopal church of the United States, making it an Anglican sect. See Cándido Fernández García, *La doctrina de la iglesia filipina independiente* (Manila, 1924), and Francis H. Wise, *The History of the Philippine Independent Church* (Manila, 1965).

At first it seemed as if the IFI might supplant Catholicism as the dominant religion in the Philippines. A major boost was given to Aglipay when the American governor of Manila and future president of the US, William Howard Taft, issued a ruling on 10 January 1903.[219] It stated that all those who occupied church property peacefully were *ipso facto* its legitimate owners. This meant that IFI priests squatting in Catholic rectories, lands, churches, and other buildings, were recognised by the American colonial administration as legitimate owners of these properties. The situation changed when a landmark case, *Barlin v. Ramirez*, was taken to the supreme court of the United States in 1906. Father Ramirez was a Catholic priest in the parish of Lagonoy. In 1903 many in his congregation and parish council converted to the IFI. Feeling the pressure, Ramirez joined them. When the diocesan vicar, Barlin, tried to oust Ramirez, he refused to vacate his parish. When the local courts upheld the IFI's right to the properties in Lagonoy, Barlin appealed to the US supreme court. On 24 November 1906 Mr Justice Willard penned the majority opinion in this case. He pronounced that the Peace of Paris of 1898 had established that the Catholic Church was the legitimate owner of its lands, parishes and hospitals in the Philippines. Therefore, the justices of the supreme court ruled that the IFI must return all property they had seized to the Catholic Church forthwith.[220]

This decision deeply damaged the viability of Aglipay's church, and allowed Rome to resume its monopoly of Christian worship in the Philippines. Although the IFI survived the blow, by 2018 fewer than 1 per cent of Filipinos were still members of this church.[221] Yet it had been a close-run thing. The Vatican had proved indecisive when it came to resolving the tensions with its Filipino clergy. By the time Rome sent a resolution in 1902, the schism had already erupted and was beyond repair. Without the supreme-court decision of 1906, one wonders if the history of Catholicism in the Philippines might not have been very different.

Leo XIII had received a burdensome inheritance from Pius IX, as he had declared war on every modern ideology. A veritable siege mentality had arisen in the wake of Rome's fall in 1870. Despite this burdensome legacy, Leo fought his own conservative instincts and tried his best to manoeuvre the church out of the storm. Peace was made with Bismarck's Germany, and *ralliement* was a genuine attempt to come to terms with republican France. Under his pontificate, the seeds were sown for a remarkable growth in the numbers of Catholics in Africa and Asia. The encyclical *Rerum novarum*, although a traditional document in many respects, demonstrated that the papacy did not approve of unrestrained capitalism and made allowances for Christian trade unions. This pontificate sought to regain the intellectual momentum by opening the Vatican archives, and encouraging biblical study and the rediscovery of Thomism.

On the other hand, very little progress was made in finding a compromise with the Italian state. Despite papal excommunications, Italy was here to stay. The reiterated condemnations of freemasonry, liberalism and socialism continued to place Catholicism on a collision course with modern politics. Any challenge to Rome's claim that it was the one true faith was met with contempt. Lord Halifax, a prominent Anglo-Catholic, and the French priest Fernand Portal sought to establish a rudimentary inter-faith dialogue between Canterbury and Rome at the start of the 1890s.[222] This early experiment in ecumenism was torn asunder, however, when Leo XIII put the cause of Christian unity back by decades when he stated categorically in the bull *Apostolicae curae* of 1896 that Anglican ordinations were absolutely null and void.[223] Thus any hope of reconciliation or official dialogue with Protestantism would have to wait until the Second Vatican Council (1962–5).

By 1903 Leo XIII was ninety-three years of age. He had confounded all expectations by living so long and his pontificate had become the fourth longest in history. Although visibly weakened, the pontiff was able to attend celebrations in St Peter's basilica for the twenty-fifth anniversary of his coronation on 3 March.[224] The next month, on 29 April the British King Edward VII was in Rome. In a spirit of cordiality, he decided to visit the pope. He would be the first reigning British monarch to do so since the Reformation. His cabinet advised that this could not be done officially, as the British monarch could hardly visit a pontiff who did not recognise him as the head of the Anglican church. It was decided that King Edward would be granted a private audience in the Vatican to avoid diplomatic awkwardness.[225] The visit was cordial and there was an exchange of gifts. Yet any discussion of Christian unity proved impossible given the toxic atmosphere created by the fallout from *Apostolicae curae*.

In July, the pope, weighed down by old age, was stricken by a chill in the Vatican gardens, where he collapsed. He would spend three weeks in slow decline, receiving cardinals and reading reports to the end. On 20 July he breathed his last.[226] The church he bequeathed to his successor was larger in terms of the souls entrusted to its care than the one he had inherited. Yet the papacy and its Curia were still psychologically incapable of accepting the loss of temporal power. This lingering nostalgia for the days of the pope-king, something which the Catholic hierarchy was never able to shake off, was to overshadow much of the twentieth century.

CONCLUSION:
THE CONCLAVE OF 1903

On 31 July 1903, sixty-two cardinals entered the Sistine chapel in solemn procession.[1] After the customary prayers, seeking inspiration and guidance from the Holy Spirit, the Master of the Papal Ceremonies proclaimed: '*Extra omnes!*' (Everyone leave!). Soon all the doors leading to the chapel and the cardinals' rooms were closed and bolted. No one would be allowed to leave until a successor to Leo XIII was elected.

Among these princes of the church only twenty-four were born outside Italy; James Gibbons, as archbishop of Baltimore, was the sole representative of a non-European church.[2] Although both Pius IX and Leo XIII had expressed the desire to create a College of Cardinals representative of global Catholicism, they had spectacularly failed to do so. As was customary, this conclave was dominated by Italians. Their hegemony would only wither away after the 1960s.

The votes cast in the opening ballots indicated that two factions were emerging, one in favour of Mariano Rampolla del Tindaro, Leo's former cardinal secretary of state, and the other supporting Cardinal Girolamo Maria Gotti, sometime prefect of the *Propaganda fide*. These two veteran politicians commanded around twenty votes each. After three ballots, it seemed that the Rampolla camp was gaining ground.[3] As the head of the Vatican diplomatic service, this cardinal had been in favour of a rapprochement with France but critical of Austria's 1882 alliance with Italy. Rumours were rife, during these first two days, that pressure was being placed on the dean of the College of Cardinals to ask Rampolla to withdraw, as he was seen as too divisive a figure by cardinals from central Europe.

After the third ballot, an astonishing event changed the course of the election decisively. Jan Puzyna de Kosielsko, a nobleman and archbishop of Krakow, stood in the Sistine chapel and asked to address the assembled princes of the church. From his crimson robes emerged a prepared statement written in courtly Latin. Many could not understand what he said in his thick Polish accent, and he was asked to reread his document several times. Once the reality of what he said was absorbed the cardinals sat in stunned silence. Puzyna informed his brethren that he had a secret mission from Count Agenor Gołuchowski, Emperor Franz-Josef's foreign minister.[4] He had been asked to exercise the *ius exclusive*,[5] or veto, against the candidate most unsuitable for the papacy. To the immense scandal of all assembled he told the cardinals that Rampolla was unacceptable to the house of Austria. Once the shock had passed, there was a noisy outcry against this interference in a papal election by the Habsburg emperor. In the modern world it was intolerable for a secular ruler to interfere in the election of a new pope. Rampolla agreed with his brother cardinals but stated, with great dignity, that Puzyna had done him a favour as he did not wish to be pontiff.[6]

Why Rampolla was unacceptable to Franz Josef has been the subject of significant speculation for over a century. His francophile and anti-Italian diplomacy did not endear him to the Ballhausplatz (the Habsburg foreign ministry). It might be speculated that his involvement in the Mayerling affair was the source of the imperial antipathy towards him. In 1889, to the immense horror of the Habsburgs, Crown Prince Rudolf had been found dead with his mistress Marie Vetsera in the hunting lodge of Mayerling.[7] It soon became clear that the young archduke in a fit of depression had shot his mistress before committing suicide himself. Whether or not this was a suicide pact remains a matter of controversy. Given the horrific head wounds found on the bodies, and the bullet trajectories, it was clear that Rudolf had taken his own life. According to the canons of the Catholic Church a person who had committed mortal sin unrepentant could not be buried in hallowed ground.

The Habsburgs were desperate to avoid a public scandal. They wanted the crown prince buried in the imperial crypt in the Capuchin convent in Vienna without the news of the suicide becoming public. The initial telegram to the Vatican announced that the crown prince had been killed. Since this note begged more questions than it answered, Franz-Josef wrote two private letters to Leo XIII – documents which, sadly, have not been located. It would appear that the emperor informed the Holy Father that his beloved son Rudolf, in a fit of insanity, had taken his life and that of his mistress. In a congregation summoned to discuss the issue, Rampolla disbelieved this story and opposed the Christian burial. Leo XII, for appearances' sake, decided to give special permission for the crown prince to be laid to rest with his ancestors. On 3 February 1889 the crown prince's body lay in state for several days. The head was so badly disfigured that it had to be replaced with a wax replica, a deep embarrassment. Over 100,000 mourners filed past the body. On glimpsing the wax head, they must have suspected that something was amiss.[8]

This event had been mortifying for the dynasty, and Franz-Josef blamed Rampolla's inflexibility for his family's embarrassment. Now, fourteen years later, the Mayerling crisis cost Leo's foreign minister the papacy. For the next two days the votes cast for Rampolla increased slightly. The cardinals wanted to make the point that the emperor could not determine the course of the election. It was the Holy Spirit who chose popes, not the Habsburgs. Yet, secretly, there were fears that Rampolla would prove controversial; at the same time, others suspected that Gotti would be an Austrian stooge. A third candidate was found in the person of the patriarch of Venice, Giuseppe Melchiorre Sarto. He was of saintly reputation, as his life had been dedicated to caring for the souls of his flock. Unlike his predecessors, he had no experience of working in the Curia and he was not a member of the Italian nobility. Slowly, the voting patterns started shifting toward Sarto's candidature. Terrified at the prospect of becoming pope the patriarch of Venice begged not to be considered for this terrible burden. The final two days of the conclave saw the dean of the College of Cardinals persuading him to accept the tiara.[9]

On 4 August 1903 the newly elected Pius X appeared inside St Peter's basilica to bless the faithful.[10] He had no intention of recognising the Italian state which had robbed his predecessors of their kingdom. This former parish priest became one of the most conservative pontiffs the Roman church has ever elected (quite an achievement!). He was determined to follow in the footsteps of Pius IX, whom he venerated. Unlike his idol, Sarto was not of the nobility – the first non-noble pope in centuries – and this trend would continue into the twentieth century. So appalled was the new pope by Cardinal Puzyna's application of the Austrian veto that he issued the apostolic constitution *Commissum nobis* on 20 January 1904.[11] This forbade any cardinals from exercising the *ius exclusive* in any future conclave on pain of excommunication. Despite Pius X's conservatism, this was a revolutionary reform. It jettisoned the final relic of the old alliance of throne and altar which had characterised the relationship between church and state during the eighteenth century. Henceforth, Catholicism abandoned monarchy and nobility to their fate on the scrap-heap of history. Only the clergy, guided by the papacy, would be allowed to determine the future of Christ's church. The *ancien régime* had passed away, silently and unmourned in the Sistine chapel during the papal election of 1903.

Yet the Curia and the papacy lived in denial of this fact for decades. Striving to regain political power and social influence, the Roman church was to make some very bad friends during the twentieth century. (But that is a story for another book...) The symbiotic relationship between church and state that had been established by Constantine's conversion to Christianity in AD 312, collapsed dramatically during the age of revolutions (it had already been compromised by the Reformation). Throughout the eighteenth century, the Catholic monarchies of Europe had slowly eroded the foundations and privileges of ecclesiastical power in Europe. Clergymen were divided on how the church should meet this challenge. Many, rather than resisting the power of the state, urged reform and modernisation. They believed in Gallican liberties and the power of neo-conciliarism to clip the wings of the papacy. A less authoritarian, more austere and pastorally committed church was their shared objective.

Their dreams seemed to be coming to fruition with the French Revolution of 1789, when the men of the National Assembly tried to create a streamlined and utilitarian church in France. To the horror of Christians throughout the continent, as the Revolution radicalised, politicians in Paris grew anticlerical in their desire to subjugate the church to the authority of the state. They had no interest in negotiation or compromise. Through their intransigence a Pandora's box was opened whose reverberations still echo down to the present day. Two popes were exiled, one died in captivity and another was forced to flee his own capital. Experiments in conciliation like the Napoleonic concordat of 1801 failed to satisfy either party. The Roman church considered that such agreements had failed to rebuild the *ancien régime* alliance of throne and altar but rather bound ecclesiastical authority to the whims of secular governments. Fearing the loss of its political independence, during the nineteenth century the church sternly committed itself to the retention of its central Italian principality. This proved to be a lost cause, which ended in abject failure in 1870 with the incorporation of Rome as the capital of the new Italian nation.

Yet all was not doom and gloom for the church in the period examined by this book. Catholicism received a notable boost in popular enthusiasm for its spiritual mission. Reeling from the blows inflicted on public worship and parish life during the 1790s, Catholics were determined to make up for lost ground and win the battle for Europe's soul. In this they looked for leadership to Rome. The nineteenth century was to be an age of religious revival. Numbers of clergy, religious and congregations grew exponentially across the rural peripheries of Europe. The parish priest continued to be a vital, though contested, community leader for southern Europeans.

In Latin America, the church made compromises with the post-imperial republics and dictatorships that emerged after the implosion of the Spanish empire. Catholicism here not merely survived but to an extent prospered. This period also witnessed Rome's rediscovery of its missionary vocation. In an unholy alliance with the imperial powers of Europe's second great age of imperialism, Catholicism spread across Africa and Asia. Rome after 1850 became a truly global religion that dwarfed any of the missionary achievements of the sixteenth or seventeenth centuries.

Another unforeseen development was the papacy's attainment of spiritual supremacy. While Rome haemorrhaged political power, paradoxically it gained unprecedented control over the church and its hierarchy. Ultramontane tendencies demanded that the pope lead the way and centralise the governance of the church. By the early twentieth century the papacy had undisputed mastery over the episcopacy and local churches. Gallicanism, reform Catholicism and neo-conciliarism were compromised through their collusion with radical revolutionary politics and the Napoleonic empire. After 1848, these ecclesiastical movements of the eighteenth century lay in ruins. The First Vatican Council proclaimed papal infallibility against the modern world. Any challenge to the pope's spiritual absolutism incurred automatic excommunication. This was a power so overwhelming that the Roman church has only deployed it a handful of times on obscure theological questions.

This book's conclusion, that the Catholic Church during the age of revolutions lost a kingdom but gained the world, merits repetition. Popes suffered the indignity of seeing their principality ripped out of their hands. Yet their spiritual authority over the largest religion in the world was beyond dispute. This move from the political toward the religious represented a great opportunity in a moment of growing individualism, capitalism and scientific progress. Often modernity offered ordinary people only a life of exploitation and isolation that was rewarded with the finality of death, a bleak outlook that caused many to turn to a nostalgic yearning for the enchanted world of Catholicism that transformed fatality into redemption. Hundreds of millions of believers turned to the saints, relics, processions and ceremonies of the church to provide comfort in a world defined by the fragility of existence. Indeed, the Virgin Mary made several unscheduled appearances during the nineteenth century to remind humanity that God had not forgotten his children despite the depredations of war, revolution and industrialisation.

Lamennais, de Mun, Grosoli, Murri, Manning, Gibbons and countless other Catholics, wanted the church to rediscover its missionary, pastoral and social imperative. For them, the reason a humble Galilean had died on the cross of Golgotha in AD 33 was not to establish the Curia, canon law or the magnificence of the Vatican. Christ died the humiliating death of a slave because he was a social and political revolutionary.[12] His church was supposed to minister to the weak not the strong. As he himself put it unforgettably in the Gospel according to Matthew:

> Come, ye blessed of my Father, inherit the kingdom prepared for you from the foundation of the world: For I was hungry, and ye gave me meat: I was thirsty, and ye gave me drink: I was a stranger, and ye took me in: Naked, and ye clothed me: I was sick, and ye visited me: I was in prison, and ye came unto me. [...] Verily I say unto you, inasmuch as ye have done it unto one of the least of these my brethren, ye have done it unto me. (Matthew 25: 34–40, KJV)

The church's true kingdom was to be found among the poor, the weak and the afflicted, not a piece of land in central Italy. Liberal and social Catholics urged the papacy to relinquish its political power and rediscover its true vocation to bring comfort to injured humanity.

When Italy wrested the kingdom out of the Catholic Church's hands in 1870, the papacy shut itself away from the modern world and sulked for sixty-eight years. Hugh MacLeod's argument that Catholicism self-ghettoised itself during the nineteenth century is incisive.[13] Beyond the forbidding Vatican walls, popes, cardinals and prelates perceived a world of sin, corruption, greed and exploitation. They were correct in their assessment. After all, modernity left much misery, violence and selfishness in its wake. Yet in shutting itself off from outsiders and sinners, the Catholic hierarchy forgot that Christ had sought the company of prostitutes, tax collectors and publicans, not the elite of Jewish society. Jesus came to bring comfort not condemnation. Safely ensconced behind the Vatican walls, the Roman church evaded its social vocation. The tragedy of the age of revolutions was not that Catholicism lost the Papal States but rather that it missed an opportunity to re-engage with society. The papacy simply did not realise that the true kingdom was to be found in the people of God.

FURTHER READING

The mixed fortunes of the Roman Catholic Church from 1700 to 1903 have received significant scholarly attention. There is no shortage of books on how the Enlightenment and revolution rocked the papacy to its core. Yet none of these works quite covers the period in its entirety, nor engages with the church's global reach as this book does. Eighteenth-century Catholicism is not well served in the English language and remains much neglected. The first port of call should be the forty volumes of Ludwig von Pastor's *History of the Popes*. Any reader interested in the period 1700–99 should turn to volumes 33–40 of this monumental history of the church. For a recent excellent collection of essays on this topic see Stewart J. Brown and Timothy Tackett (eds), *The Cambridge History of Christianity*, Vol. 7: *Enlightenment, Reawakening and Revolution 1660–1815* (Cambridge, 2006).

Although there are few general histories of the Roman church during the age of Enlightenment, there are some splendid monographs on individuals, turning-points and Catholic intellectual movements. I have found Dale van Kely's *Reform Catholicism and the International Suppression of the Jesuits in Enlightenment Europe* (New Haven, CT, 2018) inspirational. It is from these pages that the concept of reform Catholicism and its battle against the Jesuit order emerges. On the growth of Rome as a hub for art, culture and the birth of the modern museum see Christopher M. S. Johns, *Papal Art and Cultural Politics: Rome in the Age of Clement XI* (Cambridge, 1993) and Jeffrey Collins, *Papacy and Politics in Eighteenth-Century Rome: Pius VI and the Arts* (Cambridge, 2004). After much neglect by Anglo-Saxon scholars Benedict XIV has started to receive the attention which he richly deserves. Please refer to Rebecca Messbarger, Christopher M. S. Johns and Philip Gavitt (eds), *Benedict XIV and the Enlightenment: Art, Science and Spirituality* (Toronto, 2016) and Renée Haynes, *Philosopher King: The Humanist Pope, Benedict XIV* (London, 1970).

Much exemplary work on Catholicism's relationship to the Enlightenment has been produced in the past decade. I strongly recommend the studies published by the following scholars to devotees of intellectual and philosophical history: Ulrich Lehner, *The Catholic Enlightenment: The Forgotten History of a Global Movement* (Oxford, 2016); Ulrich Lehner and Michal Printy (eds), *A Companion to the Catholic Enlightenment in Europe* (Leiden, 2010); Jeffrey Burson and Ulrich Lehner (eds), *Enlightenment and Catholicism in Europe: A Transnational History* (Notre Dame, IN, 2014); Patrizia Delpiano, *Church and Censorship in Eighteenth-Century Italy: Governing Reading in the Age of Enlightenment* (London, 2019); and Shaun Blanchard, *The Synod of Pistoia and Vatican II: Jansenism and the Struggle for Catholic Reform* (Oxford, 2020). These fresh and insightful books give compelling accounts of Catholicism's struggle to conciliate religious revelation with the rationalism of Enlightenment thought. On the question of atheism in the eighteenth century one can read with much profit Charles Devellennes, *Positive Atheism: Bayle, Meslier, D'Holbach, Diderot* (Edinburgh, 2021) and Philipp Blom, *A Wicked Company: The Forgotten Radicalism of the European Enlightenment* (London, 2012). These are incisive studies on the question of nascent atheism in the age of Voltaire. Alec Ryrie's *Unbelievers: An Emotional History of Doubt* (London, 2019), gives the question a much broader analysis in his riveting study of unbelief.

France's revolution of 1789 damaged the church profoundly and many authors have treated this fascinating subject in great depth. The classic study for France is John McManners, *The French Revolution and the Church* (London, 1969). Added to this masterpiece should be Timothy Tackett, *Religion, Revolution, and Regional Culture in Eighteenth-Century France: The Ecclesiastical*

Oath of 1791 (Princeton, NJ, 1986) and Dale K. van Kley, *The Religious Origins of the French Revolution: From Calvin to the Civil Constitution, 1560–1791* (New Haven, CT, 1999). For a broader European survey and page-turner, read Owen Chadwick, *The Popes and European Revolution* (Oxford, 1981); and its sequel by the same author, *A History of the Popes 1830–1914* (Oxford, 1998). When it comes to Napoleon's relationship with Pius VII one could do worse than turn to Ambrogio A. Caiani, *To Kidnap a Pope: Napoleon and Pius VII* (London, 2021). The work of Pulitzer prize-winner David I. Kertzer is crucial to understanding the second half of the nineteenth century. His study of the Roman Revolution, *The Pope Who Would Be King: The Exile of Pius IX and the Emergence of Modern Europe* (Oxford, 2018), is vital reading. So too are his *Prisoner of the Vatican: The Pope's Secret Plot to Capture Rome from the New Italian State* (New York, 2005) and his poignant *The Kidnapping of Edgardo Mortara* (New York, 1997).

Excellent generalised studies of the Catholic Church in the nineteenth century have been published by Nicholas Atkin and Frank Tallett, *Priests, Prelates and People, A History of European Catholicism since 1750* (Oxford, 2003); Sheridan Gilley and Brian Stanley (eds), *The Cambridge History of Christianity*, Vol. 8: *World Christianities c.1815–c.1914* (Cambridge, 2006) and Frank J. Coppa, *The Modern Papacy since 1789* (London, 1998). For Marianism the best work has been done by David Blackbourn in his elegant study, *Marpingen: Apparitions of the Virgin Mary in Nineteenth Century Germany* (New York, 1993). When it comes to the resurgence of antisemitism and Catholicism's collusion with this vile movement, see David I. Kertzer, *The Popes Against the Jews: The Vatican's Role in the Rise of Modern Anti-Semitism* (New York, 2001) and Ruth Harris, *The Man on Devil's Island: Alfred Dreyfus and the Affair that Divided France* (London, 2010). Secularism only emerged late in the game to challenge religious authority. The seminal studies in this area are represented by Maurice Larkin, *Church and State after the Dreyfus Affair: The Separation Issue in France* (London, 1974) and Christopher Clark and Wolfram Kaiser (eds), *Culture Wars: Secular Catholic Conflict in Nineteenth Century Europe* (Cambridge, 2003). Catholicism's self-ghettoisation has been eloquently portrayed by Hugh McLeod in *Religion and the People of Western Europe 1789–1970* (Oxford, 1981).

Catholicism's role, and that of Christianity more generally, in the second age of European imperialism have commanded increasing attention from authors and scholars alike. The importance of missions and Christian evangelisation in propelling and catalysing imperial expansion in Africa and Asia is now understood more than ever. The most important and compendious study remains Kenneth Scott LaTourette, *A History of the Expansion of Christianity: The Great Century in the Americas, Australasia and Africa 1800–1914* (7 vols, New York, 1943). Other vital studies include Norman Etherington, *Missions and Empire* (Oxford, 2005); Adrian Hastings, *The Church in Africa 1450–1950* (Oxford, 1994); Vincent Viaene, Bram Cleys and Jan De Maeyer (eds), *Religion, Colonization and Decolonization in Congo, 1885–1960* (Leuven, 2020); and James P. Daughton, *An Empire Divided: Religion, Republicanism, and the Making of French Colonialism 1880–1914* (Oxford, 2006). For Aglipay and the Philippines the best analysis can be located in Pedro S. de Achútegui and Miguel A. Bernard, *Religious Revolution in the Philippines: The Life and Church of Gregorio Aglipay 1860–1940* (2nd edn, Manila, 1961).

LIST OF ABBREVIATIONS

AN	Archives Nationales de France (Paris)
Anon.	Anonymous
AP	*Archives Parlementaires de 1787 à 1860, 1er série*, ed. M. J. Madival and M. E. Laurant, 89 vols. (Paris, 1867–96)
ASV	Archivio Segreto Vaticano
BL, Add. Ms	British Library, Additional Manuscript (London)
Boulay	Alfred Comte Boulay de la Meurthe, *Documents sur la Négociation du Concordat et sur les Autres Rapports de la France avec le Saint-Siège en 18001 et 1801*, 6 vols. (Paris, 1891–1905)
Fasc.	Fascicolo
Ibid	Same as previous source
KJV	King James Version (Bible)
Mgr.	Monseigneur
NAP NOUV CORRES	Fondation Napoléon, *Napoléon Bonaparte, Correspondance Générale*, 15 vols. (Paris, 2004–18)

ACKNOWLEDGEMENTS

I dedicate this book to the memory of my grandparents: Ambrogio, Laura, Anna and Antonio. They were people of strong faith but in very different ways. My paternal side was fully committed to the changes wrought by the Second Vatican Council whereas my maternal *nonni* were more sceptical about its liberalising consequences. Despite these differences they were ardent and committed believers. It is a source of regret that I do not share their fervour and conviction, but I do hope that I have been fair to the faith I inherited from them. They were all marvellous and generous educators who bestowed on me a passion for history and religion. Although they passed away twenty years ago, I still miss them deeply and can only wonder what they would have made of this book.

It is a joy to thank my agent Robert Dudley who has been an indefatigable and enthusiastic supporter of my ideas. Without his encouragement and generosity in reading multiple drafts of this tome it would never have seen the light of day. A very large debt goes to Neil Belton, my editor at Head of Zeus, who originally had the idea for me to write this critical history of the Catholic Church. Neil is a wonderful, stylish and conscientious editor, with an encyclopaedic knowledge, which has saved me from several blunders. I am extremely grateful to him and his team at HoZ.

As ever I have had the privilege of working with and being inspired by many brilliant scholars in my field. Michael Broers, who decades ago wrote *Politics and Religion in Napoleonic Italy: The War Against God, 1801–1814*, remains my mentor. His patience and ability to provide good advice even when he is snowed under with his own work is a mark of his professionalism and generosity. This probably is not quite the book he would have written but the pages on Marian apparitions and popular devotions owe a great deal to his influence. It was my good fortune to discuss various aspects of this book with: Gianfranco Armando, Stephen Bann, Tim Blanning, Riccardo Benzoni, Allan Doig, Willian Doyle, Alan Forrest, Flora Fraser, Rasmus Glenthøj, Metter Harder, John Hardman, Leonie James, Colin Jones, David Laven, Giacomo Macola, Luigi Mascilli-Migliorini, Morten Nordhagen Ottosen, David Parrott, Munro Price, Mike Rapport and Geraint Thomas. I am particularly in the debt of Lady Antonia Fraser who generously read the manuscript and provided some very encouraging comments. Kelcey and Edward Wilson-Lee remain extremely dear friends; it is always blissful to enjoy their hospitality with my 'godson' Gabriel and namesake 'little' Ambrose. All these academic friends have provided much assistance and have challenged my lazier assumptions. For this I am incredibly grateful, although I must reiterate that any remaining errors or infelicities remain my own.

Very little good came from the Covid pandemic 2020–2021 but it did give me time to write (what else was there do!?). The University of Kent in Canterbury remains a very good home in which to prosper. It is with gratitude that I acknowledge the nurture received from my heads of division and school, Juliette Pattinson and Mark Connelly. I am blessed with remarkable colleagues, whom I very much thank for making the days seem very short indeed: Aurélie Basha i Novosejt, Barbara Bombi, Philip Boobbyer, Helen Brooks, Tim Bowman, Mario Draper, Gaynor Johnson, Claire Jones, Mark Lawrence (whose knowledge of Mexico was invaluable), Ben Marsh, Edward Roberts and John Wills. My biggest debt at Kent is owed to Andy Cohen and Helen Garnet who have opened their doors to me in times of crisis and joy. I often abuse their hospitality and generosity but cannot thank them enough for being there... Their northern unflappability contrasts sharply with my Mediterranean histrionics. Their disinterested friendship is among the greatest treasures of my life.

My students have had an uncanny ability to ask challenging questions and have opened my mind more than I could have expected in the past fifteen years. They may not always appreciate it, but they make me a better researcher and writer. In particular, I remember fondly the following prodigies: Drew Armstrong, Lucy Blomfield, Ana-Maria Bogdanova, Joe Boucher, Callum Bowers, Matthew Ballantine, Matthew Boyd, Angus Calder, Luke Cavanna, Greg Cooper, Kate Docking, Issy Cox-Jones, Alex Echlin, Farradeh Martin, Tom Eckett, Maria Edwards, Ben Fraser, Ryan Gatenby, Dom Gibson, Amy Harrison, Dylan Hewitt, Will Jarvis, Tom Like, Keith Minear, Stewart Murphy, Emily Parker, Barney Parr, Tom Ponzecchi, Ralph Roberts, Joe Robertson, Lucy Smith, Gemma Steer, Jack Tracey, Callum White, Lawrence White and Kesia Wills. They have made waking up in the morning and heading to the seminar room a thrill rather than a ordeal. One among them, stands out above this mighty cohort, and that is George Evans-Hulme, at the time of writing at the Department for Energy Security and Net Zero. Despite his increasingly frenetic work schedule he has offered and read a full draft of this book. His eagle eye and suggestions have made this a less flawed tome.

Parents are often taken for granted and I fear mine, Paolo and Bruna, suffer from filial neglect more than most. Despite their fear of my imminent excommunication (alas, I am not important nor eloquent enough to draw papal anathemas) they have been intensely fervent supporters of this book. My research often makes me careless about visiting and spending time with them, which is a source of regret. My father Paolo is without doubt my most shrewd and constructive critic. It is difficult to express how much it touches me that he makes the time to read my work. Without their support both moral and material my career and writing would have been impossible.

In September 2021 I met my partner Dean Smith and this improved my life more than I could have anticipated in my wildest dreams. His energy, charm, love, spicy humour and dedication make me look forward to our migrations between Canterbury and Wimbledon with anticipation. Lord knows what he sees in a conventional academic like me… but I am so grateful for his skewed vision. His presence in my life has enriched it beyond measure. Dean, you have certainly made the future seem less terrifying, thank you.

ABOUT THE AUTHOR

AMBROGIO A. CAIANI received his PhD from Sidney Sussex College, University of Cambridge in 2009. Since then he has taught at the universities of Greenwich, York and Oxford, and is currently Senior Lecturer in Modern European History at the University of Kent. Caiani's main research interests are Revolutionary France and Napoleonic Italy, and his work has been published in several leading academic journals. He is the author of *Louis XVI and the French Revolution, 1789–1792* and *To Kidnap a Pope: Napoleon and Pius VII*, which won the 2021 Franco-British Society book prize.

NOTES

Introduction

1. Charles O. Hucker, 'Ming Government', in Denis Crispin Twitchett and Frederick W. Mote (eds), *The Cambridge History of China*, Vol. 8: *The Ming Dynasty 1368–1644* (Cambridge, 1998), part 2, pp. 48–9.
2. Willard J. Peterson (ed.), *The Cambridge History of China*, Vol. 9: *The Ch'Ing Dynasty to 1800* (Cambridge, 2016), part 2; Clive Willis (ed.), *China and Macau* (London, 2002), pp. 65–74.
3. Robert C. Jenkins, *The Jesuits in China and the Legation of Cardinal Tournon: An Examination of the Conflicting Evidence and an Attempt at an Impartial Judgement* (London, 1984), pp. 38–45.
4. Ibid.
5. Evelyn S. Rawski, *The Last Emperors: A Social History of Qing Imperial Institutions* (Los Angeles, 1998), pp. 19–23.
6. R. Po-Chia-Hsia, *A Jesuit in the Forbidden City: Matteo Ricci 1552–1610* (Oxford, 2010), esp. pp. 202–23; Jonathan D. Spence, *The Memory Palace of Matteo Ricci* (London, 1984).
7. Nicolas Standaert, 'Christianity Shaped by the Chinese', in R. Po-Chia Hsia (ed.), *The Cambridge History of Christianity*, Vol. 6: *Reform and Expansion 1500–1660* (Cambridge, 2007), pp. 561–71; Tom Holland, *Dominion: The Making of the Western Mind* (London, 2019), pp. 329–35.
8. Michèle Pirazzoli-t'Serstevens, 'Giuseppe Castiglione et le renouveau du portrait impérial au XVIIIes', *Arts Asiatiques*, Vol. 60 (2005), pp. 22–30; Lucia Tripodes, 'Painting and Diplomacy at the Qianlong Court: A commemorative picture by Wang Zhicheng', *RES, Anthropology and Aesthetics*, No. 35 (1999), pp. 185–200.
9. Nicolas Standaert, 'The Edict of Tolerance 1692: A textual history and reading', in Artur K. Wardega, SJ, and Antonio Vasconcelos de Saldanha (eds), *In the Light and Shadow of an Emperor: Tomas Pereira, SJ (1645–1708), the Kangxi Emperor and the Jesuit Mission in China* (Newcastle, 2012), pp. 308–58.

10. Macabe Keliher, *The Board of Rites and the Making of Qing China* (Los Angeles, 2019).

11. Daniel K. Gardner, *Confucianism: A Very Short introduction* (Oxford, 2014), pp. 12–14.

12. Claudia von Collani, 'The Jesuits Rites Controversy', in Ines G. Županov (ed.), *The Oxford Handbook of the Jesuits* (Oxford, 2019), pp. 893–901; Rawski, *The Last Emperors*, pp. 285–90.

13. John D. Young, *Confucianism and Christianity: The First Encounter* (Hong Kong, 1983) pp. 29–34; D. E. Mungello, *The Great Encounter of China and the West, 1500-1800* (4th edn, Plymouth, 2012).

14. M. Antoni J. Üçerler, 'The Jesuits Enterprise in Sixteenth and Seventeenth Century Japan', in Thomas Worcester (ed.), *The Cambridge Companion to the Jesuits* (Cambridge, 2008), pp. 153–68, esp. pp. 161–5.

15. Edward J. Malatesta, SJ, 'A Fatal Clash of Wills: The condemnation of the Chinese rites by the papal legate Carlo Tommaso Maillard de Tournon', in D. E. Mungello (ed.), *The Chinese Rites Controversy: Its History and Meaning* (Abingdon, 2018), pp. 211–46.

16. Jonathan D. Spence, *Emperor of China: Self-Portrait of K'Ang-Hsi* (New York, 1974), pp. 76–82.

17. Ludwig von Pastor, *The History of the Popes from the Close of the Middle Ages, drawn from the secret archives of the Vatican and other original sources* (40 vols, London, 1891–1953), XXXIII, pp. 435–6.

18. Francis A. Rouleau, SJ, 'Maillard de Tournon, Papal Legate at the Court of Peking: The first imperial audience 31 December 1705,' *Archivum Historicum Societatis Iesu*, Anno XXXI, Fasc. 62 (1962), pp. 264–323, esp. p. 285.

19. Jenkins, *The Jesuits in China and the Legation of Cardinal Tournon*, p. 124.

20. Claudia von Collani, 'Charles Maigrot's Rôle in the Chinese Rites Controversy,' in D. E. Mungello (ed.), *The Chinese Rites Controversy*, pp. 149–83.

21. René Étiemble, *Les Jésuits en Chine 1552-1773: La Querelle des Rites* (Paris, 1966), pp. 111–15.

22. Rouleau, 'Maillard de Tournon', pp. 266–7.

23. Kristina Kleutghen, 'Ethnicity, Empire and Europe: Jesuit art in China during the papacy of Benedict XIV', in Rebecca Messbarger, Christopher M. S. Johns and Philip Gavitt (eds), *Benedict XIV and the Enlightenment: Art, Science and Spirituality* (Toronto, 2016), pp. 419–22; Renée Haynes, *Philosopher King: The Humanist Pope, Benedict XIV* (London, 1970), pp. 195–6.

24. Jonathan Tan, 'Encounter between Confucianism and Christianity', in Felix Wilfred (ed.), *The Oxford Handbook of Christianity in Asia* (Oxford, 2014), p. 437.

25. Nigel Aston, 'Continental Catholic Europe', in Stewart J. Brown and Timothy Tackett (eds), *The Cambridge History of Christianity*, Vol. 7: *Enlightenment, Reawakening and Revolution 1660–1815* (Cambridge, 2006), pp. 15–32.

26. William R. Ward, *Christianity under the Ancien Régime, 1648–1789* (Cambridge, 1999), pp. 147–201; Nigel Aston, *Christianity and Revolutionary Europe, 1750–1830* (Cambridge, 2003), pp. 93–133.

27. Voltaire, *Candide où l'optimisme: Traduit de l'Allemand de Mr le Docteur Ralph* (1766), esp. pp. 5–6.

28. Alec R. Vidler, *The Church in an Age of Revolution* (London, 1990).

29. Mario Caravale and Alberto Caraccioli, *Lo Stato pontificio da Martino V a Pio IX* (*Storia d'Italia*, Vol. XIV, Turin, 1978), pp. 457–67; Anthony D. Wright, *The Early Modern Papacy from the Council of Trent to the French Revolution, 1564–1789* (Harlow, 2000), pp. 231–70.

30. Joachim Whaley, *Germany and the Holy Roman Empire* (2 vols, Oxford, 2012), II, pp. 299–306; Timothy Blanning, *Reform and Revolution in Mainz 1743–1803* (Cambridge, 1974), pp. 39–69.

31. Marc R. Forster, *Catholic Revival in the Age of the Baroque: Religious Identity in Southwest Germany, 1550–1750* (Cambridge, 2001), pp. 208–40; Philip Robinson, *Die Fürstabtei Sankt. Gallen und ihr Territorium* (Saint Gall, 1995).

32. Derek Beales, *Prosperity and Plunder: European Catholic Monasteries in the Age of Revolution 1650–1815* (Cambridge, 2003), pp. 1–7; Françoise Boquillon, *Les Chanoinesses de Remiremont 1566–1790* (Remiremont, 2000); Jacques Joseph Bammert, *L'Histoire du chapitre des nobles dames de Remiremont* (Remiremont, 1972).

33. Colin Morris, *The Papal Monarchy: The Western Church from 1050 to 1250* (Oxford, 1989), esp. Ch. 9.

34. Dale Van Kley, 'Catholic Conciliar Reform in an age of Anti-Catholic Revolution: France, Italy and the Netherlands 1758–1801', in James E. Bradley and Dale Van Kley (eds), *Religion and Politics in Enlightenment Europe* (Notre Dame, IN, 2001), pp. 46–118.

35. David Sorkin, *The Religious Enlightenment: Protestants, Jews, and Catholics from London to Vienna* (Princeton, NJ, 2008), pp. 1–21.

36. James Clark, *The Dissolution of the Monasteries: A New History* (London, 2021); Owen Chadwick, *The Popes and European Revolution* (Oxford, 1981), pp. 235–52.

37. John McManners, *The French Revolution and the Church* (London, 1969), pp. 24–60.

38. Alessandro Roveri, *La Santa Sede tra rivoluzione France e Restaurazione: il cardinale Consalvi 1813–1815* (Florence, 1974), pp. 85–123.

39. Giorgio Cencetti, *Le tre legazioni: Antonio Aldini e Il Congresso di Vienna* (Bologna, 1935).

40. Miroslav Šedivý, *The Decline of the Congress System: Metternich, Italy and European Diplomacy* (London, 2018), pp. 61–79; 193–219.

41. David I. Kertzer, *The Pope Who Would Be King: The Exile of Pius IX and the Emergence of Modern Europe* (Oxford, 2018).

42. Frank J. Coppa, *The Modern Papacy since 1789* (London, 1998), pp. 111–13; David I. Kertzer, *Prisoner of the Vatican: The Pope's Secret Plot to Capture Rome from the New Italian State* (New York, 2005).

43. Owen Chadwick, *A History of the Popes, 1830–1914* (Oxford, 1998), pp. 346–59; Yves Chiron, *Pie IX, Pape Moderne* (Paris, 1995), pp. 313–53.

44. Christopher Clark and Wolfram Kaiser (eds), *Culture Wars: Secular Catholic Conflict in Nineteenth Century Europe* (Cambridge, 2003).

45. Euan Cameron, *Early Modern Europe: An Oxford History* (Oxford, 2001); Diarmaid MacCulloch, *Reformation: Europe's House Divided, 1490–1700* (London, 2004).

46. Jean-Marie Salamito, *Rerum novarum: écriture, contenu et réception d'une encyclique* (Rome, 1997).

47. August Bernhard Hasler, *How the Pope Became Infallible: Pius IX and the Politics of Persuasion* (London, 1979); Brian Tierney, *Origins of Papal Infallibility, 1150–1350: A Study on the Concepts of Infallibility, Sovereignty and Tradition in the Middle Ages* (Leiden, 1988).

48. Mary Heimann, 'Catholic Revivalism in Worship and Devotion', in Sheridan Gilley and Brian Stanley (eds), *The Cambridge History of Christianity*, Vol. 8: *World Christianities c.1815–c.1914* (Cambridge, 2006), pp. 70–83.

49. Roger Price, *Religious Renewal in France 1789–1870: The Roman Catholic Church between Catastrophe and Triumph* (Basingstoke, 2018), pp. 20–72.

50. Jürgen Osterhammel, *The Transformation of the World: A Global History of the Nineteenth Century* (Princeton, NJ, 2014), pp. 392–468.

51. Francisco Javier Ramón Solans, 'The Creation of a Latin American Catholic Church: Vatican authority and political imagination, 1854–1899', *Journal of Ecclesiastical History*, Vol.71, No.2 (2020), pp. 316–36; Angelo Mercati (ed.), *Raccolta di Concordati su matterie ecclesiastiche tra la Santa Sede e le autorita civili 1098–1914* (Rome, 1954), 1.

52. Adrian Hastings, *The Church in Africa 1450–1950* (Oxford, 1994), pp. 248–50, 253–305; Hilary M. Carey, *God's Empire: Religion and Colonialism in the British World 1801–1908* (Cambridge, 2011), pp. 114–47; J. P. Daughton, *An Empire Divided: Religion, Republicanism and the Making of French Colonialism, 1880–1914* (Oxford, 2008); Norman Etherington (ed.), *Missions and Empire* (Oxford, 2005).

1 The Alliance of Throne and Altar, 1700–73

1. Fabio Sorini, *Gli Schiavoni, le fedelissime truppe oltremarine di Venezia, tre secoli di storia 1500–1797* (Collegno, 2016).
2. Virginia Aksan, *Ottoman Wars, 1700–1870: An Empire Besieged* (London, 2014), p. 53.
3. Hans Schmidt, 'Il salvatore di Corfù: Matthias Johann von der Schulenburg (1661–1747). Una carriera militare europea al tempo dell'Alto Assolutismo', *Quaderni*, Vol. 42, Centro Tedesco di Studi Veneziani (1991), pp. 3–29.
4. Alberto Prelli and Bruno Mugnai, *L'ultima Vittoria della Serenissima, 1716 – L'assedio di Corfù* (Bassano del Grappa, 2016), pp. 141–2, 125.
5. Schmidt, 'Il salvatore di Corfù,' pp. 22–3.
6. Prelli and Mugnai, *L'ultima Vittoria della Serenissima*, pp. 127–31.
7. Peter Topping, 'Venice's Last Imperial Venture', *Proceedings of the American Philosophical Society*, Vol. 120, No. 3 (1976), pp. 159–65; William Miller, 'The Ionian Islands under Venetian Rule,' *English Historical Review*, Vol. 18, No. 70 (1903), pp. 209–39.
8. Karen-edis Barzman, *The Limits of Identity: Early Modern Venice, Dalmatia, and the Representation of Difference* (Leiden, 2017), pp. 142–3.
9. Dragoş Cosmescu, *Venetian Renaissance Fortifications in the Mediterranean* (Jefferson, NC, 2016), pp. 147–68.
10. Alice Binion, 'From Schulenburg's Gallery and Records', *Burlington Magazine*, Vol. 112, No. 806 (1970), pp. 297–303.
11. Derek Croxton, *Westphalia: The Last Christian Peace* (Basingstoke, 2013); Virgina H. Askan, *Ottoman Wars 1700–1870: Empire Besieged* (London, 2007), pp. 83–102.
12. Quoted in Pastor, *History of the Popes*, XXXVI, pp. 12–13.
13. Ibid, pp. 25–47.
14. Pamela M. Jones, Barbara Wisch and Simon Ditchfield (eds), *A Companion to Early Modern Rome, 1492–1692* (Leiden, 2019), pp. 16–19.
15. William Roosen, 'Early Modern Diplomatic Ceremonial: A systems approach', *Journal of Modern History*, Vol. 52, No. 3 (1980), pp. 452–76; Alexis Keller, 'Inter-State Arbitration in Historical Perspective', in Thomas Schultz and Federico Ortino (eds), *The Oxford Handbook of International Arbitration* (Oxford, 2020), pp. 843–73.
16. Henry Kamen, *Philip V of Spain: The King who Reigned Twice* (London, 2001), pp. 69–70.
17. Gaetano Greco, *Benedetto XIV: Un Canone per La Chiesa* (Rome, 2011), pp. 82–92.
18. Maartje Abbenhuis, *An Age of Neutrals: Great Power Politics, 1815–1914* (Cambridge, 2014), pp. 1–21.
19. Pastor, *History of the Popes*, XXXV, pp. 101–12.

20. Wł. Konopczyński, 'Early Saxon Period 1697–1733', in W. F. Reddaway, J. H. Pension, O. Halecki and R. Dyboski (eds), *The Cambridge History of Poland from Augustus II to Piłsudski, 1697–1935* (Cambridge, 1941), p.2; Kristina Friedrichs, 'Court Chapels in Saxony between 1697 and 1733: Augustus II the Strong between Catholicism and Protestantism', *Acta Poloniae Historica*, Vol. 116 (2017), pp. 93–120; Helen Watanabe-O'Kelly, *Court Culture in Dresden: From Renaissance to Baroque* (Basingstoke, 2002), pp. 195–204.

21. Peter H. Wilson, *The Holy Roman Empire: A Thousand Years of History* (London, 2016), pp. 128–31.

22. Jerzy Lukowski, *Liberty's Folly: The Polish-Lithuanian Commonwealth in the Eighteenth-Century* (London, 1991), pp. 122–9.

23. Joachim Whaley, *Germany and the Holy Roman Empire* (2 vols, Oxford, 2013), Vol. II: *The Peace of Westphalia To The Dissolution of the Reich, 1648–1806*, p. 294.

24. Patrick Milton, 'The Early Eighteenth-Century German Confessional Crisis: The juridification of religious conflict in the reconfessionalized politics of the Holy Roman Empire', *Central European History*, Vol. 49, No. 1 (2016), pp. 39–68.

25. Joachim Whaley, *Germany and the Holy Roman Empire*, II, pp. 150–7.

26. David M. Luebke, 'A Multiconfessional Empire', in Thomas Max Safley (ed.), *A Companion to Multiconfessionalism in the Early Modern World* (Leiden, 2011), pp. 129–54.

27. Alfred Burne, *The Noble Duke of York: The Military Life of Frederick Duke of York and Albany* (London, 1949).

28. Philip Mansel, *King of the World: The Life of Louis XIV* (London, 2019), pp. 424–6.

29. Edward Corp, *The Stuarts in Italy, 1719–1766: A Royal Court in Permanent Exile* (Cambridge, 2014), pp. 15–31; Edward Corp, *The Jacobites at Urbino: An Exiled Court* (Basingstoke, 2009).

30. Andreas Gestrich and Michael Schaich (eds), *The Hanoverian Succession: Dynastic Politics and Monarchical Culture* (London, 2016).

31. Daniel Szechi, *The Jacobites, Britain and Europe, 1688–1788*, (2nd edn, Manchester, 2019); Jacqueline Riding, *Jacobites: A New History of the '45 Rebellion* (London, 2016).

32. Andrew Wheatcroft, *The Enemy at the Gate: Habsburgs, Ottomans and the Battle for Europe* (London, 2009).

33. Prelli and Mugnai, *L'ultima Vittoria della Serenissima*.

34. Béla K. Király, 'The Hungarian Church', in William Callahan and David Higgs (eds), *Church and Society in Catholic Europe of the Eighteenth Century* (Cambridge, 1979), pp. 106–21.

35. Michael Hochedlinger, *Austria's Wars of Emergence, 1683–1797* (London, 2003), ch.9.

36. Robert C. Davis, *Christian Slaves, Muslim Masters: White Slavery in the Mediterranean, the Barbary Coast and Italy, 1500–1800* (Basingstoke, 2003), pp. 45–6, 110, 116–20.

37. Alain Blondy, *L'Ordre de Malte au XVIIIe des dernières splendeurs à la ruine* (Paris, 2002), pp. 47–51.

38. Davis, *Christian Slaves, Muslim Masters*, pp. 167–170, 177–9.

39. Christopher Storrs, *The Spanish Resurgence, 1713–1748* (London, 2016), p. 118.

40. Richard Bonney (ed.), *The Rise of the Fiscal State in Europe, c. 1200–1815* (Oxford, 1999); Christopher Storrs (ed.), *The Fiscal Military State in Eighteenth-Century Europe* (London, 2008); Tim Blanning, *The Pursuit of Glory: Europe 1648–1815* (London, 2007), pp. 286–304.

41. John Brewer, *The Sinews of Power: War, Money and the English State 1688–1783* (London, 1989); P. G. M. Dickson, *The Financial Revolution in England: A Study in the Development of Public Credit, 1688–1756* (London, 1993).

42. Thomas I. Crimando, 'Two French Views of the Council of Trent', *Sixteenth Century Journal*, Vol. 19, No. 2 (Summer, 1988), pp. 169–86. Geoffrey Parker, *Imprudent King: A New Life of Philip II* (London, 2014), pp. 80–99. Joachim Whaley, *Germany and the Holy Roman Empire*, II, pp. 299–306.

43. Massimo C. Giannin (ed.), *Papacy, Religious Orders, and International Politics during the Sixteenth and Seventeenth Centuries* (Rome, 2013); & Robert Bireley, *The Refashioning of Catholicism 1450–1700, A Reassessment of the Counter Reformation* (Basingstoke, 1999), pp. 43–4.

44. Wright, *The Early Modern Papacy*, pp. 258–70. For vast attempts to reform the papal economy see Franco Venturi, *Italy and the Enlightenment Studies in a Cosmopolitan Century* (New York, 1972), pp. 225–64; Donatella Strangio, 'Public Debt in the Papal States, Sixteenth to Eighteenth Century', *Journal of Interdisciplinary History*, Vol. XLIII, No. 4 (2013), pp. 511–37.

45. Joseph Bergin, *Crown, Church and Episcopate under Louis XIV* (London, 2004), pp. 232–41.

46. Ibid, p.235; Pierre Blet, *Les assemblées du clergé et Louis XIV 1670–1693* (Rome, 1972), pp. 259–60.

47. Gregory Monahan, *Let God Arise: The War and Rebellion of the Camisards* (Oxford, 2014), pp. 21–42; Janine Garrisson, *L'Edit de Nantes et sa revocation: histoire d'une intolerance* (Paris, 1985).

48. Owen Stanwood, *The Global Refuge: Huguenots in an Age of Empire* (Oxford, 2020).

49. Francis Oakley, *The Conciliarist Tradition: Constitutionalism in the Catholic Church 1300–1870* (Oxford, 2008).

50. J. H. Smith, *The Great Schism 1378: The Disintegration of the Papacy* (London 1970); and more recently, Joelle Rollo-Koster, *The Great Western Schism, 1378-1417: Performing Legitimacy, Performing Unity* (Cambridge, 2022).

51. Paul Valliere, *Conciliarism: A History of Decision Making in the Church* (Cambridge, 2012), pp. 142-8.

52. Oakley, *The Conciliarist Tradition*, pp. 81-99.

53. Pastor, *History of the Popes*, XXXVI, pp. 56-75.

54. John McManners, *Church and Society in Eighteenth Century France* (2 vols, Oxford, 1998), I, pp. 208-34.

55. Alexandre Dupilet, *Le Cardinal Dubois: le génie politique de la Régence* (Paris, 2015); Guy Chaussinand-Nogaret, *Le Cardinal de Fleury: le Richelieu de Louis XV* (Paris, 2002).

56. Massimo Solari, *Giulio Alberoni: La vita avventurosa del figlio dell'ortolano che diventò primo ministro* (Piacenza, 2013).

57. Robert Evans, *Austria, Hungary, and the Habsburgs: Central Europe c.1683-1867* (Oxford, 2006), pp. 52-3.

58. Nicole Reinhardt, *Voices of Conscience: Royal Confessors and Political Counsel in Seventeenth Century Spain and France* (Oxford, 2016); Nicole Reinhardt, 'The King's Confessors. Changing images', in Michael Schaich (ed.), *Monarchy and Religion, The Transformation of Royal Culture in Eighteenth Century Europe* (Oxford, 2007), pp. 154-85.

59. Michel Antoine, *Louis XV* (Paris, 1989), pp. 484-510.

60. Nicole Reinhardt, 'Spin Doctor of Conscience? The royal confessor and the Christian prince', *Renaissance Studies*, Vol. 23, No. 4, (2009), pp. 568-90; Reinhardt: *Voices of Conscience*, Part I.

61. McManners, *Church and Society in Eighteenth Century France*, I, 29-57; Giles Barber, '"Il a fallut meme réveiller les Suisses": Aspects of private religious practice in a public setting in eighteenth-century Versailles', in Nigel Aston (ed.), *Religious Change in Europe, 1650-1914: Essays for John McManners* (Oxford, 1997), pp. 75-101.

62. Timothy Blanning, *The Pursuit of Glory*, pp. 445-8; Antonio Àlvarez-Ossorio, 'The Ceremonial of Majesty and Aristocratic Protest: The royal chapel at the court of Charles II', in Juan José Carreras, Bernardo García-García and Tess Knighton (eds), *The Royal Chapel in the Time of the Habsburgs: Music and Ceremony in the Early Modern European Court* (Woodbridge, 2005), pp. 246-99.

63. Anne Byrne, *Death and the Crown: Ritual and Politics in France before the Revolution* (Manchester, 2019), ch.6.

64. Marc Bloch, *The Royal Touch: Monarchy and Miracles in France and England* (London, 1989); Richard A. Jackson, *Vive le Roi! A History of the French Coronation from Charles V to Charles X* (Chapel Hill, NC, 1984).

65. Dale K. Van Kley, *The Religious Origins of the French Revolution: From Calvin to the Civil Constitution 1560–1791* (London, 1996), pp. 132–4; Jeffrey W. Merrick, *The Desacralization of the French Monarchy in the Eighteenth Century* (Baton Rouge, LA, 1990), p. 20.

66. Thomas Babington Macaulay, *History of England* (5 vols, London, 1855), III, p. 431; James George Frazer, *The Golden Bough: The Magic Art and the Evolution of Kings* (12 vols, 1906), I, pp. 369–70; cf. James F. Turrell, 'The Ritual of Royal Healing in Early Modern England: Scrofula, liturgy, and politics', *Anglican and Episcopal History*, Vol. 68, No. 1 (1999), pp. 3–36.

67. Jean-Paul Garnier and Louis-Hubert Remy (eds), *Le Sacre de Charles X et l'opinion publique en 1825* (Paris, 2018).

68. Nigel Aston, *Christianity and Revolutionary Europe*, pp. 23–7.

69. Ulrich Eisenhardt, *Die Weltliche Gerichtsbarkeit der Offizialate in Köln, Bonn und Werl im 18 Jahrhundert* (Cologne, 1966); Monique Cuillieron, 'Les causes matrimoniales des officialités de Paris au Siècle des Lumières 1726–1789', *Revue historique de droit français et étranger*, Vol. 66, No. 4 (1988), pp. 527–59; Bartolomé Bennassar, *L'inquisition espagnole, XVe–XIXe siècles* (Paris, 2009); Francisco Bethencourt, *The Inquisition: A Global History, 1478–1834* (Cambridge, 2009).

70. Élisabeth Claverie, 'Sainte indignation contre indignation éclairée, L'affaire du Chevalier de La Barre', *Ethnologie française*, Vol. 22, No. 3 (1992), pp. 271–90.

71. Peter Garnsey, *Against the Death Penalty: Writings from the First Abolitionists, Giuseppe Pelli and Cesare Beccaria* (Princeton, NJ, 2020).

72. Hubert Wolf, *Storia dell'Indice, il Vaticano e i libri proibiti* (Roma, 2006).

73. James K. Farge, 'Early Censorship in Paris: A new look at the roles of the Parlement of Paris and of King Francis I', *Renaissance and Reformation/Renaissance et Réforme*, Vol. 13, No. 2 (1989), pp. 173–83; Frances E. Hammitt, 'The Burning of Books', *Library Quarterly: Information, Community, Policy*, Vol. 15, No. 4 (1945), pp. 300–12.

74. Maria Pia Donato, 'Reorder and Restore: Benedict XIY, the Index and the Holy Office', in Messbarger, Johns and Gavitt, Benedict XIV and the Enlightenment, pp. 227–52.

75. Maurice A. Finocchiaro, 'Benedict XIV and the Galileo Affair, Liberalization or Carelessness?' in Messbarger, Johns and Gavitt (eds), Benedict XIV and the Enlightenment, pp. 206–26.

76. Giuseppe Marcocci, 'Toward a History of the Portuguese Inquisition. Trends in modern historiography', *Revue de l'histoire des religions*, Vol. 227, No. 3 (2010), pp. 355–93; Christopher F. Black, *The Italian Inquisition* (London, 2009).

77. Bethencourt, *The Inquisition*, p. 252; Giuseppe Marcocci and José Pedro Paiva, *História da Inquisição Portuguesa, 1536–1821* (2 edn, Lisbon, 2016), pp. 261–80.

78. Christopher F. Black, 'Inquisitions', in Charles H. Parker and Gretchen Starr-LeBeau (eds), *Judging Faith, Punishing Sin: Inquisitions and Consistories, in the Early Modern World* (Cambridge, 2017), pp. 30–4.

79. James E. Wadsworth, 'Inquisitions', in Parker and Starr-LeBeau (eds), *Judging Faith, Punishing Sin*, pp. 317–30.

80. Bethencourt, *The Inquisition*, pp. 169–71; based on José Veiga Torres, 'Da Repressão Religiosa para a Promoção Social: A Inquisição como instância legitimadora da promoção social da burguesia mercantil', *Revista Crítica de Ciências Sociais*, Vol. 40 (1994), pp. 109–35, and Marcocci and Paiva, *História da Inquisição Portuguesa*, pp. 333–57.

81. Marcocci and Paiva, *História da inquisição portuguesa*, pp. 338, 348.

82. Mark Molesky, *This Gulf of Fire: The Great Lisbon Earthquake or Apocalypse in the Age of Science and Reason* (New York, 2016), pp. 69–116; Nicholas Shrady, *The Last Day: Wrath, Ruin and Reason in the Great Lisbon Earthquake of 1755* (London, 2008), pp. 5–24; Edward Paice, *Wrath of God: The Great Lisbon Earthquake of 1755* (London, 2008), pp. 65–116.

83. Voltaire, *Romans et Contes* (Paris, 1979), pp. 155–7.

84. Ibid, pp. 157–8

85. Kenneth Maxwell, *Pombal: Paradox of the Enlightenment* (Cambridge, 1995), pp. 79–84; Shrady, *The Last Day*, pp. 171–4; and Franklin L. Ford, 'Assassination in the Eighteenth Century: The dog that did not bark in the night', *Proceedings of the American Philosophical Society*, Vol. 120, No. 3 (1976), pp. 211–15.

86. Samuel J. Miller, *Portugal and Rome c.1748–1830: An Aspect of the Catholic Enlightenment* (Rome, 1978), pp. 107–46, esp. p.124; Marcocci and Paiva, *História da inquisição portuguesa*, pp. 336–45.

87. Wadsworth, 'Inquisitions', in Parker and Starr-LeBeau (eds), *Judging Faith, Punishing Sin*, p. 322.

88. Juan Hernández Franco, *Cultura y limpieza de sangre en la España moderna, puritate sanguinis* (Murcia, 1996); Henry Kamen, *The Spanish Inquisition: A Historical Revision* (London, 1998), pp. 234–54.

89. Wadsworth, 'Inquisitions', in Parker and Starr-LeBeau (eds), *Judging Faith, Punishing Sin*, pp. 317–19.

90. Bethencourt, *The Inquisition*, pp. 432–4.

91. Andrea Del Col, *L'inquisizione in Italia, dal XII al XXI secolo* (Rome, 2011).

92. Roderick Phillips, *Putting Asunder: A History of Divorce in Western Society* (Cambridge, 1988), pp. 9–13, 159–75.

93. Linda A. Pollock, 'Parent-Child Relations', in David I. Kertzer and

Marizio Barbagli (eds), *Family Life in Early Modern Times, 1500–1789* (London, 2001), pp. 191–220.

94. McManners, *Church and Society in Eighteenth Century France*, II, pp. 18–27; Mario Kaplan, *The Marriage Bargain: Women and Dowries in European History* (London, 1985).

95. Derek Beales, *Joseph II* (2 vols, Cambridge, 2013), II, pp. 168–213; Claude Lauriol, 'L'Édit de 1787 et la tolérance à la fin de l'Ancien Régime', *Bulletin de la Société de l'Histoire du Protestantisme Français*, Vol. 134, (Actes des Journées d'étude sur l'Édit de 1787, May–June 1988), pp. 425–33.

96. McManners, *Church and Society in Eighteenth Century France*, I, pp. 235–61.

97. Jerzy Kłoczowski, 'The Polish Church', in Callahan and Higgs (eds), *Church and Society in Catholic Europe*, pp. 122–37; John Lynch, *Bourbon Spain* (Oxford, 1989), pp. 270–2.

98. Lynch, *Bourbon Spain*, pp. 269–80; William J. Callahan, 'The Spanish Church', in Callahan and Higgs (eds), *Church and Society in Catholic Europe*, pp. 34–50.

99. Ugo Da Como, *Atti delle assemblee costituzionali italiane* (Rome, 1968), p. 599; Filiberto Agostini, *La riforma napoleonica della chiesa nella repubblica e nel regno d'italia 1802–1814* (Vicenza, 1990), pp. 114–18.

100. Whaley, *Germany and the Holy Roman Empire*, II, p. 299.

101. Richard Butterwick, *The Polish Revolution and the Catholic Church, 1788–1792* (Oxford, 2012), p. 28.

102. Whaley, *Germany and the Holy Roman Empire*, II, p. 301.

103. William Godsey, Jr, *Nobles and Nation in Central Europe: Free Imperial Knights in the Age of Revolution, 1750–1850* (Cambridge, 2004), pp. 187–97; Tim Blanning, *Reform and Revolution in Mainz, 1743–1803* (Cambridge, 1974), pp. 53–6.

104. Richard Butterwick, 'Catholicism and Enlightenment in Poland Lithuania', in Ulrich Lehner and Michal Printy (eds), *A Companion to the Catholic Enlightenment in Europe* (Leiden, 2010), pp. 297–358, esp. pp. 315–347.

105. Whaley, *Germany and the Holy Roman Empire*, II, p. 300.

106. Heribert Raab, 'Reconstruction and Constitution of the Church of the Empire', in Hubert Jedin and John Patrick Dolan (eds), *History of the Church*, Vol. VI: *The Church in the Age of Absolutism and Enlightenment* (New York, 1981), pp. 142–3.

107. Théodore Malley, 'Monseigneur Camille de Neuville et la primatie lyonnaise', *Revue d'histoire de l'Église de France*, Vol. 13 (1912), pp. 38–54.

108. M. L. Rostagnet-Latreille, 'Le Primat des Gaules et la politique religieuse du Grand Roi', *Cahiers d'histoire*, (1958), pp. 151–63, cited

in McManners, *Church and Society in Eighteenth Century France*, I, p. 187.

109. Nigel Aston, *The End of an Elite: The French Bishops and the Coming of the Revolution, 1786–1790* (Oxford, 1992).

110. McManners, *Church and Society in Eighteenth Century France*, I, pp. 476–88.

111. Richard Fetter, *Dom Perignon, Man and Myth* (Boulder, CO, 1989); and Émeline Wuilbercq, *L'ivresse de Dieu* (Paris, 2015).

112. Carolinne White (ed.), *The Rule of St Benedict* (London, 2008).

113. Henry Kamen, *The Escorial: Art and Power in the Renaissance* (London, 2010).

114. Wolfgang Christian Huber, *Das Stift Klosterneuburg: Wo sich Himmel und Erde begegnen* (Dössel, 2014).

115. Beales, *Prosperity and Plunder*, pp. 89–90.

116. McManners, *Church and Society in Eighteenth Century France*, I, p. 478.

117. Marc Venard, 'Popular Religion in the Eighteenth Century', in Callahan and Higgs (eds), *Church and Society in Catholic Europe*, pp. 138–54.

118. Po-Chia Hsia (ed.), *The World of Catholic Renewal*, pp. 109–10; Stefan d'Amico, *Spanish Milan: A City within the Empire, 1535–1706* (Basingstoke, 2012), pp. 93–123.

119. Celeste McNamara, *The Bishop's Burden: Reforming the Catholic Church in Early Modern Italy* (Washington, DC, 2020), pp. 174–210.

120. John Bossy, *Christianity in the West, 1400–1700* (Oxford, 1985), pp. 45–56.

121. John Bossy, 'The Social History of Confession in the Age of the Reformation', *Transactions of the Royal Historical Society*, Vol. 25 (1975), pp. 21–38.

122. For a fun history see John Cornwell, *The Dark Box: A Secret History of Confessional* (London, 2014), pp. 33–60; Wietse de Boer, *The Conquest of the Soul: Confession, Discipline and Public Order in Counter-Reformation Milan* (Leiden, 2000); Marc Venard, 'The Influence of Carlo Borromeo on the Church of France', in John M. Headley and John B. Tomaro (eds), *San Carlo Borromeo. Catholic Reform and Ecclesiastical Politics in the Second Half of the Sixteenth Century* (Washington, DC, 1988), pp. 208–27.

123. Stephen Haliczer, *Sexuality in the Confessional: A Sacrament Profaned* (Oxford, 1996); Karen E. Carter, *Scandal in the Parish: Priests and Parishioners Behaving Badly in Eighteenth-Century France* (Montreal, 2019), pp. 100–25.

124. Gérard Bouchard, *Le Village immobile: Sennely-en-Sologne au XVIIIe siècle* (Paris, 1972).

125. Ibid, p. 299.
126. Aston, *Christianity and Revolutionary Europe*, pp. 77–90.
127. William Doyle, *Jansenism* (Basingstoke, 2000), pp. 21–2; Thomas M. Lennon, *Sacrifice and Self-interest in Seventeenth Century France: Quietism, Jansenism, and Cartesianism* (Leiden, 2019), pp. 110–46.
128. J. D. Crichton, *Saints or Sinners? Jansenism and Jansenisers in Seventeenth-century France* (Dublin, 1996).
129. Pastor, *History of the Popes*, XXX, pp. 276–80.
130. Phillip Caraman, SJ, *Ignatius Loyola: A Biography of the Founder of the Jesuits* (London, 1979).
131. Luke Clossey, *Salvation and Globalization in the Early Jesuit Missions* (Cambridge, 2011).
132. Cristiano Casalini, 'Rise, Character and Development of Jesuit Education: Teaching the world', in Ines G. Županov (ed.), *The Oxford Handbook of the Jesuits* (Oxford, 2019), pp. 153–76; Vincent Duminuco, SJ, *The Jesuit Ratio Studiorum of 1599: 400th Anniversary Perspectives* (New York, 2000).
133. Luce Giard, 'The Jesuit College: A centre for knowledge, art and faith', trans. by Brian van Hove, *Studies in the Spirituality of the Jesuits*, Vol. 40, No. 1 (2008), pp. 1–31.
134. Philippe Girard, *Toussaint Louverture: A Revolutionary Life* (New York, 2016), p. 23.
135. Molesky, *This Gulf of Fire*, pp. 11–12.
136. Kirk MacGregor, *Luis de Molina: The Life and Theology of the Founder of Middle Knowledge* (Grand Rapids, MI, 2015).
137. Federico Palomo, 'Jesuit Interior Indias: Confession and mapping of the soul', in Županov (ed.), *The Oxford Handbook of the Jesuits*, pp. 105–27.
138. Cristiano Casalini, 'Discerning Skills: Psychological insight at the core of Jesuit identity', in Robert Aleksander Maryks, *Exploring Jesuit Distinctiveness: Interdisciplinary Perspectives on Ways of Proceeding within the Society of Jesus* (Leiden, 2016), pp. 189–21.
139. Gauvin Alexander Bailey, *Between Renaissance and Baroque: Jesuit Art in Rome, 1565–1610* (Toronto, 2009).
140. Andrew McKenzie-McHarg, '"A general murther, an universal slaughter": Strategies of anti-Jesuit defamation in reporting assassination in the early modern period', in Larissa Tracy (ed.), *Medieval and Early Modern Murder: Legal, Literary and Historical Contexts* (Woodenbridge, 2018), pp. 281–308; Geoffrey Cubitt, 'Conspiracism, Secrecy and Security in Restoration France: Denouncing the Jesuit menace', *Historical Social Research/Historische Sozialforschung*, Vol. 38, No. 1 (2013), pp. 107–28; Sabine Pavone, 'The History of Anti-Jesuitism: National and global dimensions', in Thomas

Banchoff and José Casanova (eds), *The Jesuits and Globalization: Historical Legacies and Contemporary Challenges* (Washington, DC, 2016), pp. 111–30.

141. Blaise Pascal, *The Provincial Letters* (London, 1982).

142. Joseph Bergin, *Church, Society and Religious Change in France, 1580–1730* (London, 2009), pp. 394–423.

143. Daniella Kostroun, *Feminism, Absolutism, and Jansenism: Louis XIV and the Port-Royal Nuns* (Cambridge, 2011).

144. Olivier Andurand and Sylvio H. De Franceschi (eds), *8 septembre 1713: le choc de l'Unigenitus* (Paris, 2014).

145. Kley, *The Religious Origins of the French Revolution*, p.142.

146. Doyle, *Jansenism*, pp. 41–4.

147. Dale van Kely, 'Catholic Conciliar reform in an age of anti-Catholic Revolution: France, Italy and the Netherlands, 1758–1801', in James Bradley and Dale Van Kley (eds), *Religion and Politics in Enlightenment Europe*, pp. 46–118; David Hudson, 'The Nouvelles Ecclésiastiques, Jansenism, and Conciliarism, 1717–1735', *Catholic Historical Review*, Vol. 70, No. 3 (1984), pp. 389–406.

148. Hélène Vu Thanh, 'The Jesuits in Asia under the Portuguese Padroado: India, China and Japan, sixteenth to seventeenth century', in Županov (ed.), *The Oxford Handbook of the Jesuits*, pp. 400–26.

149. Madeleine Foisil, Françoise de Noirfontaine and Isabelle Flandrois, 'Un Journal de polémique et de propagande les Nouvelles Ecclesiastiques', *Histoire, Économie et Société*, Vol. 10, No. 3 (1991), pp. 399–420.

150. Geert H. Janssen, *The Dutch Revolt and Catholic Exile in Reformation Europe* (Cambridge, 2014), pp. 33–58.

151. Pietro Stella, 'Roma e Utrecht: Dal dissidio alla rottura XVIII-XIX sec, appunti per una rilettura storiografica', *Rivista di storia della chiesa in Italia*, Vol. 65, No. 2 (2011), pp. 523–36.

152. Andre Queen, *Old Catholic: History, Ministry, Faith and Mission* (Lincoln, NE, 2003), p. 6.

153. Claude Beaufort Moss, *The Old Catholic Movement: Its Origins and History* (London, 1948).

154. Michael NeSmith, *The History and Beliefs of Old Catholicism and the Old Catholic Church of North America* (2nd edn, Tampa, FL, 2007).

155. Adalberto López, *The Colonial History of Paraguay: The Revolution of the Comuneros 1721–1735* (London, 1976) pp. 2–33.

156. William F. Jaenike, *Black Robes in Paraguay: The Success of the Guaraní Missions Hastened the Abolition of the Jesuits* (Minneapolis, MN, 2008), p. 82.

157. Alida C. Metcalf, *Go-betweens and the Colonization of Brazil 1500–1600* (Austin, TX, 2005), chs. 4 and 6; Shawn Michael Austin, *Colonial Kinship: Guaraní, Spaniards, and Africans in Paraguay* (Albuquerque,

NM, 2020); Rafael Chambouleyron and Karl Heinz Arenz, 'Indiens ou Noirs, libres ou esclaves, travail et métissage en Amazonie portugaise XVII et XVIII siècles', *Caravelle*, No. 107 (2016), pp. 15–29.

158. David Brion Davis, *Inhuman Bondage: The Rise and Fall of Slavery in the New World* (Oxford, 2006), p. 98; Fernando Cervantes, *Conquistadores: A New History* (London, 2020), p. 77.

159. John H. Elliott, *Empires of the Atlantic World: Britain and Spain in America 1492–1830* (London, 2006), pp. 35–48; Bethany Aram and Rafael Obando Andrade, 'Violenxa, Esclavitud y Encomieda en la Conquista de America, 1513–1542', *Historia Social*, No. 87 (2017), pp. 129–48; Timothy J. Yeager, 'Encomienda or Slavery? The Spanish crown's choice of labour organization in sixteenth-century Spanish America', *Journal of Economic History*, Vol. 55, No. 4 (1995), pp. 842–59.

160. John Francis Maxwell, *Slavery and the Catholic Church: The History of Catholic Teaching Concerning the Moral Legitimacy of the Institution of Slavery* (London, 1975), pp. 69–71.

161. Francisco Castilla Urbano, 'The Debate of Valladolid 1550–1551: Background, discussions and results of the debate between Juan Ginés de Sepúlveda and Bartolomé de las Cases', in Jörg Tellkamp (ed.), *A Companion to Early Modern Spanish Imperial Political and Social Thought* (Leiden, 2020), pp. 222–52; Daniel R. Brunstetter, 'Sepúlveda, Las Casas, and the Other: Exploring the tension between moral universalism and alterity', *Review of Politics*, Vol. 72, No. 3 (2010), pp. 409–35; Diego von Vacano, 'Las Casas and the Birth of Race', *History of Political Thought*, Vol. 33, No. 3 (2012), pp. 401–26.

162. Lawrence A. Clayton, *Bartolomé de Las Casas: A Biography* (Cambridge, 2012), pp. 347–76.

163. Teresa Meade, *History of Modern Latin America: 1800 to the Present* (2nd edn, Oxford, 2010), pp. 60–1; Mary E. Sommar, *The Slaves of the Churches: A History* (Oxford, 2020); Thomas Murphy, *Jesuit Slaveholding in Maryland, 1717–1838* (New York, 2001).

164. Marina Caffiero, *Gli Schiavi del papa, conversioni e libertà dei musulmani a Roma in età moderna* (Brescia, 2022).

165. Maxime Haubert, *La vie quotidienne des indiens et des Jésuites du Paraguay au Temps des Missions* (Paris, 1967), pp. 63–99.

166. James Schofield Saeger, 'The Mission and Historical Missions: Film and the writing of history', *The Americas*, Vol. 51, No. 3 (1995), pp. 393–415.

167. Cf. Roberto Caria, *Le reducciones dei Gesuiti in Paraguay, 1609–1768: un interpretazione teologica* (Cagliari, 2013), pp. 73–9.

168. Girolamo Imbruglia, *The Jesuit Missions of Paraguay and a Cultural History of Utopia, 1568–1789* (Leiden, 2017), pp. 15–18; Gianpaolo Romanato, *Gesuiti, Guaranì ed Emigranti nelle riduzioni del Paraguay* (Ravenna, 2008), pp. 37–41.

169. Robert H. Jackson, *Regional Conflict and Demographic Patterns on the Jesuit Missions among the Guaraní in the Seventeenth and Eighteenth Centuries* (Leiden, 2019), pp. 34–5.

170. Barbara Anne Ganson, *The Guaraní under Spanish Rule in the Río de la Plata* (Stanford, CA, 2003), pp. 26–48, 113.

171. Anon, *Storia di don Bernardino de Cárdenas Vescovo del Paraguai* (Lugano, 1760); Walter James Cummings, *The Career of Don Fray Bernardino de Cárdenas, the Bishop of Paraguay, 1640–1660* (Los Angeles, 1932).

172. Guillermo Wilde, 'Writing Rites in the Borderlands: Appropriation, mimesis and interaction between Jesuits and Indians in colonial South America', in Ines G. Županov and Pierre Antoine Fabre (eds), *The Rites Controversies in the Early Modern World* (Leiden, 2018), pp. 280–4; Renate Dürr, 'Reflection on Language in Christian Mission: The significance of communication in the linguistic concepts of José de Acosta, SJ and Antonio Ruiz de Montoya, SJ', in Antje Flüchter and Rouven Wirbser (eds), *Translating Catechisms, Translating Cultures: The Expansion of Catholicism in the Early Modern World* (Leiden, 2017), pp. 68–74.

173. Jaenike, *Black Robes in Paraguay*, pp. 160–2; and José Luis Mora Mérida, *Historia social de Paraguay, 1600–1650* (Seville, 1973), pp. 286–89.

174. Saeger, 'The Mission and Historical Missions: Film and the Writing of History', pp. 393–415.

175. Jaenike, *Black Robes in Paraguay*, pp. 104–24.

176. Haubert, *La vie quotidienne des indiens et des jésuites du Paraguay*, pp. 101–37, 192–236.

177. Girolamo Imbruglia, 'A Peculiar Idea of Empire: Missions and missionaries of the Society of Jesus in early modern history', in Marc André Bernier, Clorinda Donato, and Hans-Jürgen Lüsebrink (eds), *Jesuit Accounts of the Colonial Americas: Intercultural Transfers, Intellectual Disputes, and Textualities* (Toronto, 2014), pp. 21–49; Guillermo Wilde, 'The Missions of Paraguay, Rise, Expansion and Fall', in Ronnie Po-Chia Hsia (ed.), *A Companion to the Early Modern Catholic Global Missions* (Leiden, 2018), pp. 73–101.

178. Michel Leroy, *Le mythe jésuite: De Béranger à Michelet* (Paris, 1992), p. 277.

179. López, *The Colonial History of Paraguay*, chs. 6 and 7.

180. Denise Moura, 'Geographical Knowledge and Mineral Riches in the Struggle for Sovereignty and Possession of Southern Brazil, 1750–1755', *Portuguese Studies*, Vol. 35, No. 1 (2019), pp. 20–38.

181. Tamar Herzog, *Frontiers of Possession: Spain and Portugal in Europe and the Americas* (Cambridge, MA, 2015), pp. 20–32; David James

Owens, 'Spanish-Portuguese Territorial Rivalry in Colonial Río de la Plata', Conference of Latin Americanist Geographers Yearbook, Vol. 19 (1993), pp. 15–24.

182. Jeremy Adelman, *Sovereignty and Revolution in the Iberian Atlantic* (Princeton, NJ, 2006), pp. 141–74; Adrian Finucane, *The Temptations of Trade: Britain, Spain, and the Struggle for Empire* (Philadelphia, 2016).

183. Dale Van Kley, 'Jansenism and the International Suppression of the Jesuits', in Brown and Tackett (eds), *Enlightenment, Reawakening and Revolution 1660–1815*, p. 315.

184. Markus Friedrich, 'Jesuit Organisation and Legislation: Development and implementation of a normative framework', in Županov (ed.), *The Oxford Handbook of the Jesuits*, pp. 24–9.

185. Jaenike, *Black Robes in Paraguay*, p. 183; John Lynch, 'The Expulsion of the Jesuits and the Late Colonial Period', in Virginia Garrard-Burnett, Paul Preston and Stephen C. Doves (eds), *The Cambridge History of Religions in Latin America* (Cambridge, 2016), pp. 220–30.

186. Ibid, pp. 177–190; Maurice Ezran, *Une Colonisation Douce: Les missions du Paraguay, les lendemains qui ont chanté* (Paris, 1989), pp. 198–208.

187. Ibid, pp. 183–5; Maurice Whitehead, 'On the Road to Suppression: The Jesuits and their expulsion from the reductions of Paraguay', in Jeffrey D. Burson and Jonathan Wright (eds), *The Jesuit Suppression in Global Context* (Cambridge, 2015), pp. 83–99.

188. Ganson, *The Guaraní under Spanish Rule*, pp. 87–116.

189. Tau Golin, *A Guerra Guaranitica: Como os Exercitos De Portugal e Espanha Destruiram os Sete Povos dos Jesuitas e Indios Guaranis No Rio Grande Do Sul* (Rio Grande do Sul, 1998).

190. John Hemming, *Red Gold: The Conquest of the Brazilian Indians* (Cambridge, MA, 1978), pp. 472–3.

191. Ganson, *The Guaraní under Spanish Rule*, pp. 117–36.

192. David F. Marley, *Wars of the Americas: A Chronology of Armed Conflict in the Western Hemisphere* (2 edn, Santa Barbara, CA, 2008), pp. 441–3.

193. Christine Vogel, *Guerra aos jesuítas: a propaganda antijesuítica do Marquês de Pombal em Portugal e na Europa* (Lisbon, 2017).

194. Stephane Lenik, 'Mission Plantations, Space, and Social Control: Jesuits as planters in French Caribbean colonies and frontiers', *Journal of Social Archaeology*, Vol. 12, No. 1 (2012), pp. 51–71.

195. D. G. Thompson, 'The Fate of the French Jesuits' Creditors under the Ancien Régime', *English Historical Review*, Vol. 91, No. 359 (1976), pp. 255–77; Dorothy Gillian Thompson, 'The Lavalette Affair and the Jesuit Superiors', *French History*, Vol. 10, No. 2 (1996), pp. 206–39.

196. D. G. Thompson, 'French Jesuit Wealth on the Eve of the Eighteenth-century Suppression', *Studies in Church History*, Vol. 24 (1987), pp. 307–19.

197. Dale K. Van Kley, *The Damiens Affair and the Unraveling of the Ancien Régime 1750–1770* (Princeton, NJ, 1984), esp. 3–6.

198. For the best treatment of the Global Suppression see Dale K. Van Kley, *Reform Catholicism and the International Suppression of the Jesuits in Enlightenment Europe* (London, 2018), esp. pp. 154–5; Jonathan Wright, 'The Suppression and Restoration', in Worcester (ed.), *The Cambridge Companion to the Jesuits*, pp. 263–77.

199. D. G. Thompson, 'The Persecution of French Jesuits by the Parlement of Paris 1761–71', *Studies in Church History*, Vol. 21 (1984), pp. 289–301; Hamish M. Scott, 'Religion and Realpolitik: The Duc de Choiseul, the Bourbon Family Compact, and the Attack on the Society of Jesus, 1758–1775', *International History Review*, Vol. 25, No. 1 (2003), pp. 37–62. Emanuele Colombo and Niccolò Guasti, 'The Expulsion and Suppression in Portugal and Spain: An overview', in Jeffrey D. Burson and Jonathan Wright (eds), *The Jesuit Suppression in Global Context*, pp. 117–38.

200. Pastor, *History of the Popes*, XXXVI, pp. 155–62, 497–9.

201. Van Kley, *Reform Catholicism and the International Suppression of the Jesuits*, pp. 164–5.

202. Agostino Theiner, *Storia del Pontificato di Clemente XIV scritta sopra documenti inediti degli archivi segreti del Vaticano* (3 vols, Milan 1855), I, pp. 173–280.

203. Jean-Paul Desprat, *Le Cardinal Bernis 1715–1794: la belle ambition* (Paris, 2000), pp. 525–30; Bernard Marceau, 'Le Cardinal de Bernis et la suppression de la Compagnie de Jésus', in Gilles Montègre, *Le Cardinal de Bernis: le pouvoir de l'amitié* (Paris, 2019), pp. 454–7. Theiner, *Storia del Pontificato di Clemente XIV*, I, pp. 259–60.

204. Pastor, *History of the Popes*, XXXVIII, p. 73.

205. Pierre Charpenne, *Histoire des réunions temporaires d'Avignon et du Comtat Venaissin* (2 vols, Paris, 1886), II, pp. 69–81, 238–49.

206. Joseph Reinach (ed.), *Recueil des instructions données aux ambassadeurs et ministres de France depuis les Traités de Westphalie jusqu'à la Révolution Française, Naples et Parme* (32 vols, Paris, 1893), X, p. 110.

207. Niccolò Guasti, 'Clemente XIV e la diplomazia borbonica: La genesi del breve di soppressione della Compagnia di Gesù', in Mario Rosa e Marina Colonna (eds), *L'età di Papa Clemente XIV: Religione, politica, cultura* (Roma, 2010), pp. 29–77.

208. Van Kley, *Reform Catholicism and the International Suppression of the Jesuits*, pp. 238–40.

209. D. G. Thompson, 'General Ricci and the Suppression of the Jesuit Order in France 1760–4', *Journal of Ecclesiastical History*, Vol. 37, No. 3 (1986), pp. 426–41.
210. Ugo Bellocchi, *Tutte le encicliche e i principali documenti dei pontefici emanati dal 1740* (2 vols, Rome, 1994), II, pp. 101–15, esp. 106–7.
211. Adrian O'Connor, *In Pursuit of Politics: Education and Revolution in Eighteenth-century France* (Manchester, 2017), Ch. 2.
212. Beales, *Prosperity and Plunder*, pp. 143–68.
213. Stefania Nanni, 'Le Missioni nell'èta della crisis', in Rosa and Colonna (eds), *L'età di Papa Clemente XIV*, pp. 79–103; J. H. Arrowsmith-Brown (ed.), *Prutky's Travels in Ethiopia and Other Countries* (London, 1991), esp. pp. 153–75.

2 Reform Catholicism and Enlightenment, 1773–89

1. Marc Bredel, *Jean Meslier l'enragé: prêtre athée et révolutionnaire sous Louis XIV* (Paris, 1983), pp. 18–19.
2. Ibid, pp. 9–14.
3. 'Il souhaitait [...] que tous les grands de la terre et tous les nobles fussent pendus et étranglés avec des boïaux de prêtres'. Rudolf Charles (ed.), *Le Testament de Jean Meslier, Curé d'Étrepigny et de but en Champagne décédé en 1733*, 3 vols. (Amsterdam, 1864), I, p. 9.
4. Bredel, *Jean Meslier l'enragé*, esp. pp. 67–71.
5. Jonathan I. Israel, *Enlightenment Contested: Philosophy, Modernity and the Emancipation of Man, 1670–1752* (Oxford, 2006), p. 726; and M. Frontius, 'Une nouvelle copie du Testament de Meslier', in *Actes du colloque international d'Aix-en-Provence, 21 novembre 1964: études sur le Curé Meslier* (Paris, 1966), pp. 27–33.
6. Voltaire (ed.), *Extrait des sentiments de Jean Meslier adressés à ses paroissiens sur une parties des abus et erreurs en général et en particulier* (1762); and Ira O. Wade, 'The Manuscripts of Jean Meslier's Testament and Voltaire's Printed *Extrait*', *Modern Philology*, Vol. 30, No. 4 (1933), pp. 381–98.
7. Thomas Antoninus Degola (ed.), *Index Librorum Prohibtorum Sanctissimi Domini Nostri Gregorii XVI Pontificis Maximi* (Rome, 1847) p. 379.
8. René Pomeau, *La Religion de Voltaire* (Paris, 2000); Dennis C. Rasmussen, 'Burning Laws and Strangling Kings? Voltaire and Diderot on the perils of rationalism', *Review of Politics*, Vol. 73, No. 1 (2011), pp. 77–104; Peter Gay, *Voltaire's Politics: The Poet as Realist* (London, 1988).
9. S. J. Barnett, *The Enlightenment and Religion: The Myths of Modernity* (Manchester, 2003), pp. 11–44.

10. Steven Nadler, *A Book Forged in Hell: Spinoza's Scandalous Treatise and the Birth of the Secular Age* (Princeton, NJ, 2011), pp. 76–103.

11. Rudolf Charles (ed.), *Le Testament de Jean Meslier.*

12. Jonathan I. Israel, *Radical Enlightenment: Philosophy and the Making of Modernity 1650–1750* (Oxford, 2001); Jonathan I. Israel, *Revolutionary Ideas: An Intellectual History of the French Revolution from* The Rights of Man *to* Robespierre (Princeton, NJ, 2015); Charles Devellennes, 'Jean Meslier, the Exemplar of Radical Enlightenment Political Thought', in Steffen Ducheyne (ed.), *Reassessing the Radical Enlightenment* (London, 2017), pp. 160–177.

13. René Pomeau, 'Voltaire au collège', *Revue d'Histoire littéraire de la France*, Vol. 52, No. 1 (1952), pp. 1–10.

14. Ira O. Wade, *The Intellectual Development of Voltaire* (Princeton, NJ, 1969); Theodore Besterman, *Voltaire* (London, 1969), esp. pp. 360–73.

15. Derek Beales, 'Religion and Culture', in Tim Blanning (ed.), *The Eighteenth Century* (Short Oxford History of Europe, Oxford, 2000), pp. 131–77.

16. Magda Teter, *Sinners on Trial: Jews and Sacrilege after the Reformation* (Cambridge, MA, 2011), pp. 81–88 (quotation, p. 87).

17. Lucien Febvre, *Le Problème de l'incroyance au XVI siècle: la religion de Rabelais* (Paris, 1947); Gianluca Mori (ed.), *Early Modern Atheism from Spinoza to d'Holbach* (Oxford, 2021).

18. Alec Ryrie, *Unbelievers: An Emotional History of Doubt* (London, 2019).

19. Richard Popkin, *The History of Scepticism: From Savonarola to Bayle* (Oxford, 2003), pp. 239–53.

20. Alan Charles Kors, *D'Holbach's Coterie: An Enlightenment in Paris* (Princeton, NJ, 1976), esp. Part II; Philipp Blom, *A Wicked Company: The Forgotten Radicalism of the European Enlightenment* (London, 2012), pp. 55–74.

21. Aram Vartanian, *LaMettrie's L'Homme machine: A Study in the Origins of an Idea* (Princeton, NJ, 1960); Natania Meeker, 'The Materialist Tropes of La Mettrie', *The Eighteenth Century*, Vol. 48, No. 3, (2007), pp. 245–62.

22. Mark Curran, *Atheism, Religion and Enlightenment in Pre-revolutionary Europe* (Woodbridge, 2012).

23. David D. Bien, *The Calas Affair* (Princeton, NJ, 1960).

24. Jean-Jacques Rousseau, *Œuvres complètes: émile, éducation, morale, botanique* (Paris, 1969), Vol. IV: Émile, Book IV, pp. 555–634; letter to Christophe de Beaumont, pp. 927–1007.

25. Darrin MacMahon, *Enemies of the Enlightenment: The French Counter Enlightenment and the Making of Modernity* (Oxford, 2001), p. 38; Gerard Gengembre, *La Contre-revolution ou l'histoire désespérante* (Paris, 1989), pp. 122–31; Joseph de Maistre, *Against Rousseau* 'On the

State of Nature' *and* 'On the Sovereignty of the People' (Montreal, 1996), esp. pp. 34–9: 'man born evil as past of his essence.'

26. Bernard Plongeron, *Théologie et politique au siècle des lumières, 1770–1820* (Geneva, 1973), pp. 75–102; Victoria Kahn, 'Political Theology and Fiction in the King's Two Bodies', *Representations*, Vol. 106, No. 1 (2009), pp. 77–101.

27. Margaret C. Jacob, *Living the Enlightenment: Freemasonry and Politics in Eighteenth-century Europe* (Oxford, 1991).

28. David L. Gray (ed.), *The Catholic Catechism on Freemasonry: A Theological and Historical Treatment against Freemasonry and its Appendant Masonic Bodies* (Belleville, IL, 2020) pp. 51–98.

29. Jean-Marc Vivenza, *Saint-Martin, qui suis-je?* (Puiseaux, 2003), pp. 43–62.

30. Jean-Marc Vivenza, *Martinès de Pasqually et Jean-Baptiste Willermoz: vie, doctrine et pratiques théurgiques de l'ordre des chevaliers maçons élus coëns de l'univers* (Grenoble, 2020).

31. Candido Bona, *Le 'amicizie': società segrete e rinascita religiosa, 1770–1830* (Turin, 1962).

32. Augustin Barruel, *Mémoires pour server à l'histoire du Jacobinisme* (5 vols, Hamburg, 1797–9).

33. Michel Riquet, *Augustin de Barruel: un jésuite face aux jacobins francs-maçons, 1741–1820* (Paris, 1989), pp. 83–96.

34. Umberto Eco, *The Cemetery of Prague* (London, 2011).

35. Catherine Maire, 'L'entrée des lumières à l'index, le tournant de la double censure de l'encyclopédie en 1759', *Recherches sur Diderot et sur l'encyclopédie*, Vol. 42 (2007), pp. 108–39; Maria Pia Donato, 'Reorder and Restore', in Rebecca Messbarger, Christopher Johns and Philip Gavitt (eds), *Benedict XIV and the Enlightenment: Art, Science, and Spirituality* (Toronto, 2016), pp. 227–52; Patrizia Delpiano, *Church and Censorship in Eighteenth-Century Italy: Governing Reading in the Age of Enlightenment* (London, 2019).

36. Maurice A. Finocchiaro, 'Benedict XIV and the Galileo Affair: Liberalization or carelessness?' in Messbarger, Johns and Gavitt (eds), *Benedict XIV and the Enlightenment*, pp. 206–26. Michael Segre, 'The never-ending Galileo story', in Peter Machamer (ed.), *The Cambridge Companion to Galileo* (Cambridge, 1998), pp. 388–416.

37. Marta Cavazza, 'Benedict's Patronage of Learned Women', in Messbarger, Johns and Gavitt (eds), *Benedict XIV and the Enlightenment*, pp. 17–39.

38. Rebecca Messbarger, 'Faith, Science and the Modern Body in Anna Morandi's studies of human anatomy in wax', in Ulrich L. Lehner (ed.), *Women, Enlightenment and Catholicism: A Transnational Biographical History* (London, 2018), pp. 98–113.

39. Ulrich L. Lehner (ed.), *Women, Enlightenment and Catholicism*, chs. 10–16.
40. Robert Benson, Giles Constable, and Carol Lanham (eds), *Renaissance and Renewal in the Twelfth Century* (Cambridge, MA, 1982); Frederick Christian Bauerschmidt, *Thomas Aquinas: Faith, Reason, and Following Christ* (Oxford, 2015); and William Lane Craig, *Reasonable Faith: Christian Truth and Apologetics* (3rd edn, Wheaton, IL, 2008).
41. Gijsbert van den Brink, 'How Theology Stopped Being: *Regina Scientiarum* and how its story continues', *Studies in Christian Ethics*, Vol. 32, No. 4 (2019), pp. 442–54; Avihu Zakai, 'The Rise of Modern Science and the Decline of Theology as the Queen of the Sciences in the Early Modern Era', *Reformation and Renaissance Review*, Vol. 9, No. 2 (2007), pp. 125–51.
42. Sorkin, *The Religious Enlightenment*.
43. Dale K. Van Kley, *Reform Catholicism and the International Suppression of the Jesuits*, pp. 13–57.
44. Renée Haynes, *Philosopher King: The Humanist Pope Benedict XIV* (London, 1970), p. 41.
45. Maria Teresa Fattori, 'Lambertini's Treatises and the Cultural Project of Benedict XIV: Two sides of the same policy', in Messbarger, Johns and Gavitt (eds), *Benedict XIV and the Enlightenment*, pp. 255–75, esp. p. 259.
46. Haynes, *Philosopher King*, pp. 96–137.
47. Paola Vismara, 'Lodovico Antonio Muratori 1672–1750: Enlightenment in a tridentine mode', in Jeffrey Burson and Ulrich Lehner (eds), *Enlightenment and Catholicism in Europe: A Transnational History* (Notre Dame, IN, 2014), pp. 249–68.
48. Sergio Bertelli, *Erudizione e storia in Ludovico Antonio Muratori* (Naples, 1960).
49. Richard M. Tristano, 'History "Without Scruple": The Enlightenment confronts the Middle Ages in Renaissance Ferrara', *Medievalia et Humanistica: Studies in Medieval and Renaissance Culture*, Vol. 38 (2013), pp. 103–9; Eric W. Cochrane, 'The Settecento Medievalists', *Journal of the History of Ideas*, Vol. 19, No. 1 (1958), pp. 35–61.
50. Ulrich Lehner, *The Catholic Enlightenment: The Forgotten History of a Global Movement* (Oxford, 2016), pp. 130–5.
51. Jean-Yves Grenier, 'Temps de travail et fêtes religieuses au XVIIIe siècle', *Revue Historique*, Vol. 314, No. 3 (2012), pp. 609–41.
52. Vismara, 'Lodovico Antonio Muratori', in Burson and Lehner (eds), *Enlightenment and Catholicism in Europe*, pp. 254–7.
53. Paola Vismara, 'Il Buon Prete, nell'Italia del Sei-Settecento, bilanci e prospettive', *Rivista di storia della Chiesa in Italia*, Vol. 60, No. 1 (2006), pp. 49–67.

54. Pastor, *History of the Popes*, XXXV, pp. 1–22.
55. Paolo Quintili, 'Lumières de la France, de Paris à Rome: Voltaire, Galiani, Diderot, arts, tolérance, droits de l'homme', in Isabelle Moreau (ed.), *Les Lumières en mouvement: La circulation des idées au XVIIIe siècle* (Lyon, 2009), pp. 45–64.
56. Pastor, *History of the Popes*, XXXV, pp. 47–75.
57. Francis Hanus, *Church and State in Silesia under Frederick II, 1740–1786* (Washington, DC, 2013).
58. Gaetano Greco, *Benedetto XIV un canone per la chiesa* (Rome, 2011), pp. 126–31.
59. Pastor, *History of the Popes*, XXXV, pp. 396–410.
60. John Molony, 'Christian Social Thought, Catholic Social Teaching', in Brown and Tackett (eds), *Enlightenment, Reawakening and Revolution 1660–1815*, p. 141.
61. Greco, *Benedetto XIV*, pp. 81–112.
62. All translations in this book from Bellocchi's compendium of Papal Encyclicals are my own. Bellocchi, *Tutte le encicliche*, I, p. 311.
63. Ibid, I, pp. 313–14.
64. Magda Teter, *Blood Libel: On the Trail of an Antisemitic Myth* (Cambridge, MA, 2020), pp. 300–22.
65. Ibid, pp. 311–14.
66. Andrea Radasanu, 'Montesquieu on Moderation, Monarchy and Reform', *History of Political Thought*, Vol. 31, No. 2 (2010), pp. 283–307.
67. Catherine Larrère, 'Le pluralisme de Montesquieu ou le savoir de la liberté', *Revue de Métaphysique et de Morale*, No. 1 (2013), pp. 19–32.
68. Donato, 'Reorder and Restore', in Messbarger, Johns and Gavitt (eds), *Benedict XIV and the Enlightenment*, pp. 227–52.
69. Carole Paul, 'Benedict XIV's Enlightened patronage of the Capitoline Museum', in Messbarger, Johns and Gavitt (eds), *Benedict XIV and the Enlightenment*, pp. 341–66.
70. Christopher M. S. Johns, 'Papal Diplomacy and the Catholic Enlightenment: Benedict XIV's Caffeaus in the Quirinal Gardens', in Messbarger, Johns and Gavitt (eds), *Benedict XIV and the Enlightenment*, pp. 367–87.
71. J. G. Pickwell, 'Improbable Legends surrounding Sir Clowdisley Shovell', *Mariner's Mirror*, Vol. 59, No. 2 (1973), pp. 221–3; and C. V. Sölver and G. J. Marcus, 'Dead Reckoning and the Oceans Voyages of the Past', *Mariner's Mirror*, Vol. 44, No. 1 (1958), pp. 18–34.
72. Dava Sobel, *Longitude: The True Story of a Lone Genius Who Solved the Greatest Scientific Problem of His Time* (London, 2005); Jane Squire, *A Proposal for Discovering Our Longitude* (London, 1742).
73. Paula Findlen, 'The Pope and the Englishwoman: Benedict XIV, Jane Squire, the Bologna Academy and the problem of longitude',

in Messbarger, Johns and Gavitt (eds), *Benedict XIV and the Enlightenment*, pp. 40–73.

74. Jacques Parguez, *La bulle unigenitus et le jansénisme politique* (Paris, 1936); and Catherine Maire, *L'église dans l'état: Politique et religion dans la France des lumières* (Paris, 2019), pp. 175–232.

75. Philippe Godard, *La querelle des refus de sacrements, 1730–1765* (Paris, 1937); Dale K. van Key, *The Damiens Affair and the Unravelling of the Ancien Régime, 1750–1770* (Princeton, NJ, 1984), pp. 104–27; Jeffrey Merrick, 'Conscience and Citizenship in Eighteenth-Century France,' *Eighteenth-Century Studies*, Vol. 21, No. 1 (1987), pp. 48–70.

76. Julian Swann, *Politics and the Parlement of Paris, Louis XV, 1754–1774* (Cambridge, 1995), pp. 87–121; Julian Swann, 'Disgrace without Dishonour: The internal exile of french magistrates in the eighteenth century', *Past and Present*, Vol. 195, No. 1, (2007), pp. 87–126.

77. van Key, *The Damiens Affair*, pp. 142–5.

78. Lehner, *The Catholic Enlightenment*.

79. Dale van Kely, 'Catholic Conciliar Reform in an Age of Anti-Catholic Revolution: France, Italy and the Netherlands, 1758–1801', in James Bradley and Dale Van Kley (eds), *Religion and Politics in Enlightenment Europe*, pp. 46–118.

80. Ibid.

81. Hamish Scott (ed.), *Enlightened Absolutism: Reform and Reformers in Later Eighteenth-Century Europe* (Basingstoke, 1990).

82. Timothy Blanning, *Frederick the Great, King of Prussia* (London, 2016); Simon Dixon, *Catherine the Great* (London, 2010).

83. Jules Gendry, *Pie VI, sa vie, son pontificat (1717–1799)* (2 vols, Paris, 1906), I, pp. 22–3.

84. Pastor, *History of the Popes*, XXXIX, pp. 1–22.

85. Gendry, *Pie VI*, I, pp. xii–xx; Jeffrey Collins, *Papacy and Politics in Eighteenth-century Rome: Pius VI and the Arts* (Cambridge, 2004), pp. 12–14.

86. Ibid, pp. 109–20.

87. Frank M. Snowden, *The Conquest of Malaria, Italy 1900–1962* (London, 2006), ch. 6; Denis Mack Smith, *Mussolini* (London, 1981), pp. 116–23.

88. Christopher M. S. Johns, *Papal Art and Cultural Politics: Rome in the Age of Clement XI* (Cambridge, 1993).

89. Jeffrey Collins, 'Museo Pio-Clementino, Vatican City: Ideology and aesthetic in the age of the grand tour,' in Carole Paul (ed.), *The First Modern Museums of Art: The Birth of an Institution in 18th- and early-19th-Century Europe* (Los Angeles, 2012), pp. 113–43.

90. Collins, *Papacy and Politics in Eighteenth-century Rome*, pp. 132–92.

91. William Tronzo, *St. Peter's in the Vatican* (Cambridge, 2005), p. 109.

92. Collins, *Papacy and Politics in Eighteenth-century Rome*, pp. 87–131.

93. Jeffrey Collins, 'Obelisk Designs by Giovanni Stern,' *Burlington Magazine*, Vol. 142, No. 1163 (2000), pp. 90–100.

94. Franco Venturi, *The End of the Old Regime in Europe, 1776–1789*, Part II: *Republican Patriotism and the Empire of the East* (Princeton, NJ, 1991), pp. 664–70.

95. Robert Nisbet Bain, *Gustavus III and his Contemporaries 1746–1792* (2 vols, London, 1894), I, pp. 267–71.

96. Jeffrey Collins, 'Marshaling the Muses: The Vatican's Pio-Clementino museum and the Greek ideal', *Studies in the Decorative Arts*, Vol. 16, No. 1 (2009), pp. 35–63.

97. Rudolf M. Bisanz, 'The Birth of a Myth: Tischbein's "Goethe in the Roman Campagna"', *Monatshefte*, Vol. 80, No. 2 (1988), pp. 187–99.

98. Alessandro Franchi-Verney, *L'Académie de France à Rome, 1666–1903* (Paris, 1904); François Fossier, *Le séjour des grands prix de Rome à lailla Médicis* (Paris, 2018).

99. Antonio Menniti Ippolito, *Il tramonto della curia nepotista, papi, nipoti e burocrazia curiale tra XVI e XVII secolo* (Rome, 1999).

100. Niels Grüne and Tom Tölle, 'Corruption in the Ancien Régime', *Journal of Modern European History*, Vol. 11, No. 1, (2013), pp. 31–51.

101. Gendry, *Pie VI*, I, p. 160.

102. Pastor, *History of the Popes*, XXXIX, p. 40.

103. Gendry, *Pie VI*, I, pp. 164–9.

104. Ibid.

105. Carlo Pietrangeli and Armando Ravaglioli (eds), *Palazzo Braschi e il suo ambiente* (Rome, 1967); Emiliana Ricci and Palazzo Braschi, *Storia ed architettura di un edificio settecentesco* (Rome, 1989).

106. Franco Venturi, *Italy and the Enlightenment: Studies in a Cosmopolitan Century* (New York, 1972), pp. 225–64.

107. Pastor, *History of the Popes*, XXXIX, pp. 184–6.

108. Burson and Wright (eds), *The Jesuit Suppression in Global Context*, chs. 10 and 13; Marek Inglot, *Compagnia di Gesù nell'impero russo 1772–1820 e la sua parte nella restaurazione generale della compagnia* (Rome, 1997).

109. Jerzy Lukowski, *The Partitions of Poland 1772, 1793, 1795* (New York, 1999), pp. 52–81.

110. Paweł Zając, 'Le Impressioni sulla Polonia nella corrispondenza del Nunzio Apostolico Giocanni Andrea Archetti 1775–1784', *Archivum Historiae Pontificiae*, Vol. 49 (2011), pp. 91–121.

111. T. J. Shahan, 'Catharine II and the Holy See, 1772–1796', *American Catholic Quarterly Review 30* (1905), pp. 1–27.

112. Pastor, *History of the Popes*, XXXIX, pp. 276–8.

113. Giuseppe Galasso (ed.), *Il Regno di Napoli: il mezzogiorno angioino e aragonese 1266–1494* (Storia d'Italia, Volume XV/1, Turin, 1992);

Norman Housely, *The Italian Crusades: The Papal-Angevin Alliance and the Crusades Against Christian Lay Powers, 1254–1343* (Oxford, 1982).

114. Girolamo Lioy, 'L'abolizione dell'omaggio della Chinea', *Archivio Storico per le Provincie Napoletane*, Vol. VII (1882), pp. 263–92, 497–530, 713–75.

115. Rosa Mincuzzi, *Bernardo Tanucci, ministro di Ferdinando di Borbone, 1759–1776* (Bari, 1967), pp. 43–54.

116. Francesco Renda, *L'inquisizione in Sicilia, i fatti, le persone* (Palermo, 1997), p. 186.

117. Giuseppe Galasso (ed.), *Il regno di Napoli: il mezzogiorno borbonico e napoleonico 1734–1815* (Storia d'Italia, Volume XV/4, Turin, 2007), pp. 522–5.

118. Gaetano Cozzi, Michael Knapton and Giovanni Scarabello, *La repubblica di Venezia nell'atà moderna dal 1517 alla fine della repubblica* (Storia d'Italia, Volume XII/2, Turin, 1992), pp. 572–3; Raffaele Belvederi, *Il papato di fronte alla rivoluzione e alle conseguenze del congresso di Vienna, 1775–1846* (Bologna 1965), p. 37.

119. Jenifer Roberts, *The Madness of Queen Maria: The Remarkable Life of Maria I of Portugal* (Chippenham, 2009), esp. pp. 57–76.

120. Rosa Mincuzzi, *Lettere di Bernardo Tanucci a Carlo III di Borbone, 1759–1776* (Naples, 1969); Carlo Knight, 'Politics and Royal Patronage in the Neapolitan Regency: The correspondence of Charles III and the prince of San Nicandro, 1759–1767', *Studies in the History of Art*, Vol. 79 (2013), pp. 73–88.

121. John Lynch, *Bourbon Spain, 1700–1808* (Oxford, 1993), pp. 269–80; William J. Callahan, 'The Spanish Church', in Callahan and Higgs (eds), *Church and Society in Catholic Europe*, pp. 34–50.

122. Lynch, *Bourbon Spain*, p. 209.

123. William J. Callahan, *Church, Politics and Society in Spain, 1750–1874* (Cambridge, MA, 1984), pp. 52–72.

124. Andoni Artola Rendo, *De Madrid a Roma: La fidelidad del eiscopado en España, 1760–1833* (Gijón, 2013), pp. 235–9; Émile Appolis, *Les Jansénistes espagnoles* (Bordeaux, 1966), pp. 118–44.

125. Brian R. Hamnett, 'The Appropriation of Mexican Church Wealth by the Spanish Bourbon Government: The Consolidación de Vales Reales, 1805–1809', *Journal of Latin American Studies*, Vol. 1, No. 2 (1969), pp. 85–113.

126. Barbara Stollberg-Rilinger, *Maria Theresa: The Habsburg Empress in Her Time* (Princeton, NJ, 2022).

127. Elisabeth Badinter, *Le Pouvoir au féminin: Marie-Thérèse d'Autrice 1717–1780* (Paris, 2016), pp. 87–133.

128. Barbara Stollberg-Rilinger, *Maria Theresa* (Princeton, NJ, 2021).

129. Derek Beales, *Enlightenment and Reform in Eighteenth-century Europe* (London, 2005), pp. 207–26.

130. Harm Klueting, 'The Catholic Enlightenment in Austria or the Habsburg Lands', in Printy and Lehner (eds), *A Companion to the Catholic Enlightenment*, pp. 127–65, esp. 138.

131. Robert Bireley, *The Jesuits and the Thirty Years War: Kings, Courts, and Confessors* (Cambridge, 2003).

132. Beales, *Enlightenment and Reform*, pp. 223–4.

133. Derek Beales, *Joseph II*, II, pp. 13, 49–57.

134. John Hardman, *Marie Antoinette: The Making of a French Queen* (London, 2019), pp. 46–60.

135. Derek Beales, *Joseph II*, I, pp. 43–68.

136. Ibid, pp. 66, 67–84.

137. Martin Scheutz, 'Demand and Charitable Supply: Poverty and poor relief in Austria in the 18th and 19th centuries', in Ole Peter Grell (ed.), *Health Care and Poor Relief in 18th and 19th Century Southern Europe* (London, 2017), pp. 52–95; and P. P. Bernard, 'The Limits of Absolutism: Joseph II and the Allgemeines Krankenhaus', *Eighteenth-Century Studies*, Vol. 9 (1976), pp. 208–15.

138. Blanning, *Joseph II*, p. 63.

139. Cölestin Wolfsgruber, *Christoph Anton Kardinal Migazzi: Fürsterzbischof von Wien* (Saulgau, 1890).

140. Elisabeth Garms-Cornidesa, 'Giuseppismo e Riformismo Cattolico: Problemi sempre aperti nella storiografia Austrica', *Quaderni Storici*, Vol. 5, No. 15 (1970), pp. 759–72; P. G. M. Dickson, 'Joseph II's Reshaping of the Austrian Church', *Historical Journal*, Vol. 36, No. 1 (1993), pp. 89–114.

141. Beales, *Joseph II*, II, pp. 177–186, 209.

142. Ibid, II, pp. 196–208.

143. Pastor, *History of the Popes*, XXXIX, pp. 442–5.

144. Beales, *Joseph II*, II, pp. 215–17.

145. Elisabeth Kovács, 'Pius VI, bei Joseph II, zu gast: Neue aspekte zur reise des Papstes nsch Wien im Jahr 1782', *Archivum Historiae Pontificiae*, Vol. 17 (1979), pp. 241–87.

146. Beales, *Joseph II*, II, pp. 218–19.

147. Ibid, p.219.

148. Beales, *Joseph II*, II, p. 220.

149. Elisabeth Kovács, 'Der Besuch Papst Pius VI, in Wien im Spiegel Jisephinischer Broschüren', *Archivum Historiae Pontificiae*, Vol. 20 (1982), pp. 163–217.

150. Sorkin, *The Religious Enlightenment*, pp. 217–28, 241–7.

151. Ibid, pp. 228–37.

152. Kovács, 'Der Besuch Papst Pius VI'.

153. Beales, *Joseph II*, II, pp. 226–7.
154. Renate Leggatt-Hofer and Reinhold Sahl (eds), *The Vienna Hofburg: Six Centuries as a European Centre of Power* (Vienna, 2018).
155. Max Braubach, *Maria Theresias jüngster Sohn Max Franz, letzter Kurfürst von Köln und Fürstbischof von Münster* (München, 1961) p.186.
156. Pastor, *History of the Popes*, XXXIX, p. 452.
157. Beales, *Joseph II*, II, p. 229.
158. Charles O'Brien, 'Ideas of Religious Toleration at the Time of Joseph II: A study of the Enlightenment among Catholics in Austria', *Transactions of the American Philosophical Society*, Vol. 59, No. 7 (1969), pp. 1–80.
159. Gendry, *Pie VI*, I, pp. 269–73.
160. Federico Palomo, 'Jesuit Interior Indias: Confession and mapping of the soul', in Ines G. Županov (ed.), *The Oxford Handbook of the Jesuits* (Oxford, 2019), pp. 105–27.
161. Mary Heimann, 'Catholic Revivalism in Worship and Devotion', in Gilley and Stanley (eds), *World Christianities*, pp. 70–83.
162. Beales, *Joseph II*, II, pp. 233, 234.
163. Pastor, *History of the Popes*, XXXIX, pp. 472–4.
164. Beales, *Joseph II*, II, pp. 235–6.
165. Ibid, pp. 237–8.
166. Collins, *Papacy and Politics in Eighteenth Century Rome*, p. 52.
167. Beales, *Prosperity and Plunder*, pp. 179–86, 192–209.
168. Blanning, *Joseph II*, p. 96.
169. Beales, *Joseph II*, II, pp. 271–306, 320–32.
170. Ritchie Robertson, 'The Reform of Catholic Festival Culture in Eighteenth-Century Austria: A clash of mentalities', *Austrian Studies*, Vol. 25 (2017), pp. 25–41.
171. Jane C. Judge, *The United States of Belgium: The Story of the First Belgian Revolution* (Leuven, 2018), pp. 65–77.
172. Marc Venard, 'Popular Religion in the Eighteenth Century', in Callahan and Higgs (eds), *Church and Society in Catholic Europe*, pp. 138–55.
173. Adriano Prosperi, *Crime and Forgiveness: Christianizing Execution in Medieval Europe* (Cambridge, 2020), pp. 13–19, 501–2.
174. Charles A. Bolton, *Church Reform in 18th Century Italy: The Synod of Pistoia 1786* (The Hague, 1969), pp. 1–8.
175. Furio Diaz, Luigi Mascilli Migliorini and Carlo Mangio (eds), *Il Granducato di Toscana, i Lorena dalla Reggenza agli anni rivoluzionari* (Storia d'Italia Vol.XIII/2, Turin, 1997), pp. 370–85.
176. Shaun Blanchard, *The Synod of Pistoia and Vatican II: Jansenism and the Struggle for Catholic Reform* (Oxford, 2020), pp. 134–96.
177. Prospero Lambertini (Benedict XIV), *Synodo diœcesana* (2 vols, Rome, 1742).

178. Scipione de Ricci, *Atti e decreti del concilio diocesano di Pistoia dell'anno 1786* (Pistoia, 1786); Bolton, *Church Reform in 18th Century Italy*, pp. 109–12.

179. Blanchard, *The Synod of Pistoia and Vatican II*, pp. 207–10.

180. Bolton, *Church Reform in 18th Century Italy*, pp. 115–21.

181. Bellocchi, *Tutte le encicliche*, II, pp. 272–304.

182. Blanchard, *The Synod of Pistoia and Vatican II*, pp. 259–302.

183. Gerhard Benecke, 'The German Reichskirche', in Callahan and Higgs (eds), *Church and Society in Catholic Europe*, pp. 77–87.

184. Jacques Küntziger, *Fébronius et le fébronianisme: étude historique sur le mouvement réformateur provoqué dans l'église catholique au XVIIIème siècle* (Brussels, 1891), pp. 13, 24.

185. Justinus Febronius, *de statu ecclesiae et legitima potestate romani pontificis liber singularis* (4 vols, Frankfurt and Leipzig, 1773).

186. Gendry, *Pie VI*, I, pp. 187–207.

187. Pastor, *History of the Popes*, XL, pp. 28–42.

188. J. F. Maclear (ed.), *Church and State in the Modern Age: A Documentary History* (Oxford, 1995), p. 29.

189. Beales, *Joseph II*, II, pp. 422–3.

190. Joachim Whaley, *Germany and the Holy Roman Empire*, Vol. II: *The Peace of Westphalia to the Dissolution of the Reich, 1648–1806* (2 vols, Oxford, 2013), p. 423.

191. Van Kley, *Reform Catholicism and the International Suppression of the Jesuits*, pp. 13–57, 287–93; Burson and Lehner (eds), *Enlightenment and Catholicism*, pp. 1–37; Lehner, *The Catholic Enlightenment*, pp. 1–13; Lehner and Printy (eds), *A Companion to the Catholic Enlightenment*.

192. Ulrich Lehner, *On the Road to Vatican II, German Catholic Enlightenment and Reform of the Church* (Minneapolis, MN, 2016), pp. 143–70; Robert Duchon, 'De Bossuet a Febronius', *Revue d'histoire ecclésiastique*, Vol. 65, (1970), pp. 375–422; Aimé Georges Martimort, *Le Gallicanisme* (Paris, 1973).

3 Into the Maelstrom: the French Revolution, 1789–99

1. Philip Mansel, *King of the World: The Life of Louis XIV* (London, 2019), pp. 87–8.

2. Gosselin Lenotre, *La Guillotine pendant la révolution* (Paris, 2019); Paul Friedland, *Seeing Justice Done: The Age of Spectacular Capital Punishment in France* (Oxford, 2012), pp. 268–9.

3. Bruno de Jésus-Marie, *Le Sang du Carmel* (Paris, 1992), p. 475.

4. Gaspard Jauffret, *Mémoires pour server à l'histoire de la religion à la fin du XVIIIe siècle* (2 vols, Paris, 1803), II, pp. 351–72.

5. William Bush, *Apaiser la terreur: la véritable histoire des carmélites de Compiègne* (Paris, 2001), pp. 239–67.

6. Jésus-Marie, *Le Sang du Carmel*, pp. 476–7.

7. Bush, *Apaiser la terreur*, pp. 267–70.

8. Colin Jones, *The Fall of Robespierre: 24 Hours in Revolutionary Paris* (Oxford, 2021).

9. Françoise-Geneviève Philippe, *Histoire des religieuses carmélites de Compiègne, conduites à l'échafaud le 17 juillet 1794: ouvrage posthume de Sœur Marie de l'Incarnation* (Sens, 1836).

10. Maurice Larkin, *Church and State after the Dreyfus Affair: The Separation Issue in France* (London, 1974).

11. Roland G. Bonnel, 'Révolution et sainteté dans les Dialogues des Carmélites', *French Review*, Vol. 64, No. 5 (1991), pp. 784–93; Roger Nichols, *Poulenc: A Biography* (London, 2020), pp. 215–48.

12. Van Kley, *Reform Catholicism and the International Suppression of the Jesuits*.

13. Van Kley, *Religious Origins of the French Revolution*, pp. 249–302.

14. McManners, *Church and Society in Eighteenth Century France*, I, pp. 571–614.

15. Peter M. Jones, *Reform and Revolution in France: The Politics of Transitions 1774–1791* (Cambridge, 1995), pp. 107–38.

16. William Doyle, *Aristocracy and its Enemies in the Age of Revolution* (Oxford, 2009); Michael P. Fitzsimmons, *From Artisan to Worker: Guilds, the French State, and the Organization of Labour, 1776–1821* (Cambridge, 2010); George T. Matthews, *The Royal General Farms in Eighteenth Century France* (New York, 1958).

17. James F. Bosher, *French Finances 1770–1795: From Business to Bureaucracy* (Cambridge, 1970), pp. 166–182.

18. McManners, *The French Revolution and the Church*, p. 1.

19. J. Michael Hayden, *France and the Estates General of 1614* (Cambridge, 1974).

20. Gilbert Shapiro and John Markoff, *Revolutionary Demands: A Content Analysis of the 'Cahiers de Doléances' of 1789* (Stanford, CA, 1998).

21. John Markoff, *The Abolition of Feudalism: Peasants, Lords, and Legislators in the French Revolution* (Pennsylvania, 1991).

22. Ruth F. Necheles, 'The Curés in the Estates General of 1789', *Journal of Modern History*, Vol. 46, No. 3 (1974), pp. 425–44; Maurice Hutt, 'The Role of the Curés in the Estates General of 1789', *Journal of Ecclesiastical History*, Vol. 6, No. 2, (1955), pp. 190–220.

23. Claude Lauriol, 'L'Édit de 1787 et la tolérance à la fin de l'ancien régime', *Bulletin de la Société de l'Histoire du Protestantisme Français*, Vol. 134 (1988), pp. 425–33.

24. McManners, *Church and Society, in Eighteenth Century France*, II, 726–32.
25. Timothy Tackett, *Becoming a Revolutionary: The Deputies of the French National Assembly and the Emergence of a Revolutionary Culture 1789–1790* (Princeton, NJ, 1997), pp. 24–7.
26. Yann Fauchois, 'Les Jansénistes et la constitution civile du clergé', in Cathérine Maire (ed.), *Jansénisme et révolution* (Paris 1990), pp. 195–207.
27. Edna Hindie Lemay, *La Vie quotidienne des députés aux états généraux 1789* (Paris, 1987), p. 18.
28. Philippe Salvadori, *La Chasse sous l'ancien régime* (Paris, 1996), pp. 196, 228.
29. Philip Mansel, *Dressed to Rule: Royal and Court Costume from Louis XIV to Elizabeth II* (2005), pp. 65–7.
30. Robert H. Blackman, *1789: The French Revolution Begins* (Cambridge, 2019), pp. 76–83.
31. Jean-Denis Bredin, *Sieyès: la clé de la revolution française* (Paris, 1988).
32. Emmanuel Joseph Sieyès, *Qu'est-ce que le tiers-état?* (Paris, 1789).
33. William H. Sewell, *A Rhetoric of Bourgeois Revolution: The Abbé Sieyes and* What is the Third Estate? (London, 1994), pp. 66–108.
34. Michael Sonenscher, *Political Writings: Including the Debate Between Sieyes and Tom Paine in 1791* (London, 2003), pp. 136–42 and 151–4.
35. Sewell, *A Rhetoric of Bourgeois Revolution*, pp. 146–9.
36. Munro Price, *The Fall of the French Monarchy: Louis XVI, Marie Antoinette and the Baron de Breteuil* (Basingstoke, 2002), pp. 64–7.
37. Michel de Dreux-Brézé, *Les Dreux-Brézé* (Paris, 1994), pp. 326–34.
38. John Hardman, *The Life of Louis XVI* (London, 2016), pp. 318–20.
39. Keith Michael Baker, 'The Idea of a Declaration of Right', in Dale Van Kley (ed.), *The French Idea of Freedom: The Old Regime and the Declaration of Rights of 1789* (Stanford, CA, 1994), pp. 154–97.
40. Munro Price, '"The Ministry of the Hundred Hours": A Reappraisal', *French History*, Vol. 4, No. 3 (1990), pp. 317–39.
41. Jean-Christian Petitfils, *La Bastille: mystères et secrets d'une prison d'etat* (Paris, 2016).
42. Simon Schama, *Citizens: A Chronicle of the French Revolution* (London, 1989), p. 407.
43. Jacques Godechot, *The Taking of the Bastille, July 14, 1789* (London, 1970), pp. 221–7.
44. Jean Chagniot, 'Une panique: Les Gardes Français à Dettingen 27 juin 1743', *Revue d'histoire moderne et contemporaine*, Vol. 977), pp. 78–95.
45. Samuel F. Scott, *The Response of the Royal Army to the French Revolution: The Role and Development of the Line Army 1787–1793* (Oxford, 1978), pp. 59–80.

46. Ghislain de Diesbach, *Histoire de l'émigration 1789–1814* (Paris, 1984), pp. 59–75 ; José Cabanis, *Charles X roi ultra* (Paris, 1972), pp. 41–9.

47. William Doyle, *The Oxford History of the French Revolution* (2nd edn, Oxford, 2002), p. 112.

48. Georges Lefebvre, *Great Fear of 1789: Rural Panic in Revolutionary France* (London, 1989).

49. Lynn Hunt, *Inventing Human Rights: A History* (New York, 2008), pp. 113–45.

50. *Declaration of the Rights of Man* (1789), online at https://avalon.law. yale.edu/18th_century/rightsof.asp [accessed 2 March 2021].

51. Michael Goldfarb, *Emancipation: How Liberating Europe's Jews from the Ghetto Led to Revolution and Renaissance* (New York, 2009), pp. 62–90.

52. AP 8:322.

53. Charles Walton, *Policing Public Opinion in the French Revolution: The Culture of Calumny and the Problem of Free Speech* (Oxford, 2009), pp. 86–93.

54. Ibid; Michael P. Fitzsimmons, *The Night the Old Regime Ended: August 4, 1789 and the French Revolution* (Pennsylvania, 2003), esp. pp. 14–23.

55. McManners, *Church and Society in Eighteenth Century France*, I, p. 122.

56. Sewell, *A Rhetoric of Bourgeois Revolution*, p. 136.

57. Paul Chopelin, '"Pères du peuples" ou "aristocrates calotins"? La fin des chanoines-comtes de Lyon 1789–1791', in Philippe Bourdin (ed.), *Les Noblesses françaises et dans l'Europe de la révolution* (Rennes, 2010), pp. 311–32.

58. Alyssa Goldstein Sepinwall, *The Abbé Gregoire and the French Revolution: The Making of Modern Universalism* (Los Angeles, CA, 2005); Jules Charrier, *Claude Fauchet, Évêque constitutionnel du Calvados, député à l'assemblée législative et à la convention 1744–1793* (2 vols, Paris, 1909).

59. Nigel Aston, *End of an Élite*, p. 221.

60. Xavier Raduget, 'La carrière politique de l'abbé Maury de 1786 à 1791', *Revue d'histoire de l'église de France*, Vol. 17 (1912), pp. 505–15.

61. Doyle, *Oxford History of the French Revolution*, pp. 121–3.

62. Peter M. Jones, *The Peasantry in the French Revolution* (Cambridge, 1988), pp. 86–123.

63. McManners, *The French Revolution and the Church*, p.27.

64. Emmanuel de Waresquiel, *Talleyrand le prince immobile* (Paris, 2003), p. 65.

65. McManners, *Church and Society, in Eighteenth Century France*, I, pp. 97–122.

66. Alain Blondy, *L'Ordre de Malte au XVIIIième siècle des dernières splendeurs à la ruine* (Paris, 2002), pp. 286–8.

67. Tackett, *Becoming a Revolutionary*, p. 234.
68. André Latreille, *L'Église catholique et la révolution française* (2 vols, Paris, 1946), I, pp. 80–81.
69. Peter V. Conroy, Jr, 'Gender Issues in Diderot's *La Religieuse*', *Diderot Studies*, Vol. 24 (1991), pp. 47–66.
70. McManners, *The French Revolution and the Church*, p. 32.
71. Gwenaël Murphy, *L'affaire Rose Lauray, religieuse poitevine* (La Crèche, 2001), pp. 100–42, 22–30.
72. Ibid, pp. 144–68, pp. 210, 212–13.
73. Ibid, pp. 84–96.
74. Marsden, Kathryn, 'Married Nuns in the French Revolution: The sexual revolution of the 1790s' (unpublished PhD thesis, University of California, Irvine, 2014).
75. Gwenaël Murphy, *Les Religieuses dans la révolution française* (Paris, 2005), pp. 13–24.
76. Ibid, pp. 91–111.
77. Jean Leflon, *La Crise révolutionnaire 1789–1846* (Histoire de l'église, Vol. XX) (Paris, 1949), pp. 55–6.
78. Joseph Vicomte de Bonald, *François Chabot, membre de la convention 1756–1794* (Paris, 1908), pp. 6–29.
79. Marie de la Trinité Kervingant, *A Monastic Odyssey* (Kalamazoo, MN, 1999), pp. 37–64; Jean Boussoulade, *Moniales et hospitalières dans la tourmente révolutionnaire* (Paris, 1962).
80. Bruno Marguery, *La Destruction de l'Abbaye de Cluny, 1789–1823* (Cluny, 1984).
81. Hugh Willmott, *The Dissolution of the Monasteries in England and Wales* (Sheffield, 2020).
82. AP, 12:702–03.
83. Joseph F. Byrnes, *Priests of the French Revolution: Saints and Renegades in a New Politics Era* (Pennsylvania, 2014), pp. 40–2.
84. John H. Elliott, 'A Europe of Composite Monarchies', *Past and Present*, No. 137, No. 1 (1992), pp. 48–71.
85. Marie-Vic Ozouf-Marignier, *La Formation des départements: la représentation du territoire français à la fin du XVIIIe siècle* (Paris, 1989).
86. McManners, *Church and Society in Eighteenth Century France*, I, pp. 407–8; Joseph Bergin, *Crown, Church and Episcopate under Louis XIV* (London, 2004), pp. 25–7.
87. McManners, *Church and Society in Eighteenth Century France*, I, pp. 334–45.
88. Bernard Barbiche and Ségolène de Dainville-Barbiche, 'Le Schisme constitutionnel', *Archivum Historiae Pontificiae*, Vol. 46 (2008), pp. 107–30.

89. McManners, *The French Revolution and the Church*, pp. 47–60.
90. Malcolm Crook, 'Citizen Bishops: Episcopal elections in the French Revolution', *Historical Journal*, Vol. 43, No. 4 (2000), pp. 955–76.
91. Eugène Lavaquery, *Le Cardinal de Boisgelin, 1732–1804* (2 vols, Paris, 1920), I, pp. 81–2.
92. Hardman, *The Life of Louis XVI*, pp. 364–9.
93. Giuseppe Pignatelli, 'Dugnani, Antonio', in *Treccani dizionario biografico degli Italiani*, online at www.treccani.it/enciclopedia/ antonio-dugnani_(Dizionario-Biografico)/ [accessed 2 March 2021].
94. Gérard Pelletier, *Rome et la révolution française: la théologie politique et la politique du Saint-Siège devant la révolution française, 1789–1799* (Rome, 2013), pp. 118–21.
95. Joëlle Rollo-Koster, *Avignon and Its Papacy, 1309–1417: Popes, Institutions, and Society* (New York, 2015).
96. Edward Kolla, *Sovereignty, International Law, and the French Revolution* (Cambridge, 2017), pp. 90–1.
97. Pelletier Gérard '24 septembre 1790: la constitution civile du clergé devant la curie romaine', *Mélanges de l'école française de Rome*, Vol. 104, No. 2 (1992), pp. 695–735.
98. Ibid.
99. Pelletier, *Rome et la révolution française*, pp. 145–8.
100. Philippe Bourdin, 'Collégiales et chapitres cathédraux au crible de l'opinion et de la révolution', *Annales historiques de la révolution française*, No. 331 (2003), pp. 29–55.
101. Ibid, pp. 157–161.
102. Ibid, pp. 151–157, 161.
103. Bergin, *Crown, Church and Episcopate under Louis XIV*, pp. 232–60.
104. McManners, *The French Revolution and the Church*, p. 38.
105. Virginie Martin, 'Pédire et prévenir la fin d'un monde, le Cardinal Bernis face à la révolution', in Gilles Montègre (ed.), *Le Cardinal de Bernis, le pouvoir de l'amitié* (Paris, 2019), pp. 625–9.
106. McManners, *The French Revolution and the Church*, p. 47.
107. Jean-François Brière, 'Abbé Grégoire and Haitian Independence', *Research in African Literatures*, Vol. 35, No. 2 (2004), pp. 34–43.
108. Aston, *End of an Élite*, pp. 245–6.
109. Edward A. Allen, 'The "Patriot" Curés of 1789 and the "Constitutional" Curés of 1791: A comparison', *Church History*, Vol. 54, No. 4 (1985), pp. 473–81.
110. Paul Chopelin, 'Le Cardinal de Bernis et l'accueil des tantes de Louis XVI à Rome', in Montègre, *Le Cardinal de Bernis*, pp. 690–2.
111. Timothy Tackett, *Religion, Revolution, and Regional Culture in Eighteenth-Century France: The Ecclesiastical Oath of 1791* (Princeton, NJ, 1986), pp. 235–8, 292; David C. Miller, 'Armand-Gaston Camus and

the Civil Constitution of the Clergy', *Catholic Historical Review*, Vol. 76, No. 3 (1990), pp. 481–505.

112. Ugo Bellocchi, *Tutte le encicliche*, II, pp. 150–82.

113. Ibid, pp. 183–96.

114. Waresquiel, *Talleyrand*, pp. 142–4.

115. Bellocchi, *Tutte le Encicliche*, II, p. 195.

116. Mita Choudhury, *Convents and Nuns in Eighteenth-century French Politics and Culture* (Ithaca, NY, 2004), p. 172.

117. Yann Fauchois, 'La difficulté d'être libre, les droits de l'homme, l'eglise catholique et l'assemblée constituante, 1789–1791', *Revue d'histoire moderne and contemporaine*, Vol. 48, No. 1 (2001), pp. 71–101 esp. p. 95.

118. Ambrogio A. Caiani, *Louis XVI and the French Revolution 1789–1792* (Cambridge, 2012), p. 215.

119. Jean Gabriel Peltier, *Dernier Tableau de Paris ou récit historique de la Révolution du 10 Août 1792, des causes qui l'ont produit, des evénements qui l'ont précédée, et des crimes qui l'ont suivie* (2 vols, London, 1794), II, p. 244.

120. Hardman, *The Life of Louis XVI*, pp. 366–7.

121. Caiani, *Louis XVI and the French Revolution*, pp. 192–220.

122. Timothy Tackett, *When the King Took Flight* (Cambridge, MA, 2004).

123. Louis XVI, *Déclaration du roi adressée à tous les français, à sa sortie de Paris* (Paris, 1791), pp. 25–6.

124. Tackett, *When the King Took Flight*, pp. 72–6.

125. Price, *The Fall of the French Monarchy*, pp. 181–3.

126. Tackett, *When the King Took Flight*, pp. 76–85.

127. Price, *The Fall of the French Monarchy*, p. 172.

128. Blondy, *L'Ordre de Malte au XVIIIième siècle*, pp. 302–3.

129. David Armando, 'Pacca, Bartolomeo', in *Treccani dizionario biografico degli italiani*, online at www.treccani.it/enciclopedia/bartolomeo-pacca_%28Dizionario-Biografico%29/ [accessed 3 March 2021].

130. David Andress, *Massacre at the Champ de Mars: Popular Dissent and Political Culture in the French Revolution* (London, 2000).

131. Thomas E. Kaiser, 'La fin du renversement des alliances, la France, l'Autriche et la déclaration de guerre du 20 avril 1792', *Annales historiques de la révolution française*, No. 351 (2008), pp. 77–98.

132. Tim Blanning, *The Origins of the French Revolutionary Wars* (London, 1986), pp. 23–9 and 99–123.

133. Kolla, *Sovereignty, International Law, and the French Revolution*, pp. 90–2.

134. McManners, *The French Revolution and the Church*, pp. 64–5; Hardman, *The Life of Louis XVI*, pp. 409–10.

135. Frédéric Agay, 'A European Destiny: the Armée de Condé, 1792–1801', in Philip Mansel and Kirsty Carpenter (eds), *The French Emigres in*

Europe and the Struggle against Revolution 1789–1814 (Basingstoke, 1999), pp. 28–42.

136. Tim Blanning, *The French Revolutionary Wars* (London, 1996), pp. 59–63.

137. Rodney Allen, *Threshold of Terror: The Last Hours of the Monarchy in the French Revolution* (London, 1999).

138. Elizabeth Cross, 'The Myth of the Foreign Enemy? The Brunswick Manifesto and the radicalization of the French Revolution', *French History*, Vol. 25, No. 2 (2011), pp. 188–213.

139. Frédéric Bluche, *Septembre 1792, Logiques d'un Massacre* (Paris, 1986).

140. McManners, *The French Revolution and the Church*, p. 67.

141. Raymonde Monnier, 'Que signifie être républicain en septembre 1792?' in Michel Biard, Philippe Bourdin, Hervé Leuwers and Pierre Serna (eds), *1792 Entrer en République* (Paris, 2013), pp. 37–50.

142. Camille Latreille, 'Les évêques émigrés et Louis XVIII', *Revue d'histoire de l'eglise de France*, Vol. 8 (1911) pp. 162–74; Kirsty Carpenter, *Refugees of the French Revolution: Émigrés in London 1789–1802* (Basingstoke, 1999), p. 27.

143. Eric de Haynin, *Louis de Rohan le Cardinal Collier* (Paris, 1997), pp. 313–26.

144. David Goodman, 'Intellectual Life under the Spanish Inquisition: A continuing historical controversy', *History*, Vol. 90, No. 3 (2005), pp. 375–86; Richard Herr, *The Eighteenth-Century Revolution in Spain* (Princeton NJ, 1958), pp. 297–315, 407–14.

145. Donald Greer, *The Incidence of the Emigration During the French Revolution* (Cambridge, MA, 1951), pp. 111–12.

146. René Picheloup, *Les Ecclésiastiques français émigrés ou déportés dans l'État Pontifical, 1792–1800* (Toulouse, 1972), pp. 111–15.

147. Ibid, p. 124.

148. Mario Tosti, *Una costituzione per la chiesa: la proposta di concilio ecumenico negli anni della rivoluzione francese* (Florence, 2006), pp. 53–89.

149. David P. Jordan, *The King's Trial: Louis XVI vs. the French Revolution* (Los Angeles, 1979), p. 107.

150. Michael Walzer, *Regicide and Revolution: Speeches at the Trial of Louis XVI* (Cambridge, 1993), pp. 67, 123; AP 53:391.

151. AP 55:8–9.

152. Walzer, *Regicide and Revolution*, pp. 212–13.

153. Jordan, *The King's Trial*, pp. 240–1.

154. Anon, *Testament de Louis XVI, précédé des détails sur tout ce qui s'est passé avant et après l'exécution* (Paris, 1793), pp. 5–7.

155. Henry Essex Edgeworth de Firmont, *Mémoires de M. l'abbé Edgeworth de Firmont, dernier confesseur de Louis XVI* (Paris, 1815).

156. Jordan, *The King's Trial*, pp. 219–21.
157. Blanning, *The French Revolutionary Wars*, pp. 92–6.
158. Derek Beales, 'Edmund Burke and the Monasteries of France', *Historical Journal*, Vol. 48, No. 2 (2005), pp. 415–36. Jennifer Welsh, *Edmund Burke and International Relations: The Commonwealth of Europe and the Crusade against the French Revolution* (Basingstoke, 1995), pp. 115–66.
159. Bellocchi, *Tutte le encicliche*, II, pp. 267–8.
160. Alan Forrest, *Soldiers of the French Revolution* (Durham, NC, 1996), pp. 74–7.
161. Timothy Tackett, 'The West in France in 1789: The religious factor in the origins of the counterrevolution', *Journal of Modern History*, Vol. 54, No. 4 (1982), pp. 715–45.
162. Jean-Clement Martin, *La Vendée et la France* (Paris, 1987), pp. 68–79; Jean-Clement Martin, *La Vendée et la révolution* (Paris, 2007), p. 67; Reynald Secher, *A French Genocide: The Vendee* (Notre Dame, IN, 2003); Hugh Gough, 'Genocide and the Bicentenary: The French Revolution and the revenge of the Vendee', *Historical Journal*, Vol. 30, No. 4 (1987), pp. 977–88.
163. Mona Ozouf, *L'homme régénéré: essais sur la révolution française* (Paris, 1989), pp. 116–57.
164. Jean-Jacques Rousseau, *Du Contrat social ou principes du droit politique* (Amsterdam, 1762), p. 40.
165. Alain Corbin, *Village Bells: Sound and Meaning in the Nineteenth-Century French Countryside* (Oxford, 1999), pp. 3–44.
166. AP 74:550.
167. Sanja Perovic, *The Calendar in Revolutionary France: Perceptions of Time in Literature, Culture, Politics* (Cambridge, 2012), pp. 110–24.
168. Richard A. Carrigan, Jr, 'Decimal Time: Unlike the metric system of measurements, decimal time did not survive the French Revolution. But is dividing the day by tens a possibility for the future?' *American Scientist*, Vol. 66, No. 3 (1978), pp. 305–13
169. Noah Shusterman, *Religion and the Politics of Time* (Washington, DC, 2010), pp. 161–205.
170. Matthew Shaw, *Time and the French Revolution: The Republican Calendar, 1789 - Year XIV* (Woodbridge, 2011) chs. 4 and 5; Noah Shusterman, *Religion and the Politics of Time: Holidays in France from Louis XIV through Napoleon* (Washington, 2010), chs. 5 and 6.
171. Conrad Rudolph, *Artistic Change at St-Denis: Abbot Suger's Program and the Early Twelfth-Century Controversy over Art* (Princeton, NJ, 1990).
172. Louis Réau, *Histoire du vandalisme: les monuments détruits de l'art français* (Paris, 1994).

173. Bronislaw Baczko, *Ending the Terror: The French Revolution after Robespierre* (Cambridge, 1994), pp. 185–223.

174. Geneviève Bresc-Bautier and Béatrice de Chancel-Bardelot (eds), *Un Musée des monuments français d'Alexandre Lenoir* (Paris, 2016); and Christopher M. Greene, 'Alexandre Lenoir and the Musée des Monuments Français during the French Revolution', *French Historical Studies*, Vol. 12, No. 2 (1981), pp. 200–22.

175. Richard Clay, *Iconoclasm in Revolutionary Paris: The Transformation of Signs* (Oxford, 2012), pp. 217–24.

176. Michel Vovelle, *The Revolution against the Church* (Columbus, OH, 1991), pp. 46–58; Mary Kathryn Cooney, 'May the Hatchet and the Hammer Never Damage It! The fate of the cathedral of Chartres during the French Revolution', *Catholic Historical Review*, Vol. 92, No. 2 (2006) pp. 193–214.

177. Jean Edmé Auguste Gosselin, *Vie de M. Emery* (2 vols, Paris, 1862); Joseph Foncrosé de Salamon, *Correspondance secrète de l'abbé de Salamon, chargé des affaires du Saint-Siège pendant la révolution avec le Cardinal de Zelada, 1791–1792* (Paris, 1898).

178. Nicole Bossut, 'Aux origines de la déchristianisation dans la Nièvre, Fouché, Chaumette ou les jacobins nivernais?' *Annales historiques de la révolution française*, No. 264 (1986), pp. 181–202.

179. Serge Bianchi, 'Les prénoms révolutionnaires dans la Révolution française, un chantier en devenir', *annales historiques de la révolution française*, No. 322 (2000), pp. 17–38 ; Richard Cobb, *A Second Identity: Essays on France and French History* (Oxford, 1969), pp. 135–7.

180. Michel Vovelle, *Religion et révolution, la déchristianisation de l'an II* (Paris, 1976).

181. E. Claire Cage, *Unnatural Frenchmen: The Politics of Priestly Celibacy and Marriage, 1720–1815* (Charlottesville, 2015), pp. 92–129.

182. Byrnes, *Priests of the French Revolution*, p. 102.

183. Rodney Dean, *L'Abbé Grégoire et l'église constitutionnelle après la terreur, 1794–1797* (Paris, 2008), pp. 5–8.

184. Annette Chapman-Adisho, *Patriot and Priest: Jean-Baptiste Volfius and Constitutional Church in the Côte d'Or* (Montreal, 2019), p. 86; Anon, *Annales Catholiques ou suite des Annales religieuses, politiques et littéraires*, 4 vols. (Paris, 1797), III, pp. 469–70.

185. James Guillaume, *Procès-verbaux du comité d'instruction publique de la convention nationale* (Paris, 1894), II, pp. 855–6.

186. *La Depeche* newspaper, 12 July 2016 issue online at https://www. ladepeche.fr/article/2016/07/12/2383000-decouverte-revolutionnaire-dans-l-eglise.html [accessed 5 May 2018].

187. François-Alphonse Aulard, *Culte de la raison et le culte de l'être*

suprême 1793–1794: essai historique (Paris, 1892), pp. 52–67; Bossut, 'Aux origines de la déchristianisation dans la Nièvre', p. 183.

188. Robert Palmer, *Twelve Who Ruled: The Year of the Terror in the French Revolution* (Princeton, NJ, 2005).

189. Peter McPhee, *Robespierre: A Revolutionary Life* (London, 2012), pp. 174–6, 196–9.

190. Albert Mathiez, *Robespierre et la déchristianisation* (Paris, 1909).

191. René Vœltzel, 'L'Être suprême pendant la révolution française 1789–1794', *Revue d'histoire et de philosophie religieuses*, Vol. 38, No. 3 (1958), pp. 250–72.

192. Jonathan Smyth, *Robespierre and the Festival of the Supreme Being: The Search for a Republican Morality* (Manchester, 2016), pp. 24, 49–77.

193. David Andress, *The Terror: Civil War in the French Revolution* (New York, 2005), pp. 310–11.

194. Colin Jones, 'The Overthrow of Maximilien Robespierre and the "Indifference" of the People', *American Historical Review*, Vol. 119, No. 3 (2014), pp. 689–713; Jones, *The Fall of Robespierre*.

195. Richard Lyman Bushman, *Joseph Smith, Rough Stone Rolling* (New York, 2007); Spencer W. McBride, *Joseph Smith for President: The Prophet, the Assassins, and the Fight for American Religious Freedom* (Oxford, 2021).

196. Suzanne Desan, *Reclaiming the Sacred: Lay Religion and Popular Politics in Revolutionary France* (Ithaca, NY, 1990), pp. 76–121.

197. Philip Hamburger, *Separation of Church and State* (Cambridge, MA, 2004); Daniel L. Dreisbach, *Thomas Jefferson and the Wall of Separation Between Church and State* (New York, 2002).

198. Sophia H. MacLehose, 'Separation of Church and State in France in 1795', *Scottish Historical Review*, Vol. 4, No. 15 (1907), pp. 298–308.

199. McManners, *The French Revolution and the Church*, pp. 108–11.

200. Dean, *L'Abbé Grégoire et l'église constitutionnelle*, pp. 253–9, 280–307.

201. Prosper Hemon, *Audrein, Yves-Marie, député du Morbihan à l'assemblée législative et à la convention nationale, évêque constitutionnel du Finistère 1741–1800* (Paris, 1903).

202. Dean, *L'Abbé Grégoire et l'église constitutionnelle*, pp. 311–12.

203. Gosselin, *Vie de M. Emery*, I, pp. 368–450.

204. Paul Hanson, Lynn Hunt and David Lansky, 'The Failure of the Liberal Republic in France, 1795–1799: The road to Brumaire', *Journal of Modern History*, Vol. 51, No. 4 (1979), pp. 734–59.

205. Martyn Lyons, *France under the Directory* (Cambridge, 1975), pp. 105–7.

206. Jordan R. Hayworth, *Revolutionary France's War of Conquest in the Rhineland: Conquering the Natural Frontier, 1792–1797* (Cambridge, 2019); Steven T. Ross, *Quest for Victory: French Military Strategy, 1792–1799* (London, 1973).

207. Tim Blanning, *Reform and Revolution in Mainz, 1743–1803* (Cambridge, 1974), pp. 267–302.

208. Philip Dwyer, *Napoleon: The Path to Power, 1769–1799* (London, 2014).

209. Daniele Menozzi, '*Crociata*': *Storia di un'ideologia dalla rivoluzione francese a Bergoglio* (Rome, 2020), pp. 32–3.

210. Giustino Filippone, *Le relazioni tra lo Stato pontificio e la Francia rivoluzionaria: Storia diplomatica del trattato di Tolentino* (2 vols, Milan, 1961–7).

211. Patrice Gueniffey, *Bonaparte, 1769–1802* (Cambridge, MA, 2015), pp. 323–48.

212. Juan Cole, *Napoleon's Egypt: Invading the Middle East* (Cambridge, 2007).

213. Georges Boulot, *Le Général Duphot, 1769–1797* (Paris, 1909), pp. 185–232; Ferdinando Gerra, *La Morte del Générale Duphot e la Repubblica romana del 1798–99 con documenti inediti* (Rome, 1967).

214. David Potter, *Constantine the Emperor* (Oxford, 2013), pp. 137–44.

215. Robert R. Palmer, *The Age of the Democratic Revolution: A Political History of Europe and America, 1760–1800* (Princeton, NJ, 2014) pp. 642–62.

216. Antonio Cretoni, *Roma Giacobina* (Rome, 1971).

217. Owen Chadwick, *The Popes and European Revolution* (Oxford, 1981), p. 464.

218. Raffaele Belvederi, *Il papato di fronte alla rivoluzione e alle conseguenze del congresso di Vienna 1775–1846* (Bologna 1965), pp. 57–9.

219. ASV, Archivo Concistoriale, Serie Conclavi 85, No.2 Posizione delle due Rinunzie del Cardinalto fatte dai due Sig Cardinali Tommaso Antici e Vincenzo Maria Altieri.

220. Albert Dufourcq, *Le Régime jacobin en Italie: étude sur la république romaine, 1798–1799* (Paris, 1900), pp. 173–5.

221. Giovanni Sforza, 'Pio VI alla Certosa di Firenze', *Archivio storico italiano*, Serie V, Vol. 6, No. 179 (1890), pp. 311–17.

222. Sandro Totti, *Il martirio di un papa sulle tracce della deportazione di Pio VI, febbraio 1798 – agosto 1799* (Rimini, 2002), p. 22.

223. A. B. Rodger, *The War of the Second Coalition, 1798–1801: A Strategic Commentary* (Oxford, 1964), pp. 51–5.

224. Christopher Duffy, *Eagles Over the Alps: Suvorov in Italy and Switzerland, 1799* (London, 1999).

225. Totti, *Il martirio di un papa*, pp. 51–4.

226. Ibid, pp. 55, 58.

227. Robert Bornecque, *Histoire de Valence et de sa région* (1981).

228. Totti, *Il martirio di un papa*, pp. 62–5.

229. Ibid, pp. 65–7.
230. McManners, *The French Revolution and the Church*, p. 131; Chadwick, *The Popes and European Revolution*, p. 482.

4 The Eagle and the Dove: The Napoleonic Empire, 1800–1815

1. Jean Leflon, *Pie VII, ses abbayes bénédictines à la papauté* (Paris, 1958), I, pp. 189–237.
2. Barnabà Chiaramonti, *Omelia del Cittadino Cardinal Chiaramonti Vescovo d'Imola al Popolo della sua diocesi nel giorno del Santissimo Natale l'anno MDCCXCVII* (Firenze, 1859).
3. Karl. A. Roider, *Baron Thugut and Austria's Response to the French Revolution* (Princeton NJ, 1987), pp. 3–80.
4. Giovanni Vian, 'La Chiesa Veneziana nei mesi del Conclave', *Studi Veneziani*, No. 43 (2002), pp. 299–308; Tracy Elizabeth Cooper, *Palladio's Venice: Architecture and Society in a Renaissance Republic* (London, 2005), pp. 109–46.
5. Sergio Becerra, *The Papal Tiara: The Authority and Power of The Pope* (Morrisville, NC, 2013), p. 6.
6. Nina Burleigh, *Mirage: Napoleon's Scientists and the Unveiling of Egypt* (London, 2007).
7. Albert Vandal, *L'Avènement de Bonaparte* (2 vols, Paris, 1907).
8. Michael Broers, *Napoleon, Soldier of Destiny* (London, 2014), pp. 203–29.
9. Patrice Gueniffay, *Bonaparte* (Cambridge, MA, 2015), pp. 559–74, 577–600.
10. Thierry Lentz, *Le Grand Consulat, 1799–1804* (Paris, 1999), pp. 167–218.
11. Waresquiel, Talleyrand, p. 283.
12. David Chandler, *The Campaigns of Napoleon* (London, 1993), pp. 270–86.
13. Jean Tulard, *Marengo, ou l'étrange victoire de Bonaparte* (Paris, 2021); Bernard Gainot and Bruno Ciotti *Marengo, 14 juin 1800* (Paris, 2010).
14. Michel Vergé-Franceschi, *Napoléon: une enfance corse* (Paris, 2009), pp. 216–21.
15. Marie Courtemanche, *Napoleon et le Sacré: une vie spirituelle, une politique religieuse* (Paris, 2019), p. 44.
16. Geoffrey Ellis, 'Religion According to Napoleon: The limitations of Pragmatism', in Nigel Aston (ed.), *Religious Changes in Europe 1650–1914: Essays for John McManners* (London, 1997), p. 235.
17. Leflon, *Pie VII*, pp. 12–15.
18. Lentz, *Le Grand Consulat*, pp. 199–201.
19. Augustin Theiner, Histoire des *deux concordats de la république française et de la république cisalpine* (2 vols, Paris, 1869), I, 63–5.

20. ASV, Francia Epoca Napoleonica 9, Fascicolo 1: Trattative Vercelli.

21. Jules Thomas, *Le Concordat de 1516: ses origines, son histoire au XVIe siècle* (3 vols, Paris, 1910).

22. Theiner, *Histoire des deux concordats*, I, p. 68.

23. Gérard Pelletier, *Rome et la révolution française: la théologie et la politique du saint siège devant la révolution française 1789–1799* (Rome, 2004), pp. 460–1; ASV, Archivo Concistoriale, Serie Conclavi 86, No. 357: Ordres des cérémonies qui seront observé à la sépulture du pape Pie VI.

24. Waresquiel, *Talleyrand*, p. 301–4.

25. Lentz, *Le Grand Consulat*, p. 200.

26. Boulay, III, pp. 653–5.

27. Ambrogio A. Caiani, *To Kidnap a Pope: Napoleon and Pius VII* (London, 2021), p. 90.

28. E. Claire Cage, *Unnatural Frenchmen: The Politics of Priestly Celibacy and Marriage, 1720–1815* (Charlottesville, VA, 2015), pp. 130–65.

29. ASV, Francia Epoca Napoleonica 1, Fasc. 7: Talleyrand richiesta riduzione allo stato laicale.

30. Waresquiel, *Talleyrand*, pp. 307–12.

31. Boulay, I, p.114; ASV, Francia Epoca Napoleonica 11, Fasci. 5, no.35r dimissioni vescovi.

32. W. H. C. Frend, *The Early Church from the Beginning to 461* (London, 1965), pp. 198–208; David Benedict, *The History of the Donatists* (London, 1875), pp. 43–61.

33. Bernard Plongeron, 'Face au concordat 1801, résistances des évêques anciens constitutionnels', *Annales historiques de la révolution française*, No. 337 (2004), pp. 85–115, esp. p. 90.

34. August Bernhard Hasler, *How the Pope Became Infallible*, passim.

35. Boulay, III, p. 201.

36. Marie Keenan, *Child Sexual Abuse and the Catholic Church: Gender, Power, and Organizational Culture* (Oxford, 2011).

37. ASV, Francia Epoca Napoleonica 1, Fascicolo 12: Di Pietro reflections on Concordat, No. 66v. Article 1 seems to imply the supremacy of the secular state.

38. Boulay, II, pp. 459, 397.

39. John Martin Robinson, *Cardinal Consalvi, 1757–1824* (London, 1987), p. 66.

40. Ercole Consalvi, *Mémoires du Cardinal Consalvi* (2 vols, Paris, 1866), I, pp. 348–9.

41. Boulay, IV, p. 94.

42. Consalvi, *Mémoires*, I, p. 393.

43. ASV, Segreteria di Stato, Epoca Napoleonica, Francia 4, Fasc.4: Voti sulle dimissioni de Vescovi, Nos. 14 and 26; Camille Latreille, *L'Opposition au concordat de 1792 à 1803* (Paris, 1910).

44. Jany Rouger, Jean-Lois Neveu et al., *La Petite Eglise: deux siècles de dissidence* (Parthenay, 1991); Victor Bindel, *Histoire religieuse de Napoléon: l'église impériale* (2 vols, Paris, 1940), II, pp. 147–95.

45. Irene Collins, *Napoleon and His Parliaments 1800–1815* (London, 1979), p. 70.

46. Jeannine Bordas-Charon, *La Légation en France du Cardinal Caprara, 1801–1808* (Paris, 1979).

47. Thiery Lentz, 'La Proclamation du concordat à Notre-Dame le 18 avril 1802', in Jacques-Olivier Boudon (ed.), *Le Concordat et le retour de la paix religieuse* (Paris, 2008), pp. 95–112.

48. François-Auguste Chateaubriand [sic François-René de], *Génie du christianisme, ou Beautés de la religion chrétienne* (5 vols, Paris, 1802).

49. Jean-Paul Clément, *Chateaubriand: biographie morale et intellectuelle* (Paris 1998), pp. 221–7.

50. Antoine Ricard, *Le Cardinal Fesch, archevêque de Lyon 1763–1839* (Paris, 1893), pp. 23–43.

51. Jean-Paul Lyonnet, *Le Cardinal Fesch, archevêque de Lyon, primat des Gaules, etc., fragments biographiques, politiques et religieux, pour servir à l'histoire ecclésiastique contemporaine* (2 vols, Paris, 1841), I, 89–241.

52. André Latreille, *Napoléon et le Saint Siège 1801–1808: l'ambassade du Cardinal Fesch à Rome* (Paris, 1935).

53. Boulay, V, pp. 313–27.

54. Howard Brown and Judith A. Miller (eds), *Taking Liberties: Problems of a New Order from the French Revolution to Napoleon* (Manchester, 2002) p. 29.

55. Bernard Plongeron, 'Face au concordat 1801, résistances des évêques anciens constitutionnels', *Annales historiques de la révolution française*, No. 337 (2004), pp. 85–115.

56. Jean Leflon, *Étienne-Alexander de Bernier évêque d'Orléans* (2 vols, Paris, 1938), II, pp. 36–43.

57. ASV, Segreteria di Stato, Epoca Napoleonica, Francia 24, Fas.6: Vescovi costituzionali.

58. Roger Price, *Religious Renewal in France 1789–1870*, pp. 113–53.

59. Jean Leflon, 'Le Clergé de second ordre sous le consulat et le Premier Empire', *Revue d'histoire de l'église de France*, Vol. 31, No. 18 (1945), pp. 97–119; Victor Bindel, *Histoire religieuse de Napoléon: les évêques de Bonaparte* (3 vols, Paris, 1940), I, pp. 111–124.

60. ASV, Segreteria di Stato, Epoca Napoleonica Italia 10, Fasc.1: Soppressione ordini religiosi piemonte.

61. ASV, Segreteria di Stato, Epoca Napoleonica Italia 19, Fasc.1, no.23: Brief observations on Italian concordat by anon; Daniele Arru, *Il concordato italiano 1803* (Milan, 2003), pp. 457–73.

62. Thierry Lentz, *Nouvelle histoire du Premier Empire* (Paris, 2002), I, pp. 20–2; Emmanuel de Waresquiel, *Fouché, les silences de la pieuvre* (Paris, 2014), pp. 387–404; Philip Dwyer, 'Napoleon and the Foundation of the Empire', *Historical Journal*, Vol. 53, No. 2 (2010), pp. 339–58.

63. Robert Morrissey, *Charlemagne and France: A Thousand Years of Mythology* (Notre Dame, IN, 2003), pp. 250–65.

64. Michael Broers, 'Napoleon, Charlemagne, and Lotharingia: Acculturation and the boundaries of Napoleonic Europe', *Historical Journal*, Vol. 44, No. 1 (2001), pp. 135–54.

65. Rosamond McKitterick, *Charlemagne: The Formation of a European Identity* (Cambridge, 2008), p. 292. Matthias Becher, *Charlemagne* (London, 2003), pp. 7–18.

66. ASV, Segreteria di Stato, Epoca Napoleonica, Francia 5, Fasc.1: Incoronazione Napoleone, no.46, Consalvi a Caprara 2 settembre 1804.

67. Beales, *Joseph II*, II, pp. 214–38.

68. Caiani, *To Kidnap a Pope*, p. 119.

69. ASV, Segreteria di Stato, Epoca Napoleonica, Francia 5, Fasc.6: Viaggio Pio VII Parigi, nos.1–26, list of convoys.

70. Charles-Éloi Vial, *Le Grand Veneur de Napoléon Ier à Charles X* (Paris, 2016), pp. 132–3.

71. Anne Jean Marie René Savary, duc de Rovigo, *Mémoires du duc de Rovigo pour servir à l'histoire de l'empereur Napoléon* (8 vols, Paris, 1829), II, pp. 111–12.

72. Jean-Marc Ticchi, *Le Voyage de Pie VII à Paris pour le sacre de Napoléon 1804–1805* (Paris, 2013), pp. 128–31.

73. Erasmo Pistolesi, *Vita del sommo pontefice Pio VII* (4 vols, Roma, 1824), I, p. 207.

74. Broers, *Napoleon, Soldier of Destiny*, p. 425.

75. Henri Welschinger, *Le pape et l'empereur, 1804–1815* (Paris, 1905), pp. 29–31.

76. Thierry Lentz, Joseph Bonaparte (Paris, 2016), pp. 147–8, 176–7, 191, 242.

77. Jean Tulard, *Le Sacre de l'empereur Napoléon: histoire et légende* (Paris, 2004), pp. 14–20.

78. Lauren Johnson, *Shadow King: The Life and Death of Henry VI* (London, 2019).

79. Jackson, Richard, *Vive le Roi! A History of the French Coronation from Charles V to Charles X* (London, 1984).

80. Jean-Marc Ticchi, 'Le Vicaire du Christ en France: Pie VII en voyage pour le couronnement de Napoléon 1er', Archivum Historiae Pontificiae, Vol. 43 (2005), pp. 139–55, esp. p. 147.

81. David Chanteranne, *Le Sacre de Napoléon* (Paris, 2004), pp. 115–16.

82. Ibid, pp. 161–230.

83. Gemma Betros, 'Napoleon and the Revival of Female Religious Communities in Paris, 1800–1814', *Studies in Church History*, Vol. 44 (2008), pp. 185–95.

84. Leflon, Étienne-Alexander de Bernier, II, p. 238; Herbert Hömig, *Karl Theodor von Dalberg: Staatsmann und Kirchenfürst im Schatten Napoleons* (Paderborn, 2011), pp. 399–470.

85. ASV, Segreteria di Stato, Epoca Napoleonica Italia 19, Fasc.3–4: private correspondance of Pius VII, lots of letters to Scipione Chiaramonti.

86. E. E. Y. Hales, *The Emperor and the Pope* (New York, 1961), pp. 70–1.

87. *Giornale Italiano*, 1 maggio 1805, No. 52, p.213, Description of papal meeting; Ambrogio A. Caiani, 'Ornamentalism in a European Context? Napoleon's Italian coronation May 1805', *English Historical Review*, Vol. 132 (2017), pp. 41–72. Emanuele Pigni, *Armoriale del Regno Italico* (Milan, forthcoming).

88. Maarje Abbenhuis, *An Age of Neutrals: Great Power Politics 1815–1914* (Cambridge, 2014), pp. 22–38.

89. Archives Départementales du Rhône, 1F Papiers Fesch, 1F 50, Lettres Meuron Ancône 1805–1806, Meuron to Fesch, report on arrival of troops in Ancona 18 and 21 October 1805, which in May 1806 led the French to send a Franco-Neapolitan force to occupy Civitavecchia, the main papal port, ASV, Segreteria di Stato, Epoca Napoleonica, Francia 19, Fasc.3 Trattative 1806–1807, No.10 14 June 1806, protest against occupation of Civitavecchia.

90. Daniello Maria Zigarelli, *Storia di Benevento* (Naples, 1860); 'Pontecorvo', in Gaetano Moroni (ed.), Dizionario di erudizione storico-ecclesiastica da san Pietro sino ai nostri (Roma, 1852), LIV, pp. 94–104; ASV, Segreteria di Stato, Epoca Napoleonica, Francia 8, Fasc.17: Giuseppe Re di Napoli; ASV, Segreteria di Stato, Epoca Napoleonica, Francia 13, Fasc. 13: Chiusura Porti agli Inglesi, nos. 11–16; ASV, Segreteria di Stato, Epoca Napoleonica, Francia 24, Fasc. 17: Riflessioni sulle diverse note del governo Francese 1806, No. 2, Reflections di Pietro on violation of papal territory and Joseph recognition.

91. Filiberto Agostini, *La riforma Napoleonica della Chiesa nella repubblica e nel regno d'Italia* (Vicenza, 1990) pp. 170–1, 192–7; ASV, Segreteria di Stato, Epoca Napoleonica, Francia 8, Fasc. 10: Eugène de Beauharnias Correspondance, nos. 2–46, documents on Venetian sees and problems; subsequently Fasc. 12: Lettere di Eugenio a Pio VII, Nos. 1–5, 7, 8–17.

92. Francis Loraine Petre, *Napoleon's Conquest of Prussia, 1806* (London, 1977).

93. Marie-Pierre Rey, *Alexander I, The Tsar who defeated Napoleon* (Dekalb, IL, 2009), pp. 178–86.

94. André Latreille, *Le Catéchisme impérial de 1806* (Paris, 1935).

95. ASV, Segreteria di Stato, Epoca Napoleonica, Francia 7, Fasc. 1: Catechismo imperiale, 31 March 1806, preliminary approval.

96. Riccardo Benzoni, *San Napoleone: un santo per l'impero* (Brescia, 2019), pp. 40, 54.

97. Ibid, pp. 89–95.

98. ASV, Segreteria di Stato, Epoca Napoleonica, Francia 13, Fasc. 13: Chiusura porti agli inglesi, No. 69, Mgr Arezzo, archbishop of Seleucia, summoned by Napoleon in Berlin on 9 November 1806; M. J. Rouët de Journel, *Nonciatures de Russie d'après les documents authentiques: nonciature d'Arezzo 1802–1806* (2 vols, Rome, 1922).

99. ASV, Segreteria di Stato, Epoca Napoleonica, Italia 10, Fasc. 40, untitled, No. 3, Domande sulla possibile occupazione degli stati pontefici; No. 4, Di Pietro voto.

100. Carlo Zaghi, *L'Italia di Napoleone* (Turin, 1989), pp. 74–8.

101. Henri Auréas, *Un Général de Napoléon, Miollis* (Paris, 1961), pp. 138–75.

102. Louis Madelin, *La Rome de Napoléon: la domination française à Rome de 1809 à 1814* (Paris, 1906), pp. 195–6.

103. Michael Broers, *The Napoleonic Empire in Italy, 1796–1814: Cultural Imperialism in a European Context?* (Basingstoke, 2005), pp. 127–32.

104. Donatella Panzieri, 'Braschi Onesti, Luigi', in *Treccani dizionario biografico degli Italiani*, online at www.treccani.it/enciclopedia/luigi-braschi-onesti_(Dizionario-Biografico) [accessed 5 March 2021].

105. David I. Kertzer, *The Popes Against the Jews: The Vatican's Role in the Rise of Modern Anti-Semitism* (New York, 2002) Ch. 3; Carla Nardi, *Napoleone e Roma dalla consulta romana al ritorno di Pio VII 1811–1814* (Rome, 2005) pp. 63–6; Abraham Berliner, *Storia degli ebrei di Roma: dall'antichità allo smantellamento del ghetto* (Rome, 2000).

106. ASV, Segreteria di Stato, Epoca Napoleonica, Italia 9, Fasc. 20, No.1: list of cardinals ordered to leave 23 March 1808.

107. Bartolomeo Pacca, *Mémoires du Cardinal Pacca, sur le pontificat de Pie VII* (3 vols, Paris, 1860), I, pp. 5–21.

108. Madelin, *La Rome de Napoléon*, p. 192; Pacca, *Mémoires du Cardinal Pacca*, I, pp. 137–43.

109. Charles Esdaile, *The Peninsular War: A New History* (London, 2003).

110. Michael Broers, *Napoleon's Other War: Bandits, Rebels and Their Pursuers in the Age of Revolution* (Oxford, 2010).

111. José María Codón, *Biografía y crónica, del cura Merino* (Burgos 1986).

112. Pierre Daunou, *La Puissance temporelle des papes, et l'abus qu'ils ont fait de leur ministère spiritual* (Paris 2007); Jean-Antoine Llorente,

Histoire critique de l'inquisition d'Espagne, depuis l'époque de son établissement par Ferdinand V jusqu'au règne de Ferdinand VII (4 vols, Paris, 1817).

113. Charles J. Esdaile, *Fighting Napoleon: Guerrillas, Bandits and Adventurers in Spain 1808–1814* (London 2004); Milton Finley, *The Most Monstrous of Wars: The Napoleonic Guerrilla War in Southern Italy, 1806–1811* (London, 1994); Gunther Eyck, *Loyal Rebels: Andreas Hofer and the Tyrolean Uprising of 1809* (Washington, 1986).

114. Sam Mustafa, *The Long Ride of Major von Schill* (New York, 2008).

115. Pacca, *Mémoires du Cardinal Pacca*, I, p. 178.

116. Bellocchi, *Tutte le encicliche*, II, pp. 379–88.

117. Jea Leflon, *La Crise révolutionnaire, 1789–1846*, pp. 256–8.

118. Wolfram Siemann, *Metternich, Strategist and Visionary* (Cambridge, MA, 2019), pp. 242–67.

119. NAP NOUV CORRES, No.21289, Schönbrunn, 19 juin 1809, IX, pp. 745–6.

120. Dominique Rézeau, *Le Gendarme de Napoléon qui arrêta le pape* (Paris, 2012).

121. Madelin, *La Rome de Napoléon*, pp. 237–8.

122. Alexis-François Artaud de Montor, *Histoire du pape Pie VII, par Me le Chevalier Artaud, ancien chargé d'affaires de France à Rome, à Florence et à Vienne* (2 vols, Paris, 1836), II, p. 221; ASV, Segreteria di Stato, Epoca Napoleonica, Italia 7, Fasc. 17: No. 1 fo.16, report on papal abduction.

123. Pacca, *Mémoires du Cardinal Pacca*, I, pp. 188–9.

124. Ibid, I, p. 248.

125. NAP NOUV CORRES, No. 21562, Shönbrunn, 18 juillet 1809, IX, p. 885.

126. Henri de Mayol de Lupé, *La captivité de Pie VII, d'après des documents inédits* (2 vols, Paris, 1916), I, pp. 176–206.

127. Ian Verstegen (ed.), *Patronage and Dynasty: The Rise of the Della Rovere in Renaissance Italy* (Kirksville, MO, 2007).

128. Claudio Costantini, *La Repubblica di Genova nell'età moderna* (*Storia d'Italia*, Vol. IX, Turin, 1978), esp. Ch. IV; Steven A. Epstein, *Genoa and the Genoese, 958–1528* (Chapel Hill, NC, 2001), esp. Ch. 2.

129. D. Baldassarre d'Emilio, *Storia dell'apparizione di N.S. della misericordia in Savona* (Naples, 1838).

130. Giovanni Farris, *Studi e documenti su Pio VII* (Savona, 2010), pp. 79–81, 157–60.

131. Mary Heimann, 'Catholic Revivalism in Worship and Devotion', in Gilley and Stanley (eds), *World Christianities*, pp. 70–83.

132. Albert Vandal, *Napoléon et Alexander Ier, l'alliance russe sous le Premier Empire* (3 vols, Paris, 1907), II, pp. 168–97.

133. Charles-Eloi Vial, *Marie-Louise* (Paris, 2017), pp. 35–73.

134. Catherine Fletcher, *The Divorce of Henry VIII: The Untold Story* (London, 2013); Giles Tremlett, *Catherine of Aragon, Henry's Spanish Queen* (London, 2011).

135. Henri Welschinger, *Le Divorce de Napoléon* (Paris, 1889), pp. 123–39, 143–4, 165–72.

136. Victor Bindel, *Le Vatican à Paris 1809–1814* (Paris, 1942), pp. 135–53; Maria Pia Donato, *Les Archives du monde, quand Napoléon confisqua l'histoire* (Paris, 2019), pp. 37–70; Jean Mauzaize, 'Le tranfert des archives vaticanes à Paris sous le Premier Empire', *Bulletin de l'Association des archivists de l'église de France*, Vol. 8 (1977), pp. 3–14; Maria Pia Dontao, 'La Conquista della memoria: Napoleone, Galileo e gli archivi dell'impero', *Galilaena: Journal of Galilean Studies*, Vol. X (2013), pp. 187–200.

137. Bindel, *Le Vatican à Paris*, pp. 135–53.

138. Jean-Philippe Garric, *Percier et Fontaine, les architectes de Napoléon* (Paris, 2012); Charles Percier and Pierre-Francois Fontaine, *Empire Stylebook of Interior Design: All 72 Plates from the 'Recueil de Décorations Intérieures'* (Dover, 1991).

139. Geoffroy de Grandmaison, *Napoléon et les cardinaux noirs 1810–1814* (Paris, 1895); Umberto Beseghi, *I tredici Cardinali Neri* (Firenze, 1944); David Chanteranne, 'Les Cérémonies du mariage', in Thierry Lentz (ed.), *1810: le tournant de l'Empire* (Paris, 2010), pp. 37–50.

140. Anon, *Serie de documenti sulle vertenze insorte fra la Santa Sede ed il governo francese* (6 vols, Rome, 1833), II, pp. 165–6, 169–175; Francia 12, Fasc. 14, Trattative con Napoleone 1807, no. 9: Cardinal Casoni to Italian minister of religions Bovara, 11 Oct. 1806.

141. Pierre-Étienne Guillaume, *Vie épiscopale de Mgr Antoine-Eustache Osmond, évêque de Nancy* (Nancy, 1862), pp. 564–602; Jacques-Olivier Boudon, *Napoléon et les cultes: les religions en Europe à l'aube du XIXème siècle, 1800–1815* (Paris, 2002), pp. 282, 287.

142. Antoine Ricard (ed.), *Correspondance diplomatique et mémoires inédits du Cardinal Maury, 1792–1817* (2 vols, Lille, 1891), II, pp. 316–17.

143. ASV, Segreteria di Stato, Epoca Napoleonica, Italia 15, Fasc. 3, Savona, No. 6, Catena delle persone per mezzo delle quali passavano le notizie e pieghi da Parigi a Savona.

144. AN, AF IV 1048, Dos.1 Affaire d'Astros, undated 'communication avec Savone', probably a report by Savary describing the secret network; Candido Bona, *Le 'Amicizie', societe segrete e rinascita religiosa, 1770–1830* (Turin, 1962), pp. 283–300.

145. AN, AF IV 1048, Dos.1 Affaire, d'Astros, undated rapport à SM sur l'affaire d'Astros; Guillaume Bertier de Sauvigny 'Un Épisode de la résistance catholique sous le Premier Empire, l'affaire d'Astros', *Revue*

d'histoire de l'eglise de France, Vol. 35 (1949), pp. 49–58.

146. Jean Destrem, 'Déportations de prêtres sous le Premier Empire', *Revue historique*, Vol. 11, No. 2 (1879), pp. 331–88.

147. Mayol de Lupé, *La Captivité de Pie VII*, II pp. 101–7; Comte d'Haussonville, *L'Église romaine et le Premier Empire* (Paris, 1870), III, pp. 484–5.

148. Giovanni Farris, *Atti per l'inquisitio su Pio VII* (Savona, 2013); Antonio Verico, print after Vincenzo Gozzini, *The Miracle of Pope Pius VII 'Levitating' at Mass on 15 August 1811*, British Museum No. 1941, 0918.60, online at https://www.britishmuseum.org/research/collection_online/collection_object_details.aspx?objectId=3243314andpartId=1 [accessed 5 March 2021].

149. NAP NOUV CORRES, No. 26820, Saint-Cloud, 24 April 1811, XI, pp. 220–1.

150. Mayol de Lupé, *La Captivité de Pie VII*, II, pp. 217–18.

151. John O'Malley, *When Bishops Meet: An Essay Comparing Trent, Vatican I, and Vatican II* (Cambridge, MA, 2019).

152. Haussonville, *L'Église romaine et le Premier Empire*, IV, p. 125.

153. Jean Tulard, *Napoléon II* (Paris, 1996).

154. Henri Welschinger, *Le Roi de Rome 1811–1832* (Paris, 1897), Ch. 2.

155. Étienne-Antoine Boulogne, *Sermons et discours inédits de M. de Boulogne, évêque de Troyes* (3 vols, Ghent, 1827), III, pp. 338–73; AN, AF IV 1047, dossier 2, Nos 31–2: Report from Bigot to the emperor on ecclesiastical oath.

156. AN, AF IV 1047, dossier 2, No.74: Imperial address.

157. Joseph Lenfant, 'Maurice de Broglie, évêque de Gand, 1766–1821', *Revue d'histoire de l'eglise de France*, Vol. 76 (1931), pp. 312–47; Gabriel Van den Gheyn, *Maurice prince de Broglie, XIXe évêque de Gand* (Hand, 1923).

158. Lenfant, 'Maurice de Broglie', p. 325.

159. Antoine Ricard, *Le Concile national de 1811* (Paris, 1894), pp. 158–60.

160. Haussonville, *L'Église romaine et le Premier Empire*, IV, p. 325.

161. Ricard, *Le Concile national de 1811*, pp. 239–44.

162. Archives de l'Archevêché de Lyon, 2 Episcopat de Mgr Fesch 1802–1840, 2 II 16, Concile 1811 Arrestations.

163. Pacca, *Mémoires du Cardinal Pacca*, I, p. 283.

164. Haussonville, *L'Église romaine et le Premier Empire*, V, pp. 58–9.

165. Ibid, pp. 131–4.

166. Alexandre Tchoudinov, 'Russia and the Continental System: Trends in Russian historiogrpahy', in Kathrine B. Aaslestad and Johan Joor (eds), *Revisiting Napoleon's Continental System: Local Regional and European Experiences* (Basingstoke, 2015), pp. 56–60.

167. Dominic Lieven, *Russia Against Napoleon: The Battle for Europe, 1807 to 1814* (London, 2010), esp. Ch. 4.

168. NAP NOUV CORRES, No.30651, Dresde, 21 mai 1812, XII, pp. 593–4.

169. Louis de Nussac, 'Le Colonel Antoine Lagorse 1770–1842, Gardien de Pie VII', *Bulletin de la Société scientifique, historique et archéologique de la Corrèze*, Vol. 46, No. 1 (1924), pp. 97–122, 193–226.

170. Domenico and Francesco Martinengo, *Pio VII in Savona: memorie storiche* (Turin, 1888), p. 267.

171. Louis Bouvier, 'Le Mont-Cenis, souvenirs de voyage', *Revue des deux mondes*, Vol. 87 (1888), pp. 908–21.

172. BL, Add. Ms. 8389, fos. 23–27, Claraz narrative.

173. Savary, *Mémoires du duc de Rovigo*, V, pp. 287–8.

174. Haussonville, *L'Église romaine et le Premier Empire*, V, p. 165.

175. Christophe Beyeler (ed.), Pie face à Napoléon, la tiare dans les serres de l'aigle, Rome, Paris, Fontainebleau, 1796–1814 (Paris, 2015), pp. 186–7.

176. Adam Zamoyski, *1812: Napoleon's Fatal March on Moscow* (London, 2005), Ch. 13.

177. Lieven, *Russia Against Napoleon*, pp. 212–14.

178. Munro Price, *Napoleon: The End of Glory* (Oxford, 2014), p. 5.

179. Lentz, *Nouvelle Histoire du Premier Empire*, II, p. 343.

180. Pacca, *Mémoires du Cardinal Pacca*, II, p. 98.

181. François-René de Chateaubriand, *De Buonaparte et des Bourbons et de la nécessité de se rallier à nos princes légitimes pour le bonheur de la France et celui de l'Europe* (Paris, 1814), p. 12.

182. ASV, Segreteria di Stato, Epoca Napoleonica, Francia 6, Fasc. 10: Memoria Mgr Gazzola concordato di Fontainebleau, fol.85.

183. Anon, *Collection des Lois, sénatus-consultes, décrets impériaux et avis du conseil d'état relatif aux cultes, publiés depuis le concordat jusqu'au 1er janvier 1813* (Paris, 1813), ff.xx–xxi.

184. Welschinger, *Le pape et l'empereur, 1804–1815*, pp. 365–6.

185. Mayol de Lupé, *La captivité de Pie VII*, II, pp. 455–61.

186. Francis Loraine Petre, *Napoleon's Last Campaign in Germany, 1813* (London, 1912).

187. Munro Price, 'Napoleon and Metternich in 1813: Some new and some neglected evidence', *French History*, Vol. 26, No. 4 (2012), pp. 482–503.

188. Paul W. Schroeder, *The Transformation of European Politics 1763–1848* (Oxford, 1994), pp. 459–76; Wolfram Siemann, *Metternich, Strategist and Visionary* (Cambridge, MA, 2019), pp. 320–60.

189. Alan Sked, *Radetzky, Imperial Victor and Military Genius* (London, 2010), pp. 30–42.

190. Price, *Napoleon: End of Glory*, pp. 151–2.

191. Jean-Baptiste Capefigue, *Le Congrès de Vienne et les traités de 1815, précédé et suivi des actes diplomatiques* (Paris, 1863), pp. 83–7; Price, *Napoleon: The End of Glory*, pp. 187–204.

192. Jacques-Olivier Boudon, *Les Élites religieuses à l'époque de Napoléon: dictionnaire des évêques et vicaires généraux du Premier Empire* (Paris, 2002), pp. 143–4; Michael Broers, *The Politics of Religion in Napoleonic Italy: The War against God, 1801–1814* (London, 2002), pp. 90–9; Doina Pasca Harsanyi, 'Brigands or Insurgents? Napoleonic authority in Italy and the Piacentino counter-insurrection of 1805–06', *French History*, Vol. 30, No. 1 (2016) pp. 51–76.

193. AN AB XIX 4496, dos. 4, fo. 20: Fallot to duc de Bassano, draft letter for the pope, 20 janvier 1814.

194. Alan Reinerman, *Austria and the Papacy in the Age of Metternich* (2 vols, Washington, DC, 1979), I, pp. 6–7.

195. Gian Michele Gazzola, Pio VII prigioniero a Cuneo, cronache ed avvenimenti locali attorno al suo passaggio nel 1809, (2 vols, Cuneo, 2011) I, p. 19; AN F 7 6530, Plaq 1 Savone, fo. 36: Report by prefect of Montenotte, Anton Brignole Sale, 17 fevrier 1814.

196. Nussac, 'Le Colonel Antoine Lagorse', pp. 216–24; NAP NOUV CORRES, No. 38476, Chavignon 10 mars 1814, XV, p. 389.

197. Mayol de Lupé, *La captivité de Pie VII*, II, p. 520.

198. J. P. T. Bury, 'The End of the Napoleonic Senate', *Cambridge Historical Journal*, Vol. 9, No. 2 (1948), pp. 165–89.

199. Samuele Giombi, 'Leone XII (Annibale della Genga Sermattei), per un profilo biografico a partire dalla recentre storiografia', in Gilberto Piccinini (ed.), *Il Pontificato di Leone XII, restaurazione e riforme nel governo della Chiesa e dello stato* (Genga, 2011), p. 34.

200. Roberto Regoli, *Ercole Consalvi, le scelte per la Chiesa* (Rome, 2006), p. 338.

201. Bellocchi, *Tutte le encicliche*, II, p. 390.

202. Mayol de Lupé, *La captivité de Pie VII*, II, p. 525.

203. Marina Natoli, 'Raffaele Stern e l'allestimento degli appartamenti imperiali al Quirinale', in Maria Antonietta Scarpati (eds), *Il palazzo del Quirinale il mondo artistico a Roma nel periodo napoleonico* (2 vols, Rome, 1989), I, pp. 1–82.

204. ASV, Congregazione Disordini, 20 boxes, see Lajos Pásztor catalogue in archives.

205. ASV, Congregazione Particolare Disordini, 1 and 2: many lists of priests compromised with the Napoleonic regime.

206. ASV, Segreteria di Stato, Epoca Napoleonica, Italia 17, Fasc. 4 and 5: Maury affair.

207. Dominique Julia, 'La Restauration de la compagnie de Jésus', in Pierre-Antoine Fabre, Patrick Goujon and Martín M. Morales (eds), *La Compagnie de Jésus, des anciens régimes au monde contemporain, XVIIIe–XXe siècles* (Rome, 2020), pp. 51–70.

208. Robert A. Maryks and Jonathan Wright (eds), *Jesuit Survival and*

NOTES

Restoration: A Global History, 1773–1900 (Leiden, 2014); Martín M. Morales, 'The Restoration of the Society of Jesus and the Vagaries of Writing', in Zupanov (ed.), *The Oxford Handbook of the Jesuits*, pp. 953–73.

209. Geoffrey Cubitt, *The Jesuit Myth: Conspiracy Theory and Politics in Nineteenth-Century France* (Oxford, 1993); Vincenzo Gioberti, *Il Gesuita moderno* (5 vols, Lausanne, 1847).

210. Francisco Bethencourt, *The Inquisition: A Global History, 1478–1834* (Cambridge, 1995), pp. 416–39; Emilio la Parra, *Fernando VII, un rey deseado y detestado* (Barcelona, 2018), pp. 295–302.

211. Alessandro Roveri, *La Santa Sede tra rivoluzione francese e restaurazione: il Cardinale Consalvi 1813–1815* (Florence, 1974), pp. 127–8; Lucio Bigi and Mario Mareddu, *L'orologio del Duomo di Firenze, l'unico al mondo che segna l'ora italica* (Florence, 2016).

212. Camille Latreille, *Après le Concordat, l'opposition de 1803 à nos jours* (Paris, 1910), pp. 125–69; Antoine Roquette, *Le Concordat de 1817: Louis XVIII face à Pie VII* (Paris, 2010), pp. 15–46.

213. Regoli, *Ercole Consalvi*, pp. 368–71.

214. Walter W. Seton, 'The Relations of Henry Cardinal York with the British Government', *Transactions of the Royal Historical Society*, Vol. 2 (1919), pp. 94–112.

215. Christopher M. S. Johns, *Antonio Canova and the Politics of Patronage in Revolutionary and Napoleonic Europe* (London, 1998), pp. 160–3.

216. Antonia Fraser, *The King and the Catholics: The Fight for Right, 1829* (London, 2018), pp. 78–80.

217. Mark Jarret, *The Congress of Vienna and Its Legacy: War and Great Power Diplomacy after Napoleon* (London, 2013), pp. 131–41; Lentz, *Nouvelle histoire du Premier Empire*, IV, 66.

218. Alessandro Roveri, *La missione Consalvi e il congresso di Vienna* (3 vols, Rome, 1976), I, pp. 458–9.

219. Cencetti, *Le tre legazioni*.

220. Adolfo Omodeo, *Studi sull'èta della restaurazione, la cultura francese nell'èta della restaurazione, aspetti del cattolicesimo della restaurazione* (Turin, 1974), pp. 443–6.

221. Abbenhuis, *An Age of Neutrals*, pp. 39–65.

222. Pierre Branda, *La Guerre secrète de Napoléon: Île d'Elbe 1814–1815* (Paris, 2014), pp. 346–60.

223. ASV, Segreteria di Stato, Epoca Napoleonica, Italia 12, Fasc.2: Fuga dal Elba.

224. Emmanuel de Waresquiel, *Cent Jours: la tentation de l'impossible mars-juillet 1815* (Paris, 2008), pp. 306–12, 353–62.

225. Angelo and Marcello Remondini, *Pio VII P.M. in Genova e nella Liguria l'anno 1815* (Genova, 1872), pp. 19–24.

226. Giovanni Farris, *Studi e documenti su Pio VII* (Savona, 2010), pp. 79–81, 157–60.
227. Vincent Haegele, *Murat: la solitude du cavalier* (Paris, 2015), pp. 696–706.
228. AN, F 19 5597: Lettres du mois de juin 1815 relatives aux dénonciations contre les prêtres opposés au gouvernement impérial.
229. AF IV 1935: Council of state reports by Bigot on the clergy during the 100 days.
230. Alan Forrest, *Waterloo* (Oxford, 2015).
231. Thiery Lentz, *Bonaparte n'est plus! le monde apprend la mort de Napoléon Juillet-Septembre 1821* (Paris, 2019).
232. Emmanuel de Waresquiel, *Talleyrand: dernières nouvelles du diable* (Paris, 2011), pp. 159–67.
233. Roveri, *La missione Consalvi*, III, pp. 631–57.
234. Phillip Cuccia, 'Controlling the Archives: The requisition, removal, and return of the Vatican archives during the age of Napoleon', *Napoleonica: La Revue*, No. 17 (2013), pp. 66–74.
235. Massimo Petrocchi, *La restaurazione: il cardinale Consalvi e la riforma del 1816* (Florence, 1941).

5 Resurrection: The Church after the Congress of Vienna, 1815–46

1. Roberto Mares, *Miguel Hidalgo y Costilla, los grandes Mexicanos* (Mexico, 2004), p. 55.
2. Ibid. p. 56.
3. Colin M. MacLachlan and Jaime E. Rodríguez O, *The Forging of the Cosmic Race: A Reinterpretation of Colonial Mexico* (Los Angeles, CA, 1980), pp. 198–228.
4. Hugh M. Hamill, Jr., *The Hidalgo Revolt: Prelude to Mexican Independence* (Westport, CT, 1966), p. 123.
5. William H. Beezley and David E. Lorey (eds), *Viva Mexico! Viva la Independencia! Celebrations of September 16* (Wilmington, DE, 2001).
6. D. A. Brading, *Mexican Phoenix: Our Lady of Guadalupe: Image and Tradition Across Five Centuries* (Cambridge, 2001), pp. 54–95.
7. Miranda Godínez Miranda, *Dos cultos fundantes, los remedios y Guadalupe, 1521–1649: historia documental* (Michoacán, 2001), p. 21.
8. Douglas Hilt, *The Troubled Trinity: Godoy and the Spanish Monarchs* (Tuscaloosa, AB, 1987), pp. 227–42.
9. Brian R. Hamnett, *The End of Iberian Rule on the American Continent 1770–1830* (Cambridge, 2017), pp. 110–15, 119–30, 145–50.
10. Jacques Droz, *Europe between Revolutions, 1815–1848* (Glasgow, 1967), pp. 9–17.

11. Magnus Mörner, 'The Expulsion of the Jesuits from Spain and Spanish America in 1767 in Light of Eighteenth-Century Regalism', The Americas, Vol. 23, No.2 (1966), pp. 156–164.
12. Brian R. Hamnett, 'The Appropriation of Mexican Church Wealth by the Spanish Bourbon Government, the Consolidación de Vales Reales, 1805–1809', Journal of Latin American Studies, Vol.1, No.2 (1969), pp. 85–113.
13. Jean-Clement Martin, La Guerre de Vendée 1793–1800 (Paris, 2014).
14. Hamill, The Hidalgo Revolt, pp. 66–80.
15. Armando Fuentes Aguirre ('Catón'), La otra historia de México: Hidalgo e Iturbide, la gloria y el olvido (Mexico, 2008), pp. 44–5.
16. Hamill, The Hidalgo Revolt, pp. 139–40.
17. Aguirre, Hidalgo e Iturbide, pp. 46–51.
18. Lester D. Langley, The Americas in the Age of Revolution 1750–1850 (London, 1996), pp. 181–2.
19. Mares, Miguel Hidalgo y Costilla, p. 73.
20. Aguirre, Hidalgo e Iturbide, pp. 58–60.
21. Mark Lawrence, Experiences of War in Europe and the Americas, 1792–1815: Soldiers, Slaves, and Civilians (London, 2021), pp. 52, 142.
22. MacLachlan and Rodríguez, The Forging of the Cosmic Race, pp. 314–15.
23. Hamill, The Hidalgo Revolt, pp. 177–9.
24. MacLachlan and Rodríguez, The Forging of the Cosmic Race, p. 318.
25. Hamill, The Hidalgo Revolt, pp. 168–75.
26. Aguirre, Hidalgo e Iturbide, pp. 75–7.
27. Mares, Miguel Hidalgo y Costilla, pp. 117–20.
28. Hamill, The Hidalgo Revolt, pp. 212–15.
29. Alejandro Rosas, Mitos de la Historia Mexicana de Hidalgo a Zedillo (Mexico, 2006), p. 32.
30. Aguirre, Hidalgo e Iturbide, pp. 120–6.
31. William Eugene Shiels, King and Church: The Rise and Fall of the Patronato (Chicago, 1961).
32. John Lynch, New Worlds: A Religious History of Latin America (London, 2012), p. 117; Eric van Young, The Other Rebellion: Popular Violence, Ideology and the Mexican Struggle for Independence 1810–1821 (Stanford, CA, 2001), pp. 243–67.
33. Aguirre, Hidalgo e Iturbide, pp. 181–4.
34. William B. Taylor, Magistrates of the Sacred: Priests and Parishioners in Eighteenth-Century Mexico (Stanford, CA, 1996), pp. 463–65.
35. Ibid, pp. 470–2.
36. José María Morelos y Pavón, Sentimientos de la nación: El sitio de Cuautla (Mexico, 2020).
37. Taylor, Magistrates of the Sacred, p. 472.

38. Aguirre, *Hidalgo e Iturbide*, pp. 268–83.
39. MacLachlan and Rodríguez, *The Forging of the Cosmic Race*, p. 328.
40. John Lynch, *The Spanish American Revolutions 1808–1826* (2 edn, New York, 1986), pp. 53–4.
41. Lynch, *New Worlds*, p. 118.
42. Brian R. Hamnett, 'The Counter Revolution of Morillo and the Insurgent Clerics of New Granada, 1815–1820', *The Americas*, Vol. 32, No. 4 (1976), pp. 597–617.
43. Roberto María Tisnés Jiménez, *Fray Ignacio Mariño OP, capellán general del Ejército Libertador* (Bogota, 1963).
44. Enrique de Gandía, *Nueva historia de América, las épocas de libertad y antilibertad desde la independencia* (Buenos Aires, 1986), pp. 257–62.
45. Bellocchi, *Tutte le encicliche*, II, p. 400.
46. Lynch, *The Spanish American Revolutions*, pp. 207–19.
47. Richard Stites, *The Four Horsemen: Riding to Liberty in Post-Napoleonic Europe* (Oxford, 2014), pp. 65–98.
48. Hamnett, *The End of Iberian Rule*, pp. 235–44, 281–6.
49. John Lynch, *Simón Bolívar, A Life* (London, 2006), p. 248.
50. Pedro de Leturia, SJ, *Relaciones entre la Santa Sede e Hispanoamérica* (3 vols, Caracas, 1957), II, p. 174.
51. Giuseppe Tanzi, 'Documenti sulla missione pontificia al Cile e al Sudamerica di Monsignor Giovanni Muzi rinvenuti a città di castello', Archivum Historiae Pontificiae, Vol. 20 (1982), pp. 253–336, esp. p.254.
52. Leturia, *Relaciones entre la Santa Sede e Hispanoamérica*, II p. 176.
53. Maria Lupi, 'Muzi, Giovanni', in *Treccani dizionario biografico degli Italiani*, online at www.treccani.it/enciclopedia/giovanni-muzi_%28Dizionario-Biografico%29/ [accessed 19 June 2021].
54. Pedro de Leturia and Miguel Batllori (eds), *La primera misión pontificia a Hispanoamérica, 1823–1825: Relación oficial de Monsignor Giovanni Muzi* (Vatican, 1963), pp. 58–91.
55. D. F. Sarimento, *Viaje a Chile del canónigo Don Juan María Mastai-Ferreti oi sumo pontifice Pio Papa IX traducido del Italiano i seguido de un apendice* (Santiago de Chile, 1848).
56. Giacomo Martina, 'La prima missione pontificia nell'America latina', *Archivum Historiae Pontificiae*, Vol.32 (1994), pp. 149–93, esp. p. 164.
57. Alexis-François Artaud de Montor, *Storia del Pontefice Leone XI* (3 vols, Milan, 1863), I, 21–65.
58. Tanzi, 'Documenti sulla missione pontificia al Cile e al Sudamerica', p. 263.
59. Lynch, *New Worlds*, pp. 122, 124; John Lynch, *San Martín: Argentine Soldier, American Hero* (London, 2009), p. 202.
60. Leturia, *Relaciones entre la Santa Sede e Hispanoamérica*, II, pp. 211–15.
61. Lynch, *The Spanish American Revolutions*, pp. 146–7.

62. Frances Kellam Hendricks, 'The First Apostolic Mission to Chile', *Hispanic American Historical Review*, Vol. 22, No. 4 (1942), pp. 644–9, esp. p. 658.

63. Tanzi, 'Documenti sulla missione pontificia al Cile e al Sudamerica', pp. 264–5.

64. Leturia and Batllori (eds), *La primera misión pontificia a Hispanoamérica*, pp. 287–8.

65. Tanzi, 'Documenti sulla Missione Pontificia al Cile e al Sudamerica', p. 266.

66. Leturia, *Relaciones entre la Santa Sede e Hispanoamérica*, II, pp. 217–19.

67. Martina, 'La prima missione pontificia nell'America latina', p. 170.

68. Tanzi, 'Documenti sulla missione pontificia al Cile e al Sudamerica', p. 268.

69. Leturia and Batllori (eds), *La primera misión pontificia a Hispanoamérica*, pp. 442–5.

70. Martina, 'La prima missione pontificia nell'America latina', pp. 177–8.

71. Maria Lupi, 'Muzi, Giovanni'.

72. Carlo Falconi, *Il Giovane Mastai, il futuro Pio IX dall'infanzia a Senigallia alla Roma della restaurazione, 1792–1827* (Milan, 1981), pp. 525–612.

73. Yves Chiron, *Pie IX, Pape Moderne* (Paris, 1995), pp. 88–129.

74. Antoine Roquette, *La restauration et la révolution espagnole: de Cadix au Trocadéro* (Paris, 2016).

75. Bellocchi, *Tutte le encicliche*, III, p.27.

76. Leflon, *La Crise Révolutionnaire*, pp. 453–4.

77. Lynch, *New Worlds*, p. 123.

78. Emilio La Parra, *Fernando VII: un rey deseado y detestado* (Barcelona, 2018), pp. 580–97.

79. Mark Lawrence, *Spain's First Carlist War, 1833–40* (Basingstoke, 2014).

80. Angelo Mercati, *Raccolta di concordati su materie ecclesiastiche tra la Santa Sede e le autorità civili* (Rome, 1919), pp. 800–1085.

81. Langley, *The Americas in the Age of Revolution*, pp. 217–60; Anthony McFarlane, *War and Independence in Spanish America* (London, 2014), pp. 65–78.

82. Lynch, *New Worlds*, pp. 129–60; Douglass Sullivan-González, 'Religious Devotion, Rebellion and Messianic Movements: Popular Catholicism in the nineteenth century', in Virginia Garrard-Burnett, Paul Freston and Stephen C. Doves (eds), *Religions in Latin America* (Cambridge, 2016), pp. 269–85.

83. Lynch, *New Worlds*, pp. 133–4.

84. Rosas, *Mitos de la historia mexicana de Hidalgo a Zedillo*.

85. Matthew Butler, 'Liberalism, Anticlericalism and Antireligious

Currents in the Nineteenth Century', in Garrard-Burnett, Freston and Doves (eds), *Religions in Latin America*, pp. 251–68.

86. Lynch, *Simón Bolívar*, pp. 244–9.

87. Lynch, *New Worlds*, pp. 129–60.

88. Michael Broers and Ambrogio Caiani (eds), *A History of the European Restorations* (2 vols, London, 2019).

89. Joseph Scmidlin, *Histoire des papes de l'époque contemporaine*, Part II: *Léon XII, Pie VIII and Grégoire XVI, 1823–1846* (Paris, 1940).

90. Donald J. Keefe, SJ, 'Tracking a Footnote', *Fellowship of Catholic Scholars Newsletter*, Vol. 9, No. 4 (1986) pp. 6–7.

91. Yves-Marie Bercé and Jean-Claude Otteni, 'Pratique de la vaccination antivariolique dans les provinces de l'État pontifical au 19ème siècle: remarques sur le supposé interdit vaccinal de Léon XII', *Revue d'histoire ecclésiastique*, Vol. 103, No. 2 (2008), pp. 448–66.

92. Leflon, *La Crise Révolutionnaire*, pp. 385–91.

93. Hugh Honour, *Romanticism* (London, 1979).

94. Tim Blanning, *The Romantic Revolution* (London, 2011), p. 9.

95. Emile Perreau-Saussine, *Catholicism and Democracy: An Essay in the History of Political Thought* (Princeton, NJ, 2012), pp. 37–69; Alec Vidler, *A Century of Social Catholicism, 1820–1920* (London, 1964).

96. Ambrogio A. Caiani, 'The Concile National of 1811: Napoleon, Gallicanism and the failure of neo-conciliarism', *Journal of Ecclesiastical History*, Vol. 70, No. 3 (2019), pp. 546–64.

97. Carolina Armenteros, *The French Idea of History: Joseph De Maistre and His Heirs, 1794–1854* (Ithaca, NY, 2011) pp. 115–55.

98. Vidler, *A Century of Social Catholicism*.

99. Tanguy Kenec'Hdu, *Lamennais: un prêtre en recherche* (Saint-Cénéré, 1982), pp. 37–45.

100. Aimé Richardt, *Lamennais: le révolté, 1782–1854* (Paris, 2016), pp. 25–6.

101. Felicité and Jean-Marie Lamennais, *Réflexions sur l'état de l'eglise en France pendant le dix-huitième siècle et sur sa situation actuelle* (Lyon, 1808).

102. Victor Giraud, *La Vie tragique de Lamennais* (Paris, 1933), pp. 18–23.

103. Carolina Armenteros, 'Hugues-Félicité Robert de Lamennais, 1782–1854: Lost sheep of the religious enlightenment', in Jeffrey Burson and Ulrich Lehner (eds), *Enlightenment and Catholicism in Europe: A Transnational History* (Notre Dame, IN, 2014), pp. 145–164, esp. pp. 147–50.

104. Nicholas Atkin and Frank Tallett, *Priests, Prelates and People: A History of European Catholicism since 1750* (Oxford, 2003), p. 90.

105. Mary S. Hartman, 'The Sacrilege Law of 1825 in France: A study in anticlericalism and mythmaking', *Journal of Modern History*, Vol. 44, No. 1 (1972), pp. 21–37.

106. Felicité de Lamennais, *Essai sur l'indifférence en matière de religion* (7 edn, 2 vols, Paris, 1823), II, pp. 387–99, 463–72.

107. Sheryl Kroen, *Politics and Theatre: The Crisis of Legitimacy in Restoration France 1815–1830* (Los Angeles 2000), pp. 89–96, 203–16.

108. Martyn Lyons, *Reading Culture and Writing Practices in Nineteenth-century France* (Toronto, 2008), pp. 65–91.

109. Paul Dudon, *Lamennais et le Saint-Siège 1820–1834 d'après des document inédits et les archives du Vatican* (Paris, 1911), pp. 26–32.

110. Louis le Guillou, *Lamennais* (Bruges, 1969), p. 29.

111. Felicité de Lamennais, *De la religion considérée dans ses rapports avec l'ordre politique et civil* (Paris, 1826), pp. 153–82.

112. Antoine Ricard, *Lamennais* (Paris, 1883), p. 159.

113. Alfred Roussel, *Lamennais à La Chènaie, supérieur de la congrégation de Saint-Pierre, 1828–1833: le père, l'apôtre, le moraliste* (Paris, 1909).

114. Richardt, *Lamennais: le révolté*, pp. 56–8.

115. Fergus O'Ferrall, *Catholic Emancipation, Daniel O'Connell and the Birth of Irish Democracy 1820–30* (Dublin, 1985), p. 62.

116. Patrick M. Geoghegan, *Liberator: The Life and Death of Daniel O'Connell 1830–1847* (London, 2012).

117. Fraser, *The King and the Catholics*, pp. 271–81.

118. Ibid, pp. 272.

119. Vincent P. Ruddy, 'Dublin 1843: O'Connell's repeal meetings', *Dublin Historical Record*, Vol. 68, No. 1 (2015), pp. 60–70; Christine Kinealy, *Repeal and Revolution: 1848 in Ireland* (Manchester, 2013).

120. Brian Jenkins, *Irish Nationalism and the British State: From Repeal to Revolutionary Nationalism* (Montreal, 2006).

121. Pierre Joannon, 'A Romantic Hibernophile: Charles de Montalembert, 'the O'Connell of France', *Etudes Irlandaises*, special issue (1991), pp. 75–87 ; Geraldine Grogan, 'Daniel O'Connell and European Catholic Thought', *Studies: An Irish Quarterly Review*, Vol. 80, No. 317 (1991), pp. 56–64; Derek Holmes, 'Catholics and Politics at the time of Emancipation', *New Blackfriars*, Vol. 54, No. 639 (1973), pp. 365–73.

122. Felicité de Lamennais, *Des Progrès de la révolution et de la guerre contre l'église* (Paris, 1829), p. 119.

123. Charles Boutard, *Lamennais, sa vie et ses doctrines* (3 vols, Paris, 1908), II, pp. 107–36.

124. Felicité de Lamennais, *Articles de L'Avenir* (Paris, 1930), No. 53, 7 December 1830, pp. 384–5.

125. Ibid, pp. 382–9.

126. Lamennais, *Articles de L'Avenir*, No. 59, 13 December 1830, pp. 406–13: 'Aux catholiques français sur la révolution de la Belgique'.

127. Henri Comte de Merode and Marquis de Beauffort, *De l'esprit de vie et de l'esprit de mort* (Louvain, 1831), p. 105.

128. *Constitution* Belge, 1831, online at https://mjp.univ-perp.fr/constit/be1831.htm [accessed 20 June 2021].

129. Elisabeth Claude and Jacques Kuhnmunch, *Louise et Léopold: le mariage du premier roi des Belges à Compiègne le 9 août 1832* (Compiègne, 2008).

130. Rik Torfs, 'Religion and State in Belgium', *Insight Turkey*, Vol. 17, No. 1 (2015), pp. 97–119.

131. Leflon, *La Crise Révolutionnaire*, p. 455.

132. Vincent Viaene, *Belgium and the Holy See, from Gregory XVI to Pius IX, 1831–1859* (Catholic Revival Society and Politics in 19th-century Europe) (Brussels, 2001), pp. 390–404.

133. Friedrich Engel-Janosi, 'Austria and the Conclave of 1878', *Catholic Historical Review*, Vol. 39, No. 2 (1953), pp. 142–66.

134. Lillian Parker Wallace, *Leo XIII and the Rise of Socialism* (Durham, NC, 1966).

135. Henri-Xavier Arquilliere, *Lamennais et le Gallicanisme* (Paris, 1907).

136. Pamela M. Pilbeam, 'The Emergence of Opposition to the Orleanist Monarchy, August 1830–April 1831', *English Historical Review*, Vol. 85, No. 334 (1970), pp. 12–28, esp. pp. 17–20.

137. Vallery-Radot, *Lamennais, ou le prêtre malgré lui* (Paris, 1931), p. 287.

138. Atkin and Tallett, *Priests, Prelates and People*, p. 91.

139. Lino Marini, Giovanni Tocci, Cesare Mozzarelli and Aldo Stella, *I ducati padani, trento e trieste* (Storia d'Italia, Vol. XVII) (Turin, 1979), pp. 184–6.

140. Ibid, pp. 325–6.

141. Cencetti, *Le tre legazioni*.

142. Antonio Zanolini, *La rivoluzione avvenuta nello Stato Romano l'anno 1831* (Bologna, 1878).

143. Alan J. Reinerman, *Austria and the Papacy in the Age of Metternich* (2 vols, Washington, DC, 1989), II, pp. 21–34.

144. Alberto Maria Ghisalberti, 'Gregorio XVI e il Risorgimento Italiano', in Censo Costantini et al., *Gregorio XVI: miscelllanea commemorativa parte seconde* (Miscellanea Historiae Pontificiae, Vol. XIV) (Rome, 1948), pp. 123–34.

145. Daniele Menozzi, *Cattolicesimo, nazione e nazionalismo: Catholicism, nation and nationalism* (Pisa, 2015).

146. Alan J. Reinerman, 'Metternich, Pope Gregory XVI, and Revolutionary Poland, 1831–1842', *Catholic Historical Review*, Vol. 86, No. 4 (2000), pp. 603–19.

147. Vallery-Radot, *Lamennais ou le prêtre malgré lui*, p.287.

148. Lamennais, *Articles de L'Avenir* (Paris, 1832), No. 395, 15 November 1831: Suspension de l'Avenir, p. 158.

149. Boutard, *Lamennais, sa vie et ses doctrines*, II, pp. 258–61.

150. Jean-René Derré and Pierre Moisy, *Metternich et Lamennais, d'après les documents conservés aux Archives de Vienne* (Paris, 1963).

151. Carol E. Harrison, *Romantic Catholics: France's Postrevolutionary Generation in Search of a Modern Faith* (Ithaca, NY, 2014), p. 132.

152. Dudon, *Lamennais et le Saint-Siège, 1820–1834*, p. 155.

153. Reinerman, *Austria and the Papacy in the Age of Metternich*, II, pp. 81–133.

154. Miroslav Šedivý, *The Decline of the Congress System: Metternich, Italy and European Diplomacy* (London, 2018), pp. 61–4.

155. Boutard, *Lamennais, sa vie et ses doctrines*, II, p. 287.

156. Vallery-Radot, *Lamennais, ou le prêtre malgré lui*, p. 299.

157. Dudon, *Lamennais et le Saint-Siège*, pp. 159–60.

158. Vallery-Radot, *Lamennais, ou le prêtre malgré lui*, p. 302.

159. Reinerman, 'Metternich, Pope Gregory XVI, and Revolutionary Poland', pp. 609–12.

160. Vallery-Radot, *Lamennais ou le prêtre malgré lui*, pp. 304–5.

161. Paul Droulers, 'L'abbé d'Astros et l'expérience religieuse du Premier Empire', *Gregorianum*, Vol. 29, No. 2 (1948), pp. 252–87.

162. Paul-Thérèse-David d'Astros, *Censure de cinquante-six propositions extraites des divers écrits de M. De Lamennais et de ses disciples, par plusieurs evêques de France et lettre des mêmes évêques au souverain pontife Grégoire XVI* (Toulouse, 1835), pp. 59–92. Antoine Roquette, *Monseigneur Frayssinous, grand maître de l'université sous la restauration – evêque d'Hermopolis ou le chant du cygne du trône et de l'autel* (Paris, 2007), p. 333.

163. Thomas Albert Howard, *The Pope and the Professor: Pius IX, Ignaz von Döllinger, and the Quandary of the Modern Age* (Oxford, 2017), pp. 44–51.

164. Vallery-Radot, *Lamennais, ou le prêtre malgré lui*, pp. 307–8.

165. Bellocchi, *Tutte le encicliche*, III p. 177.

166. Boutard, *Lamennais, sa vie et ses doctrines*, II, p. 330.

167. Dudon, *Lamennais et le Saint-Siège*, pp. 213–41.

168. Georges Collas, 'La Chênaie', *Bulletin de l'Association Guillaume Budé*, No. 2 (1956), pp. 102–19.

169. Louis de Villefosse, *Lamennais, ou l'occasion manquée* (Paris, 1945), pp. 93–114.

170. Adam Mickiewicz, *Livre des Pèlerins Polonais* (Paris, 1833), pp. 171–6.

171. Paul Droulers, SJ, *Action Pastorale et problèmes sociaux sous la monarchie de juillet chez Mgr. d'Astros archevêque de Toulouse, censeur de Lamennais* (Paris, 1954), pp. 142–4.

172. Bellocchi, *Tutte le encicliche*, III, pp. 193–203.

173. Vallery-Radot, *Lamennais, ou le prêtre malgré lui*, pp. 341–5.

174. Dudon, *Lamennais et le Saint-Siège*, p. 419. Vallery-Radot, *Lamennais, ou le prêtre malgré lui*, p. 340.

175. Bellocchi, *Tutte le encicliche*, III, pp. 202–3.

176. Alec R. Vidler, *Prophecy and Papacy: A Study of Lamennais, the Church and the Revolution* (London, 1954), pp. 237–39.

177. Villefosse, *Lamennais, ou l'occasion manquée*, p. 113.

178. Vallery-Radot, *Lamennais, ou le prêtre malgré lui*, pp. 345–7.

179. Boutard, *Lamennais, sa vie et ses doctrines*, III, pp. 1–33.

180. Ibid, pp. 55–61.

181. Ricard, *Lamennais*, pp. 268–94.

182. Bellocchi, *Tutte le encicliche*, III, p. 211.

183. Boutard, *Lamennais, sa vie et ses doctrines*, III, pp. 195–226.

184. Pamela Pilbeam, *French Socialists before Marx* (Teddington, 2000), pp. 49, 174.

185. Vallery-Radot, *Lamennais, ou le prêtre malgré lui*, pp. 396–8.

186. Joe Holland, *Modern Catholic Social Teaching: The Popes Confront the Industrial Age, 1740–1958* (New York, 2003), pp. 71–86.

187. Christopher Guyver, *The Second French Republic, 1848–1852: A Political Reinterpretation* (Basingstoke, 2016), esp. ch. 2.

188. Anne Philibert, *Henri Lacordaire* (Paris, 2016).

189. Archibald J. Dunn, *Frederic Ozanam and the Establishment of the Society of St. Vincent de Paul* (New York, 1887).

190. Aurélien Ligneureux, *Les Impériaux: administrer et habiter l'Europe de Napoléon* (Paris, 2019), pp. 215, 327.

191. Alan S. Kahan, *Aristocratic Liberalism: The Social and Political thought of Jacob Burckhardt, John Stuart Mill and Alexis de Tocqueville* (London, 2001), pp. 115–34.

192. Alban de Villeneuve-Bargemont, *Économie politique chrétienne* (3 vols, Paris, 1834).

193. Piero Roggi, 'Il pensiero economico-sociale di Albano de Villeneuve-Bargemont', *Rivista Internazionale di Scienze Sociali*, Third series, Vol. 44. A. 81, Fasc. 3 (1973), pp. 229–51, esp. p. 245.

194. Benjamin F. Martin, Jr., *Count Albert De Mun, Paladin of the Third Republic* (Chapel Hill, NC, 2011), pp. 14–30, 295–301; Stephen D. Kale, *Legitimism and the Reconstruction of French Society, 1852–1883* (Baton Rouge, LA, 1992).

195. Šedivý, *The Decline of the Congress System*, p. 75.

196. Leflon, *La Crise Révolutionnaire*, pp. 438–40.

197. Silvana Patriarca, *Italian Vices, Nation and Character from the Risorgimento to the Republic* (Cambridge, 2010), esp. chs. 2–3.

198. Denis Mack Smith, *Mazzini* (London, 1994); Giovanna Angelini, 'Le correnti politiche del risorgimento', *Il Politico*, Vol. 76, No. 2 (2011), pp. 67–87.

199. Giorgio Rumi, *Gioberti* (Bologna, 1999), pp. 17–22.

200. Vincenzo Gioberti, *Lettre sur les doctrines philosophiques et politiques de M. de Lamennais* (Capolago, 1851).

201. Cf. Giuseppe Mazzini, *La Giovine Italia e l'abate Vincenzo Gioberti* (Turin, 1849).

202. Rumi, *Gioberti*, pp. 20–1.

203. Vincenzo Gioberti, *Il Gesuita Moderna* (6 vols, Milan, 1940), passim.

204. Vincenzo Gioberti, *Del primato morale e civile degli italiani* (2 vols, Brussels, 1843).

205. For the classic study see Oscar Browning, *Guelphs and Ghibellines: A Short History of Medieval Italy from 1250–1409* (London, 1894).

206. Alberto Mario Banti, *Nel nome dell'Italia: Il risorgimento nelle testimonianze, nei documenti e nelle immagini* (Rome, 2010), p. 148.

207. Bruce Haddock, 'Political Union without Social Revolution: Vincenzo Gioberti's Primato', *Historical Journal*, Vol. 41, No. 3 (1998), pp. 705–23.

208. Duane Koenig, 'Backdrop to Revolution: The reign of Pope Gregory XVI', *Quarterly Journal of the Florida Academy of Sciences*, Vol. 9, No. 2 (1946), pp. 131–43.

209. John Michael Hill, *Persecuted Prophet, Antonio Rosmini* (Leominster, 2014), pp. 9–42, 83, 67–8; Umberto Muratore, 'Manzoni e Rosmini: le ragioni di un'amicizie spirituale', *Rivista di Filosofia Neo-Scolastica*, Vol. 98, No. 1 (2006), pp. 131–7.

210. Umberto Muratore, *Antonio Rosmini: la società della carità* (Stresa, 2005).

211. Antonio Romsini, *Delle cinque piaghe della santa chiesa* (Milan, 1997).

212. Francesco Traniello, 'Riforma della Chiesa e utopie del '48: il caso delle cinque piaghe di Rosmini', *Contemporanea*, Vol. 1, No. 3 (1998), pp. 407–26.

213. Frank J. Coppa, *The Modern Papacy since 1789*, pp. 77–8.

214. William J. Callahan, *Church, Politics, and Society in Spain, 1750–1874* (Cambridge, MA, 1984), p.153–5.

215. Renato Lefebvre, 'Santa Sede e Russia e i colloqui dello Czar Nicola I nei documenti Vaticani 1843–1846', in Costantini et al., *Gregorio XVI*, pp. 231–93.

216. Adiren Boudou, *Le Saint-Siège et la Russie 1814–1847* (Paris, 1922), pp. 413–48.

217. James F. MacMillan, 'Catholic Christianity in France from the Restoration to the Separation of Church and State, 1815–1905', in Gilley and Stanley (eds), *World Christianities*, pp. 217–32, esp. p. 218.

218. Roger Price, *Religious Renewal in France 1789–187*, p. 41.

219. Mary Heimann, 'Catholic Revivalism in Worship and Devotion', in Gilley and Stanley (eds), *World Christianities*, pp. 70–83; Hugh

McLeod, *Religion and the People of Western Europe 1789–1970* (Oxford, 1981), pp. 47–53, esp. 76.

220. René Laurentin and C. M. P. Roche (eds), *Catherine Labouré et la médaille miraculeuse, documents authentiques 1830–1876* (Paris, 1976).
221. Censo Costantini, 'Gregorio XVI e le missioni', in Constantini et al., *Gregorio XVI*, pp. 1–28.
222. Adrian Hastings, *The Church in Africa, 1450–1950* (Oxford, 1994), pp. 408–24.
223. Bellocchi, *Tutte le encicliche*, III, pp. 271–3.
224. Patrick Wilcken, *Empire Adrift: The Portuguese Court in Rio De Janeiro, 1808–1821* (London, 2005); Kirsten Schultz, *Tropical Versailles, Empire, Monarchy, and the Portuguese Royal Court in Rio de Janeiro, 1808–1821* (London, 2001).
225. Philip D. Curtin, *The Rise and Fall of the Plantation Complex: Essays in Atlantic History* (Cambridge, 1998).
226. Lynch, *New Worlds*, pp. 157–60.

6 Revolution in Rome, Pio Nono and the Roman Republic of 1846–50

1. Christoph Luitpold Frommel, 'I chiostri di S. Ambrogio e il cortile della cancelleria a Roma, un confronto stilistico', *Arte Lombarda*, No. 79, No. 4 (1986), pp. 9–18.
2. Gustavo Brigante Colonna, *L' Uccisione di Pellegrino Rossi, 15 novembre 1848* (Milan, 1938).
3. Giuseppe Monsagrati, *Roma senza il papa, la repubblica romana del 1849* (Bari, 2014), p. 30.
4. Stefan Tomassini, *Storia avventurosa della rivoluzione romana, repubblicani, liberali e papalini nella Roma del 48* (Milan, 2008), p. 165.
5. Chadwick, *A History of the Popes*, p. 83.
6. Kertzer, *The Pope Who Would Be King*, pp. 107–8.
7. Carlo Falconi, *Il cardinale Antonelli: Vita e carriera del Richelieu italiano nella Chiesa di Pio IX* (Rome, 1983).
8. Giulio Andreotti, *La fuga di Pio IX e l'ospitalità dei Borbone* (Rome, 2003), pp. 15–20; Alberto M. Ghisalberti, 'Intorno alla fuga di Pio IX', *Archivio Storico Italiano*, Vol. 127, No. 1/2 (1969), pp. 109–40.
9. Dorothea Wiesenberger, '"Graf Spaur, Ihr Namen wird in der Geschichte glänzen…" Die Persönlichkeit des bayerischen Gesandten in Rom Karl Graf von Spaur 1794–1854 anhand von ausgewählten Quellen aus dem Stürgkh´schen Familienarchiv', *Mitteilungen des Steiermärkischen Landesarchivs*, Vol. 46 (1996), pp. 127–79, esp. pp. 132–43.
10. Teresa Giraud Spaur, *Relazione del viaggio di Pio IX. P.M. a Gaeta* (Trent, 2011), esp. 20–33.

11. Odoardo Toti, *Storia di Civitavecchia, da Pio VII alla fine del governo pontificio* (Rome, 2000).
12. Frank J. Coppa, *Cardinal Antonelli and Papal Politics in European Affairs* (New York, 1990), pp. 64–5.
13. Tomassini, *Storia avventurosa della rivoluzione romana*, p. 172; Carla Nardi, *Napoleone e Roma, dalla consulta romana al ritorno di Pio VII 1811–1814* (Rome, 2005).
14. Giacomo Martina and Wiktor Gramatowski, 'La relazione ufficiale sul conclave del 1846, nel 150° anniversario dell'elezione di Pio IX', *Archivum Historiae Pontificiae*, Vol. 34 (1996), pp. 159–212.
15. Edward E. Y. Hales, *Pio Nono: A Study in European Politics and Religion in the Nineteenth Century* (London, 1956), pp. 36–9.
16. Giovanni-Maria Mastai Ferretti, 'Pensieri relativi all'amministrazione pubblica dello Stato pontificio', in Alberto Serafini (ed.), *Pio IX: Giovanni Maria Mastai Ferretti dalla giovinezza alla morte nei suoi scritti e discorsi editi e inediti*, Vol. 1, *Le vie della divina provvidenza 1792–1846* (Vatican, 1958), pp. 1397–1406.
17. Giuseppe M. Zaccaria, 'La elezione di Pio IX 1846 nella corrispondenza diplomatica dell'archivio vaticano', *Rivista di Storia della Chiesa in Italia*, Vol. 26 (1972), pp. 421–35.
18. Luigi Salvatorelli, *Prima e dopo il Quarantotto* (Rome, 1948), esp. Ch. 4.
19. Roger Aubert, *Le Pontificat de Pie IX 1846–1878* (Paris, 1952), p. 16.
20. Ignazio Veca, *Il Mito di Pio IX: Storia di un papa liberale e nazionale* (Rome, 2018), pp. 57–94.
21. Bellocchi, *Tutte le encicliche*, IV, pp. 13–23.
22. H. Russell Williams, 'Pius IX and a Visitor in Plaid Trousers', *Catholic Historical Review*, Vol. 50, No. 2 (1964), pp. 208–10; Saho Matsumoto-Best, *Britain and the Papacy in the Age of Revolution, 1846–1851* (Woodenbridge, 2003). Massimo Franco, *Parallel Empires: The Vatican and the United States: Two Centuries of Alliance and Conflict* (New York, 2008), p. 32.
23. Robert A. Maryks and Jonathan Wright (eds), *Jesuit Survival and Restoration: A Global History, 1773–1900* (Leiden, 2014).
24. Paola Vismara, 'La Chiesa nella storia, note su alcune critiche di Carlo Maria Curci al Gesuita Moderno', *Rivista di storia della Chiesa in Italia*, Vol. 64, No. 1 (2010), pp. 55–69.
25. Aubert, *Le Pontificat de Pie IX* pp. 24–6.
26. Veca, *Il Mito di Pio IX*, pp. 103–33.
27. Pierre Rosanvallon, *La Monarchie impossible: les chartes de 1814 et de 1830* (Paris, 1994); Markus J. Prutsch, *Making Sense of Constitutional Monarchism in Post-Napoleonic France and Germany* (Basingstoke, 2013).

28. Friedrich Engel-Janosi, 'French and Austrian Political Advice to Pius IX, 1846–1848', *Catholic Historical Review*, Vol. 38, No. 1 (1952), pp. 1–20.

29. Luc Marco, 'Un économiste éclectique, Pellegrino Rossi 1787–1848', *Revue d'économie politique*, Vol. 98, No. 2 (1988), pp. 293–302; Henry d' Ideville, *Le comte Pellegrino Rossi: sa vie, son oeuvre, sa mort 1787–1848* (Paris, 1887).

30. Chadwick, *A History of the Popes*, pp. 65–8.

31. Yves Chiron, *Pie IX, Pape Moderne* (Paris, 1995), p. 169.

32. Harry Hearder, 'The Making of the Roman Republic, 1848–1849', *History*, Vol. 60, No.1 99 (1975), pp. 169–184; Robert Carocci, *La Repubblica Romana, 1849 prove di democrazia e socialismo nel risorgimento* (Rome, 2017), pp. 27–30; Anon, *Statuto del Circolo popolare nazionale in Roma approvato nelle assemblee generali de'21 maggio e 15 giugno 1848* (Rome, 1848).

33. Alberto Maria Ghisalberti, *Nuove ricerche sugli inizi del pontificato di Pio IX e sulla consulta di stato* (Rome, 1939).

34. Chadwick, *A History of the Popes*, p. 72.

35. Claudio Modena, *Ciceruacchio: Angelo Brunetti, capopopolo di Roma* (Rome, 2011).

36. Frank J. Coppa, 'Pio Nono and the Jews: From reform to reaction, 1846–1878', *Catholic Historical Review*, Vol. 89, No. 4 (2003), pp. 671–95; Paolo Colbi, 'Gli Ebrei italiani alla vigilia del risorgimento', *La Rassegna Mensile di Israel*, Vol. 29, No. 10 (1963), pp. 438–45, esp. pp. 440–1; Ignazio Veca, 'La strana emancipazione: Pio IX e gli ebrei nel lungo Quarantotto', *Contemporanea*, Vol. 17, No. 1 (2014), pp. 3–30; Sam Waagenaar, *The Pope's Jews* (London, 1974), pp. 253–71; for the broader context, see Paolo Guadagno and Banchetti Romani, *Socialità e politica dall'ascesa di Pio IX alla repubblica romana* (Rome, 2020); Michael Goldfarb, *Emancipation: How Liberating Europe's Jews from the Ghetto led to Revolution and Renaissance* (New York, 2009), pp. 195–241.

37. Chiron, *Pie IX*, pp. 179–80.

38. Tomassini, *Storia avventurosa della rivoluzione romana*, pp. 30–1.

39. Martina, *Pio IX*, Vol. I: *1846–1850* (Rome, 1974), pp. 139–41.

40. Sked, *Radetzky*, pp. 119–24.

41. Miroslav Šedivý, 'The Austrian 'occupation' of Ferrara in 1847: Its legal aspect between myth and reality', *Journal of Modern Italian Studies*, Vol. 23, No. 2 (2018), pp. 139–55.

42. Harry Hearder, *Italy in the Age of the Risorgimento, 1790–1870* (London, 2014), pp. 80–1.

43. Giuseppe Mazzini, *A Pio IX. P. O. M. Lettera* (Paris, 1848).

44. Martina, *Pio IX*, I, p. 178.

45. Kertzer, *The Pope Who Would Be King*, p. 51.

46. Michael Rapport, *1848: Year of Revolution* (London, 2010).

47. Asef Bayat, *Revolution without Revolutionaries: Making Sense of the Arab Spring* (Stanford, CA, 2017); Lin Noueihed and Alex Warren, *The Battle for the Arab Spring: Revolution, Counter-revolution and the Making of a New Era* (London, 2013).

48. Peter Jones, *The 1848 Revolutions* (London, 1991).

49. Roberto Romani, 'Reluctant Revolutionaries: Moderate liberalism in the kingdom of Sardinia 1849–1859', *Historical Journal*, Vol. 55, No. 1 (2012), pp. 45–73; Jonathan Sperber, *The European Revolutions 1848–1851* (2nd edn, Cambridge, 2005), pp. 117, 136–7.

50. Chiron, *Pie IX*, p. 183.

51. Bellocchi, *Tutte le encicliche*, IV, p. 35.

52. Ibid, pp. 34–44.

53. Horst Dippel (ed.), *Executive and Legislative Powers in the Constitutions of 1848–1849* (Berlin, 1999); Linda Colley, *The Gun, the Ship and the Pen: Warfare, Constitutions and the Making of the Modern World* (London, 2021), Ch. 4.

54. Coppa, *Cardinal Antonelli and Papal Politics*, pp. 47–52.

55. Filippo Ambrosini, *Carlo Alberto Re* (Turin, 2004), pp. 338–40.

56. Chiron, *Pie IX*, p. 185.

57. Pietro Ferrua, *Giovanni Durando, cenni biografici* (Turin, 1879); Vincenzo Fannini, 'Ferrari, Andrea', in *Treccani dizionario biografico degli italiani*, online at www.treccani.it/enciclopedia/andrea-ferrari_res-09e936f7-87ed-11dc-8e9d-0016357eee51_(Dizionario-Biografico)/ [accessed 5 July 2021].

58. Paul Ginsborg, *Daniele Manin and the Venetian Revolution of 1848–1849* (Cambridge, 1979), p. 205.

59. Chiron, *Pie IX*, p. 187.

60. Martina, *Pio IX*, I, 234–5.

61. Kertzer, *The Pope Who Would Be King*, p. 74.

62. Bellocchi *Tutte le encicliche*, IV, pp. 45–8.

63. Ibid, p. 47.

64. Domenico Gaspari, *Vita di Terenzio Mamiani Della Rovere* (Ancona, 1888).

65. Piero Pieri, *Storia militare del risorgimento* (Turin, 1962), pp. 378–90.

66. Giorgio Rumi, *Gioberti* (Bologna, 1999), pp. 21–3.

67. John Michael Hill, *Persecuted Prophet*, pp. 185–9.

68. Luciano Malusa and Stefania Zanardi (eds), *Della Missione a Roma di Antonio Rosmini-Serbati negli anni 1848–1849*, Vol.1A (Rome, 2020), pp. 387–98, 458–65; Kenelm Foster, 'Rosmini and Pius IX, 1848–49', *Blackfriars*, Vol. 36, No. 424–5 (1955), pp. 264–71.

69. Mario d'Addio, 'Rosmini e la Confederazione Italiana', *Il Politico*, Vol. 59, No. 2 (1994), pp. 189–231.

70. Frederick A. de Luna, *The French Republic under Cavaignac, 1848* (Princeton, NJ, 1969), pp. 128–73.

71. Sperber, *The European Revolutions 1848–1851*, pp. 208–9.

72. Giuseppe Campolieti, *Il re bomba: Ferdinando II, il Borbone di Napoli che per primo lottò contro l'unità d'Italia* (Rome, 2001).

73. Munro Price, *The Perilous Crown: France between Revolutions 1814–1848* (Basingstoke, 2007), pp. 326–65.

74. Charles de Mazade, 'Pellegrino Rossi, l'Italie et la Papauté', *Revue des deux mondes*, Vol. 36, No. 3 (1861), pp. 718–53.

75. Renato Mori, 'Il progetto di lega neoguelfa di Pellegrino Rossi', *Rivista di studi politici internazionali*, Vol. 24, No. 4 (1957), pp. 602–28.

76. Martina, *Pio IX*, I, pp. 279–86.

77. Ideville, *Le comte Pellegrino Rossi*, pp. 245–60.

78. Andreotti, *La fuga di Pio IX*, p. 24.

79. Chiron, *Pie IX*, p. 197.

80. Kertzer, *The Pope Who Would Be King*, pp. 117–18.

81. Andreotti, *La fuga di Pio IX*, p. 27.

82. Kertzer, *The Pope Who Would Be King*, pp. 119–21.

83. Chadwick, *A History of the Popes*, p. 85.

84. Tomassini, *Storia avventurosa della rivoluzione romana*, pp. 182–8.

85. John Bierman, *Napoleon III and his Carnival Empire* (London, 1988), pp. 70–1.

86. Roger Price, *The Church and the State in France 1789–1870* (Basingstoke, 2017), pp. 93–105.

87. Bellocchi, *Tutte le encicliche*, IV, p. 50.

88. Caiani, *To Kidnap a Pope*, pp. 281–90.

89. Hill, *Persecuted Prophet*, p. 201.

90. Kertzer, *The Pope Who Would Be King*, p. 147.

91. Tim Blanning, *The Triumph of Music: The Rise of Composers, Musicians and their Art* (Cambridge, MA, 2007), pp. 270–1.

92. Monsagrati, *Roma Senza il Papa*, pp. 53–60.

93. Daniele Arru, *La legislazione della Repubblica romana del 1849 in materia ecclesiastica* (Bari, 2012) p. 166.

94. Denis Mack Smith, *Mazzini* (London, 1994), pp. 64–70; Giuseppe Picazio, *L'altra faccia di Giuseppe Mazzini, ovvero il diavolo e l'acqua santa, Mazzini e Pio IX* (Rome, 2018).

95. Alfonso Scirocco, *Garibaldi, Citizen of the World: A Biography* (Princeton, NJ, 2007), pp. 138–167.

96. Umberto Beseghi, *Ugo Bassi*, Vol. II: *Il Martire* (Parma, 1940), pp. 64–98.

97. Rapport, *1848: Year of Revolution*, pp. 263–334.

98. Romano Paolo Coppini, *Il Granducato di Toscana, dagli anni francesi all'unità* (Storia d'Italia, Vol. XIII) (Turin 1993), pp. 394–400.

99. Ambrosini, *Carlo Alberto*, pp. 376–9; Niccolò Rodolico, *Carlo Alberto negli 1843–1849* (Florence, 1943), pp. 491–514.

100. Ambrosini, *Carlo Alberto*, pp. 381–7.

101. Jonathan Keates, *The Siege of Venice* (London, 2006).

102. Edward D. Mansfield and Jack L. Snyder, *Electing to Fight: Why Emerging Democracies Go to War* (Boston, MA, 2005), p. 185.

103. Kertzer, *The Pope Who Would Be King*, pp. 171–7.

104. Émile Bourgeois, *Rome et Napoléon III 1849–1870: Etude sur les origines et la chute du Second Empire* (Paris, 1907), pp. 3–19.

105. Anon, *Bando Difesa della Repubblica Romana 1849*, online at http://www.repubblicaromana-1849.it/index.php?7/dettaglio/andtype=documentoandid=600andbackUrl=index.php%3F5%2Fbandi%2520e%2520fogli%2520volanti%26documento_data2%3D1849%2520-%252004%26documento_data%3D1849%2520-%2520aprile%26searchFld%3Dresis%26id%3D%26type%3D%26pageNum%3D1 [accessed 6 July 2021].

106. Lucy Riall, *Garibaldi, Invention of a Hero* (London, 2007), pp. 81–97.

107. Pietro Pistelli and Marco Severini, *L'alba della democrazia: Garibaldi, Bruti e la repubblica romana* (Rome, 2004), p. 32.

108. Kertzer, *The Pope Who Would Be King*, p. 189; Francesco Maria Agnoli, *L'ultimo mito del risorgimento: storia senza retorica della repubblica romana 9 febbraio – 4 luglio 1849* (Rome, 2011), pp. 70–2.

109. Mauro Quercioli, *Le mura papali di Roma città Leonina e Gianicolo: storia, topografia, politica* (Rome, 1978).

110. Tomassini, *Storia avventurosa della rivoluzione romana*, pp. 329–45.

111. Edgar Holt, *Risorgimento: The Making of Italy, 1815–1870* (Basingstoke, 1970), p. 170.

112. Gregorio Alonso, 'Dar la vida por la contrarrevolución? Voluntarios españoles en defensa del poder temporal de Pío IX en 1850', in Pedro Rújula López and Javier Ramón Solans (eds), *El desafío de la revolución: reacciones, antiliberales y contrarrevolucionarios siglos XVIII y XIX* (Madrid, 2017), pp. 125–40.

113. George Barnett Smith, *The Life and Enterprises of Ferdinand de Lesseps* (London, 1893), pp. 18–49; and Pierre Rain, 'La Politique italienne de Napoléon III 1849–1861', *Revue des deux mondes* (1961), pp. 276–88.

114. Alberto Mario Banti, *Il risorgimento italiano* (Bari, 2013); Lucy Riall, *Risorgimento: The History of Italy from Napoleon to Nation State* (Basingstoke, 2008); Isabella Dal Fabbro, *Il contro risorgimento, gli italiani al servizio imperiale, i Lombardi, i Veneti e i Friulani nell'imperia regia armata 1814–1866* (Milan, 2010).

115. Mack Smith, *Mazzini*, pp. 71–2.

116. Inès Murat, *La Deuxième République* (Paris, 1987), pp. 388–407.

117. Tomassini, *Storia avventurosa della rivoluzione romana*, pp. 398–400.

118. Federico Torre, *Memorie storiche sull'intervento francese in Roma nel 1849 di Federico Torre* (2 vols, Turin, 1852), II, pp. 251–75; Léopold de Gaillard, *L'Expédition de Rome en 1849 avec pièces justificatives et documents inédits* (Paris, 1861), pp. 246–9.

119. Monsagrati, *Roma senza il papa*, pp. 173–81.

120. Tomassini, *Storia avventurosa della rivoluzione romana*, pp. 412–14.

121. Rapport, *1848: Year of Revolution*, pp. 360–1.

122. Kertzer, *The Pope Who Would Be King*, p. 251.

123. Giuseppe Allegri (ed.), *Le due carte che (non) fecero l'Italia* (Rome, 2013), pp. 49–66.

124. Monsagrati, *Roma senza il papa*, pp. 214–24.

125. Mack Smith, *Mazzini* pp. 73–6.

126. Kertzer, *The Pope Who Would Be King*, pp. 277–8.

127. Anthony Valerio, *Anita Garibaldi: A Biography* (London, 2000), pp. 151–69.

128. Beseghi, *Ugo Bassi*, II, pp. 169–269.

129. Patricia Tyson Stroud, *The Emperor of Nature: Charles-Lucien Bonaparte and His World* (Pennsylvania, 2000).

130. Andreotti, *La fuga di Pio IX*, pp. 95–6.

131. Martina, *Pio IX*, I, pp. 381–7.

132. Coppa, 'Pio Nono and the Jews', pp. 671–95; Kertzer, *The Popes Against the Jews*, pp. 106–30.

133. Martina, *Pio IX*, I, pp. 350–76.

134. Kertzer, *The Pope Who Would Be King*, p. 274.

135. Chiron, *Pie IX*, pp. 217–19.

136. Kertzer, *The Pope Who Would Be King*, pp. 287–94.

137. Andreotti, *La fuga di Pio IX*, p. 56.

138. Hales, *Pio Nono*, pp. 149–58.

139. Andreotti, *La fuga di Pio IX*, pp. 55–74.

140. Bellocchi, *Tutte le encicliche*, IV, pp. 71–85, *Nostis et Nobiscum*, at p. 74; Danilo Raponi, *Religion and Politics in the Risorgimento: Britain and the New Italy 1861–1875* (Basingstoke, 2014), pp. 73–111.

141. Gaetano Greco 'La Civiltà Cattolica nel decennio 1850–1859, Appunti sulla pubblicistica reazionaria durante il Risorgimento', *Annali della scuola normale superiore di Pisa, Classe di lettere e filosofia*, Vol. 6, No. 3 (1976), pp. 1051–95.

142. Chiron, *Pie IX*, p.221.

143. Kertzer, *The Popes Against the Jews*, pp. 133–51.

144. Daniela Felisini, *Le finanze pontificie e i Rothschild 1830–1870* (Rome, 1990).

145. Giuseppe Laras, 'Ansie e speranze degli ebrei di Roma durante il pontificato di Pio IX', *La Rassegna Mensile di Israel*, Vol. 39, No. 9 (1973), pp. 512–31.

146. Raffaele de Cesare, *Roma e lo Stato del Papa dal ritorno di Pio IX al XX settembre* (Vicenza, 1975), pp. 13–14.
147. Ibid, pp. 16–19.
148. Kertzer, *The Pope Who Would Be King*, pp. 325–7.
149. Coppa, *Cardinal Antonelli and Papal Politics*, pp. 73–86.
150. McLeod, *Religion and the People of Western Europe*, pp. 51–53.

7 Can the Pope Err? The First Vatican Council, 1851–78

1. David I. Kertzer, *The Kidnapping of Edgardo Mortara* (New York, 1997), pp. 3–6.
2. Ibid, pp. 7–8.
3. Marco Severini, 'Milesi Ferretti, Giuseppe', in *Treccani dizionario biografico degli italiani*, online at www.treccani.it/enciclopedia/giuseppe-milesi-ferretti_(Dizionario-Biografico) [accessed 23 July 2021].
4. Kertzer, *The Kidnapping of Edgardo Mortara*, pp. 10–12.
5. Raphael Langham, 'The reaction in England to the kidnapping of Edgardo Mortara', *Jewish Historical Studies* Vol. 39 (2004), pp. 79–101; Natalie Isser, *Antisemitism during the French Second Empire* (New York, 1991), esp. Ch. 2 on the Mortara affair.
6. Marina Caffiero, 'La caccia agli ebrei, inquisizione, casa dei catecumeni e battesimi forzati nella Roma moderna', in Conferenza della Ricerca 2001, *Le inquisizioni, cristiani e gli ebrei* (Roma, 2003), pp. 503–37.
7. Carlo Falconi, *Il cardinale Antonelli: vita e carriera del Richelieu italiano nella chiesa di Pio IX* (Milan, 1983), p. 282.
8. Giacomo Martina, *Pio IX*, Vol. II: *1851–1866* (1986), pp. 31–5.
9. Kertzer, *The Kidnapping of Edgardo Mortara*, pp. 55–73.
10. Gemma Volli, *Il caso Mortara, il bambino rapito da Pio IX* (Florence, 2016), pp. 35–7.
11. José David Lebovitch Dahl, 'The Role of the Roman Catholic Church in the Formation of Modern Anti-Semitism: La Civiltà Cattolica, 1850–1879', *Modern Judaism*, Vol. 23, No. 2 (2003), pp. 180–97.
12. Volli, *Il caso Mortara*, p. 29; Kertzer, *The Kidnapping of Edgardo Mortara*, pp. 126–8.
13. Elèna Mortara, *Writing Justice: Victor Séjour, the Kidnapping of Edgardo Mortara and the Age of Transatlantic Emancipations* (Hanover, NH, 2015), pp. 31–54, 78–126.
14. Abigail Green, 'Intervening in the Jewish Question 1840–1878', in Brendan Simms and David Trim (eds), *Humanitarian Intervention: A History* (Cambridge, 2011), pp. 139–58, esp. p. 151; Lisa Moses Leff, 'Jews, Liberals and the Civilizing Mission in Nineteenth-Century France', *Historical Reflections/Réflexions historiques*, Vol. 32, No. 1 (2006), pp. 105–28.

15. Kertzer, *The Kidnapping of Edgardo Mortara*, pp. 159–69.
16. Felisini, *Le finanze pontificie e i Rothschild*.
17. Abigail Green, *Moses Montefiore: Jewish Liberator, Imperial Hero* (Cambridge, MA, 2010), pp. 258–81.
18. Kertzer, *The Kidnapping of Edgardo Mortara*, p. 184.
19. Ibid, p.191.
20. Gianpaolo Romanato, 'Le leggi antiecclesiastiche negli anni dell'unificazione italiana', *Studi Storici dell'Ordine dei Servi di Maria*, Vol. VI–VII (2006–2007), pp. 1–120.
21. Volli, *Il caso Mortara*, pp. 31–4.
22. Kertzer, *The Kidnapping of Edgardo Mortara*, p. 255.
23. Ibid, p. 260.
24. Volli, *Il caso Mortara*, pp. 36–7.
25. Kertzer, *The Kidnapping of Edgardo Mortara*, pp. 266–94.
26. Ibid, pp. 295–8.
27. Marina Caffiero, *Battesimi forzati: Storie di ebrei, cristiani e convertiti nella Roma dei papi* (Rome, 2004).
28. De Cesare, *Roma e lo Stato del Papa*, pp. 37–52, esp. p. 46; Martina, *Pio IX*, II, pp. 16–24.
29. Derek Beales and Eugenio Biagini, *The Risorgimento and the Unification of Italy* (2nd edn, Harlow, 2002), pp. 110 and 163.
30. Martina, *Pio IX*, II, p. 25.
31. De Cesare, *Roma e lo Stato del Papa*, pp. 207–26.
32. Giuseppe Pasolini dall'Onda, *Memorie raccolte da suo figlio* (2 vols, Turin, 1887), I, p. 214.
33. Donal A. Kerr, *Peel, Priests and Politics: Sir Robert Peel's Administration and the Roman Catholic Church in Ireland, 1841–1846* (Oxford, 1983), esp. Ch. 6.
34. Raponi, *Religion and Politics in the Risorgimento*, pp. 8–10.
35. Walter Ralls, 'The Papal Aggression of 1850: A study in Victorian anti-Catholicism', *Church History*, Vol. 43, No. 2 (1974), pp. 242–56; Frank H. Wallis, *Popular Anti-Catholicism in Mid-Victorian Britain* (New York, 1993).
36. Owen Chadwick, *The Victorian Church* (2 vols, London, 1966), I, p. 440.
37. Grayson M. Ditchfield, *The Evangelical Revival* (London, 2005); David W. Bebbington, *Evangelicalism in Modern Britain: A History from the 1730s to the 1980s* (London, 2003).
38. J. L. McCracken, 'The Ecclesiastical Structure 1714–1760', in T. W. Moody and W. E. Vaughan (eds), *Eighteenth-century Ireland* (A New History of Ireland, Vol. IV) (Oxford, 1986), pp. 91–9; and Brendan Grimes, 'Funding a Roman Catholic Church in Nineteenth-Century Ireland', *Architectural History*, Vol. 52 (2009), pp. 147–68.

39. Sean J. Connolly, *Priests and People in Pre-famine Ireland, 1780–1845* (London, 1985).

40. Ciaran O'Carroll, *Paul Cardinal Cullen: Portrait of a Practical Nationalist* (Dublin, 2009); Daire Keogh and Albert McDonnell (eds), *Cardinal Paul Cullen and His World* (Dublin, 2011); and for a more hostile treatment see Desmond Bowen, *Paul Cardinal Cullen and the Shaping of Modern Irish Catholicism* (Waterloo, ON, 1983).

41. Donal A. Kerr, *A Nation of Beggars? Priests, People, and Politics in Famine Ireland, 1846–1852* (Oxford, 1998), esp. Ch. 7.

42. Emmet Larkin, 'The Devotional Revolution in Ireland, 1850–75', *American Historical Review*, Vol. 77, No. 3 (1972), pp. 625–52, esp. pp. 644, 652.

43. Colin Barr, 'Imperium in Imperio, Irish Episcopal Imperialism in the Nineteenth Century', *English Historical Review*, Vol. 123, No. 502 (2008), pp. 611–50.

44. E. D. Steele, 'Cardinal Cullen and Irish Nationality', *Irish Historical Studies*, Vol. 19, No. 75 (1975), pp. 239–60.

45. Moira Lysaght, 'Father Theobald Mathew, Apostle of Temperance', *Dublin Historical Record*, Vol. 36, No. 4 (1983), pp. 140–52; Paul Townend, 'Temperance, Father Mathew, and the Irish Clergy', *New Hibernia Review/Iris Éireannach Nua*, Vol. 3, No. 1 (1999), pp. 111–22.

46. Gerard Moran, 'Near Famine: The Roman Catholic Church and the subsistence crisis of 1879–82', *Studia Hibernica*, No. 32 (2002/2003), pp. 155–77; Laurence Marley, *Michael Davitt, Freelance Radical and Frondeur* (Dublin, 2007).

47. Larkin, 'The Devotional Revolution in Ireland, 1850–75', pp. 625–52.

48. Senia Paseta, 'The Catholic Hierarchy and the Irish University Question, 1880–1908', *History*, Vol. 85, No. 278 (2000), pp. 268–84; Donald Akenson, *The Irish Education Experiment: The National System of Education in the Nineteenth Century* (London, 2011).

49. Lawrence W. McBride, *The Greening of Dublin Castle: The Transformation of Bureaucratic and Judicial Personnel in Ireland, 1892–1922* (Washington, DC, 1991).

50. J. C. Mathew, revised Sinéad Agnew, 'Russell, Charles Arthur, Baron Russell of Killowen 1832–1900', *Oxford Dictionary of National Biography*, online at https://doi.org/10.1093/ref:odnb/24301 [accessed 20 May 2002].

51. Rosario Romeo, *Cavour e il sul tempo*, (3 vols, Bari, 1977–84), I, pp. 451–509.

52. Harry Hearder, *Cavour* (London, 1994), pp. 17–23 and 66–9; Denis Mack Smith, *Cavour: A Biography* (London, 1985); Romeo, *Cavour e il sul tempo*, III, pp. 14–23, 69–81.

53. Frank J. Coppa, 'Realpolitik and Conviction in the Conflict between

Piedmont and the Papacy during the Risorgimento', *Catholic Historical Review*, Vol. 54, No. 4 (1969), pp. 579–612.

54. Giuseppe Griseri, 'Fransoni, Luigi', in *Treccani dizionario biografico degli italiani*, online at www.treccani.it/enciclopedia/luigi-fransoni_ (Dizionario-Biografico) [accessed 23 July 2017].

55. Frank J. Coppa, *The Modern Papacy since 1789*, p. 102.

56. Chadwick, *A History of the Popes*, p. 137.

57. Mack Smith, *Cavour*, pp. 80, 114–41.

58. Chadwick, *A History of the Popes*, pp. 138–41.

59. Marilyn McCord Adams, 'The Immaculate Conception of the Blessed Virgin Mary: A thought-experiment in medieval philosophical theology', *Harvard Theological Review*, Vol. 103, No. 2 (2010), pp. 133–59.

60. Donna Spivey Ellington, *From Sacred Body to Angelic Soul: Understanding Mary in Late Medieval and Early Modern Europe* (Washington, DC, 2001), pp. 47–60.

61. Fergus Kerr, *Thomas Aquinas: A Very Short Introduction* (Oxford, 2009), p. 92.

62. Alberto Cadili, 'Conciliar Liturgy', in Gerald Christianson, Michiel Decaluwe, and Thomas M. Izbicki (eds), *A Companion to the Council of Basel* (Leiden, 2016), pp. 361–5.

63. Richard Bauckham, *Gospel Women: Studies of the Named Women in the Gospels* (London, 2002).

64. Martina, *Pio IX*, II, pp. 264–5.

65. Vito Nardin, 'Rosmini`s Contribution to the Definition of the Immaculate Conception', online at https://studylib.net/doc/7607395/ rosmini-s-contribution-to-the-definition-of-the-immaculat [accessed 23 July /2021].

66. Chiron, *Pie IX, Pape Moderne*, pp. 264–9 ; Bellocchi, *Tutte le encicliche*, IV, pp. 131–2.

67. Bellocchi, *Tutte le encicliche*, IV, p. 141.

68. Eugen Weber, *Peasants into Frenchmen: The Modernization of Rural France, 1870–1914* (Standford, CA, 1976); David Blackbourn, 'Peasants and Politics in Germany, 1871–1914', *European History Quarterly*, Vol. 14, No. 1 (1984), pp. 47–75; Michel Pigenet and Gilles Pécout (eds), *Campagnes et sociétés en Europe, France, Allemagne, Espagne, Italie 1830–1930* (Paris, 2005).

69. René Laurentin and Michel Corteville, *Découverte du secret de la Salette* (Paris, 2002).

70. François de Muizon, *Un nouveau regard sur les apparitions: le Laus, la rue du Bac, la Salette, Lourdes, Pontmain, Fatima* (Paris, 2008); Michael P. Carroll, 'The Virgin Mary at La Salette and Lourdes: Whom did the children see?' *Journal for the Scientific Study of Religion*, Vol. 24, No. 1 (1985), pp. 56–74.

71. Willy Jansen and Catrien Notermans, 'From Vision to Cult Site, A Comparative Perspective', *Archives de sciences sociales des religions*, Vol. 55, No. 151 (2010), pp. 71–90.

72. Ruth Harris, *Lourdes: Body and Spirit in the Secular Age* (London, 1999), pp. 44–51, 55–82.

73. Yvonne Estienne, *Lourdes et la Salette* (Paris, 1958), p. 112.

74. Harris, *Lourdes: Body and Spirit*, pp. 293–303.

75. Fernando Vidal, 'Modernizing the Miraculous Body in Prospero Lamberti's *de servorum Dei*', in Rebecca Messbarger, Christopher Johns and Philip Gavitt (eds), *Benedict XIV and the Enlightenment: Art, Science, and Spirituality* (Toronto, 2016), pp. 151–74.

76. Jason Szabo, 'Seeing Is Believing? The form and substance of French medical debates over Lourdes', *Bulletin of the History of Medicine*, Vol. 76, No. 2 (2002), pp. 199–230.

77. Harris, *Lourdes: Body and Spirit*, pp. 325–31.

78. David Blackbourn, *Marpingen: Apparitions of the Virgin Mary in Nineteenth-century Germany* (New York, 1993), pp. 103–30, 146–163.

79. Ibid, pp. 110–19.

80. Gordon Boyce Thompson, *The Kulturkampf: An Essay* (London, 1909); Michael B. Gross, *The War against Catholicism: Liberalism and the Anti-Catholic Imagination in Nineteenth-century Germany* (Ann Arbor, MN, 2004).

81. Blackbourn, *Marpingen: Apparitions of the Virgin Mary*, pp. 202–21.

82. Edmund Radziwiłł, *Ein Besuch in Marpingen* (Berlin, 1877); Klaus-Michael Mallmann 'Aus des Tages Last machen sie ein Kreuz des Herrn...? Bergarbeiter, Religion und sozialer Protest im Saarrevier des 19 Jahrhunderts', *Geschichte und Gesellschaft: Sonderheft*, Vol. 11, (1986), pp. 152–84; (and to be read with caution) Heinrich Tötter, *Bismarck und das Zentrum der Kampf des Zentrums und seine Anerkennung als unabhängige politische Partei in den Jahren 1878–79* (Cologne, 1936), pp. 26–7.

83. Blackbourn, *Marpingen: Apparitions of the Virgin Mary*, pp. 277–304.

84. Mona Ozouf, *L'École, l'eglise et la république, 1871–1914* (Paris, 2007); Jacques and Mona Ozouf, *La république des instituteurs* (Paris, 2001); Annie Crépin, *Histoire de la conscription* (Paris, 2009). See also Solans, 'The Creation of a Latin American Catholic Church'; Mercati (ed.), *Raccolta di Concordati*.

85. Harris, *Lourdes: Body and Spirit*, pp. 331–49.

86. Charles A. Coulombe, *The Pope's Legion: The Multinational Fighting Force that Defended the Vatican* (Basingstoke, 2008), esp. pp. 17–62.

87. Virginio Paolo Gastaldi, 'Cavour e la Strategia dell'Unificazione 1850–1861', *Il Politico*, Vol. 54, No. 3 (1989), pp. 391–407; Arnold Blumberg, *A*

Carefully Planned Accident: The Italian War of 1859 (Susquehanna, PA, 1990).

88. Harry Hearder, 'Clarendon, Cavour, and the Intervention of Sardinia in the Crimean War, 1853–1855', *International History Review*, Vol. 18, No. 4 (1996), pp. 819–36.

89. Adrien Dansette, *L'Attentat d'Orsini* (Paris 1964); Jean-Noël Tardy, 'Murder the tyrant or kill tyranny? Political attacks and plots in France from 1830 to 1870', *La Révolution française: cahiers de l'Institut d'histoire de la révolution française*, No. 1 (2012), online at https://doi.org/10.4000/lrf.438 [accessed 24 July 2021], let 2021.

90. Louis Girard, *Napoléon III* (Paris, 1986), pp. 275–8.

91. Roland Conilleau, *L'entrevue de Plombières* (Nancy, 1991); Paul Guichonnet, *Histoire de l'Annexion de la Savoie à la France et ses dossiers secrets* (Roanne, 1982); Mack Walker, *Plombieres, Secret Diplomacy and the Rebirth of Italy* (Oxford, 1969).

92. John Gooch, *The Unification of Italy* (London, 2002), pp. 26–7; Frank J. Coppa, *The Origins of the Italian Wars of Independence* (London, 1992), pp. 74–91.

93. James H. Billington, *Fire in the Minds of Men: Origins of the Revolutionary Faith* (London, 2017), p. 157.

94. Harold Carmichael Wylly, *The Campaign of Magenta and Solferino 1859: The Decisive Conflict for the Unification of Italy* (London, 2009).

95. A. J. P. Taylor, 'European Mediation and the Agreement of Villafranca, 1859', *English Historical Review*, Vol. 51, No. 201 (1936), pp. 52–78.

96. Mack Smith, *Cavour*, pp. 174–5; Romeo, *Cavour e il sul tempo*, III, pp. 622–77.

97. Gian Savino Pene Vidari, *I plebisciti del 1860 e il governo Sabaudo* (Turin, 2016).

98. Walker, *Plombieres, Secret Diplomacy*.

99. Scirocco, *Garibaldi, Citizen of the World*, pp. 236–86.

100. Derek Beales, *England and Italy 1859–1860* (London, 1961); Alfredo Signoretti, *Italia e Inghilterra durante il risorgimento* (Milan, 1940).

101. Denis Mack Smith, *Cavour and Garibaldi, 1860: A Study in Political Conflict* (Cambridge, 1954).

102. Raffaelle De Cesare, *La fine di un regno* (2 vols, Città di Castello, 1909), II, pp. 340–50.

103. Riall, *Garibaldi, Invention of a Hero*, p. 221.

104. Gigi di Fiore, *L'ultimo re di Napoli: l'esilio di Francesco II di Borbone nell'Italia dei Savoia* (Turin, 2018).

105. David Alvarez, *The Pope's Soldiers: A Military History of the Modern Vatican* (Kansas, 2011), pp. 103–7.

106. Coulombe, *The Pope's Legion*, pp. 51–4.

107. Gerard Anthony Hayes-McCoy, *Captain Myles Walter Keogh: United States Army 1840–1876* (Dublin, 1965).

108. Hearder, *Cavour*, pp. 165–6.

109. Alvarez, *The Pope's Soldiers*, pp. 94–8.

110. Coulombe, *The Pope's Legion*, pp. 76–89.

111. Roger Aubert, *Le Pontificat de Pie IX*, p. 92.

112. Bellocchi, *Tutte le encicliche*, IV, pp. 200, 201.

113. Romeo, *Cavour e il sul tempo*, III, pp. 928–38; Mack Smith, *Cavour*, pp. 270–3.

114. Carlo M. Fiorentino, 'Da Poirino, Giacomo', in *Treccani dizionario biografico degli italiani*, online at www.treccani.it/enciclopedia/ giacomo-da-poirino_%28Dizionario-Biografico%29/ [accessed 24 July 2021].

115. Arnold Blumberg, 'The Demise of Italian Federalism: 1859', *The Historian*, Vol. 18, No. 1 (1955), pp. 57–82.

116. Martina, *Pio IX*, II, pp. 22–4.

117. Géraldine Djament-Tran, 'Le débat sur Rome capitale 1861–1871, choix de localisation et achèvement de la construction nationale italienne', *Revue historique*, Vol. 311, No. 1 (2009), pp. 99–118.

118. Gian Luca Fruci, 'Mitografia e storia dei plebisciti di unificazione nelle Due Sicilie', *Meridiana*, No. 95 (2019), pp. 113–38; Alessandro Capone, 'Legittimismo popolare e questione demaniale, i repertori della protesta nella Capitanata del 1860–61', *Meridiana*, No. 84 (2015), pp. 213–35; Marco Vigna, *Brigantaggio italiano: considerazioni e studi nell'Italia unita* (Rome, 2020); Enzo Ciconte, *La grande mattanza: storia della guerra al brigantaggio* (Bari, 2020); Rocco Biondi, *Storiografia del brigantaggio postunitario* (Rome, 2018).

119. Bourgeois, *Rome et Napoléon III*, pp. 200–7.

120. Coppa, *The Modern Papacy since 1789*, p. 106.

121. Harrison, *Romantic Catholics*, pp. 251–6; Philibert, *Henri Lacordaire*, pp. 644–56.

122. Girard, *Napoléon III*, pp. 398–9.

123. Scirocco, *Garibaldi, Citizen of the World*, pp. 388–99; Fulvio Conti and Benjamin Ginsborg, 'The Religion of the Homeland: The Cult of Martyrs of Freedom in Nineteenth-century Italy', *Journal of Modern European History/Zeitschrift für moderne europäische Geschichte/ Revue d'histoire européenne contemporaine*, Vol. 12, No. 3 (2014), pp. 398–418.

124. Daniel Pick, 'Roma o morte! Garibaldi, nationalism and the problem of psycho-biography', *History Workshop Journal*, No. 57 (2004), pp. 1–33.

125. Giuseppe Monsagrati, 'Garibaldi e il culto vittoriano dell'eroe', *Studi Storici*, Vol. 42, No. 1 (2001), pp. 165–180.

126. De Cesare, *Roma e lo Stato del Papa*, pp. 510–25.

127. Martina, *Pio IX*, II, pp. 299–310.

128. Chiron, *Pie IX, Pape Moderne*, pp. 324–6.

129. Martina, *Pio IX*, II, p. 306.

130. Chiron, *Pie IX, Pape Moderne*, pp. 324–6.

131. Chadwick, *A History of the Popes*, p. 170.

132. Charles Forbes, comte de Montalembert, *L'église libre dans l'état libre: discours prononcés au Congrès catholique de Malines, par le comte de Montalembert* (Paris, 1863).

133. Howard, *The Pope and the Professor*, pp. 95–114.

134. Bellocchi, *Tutte le encicliche*, IV, pp. 265–8.

135. Articles 65–74, ibid, pp. 281–2; Article 80, p. 283.

136. Roland Hill, *Lord Acton* (London, 2000), pp. 173–91.

137. Waresquiel, *Talleyrand*, pp. 608–10; François Lagrange, *Vie de Mgr Dupanloup, Évêque d'Orléans, membre de l'académie française* (3 vols, Paris, 1886), I, pp. 196–235.

138. Félix Dupanloup, *La Convention du 15 septembre et l'encyclique du 8 décembre* (Paris, 1865); and Lagrange, *Vie de Mgr Dupanloup*, II, 288–309.

139. Marvin R. O'Connell, 'Ultramontanism and Dupanloup: The compromise of 1865', *Church History*, Vol. 53, No. 2 (1984), pp. 200–17.

140. Aubert, *Le pontificat de Pie IX*, p. 257.

141. Elizabeth R. Varon, *Armies of Deliverance: A New History of the Civil War* (Oxford, 2019).

142. Murphy, *Jesuit Slaveholding in Maryland*.

143. Kraszewski, *Catholic Confederates*, pp. 8–9.

144. Charles M. Hubbard, *The Burden of Confederate Diplomacy* (Tennessee, 1998); Frank Lawrence Owsley, *King Cotton Diplomacy: Foreign Relations of the Confederate States of America* (Alabama, 2008).

145. Kraszewski, *Catholic Confederates*, p. 112.

146. Franco, *Parallel Empires*, pp. 34–5.

147. David J. Alvarez, 'The Papacy in the Diplomacy of the American Civil War', *Catholic Historical Review*, Vol. 69, No. 2 (1983), pp. 227–48.

148. Joseph O. Baylen and William W. White, 'A. Dudley Mann's Mission in Europe, 1863–1864: An unpublished letter to Jefferson Davis', *Virginia Magazine of History and Biography*, Vol. 69, No. 3 (1961), pp. 324–8; Kraszewski, *Catholic Confederates*, p. 113.

149. Kraszewski, *Catholic Confederates*, pp. 120–31.

150. Ibid, p. 127.

151. Peter Bridges, 'Civil War in America, Unification in Italy and a developing relationship', *Il Politico*, Vol. 78, No. 2 (2013), pp. 5–21.

152. Steven Conn, 'Political Romanism: Re-evaluating American anti-Catholicism in the age of Italian revolution', *Journal of the Early Republic*,

Vol. 36, No. 3 (2016), pp. 521–48; Howard R. Marraro, 'The Closing of the American Diplomatic Mission to the Vatican and Efforts to Revive it, 1868–1870', *Catholic Historical Review*, Vol. 33, No. 4 (1948), pp. 423–47.

153. Geoffrey Wawro, *The Austro-Prussian War: Austria's War with Prussia and Italy in 1866* (Cambridge, 1996), pp. 82–123.

154. Pierluigi Romeo di Colloredo Mels, *Mentana 1867, la disfatta di Garibaldi Copertina* (Rome, 2020).

155. Piero Crociani, 'Kanzler, Hermann', in *Treccani dizionario biografico degli italiani,* online at www.treccani.it/enciclopedia/hermann-kanzler_%28Dizionario-Biografico%29/ [accessed 24 July 2021].

156. Alvarez, *The Pope's Soldiers,* p. 170.

157. Martina, *Pio IX,* Vol. III: *1867–1878* (Rome 1990), p.42.

158. Anon, *Relazione degli ultimi giorni di Giuseppe Monti e di Gaetano Tognetti giustiziati in Roma il dì 24 novembre* 1868 (Rome, 1868).

159. Bourgeois, *Rome et Napoléon III,* pp. 216–17. Adriano Sconocchia, *Le camicie rosse alle porte di Roma: Il tentativo garibaldino del 1867 a Roma e nello Stato Pontificio* (Rome, 2016).

160. Gervase Phillips, 'Military Morality Transformed: Weapons and soldiers on the nineteenth-century battlefield', *Journal of Interdisciplinary History,* Vol. 41, No. 4 (2011), pp. 565–90.

161. Alvarez, *The Pope's Soldiers,* pp. 182–192.

162. Hermann Kanzler, *Rapporto alla santità di nostro signore papa Pio IX felicemente regnante del generale Kanzler pro-ministro alle armi sulla invasione dello Stato Pontificio nell'autunno 1867* (Rome, 1868).

163. Riall, *Garibaldi: Invention of a Hero,* pp. 350–1.

164. John W. O'Malley, *Trent: What Happened at the Council* (Cambridge, MA, 2012).

165. Frank Welsh, *The Battle for Christendom: The Council of Constance 1415, and the Struggle to Unite Against Islam* (London, 2008).

166. Ambrogio A. Caiani, 'The Concile National of 1811', pp. 546–64.

167. Brian Tierney, *Origins of Papal Infallibility, 1150–1350: A Study on the Concepts of Infallibility, Sovereignty and Tradition in the Middle Ages* (Leiden, 1972), pp. 58–92.

168. Austin Gough, *Paris and Rome: The Gallican Church and the Ultramontane Campaign 1848–1853* (Oxford, 1986).

169. Martina, *Pio IX,* III, pp. 136–45.

170. Donato, *Les Archives du Monde.*

171. Achille Mauri, 'Agostino Theiner', *Archivio Storico Italiano,* Vol. 21, No. 86 (1875), pp. 350–91.

172. Owen Chadwick, *Catholicism and History: The Opening of the Vatican Archives* (Cambridge, 1978), pp. 46–53.

173. Hill, *Lord Acton,* pp. 209–10.

174. Chadwick, *Catholicism and History,* pp. 53–66.

175. John W. O'Malley, *Vatican I: The Council and the Making of the Ultramontane* (Cambridge, MA, 2018), p. 111.

176. Ibid, p.119.

177. Bellocchi, *Tutte le encicliche*, IV, p. 295.

178. Ibid, p. 296.

179. Timothy Verhoeven, 'Transatlantic Connections: American anti-Catholicism and the First Vatican Council 1869–70', *Catholic Historical Review*, Vol. 100, No. 4 (2014), pp. 695–720; James H. Smylie, 'American Protestants Interpret Vatican Council I', *Church History*, Vol. 38, No. 4 (1969), pp. 459–74.

180. O'Malley, *When Bishops Meet*, pp. 90–6.

181. O'Malley, *Vatican I*, pp. 139–52.

182. Hasler, *How the Pope Became Infallible*, pp. 41–67.

183. Martina, *Pio IX*, III, pp. 166–8.

184. O'Malley, *Vatican I*, p. 134.

185. Claude Bressolette, *Le pouvoir dans la société et dans l'eglise: l'ecclésiologie politique de Mgr. Maret, dernier doyen de la faculté de théologie de la Sorbonne* (Paris, 1984).

186. Chadwick, *A History of the Popes*, pp. 197–201.

187. Owen Chadwick, 'Lord Acton at the First Vatican Council', *Journal of Theological Studies*, Vol. 28, No. 2 (1977), pp. 465–97; Hill, *Lord Acton*, pp. 192–225.

188. James F. McMillan, 'Remaking Catholic Europe: Louis Veuillot and the ultramontane project', *Kirchliche Zeitgeschicht*, Vol. 14, No. 1 (2001), pp. 112–22.

189. O'Malley, *Vatican I*, p. 146.

190. Hasler, *How the Pope Became Infallible*, p. 85.

191. Ibid, pp. 70–4.

192. Bellocchi, *Tutte le encicliche*, IV, pp. 326–7.

193. Howard, *The Pope and the Professor*, pp. 117–38.

194. Ibid, pp. 138–52.

195. Michał Chaberek, *Catholicism and Evolution: A History from Darwin to Pope Francis* (Ohio, 2015).

196. Martina, *Pio IX*, III, pp. 190–9.

197. O'Malley, *Vatican I*, p. 186.

198. Hasler, *How the Pope Became Infallible*, pp. 173–4.

199. Fergus Kerr, 'Vatican I and the papacy: Defining "defining"', *New Blackfriars*, Vol. 60, No. 712 (1979), pp. 356–366; Rosamond McKitterick, 'The Papacy and Byzantium in the Seventh and Early Eighth-century Section of the *Liber Pontificalis*', *Papers of the British School at Rome*, Vol. 84 (2016), pp. 241–73.

200. O'Malley, *Vatican I*, pp. 202–4.

201. Martina, *Pio IX*, III, pp. 205–9.

202. O'Malley, *Vatican I*, p. 212.
203. Chiron, *Pie IX, Pape Moderne*, pp. 426–45.
204. O'Malley, *Vatican I*, pp. 220–21.
205. Price, *Religious Renewal in France 1789-1870*, pp. 78–82.
206. Hasler, *How the Pope Became Infallible*, pp. 187–99; O'Malley, *Vatican I*, pp. 221–2.
207. Bellocchi, *Tutte le encicliche*, IV, p. 339.
208. Ibid, pp. 339–40.
209. Paul E. Duggan, *The Assumption Dogma: Some Reactions and Ecumenical Implications in the thought of English-speaking Theologians* (Cleveland, OH, 1989).
210. Geoffrey Wawro, *The Franco-Prussian War: The German Conquest of France in 1870-1871* (Cambridge, 2003), pp. 211–29.
211. Giuseppe Guerzoni, *La vita di Nino Bixio, con lettere e documenti* (Florence, 1875), pp. 372–416.
212. Alvarez, *The Pope's Soldiers*, pp. 223–4.
213. Martina, *Pio IX*, III, p. 242.
214. Chadwick, *A History of the Popes*, p. 217.
215. Kertzer, *Prisoner of the Vatican*, p. 45.
216. Ibid, pp. 50–1; Falconi, *Il cardinale Antonelli*, pp. 459–64.
217. Martina, *Pio IX*, III, p. 243.
218. Alvarez, *The Pope's Soldiers*, pp. 236–51; Carol E. Harrison, 'Zouave Stories: Gender, Catholic spirituality, and French responses to the Roman question', *Journal of Modern History*, Vol. 79, No. 2 (2007), pp. 274–305.
219. Carlo Maria Fiorentino, 'Dalle Stanze del Vaticano, il venti settembre e la protesta della Santa Sede 1870-1871', *Archivum Historiae Pontificiae*, Vol. 28 (1990), pp. 285–333.
220. Martina, *Pio IX*, III, pp. 216–32.
221. Chadwick, *A History of the Popes*, p. 218.
222. Kertzer, *Prisoner of the Vatican*, pp. 62–3.
223. Emilia Morelli, 'Il palazzo del Quirinale da Pio IX a Vittorio Emanuele II', *Archivum Historiae Pontificiae*, Vol. 8 (1970), pp. 239–300.
224. Denis Mack Smith, *Italy and its Monarchy* (London, 1989), pp. 48–54.
225. Bellocchi, *Tutte le encicliche*, IV, pp. 341–8.
226. Francesco Scaduto, *Guarentigie pontificie e relazioni fra stato e chiesa, legge 13 Maggio 1871: storia, esposizione e giurisprudenza, critica, documenti, bibliografia* (Turin, 1889).
227. Bellocchi, *Tutte le encicliche*, IV, pp. 355–60.
228. Saretta Marotta, L'Evoluzione del Dibattito sul "non expedit" all'interno della Curia Romana tra il 1860 e il 1889', *Rivista di storia della Chiesa in Italia*, Vol. 68, No. 1 (2014), pp. 95–164.
229. Chadwick, *A History of the Popes*, pp. 247–54.

230. Martina, *Pio IX*, III, pp. 418–34; Waagenaar, *The Pope's Jews*, pp. 273–7.
231. William J. Callahan, *Church, Politics, and Society in Spain 1750–1874* (Cambridge, MA, 1984), pp. 255–73; Gregoerio Alonso, *La Nación en Capilla: Ciudanía Católica y cuestión religiosa en España 1793–1874* (Granada, 2014), pp. 255–325.
232. Katja Hoyer, *Blood and Iron: The Rise and Fall of the German Empire 1871–1918* (Cheltenham, 2021), esp. Ch. 1; Helmut Walser Smith, *Germany, a Nation in its Time: Before, During and After Nationalism, 1500–2000* (New York, 2020), pp. 234–60.
233. David Blackbourn, *History of Germany 1780–1918: The Long Nineteenth Century* (2nd edn, Oxford, 2003), pp. 222–7.
234. Gross, *The War against Catholicism*, p. 197.
235. Massimiliano Valente, *Diplomazia Pontificia e Kulturkampf, La Santa Sede e la Prussia tra Pio IX e Bismarck 1862–1878* (Rome,2004), pp. 163–5.
236. Howard, *The Pope and the Professor*, pp. 152–77.
237. Rebecca Ayako Bennette, *Fighting for the Soul of Germany: The Catholic Struggle for Inclusion after Unification* (Cambridge, MA, 2012), pp. 122–56.
238. Blackbourn, *Marpingen*, pp. 202–21.
239. Atkin and Tallett, *Priests, Prelates and People*, p. 146.
240. Chadwick, *A History of the Popes*, pp. 264–5.
241. Martina, *Pio IX*, III, pp. 522–3.
242. Ibid, pp. 524–6.
243. Kertzer, *Prisoner of the Vatican*, pp. 134–6.
244. Daniela Mondini, *San Lorenzo fuori le mura: storia del complesso monumentale nel medioevo* (Rome, 2016).
245. Chadwick, *A History of the Popes*, pp. 271–2; Chiron, *Pie IX, Pape Moderne*, pp. 496–7.

8 'The New Things': Leo XIII and the Social Question, 1878–1903

1. Tim Jeal, *Stanley: the Impossible Life of Africa's Greatest Explorer* (London, 2007), p. 173.
2. Richard J. Reid, *A History of Modern Uganda* (Cambridge, 2017), pp. 175–6.
3. Jocelyn Murray, *Proclaim the Good News: A Short History of the Church Missionary Society* (London, 1985).
4. C. Duncan Rice, 'The Missionary Context of the British Anti-slavery Movement', in James Walvin (ed.), *Slavery and British Society, 1776–1846* (London, 1982), pp. 150–63.
5. ASV, Francia Epoca Napoleonica 8 fol.169r; ASV Francia Epoca Napoleonica 12 Fasc. 12 Missioni Francesi.
6. Costantini, 'Gregorio XVI e le missioni'.

7. Jean-Marie Mayeur, Luce Pietri and André Vauchez (eds), *Histoire du Christianisme: Libéralisme, Industrialisation, Expansion Européenne 1830–1914* (14 vols, Paris, 1995), XI, pp. 161–7.

8. Jennifer E. Sessions, *By Sword and Plow: France and the Conquest of Algeria* (Cornell, NY, 2017).

9. Norman Etherington, *Missions and Empire* (Oxford, 2005), pp. 1–8.

10. Ronald Robinson, Stig Förster and Wolfgang J. Mommsen (eds), *Bismarck, Europe, and Africa: The Berlin Africa Conference 1884–1885 and the Onset of Partition* (Oxford, 1988).

11. John Kelly Thornton, *The Kingdom of Kongo: Civil War and Transition, 1641–1718* (Madison, WI, 1983).

12. General Act of the Berlin Conference on West Africa 1885, online at https://jusmundi.com/en/document/treaty/en-general-act-of-the-berlin-conference-on-west-africa-1885-general-act-of-the-berlin-conference-on-west-africa-1885-thursday-26th-february-1885 [accessed 15 August 2021].

13. Adrian Hastings, *The Church in Africa 1450–1950* (Oxford, 1994), p. 419.

14. Michael Meeuwis 'The White Fathers and Luganda: To the origins of French missionary linguistics in the Lake Victoria region', *Annales Aequatoria*, Vol. 20 (1999), pp. 413–43; Anton Quack, 'Anthropology and Missionaries: A review essay', *Anthropos*, Vol. 103, No. 2. (2008), pp. 560–67; Fanny Wonu Veys, 'Missionary Attitudes towards Tongan Material Culture', *Paideuma: Mitteilungen zur Kulturkunde*, Vol. 63 (2017), pp. 159–182.

15. Ruth Slade, 'English Missionaries and the Beginning of the Anti-Congolese Campaign in England', *Revue belge de Philologie et d'Histoire*, Vol. 33, No. 1 (1955), pp. 37–73; Andrew Porter, 'Cultural Imperialism and Protestant Missionary Enterprise, 1780–1914', *Journal of Imperial and Commonwealth History*, Vol. 25, No. 3 (1997), pp. 367–91; Andrew Porter, 'Religion versus Empire? British Protestant missionaries and overseas expansion, 1700–1914', (Manchester, 2004).

16. Hastings, *The Church in Africa 1450–1950*, p. 433.

17. James Patrick Tudesco, 'Missionaries and French Imperialism: The role of Catholic missionaries in French colonial expansion, 1880–1905' (unpublished PhD Thesis, University of Connecticut, 1980).

18. Charles Lavigerie, *Souscription recuillie en faveur des chrétiens de Syrie: voyage en Orient exposé de l'état actuel des chrétiens du Liban* (Paris, 1861).

19. Orlando Figes, *Crimea, the Last Crusade* (London, 2011), pp. 1–22.

20. Federico Cresti, 'Il ristabilimento del patriarcato latino di Gerusalemme e la custodia di terra santa 1847–1872', *Studi Storici*, Vol. 48, No. 2 (2007), pp. 569–79.

21. Ronald E. Prosser, *The Equestrian Order of the Holy Sepulchre of Jerusalem: History and Insignia* (London, 1981).

22. Heleen Murre-Van den Berg, 'The Midde East: Western missions and the Eastern churches, Islam and Judaism', in Gilley and Stanley (eds), *World Christianities*, pp. 443–57.

23. Jean-Claude Ceillier, *Histoire des missionnaires d'Afrique: pères blancs, de la fondation par Mgr Lavigerie à la mort du fondateur, 1868–1892* (Paris, 2008).

24. Bertrand Taithe, 'Missionary Hubris in Colonial Algeria? Founding and governing Christian Arab villages, 1868–1930', in Inger Marie Okkenhaug and Karène Sanchez Summerer (eds), *Christian Missions and Humanitarianism in the Middle East, 1850–1950: Ideologies, Rhetoric, and Practices* (Leiden 2020), pp. 133–54.

25. Marcel Émerit, 'Le problème de la conversion des musulmans d'Algérie sous le Second Empire: le conflit entre Mac-Mahon et Lavigerie', *Revue historique*, Vol. 223, No. 1 (1960), pp. 63–84; J. Dean O'Donnell, 'Cardinal Charles Lavigerie: The politics of getting a red hat', *Catholic Historical Review*, Vol. 63, No. 2 (1977), pp. 185–203.

26. Georges Goyau, 'Un Grand Missionnaire: Le Cardinal Lavigerie, la croisade contre l'esclavagisme les dernières années', *Revue des deux mondes*, Vol. 27, No. 1 (1925), pp. 149–86; François Renault, Le Cardinal Lavigerie: l'eglise, l'Afrique et la France 1825–1892 (Paris, 1992), pp. 554–80.

27. Renault, *Le Cardinal Lavigerie*, p. 359.

28. Jean-Michel Vasquez, *La Cartographie missionnaire en Afrique: science, religion et conquête, 1870–1930* (Paris, 2011), pp. 245–60.

29. Hastings, *The Church in Africa*, p. 410.

30. Aylward Shorter, *Les Pères blancs au temps de la conquête coloniale: histoire des missionnaires d'Afrique 1892–1914* (Paris, 2011), pp. 15–21.

31. Armand Duval, *Le père Siméon Lourdel, apôtre de l'Ouganda* (Paris, 2004).

32. Augustin Nicq, *Le Père Siméon Lourdel de la société des pères blancs et les premières années de la mission de l'Ouganda* (2nd edn, Algiers, 1906), pp. 86, 94.

33. Zachary Karabell, *Parting the Desert: The Creation of the Suez Canal* (New York, 2003).

34. Anon., *Vers les grands lacs: journal de la première caravane des pères blancs d'Afrique 1878–1879* (Namur, 1954), pp. 225–34.

35. John B. Kabeya, *King Mirambo, One of the Heroes of Tanzania* (Kampala, 1976), pp. 64–9.

36. Nicq, *Le Père Siméon Lourdel*, pp. 120–1.

37. Christopher Wrigley, *Kingship and State: The Buganda dynasty* (Cambridge, 1996), pp. 20–4; J. W. Harrison, *A. M. Mackay: Pioneer Missionary of the Church Missionary Society in Uganda* (New York, 1895), p. 192; Nicq, *Le Père Siméon Lourdel*, pp. 133–5.

38. Harrison, *A. M. Mackay*, pp. 9–34.
39. Nicq, *Le Père Siméon Lourdel*, pp. 135–6.
40. Richard Reid, 'Images of an African Ruler: Kabaka Mutesa of Buganda, ca.1857–1884', *History in Africa*, Vol. 26 (1999), pp. 269–98.
41. Nicq, *Le Père Siméon Lourdel*, pp. 148–50.
42. Ibid, p. 197.
43. Jean Brierley and Thomas Spear, 'Mutesa, the Missionaries, and Christian Conversion in Buganda', *International Journal of African Historical Studies*, Vol. 21, No. 4 (1988), pp. 601–18.
44. Pawlíková-Vilhanová Viera, 'The Role of Early Missionaries of Africa, or White Fathers in the Study and development of African languages', *Journal of Asian and African Studies*, Vol. 20, No. 2 (2011), pp. 267–88.
45. Henri Médard, 'État et conversion au Buganda (1875–1900): politique et héros missionnaires dans un grand royaume est-africain', *Histoire et missions chrétiennes*, Vol. 4, No. 4 (2007), pp. 25–46; William Burridge, *Destiny Africa: Cardinal Lavigerie and the Making of the White Fathers* (London, 1966), pp. 100–32.
46. Reid, *A History of Modern Uganda*, pp. 154–5.
47. James Tumusiime, *Uganda, A Picture History, 1857–2007* (Kampala, 2009), p. 5.
48. Nicq, *Le Père Siméon Lourdel*, pp. 281, 289–93.
49. Reid, *A History of Modern Uganda*, p. 101.
50. Edwin Collas Dawson, *James Hannington, D.D., F.L.S., E.R.G.S., First Bishop of Eastern Equatorial Africa: A History of His Life and Work, 1847–1885* (New York, 1969).
51. Nicq, *Le Père Siméon Lourdel*, p. 388.
52. J. A. Rowe, 'The Purge of Christians at Mwanga's Court: A reassessment of this episode in Buganda history', *Journal of African History*, Vol. 5, No. 1 (1964), pp. 55–72.
53. Cf., John F. Faupel, *African Holocaust: The Story of the Uganda Martyrs* (London, 1962); Francis Marion, *New African Saints: The Twenty-two Martyrs of Uganda* (Nairobi, 1985).
54. John Gray and Carl Peters, 'Anglo-German Relations in Uganda, 1890–1892', *Journal of African History*, Vol. 1, No. 2 (1960), pp. 281–97.
55. Michael Twaddle, 'The Muslim Revolution in Buganda', *African Affairs*, Vol. 71, No. 282 (1972), pp. 54–72.
56. D. A. Low, *Fabrication of Empire: The British and Uganda Kingdoms 1890–1902* (Cambridge, 2009), pp. 65–7; Roland Oliver, *The Missionary Factor in East Africa* (London, 1952), pp. 103–6.
57. Low, *Fabrication of Empire*, pp. 68–75, 176–214.
58. Samwiri Lwanga-Lunyiigo, *Mwanga II: Resistance to Imposition of British Colonial Rule in Buganda, 1884–1899* (Kampala, 2011).

59. Kenneth Scott LaTourette, *A History of the Expansion of Christianity*, Vol. 5: *The Great Century in the Americas, Australasia and Africa 1800–1914* (New York, 1943), pp. 418–19; Yves Tourigny, *St. Mary's Cathedral, Lubaga: The Cathedral in Details* (Entebbe, 1986).

60. James P. Daughton, *An Empire Divided: Religion, Republicanism, and the Making of French Colonialism 1880–1914* (Oxford, 2006), pp. 25–7.

61. Jairzinho Lopes-Pereira, 'The Catholic Church and the Early Stages of King Leopold II's Colonial Projects in the Congo 1876–1886', *Social Sciences and Missions*, Vol. 32, Nos. 1–2 (2019), pp. 82–104.

62. Vincent Viaene, 'King Leopold's Imperialism and the Origins of the Belgian Colonial Party, 1860–1905', *Journal of Modern History*, Vol. 80, No. 4 (2008), pp. 741–90.

63. Aldwin Roes, 'Towards a History of Mass Violence in the Etat Indépendant du Congo, 1885–1908', *South African Historical Journal*, Vol. 62, No. 4 (2010), pp. 634–70.

64. Robert G. Weisbord, 'The King, the Cardinal and the Pope: Leopold II's genocide in the Congo and the Vatican', *Journal of Genocide Research*, Vol. 5, No. 1 (2003), pp. 35–45.

65. Helena Concannon, 'Apostles of the Congo', *Studies, An Irish Quarterly Review*, Vol. 16, No. 64 (1927), pp. 641–52; Vincent Viaene, Bram Cleys and Jan De Maeyer (eds), *Religion, Colonization and Decolonization in Congo, 1885–1960* (Leuven, 2020); Zana Etambala Mathieu, 'Patrimoines missionnaire et colonial: des images médiévales à l'époque du Congo Belge 1890–1940', *Annales Aequatoria*, Vol. 30 (2009), pp. 989–1047.

66. LaTourette, *A History of the Expansion of Christianity*, V, p. 422; Marvin D. Markowitz, 'The Missions and Political Development in the Congo', *Africa: Journal of the International African Institute*, Vol. 40, No. 3 (1970), pp. 234–47.

67. Catherine Ann Cline, 'The Church and the Movement for Congo Reform', *Church History*, Vol. 32, No. 1 (1963), pp. 46–56, esp. pp. 50–1; William Roger Louis, 'Roger Casement and the Congo', *Journal of African History*, Vol. 5, No. 1 (1964), pp. 99–120.

68. Jairzinho Lopes-Pereira, 'Slavery and Other Atrocities in the Relations between the Catholic Church and the Congo Free State 1889–1908', in Jairzinho Lopes-Pereira ed., *Church-State Relations in the Nineteenth and Twentieth Centuries, Mission, Empire and the Holy See* (Basingtoke, 2022), pp. 59–92.

69. Adam Hochschild, *King Leopold's Ghost: A Story of Greed, Terror and Heroism in Colonial Africa* (London, 1998), pp. 253–9.

70. Arthur Vermeersch, *La Question congolaise* (Brussels, 1906).

71. Angelo Mercati (ed.), *Raccolta di concordati su materie ecclesiastiche tra la Santa Sede e le autorita civili*, Vol. I: *1098–1914* (Rome, 1954), pp. 1096–7.

72. Georges-Henri Dumont, *Léopold II* (Paris, 1990).

73. Barbara A. Yates, 'White Views of Black Minds: Schooling in King Leopold's Congo', *History of Education Quarterly*, Vol. 20, No. 1 (1980), pp. 27–50; Guy Vanthemsche, *Belgium and the Congo 1885–1980* (Cambridge, 2012), pp. 27–32.

74. Owen Chadwick, *The Secularization of the European Mind in the Nineteenth Century* (Cambridge, 1978); Hugh Mcleod, *Secularisation in Western Europe, 1848–1914* (Basingstoke, 2000).

75. Susan K. Foley and Charles Sowerwine, *A Political Romance: Léon Gambetta, Léonie Léon and the Making of the French Republic, 1872–1882* (Basingstoke, 2012), p. 145.

76. Martin Thomas, *The French Colonial Mind: Mental Maps of Empire and Colonial Encounters* (London, 2011), p. 136; Nicole-Dominique Lê, *Les Missions-étrangères et la pénétration française au Viêt-Nam* (Paris, 1975).

77. Haijian Mao, *The Qing Empire and the Opium War: The Collapse of the Heavenly Dynasty* (Cambridge, 2016).

78. Charles Keith, *Catholic Vietnam: A Church from Empire to Nation* (Los Angeles, CA, 2012), pp. 18–54.

79. Jacob Ramsay, *Mandarins and Martyrs: The Church and the Nguyen Dynasty in Early Nineteenth-Century Vietnam* (Stanford, CA, 2008), pp. 68–91.

80. R. Stanley Thomson, 'France in Cohinchina: The Question of Retrocession 1862–1865', *Far Eastern Quarterly*, Vol. 6, No. 4 (1947), pp. 364–78.

81. Peter C. Phan, 'Christianity in Indochina', in Gilley and Stanley (eds), *World Christianities*, pp. 513–27, esp. p. 516.

82. Lloyd Eastman, *Throne and Mandarins: China's Search for a Policy during the Sino-French Controversy, 1880–1885* (Cambridge, MA, 1967), esp. Ch. 7.

83. Antoine Michelland, *Marie Ier, le dernier roi français: la conquête d'un aventurier en Indochine* (Paris, 2012).

84. Daughton, *An Empire Divided*, pp. 73–7.

85. Henry James Lethbridge, 'Adventures in Hong Kong: The Marquis de Mores and David de Mayréna', *Journal of the Hong Kong Branch of the Royal Asiatic Society*, Vol. 14 (1974), pp. 28–57.

86. Lionel Lecourt, *Marie 1er, roi des sédangs en Indochine* (Paris, 2012), pp. 215–60.

87. Daughton, *An Empire Divided*, pp. 80–4.

88. For a case study see Elizabeth A. Foster, *Faith in Empire: Religion, Politics, and Colonial Rule in French Senegal, 1880–1940* (Stanford, CA, 2013), pp. 69–94; Maurice Larkin, *Religion, Politics and Preferment in France 1890: La Belle Epoque and Its Legacy* (Cambridge, 1995), pp. 88–106.

89. Bruno Étienne, 'Laïcité et Maçonnerie, le cas du grand orient de France', *Revue des deux mondes* (2002), pp. 9–25.

90. Larkin, *Religion, Politics and Preferment*, pp. 107–18.

91. Claude Prudhomme, *Stratégie Missionnaire du Saint-Siège sous Léon XIII 1878–1903* (Rome, 1994), pp. 1–19.

92. Ian Linden, *Global Catholicism: Toward a Networked Church* (London, 2012), pp. 11–15.

93. Stephen Niell, *A History of Christian Missions* (London, 1964), pp. 344–53.

94. Edward Laxton, *The Famine Ships* (London, 1997); Christine Kinealy, *This Great Calamity: The Great Irish Famine, 1845–52* (2nd edn, London, 2006), esp. ch. 8.

95. Tyler G. Anbinder, *Nativism and Slavery: The Northern Know Nothings and the Politics of the 1850's* (Oxford, 1992); Katie Oxx, *The Nativist Movement in America: Religious Conflict in the 19th Century* (London, 2013).

96. Jay P. Dolan, *The Immigrant Church: New York's Irish and German Catholics, 1815–65* (Notre Dame, IN, 1983); Mayeur, Pietri and Vauchez (eds), *Histoire du Christianisme*, XI, p. 904.

97. Hugh J. Kelly, *Honest John Kelly, Truth or Satire* (New York, 2016); Terry Golway, *Machine Made: Tammany Hall and the Creation of Modern American Politics* (New York, 2017).

98. Richard Panchyk, *Catholic New York City* (Chicago, 2009), pp. 34–6; Mary C. Kelly, *The Shamrock and the Lily: The New York Irish and the Creation of a Transatlantic Identity, 1845–1921* (New York, 2005), p. 124.

99. Mayeur, Pietri and Vauchez (eds), *Histoire du Christianisme*, XI, p. 906.

100. Hieronim Kubiak, *The Polish National Catholic Church in the United States of America from 1897 to 1980, its Social Conditioning and Social Functions* (Warsaw, 1982).

101. Kim Voss, *The Making of American Exceptionalism: Knights of Labour and Class Formation in the Nineteenth Century* (Cornell, NY, 1994).

102. Bernadette Brex, *The Knights of Labour and the Haymarket Riot: The Fight for an Eight-Hour Workday* (New York, 2003).

103. Margaret M. McGuinness and James T. Fisher (eds), *Roman Catholicism in the United States: A Thematic History* (Fordham, NY, 2019).

104. Mayeur, Pietri and Vauchez (eds), *Histoire du Christianisme*, XI, pp. 905–6.

105. John J. Meng, 'Cahenslyism: The second chapter, 1891–1910', *Catholic Historical Review*, Vol. 32, No. 3 (1946), pp. 302–40.

106. Gerald Fogarty, SJ, 'Leo XIII and the Church in the Unitied States', in Philippe Levillain and Jean-Marc Ticchi (eds), *Le Pontificat de Léon XIII: renaissances du Saint-Siège?* (Rome, 2006), pp. 351–68, esp. pp. 351–4.

107. Chester Hearn, *Circuits in the Sea: The Men, the Ships, and the Atlantic Cable* (Westport, CT, 2004).
108. Bellocchi, *Tutte le encicliche*, V, pp. 300–12.
109. James McMurray Longo, *Isabel Orléans-Bragança, the Brazilian Princess Who Freed the Slaves* (London, 2008), pp. 212–30.
110. Roderick J. Barman, *Citizen Emperor: Pedro II and the Making of Brazil, 1825–1891* (Stanford, CA, 1999), pp. 335–63.
111. John Lynch, *New Worlds: A Religious History of Latin America* (London, 2012), pp. 191–4.
112. Friedrich Engel-Janosi, 'Austria and the Conclave of 1878', *Catholic Historical Review*, Vol. 39, No. 2 (1953), pp. 142–66.
113. R. de Cesare, *Il conclave di Leone XIII con aggiunte e nuovi documenti, il futuro conclave* (Citta di Castello 1888); Owen Chadwick, *A History of the Popes* (Oxford, 1998), pp. 278–83.
114. Falconi, Il cardinale Antonelli, pp. 274–5.
115. Paul Spehr, *The Man Who Made Movies: W. K. L. Dickson* (Bloomington, IN, 2008), pp. 508–9.
116. Santiago Casas, *Léon XIII, un papado entre modernidad y tradición* (Barañáin, 2014), p. 58.
117. Gross, The War against Catholicism, pp. 288–91.
118. Robert Tombs, *The Paris Commune 1871* (London, 1999), pp. 123–5.
119. Jean-Marie Mayeur and Madeleine Rebérioux, trans. J. R. Foster, *The Third Republic from Its Origins to the Great War, 1871–1914* (Cambridge, 1987), pp. 18–36.
120. David Harvey, 'Monument and Myth', *Annals of the Association of American Geographers*, Vol. 69, No. 3 (1979), pp. 362–81.
121. Benjamin F. Martin, *Count Albert de Mun, Paladin of the Third Republic* (Chapel Hill, NC, 1978), pp. 13–27; François Veuillot, 'La Pensée sociale d'Albert de Mun', *Studies: An Irish Quarterly Review*, Vol. 4, No. 13 (1915), pp. 72–87.
122. Adrien Dansette, 'Le catholicisme social et la III e République', *Hommes et mondes*, No. 63 (1951), pp. 95–108; Angelo Gambasin, *Il movimento sociale nell'opera dei Congressi 1874–1904: contributo per la storia del cattolicesimo in Italia condividi* (Rome, 1958).
123. David Seawright, *The British Conservative Party and One Nation Politics* (London, 2011).
124. Stephen D. Kale, *Legitimism and the Reconstruction of French Society, 1852–1883* (Baton Rouge, LA, 1992).
125. Marvin Luther Brown, *The Comte de Chambord: The Third Republic's Uncompromising King* (Durham, NC, 1967), pp. 127, 137; Samuel M. Osgood, *French Royalism under the Third and Fourth Republics* (The Hague, 2012), pp. 27–36.
126. Mayeur and Rebérioux, *The Third Republic*, p. 23.

127. Renault, *Le Cardinal Lavigerie*, pp. 590–1.
128. Roberto de Mattei, *Le Ralliement de Léon XIII, l'échec d'un projet pastoral* (Paris, 2016), pp. 129–31.
129. Bellocchi, *Tutte le encicliche*, VI, pp. 7–17.
130. Parker Thomas Moon, 'The Social Catholic Movement in France under the Third Republic', *Catholic Historical Review*, Vol. 7, No. 1 (1921), pp. 24–34.
131. Mayeur and Rebérioux, *The Third Republic*, pp. 72–90; Theresa McBride, 'Public Authority and Private Lives: Divorce after the French Revolution', *French Historical Studies*, Vol. 17, No. 3 (1992), pp. 747–68.
132. Murat Akan, *The Politics of Secularism: Religion, Diversity, and Institutional Change in France and Turkey* (New York, 2017), pp. 30–96; Eoin Daly, 'The Ambiguous Reach of Constitutional Secularism in Republican France: Revisiting the idea of laïcité and political liberalism as alternatives', *Oxford Journal of Legal Studies*, Vol. 32, No. 3 (2012), pp. 583–608.
133. Walter Maturi 'Tosti, Luigi, in *Treccani dizionario biografico degli italiani*, online at www.treccani.it/enciclopedia/luigi-tosti_%28Enciclopedia-Italiana%29/ [accessed 16 August 2021].
134. Virgilio Procacci, *La questione romana, le vicende del tentativo di conciliazione del 1887* (Florence, 1929).
135. Kertzer, *Prisoner of the Vatican*, pp. 219–21.
136. Calorgero Cerami, *La figura e l'opera del Cardinale Mariano Rampolla del Tindaro* (Palermo, 2006).
137. Giuseppe Gallina, Il Problema religioso nel risorgimento e il pensiero di Geremia Bonomelli (Rome, 1974), pp. 266–79.
138. John A. C. Conybeare, 'A Portfolio Diversification Model of Alliances: The Triple Alliance and Triple Entente, 1879–1914', *Journal of Conflict Resolution*, Vol. 36, No. 1 (1992), pp. 53–85.
139. James E. Ward, 'Leo XIII and Bismarck: The Kaiser's vatican visit of 1888', *Review of Politics*, Vol. 24, No. 3 (1962), pp. 392–414.
140. Christopher Duggan, *The Force of Destiny: A History of Italy Since 1796* (New York, 2008), p. 330.
141. Giuseppe Pipitone-Federico, *Francesco Crispi e la spedizione dei mille* (Palermo, 1910).
142. Chadwick, *A History of the Popes*, pp. 302–3.
143. Frances Yates, *Giordano Bruno and the Hermetic tradtion* (London, 2015); Michael White, *The Pope and the Heretic: The True Story of Giordano Bruno, the Man Who Dared to Defy the Roman Inquisition* (New York, 2009).
144. Kertzer, *Prisoner of the Vatican*, pp. 272–8.
145. Primo Levi, *Il cardinale d'Hohenlohe nella vita italiana, da Leone XIII a Francesco Crispi* (Turin, 1907).

146. Kertzer, *Prisoner of the Vatican*, p. 279.

147. Christopher Duggan, *Francesco Crispi: From Nation to Nationalism* (Oxford, 2002), pp. 561–8.

148. Raymond Jonas, *The Battle of Adwa: African Victory in the Age of Empire* (Cambridge, MA, 2011).

149. Owen Chadwick, *Catholicism and History: The Opening of the Vatican Archives* (Cambridge, 1978), pp. 72–109; Joseph G. Prior, *The Historical Critical Method in Catholic Exegesis* (Rome, 2001), pp. 90–101.

150. Chadwick, *A History of the Popes*, pp. 281–3.

151. Bellocchi, *Tutte le encicliche*, V, pp. 202–18.

152. Ibid, V, pp. 313–30.

153. Lillian Parker Wallace, *Leo XIII and the Rise of Socialism* (Durham, NC, 1966), pp. 397–9.

154. Margaret Lavinia Anderson, 'The Limits of Secularization: On the problem of the Catholic revival in nineteenth-century Germany', *Historical Journal*, Vol. 38, No. 3 (1995), pp. 647–70; Larkin, 'The Devotional Revolution in Ireland', pp. 625–52.

155. Clark and Kaiser (eds), *Culture Wars*, pp. 47–76.

156. Jutta Scharzkopt, 'The Social Condition of the Working Class', in Stefan Berger (ed.), *A Companion to Nineteenth-Century Europe, 1789–1914* (Oxford, 2008), pp. 109–21.

157. Chadwick, *A History of the Popes*, pp. 307–11.

158. Philippe Boutry (ed.), *Rerum novarum: écriture, contenu et réception d'une encyclique* (Rome, 1997).

159. David Wasp, *The Great Dock Strike, 1889* (London, 1974), esp. pp. 96–8.

160. Bellocchi, *Tutte le encicliche*, V, p. 454.

161. Gabriele De Rosa, *I tempi della rerum novarum* (Rome, 2002), pp. 297, 378.

162. Bellocchi, *Tutte le encicliche*, V, pp. 451, 455–58; Roberto A. Sirico and Beniamino di Martino, *Rerum novarum, due prospettive liberali sulla proprietà e la libertà* (Plano, TX, 2018), pp. 9–24.

163. Edward Hadas, *Counsels of Imperfections: Thinking through Catholic Social Thinking* (Washington, DC, 2021), pp. 96–126, 276–310.

164. Frédéric Cépède, 'Les socialistes français et l'encyclique rerum novarum', in Boutry (ed.), *Rerum novarum*, pp. 357–66; Peter Doyle, 'Nothing New and Nothing True: Some socialist reactions to Rerum novarum', in Boutry (ed.), *Rerum novarum*, pp. 357–82.

165. Chadwick, *A History of the Popes*, pp. 316–18.

166. Paolo Giovannini, 'La democrazia cristiana e la crisi finale dell'opera dei congressi 1902–1904', *Studi Storici*, Vol. 43, No. 1 (2002), pp. 5–39.

167. Marvin R. O'Connell, *John Ireland and the American Catholic Church* (St Paul, MN, 1988), pp. 286–347.

168. Maurice Nédoncelle, *L'abbé Félix Klein, professeur honoraire à l'institut catholique de Paris 1862–1953* (Paris, 1954).

169. De Mattei, *Le Ralliement de Léon XIII*, p. 190.

170. Walter Elliott, *Life of Father Hecker* (New York, 1891), French edition, *Le Père Hecker: traduit et adapté de l'anglais, introduit par Mgr Ireland, avec un oréface par l'abbé Félix Klein* (6th edn, Paris, 1989, originally pub, 1898).

171. Solange Hertz, *The Star-Spangled Heresy: Americanism* (Arcadia, CA, 2012); Franco, *Parallel Empires*, pp. 39–44.

172. Norman Bolotin and Christine Laing, *The World's Columbian Exposition: The Chicago World's Fair of 1893* (Chicago, 1992).

173. David R. M. Beck, *Unfair Labour? American Indians and the 1893 World's Columbian Exposition in Chicago* (Lincoln, NE, 2019); Anna R. Paddon and Sally Turner, 'African Americans and the World's Columbian Exposition', *Illinois Historical Journal*, Vol. 88, No. 1 (1995), pp. 19–36.

174. Egal Feldman, 'American Ecumenicism: Chicago's world's parliament of religions of 1893', *Journal of Church and State*, Vol. 9, No. 2 (1967), pp. 180–99.

175. Charles Maignen, *Le père Hecker, est-il un saint?* (Paris, 1898).

176. Gerald P. Fogarty, 'Reflections on the Centennial of Testem Benevolentiae', *US Catholic Historian*, Vol. 17, No. 1 (1999), pp. 1–12; Samuel J. Thomas, 'The American Periodical Press and the Apostolic Letter Testem Benevolentiae', *Catholic Historical Review*, Vol. 62, No. 3 (1976), pp. 408–23.

177. John Tracy Ellis, *The Life of James Cardinal Gibbons, Archbishop of Baltimore, 1834–1921* (2 vols, New York, 1952), II, pp. 66–73.

178. Alex Bein, *Modern Anti-semitism and Its Place in the History of the Jewish Question* (London, 1958); William I. Brustein, *Roots of Hate: Anti-semitism in Europe before the Holocaust* (Cambridge, 2003).

179. Michael D. Biddiss, *Father of Racist Ideology: Social and Political Thought of Count Gobineau* (New York, 1970); Thomas P. Anderson, 'Édouard Drumont and the Origins of Modern Anti-semitism', *Catholic Historical Review*, Vol. 53, No. 1 (1967), pp. 28–42; Vicki Caron, 'Catholic Political Mobilization and Antisemitic Violence in Fin de Siècle France: The case of the union nationale,' *Journal of Modern History*, Vol. 81, No. 2 (2009), pp. 294–346; Nina Valbousquet, 'Tradition catholique et matrice de l'antisémitisme à l'époque contemporaine', *Revue d'histoire moderne et contemporaine*, Vol. 62, Nos. 2–3 (2015), pp 63–88.

180. J. Verdès-Leroux, 'Un prototype des scandales politico-financiers, le krach de l'union générale 1882', *Le Mouvement social*, No. 66 (1969), pp. 89–103; Jeannine Verdès, 'La presse devant le krach d'une banque catholique: l'union génerale 1882', *Archives de sociologie des religions*, Vol. 10, No. 19 (1965), pp. 125–56.

181. Jean-Yves Mollier, *Le Scandale de Panama* (Paris, 1991).

182. Lucien Guissard, *Les assomptionnistes d'hier à aujourd'hui* (Paris, 2000).

183. Jacqueline and Philippe Godfrin, *Une Centrale de presse catholique, la maison de la bonne presse et ses publications* (Paris, 1965).

184. Maurice Larkin, *Church and State after the Dreyfus Affair: The Separation Issue in France* (London, 1974), p. 65; Bertrand Joly, 'Le parti royaliste et l'affaire Dreyfus 1898–1900', *Revue historique*, Vol. 269, No. 2 (1983), pp. 311–64.

185. Kertzer, *The Popes Against the Jews*, pp. 135–41.

186. Ruth Harris, *The Man on Devil's Island: Alfred Dreyfus and the Affair that Divided France* (London, 2010), pp. 226–9.

187. Jill Jonnes, *Eiffel's Tower: And the World's Fair Where Buffalo Bill Beguiled Paris, the Artists Quarrelled, and Thomas Edison Became a Count* (New York, 2009).

188. Harris, *The Man on Devil's Island*, pp. 15–41.

189. Christian Vigouroux, *Georges Picquart, un héros méconnu de l'affaire Dreyfus, le choix de la vérité dans l'affaire Dreyfus* (Paris, 2020).

190. Martin Phillip Johnson, *The Dreyfus Affair: Honour and Politics in the Belle Époque* (Basingstoke, 1999), pp. 45–60.

191. Harris, *The Man on Devil's Island*, pp. 81–104.

192. Émile Zola *'J'Accuse…!'* (pocketbook edn, Paris 2017), originally published as an article in *L'Aurore*, 13 January 1898.

193. Harris, *The Man on Devil's Island*, p. 224; Ruth Harris, 'The Assumptionists and the Dreyfus Affair', *Past and Present*, No. 194 (2007), pp. 175–211.

194. Alan Schom, *Émile Zola: A Biography* (London, 1987), chs. 19–21; Stephen Wilson, 'The Antisemitic Riots of 1898 in France', *Historical Journal*, Vol. 16, No. 4 (1973), pp. 789–806.

195. Mayeur and Rebérioux, *The Third Republic*, pp. 185–208.

196. Johnson, *The Dreyfus Affair*, pp. 107–12.

197. Maurice Larkin, 'La République en danger? The pretenders, the army and Déroulède, 1898–1899', *English Historical Review*, Vol. 100, No. 394 (1985), pp. 85–105; Zeev Sternhell, 'Paul Deroulede and the Origins of Modern French Nationalism', *Journal of Contemporary History*, Vol. 6, No. 4 (1971), pp. 46–70.

198. Harris, *The Man on Devil's Island*, pp. 322–61.

199. Cesare Silva, *La separazione dello stato dalla Chiesa in Francia del 1905* (Rome, 2020).

200. Harris, *The Man on Devil's Island*, pp. 371–85, esp. pp. 380–1.

201. Kertzer, *The Popes Against the Jews*, pp. 182–5.

202. Esther Benbassa, *The Jews of France: A History from Antiquity to the Present* (Princeton, NJ, 2001), esp. ch. 11.

203. Ada Ferrer, *Insurgent Cuba: Race, Nation, and Revolution, 1868–1898* (Chapel Hill, NC, 1999); Glenn Anthony May, 'Warfare by Pulong: Bonifacio, Aguinaldo, and the Philippine revolution against Spain',

Philippine Studies, Vol. 55, No. 4 (2007), pp. 449–77.

204. Edmund Morris, *The Rise of Theodore Roosevelt* (New York, 2001), pp. 588–616.

205. Thomas G. Paterson, 'United States Intervention in Cuba, 1898: Interpretations of the Spanish–American–Cuban–Filipino war', *History Teacher*, Vol. 29, No. 3 (1996), pp. 341–61.

206. Daniel Immerwahr, *How to Hide an Empire: A Short History of the United States* (London, 2019), p. 74.

207. Joseph Smith, *The Spanish–American War 1895–1902* (London, 1994), ch. 4.

208. Stuart Creighton Miller, *Benevolent Assimilation: The American Conquest of the Philippines, 1899–1903* (London, 1984), pp. 36–8; Reynaldo Clemeña Ileto, *Payson and the Revolution: Popular Movements in the Philippines, 1840–1910* (Manila, 1979), pp. 115–26; Nicole Cuunjieng Aboitiz, *Asian Place, Filipino Nation: A Global Intellectual History of the Philippine Revolution 1887–1912* (New York, 2020), pp. 74–97.

209. David J. Silbey, *A War of Frontier and Empire: The Philippine-American War, 1899–1902* (New York, 2008), pp. 63–78.

210. Pedro S. de Achútegui and Miguel A. Bernard, *Religious Revolution in the Philippines: The Life and Church of Gregorio Aglipay 1860–1940* (2nd edn, Manila, 1961), pp. 146–7.

211. Miller, *Benevolent Assimilation*, chs. 3 and 4.

212. Immerwahr, *How to Hide an Empire*, p. 90.

213. Miller, *Benevolent Assimilation*, chs. 7–11.

214. Achútegui and Bernard, *Religious Revolution in the Philippines*, pp. 104–14, 128.

215. Isabelo de los Reyes, Jr, 'The Iglesia Filipina Independiente', *Historical Magazine of the Protestant Episcopal Church*, Vol. 7, No. 2, (1948), pp. 132–7; William Henry Scott, 'A Minority Reaction to American Imperialism: Isabelo de los Reyes', *Philippine Quarterly of Culture and Society*, Vol. 10, Nos. 1–2 (1982), pp. 1–11.

216. Achútegui and Bernard, *Religious Revolution in the Philippines*, pp. 187, 199–202.

217. Ibid, pp. 203–6; Daniel F. Pilario and Gerardo Vibar, *Philippine Local Churches under the Spanish Regime: Quae Mari Sinico and Beyond* (Ozamiz, 2010), pp. 1–17.

218. Pilario and Vibar, *Philippine Local Churches under the Spanish Regime*, p. 225.

219. Achútegui and Bernard, *Religious Revolution in the Philippines*, p. 328.

220. Justice J. Willards' opinion G.R. No. L-2832, in *Barlin vs. Ramirez*, 24 November 1906, online at www.chanrobles.com/scdecisions/jurisprudence1906/nov1906/gr_l-2832_1906.php [accessed 17 August 2021].

221. *Philippines in Figures* 2018, p. 23, online at https://psa.gov.ph/sites/default/files/PIF%202018.pdf [accessed 17 July 2021].

222. Francis Clark, 'Les ordinations anglicanes: problème œcuménique', *Gregorianum*, Vol. 45, No. 1 (1964), pp. 60–93 ; R. J. Lahey, 'The Origins and Approval of the Malines Conversations', *Church History*, Vol. 43, No. 3 (1974), pp. 366–84.

223. Simon Francis Gaine, 'Defect of Sacramental Intention: The background of "Apostolicae Curae"', *New Blackfriars*, Vol. 82, No. 959 (2001), pp. 4–23.

224. Chadwick, *A History of the Popes*, pp. 330–1.

225. Matthew Glencross, *The State Visits of Edward VII: Reinventing Royal Diplomacy for the Twentieth Century* (Basingstoke, 2015), Ch. 3.

226. Jean-Baptiste Noé, *Léon XIII, le semeur de Dieu* (Suresnes, 2013), p. 213.

Conclusion: The Conclave of 1903

1. Owen Chadwick, *A History of the Popes* (Oxford, 1998), pp. 332–41.

2. Frederick J. Baumgartner, *Behind Locked Doors: A History of the Papal Elections* (Basingstoke, 2003), p. 202.

3. Francisco Martín Hernández, 'El conclave de 1903, unas notas acerca de la elección del papa S. Pio X', *Salmanticensis*, Vol. 36, No. 2 (1989), pp. 193–208; Eduardo Brazão, 'O conclave de 1903 e o veto da exclusão', *Lusitania Sacra*, Vol. 6 (1962), pp. 177–237.

4. Friedrich Engel-Janosi 'L'Autriche au conclave de 1903', *Revue belge de philologie et d'histoire*, Vol. 29, No. 4 (1951), pp. 1119–41.

5. Matteo Lamacchia, 'Ius exclusivae e conclave, il diritto di veto delle potenze cattoliche nella storia delle elezioni pontificie', *Eunomia*, Vol. 7, No. 2 (2018), pp. 105–30.

6. Anon, 'Les Derniers Jours de Léon XIII et le conclave de 1903', *Revue des deux mondes*, Vol. 20, No. 2 (1904), pp. 241–85.

7. Greg King and Penny Wilson, *Twilight of Empire: The Tragedy at Mayerling and the End of the Habsburgs* (New York, 2017), pp. 111–32.

8. Ibid, pp. 158–63.

9. Igino Giordani, *Pius X, A Country Priest* (Milwaukee, WI, 1954), pp. 59–66.

10. Frank J. Coppa, *The Modern Papacy since 1789* (New York, 1998), pp. 115–17.

11. Drahomír Suchánek, 'The End of the Right of Exclusion: Conclave of 1903 and the new legislative of Pope Pius X', *Dvacáté století/The Twentieth Century*, Vol. 5, No. 2 (2013), pp. 126–37.

12. Holland, *Dominion: The Making of the Western Mind*.

13. McLeod, *Religion and the People of Western Europe*, pp. 36–53.

IMAGE CREDITS

Page 9

(*top left*) Photo by Heritage Art/Heritage Images via Getty Images
(*middle right*) colaimages / Alamy Stock Photo
(*bottom*) Photo by Luigi Baldin/Electa/Mondadori Portfolio via Getty
  Images

Page 10

(*top*) Photo by Illustrated London News/Hulton Archive/Getty Images
(*middle left*) © Bradford Museums & Galleries / Bridgeman Images
(*bottom right*) Ambrogio A. Caiani

Page 11

(*top*) adam eastland / Alamy Stock Photo
(*middle left*) Yogi Black / Alamy Stock Photo
(*bottom right*) Photo by Rabatti&Domingie/Mondadori Portfolio via
  Getty Images

Page 12

(*top*) Photo by Fine Art Images/Heritage Images/Getty Images
(*bottom*) The Picture Art Collection / Alamy Stock Photo

Page 13

(*top*) Recall Pictures / Alamy Stock Photo
(*bottom*) Album / Alamy Stock Photo

Page 14

(*top*) The History Collection / Alamy Stock Photo
(*middle*) Livioandronico2013 / Wikimedia Commons
(*bottom*) Chronicle / Alamy Stock Photo

Page 15

(*top*) atreyu / Wikimedia Commons
(*middle*) Photo by: Universal History Archive/Universal Images Group
  via Getty Images
(*bottom*) Art Collection 4 / Alamy Stock Photo

Page 16

(*top*) Photo by The Print Collector/Getty Images
(*bottom*) Album / Alamy Stock Photo

INDEX